A Practical Guide to
Early Childhood Curriculum

Seventh Edition

A Practical Guide to Early Childhood Curriculum

Claudia Eliason

Loa Jenkins

Merrill
Prentice Hall

Upper Saddle River, New Jersey
Columbus, Ohio

Library of Congress Cataloging-in-Publication Data

Eliason, Claudia Fuhriman
  A practical guide to early childhood curriculum / Claudia Eliason, Loa Jenkins.—7th ed.
     p. cm.
  Includes bibliographical references (p.) and index.
  ISBN 0-13-094518-8
  1. Early childhood education—Curricula. I. Jenkins, Loa Thomson, 1942- II. Title.
LB1139.4 .E54 2003
372.19—dc21

                         2002019867

Vice President and Publisher: Jeffery W. Johnston
Executive Editor: Kevin M. Davis
Associate Editor: Christina M. Tawney
Editorial Assistant: Autumn Crisp
Production Editor: Sheryl Glicker Langner
Production Coordination: Linda Zuk, WordCrafters Editorial Services, Inc.
Design Coordinator: Diane C. Lorenzo
Cover Designer: Linda Sorrells-Smith
Cover Photo: Corbis Stock Market
Production Manager: Laura Messerly
Director of Marketing: Ann Castel Davis
Marketing Manager: Amy June
Marketing Coordinator: Tyra Cooper

This book was set in ITC Garamond 1 and Lucida Sans by BookMasters, Inc. It was printed and bound by R.R. Donnelley & Sons Company, Harrisonburg, VA. The cover was printed by The Lehigh Press, Inc.

Photo Credits: All photos by Paul L. Jenkins.

Pearson Education LTD
Pearson Education Australia PTY, Limited
Pearson Education Singapore, Pte. Ltd.
Pearson Education North Asia Ltd.
Pearson Education Canada, Ltd.
Pearson Educacion de Mexico, S.A. de C.V.
Pearson Education–Japan
Pearson Education Malaysia, Pte. Ltd.
Pearson Education, *Upper Saddle River, New Jersey*

Preface

Many are the times
we will teach.
Many are the times
we will be taught.
. . . But only once, a child.

PHILOSOPHY AND PURPOSE

While preparing to teach, students become imbued with educational theories, but then often find themselves in the classroom as student teachers or professional teachers without practical knowledge of what and how to teach. They understand the theories of learning, but they often are unable to blend these theories with practical application appropriate for young children. Curriculum books for early childhood education abound, but they are frequently general, rather than specific, in content and direction.

In this textbook, we not only emphasize the application aspect of teaching, but we also provide a solid foundation for the theoretical basis of the concepts being applied. We want students and teachers to understand what can be taught to young children, why it is important, and how it can be accomplished. We also emphasize the importance of a child-centered curriculum that encompasses the whole child—physical, social, emotional, creative, and cognitive. This book focuses on cognitive areas of the curriculum and effective methods of curriculum implementation.

A Practical Guide to Early Childhood Curriculum evolved from the constant inquiry and search for meaningful teaching ideas by students and professional teachers. It also evolved from our teaching experiences in the primary grades, in Head Start, and in college and university class-rooms and laboratories. The concepts selected for inclusion are those that most often meet the needs, interests, and developmental levels of children ages 3 through 8 years. However, they should not limit your thinking, planning, and imagination, but rather should serve as a springboard for you and your students as you select projects and themes to explore.

This book is designed for those in the process of preparing to teach young children, as well as for those currently teaching: teachers, teacher's aides, parents, grandparents, church leaders, administrators, supervisors, and other care givers. Its purpose is to explore how children learn; what children can learn; and the specific concepts, ideas, and strategies that are developmentally appropriate for young children.

CHAPTER PEDAGOGY

The unified pedagogy follows a specific format for most chapters: introductory comments, including content information; approach to teaching; chapter summary; student learning activities; and suggested resources. The introduction provides an overview of the chapter as well as specific background and guidelines on the concept or concepts, and the summary reviews the important notions presented. The approach to teaching provides very specific content information, precise concepts, and ideas that are developmentally appropriate for young children, and many explicit ideas for classroom activities and experiences for young children. In addition, as appropriate, unit plans or webs are shared or illustrated within the approach to teaching section. Occasionally within the chapters, also as a part of the approach to teaching section, a lesson plan is included to allow students the opportunity of seeing how one teacher might apply the concepts in the chapter. However, most lesson plan illustrations appear in Appendix A.

To make the text more readable, we have included some boxed content in every chapter. In addition, in the chapters that include sections titled "Concepts and Ideas for Teaching," we have consistently boxed this section. The student learning activities offer discussion questions and many suggestions for applying the concepts presented in the chapter within the university or college classroom. Included in each chapter are current references and research on the specific areas discussed in the chapter. The full reference citations are listed alphabetically at the end of the book. The suggested resources at the end of the chapter provide updated lists of children's books, tapes, compact discs, pictures, multimedia kits, videos, and other audiovisual and technology aids. Literally hundreds of new works are published each month in early childhood education alone. Based on the kind of computer that you have and your budget, we suggest that you evaluate new software choices for your school, classroom, or center on an ongoing basis. We emphasize that the software selected should be developmentally appropriate, utilize a variety of approaches, emphasize a variety of concepts, and encourage problem solving.

CONTENT COVERAGE AND ORGANIZATION

Writing this seventh edition of *A Practical Guide to Early Childhood Curriculum* has been both exciting and challenging. Determining what information to add, expand on, or delete has required research, assessment, and introspection. In this current edition, a number of major changes have been made, including some reorganization of the chapters. The text is divided into four parts, each presenting a solid theoretical discussion and rationale.

Part One includes four chapters and provides an introduction and framework for the text. Chapter 1 is an overview of early childhood education and addresses its past, present, and future. The importance of early childhood education is also considered in depth. Chapter 2 concerns the developmental appropriateness of early academics, play, assessment, curriculum, and the physical setting. Theories of learning and children's excitement for learning are also included. Chapter 3 provides direction for developing partnerships between the school and parents, and a detailed discussion on curriculum planning is presented in Chapter 4.

Part Two presents skills and concepts related to understanding and dealing with the self and others. Helping children to learn about people and their diversities, focusing more on similarities than differences, is presented in Chapter 5. Although multicultural and antibias education is integrated throughout the text, it is also considered in greater depth in this chapter. Helping children to learn more about their families and themselves is the focus of Chapter 6, which includes a discussion of character education and resiliency. Information regarding physical and nutritional fitness and general health issues is the focus of Chapter 7.

Part Three includes five chapters that directly relate to cognitive development in the early childhood years. All curriculum development rests on the child's literacy ability, and Chapter 8 reflects our beliefs regarding the importance of balanced literacy development. Many new sections and much new information have been added to this chapter. Young children should not only be taught to learn, memorize, and take in facts; more importantly, they must also learn to think deeply—to classify, explain, investigate, question, observe, sort, wonder, synthesize, communicate, analyze, compare, hypothesize, and predict. Science concepts and ideas for incorporation in the curriculum are discussed in Chapters 9, 10, and 11. These chapters have been reorganized in such a manner that Chapter 9 is "Physical Science Experiences," Chapter 10 is "Earth Science Experiences," and Chapter 11 is "Life Science Experiences." Chapter 12 relates to math concepts and emphasizes problem-solving skills. Children should learn to solve problems initially by working with concrete ideas; then, equipped with some process skills, they become able to generalize and handle more abstract problems.

Finally, Part Four includes chapters on music and movement (Chapter 13), and also creativity, art, and dramatic activities (Chapter 14). These vital experiences should be incorporated frequently throughout the curriculum, and not planned as only occasional endeavors.

We emphasize that we take a developmental approach to teaching young children; that is, experiences are planned in accordance with the developmental needs of the children in the classroom or center. Although some lesson plans supporting the specific chapters are included throughout the text, Appendix A contains additional lesson plans that will expand the concepts and subjects presented in the book. Recipes have generally been moved from the body of the text and are now included in Appendix B.

Occasionally, we suggest the use of foods as art media; but we consider it imperative that children learn early the value of using and preserving, rather than wasting, food. Sometimes a food item, such as macaroni, may be more economical than purchasing beads for stringing necklaces. Also, discarded items such as oranges and potatoes from the produce department of the grocery store often expand the possibilities of creative art activities.

In the process of formulating the preface for this seventh edition, we read a statement that delightfully supports our own feelings regarding working with children: "Young children keep us from stalling in neutral gear. They make us drive in the heart of the center lane of life" (Chenfeld, 1995, p. 71). We find that working with young children is refreshing and helps to keep us focused on the importance of the early childhood years. Our desire is that this text, which supports the child-centered and constructivist points of view, will assist you in planning and implementing a fully integrated, developmentally appropriate early childhood curriculum.

ACKNOWLEDGMENTS

We express appreciation to the many people who have assisted, supported, and encouraged us in this project. We are indebted to Paul Jenkins for the photographs throughout the book. We appreciate his sensitivity, skill, time, and effort. We also thank the many children and adults who cooperated in the photography, including various elementary schools in Bonneville Joint School District Number 93, Idaho Falls, Idaho, and Carol Duncan, day-care provider, Idaho Falls, Idaho. In addition, we thank the Lewis School in the Ogden City School District (Ogden, Utah), with Principal Catherine Montgomery and teachers.

A special thanks to Jana Jones for her assistance in providing information on teaching children with special needs. We also express our appreciation to the publisher's reviewers for their valued contributions to the completion of this book: Alice Beyrent, Hesser College; Pamela Kramer, East Stroudsburg University of Pennsylvania; Rosanne Morel, Mount Wachusett Community College; and Patricia Weaver, Fayetteville Technical Community College.

Lisa Warner, of Eastern Kentucky University, shared materials with us, and Patrice Liljenquist Boerens contributed her graphics and artistic talents.

For editorial assistance, we thank Ann Davis, Christina Tawney, Keli Gemrich, and Pat Grogg at Prentice Hall; their wise direction, patient prodding, and demand for excellence were valued. Linda Zuk provided comprehensive guidance throughout the production cycle. Carol Sykes was especially helpful with photo coordination.

We are grateful for our interaction with the children, parents, and students we have taught. Their inspiration, incentive, behavior, and thoughts have influenced whatever understandings we have.

We are indebted to our friends and families, especially to our husbands, Paul and Glen, whose patient support, interest, and encouragement were vital to the completion of this new edition. We express thanks to our children, Jason, Cathrine, Anne, Matthew, Megan, Eric, Erin, Kyle, Kristen, and Catherine, whose examples have enlightened our understanding of the truths of childhood.

Discover the Companion Website Accompanying This Book

THE PRENTICE HALL COMPANION WEBSITE: A VIRTUAL LEARNING ENVIRONMENT

Technology is a constantly growing and changing aspect of our field that is creating a need for content and resources. To address this emerging need, Prentice Hall has developed an online learning environment for students and professors alike—Companion Websites—to support our textbooks.

In creating a Companion Website, our goal is to build on and enhance what the textbook already offers. For this reason, the content for each user-friendly website is organized by topic and provides the professor and student with a variety of meaningful resources. Common features of a Companion Website include:

FOR THE PROFESSOR—

Every Companion Website integrates **Syllabus Manager**™, an online syllabus creation and management utility.

- **Syllabus Manager**™ provides you, the instructor, with an easy, step-by-step process to create and revise syllabi, with direct links into Companion Website and other online content without having to learn HTML.

- Students may log on to your syllabus during any study session. All they need to know is the web address for the Companion Website and the password you've assigned to your syllabus.

- After you have created a syllabus using **Syllabus Manager**™, students may enter the syllabus for their course section from any point in the Companion Website.

- Clicking on a date, the student is shown the list of activities for the assignment. The activities for each assignment are linked directly to actual content, saving time for students.

- Adding assignments consists of clicking on the desired due date, then filling in the details of the assignment—name of the assignment, instructions, and whether or not it is a one-time or repeating assignment.

- In addition, links to other activities can be created easily. If the activity is online, a URL can be entered in the space provided, and it will be linked automatically in the final syllabus.

- Your completed syllabus is hosted on our servers, allowing convenient updates from any computer on the Internet. Changes you make to your syllabus are immediately available to your students at their next logon.

FOR THE STUDENT—

- **Topic Overviews**—outline key concepts in topic areas

- **Web Links**—general websites related to topic areas as well as associations and professional organizations

- **Read About It**—timely articles that enable you to become more aware of important issues in early childhood education

- **Learn by Doing**—put concepts into action, participate in activities, complete lesson plans, examine strategies, and more

- **For Teachers**—access information that you will need to know as an in-service teacher, including information on materials, activities, lessons, curriculum, and state standards
- **Visit a School**—visit a school's website to see concepts, theories, and strategies in action
- **Electronic Bluebook**—send homework or essays directly to your instructor's email with this paperless form
- **Message Board**—serves as a virtual bulletin board to post—or respond to—

questions or comments to/from a national audience
- **Chat**—real-time chat with anyone who is using the text anywhere in the country—ideal for discussion and study groups, class projects, etc.

To take advantage of these and other resources, please visit the *A Practical Guide to Early Childhood Curriculum*, Seventh Edition, Companion Website at

www.prenhall.com/eliason

Brief Contents

Contents

6 Myself and My Family   170

7 Myself and My Body   196

PART THREE
COGNITIVE AND LITERACY
DEVELOPMENT   229

8 Language and Literacy Development   232

Part One

Introduction to Early Childhood Education

The four chapters in Part One provide an introduction to and overview of this textbook. The
focus of this book is on children ages 3 to 8 years
or prekindergarten through third grade, and the
curriculum emphasis is on play. During early childhood, it is suggested that more concepts and struc-

ture be added to the curriculum very gradually;
however, we emphasize that even though there
have been major sociological and technological
changes in our society over the past years, developmental rates have not accelerated (Scherer,
1996). Children need environments and learning

experiences that are geared to their needs, not highly academic curricula planned around what adults think children ought to be learning and doing. Young children need child-centered environments that offer many opportunities for choices and encourage learning through play, exploration, and discovery. They need cognitive challenges that facilitate their overall development (Meyer, 2001). In addition, because children acquire competencies and abilities at different rates, it is suggested that a set or standardized curriculum be avoided during these years (Elkind, 1996).

Chapter 1 gives a historical perspective on early childhood education, discusses why it is important, and includes current trends and considerations as well as a look at the future of early childhood education. The field of early childhood education is a dynamic, changing discipline that has strong roots but is presently blossoming in new and exciting ways. Perhaps the greatest change in early childhood education is the movement for preschool public education programs. Where they are available they give all children an equitable chance for quality early education. Chapter 2 gives an overview of developmentally appropriate practices (DAP) for early childhood. One of the important strands in the DAP perspective is play; it is respected both for its value and as an appropriate learning medium during early childhood. The importance of the physical environment is discussed as another strand in the DAP program. The value of various areas of the room or various play activities is considered, and criteria for selecting materials and toys are given. Teacher-made learning materials are also discussed. Other significant strands in developmentally appropriate practice are its approach to teaching and learning and the way learning is assessed. Because early childhood is a unique and distinctive stage in human development, programs need to adopt teaching practices that adjust to the way young children learn and to appropriate ways of assessing their learning and growth.

Still another significant strand is collaborating with parents. Chapter 3, Developing Partnerships with Parents, considers the relevance of the parent–school alliance and presents innovative ways for achieving optimum involvement of parents in our schools. It explores far beyond the singular traditional idea of parents volunteering in the classroom. Effective school–home partnership programs help parents realize that their participation has a positive influence on their children's success now and in the future (Brand, 1996; Washington, Johnson, & McCracken, 1995). Political leaders have sensed the impact of parent involvement in schools and focused on the issue in a variety of ways. Every school is encouraged to promote partnerships that will increase parental involvement and participation in promoting needs of children. In order for children to integrate both the home and school experiences, it is imperative that children, their families, and their schools work as partners with one another.

There are many ways and approaches to curriculum planning. Chapter 4 presents an overview of curriculum planning and gives examples using themes and units and also the "Project Approach" (Chard, 1992; 1994). It is hoped that those who use this book will learn the concepts, methods, and strategies that best meet the needs of young children and how to plan in such a way that children have age-appropriate, child-centered educational experiences. We emphasize that various levels of ability and development in each early childhood classroom should be expected, valued, accepted, and planned for; in fact, appropriate plans can be made only with the needs of children in mind. We address their diverse needs best when our perspective is one that regards early education as "a liberating, rather than a remedial, enterprise" (Elkind, 1996, p. 13). Whatever the planning model or schedule configuration, the question constantly addressed should be, "How can we best provide a high-quality program for the children we serve?" (Graue, 2001).

Chapter 1

Early Childhood Education

The beliefs of many philosophers, psychologists, and educators dating back to the 17th century have influenced early childhood education as it is practiced in the 21st century.

In order to know where early childhood education is going, it is important to know where it has come from.

The needs and values of early childhood education are many faceted, and caring, qualified early childhood teachers are paramount to the learning of the developing child. To implement developmentally appropriate teaching practices in the child's early years, it is vital for teachers and caregivers to be aware of the developmental characteristics of the children with whom they are working. It is also essential that teachers and caregivers gain an understanding of the needs of children as they progress toward becoming well adjusted, confident, and thoughtful learners.

A HISTORICAL LOOK AT EARLY CHILDHOOD EDUCATION

Early childhood education has historical roots dating back for centuries, although it has experienced a renewal in the past few decades. Various philosophers and unique philosophies have influenced early childhood education, but one's own, individual perspective is what has the greatest influence on actions, teaching, and the curriculum.

A Glimpse at Some of the Philosophers and Educators of the Past Three Centuries Who Have Influenced Early Childhood

John Locke (1632–1704)

Individual differences and play important

Children should be treated with kindness and sensitivity

Children progress through developmental stages

Children learn from interaction with their environment

Johann Pestalozzi (1746–1827)

The purpose of education is to develop physical, moral, and intellectual skills and powers

Positive teacher–child relationships are important

Friedrich Froebel (1782–1852)

Originated first kindergarten; it was based on play and materials

Children have innate gifts to be developed

Elizabeth Peabody (1804–1894)

Established first United States kindergarten in Boston in 1860

Margaret McMillan (1860–1931)

Established first nursery school in London in 1911

Patty Smith Hill (1868–1946)

Early pioneer in kindergarten education in United States

John Dewey (1859–1952)

American educator who emphasized experimentation and discovery learning

Maria Montessori (1870–1952)

Italian educator who developed the Montessori method, which focuses on development of the intellect through the exploration of materials

Arnold Gesell (1880–1961)

Developed norms of children's growth

Jean Piaget (1896–1980)

Proposed theory of children's cognitive development

Children learn through experimentation

Described periods of cognitive development

Lev Vygotsky (1896–1934)

Theory of development describing social process of learning and impact of development of language

Erik Erikson (1902–1994)

Theory of personality development

Highlights of the 17th and 18th Centuries

Prior to the 1900s, childhood was not looked on as an important, valuable, and viable part of the total life-span. Around 1690, the English philosopher John Locke (1632–1704) was one of the first to emphasize the importance of individual differences, the early years and experiences, and play. Jean-Jaques Rousseau (1712–1778), a French philosopher, suggested that society has a corrupting influence on children and that children should be treated with sympathy and compassion. In his classic work *Emile* (1762), Rousseau addressed the value of early childhood education, proposing that education begins at birth and children move through a succession of developmental stages. Rousseau was resolute in his belief that children learn through direct interaction with their environment, rather than through abstractions of the written word (Williams, 1999). He recognized play as a medium for learning and suggested that sensory-based processes also play a role in learning. The Swiss educator Johann Pestalozzi (1746–1827) maintained that all persons have the right to an education—to develop skills and learn those things that will help them to be successful. The purpose of education, according to Pestalozzi, was to develop children's moral, physical, and intellectual powers (Williams, 1999). He believed that children learn best through self-discovery. He advocated that teaching be of the highest moral character for young children and recognized the importance of the emotional climate of the classroom and home. He modeled, as a teacher himself, the importance of positive teacher–child relationships that are still recognized as being significant in the teaching–learning arena. He founded one of the first European schools that focused on children's developmental characteristics and used older children as tutors of younger ones.

Development of Kindergarten and Nursery School

Friedrick Froebel (1782–1852) originated the first kindergarten, around 1837, in Germany. To achieve his proposed objectives, he designed a curriculum based on play and materials. In Froebel's kindergarten, children used manipulatives to develop skills and learn concepts. He was the first to design a curriculum to meet the specific needs of young children. Froebel's notion of play was very different from our present philosophy. He perceived play as a more structured, teacher-directed activity, but it could also be a more creative self-expression. Froebel believed that children have innate gifts that need to be developed and that they will cultivate these gifts by choosing activities that interest them. Froebel's interest in the teacher's role in classroom talk through asking questions, prompting, and coaching has been reaffirmed by researchers such as Katz and Chard (1989), as well as his emphasis on the teacher–child relationship.

Elisabeth Peabody (1804–1894) established the first English-speaking kindergarten in 1860 in Boston. Beginning in 1870 in the United States and by World War I, kindergarten was incorporated into public schools in large cities. Today, kindergarten education is nearly as universal as elementary education.

In 1911, Margaret McMillan (1860–1931) established the first nursery school in London. In the United States, Patty Smith Hill (1868–1946) was one of the early pioneers in kindergarten education. After observing the McMillan nursery school, she also became a pioneer in nursery or preschool education. The early nursery schools were geared primarily for children who were poor, with a focus on nurturing them and preventing both mental and physical illness. As the movement spread, they became more concerned with educating children.

Other Historical Contributors to Early Childhood Education

John Dewey (1859–1952), an American educator and philosopher, developed the idea of pragmatism and maintained that children should experiment and discover. He did not like rote teaching, but believed in natural materials and presumed that children should explore in a free-play environment, with much activity and freedom, geared to their own interests. Dewey and other progressive followers suggested a curriculum for young children that focused on the challenges and situations that children faced as members of a democratic society. They promoted problem solving based on real-life circumstances, sociodramatic play, and cooperative learning activities. In the United States following World War I, the ideas of Sigmund Freud (1856–1939) affected education. His theory emphasized unconscious motivation, conflicts between social

Opportunities for children to play with a variety of materials and equipment foster enjoyment of learning and support development of age-appropriate concepts.

expectations and spontaneous behaviors, and the impact of emotions on behaviors.

Maria Montessori (1870–1952), the first woman in Italy to be granted a medical degree, is best known for the teaching method that bears her name, the Montessori method. She opened the Casa dei Bambini (children's home) in a tenement area of Rome in 1907. There has been a resurgence of interest in the Montessori method since the reintroduction of her work by Rambusch (1962). Among Montessori's key ideas was her belief that the senses are the source of all intellectual growth and that intellectual development is, therefore, dependent on the training of the senses. She developed a set of physical materials, autotelic or self-correcting in nature, to be used by the teacher in a prescribed manner. Self-discipline and autonomy were also key ingredients in her philosophy. She emphasized the importance of the school and family working together. Parents and teachers were to observe children's behavior to assist their correct choices of materials and also to understand children and refine the curriculum.

Arnold Gesell (1880–1961) played a key role in the early childhood movement and is particularly known for his research in establishing norms of the types of behavior likely to occur in children at specific ages. However, he still emphasized the concept of individual differences and cautioned against using the norms literally.

Jean Piaget (1896–1980) is noted for his interest in and theory of children's cognitive development. The impact of his works on present-day education, psychology, and child development is increasingly evident. Piaget's work and writing have generated more interest and research in education and developmental psychology in the last 50 years than those of any other person. His research also radically changed our thinking about the growth of human intelligence. He had great love, empathy, and appreciation for children. Programs that adapt a Piagetian model emphasize that children learn through experimentation and initiative and construct their own knowledge and understanding through adaptation to the environment. His theory gave strong impetus for including play in the early childhood curriculum. He described children as moving through four stages or periods of intellectual development (sensorimotor, preoperational, concrete operational, and formal operational) and that time and experience were needed for maturation. Piaget's theory further suggested that children need ample time and plenty of manipulative materials as they interact and move through the various cognitive stages. His theory was the result of observation of his own children, and he advocated teacher observation to determine children's needs, developmental stages, and as a means of deriving the curriculum.

The work of Lev Vygotsky (1896–1934), Russian psychologist, has recently taken root in the United States. Because of political circumstances, his work was not dispersed in Russia or any part of the world during the first half of the 20th century. However, by the 1960s, well after his death, his writing was translated into English. His work presently has received widespread acceptance, and early childhood educators often compare him to Piaget. Vygotsky alleged that development proceeded through a social process and that learning is affected by the social occurrence of language. This was in contrast to the Piagetian perspective that development leads language and everything rests on an internal schedule of maturation. For Vygotsky, learning is viewed as a social construction, with adults and peers strongly influencing what children know and do. Through scaffolding and support from capable peers and adults, the child can move to higher levels of understanding and achievement. Vygotsky called this area of psychological influence the "zone of proximal development" (ZPD). Thus, in early childhood Vygotsky's work has emphasized the importance of language and social contexts as primary sources of development and learning (Williams, 1999).

The focus in the 1920s and 1930s was on physical and intellectual development. During the 1930s, early education programs were based on the works of Froebel, Montessori, McMillan, and a few other pioneers of early childhood education. Between 1940 and 1950, the emphasis was on physical, social, and emotional growth. At the 1950 White House Conference on Youth, Erik Erikson (1902–1994) presented his theory on personality development, which was to gain widespread acceptance and favor among educators and swing the emphasis in early childhood education to the social and emotional side. The socioemotional development of children, according to Erikson, results from the consequences of a series of conflicts, each of which addresses an essential concern of the human mind (Williams, 1999).

In the 1960s, research gave evidence that the early environment has a profound effect on the child's development. As a result, parents from lower economic environments obtained greater opportunity for involvement and decision making in the education of their children. Project Head Start, a composite of federally funded preschool programs for children from impoverished backgrounds, was established in 1965. With the organization of Head Start, preschool education moved to the national level and programs became available for all children. The inception of Head Start presented a major change in early childhood education in the United States. It was hoped that by offering an enriched program for children from lower incomes, this "head start" would reverse the cycle of poverty, children would enter public school ready for the prescribed content, and children would not fail. This program also emphasized the family and community. Perhaps its foremost accomplishment, however, was awakening in the public a sense of the profound importance of the early years and of education for the young. Currently, many Head Start programs are housed in public schools, giving children an early opportunity to acclimate to the school environment as well as ensuring a quality program for children and parents.

The pressures of the 1960s were for openness, humanistic approaches to education, acceptance of individual learning styles, and education for the impoverished. Directions in the 1970s emphasized literacy, discipline, achievement in the "basics," conformity, and demands for accountability. During the late 1960s and the 1970s, many program models received attention. For example, Ira Gordon developed home-based education focusing on teaching and working with parents.

Another significant event in the 1970s was the enactment of Public Law 94–142, the Education for All Handicapped Children Act of 1975 (renamed the Individuals with Disabilities Education Act in 1990). This law required that all children be given the opportunity to reach their fullest potential and that children with special needs be included in regular public school programs when possible. During the 1970s, much more emphasis was placed on understanding children with special needs or disabilities.

During the 1980s the importance of early education continued. The Ypsilanti, Michigan, Early Training Project is a research study based on Piaget's theorizing, with the aim of promoting total cognitive development. The program developers believe that preventive preschool programs must begin earlier than traditional preschool programs, because the critical years for early learning are age 3 and under. They also maintain that early intervention programs will be much more effective if they involve both the mother and the child. The Ypsilanti research project has presented solid evidence that preschool education does make a difference for children (Schweinhart & Weikart, 1996; Schweinhart & Weikart, 1992; Schweinhart, Weikart, & Larner, 1986).

During the end of the 20th century, debate centering on curriculum in early childhood programs created controversy, confusion, and even contention. Some curriculum programs stressed content skills such as math, language, reading, and science. These programs advocated direct instruction, workbook exercises, drill and practice, and in general emphasis on children's achievement on standardized IQ and readiness tests. On the other hand, other curriculum developers supported developmentally appropriate practice (DAP), which they believe is in harmony with Piaget's theory and does not rush children into academically rigorous learning before they are ready. This is the child development approach in which work with manipulatives, social interaction, and a more traditional method is advocated. Developmentally appropriate practice considers the whole child, while taking into account the individual child's needs (Bredekamp, 1997; Hart, Burts, & Charlesworth, 1997).

Developmentalists maintain that play should not be abandoned in early childhood programs and classes in favor of more direct instruction and formal, academic skills. So heated did the debate become between these two opposing perspectives that the National Association for the Education of Young Children (NAEYC, the largest professional association for early childhood educators) issued a policy statement defining its position (Bredekamp & Copple, 1997). This position paper has become known as the DAP (developmentally appropriate practice) guidelines for the developmentalists and the debate between the two opposing camps continues into the new century.

Program models differ in their curriculum emphasis, structure, reinforcement methods, teacher role, activities, and materials, but no program has been found to be the best for all children, and the children in any program show improvements in the areas emphasized in that particular program. Many early childhood programs in the United States have taken an eclectic philosophical approach and drawn from many philosophers and theorists to form the perspective that drives their actions and curriculum.

Federal legislation has also greatly influenced early childhood programs today. Legislation on behalf of children with special needs continued in the 1980s with passage of the Education of the Handicapped Act Amendments of 1986 (P.L. 99–457). This legislation represents far-reaching federal policy supporting early childhood intervention for children 3 to 5 years of age.

During the 1980s, the importance of high standards and excellence in education became a focus, in part because of a widely quoted report from the National Commission on Excellence in Education (1983). The report, *A Nation at Risk: The Imperative for Educational Reform*, discussed in detail the "rising tide of mediocrity" in the educational foundations of our country (p. 5). Following the release of this report, reform became the byword and focus of educational programs throughout the country.

Early Childhood Education in the 1990s

More and more children are receiving the benefits of early childhood education. During the 1990s the number of children enrolled in preprimary programs continued to increase. Between 1990 and 1999, the number of children in preprimary programs rose by 7 percent (U.S. Department of Education, 2001). The growing phenomenon that is most influencing this trend in prekindergarten education is that more and more elementary schools are offering programs for 3- and 4-year-old children as a part of their regular academic programs. By 1992, 48 states offered publicly funded programs for all children age 5. In 1999, 53 percent

of 3- and 4-year-olds and 96 percent of 5- and 6-year-olds were enrolled in school (U.S. Department of Education, 2001). Growing numbers (53 percent in 1999) attend preprimary all day (U.S. Department of Education, 2001). There are also national initiatives to provide all-day or full-day kindergartens in public schools. The developmentalists are concerned that many children are not ready for a full day of learning and, in addition, are apprehensive that traditional school skills and content areas taught the full day in kindergarten will put additional pressure on young children for academic achievement.

Early Childhood School Enrollment 1970–1997

	1970	1980	1990	1999
3- and 4-year-olds	21%	37%	44%	52%
5- and 6-year-olds	90%	96%	97%	96%

U.S. Census Bureau, *Statistical Abstracts of the United States*, 2000, p. 155.

Excellence and high-quality standards continue to be a focus as a significant program variable in early childhood education (Fuerst & Petty, 1996; Katz, 1994; NAESP, 1990). In an article on early childhood reform, Schultz and Lopez (1995) suggest that the system for educating young children is flawed primarily because of a lack of overall quality in programs, a funding crisis, and staffing problems often caused by low wages. They assert that most early childhood programs fail to provide a high-quality education that would optimize young childrens' learning and development.

Quality in early childhood programs is often difficult to assess because program goals are by necessity less specific, and the evaluation of quality cannot be determined by standardized achievement tests because they are developmentally inappropriate for children less than 6 years of age (Katz, 1994). Katz suggests five perspectives on quality. They include a top-down perspective that looks at the setting, equipment, teacher–child ratio, and the program's provisions for health and safety. A second perspective, bottom-up, assesses the child's experience in the program through child-focused questions such as whether the provided activities are meaningful rather than

Early childhood programs provide many opportunities for children to develop positive feelings about themselves and others.

mindless. In this bottom-up assessment, the staff becomes accountable for positive and relevant experiences. A third perspective on quality, the outside–inside perspective, takes into account the parent's perception of the program. A fourth indicator of quality is the inside perspective of the staff. The fifth assessment, the ultimate perspective, is the wider community. When taken seriously, these five contributing perspectives should be considered when assessing or determining a program's quality.

Elkind (1996) used the term *character* to describe the effectiveness of early childhood programs and suggested that each program's character is determined by factors such as the teachers' training, materials, teacher–child ratio, and physical facilities. Quality in early childhood programs was also addressed by the NAESP. With the movement for more and more school districts across the country to include classes for 4-year-olds and in some cases 3-year-olds, this group offered guidelines for establishing quality educational programs for young children and for assessing those programs already established (NAESP, 1990). According to NAESP (1990), quality programs enhance

the child's self-image, strengthen social and emotional development, expand communication skills, and stimulate an interest in the world's surroundings. In addition, a quality program expands concepts and notions, encourages independent thinking, and develops problem-solving skills. Furthermore, a quality program advances motor skills, identifies special needs, reinforces respect for others and for the rights of others, promotes creativity and aesthetic appreciation and expression, and increases the child's capacity for self-control and self-discipline.

> Quality programs are child centered and keep the needs of children at the center of the teaching and learning process.

The education of the whole child continued to be emphasized in the 1990s, with the need to meet each child's individual needs again being stressed by both the public and educators. A major impetus in sensitizing educators to the needs of *all* children was the understandings gleaned from the multicultural approach to education. Teachers became aware of direct and subtle things that they do that may be demeaning to some children. The concept of multicultural education broadened during the past decade from viewing multicultural education through issues such as culture, language, race, gender, class, and sexual orientation to issues of inclusion of children with special educational needs (Williams, 1999). Culturally appropriate practices were called into question and teachers were encouraged to evaluate their personal attitudes relating to diversity. Educators can learn about diversity by moving outside their own cultural perspective; their vision of the way things are may not be the same for another person. Teachers can understand that their own approach is not the "only way" or even the "right way," but simply "one way" of doing things. They may also realize how their students' culture outside the classroom may influence what happens inside it (Chipman, 1997). The impact of diverse culture and language on development was brought more clearly into focus.

There was increasing focus on the positive aspects of child-centered instruction, talk, and interaction in the learning process; but, in reality, most classrooms were still teacher centered, with children seldom becoming active participants in their own learning (Bracey, 1996a; Garmston & Wellman, 1994; Heckman, Confer, & Hakim, 1994; Kohn, 1993a; Levin, 1994). Change and action require initiative, planning, thinking, and organization and are at the heart of the child-centered curriculum movement proposed by Chard (1992, 1994), Clark (1997), Kohn (1993) and others. If students are to learn more, their ideas, interests, and preferences need to be attended to in the organization of the classroom and the teaching and learning process (Levin, 1994). Teachers can empower and motivate students and accelerate their achievement by allowing them to make their own decisions about their learning (Glasser, 1997; Kohn, 1993; Ohanian, 1996). Thus far, however, it appears that the gap between theory and practice is wide.

Children grow in esteem, confidence, and skill as they accomplish new developmental tasks. Accentuating the developmental approach, researchers affirmed the notion that children's developmental rates have not accelerated over time, although in practice programs and teachers have tried to accelerate their learning. Those concerned with early childhood education realize that early childhood programs should be concerned with *all* areas of the child's growth, should be action oriented, and should include educating children in ethics, values, and morals. One concern in this broad-based educational approach is that we may be trying to do too much. When early childhood programs become responsible for meeting all the child's needs, resources and teaching time are used to meet nonacademic needs formerly met by families. As a result, students may not achieve academically as well as in the past, and schools and programs may then be criticized for a decrease in achievement (Elkind, 1995).

SOCIAL CONCERNS AFFECTING EARLY CHILDHOOD EDUCATION

Primary Social Concerns Affecting Young Children

Child abuse

Poverty

Violence

Homelessness

Drug abuse

During the 1990s, although we became increasingly sensitized to what was right for young children, many social ills and problems emphasized what was wrong for our young children. The family, as already noted, has changed dramatically in the past century. Divorce, single-parent families, blended families, women employed full time, parents returning to higher education and training programs, out-of-home child care, afterschool child care, and movement away from extended families have all given adults relief from family functions and constraints of the past. Such changes have been disconcerting and even harmful to the children affected by these changes (Elkind, 1994). Recognizing this diversity in family structure and function, early childhood programs have to assume responsibility for children in ways once thought to be the exclusive accountability of families.

In this new millennium, concern for social justice issues for young children continues in the forefront. Child abuse continues to increase and has become a social disgrace. In 1994, there were over a million child victims in cases of substantiated maltreatment and neglect (U.S. Department of Commerce, 1996, p. 217). In 1995, the National Committee to Prevent Child Abuse reported that more than 2,700 children per day (or 996,000 a year) were neglected or abused (Children's Defense Fund, 1997, p. 51). Perhaps because of our increased awareness, more abuse is reported than in previous decades, but the reality of the numbers tells us that child abuse continues to increase significantly every year. Most abuse of children is committed by family members (U.S. Department of Health and Human Services, National Center on Child Abuse and Neglect, 1996). More and more children from every economic and racial group are being neglected and mistreated. Their troubles pose a threat to U.S. security, values, and ideals and to a prosperous, happy future for every U.S. citizen. Early childhood educators can help to mitigate child abuse by supporting families and making referrals to appropriate service agencies as needed (NAEYC, 1997b).

In this new era there is increased wealth for the affluent and increased poverty for America's poor. Child poverty continues to rise. Table 1–1 shows the dramatic changes that have occurred in the past two decades. The data illustrate that poverty continues to increase and that children are its victims.

Our national child poverty rate is well above that of other developed nations (Annie E. Casey Foundation, 2001). Despite the healthy economy of the last several years, the proportion of children in poverty has remained between 17 and 23 per-

cent in the last decade (Annie E. Casey Foundation, 2001). The percent of children in poverty is one of the most widely used indicators of child well-being, perhaps because it is closely tied to a number of other undesirable outcomes in areas such as education and health. Children who spend their lives in homes that are poor are more likely to lack proper nutrition, quality housing, and geographical stability. The consequences of poverty, to name a few, are that these children are more likely to become teen-aged parents, drop out of high school, and be unemployed (Annie E. Casey Foundation, 2001). The costs of poverty are economic and social. In a country with so much wealth, one in five American children lives at or below the poverty level. Surely we can discover a way to reverse this upward trend and find the means by which we can create a better future for all our children.

On the threshold of a new millennium, America continues to manifest signs of growing violence

Variety in early childhood activities provides opportunities to expand social, cognitive, emotional, adaptive, and physical skills.

TABLE 1–1
Percent of Families with Children under 18 Years of Age Who Were below the Poverty Level

1970	15%
1980	18%
1990	20%
1999	21%

U.S. Department of Education, 2001, p. 28.

(Brendtro & Long, 1995; Curwin, 1995; Watson, 1995). There has been increased family, gang, and individual violence, often directed toward children. Consider the following:

- In 1994, 1.6 million 12- to 17-year-olds reported that they had been victims of violent crimes other than those involving murder. The same year, 2,661 children under 18 were homicide victims (Children's Defense Fund, 1997, p. 62).

- Children were killed as they waited in line at the movie theater, at the park, in their front yards, and in their neighborhoods and schools.

- Many children and youth went to school armed. Every day in the United States, 135,000 children take guns to school (Children's Defense Fund, 1991, p. 5).

We have created a culture of violence that has engendered children of violence; for many children, childhood has become a war zone, and children are often perpetrators (Sautter, 1995). Today children are more violent at earlier ages and commit more violent crimes (Sautter, 1995). As a result, safety issues are at the forefront in our schools, and many schools are now including conflict resolution and antiviolence programs within their curricula. Successful antiviolence programs help students to change habits, attitudes, and values and replace violent behavior with more positive behaviors (Johnson & Johnson, 1995). Others suggest that, in addition to programs for controlling violence, we must address its root causes (poverty and lack of individual responsibility and family support) and its risk factors (guns, media, drugs, observing violent acts, and community deterioration) (Isenberg and Brown, 1997).

The plight of the homeless has also invaded our conscience. The homeless are not all middle-aged, single men; many are women and children. In fact, 850,000 American children and youth are homeless each night, and it is estimated that children make up one-third of the nation's homeless population (Children's Defense Fund, 2000). In 29 cities surveyed by the U.S. Conference of Mayors, families with children made up 38 percent of the homeless (Children's Defense Fund, 1997, p. 14). A single parent, usually the mother, heads most homeless families. Some researchers estimate that

> ### Antiviolence Suggestions for Parent and Teachers
>
> Provide daily experiences that:
>
> - Help to build and foster relationships that support learning
> - Promote social and emotional competency
> - Provide frequent and positive interactions with children
> - Strengthen children's skills to interact meaningfully and inclusively with others
> - Demonstrate positive role models
> - Cultivate problem solving with respectful words, actions, and attitudes
>
> Adapted from Anderson, 2001.

single mothers head approximately 90 percent of homeless families. Many homeless children come from backgrounds that include dysfunctional families, early deprivation, and abuse (Gracenin, 1994). Homeless children have a difficult time attending to learning; their minds are elsewhere because they are focused on the basics of survival (Gracenin, 1994).

Schools can and should help to expand local, state, and national efforts to support homeless children who are victimized by their living situations. As caregivers of these children, we must not single them out, but must stress their similarities with others, as we must emphasize that *all* children have more similarities than differences.

The percent of families headed by a single parent in 2000 is 28 percent (Annie E. Casey Foundation, 2001). The phenomenon of fathers who head single-parent households is increasing, with more than 900,000 fathers in the United States raising children on their own (Osborn, 1991); however, most children who are in single-parent homes live with their mothers.

During the past decade, the trend toward more women working outside the home continued. An increasing number of women enter the workforce because of economic necessity or personal desire or because they are the head of the household. Many mothers in the workforce are also heads of households. In 1980, 18 percent of children under 18 years of age were living with their mother only. By 1990 this figure grew to 22 percent, and in 1998, 23 percent of children were living with their mother only (U.S. Census Bureau, 2000, p. 58). In 1999, 64 percent of children under 6 years of age had mothers in the workforce (U.S. Census Bureau, 2000, p. 410). About three-fourths of mothers with children 6 to 17 years of age are employed (U.S. Census Bureau, 2000, p. 409).

With so many women with young children employed outside the home, high-quality, affordable child care is a major concern. Although many children ages 3 to 6 years whose mothers are employed are cared for in their own homes or in other homes by relatives, neighbors, or friends, a growing percentage of preschool children are receiving care in center-based programs (Snyder, 1996). The trend in the 1990s was toward child care in organized facilities; about three-fourths of all preschool children spend some portion of their day in a center or with a day-care provider (Snyder, 1996). It is estimated that working parents spend over $16 billion dollars on day care each year. The cost of high-quality care increases disproportionately for the low-income family. The child-care portion of the family budget for poor families may be 25 percent, but for middle-income families it may be 10 percent (Osborn, 1991). It can cost $4,000 a year to have a youngster in child care (Children's Defense Fund, 1997, p. 34). When child care takes a large portion of the family budget, parents often try to save money and compromise by putting children in places that do not meet high standards.

With so many parents now working outside the home, it has become necessary for businesses and agencies to provide high-quality early childhood programs. More and more businesses, corporations, and local, state, and federal government agencies are offering child-care services for their employees. This approach allows the parent and child to interact during the day and tends to involve high-quality care. The business is often concerned about the quality of the program and the facility and pays for part of its cost as a benefit to employees.

With parents working full time, another problem is caring for children after school hours. The care and developmental needs of school-aged children differ from those of younger children, and the type of care that they receive will affect their social, emotional, and cognitive development, as well as their school performance. There may be positive or negative effects of before and after school care depending on the characteristics of the care arrangements. Approximately 39 percent of the nations primary school children (K to grade 3) receive some kind of nonparental care before and/or after school on a weekly basis (U.S. Department of Education, 1999).

The 21st Century Community Learning Centers is a government-sponsored program to keep children safe and help them to learn after school. Congress supported this initiative by appropriating $200 million for afterschool programs in 1999, up from $40 million in 1998. The program appears justified by recent reports by the U.S. Departments of Education and Justice on the effectiveness of afterschool programs (U.S. Department of Education, 1999, p. 1).

Other social concerns presently are drug abuse and teen-age suicide, and programs were begun

Reasons Public Supports Providing School-Based After-School Programs for Children

Over 28 million school-aged children have both parents or their only parent in the workforce.

At least 5 million children, and possibly as many as 15 million, are left alone at home each week.

Many children, especially low-income children, lose ground in reading if they are not engaged in organized learning over the summer.

Experts agree that school-aged children who are unsupervised during the hours after school are more likely to receive poor grades and drop out of school than those who are involved in supervised, constructive activities.

Statistics show that most juvenile crime takes place between the hours of 2:00 and 8:00 P.M. and that children are also at much greater risk of being the victims of crime during the hours after school.

U.S. Department of Education, 1999, p. 1.

with very young children to prevent these social problems from growing. "We lose 5,000 kids a year in suicide" (Scherer, 1996, p. 7). The government reported an increase in illicit drug use among 12- to 17-year-olds from 8.2 percent in 1994 to 10.9 percent in 1995 (Children's Defense Fund, 1997, p. 87).

Another growing social problem that affects our children is the number of infants born to unmarried women. In the United States, one in three infants is born to an unmarried mother, a statistic that has changed drastically during the past decades (Children's Defense Fund, 1997, p. x). For example, in 1950 only 4 percent of infants were born to unmarried women (Osborn, 1991). This increasing percentage means that there is a growing group of babies who will have to overcome great problems to thrive and even survive (Annie E. Casey Foundation, 2001). This concern affects the single-parent household statistic and also the issues of poverty, homelessness, and child abuse. "Eight to 12 years after birth, a child born to an unmarried, teenage, high school dropout is 10 times as likely to be living in poverty as a child born to a mother with none of these three characteristics" (Annie E. Casey Foundation, 2001, p. 16).

Politically, during the 1990s attention focused on still another concern for our young children: the lack of medical insurance, resulting in a lack of regular medical care for millions of our children. It is estimated that about 12 million children do not have health insurance, a figure that has been increasing by an average of 1.2 million each year (Children's Defense Fund, 2000).

Social problems affect our children and their education. The problems will not disappear overnight, but with many people working for the sake of our children, together we can make a difference in their future. It will take more than money; it will take time, work, effort, and a sincere caring for the welfare and needs of our children. We must not give up on them or on a brighter future for all.

EARLY CHILDHOOD PERSPECTIVE FOR THE 21ST CENTURY

As we evaluate the current status of America's young children and look to their future, we see some events that are hopeful and others that are cause for great alarm. Historically, children have

The early childhood teacher must recognize the need for providing support and security when a child is fearful.

moved from having no value or importance, to being looked on as miniature adults, to our present-day mainstreaming, which attempts to provide *all* children with the opportunity to reach their fullest potential. Over time we have witnessed cultures that have ignored children, whipped them, spoiled them, and overindulged and pampered them. We have observed teachers who have provided catechisms, resting mats, candy rewards, interest centers, ditto and work sheets, and projects. Over the years, parents and teachers have changed their perspective and teaching focus variously among the child's religious development, character and moral development, self-esteem, physical development, social development, emotional well-being, and cognitive and academic achievement. Most recently, professionals have emphasized total development or the whole child, and when teachers focus first on the child's development, this then can guide curriculum, instruction, and assessment (Goldberg, 1997). Early childhood professionals have benefited from Rousseau, Froebel, Montessori, Dewey, Gesell, Freud, and Erikson, but it is from Piaget that the current philosophy of developmentally appropriate practice has emerged. From Piaget, early educators have learned the importance of development and the limits it sets on learning. They have learned that from rich, developmentally appropriate experiences the child can construct his or her own knowledge and understanding. The aim is to provide the kind of environment and stimuli that will stir children to be curious, active, and thoughtful learners.

Development of the Whole Child

Political, social, and economic changes in our society have made families increasingly dependent on outside social institutions to aid not only in educating young children, but also in providing for all their needs. The demand for quality child care has far exceeded the availability and economic feasibility of providing it for all children. "Although the costs of good early childhood programs for the nation are great, the eventual costs of not providing them, in money and in decreased quality of life, are greater" (Schweinhart & Weikart, 1992, p. 83). Some strongly advocate the expansion of the federal Head Start program into a 4- to 6-year program that would start at an earlier age for disadvantaged children, proposing that the long-term benefits would outweigh the costs (Fuerst & Petty, 1996). A variety of studies now shows that more extended periods of early childhood education, meaning more years of preschool training, do produce long-term improvements (Bracey, 1996b; Fuerst & Petty, 1996; Schweinhart & Weikart, 1996). Others believe that what is needed for disadvantaged children is earlier intervention, perhaps beginning at birth (Fuerst & Petty, 1996).

There is a renewal of interest in strengthening the American family, particularly to help families to develop a moral orientation and to build stronger values within the family unit. It is recognized that for our country to be strong our families need rejuvenating. To this end, parents must have a genuine desire to learn and make changes, must be committed to their families, and must take charge of themselves and their children. They need eyes, hearts, and minds focused on high family standards and values. Integrity needs to be prized. They need to put into practice behaviors drawing on traditions, experiences, and expectations that will bring them to a higher ground and enable them to mold and guide children to do better, think better, and *be* better individuals.

Businesses are recognizing the importance of contributing to schools and early childhood programs to ensure a strong and capable workforce for the future and of providing child-care options for employees. However, we need more businesses willing to provide business-based child-care centers and to develop partnerships with schools and centers (Galinsky, 1992). Many agencies and businesses are involved in school partnerships, providing financial help, administrative assistance, or employees' volunteer time as tutors or mentors.

Public schools have expanded the number of safe, affordable child-care options for parents by administering Head Start, child-care, or other school-based programs. For example, schools are often used for afterschool programs for those who would otherwise be latchkey children. However, when child-care programs are planned in public schools, teachers must be cautioned not to emphasize formal, structured, academic instruction for young children. When they do, miseducation results (Elkind, 1986). Young children learn best through firsthand experience and concrete encounters. Their learning emerges through active exploration and guided discovery (NAESP, 1990). Administrators need to make every effort to ensure that guidelines proposed for group sizes by professional associations such as the NAEYC be adhered to. Advocates of developmentally appropriate practice (DAP) need to articulate its principles and implement its vision in public schools (Schultz, 1992).

Ratios and Group Size Recommended by NAEYC		
Age	Ratio	Maximum Group Size
30–36 months	1:7	14
Preschool	1:10	20
Kindergarten	1:12	24
Primary	1:15	30

Greenberg, 2001, pp. 7, 10.

The public, as well as parents, must demand excellence in the education of administrators and teachers. The Weikart and Schweinhart studies (Schweinhart & Weikart, 1996; Schweinhart & Weikart, 1992; Schweinhart, Weikart, & Larner, 1986) equated excellence with the terms *effective* and *high quality* the key to the lasting effects of their projects.

Research on the long-term effects of quality child-care programs has been well documented and indicates that children demonstrate positive outcomes as a result (Bredekamp & Copple, 1997; Layzer, Goodson & Moss, 1993). However, several studies have found that high-quality child-care programs are not the norm (Bredekamp & Copple, 1997; Layzer, Goodson, & Moss, 1993). Those working with young children should plan and implement experiences to meet the basic needs of each individual child, no matter what the child's gender, social class, or cultural or ethnic background. Early childhood education should be seen as an integrated experience for the child from 3 to 8 years of age. This means that each grade level should be built on the preceding one, with the needs of the child being met at each level. Providing quality early childhood education is not an easy task and requires a well-trained, committed staff, a rich cur-

Standards for high-quality, effective programs include the following characteristics:

- The curriculum is specifically stated and adheres to developmentally appropriate practice that supports children's self-initiated learning.
- Teachers or caregivers are trained in the curriculum through ongoing in-service training, and staff turnover is low.
- Administrators provide training and support for staff.
- To allow for a high degree of adult–child interaction, there is a ratio of two adults for every 20 or fewer 3- to 5-year-old children.
- Parents become partners with teachers in educating the child, and home visits are made at least monthly.

Schweinhart & Weikart, 1996; Schweinhart & Weikart, 1992.

riculum, and adequate resources. The term *quality* is used to describe what we are seeking in our classrooms (Sarison, 1995; Schultz & Lopez, 1995). The early years are crucial in determining the child's success as a student and as a future contributing member of society. Adams and Poersch (1997, p. 67) state, "Good-quality programs can help children succeed in school, lessen the likelihood that they will come into contact with the criminal justice system, and help them become more productive citizens." Thus, providing a great start is well worth the effort!

Goals for Early Childhood Education

Educators and other concerned people need to determine how to best provide for the needs of young children and enable *all* children to reach their full potential.

Educators need to be competent and have a sound set of beliefs on which policies, goals, and actions are based (Darling-Hammond, 1996, 1997). Early childhood professionals need to be accountable and to keep focused on accomplishing their

Goals for Early Childhood Professionals

1. Understand the nature of development and learning as well as the individual nature and characteristics of each child.
2. Know what to teach, how to teach, and how to assess what children have learned, as well as how to adapt the curriculum to the needs and interests of individual children.
3. Create a caring and responsive learning environment that is inclusive of the diverse cultural and linguistic backgrounds of all children.
4. Establish positive, mutual relationships of trust and respect with families, recognizing that shared goals benefit children and their education.
5. Seek ongoing and professional knowledge and training, recognizing that quality programs and classrooms have teachers who are lifelong learners.
6. Treat every child with respect, dignity, and positive regard, recognizing that every child has great potential.

Young children must have opportunities to move into activities as they feel comfortable, which oftentimes involves observing from a distance.

goals as they relate to the children that they serve. Schools, programs, and caring individuals can positively influence troubled children; and although they cannot do everything at once, reducing any risk factor can make a difference between failure and success (Coontz, 1995). Consistent changes and daily efforts work.

Another priority for the future is to continue the impetus to involve the family more in early childhood programs. The more that teachers collaborate with the family, the greater the child's strides. Until we embrace family diversity, share power with families in significant ways, and strive for agreement on what understanding is of most value, the reform that the field of early childhood education so desperately needs will only be a hope and not a reality (Briggs, Jalongo, & Brown, 1997).

Still another priority is to improve our professional image by educating the public about the importance of high-quality early childhood programs and seeking to protect and strengthen licensing in states and local communities. Program standards, regulations, and expectations need to

be closely monitored and enforced (Schultz & Lopez, 1995). In a study of states' commitment to child care and early education, it was suggested that this commitment "depended more on state 'will' than state 'wallet'" (Adams & Poersch, 1997, p. 67). Greater resources did not necessarily mean greater commitment.

When a child has rich, high-quality early childhood experiences with stimulating activities enhancing his or her development, the effect will likely be lasting. It is exciting, indeed, to envision the results of providing high-quality programs for all children ages 3 to 8 years with excellent, well-trained teachers who enjoy working with children and provide them with first-rate facilities and materials. The vision does not have to stop in the imagination; it can become a reality.

The fabric of our society is woven of strong family values and ideals. The threads are strong individuals who have hope and enthusiasm for the opportunities on the horizon and a desire to become educated. Our children must be strong threads—responsible, unselfish, and self-disciplined and holding positive attitudes.

IMPORTANCE OF EARLY CHILDHOOD EDUCATION

Factors Influencing the Need for Early Childhood Education

All children deserve, and children who are poor need, the promise and boost of high-quality early childhood education. The work of many psychologists and researchers has influenced both the growth of and the need for early childhood education. Bredekamp and Rosegrant (1992), Elkind (1991a, b, 1996), Fuerst and Petty (1996), National Association for the Education of Young Children (1997a), National Association of State Boards of Education (1988), and others have supported the importance of environmental factors in influencing the early development of the child. Effective preschool experiences help children to overcome the influences of poverty (Bracey, 1996b; Fuerst & Petty, 1996).

Children suffering poverty need the benefit of quality early childhood education. If the trend of increasing poverty continues, soon one in four will be living below the poverty level. We can and must respond by providing high-quality child care and enriching preschool experiences for our poor children, both for them and for our own future.

Children from homes where both parents work or from single-parent homes need child care. The primary factor forcing early childhood education on the national agenda is the number of women in the workforce. There is a need not only for more places for child care, but also for upgrading the quality of the care given. Based on the fact that many young children are still cared for by untrained caregivers, our efforts should be toward not just training those individuals in centers who are untrained, but also providing some means and incentive to reach the large number of people who are caring for our nation's young children. Community agencies, churches, clubs, and any other groups who might reach and teach those caring for young children have a charge and responsibility to provide quality training.

Children with special needs benefit from early childhood education, as do the children who have the opportunity to play and work with exceptional children. Early education can be viewed as the time to alleviate problems by providing special programs: programs focusing on children who are economically disadvantaged and the problems often associated with poverty, programs treating learning disabilities at an early age, programs in special education, or programs reaching children with emotional difficulties at a time when negative behaviors have had little time to become ingrained. All children need the opportunity to learn at their highest potential in an inclusive environment.

Developmental Need for Early Childhood Education

Several aspects of young children's growth point to the need for early childhood education; and to foster a balanced human being, it is important to pay attention to all aspects of a child's growth, including social, emotional, physical, moral, and academic development (Howe, 1993). *Socialization* takes place in the early years, with the family being the first and most important group to which the child belongs. The early childhood group, in which children relate to other children of their own age, is an ideal situation for furthering social skill and development. Through their play, children learn to develop friendships that enable them to refine their social behavior. Sharing, listening to others, developing leadership skills, learning to follow others, gaining confidence in dealing with others, and learning to conform to the rules of the group are all examples of by-products of early childhood socialization.

The *emotional development* of the child has long been of paramount concern; children need schools that foster warm, supportive relationships (Glasser, 1997). This aspect relates closely to the development of either a positive or a negative self-image. Children must like themselves. The feelings of being "okay" and important and of having strengths and direction make up the positive self-image.

Although these feelings are generated from within, they are influenced from outside the child. It is hoped that in the early years teachers and parents will begin to tap into and encourage these kinds of feelings in children and eliminate the opposite kinds of feelings: of no one caring, unimportance, lack of worth and significance. Positive feelings provide motivation and encourage growth, whereas negative feelings stimulate failure and engender bitterness and resentment. The significant people in children's early environment reflect back to the children how they are viewed, and the children, in turn, decide how to see themselves. These views of themselves will form their self-concepts, which in turn will determine their behaviors, attitudes, values, feelings, experiences, and success. "A child loved by us at two will reflect that love at seven. A child encouraged by us at age three will show confidence at age seven. A child affirmed by us at four will demonstrate self-esteem at seven" (Bakley, 1997, p. 21).

Generally, children who feel good about themselves also feel good about their world; their emotions are characterized by spontaneity, enthusiasm, joy, interest, and happiness. On the other hand, children who do not feel good about themselves view the world with disappointment, anger, resentment, prejudice, and fear. Children cannot be protected from negative emotions and situations, but to be emotionally healthy, they should be equipped to cope with these feelings. Early childhood programs offer experiences that help to develop this coping ability, which is necessary to emotional health. Much depends on the classroom atmosphere, and a positive, joyful classroom makes students more apt to learn how to solve problems in stressful situations, as well as increasing their ability to learn (Sylvester, 1994). A child's emotional well-being is an indicator or predictor of academic success (Pool, 1997).

Success, accomplishment, trust, belonging, and achievement create positive feelings. The child's early experiences must provide and generate many such feelings in building a framework for healthy emotional development. A basic ingredient in the development of a healthy self-concept and emotional foundation is love.

The power of love in the very early years of life is strong enough to make sick children well, and the lack of it can make well children sick. Love has such a positive force that it can decrease the child's inevitable moments of pain, frustration, and anger. Love can change, modify, and channel negative feelings into constructive actions and later in life toward success and achievement. Katz (1985) suggests that it is important for the child not just to *be* loved but also to *feel* loved. The child must feel that "what he [or she] does, or does not do,

really matters to others" (p. 13). Some programs, because of liability concerns amid allegations of child abuse in child-care settings, have instituted policies that do not allow physical displays of affection toward young children. "No-touch policies are misguided efforts that fail to recognize the importance of touch" to the healthy development of children, especially to infants and toddlers (NAEYC, 1997a, p. 43). Warm responses such as pats on the back, hugs, face touches, or ruffling a child's hair show care, concern, and love. However, these should always be appropriate, considering each child's individual needs, and should always be acceptable to the child (NAEYC, 1997a).

The early childhood experiences also aid in the *development of physical and motor functions*. Materials and apparatus should be provided that enable the child to use and exercise both large and small muscles. Large-muscle equipment and activities include climbing apparatus, tricycles, wagons, rocking boats, tumble tubs, and locomotor and rhythmic activities. Small-muscle apparatus and activities include puzzles, lacing games and toys, scissors, and crayons, as well as fingerplays and any other activities and materials that encourage the use of the hands and fingers. There are also many appropriate physical–motor games for children in the early childhood years. They should be simple to play and noncompetitive.

The term *early childhood education* implies teaching the child. Thus *intellectual* or *cognitive* aspects become an ingredient in the growth and development of the young child. It is well documented that the early years are of crucial importance to the child's intellectual growth. Early childhood education opens up a world to young children through experiences with people, events, animals, places, and other things. A child cannot have an understanding of what a strawberry is, for example, without some experience with it—either a real experience or a vicarious experience through a picture or an explanation, in specific detail, of what a strawberry is. The richest and most meaningful experiences for children are firsthand, concrete, or sensory. These experiences may be within the school or on field trips outside the school.

Although young children need opportunities for learning, mastering skills, and thinking, the process must be slow and organized. Young children must be given time to experience who they

As children experiment with various materials, they acquire skills that provide the basis for success in the development of literacy.

development of the child's IQ. However, the individual child should be the focus, and the curriculum should be planned to help each child to reach his or her fullest potential. Basic concepts presented in an exciting way are stimulating, fun, interesting, and involving, and they provide the foundations for both learning and initial attitudes toward learning. Teachers of young children thus have the challenge of providing a curriculum that meets their needs and is relevant for them.

Early childhood educators seek to educate children not only to think, but also to feel and act. As lessons are planned and objectives written, teachers should ask, "What is it that I want these students to know, do, and feel as a result of this lesson?" Teachers should not separate the cognitive from the affective; rather, they should see these domains as integrated parts of the whole and try to gear their instruction to build on this interdependence.

Early childhood education can thus be one of the primary means for meeting and satisfying some of the basic needs of young children: social, emotional, physical, intellectual, and linguistic. The early years are times for the development of language, creativity, thinking, and self-concept. Therefore, the importance of high-quality education during this period cannot be overemphasized.

The Early Childhood Teacher

Providing a quality program in early childhood requires excellent teachers (Gatzke, 1991). In a report by the National Commission on Teaching and America's Future (1996), the authors contend that every child should have a caring, competent, and qualified teacher. Early childhood education may lose its intellectual thrust and its affirmative status and reputation in our society if it is unable to provide teachers who are specialists and experts in both theory and practice. In one study of child-care staff, it was found that

are on their road to becoming. It has been suggested that pressures for early achievement and academic learning have intensified, but the way that young children grow and learn has not changed.

Issues relating to depth versus breadth remain unresolved in early childhood education. It is believed that for most children elaboration of basic concepts is preferred to rapid and accelerated learning in the cognitive domain (Hanson & Reynolds, 1991; Raines, 1997). Some cognitively oriented programs focus simply on accelerating

---

Demonstrated Qualities of Effective Early Childhood Teachers

caring	competent	qualified	educated
credentialed	enthusiastic	positive attitude	creative
empathy	tolerance	understanding	communicator
learner	nurturing	sensitive	high expectations
cultivate thinking	patience	high energy	awareness
teaching strengths	planning strengths	flexible	curriculum awareness

38 percent of those working with children had no education at all relating to the field (Phillips, 1994). Well-trained teachers are necessary for excellent programs; teachers should be certified in early childhood education or child development. Other staff working with children should have training, experience, and credentials for understanding and working with young children. Teacher education institutions need to provide high-quality training from which prospective teachers can gain knowledge of young children, skill in teaching techniques, and a sense of responsibility for the whole child. Darling-Hammond contends that "my research and personal experience tell me that the single most important determinant of success for a student is the knowledge and skills of that child's teacher" (Goldberg, 2001, p. 689). It has been argued that high-quality teachers ought to be the main investment of any school or program (Darling-Hammond, 1996; Goldberg, 2001). Darling-Hammond advocates that teachers need to know how children learn, that different children learn in a variety of ways, and that teachers must know how to use a variety of teaching methods and strategies that will take children through substantive content (Goldberg, 2001). Teachers cannot succeed without content knowledge, strategies for teaching that content, and an understanding of the children that they teach.

Piaget (1970b) believed that a teacher of young children should be highly intelligent and highly trained. When teachers have quality training and education, they are more likely to make a significant impact on children's development and learning. Professional teachers must use judgment and insight that is based on knowledge and wisdom.

The teacher is the person who implements the model or program. The teacher is also the decision maker and most often determines whether a day is successful or unsuccessful. The attitudes of the teacher and the teaching staff influence every aspect of the program; their attitudes should reflect interest, enthusiasm, creativity, empathy, hope, tolerance, understanding, and care. Research on teaching effectiveness indicates that some of these qualities, in addition to flexibility, communication skills, a secure self-image, and the ability to involve children actively in learning activities, are the most desirable assets in early childhood education teachers.

Thinking teachers are people who reflect and think deeply while helping and inviting others to

> Early childhood educators must strive to be *learners* who are willing to continually study, grow, and change and to think and solve problems.

think well. The term *thoughtful teaching* is prevalent in the literature today, and it has a double meaning. Thoughtful teachers are those who are caring and sensitive to the needs of young children, on the one hand, and also demand deep thinking, problem solving, study, and decision making of themselves and those that they teach. Thoughtful teachers do everything in their power to cultivate thoughtful teaching; they raise their own standards and expectations to the highest level.

Teachers who are successful in working with young children are likely to have warm and nurturing personalities. Children do not tune in or develop a rapport with cold, uncaring teachers; warmth and love are musts for successful early childhood teachers (Greenberg, 1995). Children flourish in a classroom where they sense that the teacher deeply *cares* about them as people, about what they are learning, and about the skills that they are developing (Bosworth, 1995). When they know that the teacher genuinely cares for them, children usually strive to live up to the teacher's expectations. In addition, when they see a teacher working very hard to provide good teaching, they, in turn, have a drive to do good work (Glasser, 1990). Caring teachers create caring kids (Kohn, 1997).

Another vital quality for effective early childhood teachers is patience, because children make mistakes as they learn. Energy and enthusiasm are also important characteristics. The excellent early childhood teacher must be on the move frequently, and often very quickly, for most of the day. Enthusiasm must highlight the teacher's personality and illuminate every activity, for enthusiasm is caught, not taught. The more excited and enthusiastic the teacher is, the more eager, enthusiastic, and positive the children will be. It should also be noted that both men and women can be excellent early childhood teachers. The total personality and overall characteristics of the teacher are the critical factors, not the gender.

In addition to personal qualities that provide educational benefits for young children, teachers can also acquire skills and learn to improve their

Effective early childhood programs provide opportunities for children to solve problems that frequently arise during play activities.

teaching abilities through the development of teaching competencies. For example, to earn a CDA credential (Child Development Associate), candidates must demonstrate competency in six general areas, such as organizing the physical environment; promoting the physical and intellectual competence of children; building personal strength in children; facilitating group interaction; working with parents; and working with other staff members concerning plans, activities, and policies relating to the program. Teachers need *know-how*. They need to know how children develop and how they learn; in addi-

tion, they need to know what children actually understand and what they can do (Darling-Hammond, 1997). Knowledge in the following general areas provides a framework for competencies and is important for early childhood teachers: early childhood curriculum, planning and implementing activities, safety and health, classroom management, and teaching techniques.

> Teaching in early childhood is a complex task and requires teachers with positive teaching strengths and qualities, as well as excellent teacher preparation and practice.

To encourage high-quality teaching and competent teachers, the following appear to be significant (Darling-Hammond, 1996, 1997):

- Teachers should have standards of practice.
- Beginning teachers need a mentoring program.
- Schools need to be organized for both student and teacher learning.
- Teachers should be regularly evaluated on their teaching strengths, weaknesses, and skills.
- Professional development is a must. It needs to be a part of a teacher's daily work.
- Competent teachers need to be encouraged and rewarded for their knowledge, skills, and quality teaching.

In the right kind of environment, one that is planned to include materials and firsthand experiences, coupled with an atmosphere of teacher competency, warmth, and concern, children are likely to flourish and have the groundwork laid for positive educational attitudes. Their needs will be met in such a way that they can proceed successfully to the next level of development.

Summary

We have looked at early childhood education historically and have found that its roots go back for centuries. The early childhood education perspective dates back to the 17th century, with the beliefs

of such people as Locke, Rousseau, Pestalozzi, and Froebel. Others who have influenced early childhood education as it is practiced today include McMillan, Hill, Dewey, Freud, Montessori, Gesell,

Piaget, Vygotsky, and Erikson. Many early childhood education programs are patterned after the beliefs of particular individuals, although most programs are eclectic in nature and therefore influenced by a variety of philosophies and ideologies.

We have examined early childhood education today and have found that, perhaps more than any other aspect of education, it is characterized by variety. Demographics relating to early childhood education have been discussed, as well as some of the sociological influences. In the new millennium, early childhood concerns have focused on such social changes as abuse, poverty, violence, homelessness, working women, single-parent families, suicide, discipline, and financial support for early education and how they affect young children.

Although early childhood education has made great strides in the past and is presently moving forward, we have seen that even greater advances are necessary for the future. Few children are receiving the benefits of high-quality early childhood education. The challenge in the new century is to address these social concerns and direct our efforts toward positive influences on young children. All children should be provided with high-quality child care, regardless of their gender, race, religion, or economic situation. There needs to be increased support for the strengthening of family values, standards, traditions, experiences, and expectations.

In addition, our concern is for the quality of kindergarten and primary-grade education, which too often have an academic focus, with the main activities each day being completion of worksheets. Early childhood education should be different from other kinds of education. We need to determine how to best provide experiences that contribute to the development of the whole child, and these experiences should be available for *all* children to help them to reach their full potential.

Early childhood teachers should be highly trained and reflect thoughtfulness, enthusiasm, creativity, empathy, hope, tolerance, understanding, warmth, and nurturance. Teachers should be trained to work with children whose needs vary from those of other children.

Student Learning Activities

1. Describe your own feelings regarding early childhood education. When do you believe children should begin to receive formalized instruction? What kind of program do you prefer at this point? What kinds of early childhood education experiences did you have? Do you have positive memories?

2. Make an early childhood historical time line. It may include both people and events. What people and/or events do you personally feel have made the most significant contributions to early childhood education?

3. From your reading and observation, make a summary chart of the characteristics of children ages 3 to 8 years. Why is it important that teachers of early childhood education be aware of these characteristics in the children that they teach? What precautions should be taken in applying developmental characteristics?

4. Visit an early childhood classroom or center and write a brief report of your visit. Answer as many of the following questions as possible: In what activities were the children involved? What is the nature of the facilities, both indoors and outdoors? What kinds of resources did you observe? What kind of program is offered? How many children were there? How many teachers were there? Based on your visit, what are your feelings about early childhood education? In terms of your visit, evaluate the program with regard to advantages and/or disadvantages for the young children it serves.

5. Visit a public school that has an afterschool program for children who would otherwise have no place to go. Evaluate the program to determine whether it is developmentally appropriate. Does it emphasize formal, academic structure? If you were designing an afterschool program, how would you do it and what would it include?

6. Develop a prototype for a great early childhood teacher. Observe an early childhood teacher and describe some of her or his qualities and

characteristics. Describe some of the qualities that you have that will make you a great early childhood teacher. What qualities and competencies do you need to work to develop? How will you do this?

7. Do further in-depth research and study of the social problems that young children encounter. You may wish to select one and do a critical issues reporting of it.

Teaching Videos

Classic Piaget (six-tape series). Child Development Media, Inc.

Effective Teaching. Insight Media.

Erik H. Erikson: A Life's Work. Davidson Films.

Evaluating Preschool Education. Films for the Humanities & Sciences.

Growth of Intelligence in the Preschool Years. Davidson Films.

Learning in Context: Probing the Theories of Piaget and Vygotsky. Films for the Humanities & Sciences.

Pediatric Brain Development: The Importance of a Head Start. Films for the Humanities & Sciences.

Piaget's Developmental Theory: An Overview. Davidson Films.

Play: A Vygotskian Approach. Davidson Films.

Scaffolding Self Regulated Learning in the Primary Grades. Davidson Films.

The Seven Habits of Highly Ineffective Educators. Insight Media.

Using What We Know: Applying Piaget's Developmental Theory in Primary Classrooms. Davidson Films.

Voices from the Classroom: Dimensions of Good Teaching. Insight Media.

Vygotsky's Developmental Theory: "An" Introduction. Davidson Films.

Chapter 2

A *Developmentally Appropriate Early Childhood Program*

Developmentally appropriate practice is based on knowledge about how children develop and learn. (Bredekamp & Copple, 1997, p. 9)

Developmentally appropriate teaching means that we approach children from where they are and not from where we think they ought to be.

It is necessary for teachers to understand the developmental needs and characteristics of each age group as well as of each individual child. Developmentally appropriate practice (DAP) focuses on the whole child "while taking into account gender, culture, disabilities, and other factors that require varied applications of curriculum to meet both group and individual child needs and learning styles" (Hart, Burts, & Charlesworth, 1997, p. 4).

The curriculum is adjusted to meet the child's needs in developmentally appropriate practice. Learning activities and goals match children's development, and adequate time is provided for exploring during the various stages of learning. Teaching is not simply a matter of collecting materials and toys and selecting projects and activities for children; rather, deciding what to do and when to do it requires a sensitivity and understanding of who the children are, who their parents are, and of the developmentally appropriate

practices (Phillips, 1994). As teachers plan developmentally appropriate activities, they should ask three questions: Is this activity right for a child this age? Is this activity right for this child? Does this activity match the social and cultural contexts in which the children in this class live? (Bredekamp & Copple, 1997). In other words, the concept of developmentally appropriate practice has three components: age appropriateness, individual appropriateness, and social and cultural relevance (Bredekamp, 1997).

Everything teachers plan and do should focus on the individual child. They tailor, adjust, and adapt the curriculum to fit each child in the program, rather than expecting children to fit the program (Charlesworth et al., 1993; Elkind, 1987; Gullo, 1992). It is imperative in a developmentally appropriate perspective that the curriculum and teaching methods be age appropriate, individually appropriate, and culturally appropriate (Bredekamp, 1997). This means that similarities within an age group are considered and understood, but also that each child's individual differences are recognized. In a developmentally appropriate classroom, children are allowed to progress at their own rate, and both the curriculum and teaching strategies are relevant for all the children in the classroom (Gullo, 1992). Thus, a great deal of flexibility is required, but this does not mean a total lack of structure and academics; rather, it means that the structure and academics of the

Developmentally appropriate early childhood programs allow children opportunities to explore with a variety of toys and materials.

program are based on individual and group needs and current understanding of child development (Charlesworth et al., 1993; Raines, 1997).

Characteristics of Developmentally Appropriate Practice (DAP)

- Age and developmentally appropriate.
- Individually appropriate.
- Culturally and linguistically appropriate.
- Authentic instruction and assessment are more typical.
- Children construct knowledge based on what they already know as well as what they want to know.
- Hands-on learning experiences.
- Students have choices, although there are teacher-directed experiences.
- Students are encouraged to develop autonomy as learners and also socially.
- Play is a central ingredient in the curriculum.

- Adequate time is provided for exploring, questioning, and problem solving.
- The curriculum and school experiences are adjusted to meet the needs of the children in the classroom.
- Children progress at their own rate.
- Curriculum is dynamic and ever-changing.
- Families are important.
- A caring community is relevant to learning and development.

Children should be encouraged to engage in each stage of development fully. Their learning should be a pleasant and fascinating journey, with their motivation for learning emerging from their "natural curiosity and desire to make sense of their world" (Hart, Burts, & Charlesworth, 1997, p. 5). Teachers are viewed as facilitators and play an active role in helping children to construct their knowledge and understanding (Charlesworth et al., 1993; Raines, 1997). Recognizing the diversity in rates of intellectual attainment and mental abilities requires constant accommodation and flexibility on the part of the teacher and is a hallmark of developmentally appropriate education (Elkind, 1996). "Teachers must maintain the interest and promote the growth of children who have already demonstrated signs of early literacy and numeracy, while simultaneously encouraging the development of these behaviors in children who have not yet acquired them" (Zill & Collins, 1996, p. 17). Teachers thus need to meet the needs of children at various levels of development and view the early childhood age range as a "continuum of development rather than as discrete grade levels" (Gullo, 1992, p. 11).

Even though many educators understand and support developmentally appropriate practice, research tells us that as little as one-third to one-fifth of the early childhood programs studied actually exemplified the philosophy (Bredekamp, 1997; Bryant, Clifford, & Peisner, 1991; Hatch & Freeman, 1988; Kontos & Dunn, 1993; Oakes & Caruso, 1990; Sherman & Mueller, 1996). "Many teachers who say they believe in developmentally appropriate practice do not have developmentally appropriate classrooms" (Dunn & Kontos, 1997, p. 7). In addition, DAP is being challenged from some within the field (Raines, 1997). We have come far . . . we have a ways to go!

Some common misconceptions relating to DAP include the following:

- The teacher is not in charge.
- There is no structure in the curriculum or the classroom.
- Few skills and concepts are taught.
- DAP is a set curriculum. (Raines, 1997)

Although the teacher is in charge in a DAP classroom, children do have choices and many hands-on learning activities. There are teacher-directed experiences, but the many opportunities for choice build independence and responsibility in the young learners. There is structure in the classroom in terms of the curriculum, the space, the time, and the schedule, but this organization is sometimes hard to detect to an observer who sees children in play and making choices of various activities. Skills are learned in authentic play experiences and activities, rather than with drill and worksheets. Children can and should develop as knowledgeable, skillful, and active problem solvers, not passive, inactive, fill-the-vessel learners.

Developmentally appropriate practice is reflected not in one particular curriculum, but in the way the curriculum is carried out (Raines, 1997). Teachers practicing DAP are influenced by the constructivist approach in encouraging students' points of view and supporting the learner working in an authentic environment, making choices, and solving problems (Torp & Sage, 1998).

Bredekamp and Copple (1997, pp. 16–22) address five interrelated dimensions of incorporating developmentally appropriate practice:

- Creating a caring community of learners
- Teaching to enhance development and learning
- Constructing appropriate curriculum
- Assessing children's learning and development
- Establishing reciprocal relationships with families

Our philosophy of early childhood education has included these dimensions throughout this text, and their incorporation into classroom teaching results in successful, high-quality, developmentally appropriate classrooms and programs.

THE INAPPROPRIATENESS OF EARLY ACADEMICS

Generally, *how* we teach influences success or failure more than *what* we teach. Curriculum content, strategies, or teaching methods that put too much emphasis on intellectual achievement can misuse these early years (Elkind, 1987). There is pervasive acceptance of the proposition that young children are not smaller versions of older children (NAESP, 1990). However, there is a dangerous trend toward teaching skills earlier and earlier in educational settings, increasing the stresses and failures felt by our youth. The college curriculum is being taught in senior high school, the senior high school curriculum in junior high, the junior high in later elementary grades, the later elementary in early elementary classes, the early elementary in kindergarten, and the kindergarten in preschool.

Ten Boom (1971) writes that her father would not allow her to learn too much, too soon, too fast. She had asked him a question, the answer to which he felt she was not yet able to fully understand. He responded by asking her to carry his luggage from the train, which she was unable to do, and she said, "It's too heavy." He answered that it is the same way with knowledge. "Some knowledge is too heavy for children. When you are older and stronger you can hear it. For now you must trust me to carry it for you" (pp. 26–27). In our sometimes faulty evaluations of where children are at a specific stage of development and what they seem capable of handling, we often believe that they can "carry it." We need to consider seriously, can they? And if they can carry it right now, how long will they be able to carry it? Is it necessary for them to carry it at this point in time?

Elkind (1987, 1996) believes that the national trend toward pushing young children to achieve academically has led to using inappropriate teaching methods and developing unreasonable expectations, particularly for kindergarten and prekindergarten children. The end result has been that many of these children are pressured with too much, too soon, too fast, and they face stress and burnout early in their lives. "Parents or care givers who push children too fast or too hard can do as much damage as those who do not challenge children at all" (Newberger, 1997, p. 4).

The kindergarten scene of years gone by, of children building with blocks, painting at the easel, and dressing up, has been replaced with one of formal education practices, including workbooks, ditto sheets, paper and pencil work, and basal-based instruction (Charlesworth et al., 1993). Children who are pushed too fast, too far, too soon lose interest in learning, experience failure, are unable to think for themselves, cannot deal with stress, and often find it difficult to relate to peers.

DEVELOPMENTALLY APPROPRIATE ASSESSMENT

Educational reform and concerns about accountability have fueled a testing mania in our country that is affecting early childhood. There is increased use of standardized testing at all levels of education, as well as state-level achievement tests mandated in many states. Tests are driving teaching and the curriculum and determining the success of a particular program. It is believed that this measurement-driven curriculum is resulting in a more academic approach to early childhood curriculum (Wortham, 1997). Young children in any class do not begin the year at the same place, they certainly do not learn in the same way, and they do not learn at the same pace.

Developmentally appropriate assessment is using knowledge of age-appropriate, individually appropriate, and culturally appropriate expectations as a context for individual children's growth and learning (Bredekamp & Copple, 1997). From the perspective of developmentally appropriate practice, children are assessed or evaluated to determine curriculum needs, and the curriculum is adjusted to accommodate to these needs, to determine and diagnose the individual special needs of children, and to communicate effectively with parents (Bredekamp, 1987; Gullo, 1992; NAEYC & NAECS/SDE, 1991; Shepard, 1994). Assessment includes all the strategies and methods used to measure learning and development that affect decisions and planning on behalf of all the students (Wortham, 1997). Assessment, or the process of observing, measuring, or recording what learning has occurred or documenting the work of the child for the purpose of making educational decisions about the child, is an important part of developmentally appropriate curriculum and instruction (Bredekamp & Copple, 1997; Fleege, 1997; NAEYC & NAECS/SDE, 1991). Helm, Beneke, and Steinheimer (1997, p. 200), suggest, "documenting children's learning may be one of the most valuable skills a teacher can learn." Not only are teachers more able to understand how children learn, but they can also help others to recognize this learning as they collect, interpret, analyze, and display various evidences of learning (Helm, Beneke, & Steinheimer, 1997). One of the keys to suitable assessment is that it be used to benefit children and not to retain, track, or segregate them (Bredekamp & Shepard, 1989; NAEYC & NAECS/SDE, 1991).

A number of authors have cautioned against the use of entrance tests to determine readiness and admittance to kindergarten and suggest that these tests are often a form of bias and are abusive (Gullo, 1992; Shepard, 1994). A child's score on a developmental readiness test may be the result of inadequate social and physical experiences in his or her home environment, and the kindergarten environment may be the only place that this child could obtain these kinds of experiences (Gullo, 1992; Shepard, 1994). Our focus should be on making schools more ready for children, rather than children ready for schools or classes. Too often these kinds of tests deny the child the opportunity of having the kinds of developmental experiences

Purposes of Assessment in Early Childhood

Benefit students

Inform instruction

Diagnose individual special needs

Communicate effectively with parents

Document children's learning and progress

Monitor development of the whole child: physical, cognitive, socioemotional

Identify and serve youngsters who are at risk for development and learning

Identify those who need early intervention

Evaluate the program: evidence of the child's growth, learning, and progress also reflect success in meeting program goals

which ones should be held back (Scherer, 1996). In a longitudinal study of retention, Allington and McGill-Franzen (1995) concluded that both retention and transitional classrooms do not benefit children. "Redshirting and retention are outmoded tools that should be replaced by more appropriate practice" (Graue, 2001, p. 69).

Guidelines from the National Association for the Education of Young Children and the National Association of Early Childhood Specialists in State Departments of Education (NAEYC, 1988a & b; NAEYC & NAECS/SDE, 1991) for assessing and testing young children include the following suggestions:

- Children should enter school on the basis of their chronological age and actual legal right to enter school, rather than on what they know.
- Assessment relates to the goals of the program and should be integrated through the program.
- Assessment is used to benefit the child.
- All domains of learning and development, including physical, social, emotional, and cognitive, are routinely and informally assessed.
- Assessment recognizes and welcomes individual differences in learning styles, experiences, and rates of learning.
- Assessment focuses on what children can do, on their strengths and progress in learning and development.
- Assessment relies on a variety of processes, such as observations, interviews, portfolios, anecdotal records, and teachers' summaries of children's development and progress.
- Teacher–child ratios should be such that children have individualized instruction and children are not all doing the same thing at the same time.
- If grouping occurs, it should be flexible.
- Children should progress at their own rate and pace through the curriculum.
- Teaching methods should be appropriate for the age and developmental level of the children in the class.

that he or she needs, which is considered developmentally inappropriate practice. Tests mandated for accountability purposes have been used at all levels of education, including early childhood, to determine what is to be taught; thus, the tests at every level are driving the curriculum (Shepard, 1999). Some believe that the effort to use testing in tandem with raising standards has actually lowered the standards (Shepard, 1999). "Massive effort has produced small gains in rote skills at the expense of teaching students to reason and apply what they have learned" (Shepard, 1999, p. 171). Meisels (1993) cautions that standardized achievement group tests are especially inappropriate for assessing learning in children younger than third grade.

Far too often, when children do not measure up to preconceived readiness standards on a standardized assessment in early years, they are held back for remedial work or intervention. Individual growth rates are pronounced during these early years. The different rates at which they acquire various abilities are independent of their IQ and should not be used as a judgment for retention (Scherer, 1996). When we understand these important principles and accommodate to children's vast diversity in competencies, we focus on creating a liberating, active, and engaging program, rather than on assessing children to determine

Shepard (1994) also delineates principles for testing and assessment; and in addition to sharing some of the guidelines suggested by NAEYC and NAECS/SDE, Shepard proposes that assessments should be planned for specific purposes and the methods used in assessing should be appropriate for the experiences and developmental levels of the children being tested. Early childhood assessment should be "nonintrusive, nonstressful, and available to the child and the family" (Wortham, 1997, p. 109). Too often the testing that is done in early childhood creates the opposite effect: it is intrusive, stressful, and unavailable to family members.

As children proceed developmentally, teachers should also be cautious about judging the success of a program or activity solely on the basis of children's performance on standardized tests. Too often when children do not measure up on standardized tests, they are held back to repeat a grade (Bredekamp & Shepard, 1989; NAESP, 1990). The best measure of children's success is through careful observations by teachers and professionals who are trained observers and know the children and their developmental characteristics well (Elkind, 1987; Fleege, 1997). When standardized tests are used, they need to be valid, reliable, and used only for the purpose for which they were designed (Bredekamp & Shepard, 1989). Standardized tests are used appropriately when they are used for identification and diagnosis of delays and/or disabilities, which then lead to essential intervention services for children. Decisions that affect children educationally should be based on multiple sources of data or information and not on one test (Bredekamp & Shepard, 1989).

In developmentally appropriate practice, children do not compete for grades or scores; letter or numerical grades are not used in reporting progress to parents. Rather, in regular, intermittent sessions, progress is reported with detailed information using documented sources, and the focus is on what the child can do (NAEYC & NAECS/SDE, 1991). Another important guideline for appropriate assessment is that the whole child is considered, not just the child's academic abilities. The child's physical, social, emotional, as well as cognitive development is routinely assessed through appropriate means, including observations of what they do and listening to what they say (Fleege, 1997; NAEYC & NAECS/SDE, 1991).

Inappropriate Uses of Assessments in Early Childhood Education

Use of entrance tests to determine readiness and admittance to kindergarten

Judging the success of a program on the basis of children's performance on standardized tests

Use of tests to determine retention of children

Use of tests to compare teachers, schools, and school districts

Use of test material to determine what should be taught

Use of tests to accelerate learning

Authentic and Performance Assessment of Young Children

While standardized tests and other traditional types of assessment have as their purpose to assess what the child knows, authentic assessment appraises what the child can do or apply. It is conducted in the meaningful context of the child's work and play environment. The documentation focuses on children's experiences, thinking, ideas, and memories (Jones, 1997; Katz & Chard, 1997). The documentation may be in the form of a checklist; a portfolio that would include such things as writing, art, or other work samples; disk, tape, or video recordings of discussions with the child and showing the child at work and play or discussing opinions or understandings; photographs; detailed observations or anecdotal records; journal entries; interviews with children about their progress, including notes from the interviews; and letters or notes from teachers or parents (Collinson, 1995; Fleege, 1997; Katz & Chard, 1997; NAEYC & NAECS/SDE, 1991). Portfolios allow students the opportunity of seeing their progress and also telling the stories associated with their learning; the assessment, therefore, should focus on *potential* and not just *performance* (Chipman, 1997; Herbert & Schultz, 1996). Portfolios provide a means of organizing various types of resources and materials into a collection that can then be used to evaluate the child's progress. They can be organized by units or projects, developmental domains, content areas, or a combination of topics or themes. Current practices in how young children should be assessed favor authentic assessments (Wortham, 1997). When authentic assessments are combined with written summary reports and an organized record-keeping system, a clear picture of each child's progress and learning can be obtained and shared with parents.

Strategies for Authentic and Performance Assessment of Young Children

Portfolio collections or work samples with a specific purpose

Interviews

Projects and presentations

Games

Anecdotal records and observations

Self-assessments

Narratives

Observations and anecdotal records are one of the most effective means of assessment in early childhood. The traditional street-crossing safety reminder, "Stop, look, and listen," can help us to identify developmentally appropriate practices in assessing the development of young children. Very often we should stop what we are doing, look around to see where the children and we are, and listen for feedback, or what is being said. Then, with caution, we can go ahead. The education of young children is influenced by the quality of the assessments used.

PLAY

In a developmentally appropriate program, both the curriculum and the environment should reflect the teacher's knowledge and acceptance of the value and importance of play in early childhood. "Play is not just for recess and for fun after 'work' is finished; it's a medium through which a great deal of learning takes place" (Greenberg, 1995, p. 12). Play shapes and guides the child's

world, and is an organizing force in the child's life (Hillman, 1995). To help us to direct our thinking more toward the importance of the play environment, Rivkin (1995) suggests that we remember the places where we liked to play when we were young. Did they allow privacy, independence, or materials to arrange? Could we revisit those places now? Are they still accessible to children, or do they no longer exist? What can we do about providing "memory" places for children today? Play should be the very heart of the early childhood curriculum (Berk, 1994; Bredekamp & Copple, 1997; Brewer & Kieff, 1996/1997; Fromberg, 1999; Greenberg, 1995; Isenberg & Jalongo, 2001; Jones, 1997; NAESP, 1990; Pellegrini & Boyd, 1993; VanHorn, Nourat, Scales, & Alward, 1999). Play provides a way for young children to reinforce worthwhile, meaningful learning and cooperation with others, rather than just acquiring facts and information alone (Fromberg, 1999). Children need time, materials, and a place to explore their ideas and feelings, experience self-initiated problem solving, and experiment in an atmosphere of success. Theoretically, there is widespread acceptance of the idea that play is important—that it is serious business for the young child. However, this is a time when the push for academics in early childhood is pressing, and at the practical level, play is too often being replaced with worksheets and highly structured learning.

Children constantly remind us, through their behavior and interest, how compelling and essential play is to them.

The very word *play* is misleading. To some, it suggests frivolous leisure activities, "killing time," and recreational activities. Play does not provide a concrete, tangible, or academic end product that can be displayed to parents. It is not teacher directed. However, research verifies that play is a vehicle to enhance children's development (Bordner & Berkley, 1992; Fromberg, 1999; NAEYC & NAECS/SDE, 1991). "Play may well be the ultimate relativist integrator of development" (Fromberg, 1999, p. 45).

Good play experiences unite and blend all aspects of development, reaping social, emotional, physical, intellectual, moral, creative, and cultural benefits for young children. Good play strengthens skills and deepens understanding of concepts. It gives children opportunities to explore, experiment, create, and imagine (NAEYC & NAECS/SDE, 1991). As educators, we must recognize our responsibility to educate parents in the values and purposes of play for young children. This can be done through workshops, orientation meetings, newsletter articles, and by providing resource materials that teach the values of play.

Features of Early Childhood Play

Integrative

Meaningful

Worthwhile

Solitary or cooperative

Satisfying and personally motivating

Active

Imaginative

Symbolic (it represents reality)

Rule governed

Episodic (emerging and shifting goals)

Adapted from Fromberg, 1999, p. 28.

Play encourages positive curiosity and initiative as children become able to explore and experiment with a variety of materials. As this child fits parts of a marble game together, he discovers that it can also be used as a telescope.

Values of Play

Much has been written about the values or purposes of play. Here we discuss various purposes for play to help you to recognize its inherent values. This information will aid you in responding clearly and wisely to such queries as "Is that all my child does? Just play?" Some parents may believe that play is an important part of the home environment but question its value in school. They often feel that the school curriculum should be more involved in academics (Brewer & Kieff, 1996/1997). We need to be sensitive to these parental concerns and help parents to understand the value of play in a curriculum that fosters learning and development of children.

Play promotes significant mental or cognitive skills (Cooper and Dever, 2001). Play gives the

child opportunities to express thoughts and ideas. It provides occasions to organize, plan, discover problems, reason, try out solutions and skills, create, and explore. According to the work of Piaget (1962), play allows children to construct knowledge through assimilation, acquiring information through experiences, as well as through accommodation, or modification of an existing point of view because information cannot be integrated into a particular scheme of understanding. Play contributes to the child's development of imaginative thinking (Fromberg, 1999). Play enables children to formulate ideas and then to test them. Much skill development occurs through play. During play, children have the opportunity to develop their senses of touch, taste, smell, sound, and sight—to assimilate new stimuli (Isenberg & Jalongo, 2001). In addition, their attention spans are expanded as they stay on task and remain attentive to activities in which they are involved.

Play facilitates both divergent thinking and convergent thinking. Convergent tasks have a single answer, while divergent tasks have multiple solutions or approaches. Both kinds of thinking are important, and play provides the opportunity to practice both. Even though it is a vigorous intellectual exercise, play does not create the pressure or tension that is often associated with more structured learning approaches.

Piaget (1973) maintained that play is one of the most important functions of childhood, permitting the child to assimilate reality to self and self to reality. Many researchers feel that communication skills are developed in part through peer play and the need for children to communicate with each other in their play (Chenfeld, 1991). Play stretches the vocabulary and expands language development by providing opportunities to use new words, converse with playmates, listen to another's language and point of view, learn new semantics (meanings of words), and hear and subsequently use new syntax (parts of speech). Play synthesizes or brings together previous experiences and thinking, allowing children to piece them together. Because children communicate, listen, read, and write in their play, it offers the right condition for learning language and literacy skills (Cooper & Dever, 2001). Play also fosters creativity and aesthetic appreciation, which can influence the way children think and solve problems.

Play promotes physical–motor development. Play is active; children are never passive recipients (Jones, 1997). Children use their bodies and increase large-muscle dexterity as they run, climb, skip, hop, jump, throw, and catch. Play, therefore, provides the exercise and physical activity needed to strengthen and coordinate children's muscles and bodies. Through physical play, children can learn appropriate ways to display aggression and other assertive behaviors without hurting themselves or others. When a group of kindergarten children was quizzed about their favorite part of school, a large majority stated that they liked recess best of all. During recess, the spontaneous, self-directed activities involve mostly physical–motor play.

Play encourages positive emotional development. Play is the means for fostering a healthy personality, and it provides the opportunity for each child to discover the self. Play provides the opportunity to express thoughts and ideas and to try out ways of behaving and feeling. Play experiences provide children safe avenues for expressing both positive and negative emotions. As they express thoughts and ideas, children can learn and be directed to the most positive ways of handling their emotions. This will come through support and reinforcement by both peers and teachers.

Play is pleasurable and enjoyable (Garvey, 1990). Children use play to make up for unkindness, defects, and disappointments, as well as to play out frustrations, sufferings, fears, anxieties, and anger. In addition, play allows children to be powerful, in control, and assertive, depending on the choices and decisions made in particular play situations. Play enables children to translate feelings, thoughts, fantasies, and inclinations into action, to literally be in control and in charge of their world and feelings. Perhaps the greatest asset of self-directed, self-discovery, or spontaneous play is the satisfaction it gives children of making choices based on interests, of attaining some control over their own learning.

Freedom to experiment with materials, feelings, words, and ideas gives impetus to the development of creativity. Through carefree, unpressured play, children's imaginations invent new solutions, different approaches, and unique ideas. Even though ideas are "pretend," it is important that the ideas are created; and, one day, children will realize that their ideas must be compatible with reality.

Play allows children to develop into social human beings. Piaget (1970a) considered the theoretical relationship between play and socialization. He believed that children are naturally motivated to interact with other children and, as they do so, they become less egocentric and more aware of others. Solitary play is valuable, but in early childhood play usually means people. In play experiences, children learn to be both leaders (telling others what to do) and followers (being told what to do). They learn to try different roles and think of other possibilities (Chenfeld, 1991). They learn to give and take, to put themselves in another's position, to sense another's feelings, to hear another's point of view. They learn to share, cope with disappointment, and resolve differences (Brewer & Kieff, 1996/1997). Play provides practice in the social skills that society demands for success. It also provides practice in being less bossy, less selfish, less meek, or less shy. Play encourages a child to be a friend and a contributor, to cooperate, and to be flexible.

As teachers plan the time that children spend in their classrooms, they must remember the inherent values of play for its own sake and for the behaviors it directly affects. They must not structure and arrange so much of the school time that inadequate time is left for spontaneous, self-directed free-play periods. In terms of values and benefits, these periods may well be the most important times of the day, and children should not be robbed of them. Every day should have one or more blocks of time for spontaneous play.

The lesson plans suggested in this book are activity oriented, and many of the activities listed are to be included in the free-play or self-directed, spontaneous play period, in addition to the centers that are a regular part of the room environment.

Play facilitates:

Learning

Development

Thinking and problem solving

Social development

Skill development

Sensory awareness

Attention span and listening

Language acquisition and communication

Physical and motor development

Healthy emotional development

Autonomy

Imagination

Metacognition (thinking about one's own thinking)

Developmental Play Stages

Like other aspects of development, play progresses through stages, with one stage preparing the way for the next. Observing play behavior is an important aspect of gaining an understanding of children's development. Play is a manifestation of the child's social development. As one understands the stage of play in which each child is primarily functioning, appropriate social and group experiences can be determined. For example, if the majority of children in the group are toddlers and observation determines that their play behavior is primarily solitary, onlooking, and parallel, this indicates a need for most of the classroom play to be spontaneous or free play. Group activities should be short and few in number. [It should be noted that children with disabilities progress through the same stages of play as other children, but at their own rate (Bordner & Berkley, 1992)].

Parten (1932, 1933) suggested dividing play by the social interaction that takes place among children during their play. During solitary play, the child acts alone and independently of others. Children, as they mature, may still seek solitary play as a means of getting away from it all or because they are goal directed and have something they desire to accomplish. In onlooking play, the child spends much time watching others play. In parallel play, the child individually plays with toys similar to those used by nearby children. Its purpose may be to allow children to become acquainted with one another or to gain social acceptance, or it may serve as a transition between solitary and more cooperative, interactive play. During associative play, children engage in basically the same activity, but no attempt is made to divide the play tasks or to organize the activity. In cooperative play, children organize in a group for some purpose. In this give-and-take interaction, they share not only materials and equipment, but also ideas and goals. Cooperative play is the ultimate play behavior that parents and early childhood teachers seek. Generally, solitary and parallel play decline during the preschool years, while associative and cooperative play tend to increase as children approach kindergarten.

Play experiences provide an opportunity to try out social behaviors, that is, to put social development and thought into action. They build social skills that allow the child to move to higher levels or stages of play. However, it is still developmentally appropriate for children who have reached the cooperative stage of play to occasionally enjoy solitary, parallel, and associative play.

Play Stages

Solitary play: child acts alone

Onlooking play: child watches others

Parallel play: child individually plays with toys and materials similar to those used by children who are nearby

Associative play: child engages in the same activity as other children, but in an unorganized, disassociated way

Cooperative play: child organizes in a group for some purpose and with other children shares materials, equipment, ideas, and goals

Partin 1932, 1933.

Fostering Positive and Meaningful Play Experiences

Contact with others, both adults and children, is more important in fostering positive play experiences than materials and toys. Children develop empathy, understanding, and sensitivity to each other by relating to each other. Human relationship skills come from firsthand experiences of learning to give and take, to sense another's feelings and needs, to share kindnesses in words and deeds (Glasser, 1997). Teachers provide models of these human qualities and encourage their development during play situations. The teacher's positive attitude, interest in individual children and groups, and enthusiasm for play experiences will be transferred to the children and influence their attitudes toward play and the meaning that they draw from their play experiences.

The Teacher's Role in Play Experiences

The teacher's role is to value, provide for, encourage, guide, and supervise the play of young children. However, the teacher does not become the object of the play or the center of attraction or dictate what the child can or should do in the play activity. Teachers should be available to support, assist, observe, interact when appropriate to do so, and indirectly channel misbehavior, as well as to

Creative arts areas in the early childhood classroom include paints and brushes, glue, scissors, crayons, and markers.

direct and encourage positive behaviors. Teachers encourage play by modeling, planning with children, and playing with language (Fromberg, 1999). In order for play to be sustained or extended, children often need adult suggestion, intervention, or stimulation, but once limits have been established and children are comfortable with their environment, adults should interfere as little as possible.

Teachers can make suggestions for play activity and, through play, expand the children's language development, increase conceptual understanding, answer questions, and encourage new social interactions and friendships (Saracho, 1999). Perhaps the most important contribution that they can make to foster children's play is to provide ample time for play and create adequate protected space for playing (Balke, 1997).

During their play, children need opportunity for making choices; this is student-centered learning. One of the best means for creating student engagement in learning is to allow children the opportunity to make decisions (Kohn, 1993a). As they make choices, they feel in control, which results in their being able to accept responsibility (Kelman, 1990). However, children's interest will dwindle, and they may even stop playing, if teachers interfere too much or try to structure their play for them. Play is more valuable when children plan, define, shape, and carry out their own play activities (Kohn, 1993a). However, the teacher's role must not be diminished. Play should not be used as a reward for children who finish their work. Rather, it has to be planned for by the teacher, expected of all children, and encouraged and understood by parents. Well-planned play during early childhood is more important than adult instruction or formal, structured learning activities. Play comes from within the child and is natural. Children are intrinsically motivated to play, and it is enjoyable to them (Gullo, 1992).

Although the teacher is important, other children provide the greatest source of complex play. Toys and materials do not sustain play as well as other children. Peers are thus an important part of the play environment.

No matter how elaborate the physical facilities are with regard to play, the quality of these environments is determined by the caregivers. They are the ones who evaluate the function of materials, space, time, and people and determine how to appropriately meet the needs of the children (Zeavin, 1997).

PROVIDING DEVELOPMENTALLY APPROPRIATE MATERIALS

Children need carefully selected, developmentally appropriate materials that meet the age range of children in the classroom (Bredekamp, 1986). A particular piece of equipment can be enjoyed by children ages 3 to 8, but the older the child, the more advanced and complex it must be. The structure, as well as the style, of children's play and play materials becomes more diverse and complex as children mature. Teachers should be aware of developmental age characteristics and learn to sense what comes next. For example, puzzles and matching materials are enjoyed by a broad age range of children; however, younger children need fewer pieces in order to prevent frustration and foster success. Older children can manage more puzzle or matching pieces; however, age is not the determining factor here, but the developmental abilities of the child. For younger children, simple concepts such as shape and color should be presented, rather than concepts such as time, money, and more complex shapes. Age-appropriate materials, equipment, and toys are suitable for the child's interests and abilities, and children gain most from materials matched to their stage of development. We need to consider the kinds of interests, motivation, and skills that we want children to pursue when we select play materials. These materials should support future development in young children and have lasting play value (Bronson, 1995).

Selecting and Using High-Quality Commercial Toys and Equipment

The market is saturated with toys and early childhood equipment, and it is imperative that in a developmentally appropriate classroom educators make wise and careful selections.

Teacher-Made Learning Materials

In many instances, limited budgets determine the quantity and quality of the equipment and materials that can be purchased. In addition, many com-

General Criteria for Selecting Commercial Equipment, Toys, and Other Materials

1. The equipment should be appropriate for the children's ages, levels of development, abilities, needs, and interests.
2. A good piece of equipment encourages participation and involvement, not just observation and entertainment. It should stimulate independent activity.
3. The equipment should be versatile or open ended, allowing for additional creative and inventive potential.
4. The equipment should be simple and as free of detail as possible. This encourages versatility, imagination, variety, and appeal.
5. The equipment should be durable, safe, and sanitary and be repaired immediately when broken. When purchasing equipment, it is wise to find out whether extra pieces or parts are available to replace those that may be lost or broken.

mercial toys are restricted in terms of their learning potential. Equipment, materials, and games can easily be made from accessible and inexpensive supplies. This section focuses on materials that contribute to conceptual, perceptual, and language development, in addition to supporting the concepts presented throughout this book.

Equipment and materials are tools for the teacher to use in teaching and reinforcing learning, as well as for the child to enjoy through play. They provide the child with the opportunity to develop concepts such as color, shape, and number, as well as visual perception and eye–hand coordination. Children also use skills that provide the foundation for developing abilities and understanding in reading, writing, and mathematical operations.

Wisely selected equipment and materials can be used in a variety of ways, including child-initiated and teacher-initiated activities. Frequently, when the child initiates the play, it may simply (but importantly) involve exploration. Teachers can suggest, model, or prod, but ultimately the children should determine how they want to use equipment and materials (Kohn, 1993a; Levin, 1994).

To sustain and extend play, a teacher could suggest additional ways of working with a material. The teacher could ask, "Have you ever thought about how the beads would look on the string if they were strung in a pattern such as two reds and then one blue, two reds and then one yellow, and so on?" In teacher-initiated play, a teacher usually invites the child to play with the equipment and may suggest ways of using the materials or even establish rules for games such as dominoes. Both kinds of play, child initiated and teacher initiated, are valuable, and the selection of either depends on the individual situation and children.

It should be emphasized that, although many materials themselves stimulate children's imaginations for use, guided help and teacher assistance are needed in order to focus on the concept being emphasized. A set of shape dominoes may be used as blocks or for building corrals and fences. This is important and of great value. However, as play progresses, the children should be shown how to play shape dominoes with the blocks. Teachers do not always need to play with and near children, but there are both intellectual and emotional advantages in doing so. Positive teacher–child relationships can be strengthened when teachers enjoy focusing on the use of materials and discussing basic concepts with the children.

A teacher understands the learning potential and use of manipulative materials by playing with and using them with the children. This provides a valuable opportunity for learning about each child's conceptual development. It is also an excellent time for visiting personally with children and becoming better acquainted with their needs, emotions, desires, and interests.

In deciding which equipment to make for enhancing classroom learning, remember that teacher-made materials should be prepared using basically the same criteria used in selecting commercial materials and equipment. Be flexible in considering the various ways that each material can be used. Many materials adapt to play by one child, many children, child and teacher, or children and teacher. Figure 2–1 shows some examples of teacher-made materials.

(Appendix A includes lists of suggested materials for use in preparing teacher-made learning materials.)

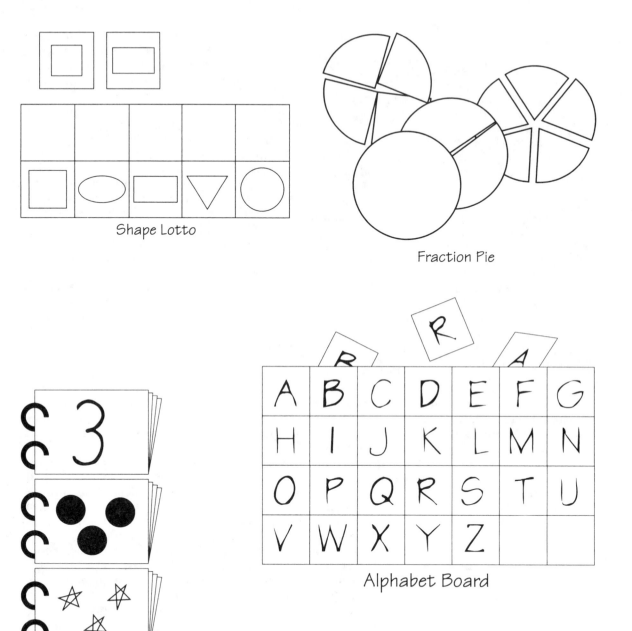

Shape Lotto

Fraction Pie

Number Book

Alphabet Board

FIGURE 2–1
Examples of Teacher-Made Materials

Properly chosen toys and materials facilitate the children's play as well as foster a developmentally appropriate program. Wisely selected teacher-made learning materials contribute to conceptual, perceptual, and language development. The effectiveness of the equipment depends on its arrangement, display, and organization; periodic rotation; and care and maintenance. Play is of value whether it is child initiated or teacher initiated when the materials have been selected wisely, with care and understanding of young children's developmental needs.

PREPARING A DEVELOPMENTALLY APPROPRIATE AND CURRICULUM SUPPORTIVE PHYSICAL SETTING

When a teacher recognizes and understands the developmental needs of young children, planning appropriate play experiences and organizing a suitable curriculum are facilitated. This knowledge also positively influences the physical setting, which includes both the outdoor play area and the indoor classroom. These two areas must be planned to focus on the needs of the children, while supporting the curriculum and what is being taught. With regard to providing developmentally appropriate play environments, Rivkin (1995, pp. 9, 10) proposes a couple of thought-provoking questions: Is it possible that hyperactivity, in part, could be a "cultural disease" and "that if children were not as confined as they are, their activity level would not be so disruptive? Would active play, if in an outdoor setting rather than indoors, be more tolerated?"

Teachers should know and understand the age characteristics of children so that they can identify developmental changes and needs at different stages in order to select the proper equipment, materials, toys, furniture, and other learning aids. Then, through needs assessment and careful observation, materials can be added or deleted, depending on their appropriateness for the children.

The physical setting or environment has a great impact on the child in both an affective and a cognitive way. Feelings engendered in the child by the environment should include a sense of order, enthusiasm, interest, curiosity, cleanliness, and safety. The environment contributes to setting the tone of the school day for both the children and the teacher. An organized, attractive, clean, and cheerful or "warm" setting results in more positive behaviors and attitudes. In addition, the environment should offer opportunities for learning and increasing skill in all developmental areas: physical, social, emotional, cognitive, and language. Children need and deserve an environment conducive to learning, growing, positive behavior, and good play.

Guidelines for Arranging the Early Childhood Classroom

The materials and equipment should be appropriate for the developmental level of the children in the class (NAESP, 1990). Indoor and outdoor environments should be set up and arranged to avoid situations that naturally frustrate or anger children. For example, a mixture of toys or materials should not be stored in the same box. If a child desires to play with a soldier that happens to be in the bottom of the box and dumps out the whole box of toys in order to obtain the soldier, the child may become angry or frustrated when told to pick up all the other toys. The child may honestly say, "But I didn't play with all the toys, only the soldier." Also, toys and equipment should be complete and in good repair. It is frustrating to put a puzzle together only to find that a piece is missing. Some incomplete or unrepaired materials are unsafe. For example, worn, rough wooden blocks can cause slivers; vehicles missing wheels or broken parts can be dangerously sharp.

When the physical setting is arranged with the needs of the children in mind and combined with planning, thought, and purpose, learning opportunities increase and a more orderly environment results. The physical setting strongly influences the behavior and learning activities of children.

Guidelines for a Developmentally Appropriate Physical Setting

1. Equipment and materials must be the correct size and height for children. This means that pictures and bulletin boards should be placed at the child's eye level, not the teacher's. Coathooks, cupboards, shelves, and other materials or items should be where the children can reach them. For comfort

and availability, chairs and other furniture pieces should be the appropriate size.

2. The room should be organized and uncluttered. A disorderly environment frequently ignites similar behavior in children. Classrooms are more orderly and interesting when teachers avoid putting everything out at once. For example, if your classroom has six puzzles, put only one or two out at a time. However, there must be enough toys for all children to have something to play with. Material for specific areas or learning centers in the room should be kept separate. As part of cleanup, children should be encouraged to put toys and materials away where they belong.

3. Make certain the room is free of stereotypes. Pictures, toys, materials, dress-up clothes, and other objects should reflect the diversity of people and genders.

4. Consider the traffic flow when planning the room arrangement. Eliminate long corridors or "running spaces" that encourage children to run. Break up long spaces, for example, with a trough filled with sensory media. Arrange art areas near a sink for easy access to cleanup. By wisely planning the environment, teachers can indirectly manage behavior; this is referred to as behavior prevention.

5. Where possible, keep noisy areas close together and apart from quiet areas. For example, it would not be wise to put a music area with a rhythm band right next to the story area (Crosser, 1992).

6. The classroom and outdoor areas must be clean, neat, and cheerful. The physical environment must be clean for health and sanitary reasons alone. Cheerful, bright touches, combined with carefully selected bulletin board pictures, can support the unit theme being studied. Photographs of the children at work on projects and activities should be placed at a level for them to enjoy. Their pictures and work should also be displayed in the room, and a comment or question a child makes during an activity can be placed alongside the child's work (Katz, 1990). Be careful not to add too many displays; simplicity is a guideline for the entire physical setting, including the bulletin boards.

7. The organization and setup of the room should encourage children to keep the room orderly while developing classifying, categorizing, or matching skills. In the block area, for example, trace a pattern for each size and shape of the small unit blocks on solid-colored, adhesive-backed paper. Then organize and sequence these patterns on the block shelf so that the children can match the blocks to the pattern and, at the same time, organize the block area. Another possibility is to put hooks in the housekeeping area and then place a picture of a hat, dress, or slacks above specific hooks. This encourages children to sense that objects have a place to be put and facilitates matching and classifying. Pictures of fruits, vegetables, and dairy products can be glued in specific locations of the refrigerator. A similar method can be used in the stove and cupboard by gluing pictures that will help children to classify and match items to be placed in these areas. Tools can be hung on a pegboard and matched to their shape (Crosser, 1992).

8. Teachers should be able to see and supervise all areas of the room. Place tall cabinets and shelves against the wall, and use shorter cabinets and shelves as area dividers.

9. Consider the care and storage of equipment and materials. For example, to facilitate the cleanup of paint or glue brushes, have some cans or containers of water to put brushes into immediately after use so that the paint or glue will not harden. Ideally, there will be clean, orderly, organized storage areas outside the classroom, or higher than the children's reach, where some materials can be stored. Other materials and supplies such as paints, paper, pencils, and paint shirts should be accessible to children so that they can take responsibility for getting them and putting them away (Casey & Lippman, 1991; Crosser, 1992).

10. Rotating and changing areas and materials often create interest and predictable be-

havior changes. You may ask, "Will children be secure in an environment that is frequently changed?" The answer is yes. The teacher provides the security, while the changing environment encourages interest, learning, fun, and interaction among children. Children need variety and become bored with toys that are not rotated (Rogers & Sawyers, 1988).

11. Each area, piece of equipment, and material should have purpose and meaning. In evaluating areas and equipment, ask such questions as "Why am I using this?" and "What am I trying to accomplish?" Remember that the physical setting should serve the needs and interests of the children in the classroom.

12. Materials and equipment should be versatile in order to lend themselves to a variety of uses and activities.

Arranging the Environment with Areas to Meet Developmental Needs

The room should be divided into areas, with each area providing opportunities to satisfy the developmental needs of children. If a child avoids a particular area over a period of time, the teacher should encourage the child to use this area. Avoidance may be an indication of insecurity or unsureness with the particular area.

Kindergarten and first- and second-grade children may find a contract helpful to promote on-task behavior. A contract is an individualized activity plan that incorporates both teacher guidance and student interests. Contracts can also effectively guide children to all learning areas. Figure 2–2 includes examples of sample contracts for use with young children. As a child participates in each activity or area, he or she colors in the square or checks in the box. Study of individual contracts for several days alerts teachers to areas or activities that the children are not participating in as well as those in which they are interested. Contracts also serve as a means of assessment and as a springboard for parent–teacher discussions and conferences. The first example would be used for children 3, 4, and 5 years of age,

and the second example would be used for 6-, 7-, and 8-year-old children.

Children can be enabled to choose areas or centers by placing pictures or names of the centers on a board and hooks under each that determine how many children can be in this center. When children want to go to a particular center, they put their name or picture on the hook under the name or picture of the center. It has been shown that even preschool children can be effective planners, and approaches such as this help them to focus on their choices (Casey & Lippman, 1991).

Because these areas of the room satisfy various needs, they should be organized, orderly, inviting, and on the child's level. Areas can occasionally be changed or modified to maintain motivation and interest. For example, weekly rotation of toys in the manipulative area will stimulate new exploration. Sensory and creative areas can be changed more frequently, depending on the space, the theme or project, and the balance of planned activities.

The physical setting should support the curriculum whenever possible, with the room setup and outdoor playground correlating with the unit theme being presented. For example, if the current theme is "fish," the block area could be converted into a large fishing pond, with the large hollow blocks set up as the banks of the pond. Fish cutouts with attached paper clips could be caught in the pond, using fishing pole magnets. Also, an aquarium or trough containing live fish could be used as a learning area. Bulletin boards could feature fish and fishing. Another example of adapting a room area to a theme, in this case "mail and the mail carrier," is to convert the jungle gym into a mail truck by using colored butcher paper and a little imagination.

The following areas are suggested for early childhood classrooms. The size of the room may limit the use of all areas at one time, and the more areas in a classroom, the more complex the physical setting.

Outside play areas   will be determined by the facility and what is available. The playground should have appropriate permanent pieces of equipment such as domes, slides, various climbing apparatus, nesting climbers with boards and bridges, and an adjustable basketball standard and backboard.

FIGURE 2–2
Sample Contracts

NAME:

- ☐ READING
- ☐ CREATIVE ARTS
- ☐ LISTENING
- ☐ BLOCKS
- ☐ WRITING — Once upon a time
- ☐ SCIENCE
- ☐ MATH — $X > 27$ $X = \boxed{?}$
- ☐ MUSIC
- ☐ SOCIAL STUDIES
- ☐ MANIPULATIVE
- ☐ OUTDOOR PLAY

Items such as barrels, inner tubes, and other salvage pieces can often be purchased inexpensively. Versatile modular gym systems can be set up in a variety of ways for use both indoors and outdoors.

Large-muscle areas include equipment for large-muscle development. Dome climbers or jungle gyms are ideal for large rooms because they can be moved to different areas. Other large-muscle development equipment includes balance beams, slides, indoor jumping trampolines, and nesting climbers set up in a variety of ways. It is important to plan *how* the equipment will be set up each day and to plan in such a way as to facilitate the physical and motor needs of both the group and individual children (Poest et al., 1990). Some types of smaller jungle gyms fold flat for easy storage and are more appropriate in smaller areas.

Dramatic play areas provide opportunities for role playing, trying out, pretending, and acting out familiar and imaginary experiences. "Preparing for and engaging in sociodramatic play provides a nonthreatening, child-centered environment where children teach, learn, and experience real-life roles" (Cooper & Dever, 2001, p. 62). Playing house seems to be the most often preferred theme for young children; grocery stores and doctor's offices also spark interest. Teachers or other adults can function in a variety of roles, including onlooker, stage manager, supporter, or play leader (Cooper & Dever, 2001). Additional possibilities are suggested later in the chapter.

Sensory play areas may include a trough, tubs, or other possible methods of setting up media for sensory exploration. Such media might include water, sand, clay, wheat, Styrofoam packing pieces, sawdust, or other available material. Such tools as funnels, bottles, shovels, scoops, cups, beaters, or other items also add occasional interest.

Creative arts areas provide media from paints, collage materials, chalk, charcoal, crayons, felt-tipped markers, colored pencils, and other sources to be used with paper on easels, tables, floors, or walls.

Block areas are often near or part of the large-muscle area. Many classrooms are large enough to accommodate both large and small unit blocks.

The block area (especially when it includes large, hollow blocks), the large-muscle area, and sometimes the outdoor play area give children opportunities to develop strength, coordination, and balance. Manipulative and creative toys such as small cars, farm animals, zoo animals, or human figures used together with blocks can stimulate block play and provide variety. If you use human figures, make sure that they reflect diverse people.

Science areas or interest centers are often part of the early childhood classroom, especially for supporting science unit themes. For example, during a theme on "color," provide different activities such as color mixing. The science area could be a table with items, displays, or simple experiments that focus on helping children to explore their environment. Magnifying glasses or microscopes encourage additional exploration and study. Also include items involving math and measuring.

A "book nook" or library area provides a place to explore the world through books. Books should be selected to meet the developmental needs of the children and can support the theme or concepts being taught. The entire book supply should not be displayed at one time; occasional book rotation stimulates renewed interest. When a book is selected, there should always be a rug, chair, or table nearby for reading or being read to. Some of their favorite books will be those that they author; these may be individual or class projects and may or may not relate to the theme or project being explored. Also include magazines, newspapers, puppets, flannel board stories, paper, and writing implements.

Music areas are places where children listen to music, sing, play musical instruments, or perform creative dances. Additional equipment should include appropriate tapes or records and/or rhythm band instruments.

Manipulative play areas include small blocks, pegboards, puzzles, number games, bead-stringing activities, magnetic games, and other like equipment. Puzzles and other toys should show diversity and should not have any stereotypic images (Derman-Sparks & A.B.C. Task Force, 1989). Display shelves, tables, and chairs help to extend interest spans.

Opportunities to explore musical experiences and equipment encourage social interactions, and the ability to follow instructions.

Computer or technology area includes computers with developmentally appropriate software. Carefully selected hardware and software require teachers with technology training.

Lockers or cubbies may be inside or outside the classroom. Individual children should have a place with their name for storing belongings and hanging outerwear. If these spaces are inside the classroom, they could also serve as places for children to sit for quiet meditation or solitude. These areas need to be carefully and appropriately selected according to the developmental needs of the children and the concepts being taught and reinforced. Although we have not attempted to list the room areas in the daily plans and lesson plans, we assume that they will be well thought out. Remember to vary these areas and change them often to ensure continued interest and variety. In the plans suggested in this book, we have included

individual activities that could be used on specific days and for theme reinforcement.

Learning centers are designed to promote concepts and competencies to be explored independently and are planned according to the developmental needs and abilities of the children in the group.

Interest centers are based on the interests of the children in the classroom. For example, if a child brings in a rock, this may be the stimulus for an interest center on rocks that could include materials, books, and other rocks brought by the children.

THEORIES OF LEARNING

The early years are learning years. The learning and development in the early years are critical to the child's long-term well-being. Young children do not learn the same way as older children and adults. Developmentally, children these ages have short attention spans; their thinking is egocentric and often illogical. They learn best from concrete, manipulative, sensory, and firsthand experiences. Young children are in a unique period of development and need learning experiences that match their level of development. Developmentally appropriate classrooms pay attention to how children best learn (Heckman, Confer, & Hakim, 1994; Perrone, 1994). In many classrooms, curriculum goals and expectations do not match the developmental level of the children. Rather than change the curriculum, they retain children, raise the entrance age for the program, or provide a transitional year between two levels or grades.

There is an established theoretical base in early childhood education today that guides thinking and provides a framework of understanding for how children learn. Since the 1950s and 1960s the field has been particularly influenced by the constructivist perspective, a view that is based on the theories of Piaget (1896–1980) and Vygotsky (1896–1934). The *constructivist* point of view supposes that children construct their own knowledge through their own experiences, with much of the learning originating from inside the child (Kamii & Ewing, 1996). Constructivist theory puts the learner in the center and believes that teachers should provide "experiences that allow learners to link prior knowledge to the topic at hand, dispel misconceptions, and enrich their knowledge base" (Garmston & Wellman, 1994, p. 84). The constructivist teacher organizes the classroom with children's stages of development in mind (Raines, 1997).

Piaget (1952, 1955) proposed that all people are active organisms who go through a series of developmental stages and who learn from their experiences. Each child constructs, organizes, and modifies an elaborate network of ideas and concepts called cognitive structures or schemata. He defined four stages of development (see the box). Because of Piaget's work, learning is viewed as an active, constructive process in which students seek organization and meaning in their worlds. The curriculum is designed with concrete experiences presented first, followed in later years with more abstract and detailed ideas.

Piaget's Four Stages of Cognitive Development

1. Sensorimotor (1–2 years). Preverbal stage. Infant is active imitator and initiator of behavior. Learns through muscles and senses.
2. Preoperational or representation stage (2–7 years). Language becomes a primary tool for learning. Labels or words become linked to experiences; although they are abstract symbols, they stand for concrete things. Child is concrete, nonevaluative thinker who takes things as they are or as they look; therefore, firsthand, manipulative experiences are needed. Have difficulty taking another perspective. Abstract concepts should be avoided.
3. Concrete operational (7–11 years).
4. Formal operation (11–15+ years).

Vygotsky's (1962, 1978) basic assumption is that children's knowledge, ideas, attitudes, and values are developed from interaction with others. The social context of the child's learning therefore becomes significant; children learn when they collaborate with others, discussing and talking about the how and why of things. Also then, for Vygot-

sky, the role of language is critical in cognitive development and learning (Raines, 1997). It is the means for expressing ideas, asking questions, and providing concepts for thinking.

In still another theoretical view, Abraham Maslow (1968, 1970) focused on human potential and proposed that all persons strive to reach the highest within them. His theory also asserts that children learn best when their physical needs are met and they feel a sense of psychological safety and security. Curriculum then understands and respects these basic needs in order to be most effective.

The *behaviorist* theory emphasizes the roles of environmental conditions (stimuli) and overt behaviors (responses) in learning. The behaviorist teacher seeks to arrange the environment to structure and help children to learn. The basic assumption of this theory, whose primary architect was B. F. Skinner (1904–1990), is that children learn through the effects of their own intentional responses. According to this theory (Skinner, 1953), consequences determine whether a person will repeat a particular behavior that led to the consequences. The effect of these consequences may serve as a punishment or a reward.

Although we recognize the complexity of learning, we propose a variety of ingredients that are all a part of the process by which young children acquire knowledge, meaning, and understanding: (1) experiences, (2) choices and decisions, (3) curiosity and questioning, (4) communication and talking, (5) modeling and scaffolding, (6) stories, and (7) interaction with others. Delineating these specific ingredients is not to say that there are not other ingredients in the learning mix. From our experiences, observations, and reading, we feel that these are some of the key ingredients and need the attention and understanding of early childhood educators. Through these ingredients children can acquire process skills such as observing, inferring, reasoning, rationalizing, exploring, and classifying, in addition to developing the abilities to think or thoughtfully approach ideas and problems. While studying these ingredients as discussed in the following section, keep in mind the earlier discussion on the need to avoid pushing academics, thereby eliminating unnecessary pressure from teaching too much, too soon, too fast.

THE EXCITEMENT OF EARLY CHILDHOOD LEARNING

We need only follow the daily paths of children and experience their enthusiasm for learning to realize that the acquisition of knowledge is exciting. There is spontaneity in children as they gain new understandings: their bodies move, their faces smile, their eyes dance with anticipation. This zest for learning is often lost as an individual matures. A new discovery made at any age should stimulate an intrinsic sense of fulfillment within oneself. The challenge is therefore to preserve and foster the curiosity and inquisitiveness of the young child. They need active, experiential learning that provides them with many opportunities for questioning. Children's own questions can serve as springboards to curriculum study and guide the learning (Clark, 1997; Dillon, 1988; Eliason, 1996).

Much of the learning taking place in today's classrooms and early childhood centers results from planned curriculum experiences and activities based on children's needs. However, opportunities for learning abound in the child's environment beyond that which is teacher prepared. *Incidental* or *spontaneous learning* is constantly taking place as the child gives to and receives from the existing resources of the world. "Sometimes these incidental, in-between, hang-loose, unstructured, spontaneous times together are our *best* times. Perhaps these times will be remembered longest and with the most fondness by the child, and by ourselves" (Chenfeld, 1997, p. 475). Vygotsky (1978) described spontaneous concepts as those that the child discovers in contrast to school-learned concepts that emerge from the social experience the school provides. It is refreshing to observe, as in the following illustration, a young child in the process of discovery during a spontaneous learning experience.

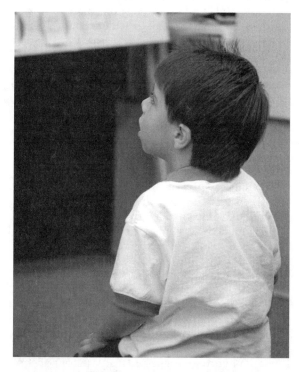

Awe and anticipation are evident as this boy watches while a visitor demonstrates how pizza dough is made, tossed into the air, and spread with toppings for eating during snack.

> Jalana painted with horizontal strokes of alternating black and white paint that had been placed at the easel. As the two colors ran together, her eyes expressed discovery, and she exclaimed, "I made gray!"

Experiences

Children in the stage of early childhood need a strong and sound base of experiences that will provide a foundation for later learning. Children in this stage develop meaning and understanding as a result of concrete, real experiences (NAESP, 1990). They need a variety of experiences around a single notion. One idea should be approached from different angles, remembering that a single experience is not usually enough to build a reliable intellectual concept. Children need experiences that encourage them to manipulate, explore, use their senses, build, create, discover, construct, take apart, question, and ultimately understand the world in which they are living. Children use their experiences to provide the basis for interpreting, conceptualizing, and categorizing into meaningful ideas. They must be active, engaged, and involved in their learning (Sylvester, 1995).

Children do not think the same way that adults or older children do, and they learn in many different ways (Elkind, 1982, 1996). They absorb information through concrete experiences involving smelling, tasting, hearing, seeing, and touching; they are sensory learners. Children are constantly absorbing meaning by observing their environment. As important as the sense of sight is, one must realize that children also need numerous other sensory experiences. Activities involving all the senses provide firsthand experiences from which the child selects and incorporates information into the development of concepts.

Young children learn and construct their knowledge through many different experiences with the objects, people, and events of the world in which they live. As these odd bits of knowledge collected through this variety of experiences are combined, meaning results. These become the bits and pieces that make up children's "maps" or understanding of their world and dictate to them how to behave. The larger the stock of experiences, the more meaning that they develop and the more elaborate is their map and, ultimately, the clearer their thinking.

Participation provides concrete knowledge from which clear understanding evolves.

Mrs. Harris, in her Head Start center, told the children a story about a donkey. When she asked what a donkey looked like, she realized that the children had never actually seen one. The next day when school began, Mrs. Harris confidently walked into the classroom, leading behind her a reluctant donkey—one which the children could experience firsthand.

Learning and information must be congruous with what has already been understood (Gullo, 1992). Teachers must start where the learner is. When a notion is understood by the child, it is stored in the mind to be added to the collection of other concepts. In further experiences, the child calls on the material already compiled to help to understand the new ideas. Teachers need to accept the individualized approach to education by being cognizant of their responsibility to make the information that they teach compatible with what

each child already knows. To provide for each child at each point in development the most stimulating circumstances is their challenge; this is developmentally appropriate practice.

Children make generalizations as they build relationships among concepts by relying on information previously accumulated. Without a broad base of direct encounters from which to generalize, children cannot move toward abstract reasoning. Before certain conceptual strategies can be learned, specific levels of cognitive development must be achieved. Learning needs to be continuous; new material encountered must correspond with skills previously assimilated. Children can understand only the things that past knowledge has prepared them to grasp.

Choices and Decisions

Child-centered or child-oriented learning engages the student in the learning process more deeply because the child takes more responsibility for his or her own learning. The call for child-centered learning is becoming ubiquitous, with many suggesting that this teaching practice is a key ingredient in improving educational productivity (Chard, 1992, 1994; Garmston & Wellman, 1994; Glasser, 1997; Heckman, Confer, & Hakim, 1994; Kohn, 1997; Levin, 1994; Lopez & Schultz, 1996; Perrone, 1994; Smith, 1993; Wolk, 1994). Allowing children to control as well as to construct their own learning is the central perspective in the constructivist philosophy of teaching (Schifter, 1996; Zahorik, 1995). Glasser (1997) suggests that a primary need in school reform is to focus on the students and their needs, rather than on the curriculum. He proposes that students work at their own pace and be given choices, rather than being coerced into their work. There should be at least one block of time in the school day in which children can decide what to do (Kohn, 1993a). It has also been suggested that students would be more engaged in their learning if teachers would give them choices of topics to be studied or at least choices about the specific ideas and questions within a general topic to be explored (Kohn, 1993a). Others have suggested that, with our diverse classrooms, more complex learning problems are created, and this creates a shift toward more student-centered learning (Newby, Stepich, Lehman, & Russell, 2000).

One key event in the "project approach" as outlined by Chard (1992, 1994) is the involvement of children in directing the course of the learning during a project study. The children's questions guide the learning and what is to be studied, and they are involved in all phases of the project. Their past experiences are used as relevant information, and their choices and interests determine what they do throughout the project.

When projects and activities are child chosen, they stem from the child's own interests and therefore have purpose. Projects often are directed by questions the students want answered. "When children are allowed to choose what to explore, they become intrinsically motivated—more than happy to work hard and strive for the highest quality" (Wolk, 1994, p. 43). When teachers capitalize on this ingredient in the learning process, their role changes from filling the vessel to facilitating learning. Teachers, rather than telling and asking questions, watch, listen, challenge, offer suggestions, or lend support; they become guides and resources (Wolk, 1994).

Curiosity and Questioning

Curiosity, another important element in early cognitive development, impels a child to reach out to the environment. An adult can help foster children's curiosity by encouraging them to explore, answering their questions, and being an example of a curious person. Children's surroundings should be kept rich with concrete, sensory, manipulative experiences that allow them to satisfy their curiosity through their senses.

Most people are born with an intrinsic drive to learn about and explore their world. Curiosity is the drive to learn. To touch, observe, listen, think about, and evaluate the things around them is the way young children learn. To take apart and put together, to explore and look for alternatives, to try and fail and try again and again until they succeed are all ways that a child learns through curiosity. The purpose of schooling is "to stimulate, capitalize on, and sustain the kind of motivation, intellectual curiosity, awe, and wonder that a child possesses when he or she begins schooling" (Sarison, 1995, p. 85).

Learning opportunities, many of them resulting from formal teaching and planning, saturate

As children are exposed to animals in a safe and secure atmosphere, they are able to move from fear to caution, then to acceptance and wonder. When this little boy became brave enough to move near the chicken, he then enjoyed walking along as the chicken followed.

the child's environment. Much more significant, however, are the "teachable moments," when a child's curiosity and initial interest in a subject provide fertile ground for the planting and nurturing of clear understandings. Adults must be alert to the ever-questioning and investigating young mind and prepared to assist the child in furthering knowledge and comprehension of the surrounding world. Having correctly interpreted ideas, the child is then prepared and eager to reach toward new galaxies of understanding.

Since the time of Plato and Socrates, questioning has been considered an important part of learning. To ask "why" and "how" questions of those around them is a means for coming to know and learn. When children question, this leads to reflection, wonder, wanting to know, grappling with ideas and issues, and to answers. An environment for student questioning is created when learners are trusted with asking their own questions, given the opportunity to question, expected to frame questions, and given the time it takes to formulate them (Dillon, 1988). Much has been written about student-centered curriculum, and student questions can be the means for designing this kind of curriculum (Commeyras, 1995; Heckman, Confer, & Hakim, 1994). However, in most classrooms today, early childhood or otherwise, teacher questioning is the norm and there is a paucity of questioning by students (Morgan & Saxton, 1995). To encourage meaning making, we must change what happens in classrooms so that more of children's learning will be based on questions that they themselves ask, rather than on questions asked by the teacher.

Early childhood educators should be especially interested in the questions that young children generate, for they are tenacious questioners before they enter formal schooling and ask many of the questions raised at home. However, something happens when they begin their formal schooling that inhibits their natural questioning, and they learn to answer the teacher's questions, but not to ask. Perhaps they are conditioned early in their education to *know* information, rather than to *question* ideas. In a study on questioning (Eliason, 1996), it was found that kindergarten teachers felt positive toward student questioning, but the gap between theory and practice was wide. Student questions in this study were seldom verbally invited, and few students in the study raised questions, particularly those of an inquisitive nature. It appears that even in early childhood classrooms the authority for knowledge and learning rests with the teacher. If we desire child-centered early childhood classrooms, we need to discipline our teaching behavior to expect, welcome, wait for, and support inquiry from children and use their questions as a springboard for planning projects, activities, and learning episodes.

Communication and Talking

Another ingredient in learning is communication or talking. As young children talk, they provide the adult or teacher with a window to their level of comprehension. In addition, as the adult responds and communicates with the child, it furthers the development of concept understandings. Therefore, communication is a two-way process in which there is a constant flow of information and questions between adults and children. Concepts broaden as they are explored and discussed in the context of another person's ideas and experiences. This is the great value of cooperative learning; we learn from one another through intercommunication.

Simply because an experience has allowed a child to become familiar with an idea, it must not be assumed that the correct information has been assimilated. In the quest for meaning, a child often misunderstands; thus, an adult or peer needs to listen constantly to determine the functioning level of discernment. Through communication and feedback from the teacher, a vital consideration in providing information, the child learns to focus on particular stimuli. In the following examples, it is evident that communication from the child is also an important aspect in the learning process.

A child who had been encouraged to keep her shoes on commented to her teacher at the end of the day: "I wore my shoes all day today, but sometimes I wore my bare feet!" During an excursion, various drums were shown to the children. It was explained that the kettledrum was so named because of its resemblance to a large pot or kettle that might be used on the stove for cooking. Later, as the concepts were being reviewed and reinforced, the children were shown a picture and asked the name of the kettledrum. Peter confidently replied, "Oh, that's a stove drum!"

Talking, reinforcement, and review are constantly needed to correct, strengthen, and expand a child's understandings. As adults prepare to be receptive to the child's communications, they must be willing to listen (not just hear) and observe (not just see). Teaching entails much more than disseminating information. It involves listening and observing not only for the obvious, but also for the subtle ways in which the child makes perceptions and understandings known.

Questioning is significant to learning, and it should be encouraged as a part of communication. The child asks a question, and the teacher listens to determine whether the information has been correctly interpreted. Then the teacher either reinforces and praises the child for the right information or corrects the misconception. A child's questions may lead the discussion in a direction unplanned by the teacher and provide feedback for concepts not understood. Following a story and discussion about watermelons, the children observed a real watermelon that was quite small. Joanna asked, "Why don't you water that thing?" and then pointed out that the teacher should "dump it in water." The teacher wisely sustained the inquiry and through feedback from the children learned that many of them thought that if they put the watermelon in water it would grow bigger. After a lengthy, unplanned discussion, the children learned the valuable notion that because the watermelon had already been picked from the vine it could not grow any more.

Listening and responding to a child's questions are accepted as important aspects of communication. Since children learn through asking questions, their questions should not be stifled but rather sustained and seen as an asset to thinking and problem solving.

Through communication received from the child, many misconceptions are identified. These misunderstandings must be clarified and corrected. Only then is a child able to obtain further knowledge of concepts in the continuing search for meaningful relationships in the environment. Thus, student questions become a means of early childhood assessment; teachers determine what students know and understand about that which has been studied, taught, and examined. An example of a child's misconception follows.

> The children had spent a week exploring the theme of the dairy cow. A number of concepts and a variety of activities had been included as the children explored the theme. On the last day of the theme study the children visited a dairy farm. The children observed some cows being machine-milked and watched the milk flowing through clear, plastic tubing. As one group was leaving, a child asked the teacher, "How can they tell when the cow is full?"

A child's questions and comments provided the necessary communication feedback to the teacher about that child's understanding. Additional experiences may need to be planned and concepts retaught, perhaps in different ways, to correct misconceptions or to extend meaning.

Many of the phrases and words in our common language usage are idioms. Until the child has experiences that will clarify meanings, the phrases are interpreted incorrectly and the literal definitions are assumed. Examples include *just pulling your leg, all tied up, on the tip of my tongue, all ears, swing shift, graveyard shift*, and *tongue-tied*. In addition, a word or phrase that has more than one meaning often causes misunderstanding for the child who is familiar with only one definition for that word. Examples include *fork in the road, catching a cold, pinch hitter, broken up, broken down, rat race*, and *wring your neck*.

Children often become needlessly concerned over statements that adults make because they interpret them by relying on the information previously stored and understood, as the following two illustrations show.

> Two-year-old Christy became upset every time her parents mentioned their forthcoming flight to New York, where they would visit Christy's grandparents. On one of these occasions when they were discussing their plans, Christy exclaimed, "But I don't know how to fly!"

> The children had observed a rooster in their classroom for several days, and they anxiously waited for it to crow. Each day just after the children left, the rooster would crow. One day while they were outside playing, the rooster began to crow. One of the teachers hurried to another teacher and suggested that she take the children inside because the rooster was "crowing its head off." A child who was nearby asked with alarm, "You mean his head is coming off?"

Children often develop misconceptions through misunderstanding a word, especially when the word is one with which they are unfamiliar, as observed in the following illustrations.

> As a group of children was leaving for an excursion to ride an elevator, a passerby asked Mike where they were going. "We're going to ride an alligator," he replied.

After being told that he would be going on an excursion that day, James informed the other children that they would be going on an "explosion."

Kyle unwrapped a birthday present, observed the toy, and said, "I wonder where the 'constructions' are."

Important ingredients in learning during early childhood are to listen and observe well enough that we have a clear understanding of young children's interpretations. Then the challenge as teachers seek to build increased meaning and knowledge is to communicate carefully, clarify concepts misunderstood, and extend and expand on children's understandings.

Modeling and Scaffolding

Modeling is another aspect of learning that is important in early childhood education. The teacher models both concepts that are to be understood and correct language usage. In addition, teachers model attitudes; enthusiasm is caught, not taught. All teachers should model an enthusiasm and excitement for learning. Prosocial behaviors are often best learned when they are modeled or when children can observe them in others. Other behaviors and attitudes that influence learning are also modeled for the young child. Teachers who are caring, questioning, and thoughtful learners, for example, are more likely to have students with these same academic qualities. One need only watch and listen to young children for a short time to understand the power of learning through modeling or imitation. Skills and behaviors are particularly learned through imitation or modeling. To tie a bow based on a word description of that skill would be very difficult, but when the skill is modeled, if the child is developmentally ready, with practice it can be learned. If a child is praised for work, efforts, or a particular behavior, the praise serves as reinforcement for that child. In addition, other children will desire to receive the praise, so they too will try to accomplish the work or skill. This is observational learning; children observe others and then model or imitate that person's efforts, skills, or work. All people model things that

they see or hear; their behavior, thinking, and language are all influenced by this important ingredient of learning.

Scaffolding is adult assistance or support to young children as they build a firm understanding. It is building bridges to higher levels of thinking and learning (Berk & Winsler, 1995). Scaffolding consists of giving clues, reminders, encouragement, support; breaking problems or challenges into steps; or anything else that allows the child to grow in independence as a learner. It is always built on the child's previous knowledge (Zahorik, 1995). Scaffolding includes the following goals and components (Berk & Winsler, 1995):

- Joint problem solving
- Intersubjectivity (two participants with different understandings begin a task and then finish with a shared understanding)
- Warmth and responsiveness
- Keeping the child in the ZPD (zone of proximal development)
- Promoting self-regulation

In assisted learning or scaffolding, the teacher or adult watches and listens to see how or what he or she might do to support the children in their learning journey.

Stories

There are many meaningful and remarkable benefits of stories in our lives; they open minds to understanding, touch hearts, and capture imaginations. Stories help children to make sense and meaning of the things that they are taught. Smith (1990, pp. 62, 63) writes in descriptive terms about the connection between stories and thinking:

> Thought flows in terms of stories—stories about events, stories about people, and stories about intentions and achievements. The best teachers are the best storytellers. We learn in the form of stories. We construct stories to make sense of events. . . . The brain is a story-seeking, story-creating instrument.

When ideas and concepts are taught with stories, they are remembered. Events, facts, and

Appropriate equipment is an integral part of the play of young children. Balancing two large balls and walking at the same time are challenging, but it encourages problem solving.

bits of information in and of themselves are not meaningful and not remembered, but in the context of the story they become understood, intelligible, and retained. Children, and all people, express themselves through sharing the stories of their lives.

Stories have a powerful effect because they not only impart ideas, concepts, and information and describe people, events, and places, but they also engage emotions. Through stories we exchange experiences and feelings with one another and we learn. Stories clarify what is being taught and enable children to make sense and meaning of that which the teacher is trying to teach. Storytellers weave a story in their own words, create images, and stir emotions, but the listeners or readers are also weaving their individual designs from the characters, situations, and actions in the story. The listeners or readers bring

their own experiences and imaginations into play to make meaning.

Rich Sociocultural Heritage

Both *what* and *how* young children learn depends partially on the sociocultural base, the context, of their experiences and lives. Their knowledge is not just individually constructed, as the constructivists believe, but is also greatly influenced by their particular families and the culture from which they come. Cultural habits and traditions in homes and communities serve as contexts for children's development; they also provide content as well as opportunities for learning (New, 1999). Learning takes place through children's active participation in the traditions, routines, and rituals of their culture, lives, and contexts. As they interact with the significant people in their environment, the shared understandings between child and others will eventually become internalized knowledge, skills, and attitudes (New, 1999). The broad range of various experiences and perspectives that come to school with diverse students is a powerful way for all children to learn more (Cole, 1995). Thus, students' individual differences are a resource for all others from which to learn.

Interaction with Others

Children learn from one another, and this learning includes both cognitive and affective perceptions. The interpersonal intelligence is one of Gardner's eight suggested intelligences and is the capacity to discern and respond appropriately to the moods, temperaments, motivations, and desires of other people (Gardner, 1983). When children learn in small groups from their peers, it satisfies their needs more than when they learn alone (Glasser, 1990). Many academic and prosocial skills are the outcome of peer interaction. Children's analytical and academic skills are sharpened, and they develop both oral and listening abilities. They learn to be sensitive to others and understand another person's point of view. Because no student in the group succeeds without the cooperation and support of the other group members, interdependence and bonding result from this type of learning.

Children in today's society will be required to be thoughtful and to have technical, relationship, and communication skills. The most effective way to develop these kinds of competencies is in small groups, where the focus is on a team effort, on helping and learning from one another, as opposed to a competitive approach.

Cooperative learning fosters higher achievement in children, especially when groups are rewarded for individual achievement (Kagan, 1992).

In other words, children achieve the most when their learning is characterized by the team members' having a positive, interdependent goal with individual accountability (Johnson, Johnson, & Holubec, 1987).

Children learn in cooperative groups when they talk and share with one another and their talk is directed toward academic concepts and achievement. When peers work to support, recognize, and build up one another, enhanced learning occurs and self-esteem is nurtured.

Summary

Developmentally appropriate early childhood education means providing a curriculum and environment that are right for the developmental needs of children. The developmental needs and characteristics of age groups and individual children need to be understood, and learning activities and goals should be based on the knowledge that children in early childhood are ready for learning through their senses, utilizing experiences, materials, and concrete activities.

Teachers should assess young children to guide and plan for their learning and to communicate in a knowledgeable way with parents. Using documentation in our assessment benefits the children, school, and parents (Fleege, 1997; Helm, Beneke, & Steinheimer, 1997). However, any assessment should be used for the benefit of children and should never be used to keep students out of a program or retain them in a particular grade. In early childhood, authentic assessments such as observations, interviews, projects, presentations or performances, and portfolios are used to determine needs, evaluate growth and learning, guide the curriculum, and evaluate the program.

Play is an integral part of the early childhood environment and curriculum. It is imperative that teachers recognize the inherent values in play, organize an environment that reflects these values, and plan a curriculum based on play. Play is developmentally right for children 3 to 8 years of age; it is what they need, based on our understanding of their developmental characteristics. Play "offers the child the opportunity to make sense out of the world by using available tools. . . . Through play, the child comes to understand the world and the adult comes to understand the child" (Chaillé & Silvern, 1996, p. 274). Not only is play fun, "but it is serious business that pays big dividends to its eager, young investors" (Diffily & Morrison, 1996, p. 4).

The physical environment is an important ingredient in determining the feeling or tone of the classroom or center. It shows the children what they will learn, how they should behave, and what they should feel about their education. It influences how they act, what they think, and how they feel. Early childhood educators must recognize their responsibility in creating a physical environment that has positive influences on the learning and growth of the children who use the environment. Toys and materials must be properly selected, used, stored, and cared for. They too influence the child's learning, behavior, and feelings. The time spent creating an appropriate and inviting environment that offers many opportunities for play will be well worth the effort.

In a developmentally appropriate program or classroom, we recognize that young children learn in a different way than older children or adults. The ingredients of learning, experiences, choices and decisions, curiosity and questioning, sociocultural background, communication and talking, modeling and scaffolding, stories, and peer interactions, are significant considerations leading to meaning and understanding. There is an excitement and enthusiasm in learning that should be preserved and fostered throughout an individual's lifetime. However, we have cautioned against inappropriate, pressurized early learning. We propose that children want to learn and that successful developmentally appropriate teaching begins with and builds on concepts and ideas that are relevant during the early years of childhood.

Student Learning Activities

1. Describe characteristics of developmentally appropriate practice (DAP). Visit at least three different early childhood classrooms or centers and evaluate them on the basis of DAP. What have you learned?

2. Why do you think play is important? Visit an early childhood classroom and evaluate the kinds of and opportunities for play.

3. Using the criteria for room arrangement suggested in this chapter, draw a sample room arrangement. Describe the intended age group. Tell why you included the specific areas. Does the arrangement support a particular curriculum theme?

4. Visit an early childhood classroom and evaluate its physical arrangement. Are there different areas of play in the room? Describe each section of the room. (You may also wish to draw a plan of the room to facilitate your description.) Describe any interest centers.

5. Visit with several early childhood teachers and discuss the forms of assessment that they use. How do they use them? Are the examples developmentally appropriate? What suggestions would you have for these teachers?

6. Visit a toy store and evaluate three early childhood toys that might be purchased for use in a classroom, using the criteria suggested in this chapter.

7. Using the criteria suggested in this chapter for selecting appropriate learning materials for young children, visit an early childhood classroom and make a list of the teacher-made learning materials. Then make a checksheet similar to the one that follows:

Equipment	Appro-priate	Not Appro-priate	Reason
Shape stacking cans		×	Sharp edges
Color lotto game	×		
Manipulative boards (lacing, buttoning, zipping)	×		
Dominoes		×	Not durable

8. Develop a list of materials that could be collected from your home and the homes of children in your classroom to be used in an early childhood situation, for example, padlock and keys; old camera; empty spools; materials for counting, sorting, grouping, ordering, and pattern making (e.g., shells, stones, marbles, straws, washers, canceled stamps).

9. Organize a list of teacher-made materials to begin working on. You may wish to organize your list into areas such as materials for teaching about colors, shapes, people, and textures. Also include science, music, and language and literacy materials. Use your list as an action, to-do list!

10. Make at least three teacher-made learning materials.

11. Write a short essay on what you believe are the significant ingredients in early childhood learning. Compare your beliefs to those of prominent theorists and also the authors of this text.

12. Do you believe most early childhood teachers provide developmentally appropriate learning? Why or why not?

Suggested Resources

Cognitive Development: Representation in Three- to Five-Year-Old Children. Films for the Humanities & Sciences.

A Day at the Beach: Barney and the Backyard Gang. The Lyons Group.

Performance Assessment in the Classroom. The Video Journal of Education.

Play: A Vygotskian Approach. Davidson Films.

Portfolio Assessment. The Video Journal of Education.

Chapter 3

Developing Partnerships with Parents

Increasing attention has recently been given to the importance of parent involvement in young children's learning (DeSteno, 2000; File, 2001; Freeman, 1998; Hurt, 2000). To meet the challenges facing families in today's rapidly changing society and to avoid the potential ill effects, a clarion call has gone out to all parents to provide learning opportunities for children in the home, to become more involved in their children's schooling, to form partnerships with their children's teachers, and to participate in parent education (Larsen & Haupt, 1997, p. 389).

Although teachers and administrators recognize the need for developing partnerships with families in the early childhood programs, there is still a significant lack of actual family involvement in the schools (Kieff & Wellhousen, 2000). This chapter will explore many of the barriers that prevent effective partnerships and how we can turn these barriers into avenues of success.

Even though the importance of school–parent partnerships is generally accepted, there is often little or no training for helping teachers to implement this valuable relationship. Partnerships and collaboration are frequently mentioned when discussing the importance of teacher–parent relationships, but putting them into actual practice becomes a more difficult task. The ideal is not always the reality! So often the parental involvement is limited to back-to-school events at the beginning of the year, occasional help with scheduled parties and field trips, or periodic parent–teacher conferences, often formal

in nature and with a set time limit. Teachers often view "parent involvement practices as another burden needlessly imposed upon them" (Brand, 1996). Parents and teachers may not feel secure working with each other; attitudes, ideas, values, previous experiences, cultures, and other influences may all make communication with one another difficult. Still, teachers are expected to involve parents, and parents are expected to become involved, and so the partnership needs to begin with building a trusting relationship. Teachers and parents must search for common ground in order for a child to achieve optimum academic, emotional, speech–language, social, moral, and physical development (Coleman & Wallinga, 2000; Hurt, 2000).

Families and schools share a mutual responsibility in helping children to learn (Coleman, 1997; Larsen & Haupt, 1997). Every effort must therefore be made to strengthen this important link and help parents and teachers to see each other as playing an important role in the education of the child. These desired relationships must include a basic concept of equality and shared responsibility (File, 2001). Powell (1998) refers to an imagined common woven fabric that is typically made when the child and staff of an early childhood program are woven together, and the threads of the parent are woven into a separate parent involvement section. He suggests that a much better design results when the parent involvement threads are interwoven with the child and staff throughout the fabric pattern. "In this pattern, programs are meant to work with children and parents within their family contexts" (Powell, 1998, p. 60).

The NAEYC's Code of Ethical Conduct helps teachers to clarify their professional responsibilities. There needs to be mutual trust, respect for the family's values, and involvement of the family when important decisions are being made. It is imperative that teachers be familiar with and base their program practices on current knowledge in the fields relating to child development, recognize and respect the uniqueness and potential of each child, and recognize the special vulnerability of children (NAEYC, 1998). Failing to incorporate these personal ethical responsibilities often results in breakdowns to the relationships and partnerships between schools and parents (Freeman, 1998).

The family is the young child's earliest educator, and parents have a lasting influence on their child's attitudes, values, learning, concepts, emotions, and ideas. They have the right, responsibility, and oppor-

When this mother visited the classroom, she wore a visitor's badge. Her daughter studied the badge, then asked: "What does this say?"

tunity to influence their child's education (Newman, 1995a; Workman & Gage, 1997). Even though many parents are not aware of how important they are in their child's education, there is extensive and convincing evidence regarding the benefit of parent involvement in the development and education of their child (Akaran & Fields, 1997; Brand, 1996; Brewer & Kieff, 1996/1997; Coleman & Churchill, 1997; Kieff & Wellhousen, 2000; Lakey, 1997; Murphy, 1997; Newman, 1995a; Powell, 1998; Rosenthal & Sawyers, 1996; Swick, Boutte, & VanScoy, 1995/1996; Webb, 1997; Workman & Gage, 1997).

Educators believe that parents make the difference between a mediocre school and a great school. Everyone benefits when parents are involved in their child's education, and all parents have competencies that will help their child to succeed in school. In order for the teaching of young children to be effective, a positive link must be made between the school and the home; the two must be partners, since they are both vital parts of the child's life and education. Involving parents in children's education improves the children's achievements and the overall level of success in our schools. The earlier we involve parents in their child's learning, the greater are the benefits. It is important for children to feel secure and comfortable in their home and school environments. A two-way flow of support and information between home and school strengthens the child's experiences in both (Kieff & Wellhousen, 2000). "Every child in my class leaves someone to come to school each day, and each child returns home to someone. I will fully know and teach that child only when I connect with that someone" (Hurt, 2000, p. 88).

Both parents and teachers can contribute to the growth and development of children. In addition, parents have much to offer teachers and the school, and teachers have much to offer parents. Parents can become better acquainted with the school's programs, and teachers can become more aware of children's home situations. As they learn each other's values and goals, they are able to be more supportive of each other in working together with their children. "Teamwork and collaboration are more likely to achieve positive results than when school systems and families work alone" (Rosenthal & Sawyers, 1996, p. 194).

It has been found that there are both parent and teacher attributes that promote partnerships. Qualities that appear especially germane for parents are their self-image, warmth, parent efficacy, nurturance, sensitivity, and strength of interpersonal involvements (Swick, 1991). Relevant attributes for teachers that promote partnerships are accessibility, reliability, sensitivity, and flexibility (Swick, 1991).

> Teachers need to develop the following skills when working with families (Kaufman, 2001):
>
> - Respect families, their ideas, decisions, values, and priorities
> - Use empathy and patience
> - Establish strong relationships between home and school
> - Validate, without judging, questions and concerns
> - Link families with needed resources
> - Use varied communication techniques
> - Collaborate with other community agencies when necessary

It therefore becomes a challenge for teachers to work to develop the qualities within themselves that foster positive relationships with parents. Teachers can also seek, through parent education and involvement programs, to strengthen the qualities in parents that appear to be particularly apropos for partnerships.

Some teachers believe that planning for parent involvement takes too much time. However, despite the difficulties, the accumulating research on the positive effects of parent participation in educational programs has created continuing interest in parent involvement. Teachers need to accept that parents' attitudes toward involvement are important. DeSteno (2000) refers to "the fine line" of finding the balance when there is some discomfort between both sides of the school–family relationship. She reminds us that, although many parents want to become involved in the classroom, some prefer not to become involved; and we must make both of them feel comfortable in their preferences. Often those who do not want to be in the classroom will change their perspective as they become more familiar with the curriculum and environment. Often teachers begin by developing positive attitudes toward parent involvement, helping parents and staff to understand the benefits that will come from parent participation and involvement (Lopez & Schultz, 1996). There is a clear relationship between the teacher's attitude toward parent involvement and the actual level of involvement; the more positive a teacher feels about involving parents, the higher the level of parent involvement.

Many strategies and techniques will assist schools and homes in developing partnerships that benefit everyone involved and help parents to realize that their participation makes a difference. Developing a positive attitude toward working with families is a major step in developing good relationships with parents.

For clarity and continuity in writing, *parents* in this chapter includes single parents, grandparents, guardians, and foster parents. By keeping this in mind, you will be able to adapt the activities and suggestions to the needs of those with whom you associate. A note of caution: Typically, the mothers' concerns and priorities are the focus when educators and other professionals work with families. Fathers are critical members of the family system and must be included in our efforts to achieve successful partnerships (Flynn & Wilson, 1998; Turbiville, Umbarger, & Guthrie, 2000). Research suggests that fathers want to be involved in their children's programs and that this involvement results in more positive outcomes for the children and the rest of the family (Frey, Fewell, & Meyer, 1989).

> **When Fathers Are Involved in School**
>
> Children are more likely to:
>
> - Enjoy school (U.S. Department of Education, 1997)
> - Achieve higher grades (U.S. Department of Education, 1997)
> - Participate in extracurricular activities (U.S. Department of Education, 1997)
>
> Children are less likely to:
>
> - Repeat a grade (U.S. Department of Education, 1997)
> - Be suspended or expelled from school (U.S. Department of Education, 1997)

- Behave violently in school (Smith, 1995)
- Be involved in acts of juvenile delinquency (Elias, 1996)

Adapted from Turbiville, Umbarger, & Guthrie, 2000.

IMPORTANCE OF ACTIVE PARENT INVOLVEMENT

Programs vary in the kind and amount of parent involvement, but we do know that schools cannot work in isolation. If programs in early childhood education are to succeed, parental support and participation are significant factors, and children need to continue to receive stimulation from parents (Fitzgerald, 1995; Glasser, 1997; Rosenthal & Sawyers, 1996; Washington, Johnson, & McCracken, 1995). It has also been found that the early, formative partnerships of families and teachers affect the connections between families and schools later in the child's schooling. Principles that need to be recognized are the following (Epstein & Sanders, 1998; Finders & Lewis, 1994; Fitzgerald, 1995; Hurt, 2000; Rock, 2000):

- All parents have strengths and can contribute.
- Almost everyone understands the value of partnerships.
- Each parent has a perspective that is significant.
- All parents care about their children.
- Parent absence should not imply noncaring.

Even though as educators we are aware of these principles, we are not always sure how to achieve positive and effective relationships.

If parents are not involved when schools are developing standards and implementing new teaching methods and strategies, plans will likely end in conflict, failure, and gridlock (Dodd, 1996). Teachers need to appeal to parents' interest, strengths, experience, and knowledge in order to have them become involved; parents need to sense and know that they are needed before they will be involved.

Traditionally, teachers have met with parents twice yearly for parent-teacher conferences and report sessions. Today, however, teachers realize that more interactions between parents and teachers are necessary, with much more communication between the two. Parents should feel

As mother intently watches, this boy proudly demonstrates that he is learning to write his name.

welcome not only at school and program activities, but also in the classroom. They must realize that they have a direct influence on their child's education (Brand, 1996; Newman, 1995a). Children should be made to feel safe and secure as they move back and forth each day between their two worlds of home and school. "Both home and school affect a child's academic performance" (Rosenthal & Sawyers, 1996, p. 196).

Parent involvement takes many forms, and it ought to encompass a broad range of activities.

Parents can provide resources for the classroom and *be* resources for particular units of study, but it is

---

Activities for Involving Parents

- Help on field trips
- Assist with art and craft projects in the classroom
- Do work at home: sewing, mending, cutting out materials, and so on
- Share their careers or hobbies with the students
- Bring in a pet or other animal
- Become a special friend to a particular child
- Read to the students
- Share a food, game, or book from particular cultures
- Assist with music and recreational activities
- Help to plan curriculum activities
- Help in planning and evaluating involvement activities
- Be a room parent
- Serve as members of committees and governing boards
- Contribute to newsletters
- Help with support groups
- Mentor in the classroom
- Assist in learning and computer centers
- Help to reach and involve other parents

Adapted from DeSteno, 2000; Halford, 1996; Parette & Petch-Hogan, 2000.

---

up to the teacher to capitalize on and use parent expertise. Parents can be assistant teachers or teacher's aides working in the classroom with the children. One teacher found that a successful way to involve parents is to invite them into the classroom to talk one-on-one about the books that the children are reading.

In addition, parent involvement helps parents to become effective teachers of their own children. Parents' involvement may be as simple as letting their child know that they value education, reading to their child at home, encouraging their child with homework, and supporting at-home projects.

Teachers and parents seek to be sensitive to one another's needs; there should be mutual understanding, trust, and respect (Berger, 1995; Newman, 1995a). In effect, teachers should seek to understand what each parent in their class or program wants or expects from their child. Teachers are accountable to parents; they feel a responsibility to answer parents' questions regarding their children's education and to satisfy parents' wishes and goals for their children.

Another current trend is that of extending the curriculum into the home through the support of parents. Teachers are realizing that school hours pass quickly and that children have an added advantage if their parents can support what is being taught at school by teaching, reinforcing, and extending these same ideas and concepts at home. What parents *do* certainly does make a difference in the child's life. In a research review, Finn (1998) described four specific parental interactions that are found to have particular influence on students' academic performance:

1. Structuring and monitoring children's time
2. Assisting children with homework
3. Talking about school matters with children
4. Reading in the home

Teachers should also consider the following when assigning homework (adapted from Bermudez, 1994; Sosa, 1993):

1. Avoid busywork and unnecessary homework assignments
2. Explain homework clearly, and give ample time for students to ask any questions relating to their homework
3. Make certain that parents and students understand homework expectations and due dates

In addition, schools and teachers are realizing that they are one of the best support systems for the family. Recognizing that parenting is a difficult task and one in which many persons have had limited training, schools frequently offer parenting classes (Lopez & Schultz, 1996). These classes allow parents to participate in discussions, lectures, and demonstrations that focus on parenting skills, guidance and discipline, child-rearing practices, home-based learning activities, and family relationships. Teachers can also suggest sources of assistance to parents who are coping with crises. Sometimes teachers can be of great help by listening and demonstrating concern. It is also imperative that teachers remember the diversified nature of the family today and find ways of encompassing and communicating with parents from diverse cultures, working parents, grandparents, single parents, guardians, and foster parents (Swick, Boutte, & VanScoy, 1995/1996). Just as each child is unique, so is each child's family situation; therefore, the teacher's method of handling each individual circumstance must be unique.

Recognizing the diversity of parents, teachers must offer a variety of strategies for involving and supporting parents and children. Teachers should realize that their own patterns of child rearing and attitudes regarding education might differ from those of the parents with whom they work (NAEYC, 1996a). This is especially apparent when children of various cultural backgrounds are in the classrooms. It is then imperative that "intercultural communication" be involved so that teachers become familiar with each child's values and traditions. Children need to know that their parents are valued and respected by the teacher, which leads to acceptance and unity in the partnership (Sturm, 1997). With ongoing and interactive communication, *all* parents can contribute to the classroom. Technology can be used as a link between school and home (*Learning*, 1995). As educators, when we develop good relationships with the families of our students, parents become our greatest ally.

GUIDELINES FOR WORKING EFFECTIVELY WITH PARENTS

The first step in working effectively with parents is to establish a warm and supportive relationship. Frequently, there are barriers to overcome. In any

Benefits of Active Parent Involvement for Children

- Make greater gains in reading
- Have a more positive attitude about school
- Have higher attendance
- Have better homework habits
- Make better home–school connections
- See parents as important part of education

Adapted from Epstein, 2000; Epstein et al., 1997.

Benefits of Parent Involvement for Parents

- More willing to help students at home with their homework
- Have more positive attitudes toward involvement at school
- Tend to rate teachers higher
- Support teachers' efforts more consistently
- More familiar with what children are being taught
- Understand better the functioning of the school and its programs
- Have more confidence in their parenting skills
- Have more understanding of child growth and development

Adapted from Eldridge, 2001.

Benefits of Parent Involvement for Teachers

- Have more time to spend with individual children
- Appreciate parents' involvement
- Respect parents' time and abilities
- Are more respected and appreciated by parents
- Feel more comfortable having parents involved in school

Adapted from Eldridge, 2001.

job involving human relationships, forming positive and constructive associations is often the most challenging aspect. When establishing partnerships, the most difficult task may not be planning and doing, but establishing and maintaining warm relationships with parents. Because some parents' contacts with schools and teachers have not been positive, teachers often have to work diligently to combat negative attitudes. Some teachers view parents as threats, and some parents develop the same view of teachers. Keep in mind the challenge to serve families and not just children. Remember that children come from families and spend much time within those families.

Be careful not to appear too strong or too authoritarian. You are a professional, and you do have much skill and expertise. However, some teachers give parents the feeling that they "know it all" and that they consider their ways and values to be the best. This attitude almost immediately breaks down relationships with parents.

Social, linguistic, or cultural barriers may interfere with effective communication and work with parents (Finders & Lewis, 1994; Larsen & Haupt, 1997). These barriers may involve differences in values, approved child-rearing methods, behavior standards, accepted foods, and many other areas. Complete agreement on everything is unrealistic, but through communication and daily contact, effective parent–teacher partnerships can be formed.

Common Barriers to Effective Partnerships with Families

- Type of household (two parent, single parent, foster parent, grandparent, divorced parent, legal guardian, same-sex parent, other relative, teen or much older parent, blended or split family, extended family)
- Life-style and culture of family (language, dress, traditions and holidays, norms, rules, foods, employment, education level, economic level, siblings, religion, attitudes toward child rearing and discipline, expectations *for* teachers and school, expectations *of* teachers and school, housing, nutrition, health, amount of support for academic practices in home)
- Time and work schedules (of teachers and families)
- Transportation (have access to car or bus, ability to drive)
- School (distance, ease of finding location, adequate parking, parents' level of comfort in situation)
- Communication (ability to understand and/or read information from teacher, and ability to respond verbally or in writing; need of interpreter)
- Siblings (need for child care, any with disabilities)
- Misunderstandings and unclear expectations between parent and school
- Attitudes and feelings of parents and teachers (discomfort, awkwardness, insecurity, lack of mutual trust)
- Parents not involved in mutual decision making
- Strengths and abilities of parents not recognized or utilized
- Previous negative school experiences of parents

Adapted from Bermudez & Marquez, 1996; File, 2001; Kieff & Wellhousen, 2000.

In working to overcome some of the barriers to effective relationships with parents, showing interest and respect will frequently assist in achieving positive relationships. Teachers must respect cultural differences and variations in family values, just as these must be respected in children. As differences in children are accepted, it becomes much easier to understand these differences in their parents; they will sense acceptance or rejection. More time should be spent listening to parents and learning about their feelings, values, and culture. Becoming effective at cross-cultural communication will minimize misinterpretations and biases.

All parents need to know that they have something to contribute to the classroom, and they need to be encouraged to share these valuable contributions (Fitzgerald, 1995). Request the help

After her mother had visited in the classroom, this girl's role playing involved the mother and the activities the two of them had worked on together.

of parents in singing songs, leading dances, supervising ethnic food preparations, or making costumes or decorations. Invite them to play music, recite poetry, or help to portray celebrations or cultural events. Barriers usually disappear when parents sense honesty, sincerity, and a feeling of professionalism. In addition, parents need to feel appreciated and be recognized for their contributions and efforts (Larsen & Haupt, 1997).

The importance of listening as a means of building effective teacher–parent relationships cannot be stressed enough. "Teachers are eager to listen to and learn from parents, because parents are especially knowledgable about the past development and current attributes of their children" (NAEYC, 1996a, p. 95). Frequently, parents will have insights into their child's behavior that the teacher could not possibly know from associating with the child only in the school setting. The parents may have developed methods for handling the child's behavior challenges at home that would work equally well for the teacher in the classroom. Perhaps the parents have deep concerns, complaints, or irritations that can be resolved through

listening and effective communication. Sometimes simply airing concerns to sensitive and understanding teachers helps parents to feel more comfortable in the relationship. Parents should be provided with a constant opportunity to share these feelings, and there are many ways to do this. An open communication line for very young children can be established through daily contact as parents pick up their children from preschool. Teachers should remind parents that their feelings and suggestions are welcomed by making such comments as "How are you feeling about (child's name's) school experience? Is there any way I can be more supportive?" At the initial meeting or conference, teachers can indicate a certain time of day when they can be contacted. In addition, teachers should encourage parents with concerns to call them. Parents will sense the sincerity and honesty of the suggestion; they will know whether or not the teacher really meant what he or she said. Begin developing this relationship before a need actually arises for problem solving. We are reminded to "develop a trusting relationship from the start" (Manning & Schindler, 1997, p. 28). To summarize, here are some specific suggestions for working effectively with parents:

1. Listen. Set up a specific open time when parents know that you will be available for listening and communicating. Sense their needs to share and discuss, and find some time—lunchtime, after school, a home visit, an evening telephone conversation—for meeting these needs by being an effective listener.

2. Treat all children and their families with respect and caring concern. Take advantage of the little opportunities that occur almost daily for showing concern and interest in children and their families. Possibly, send home a short note apprising the parents of a particular skill that the child mastered that day or telling them something the child said or did that you enjoyed. A quick phone call on the day a child is absent lets the parents and the child know that they are important and cared for. Treat the parents with the kind of respect that conveys the belief that "I see you as an equal partner, having more and superior understanding of the child in some areas than I, the child's teacher."

3. Be sure to know the child well enough to relate specific information about him or her to the parents. Record keeping is important, and a list or chart of the items that you wish to discuss will be helpful for both you and the parents. Anecdotes or other kinds of dated observation notes can also be supportive. In addition, it is helpful for the parents to see samples of the child's work; over a period of time, progress in specific areas can be observed. For the preschool child, even progress in art stages is easily apparent from selected samples of the child's artwork.

4. Convey to the parents positive and warm feelings regarding their child. Make sure that they know how much you like the child and how interested you are in the child's growth and development.

5. Be objective and realistic about goals for working with the child. Involve parents in determining appropriate goals for their child (*Learning*, 1995). Where necessary, make ap-

propriate referrals for assistance from such professionals as speech therapists, psychologists, and medical doctors.

6. Be a source of help in many parenting areas and help to extend what you are teaching into the home. Parents may need suggestions for age-appropriate good books, meaningful learning activities that can be done at home, toy selection, and where to find helpful materials on guidance. Remember, too, that the school and family alone may not be able to handle the range of children's needs. Schools should seek to help families to access community services that they need; teachers should draw on the full range of community resources to strengthen the child, and they should focus on preventive strategies (Lopez & Schultz, 1996). What does your local library offer for parents who indicate a particular need? If you have a nearby college or university, what particular services could be recommended to parents? It may be advisable to keep a current file of resources appropriate for the parents of the children that you teach.

7. Remember that it will take numerous encounters and meetings to build positive and supportive relationships with parents.

To work effectively with parents, the same attitudes used in working with children should be applied. Be positive, supportive, interested, caring, objective, friendly, and warm. Work hard, using a variety of techniques to motivate, teach, build, and strengthen.

Checklist for Effective Parent Involvement

1. Provide opportunities for parent association and training: practical skills workshops, support groups and social events, school policies and procedures, how to help with homework, developing language and communication skills, basic child development and learning, discipline and guidance, career planning
2. Conduct conferences and meetings in family-friendly settings

3. Make initial contacts friendly and inviting
4. Involve parents in ongoing assessment and evaluation of involvement opportunities
5. Administration, teachers, and other staff receive training in developing skills for relating to parents and families
6. Recognize that early childhood programs serve families, not children alone
7. Clearly define expectations and objectives (teacher's and school's—parents knowing what they should do, why it should be done, and how they should do it)
8. Involve families in choices and decision making
9. Work toward positive relationships of mutual trust, confidence, understanding, acceptance, and cooperation
10. Determine and build on strengths, skills, expertise, and abilities of the child and family
11. Maintain frequent, open, two-way communication with parents (interpreter, if needed)
12. Open and accepting classroom environment
13. Meaningful and appropriate parental involvement
14. Accept and respect uniqueness and diversity of families
15. Consider needs of family (transportation, concerns, priorities, important issues, work schedules, child care)

Sources: Bermudez, 1994; Chavkin, 1996; Chavkin & Gonzales, 1995; Eldridge, 2001; File, 2001; Finn, 1998; Henderson & Berla, 1994; Hoover-Dempsey & Sandler, 1997; Inger, 1992; Kaufman, 2001; Link, Beggs, & Seiderman, 1997; McBride, 1999; Parette & Petch-Hogan, 2000; Powell, 1998; Sosa, 1993; Williams & Chavkin, 1990.

STRATEGIES FOR ACHIEVING FAMILY-FRIENDLY SCHOOLS AND SCHOOL-FRIENDLY HOMES

Now that some guidelines for working with parents have been established, we need to focus on strategies for developing the desired partnerships between schools and homes. Parent involvement works best when parents are invited to play a variety of roles; their involvement will take different

forms depending on their needs and interests (Larsen & Haupt, 1997).

Coleman & Wallinga (2000) suggest that we develop family involvement webs. Family involvement webs, like curriculum webs (see Chapter 4), provide direction and organization for addressing specific ideas or tasks. The steps involved in developing a family involvement web include:

Identifying a theme

Brainstorming family involvement activities

Identifying family roles

Implementing the web

Evaluating the outcome

How much more effectively children will learn if parents and teachers are partners in the teaching process! Since learning occurs through repetition and many experiences, children will learn more successfully if what is being taught in the classroom is extended into the home. The following sections discuss ways for the teacher to support the development of partnerships between home and school.

Written Communication

Written communications can take many forms and are a vital link between home and school. It may take repeated invitations to motivate parents to become involved (Larsen & Haupt, 1997). Upcoming events and activities, as well as snack assignments or main-course lunch menu items, can be included on a monthly or weekly newsletter–calendar. A few specific guidance or management hints might be shared. Child quotes or anecdotes from recent activities might also be included.

Teachers can make a list of simple activities that parents can do in their homes to be actively involved in their child's learning. For example, activities listed in any chapter in this text could be shared with parents. Or, for each general curriculum area (that is, math, science, language and literacy, music, art), choose several activities that could easily be done at home and share them with parents. For example, for math children:

- Sort laundry and match socks. When finished, they can count pairs of socks for each family member and then add them together.

- Make a number lotto game and play it together.
- Circle numerals in the newspaper beginning with 1 and going to 10, or as far as the child can recognize.
- Estimate the weight of several household objects such as a ball, a gallon of milk, and so on. Once the items are weighed, have the child order them from lightest to heaviest.
- Do matching, sorting, and categorizing activities using beans, buttons, groceries, cards, and newspaper pictures or photographs.
- Use calendars for matching or for counting days until specific events, days in week, days in month, weeks in month, months in year, and so on.

Find time each week to send a note or newsletter home with the children in order to tell parents what concepts or ideas are being focused on that week, as well as to provide an overview of planned activities. In addition, write down any individual notes that may be helpful or enjoyed by the parents regarding their child. Parents will be interested in knowing when field trips are being taken. Include words to new finger plays they can teach their child. Children will also enjoy having their parents tell them of the activities planned for the next week or the next day in school; it creates interest, enthusiasm, and eagerness. For example, if parents are aware of the upcoming unit on color, they can add support by reinforcing color concepts at home, even during spontaneous experiences such as eating dinner or going to the grocery store. Also, parents frequently ask children what they did at school, and it is often difficult for young children to remember or to single out the concept being studied. It is helpful to the child for the parent to ask something like "What did you learn about color today?" or "What did the policeman tell you when he visited your classroom today?" An excellent practice to encourage inquiry is for parents to ask children what questions they asked at school that day.

Notes are also appropriate when the children have enjoyed a particular food, music, or science experience: "Today the children were amazed with the 'growth' of the chemical gardens we made in class yesterday. You may wish to make them at home. The recipe is . . . ." or "Today the children en-joyed the playdough we used. The recipe is . . . ." Parents appreciate these ideas, and knowing that activities will be enjoyed by their children, they will often do them at home.

Notes of appreciation should also be sent to parents. When parents participate in a field trip, they have donated several hours of valuable home or work time and should know that their efforts are appreciated. These short notes help to build warm parent–teacher relationships. Also, if a parent sends a snack or assists in the classroom in any way, a short note should be sent. It is helpful to keep thank-you notes and cards readily available so that they can be sent soon after the parent has participated. A bulletin board is a source of information for parents that might include general school information, lesson or activity schedules, parenting classes, upcoming events, meeting new people, and messages for children and teachers. Another effective avenue for two-way dialogue is the idea of writing journal entries. Teachers and/or children write in journals that are then taken home to the parents. Parents can also be encouraged to send return notes or messages with their children to the teacher (Harding, 1996; Rosenthal & Sawyers, 1996). For preschool and kindergarten children, their journal "writing" may actually be pictures or picture stories, and they might also dictate to a teacher or assistant words for their entries.

Parent Conferences or Conversations

Parent–teacher conferences require trust and goodwill (Newman, 1997/98), even though the backgrounds and personalities of the teachers and parents are not always compatible. Face-to-face encounters with parents contribute to student success and should be planned frequently. For some parents, the most convenient direct encounter is at the parent's place of work (*Learning*, 1995). It is unrealistic to predetermine the exact number of times per year that these conferences should be held, because some parents may need them every 6 to 8 weeks, while once every 3 or 4 months may be sufficient for others. The important thing to remember is to meet with parents as often as is necessary to maintain close contact and to be an advocate for the child and his or her best interests. Conferences, to be successful, should be well prepared for and also relate to the parents'

This boy peers through the slats in the indoor treehouse as his parents visit with the teacher during a conference.

needs and facilitate the cooperation between home and school (Rosenthal & Sawyers, 1996). When parent–teacher conferences are well planned and conducted, parents feel more comfortable in becoming involved (Morrison, 1997).

The teacher should begin and end the parent conference with something positive about the child. Once something positive has been said by the teacher, the parent should be allowed to talk. As a teacher, you gain much knowledge and understanding from parents by listening to them. This encourages information sharing and discourages confrontation between parent and teacher. Glascoe (1999, p. 18) provides the following information relating to communicating with parents:

1. Many parents do not share their concerns unless asked.

2. Parents derive their concerns by comparing their child to others.

3. Parents, regardless of educational level or parenting experience, can share concerns that are often accurate indicators of children's development.

4. Parents' concerns can be useful in developmental or behavioral screening when necessary.

5. By carefully interpreting parents' concerns, professionals can make evidenced-based decisions about any services families may need.

One way of gaining information from parents is to have them complete a preconference worksheet designed to get feedback from them about concerns that they would like to discuss and also what primary successes they believe their child is experiencing (Spaulding, 1994). Parents should feel supported, relaxed, comfortable, and wanted. They should be made aware of the child's strengths and needs and of specific ways that they can help their child at home. A postconference worksheet can be filled out in collaboration by the teacher and parent. Desired actions and steps to reach goals can be specifically delineated (Spaulding, 1994).

Teachers should be sensitive to the strong emotional investment parents have in their child, which may manifest itself as defensiveness, anger, denial, or anxiety (Morgan, 1989). Tension during conferences and interfacing with parents can be reduced as teachers use "I" messages, seek parents' suggestions, and stress positive aspects. What is best for the child should always be paramount. Be cautious with criticism, and instead of giving advice, give suggestions or guidelines. Never betray a confidence; this applies to children as well as to parents.

A suggestion regarding the physical setting for the conference: Sometimes chairs set side by side or at right angles to each other are more conducive to successful parent conferences than chairs set facing each other. This is especially true when a particular problem is being discussed and the teacher is able to show the parent related paperwork. Focusing on something physical frequently diminishes defensiveness or discomfort by diverting direct eye-to-eye contact.

The initial conference of the year may consist primarily of questions. Many schools distribute questionnaires with which the parents can become familiar before the first conference: How does your child feel about himself or herself? What expectations do you have for your child during the coming school experience? What kinds of learning experiences or activities does your child enjoy most? Is the child developing a particular talent or interest? How does your child relate to and get along with siblings and/or neighborhood friends? These questions allow parents to become familiar with some areas of discussion that are often difficult to think about without prior preparation. They generally provide the teacher with much more feedback and also open the lines of communication, because the parents have had time beforehand to think about something that they want to discuss.

Once the child is in school and conferences are scheduled, the teacher should be well prepared with ideas and materials to share with the parents. Portfolios with a sampling of the child's work can show progress being made in specific curriculum areas. The teacher should be able to discuss the child's progress in a number of areas: socially, emotionally, physically (both large- and small-motor areas), and intellectually. Parents are anxious to know of their child's progress in each of these areas and need to see materials that validate the teacher's appraisals. Anecdotal records can strengthen the teacher's evaluations and help parents to appreciate individual attention. Parents are usually anxious to hear about any ideas and activities that they can do at home in order to help their child to improve. Especially when a child is having difficulties in one or more areas, it is helpful for the teacher to give the parents concrete suggestions for helping the child to progress.

The essential ingredients for effective school–parent relationships are frequent, informal contact and warm, respectful, candid conversation. Omitting relevant information is not being honest with parents. Again, it is important for the teacher to listen to the parents—to their suggestions for working with the child or about strategies and activities that work in the home. The skills found to be important in parent–teacher relationships are valuing, accepting, listening, perceiving, guiding, understanding, helping, responding, and empowering (Lopez & Schultz, 1996).

In addition to formal scheduled conferences, teachers should take advantage of informal daily or weekly opportunities for brief but friendly conversations. These may occur when the parent

Spinelli (1998, pp. 22–23) suggests the following guidelines relating to planning the parent conferences:

1. Provide advance notice of meetings.
2. Contact parents before scheduling a meeting to determine a convenient time for everyone.
3. Ask parents what they would like to discuss or accomplish at the meeting.
4. Send a follow-up letter as a reminder (date, time to start and end, location, purpose, agenda, and who will or may be attending).
5. Schedule the conference in a private location that is convenient to the parents and conducive to good communication. The room should be physically and psychologically inviting. Group adult-sized chairs so that everyone is comfortable and at eye level, with no physical barriers between them.
6. Invite parents to bring a support person, if they desire.
7. Allow sufficient time for resolution of ordering concerns and problems.
8. Serve refreshments to help to break the ice.

Spinelli (1998, p. 25) also provides the following guidelines for the teacher:

- Use diplomacy and sensitivity.
- Provide clear, precise examples.
- Keep language simple and direct.
- Avoid educational and/or psychological jargon.
- Observe nonverbal or indirect communication.
- Encourage expression of parental concerns.
- Allow parents to vent.
- Use active listening and reflection.
- Clarify parents' meaning.
- Summarize the conference.

picks the child up from school or when the teacher and parent meet casually in the grocery store. Regardless of how the situation develops, the teacher should make good use of any opportunity for free discussions and for answering any questions that the parent may have. These informal conversations are often the building blocks to effective home–school relationships. School administrators could also schedule lunch meetings with parents to address concerns and suggestions (Rosenthal & Sawyers, 1996).

Tips for Parents Relating to Parent–Teacher Conferences

1. Get to know your child's teacher when school begins.
2. Talk to your child about the upcoming conference, and write down any questions.
3. Be familiar with the child's schoolbooks and homework.
4. Try to have both parents at the conference.
5. Remember the appointment, and be on time.
6. Find out what the teacher expects, and ask questions about various aspects of the curriculum.
7. Find out if there are any scheduled tests; and if there are, what can you do to help your child?
8. Ask about your child's relationship with both adults and peers.
9. Share any information about your child that might help the teacher.
10. Find out ways you can help your child at home to be successful in school.

Adapted from Newman, 1997/98.

There are numerous benefits that result from effective parent conferences and conversations: school programs and climate improve; parents' knowledge and leadership skills increase; family support is maintained; family, school, and community connections are built; and there is more family support of teachers. However, the most important benefit is the impact that the partnerships have on students (Spinelli, 1998)!

Parent Meetings or Parent Education Programs

Parenting classes and workshops have been found to ease parents' tensions and anxieties, improve skills, and teach child development concepts. Parent education programs that actively involve parents and require several sessions have been found to be more effective than single sessions. These meetings, workshops, or programs are planned by the teachers, by the parents, or by the two in collaboration. Since the focus is on parent education, it is advisable to take a poll of the parents' interests and then strive to meet these needs as meetings are planned. The number of meetings per year will depend on parental support and interest. Topics for these meetings could include guidance, facilitating antibias development, and making home learning materials, and curriculum topics such as art activities, science at home, or nutritious food activities.

A variation in parental meetings could involve children in both the planning and presentation. An open house could be planned, with the children acting as hosts and hostesses. A display of some of their work and activities would be shown, with the children acting as chefs for the refreshments. Parent evenings or afternoons could focus on a single topic, such as "Foods We Like to Make and Eat" or a "Science Fair." The children enjoy the preparation and planning involved in these events, but they especially look forward to sharing their school and activities with their parents. One teacher found that he was able to encourage parent involvement in his classroom by sponsoring a simple breakfast in his classroom several times a year. He planned a "Moms and Muffins" or a "Dads and Doughnuts" breakfast; for the latter, he encouraged a dad, uncle, grandpa, neighbor, or friend to share a doughnut and juice with the child, learn what was happening at school, and visit with other parents (*Learning*, 1994c, p. 37). Parent meetings, workshops, and programs can be very beneficial in enhancing parents' skills, knowledge, and attitudes toward their children.

Technology and Telephone Calls

Recent computer and telephone technology affords opportunities for quick and open communication. Parents should feel free to contact teachers and teachers to contact parents. Telephoning need not be only a means of conveying emergencies or reporting negative behavior and problem situations. It also provides a valuable opportunity to let parents know of positive things that occur in the classroom. Technology now enables some communication barriers to be overcome. For example, the use of electronic mail and telephone answering machines enables parents to leave messages for teachers and teachers to transmit general class or curriculum information and homework assignments to parents (*Learning*, 1995).

If a child has had particular success with a concept or curriculum activity, this information can be conveyed to the parents by telephone. For example, a telephone message conveyed by the teacher might be: Today we mixed the three primary colors together to make the secondary colors. We used water colored with food coloring, a white Styrofoam egg carton, and an eyedropper. You should have seen how much Christopher enjoyed this activity! For 30 minutes he continued to experiment with mixing the colors. I am sure he would enjoy doing this activity in your home.

Or, if a child is having particular difficulty with a concept presented at school, do not wait until the formal parent–teacher conference to alert the parents. A phone call can suggest, in a warm and positive way, what the difficulty is and how the parents can help. For example, in a first-grade classroom, the children have had their first activity involving concepts related to money. Rachel has difficulty understanding the values of coins and becomes very frustrated with the activity. In a call that day to the home, the teacher might say: Today we began work with the values of money and coins. Rachel seemed unusually concerned, and I plan to give her individual help at school, but you may wish to work with her at home, too. You may want to role play store situations in giving change or develop simple games to match equal values. For example, if you lay down 10 cents, from the change Rachel has at hand she needs to come up with another combination representing 10 cents. You may also want to encourage her in making actual purchases at stores, such as allowing her to purchase a pound of margarine, giving the grocer the dollar bill, and receiving the change. These kinds of suggestions are usually eagerly welcomed by the parents. It is not as helpful simply to state the learning difficulty, offering no suggestions for action. Technology can and does serve as a bridge between home and school, and it can strengthen the partnership between them.

Home Visits

Through child-centered home visits, a teacher can gain insights about the child that can be obtained in no other way. These visits provide the opportunity to relate to families in their own familiar surroundings and to gain valuable information about the child's needs and his or her interaction in the home environment. Home visits build closer ties between parents and teacher, strengthen the child's self-esteem, and communicate to the family that the child is important to the teacher. To be successful at home visits, the teacher must be able to accept different homes, the diversity of families, and the variations in values, beliefs, and attitudes. Some particularly enlightening information relating to curriculum planning can occur naturally and spontaneously in a home visit.

A Head Start teacher visited a home where the mother was just preparing dinner. She was preparing peas and happened to mention that she never made Rebecca eat them; as a family, they had learned that the texture of peas made Rebecca sick. The Head Start teacher recalled one lunchtime when peas were being served, and Rebecca had been rather persistently made to taste at least some of them. Reserved Rebecca had sat at the lunch table longer than the other children, and the teacher thought Rebecca was just testing to see if she really must taste at least some of the peas!

A kindergarten teacher was making a home visit and discovered that Stephen, with the help of his geologist father, had assembled a collection of rocks and knew many interesting facts and concepts relating to them. This began a unit on rocks, and Stephen proudly brought his specimens and shared his information with the other children.

When arranging for home visits, teachers need to request a visit to the home. Parents should be informed that the teacher is visiting to learn more about the child, to have an opportunity to spend some time with the child, to meet the family, and to allow the family to become better acquainted with the teacher. Pressure should not be put on the parents to have the teacher in their home. There may be special problems in the home at that time, and the parents may view a teacher's visit as one more problem or pressure to be handled. Most often, teachers can sense whether the time is appropriate for a home visit and if they are welcome.

When making a home visit, the teacher must be relaxed, friendly, and alert to the needs and responses of the family. The length of the visit should be determined by the needs of both the family and the teacher. Generally, home visits should not be lengthy unless the teacher has been invited for a special occasion, such as a family meal or a birthday party. Home visits also provide an opportunity for the teacher to introduce into the home a game, activity, or book that the child has enjoyed in the classroom, to be shared with the child and perhaps other family members. Depending on the receptiveness of the parents, the visit may be a good time for giving suggestions about learning activities, materials, or equipment appropriate for home use by the child. When making home visits, some teachers prefer to leave a newsletter or handout relating to learning ideas for home use with the parents. If home visits for a particular child do not seem to be appropriate, the teacher may consider visiting a parent at work.

Swinging is twice as much fun at school when the person doing the pushing is your grandmother!

Parent Involvement and Observation in the Classroom

There are many ways of involving parents in the classroom, and probably a great advantage exists in doing so. Gains made by children in early childhood education programs are maintained to a greater extent when parents are involved in the program than when they are not. When parents take the time to be involved in the classroom, this acts as a teaching experience for them, giving new ideas for home activities and guidance principles and helping them to observe and learn about the child in the school situation. It is also valuable for the child to know that he or she is important enough for the parent to spend time in the classroom. Parent–teacher rapport is strengthened as the "team" works together in the classroom. Parents become more understanding of the teacher's role as they view the teaching situation from the inside. This results in more positive attitudes toward the school and the staff.

Many teachers prepare a parent-involvement calendar at the beginning of the year, quarter, or month based on parents' needs and schedules and inviting all parents who are able into the classroom as volunteers. This is preceded by a parent meeting scheduled at the beginning of the year to help parents to understand their responsibilities and opportunities in the classroom. Teachers should convey to the parents the value of their participation, helping parents to understand that they have expertise and skills that will contribute greatly to the classroom. Most working parents, if they have adequate advance notice, are able to arrange time to be in the classroom. When parents are aware of the projects and activities at school, they can more often contribute with shared expertise or experiences (Katz & Chard, 1997).

Expectations and responsibilities need to be very clear when parents are assisting in the classroom; duties assigned to them should be important and relevant (Finders & Lewis, 1994). Parents should view themselves as participators, and not just as cleanup persons. They can become involved with the children in the various activities and experiences. For example, parents could sit at the manipulative table and visit with the children while helping them with the play materials. Parents might also read to children, sing with them, participate in their games, eat with them, build with them, and otherwise interact with them. Where cleanup is necessary or when assistance in dressing or undressing is needed, they will do it! In primary-grade classes, teachers should give parents the opportunity of working with their own children, hearing them read, helping them to write a story, completing an assignment, or working on a project. Parent volunteers in the primary grades are especially valuable when working with children who have emotional, social, physical, or academic problems.

To interact with parents more, one teacher did a unit titled "What Do Grown-ups Do All Day? The World of Work." The unit lasted all year and integrated many curriculum areas. The unit included parent questionnaires; field trips to some parents' workplaces; and activities such as mapping where parents ate lunch, having parent visitors who described what they did, and having children draw their parents at work (Nachbar, 1992, p. 6). Parent visits to the classroom may also be for the purpose of observation. Many early childhood programs in colleges and universities have observation booths with one-way viewing mirrors for student and parent observation. In other classrooms, the teachers also encourage the parents to visit and observe their child in action.

Another occasion for parent involvement in the classroom is when extra help is needed. For example, food activities and field trips may require additional help or supervision. Perhaps a parent has a particular skill that lends itself to a unit of study. During a unit on fish, a father who was an avid fisherman visited the class and brought his fishing gear to demonstrate. He showed the children how to prepare the fishing pole, how to use the many different kinds of flies and other gear in his tackle box, and then how to cast. Slides were brought of a fishing trip that he and his son had taken and of his young son catching a fish. The children watched as he demonstrated how to fillet a fish. Then, with a skillet in the middle of the circle, the fish was cooked and served to the children. Teachers should find out parents' hobbies and professions in order to learn of special skills or talents that can be shared with the children.

Sensitive teachers and staff should recognize that the needs, schedules, backgrounds, time, skills, and values of parents are all unique, so the participation of parents should also be geared to their individual capabilities.

Policy Planning, Decision Making, and Evaluation

Positive effects will be felt when parents are included as members of policy-planning committees or boards involved in decision making and/or evaluations related to the children, school, homes, programs, and policies (Dodd, 1996). However, parents must have information in order to participate in a meaningful and rational way in policy-making decisions. When parents are invited to be involved, their thinking and suggestions must have merit and be a meaningful part of the decisions made.

Parent Resource Centers

Facilities should be set up to allow parents to visit the classroom and benefit from school resources offering parenting help and methods for extending what is being taught into the home. A parent room or parents' area can be organized to include books on child development; materials, books, and toys that can be checked out for home use; videos; and other resources such as free pamphlets and brochures. Parents must be introduced to this resource and made aware of what is available in order for them to make use of the program. Programs usually include books, materials, games, and resources on particular topics. In one community, the school puts together age-appropriate materials into packets that are given out by the hospital when the child is born and then are sent to the family on each child's birthday until the child enters school. This project ties the family to the school before the child even enters school (Spewock, 1991).

Many school districts are now providing parent resource centers, which supply these same kinds of services. Even a small private preschool or a single kindergarten can make available materials and equipment to support parents in teaching their children at home. Parent bulletin boards or displays can be set up, and parents will automatically check for parent education, information, or handouts.

Summary

Effective work and communication with parents are necessary in any good early childhood program, and we must look to parents as friends and helpers. The child is in school for only a limited time each day. It is vital that a positive partnership between the home and the school be established and that parents and teachers see each other as playing an important role in the education of the child. We must develop the ability to understand and work with all different types of families. When we become familiar with the families of the children, it is easier for us to make appropriate adjustments to barriers and provide opportunities for successful family partnerships and involvement. "One of the greatest challenges to teachers striving for successful family involvement is knowing and understanding families so as to eliminate erroneous assumptions and barriers that may prevent full participation" (Kieff & Wellhousen, 2000, pp. 19, 20).

The teacher's purpose, in part, must be to help parents to utilize their potential, discover their strengths and talents, and then use these for the benefit of the children themselves and their family. In addition, the purpose of any parent-teacher or parent-school activity is to develop school-home relationships, to promote school-community activities, and, most of all, to strengthen the child. We must understand family priorities, needs, and resources if we are to effectively develop school-home partnerships. Often our perceptions of the needs of children differ from the perceptions of the families (Judge & Parette, 1998). It is hoped that any relationship or meeting with the parents will help the child. Parent involvement can be the catalyst whereby more changes and better things can emerge in the future. Changes in attitudes and behaviors between parents and their children offer great potential for lasting beneficial effects.

Teachers must recognize their responsibility in planning for parent participation and involvement. They are responsible for building trust, making the initial contacts, inviting parent participation, and providing positive reinforcement. Although planning for parent partnerships takes time and can be challenging, the positive effects and outcomes are well worth it and are causing the interest in parent involvement to continue to grow. As professionals, teachers are able to develop good relationships with students' families through class activities, conferences, telephone calls, notes, home visits, casual conversations, and actively involving parents in the program (Berger, 1995). It is important for teachers to recognize that all parents can make valuable contributions to programs. Teachers can begin by developing positive attitudes toward parent involvement and helping parents to understand the benefits that will come from their participation and involvement.

Parents and teachers need to nurture and build one another in partnerships that draw on one another's strengths. Without parent involvement, programs or schools cannot achieve the ultimate objective of excellence for which both are striving. Partnerships with parents must be built on positive approaches, with patience and confidence that the efforts will result in strong and supportive relationships among children, parents, and teachers. The rippling effect of these benefits will be evidenced in more successful school-home encounters.

Student Learning Activities

1. Find out whether arrangements could be made for you to observe during a professional teacher's home visit, the purpose of which is to encourage the development of a partnership with the family.

2. Interview an early childhood teacher and find out what methods are being incorporated for developing a partnership with the family and extending the curriculum into the home. Ask which methods the teacher feels are most valuable for helping parents to carry out learning activities in the home.

3. Visit the home of a child between the ages of 3 and 8 years. It may be a child in your neighbor-

hood, or your instructor may provide a list of parents who would enjoy having you in their home to teach a home-learning activity. Plan a learning activity that would be appropriate for the child's age; there are many suggestions throughout this book. Call the home and arrange for the visit, and then evaluate the visit and the experience. What went well? Were the parents and the child interested in the learning activity that you presented? Did the child become involved? What would you do differently on your next visit?

4. Select an early childhood grade level, such as kindergarten, and establish two concepts that would be taught at this age level. For each of these concepts, write three different learning activities that could be suggested or shared with parents for home use and learning.

5. Based on your studies and observations of various programs for young children, describe how you would be able to involve the families of the children in ways that would help to meet the needs of the children. What are some kinds of family involvement that you have observed in various programs?

6. Read at least one of the resources suggested at the end of this chapter and make a list of the most meaningful things you learned about developing home–school partnerships and extending the curriculum into the home.

7. Visit a parent resource center in a local school district and list some of the materials in which you were particularly interested. Discuss how you would use them with parents.

8. Visit your local library and make a list of some of the services it offers parents. Summarize the good parenting material available and also some of the materials that you would suggest to parents for providing meaningful learning activities in the home.

9. Plan an informal potluck picnic or dinner and describe how you would begin to develop a positive relationship with the parents and children.

10. Make a detailed list of possible topics for parent workshops and meetings.

11. Attend a parent–school meeting in a school district or center and evaluate it in terms of the ideas that you read about in this chapter.

Suggested Resources

For Teachers

Barclay, K., & E. Boone (1995). *Building a three-way partnership: The leader's role in linking school, family, and community.* New York: Scholastic.

Berger, E. H. (1994). *Parents as partners in education: Families and schools working together* (4th ed.) Upper Saddle River, NJ: Merrill/ Prentice Hall.

Chira, S. (1993). What do teachers want most? Help from parents. *New York Times,* June 23, 1993, p. 7.

Cryer, D., & M. Burchinal (1997). Parents as child care consumers. *Early Childhood Research Quarterly 12,* 35-38.

Decker, L. E., & V. A. Decker (1994). *Getting parents involved in their children's education.* Arlington, VA: American Association of School Administrators.

DeShazer, S. (1994). *Words were originally magic.* New York: Norton.

Developmental Studies Center (1994). *At home in our schools: Schoolwide activities to build community.* Oakland, CA: Author. (Can be ordered at 1-800-666-7270.)

Diffily, D., & K. Morrison (eds.) (1996). *Family-friendly communication for early childhood programs.* Washington, DC: NAEYC.

Eggbeer, L., & E. Fenichel (1994). Educating and supporting the infant family work force: Models, methods, and materials. *Zero to Three 15*(3).

Families and Work Institute (1994). *Employers, families, and education: Facilitating family involvement in learning.* New York: Author.

Finders, M., & C. Lewis (1994). Why some parents don't come to school. *Educational Leadership 51*(8): 50-54.

Foster, S. M. (1994). Successful parent meetings. *Young Children 50*(1): 78-80.

Freedman, J., & G. Combs (1996). *Narrative therapy: The social construction of preferred realities.* New York: Norton.

Gage, J., & S. Workman (1994). Creating family support systems: In Head Start and beyond. *Young Children 50*(1): 74-77.

Goodman, J. (1995). Change without a difference: School restructuring in historical perspective. *Harvard Educational Review 65*(1): 1-29.

Gorham, P. J., & P. N. Nason (1994). Why make teachers' work more visible to parents? *Young Children 52*(5): 22-26.

Greenwood, D. (1995). Home-school communication via video. *Young Children 50*(6): 66.

Hauser-Cram, P. (1994). Backing away helpfully: Some roles teachers shouldn't fill. *Child Care Information Exchange*, May/June 1994, pp. 73-77.

Helm, J. (1994). Family theme bags: An innovative approach to family involvement in the school. *Young Children 49*(4): 48-52.

Henderson, A. T., & N. Berla (1994). *A new generation of evidence: The family is critical to student achievement.* Washington, DC: National Committee for Citizens in Education.

Kokoski, T., & N. Downing-Leffler (1995). Boosting your science and home–school connection. *Young Children 50*(5): 35-39.

Kristeller, J. (1994). Creating curriculum as a workshop: An interactive process involving children, teachers, and families. *Early Childhood Today 9*(3): 58-60.

Lee, F. Y. (1995). Asian parents as partners. *Young Children 50*(3): 4-9.

Manning, D., & P.J. Schindler (1997). Communicating with parents when their children have difficulties. *Young Children 52*(5): 27-33.

Manning, M., G. Manning, & G. Morrison (1995). Letter-writing connections: A teacher, first-graders, and their parents. *Young Children 50*(6): 34-38.

Marcon, R. A. (1993). *Parental involvement and early school success: Following the "Class of 2000" at year five.* Paper presented at the Biennial Meeting of the Society for Research in Child Development, New Orleans, LA (ERIC Document Reproduction Service No. ED357-881).

Montanari, E. (1993). Keeping families happy: Communication is the key. *Child Care Information Exchange 90*(3): 21-23.

National Association for the Education of Young Children (1996). Be

a children's champion. Public policy report. *Young Children 51*(2): 58-60.

National Education Association (1996). *Building parent partnerships.* Washington, DC: Author.

Neilsen, L. E., & J. M. Finkelstein (1993). A new approach to parent conferences. *Teaching K-8, 24*(1): 90-92.

O'Callaghan, J. B. (1993). *School-based collaboration with families.* San Francisco: Jossey-Bass.

O'Hanlon, W. (1996). Basics of postmodern thinking. Presentation at the Therapeutic Conversations 3 Conference, 27-30 June, Denver, CO.

Ramirez-Smith, C. (1995). Stopping the cycle of failure: The Comer model. *Educational Leadership 52*(5): 14-19.

Sexton, D., J. Aldridge, & P. Snyder (1994). Family-driven early intervention. *Dimensions 22*: 14-18.

Spiegel, D., J. Fitzgerald, & J. Cunningham (1993). Parental perceptions of preschoolers' literacy development: Implications for home-school partnerships. *Young Children 48*(5): 74-79.

Stipek, D., L. Rosenblatt, & L. DiRocco (1994). Making parents your allies. *Young Children 49*(3): 4-9.

Swick, K. J. (1994). Family involvement: An empowerment perspective. *Dimensions of early childhood 22*(2): 5-9.

Swick, K. J., & S. B. Graves (1993). *Empowering at-risk families during the early childhood years.* Washington, DC: NEA.

Topping, K. (1995). Cued spelling: A powerful technique for parent and peer tutoring. *Reading Teacher 48*(5): 374-383.

Weissbourd, B., & S. Kagan (1994). *Putting families first.* San Francisco: Jossey-Bass.

Workman, S. H., & J. A. Gage (1997). Family-school partnerships: A family-strengths approach. *Young Children 52*(4), 10-19.

For Parents (only a few of the many offered)

Bellanca, J., C. Castagna, & S. Archibald Marcus (1990). *Star parents training manual: Skills for effective parenting.* Palatine, IL: Skylight.

Berger, E. H. (1994). *Parents as partners in education: Families and schools working together* (4th ed.). Upper Saddle River, NJ: Merrill/Prentice Hall.

Brazelton, T. B. (1992). *To listen to a child: Understanding the normal problems of growing up.* Reading, MA: Addison-Wesley.

Brooks, J. B. (1991). *The process of parenting* (3rd ed.). Palo Alto, CA: Mayfield.

Dinkmeyer, D., Sr., & D. Dinkmeyer, Jr. (1989). *Parenting young children: Parent's handbook.* Circle Pines, MN: American Guidance Service.

Dobson, J. (1992). *The new dare to discipline.* Wheaton, IL: Tyndale.

Rothenberg, B. A., S. Dubin, K. Merilo, R. Beacom, J. Hilliard, & L. Sarnat (1993). *Parentmaking: Educators training program.* Menlo Park, CA: Banster.

Szykula, S. A. (1991). *The parenting cookbook: Recipes for raising successful children.* Salt Lake City, UT: Family First.

Videos and Other Resource Materials

Ammon, M. S., & J. Collier (1994). *Leamos junto: Let's read together.* Berkeley: University of California Cooperative Extension Family Development (booklet). *The art of building and maintaining relationships with parents.* New York: Insight Media (video).

California State PTA (1991). *Parents empowering parents: The California State PTA parent education manual.* Los Angeles: Author (manual).

Community involvement: Working together to improve schools (with James P. Comer). Salt Lake City, UT: Video Journal of Education (video).

Conducting effective conferences with parents. New York: Insight Media (video).

Connecting with students and parents. New York: Insight Media (video).

ETN parent education series. Los Angeles: Los Angeles County Office of Education (8 videos).

Friendship Is Fundamental, poster #440; Nurture Negotiating Skills, poster #410; Volunteers Are Valuable, poster #442. Washington, DC: NAEYC, 1997.

Gordon, T. (1989). *Parent effectiveness training*. Washington, DC: Educational Services (cassette tape).

How families can help children learn. Salt Lake City, UT: Video Journal of Education (video).

How to create successful parent-student conferences. New York: Insight Media (video).

Jones, J. J. (1997). *Let's fix the kids* (6th ed.). Westminister, CA: Jones Publishing (a series of parenting seminars; contact at 1-800-349-2543; Web site: http://www.fixakid.com).

Parent-teacher conferences: Resolving conflicts peacefully. New York: Insight Media (video).

Parental involvement (Episode #34). Washington, DC: NEA, 1994 (video).

Parents as partners (Episode #5). Washington, DC: NEA, 1992 (video).

Partnerships with parents. Washington, DC: NAEYC, 1997 (video).

Chapter 4

Planning the Curriculum

The early childhood curriculum should be planned around the developmental needs of the children in the classroom. Many early childhood educators associate curriculum with the "whole child" (Williams, 1999).

> The goals and objectives of the curriculum need to be designed to strengthen all aspects of the children's development, including cognitive, language, emotional, social, and physical capabilities.

"The task of determining the early childhood curriculum, therefore, hinges to a certain extent on discovering the nature of children" (Williams, 1999, p. 1). Units should be based on themes that will be both interesting and developmentally beneficial. On the other hand, "projects" may be based on the interests or passions of the children in the classroom (Ferguson, 2001).

In a position statement by the National Association for the Education of Young Children (NAEYC) and the National Association of Early Childhood Specialists in State Departments of Education (NAECS/SDE), curriculum is defined as "an organized framework that delineates the content children are to learn, the processes through which children achieve the identified curricular goals, what teachers do to help children achieve these goals, and the context in which teaching and learning occur" (NAEYC & NAECS/SDE, 1991, p. 21). Curriculum is what happens in the classroom. However, Beatty (1995) submits that, even though nearly all early educators advocate a developmentally appropriate curriculum, definitions are most often broad and vague. "Providing plenty of time for free play with toys of the right size for little fingers, not forcing children to sit still for long periods of time doing paper and pencil schoolwork, and having teachers who understand young children's emotional needs are basic requirements" (Beatty, 1995, p. 205).

Developmentally appropriate curriculum also needs to be compatible with the individual needs and interests of each child in the program and also be culturally adapted to those involved (Bredekamp & Copple, 1997; NAEYC & NAECS/SDE, 1991). There is great diversity in children with regard to their experiences, maturation rates, interests, needs, parent support, and learning styles (NAEYC & NAECS/SDE, 1991). When our curriculum is culturally sensitive, it helps children to make sense of their world, creates harmony between the home and school, and helps to make the concept of diversity and acceptance a natural part of their understanding. A well-planned curriculum takes this diversity into account.

When schools adopt rigid, uniform, and structured interpretations of developmental appropriateness, this can lead to insensitivity to multicultural issues (Lubeck, 1994; New & Malory, 1994). Sometimes our perceptions, images, expectations, and covert biases unfairly influence children's educational potential and opportunities. This is why it is important to do a needs assessment and to evaluate throughout the program. One source suggests that curriculum development should draw from many sources: "child development knowledge, individual characteristics of children, the knowledge base of various disciplines, the values of our culture, parents' desires, and the knowledge children need to function competently in our society" (NAEYC & NAECS/SDE, 1991, p. 23).

Principles that guide effective teaching are the following:

1. Effective learners actively process lesson content.
2. Presenting information from multiple perspectives increases the durability of instruction.
3. Effective instruction should build upon students' knowledge and experiences and be grounded in meaningful contexts (Ornstein & Behar-Horenstein, 1999).

Experiences should be developed to help young children to improve their skills in problem solving, thinking, reasoning, and creating, not just their skill in memorizing what is taught by the teacher. Too often the curriculum and the way it is taught encourage children to become expert rote memorizers, rather than creative, reflective, involved learners. Facts may eventually become outdated, but the skills of thinking, making meaning, developing understanding, and problem solving never will. An old proverb says, "Give me a fish, and I will be fed today. Teach me how to fish, and I will be fed forever." Simply, how to solve a problem is more important than the solution.

Recent research on brain development indicates that the more active children are, the better they learn (Jensen, 2000b). Howard Gardner advocates: "I believe in action and activity. The brain learns best and retains most when the organism is actively involved in exploring physical sites and materials and asking questions to which it actually craves answers. Merely passive experiences tend to attenuate and have little lasting impact" (Gardner, 1999, p. 82). Therefore, learning should

Flexible curriculum planning adjusts to the various developmental levels of children. During this musical activity, some of the children are doing the actions, while others are choosing to observe for a while.

be a process of active involvement, with rich, meaningful content, using developmentally appropriate practices and approaches, not just focusing on an end result.

Learning should be engaging and active, and it should include many hands-on experiences. The many kinds of active learning experiences include role playing, creative dramatics, simulations, pantomime, games, art activities, and storytelling (Kline, 1995). Curriculum has deeper meaning for children when it connects them to real-world experiences, including their culture (Patton & Kokoski, 1996). The more input we have from the children in curriculum planning, the closer we come to achieving that direction. One approach is to begin units or lessons with the K–W–L chart (Ogle, 1986). The chart is divided into three columns. The first column is K: what do we know; the second is W: what do we want to know or wonder about; and the third is L: what we learned. Williams (1997, pp. 78–80) suggests four similar questions to ask children when we involve them in curriculum planning:

- What do you wonder or want to know about?

- What can we do to find out?

- What materials do we need?

- What will you bring? What would you like me to bring?

Then proceed! "Everyone wins when children are involved in curriculum planning" (Williams, 1997, p. 80).

The curriculum will provide opportunities for development in areas besides intellectual or cognitive growth. It should provide encouragement of, and opportunities for, healthy social, emotional, physical, and intellectual development. Most early childhood educators and parents think preschool education should strengthen children's social competence and language skills (Beatty, 1995). It should allow adequate time and opportunity for children to express themselves freely through various media: creative materials, large- and small-muscle materials, dramatic or role-playing materials, manipulative toys and materials, books and other literature, sensory media, and resource people.

There is no such thing as a universal curriculum that is appropriate for all. One characteristic

"of preschool education compared to elementary and secondary education is that it has been relatively nonuniform: There are many different kinds of good preschools, just as there are many different kinds of good parents" (Beatty, 1995, p. 205). To create a meaningful curriculum with respect to how children learn and what children know, VanScoy (1995) has suggested that we trade the three R's (reading, 'riting, and 'rithmetic) for the four E's: experience, extension, expression, and evaluation. Even the various approaches that we have taken in this text need to be tailored to fit children, teachers, and program goals. By suggesting a variety of ways to plan and implement curriculum, our intention is to emphasize the need for flexibility and make it easier to accomplish.

A variety of play and learning activities is included throughout the text and discussed in greater detail elsewhere, such as stories, art, music, dramatic play, science, physical fitness activities and games, and other kinds of experiences. Examples of these are included in lesson, activity, and unit plans. In this chapter we include a discussion of two types of learning activities, field trips and visitors, and then throughout the text you will find specific examples for field trips and visitors as they relate to the themes and topics discussed.

PLANNING BASED ON NEEDS

As a teacher answers the questions "What are my objectives?" "What will I do?" "Why will I do it?" "How will I do it?" and "How will I assess it?" the curriculum is determined. Particular models prescribe, in specific terms, the answers to these questions. However, in most classrooms the curriculum is more traditional, and answers to these questions depend on the teacher's training, the materials available, and the purposes or long-range goals, based on the needs of the children. These directions are established for the program by the teacher, administrators, parents, or, ideally, all these people together. In addition, children should be a part of the planning (Chard, 1992, 1994; Kohn, 1993a; Levin, 1994). They can make suggestions for themes or topics to investigate; or once a theme is selected, they can help to select specific aspects or activities to study. In the "project approach," children work individually or in groups with the teacher guiding the child's work (Chard, 1992, 1994). A project could be defined as "children's in-depth investigations of topics that interest them" (Hartman & Eckerty, 1995, p. 141). Projects may be initiated by either children or teachers, but the children provide the main impetus for direction and depth. The subjects are generally related to events and ideas with which the children are familiar. Children tend to stay focused and motivated on projects for longer periods of time when they have a personal invested interest in their learning (Barbour & Seefeldt, 1993). Projects or curriculum may emerge from a child's question (Heckman, Confer, & Hakim, 1994). When children are pressed to think beyond what they already know, this inspires understanding (Perkins & Blythe, 1994). As children realize that their ideas result in action, their self-esteem and initiative are enhanced (Nunnelley, 1990).

Goals are absolutely essential to each program. They give something to move toward, a larger framework from which to plan. Every center or program should make a list of purposes or long-range goals: What is the mission of this program or classroom? What should a parent expect a child to achieve by attending this school or program for a given length of time? What is the approach, and where is the emphasis? These goals should be posted so that parents, teachers, and administrators can read them—and read them often! Some programs or schools offer them in the form of a mission statement. The mission statement provides an overall direction for the program or school. It allows stakeholders a clear vision of the intent of the program or school.

Why?

Goals and objectives constitute the *why* of the curriculum. They provide the reasoning behind the program—the purposes of the teaching. *Why* questions must be asked constantly: Why should we have this particular activity? Why should we have this activity at the time it is planned? Why is it of value to the children? Why will it benefit the child? If there are no purposeful goals or objectives, reevaluation and redirection are needed.

It is necessary to make a distinction between the terms *objectives* and *goals*. Too often the terms *goals, objectives, values,* and *purposes* are used interchangeably. From the long-term goals, the teacher is able to make short-term objectives that will guide the curriculum. When we talk about the long-term desires of a program, we are referring to goals; when we talk about short-term desires, we are referring to objectives. Specific daily objectives add up to the long-term goals that the teacher is trying to reach. Objectives should be specific, clearly state the purpose of the unit, lesson, or activity, and suggest the desired behavior or what should be learned by the child as a result of participation.

> Objectives should be planned and written from the perspective of "What do I want my students to *know, do,* and/or *feel* as a result of this unit or lesson?

Objectives are student centered and guide learning activities and assessments. Curriculum alignment occurs when objectives, learning activities, and assessments match one another. For most teachers, Bloom's taxonomy (Bloom, 1956) is helpful in designing objectives that move children into higher-level thinking activities and projects by the very nature of the verb selected. In early childhood, teachers rarely go beyond application and analysis, but by third grade many students are able to synthesize and evaluate and should be encouraged to do so by the objectives and outcomes expected.

Besides carefully observing children and determining their needs, support in planning and writing objectives for units and lessons also comes from national content standards, such as those in mathematics and social studies, and from state core standards and objectives. This is especially true for teachers teaching K–3rd grade in public school settings. Therefore, as part of curriculum planning, teachers review the national standards and those of their state. These are found on state Web sites, and teachers are expected to align their teaching to these standards.

In some cases, it may be both helpful and necessary to make individual plans for a child and write specific *performance objectives.* These

Bloom's Taxonomy		
Competence	Skills Demonstrated	Verbs
Knowledge	Observe and recall information	list, define, describe, identify show, examine, name
Comprehension	Understand information or ideas, grasp meaning	describe, summarize, interpret, contrast, predict, discuss, illustrate
Application	Use information or use methods in new situations	apply, demonstrate, complete, illustrate, change, experiment, discover
Analysis	See patterns and relationships	analyze, compare, contrast, separate, order, classify, infer, explain
Synthesis	Combine ideas to form a new whole	create, invent, develop, design, plan
Evaluation	Compare and discriminate between ideas	judge, critique, decide, assess, conclude

Adapted from Bloom, Englehart, Furst, Hill & Krathwohl, 1956.

statements describe the desired behavior and the performance expected. At times the teacher has specific learning in mind that will result from the child's experiences in the classroom. Therefore, a performance objective is a description of that learning. It describes the way the child will demonstrate what he or she has learned. Many educators consider performance objectives too rigid and structured, forcing the child to perform certain skills simply to satisfy the goal. We believe that in some cases this kind of objective is appropriate when a specific behavior is being sought or encouraged.

What?

What activities and materials are needed to carry out the desired goals and objectives? In effect, what will be done? The curriculum is planned with the themes, projects, and activities that are developmentally appropriate, that answer the *what* question. The activities need to be aligned to or match the learning objectives or desired outcomes of the unit or lesson.

In addition to making a list of the broad program goals or purposes of the center or program, based on children's needs, some teachers plan themes for the entire year to provide direction

and meaningful sequencing of themes and concepts; however, if we are to direct our curriculum to the needs of children, this practice should either be approached with flexibility or should be avoided. Others, taking a more child-centered approach, seek to learn what experiences the children in the class bring with them and use these experiences along with their questions and interests to guide the curriculum (Chard, 1992, 1994). Through careful selection of themes, projects, units, and daily activities (some supporting the theme), days will be balanced with varied experiences, and the question "What will we do?" is answered.

How?

How will the selected activities (*what*) be presented and carried out for the desired goals and objectives (*why*) to be achieved? Answering this question includes preparing and planning materials and procedures, as well as gathering needed supplies and determining the approach for following through. It encourages the teacher not only to plan the activity, but also to organize work. In the approach to lesson planning suggested in this book, the Procedures sections answer this *how* question. With this question answered, the teacher knows the procedures or sequence for the activity, from beginning to completion.

As a teacher carefully thinks through these three questions, the curriculum becomes stronger. Teachers should know *why* they are doing *what* they are doing and *how*, specifically, they will accomplish their plans.

ASSESSING CHILDREN'S NEEDS

Teacher's Role

The abilities and needs of the children, both individually and collectively, must be assessed by the teacher. Without this preassessment, desired goals of teaching may never be realized. With this objective reached, the teacher is able to plan, set up, and create a learning environment suited to the developing child.

As the curriculum is organized and carried out, a knowledge of what the child needs and is able to do assists the teacher in captivating and motivating the child. In addition, it allows the teacher to promote self-direction and intrinsic rewards in learning. In "learning-centered classrooms, the teacher moves away from dispensing information and toward guiding students' efforts to make sense of their work" (Heuwinkel, 1996, p. 30). When children are allowed the luxury of defining curriculum content, when they are able to move in academic directions that interest them, and when they actually *do* something, they become engaged in their learning (Perrone, 1994). Ultimately, the teacher is accountable for determining what is best for the individual child, as well as the whole class, and then doing it; however, what is usually best for the child is to allow the child agency and responsibility for his or her own learning.

Hart, Burts, and Charlesworth (1997) list questions that educators can ask to assist in the development of assessment tools:

- What is considered typical development for the age level that I teach?

- What do I want the children to know and be able to do when they leave my classroom (program)?

- What will be assessed in each developmental domain and content area?

- What methods will I use to assess and document the progress of each child?

These reflective questions can encourage teachers to really think about their assessment of young children and recognize that assessment needs to be thought of in the planning stage and not at the end of a lesson or unit.

Planning Based on Developmental Needs

What we know about children should be at the center of our work with children (Goldberg, 1997). We know from research that all children pass through stages of growth in the various developmental areas; however, children do not pass through these stages at the same rate (Elkind, 1991b, 1996; NAEYC & NAECS/SDE, 1991). In a classroom of children within a 1-year age range, there may actually be a developmental range of several years in cognitive, social, emotional, and physical areas. Teachers must expect a wide range of individual differences (Elkind, 1996; NAEYC & NAECS/SDE, 1991). The challenge comes in determining where each child is developmentally and then matching appropriate learning activities and curriculum to that developmental stage. This requires observation, listening, planning, organization, assessment, and often help from other professionals.

If all children are asked to do the same things, in the same way, and all at the same time, we are not honoring their distinct, individual learning styles, abilities, and interests (Cartwright, 1991). When programs are geared to individual children, the teacher cannot *control* all the children all the time; on the contrary, children become self-disciplined as they take responsibility for their own learning. Then they learn from their own initiative and action. From the constructivist perspective, autonomy should be the aim of education; to foster autonomy in the classroom, children need encouragement to make their own decisions and also to enforce their own rules (Kamii, Clark, & Dominick, 1994).

Frequently, we find that teachers have planned the curriculum for an entire school year before they have even met the children that they will be teaching. Too often the teaching focus considers only the scope and sequence guides established by national, state, and local organizations and pays little attention to the developmental needs of individual children in the classroom. It is more effective to begin the year with a needs assessment that determines the strengths, developmental levels, and needs of the children; this also identifies the best place to begin and the competencies that should be stressed. Throughout the year, additional observations and performance assessments or alternative assessments determine the child's progress and help to select appropriate curricula.

In addition, nearly every classroom has children who have learning difficulties. More and more, schools are utilizing programs for early recognition of children who may be displaying signs of impending special needs. Screening and assessment can alert the school or program to the existence of developmental deviations that may be due to physical, psychological, or neurological circumstances. Early diagnosis decreases the possibility of the conditions becoming more severe and increases the opportunity for successful corrective treatment.

As a reminder, we stress again that programs should be developmentally appropriate and based on the needs of children. It is far more beneficial and successful to design programs to fit the children than to expect children to fit the program or curriculum. Therefore, assessment testing should not be a diagnosis for success or failure, advancement or retention, but a means of determining the needs and goals of individual children (McAfee & Leong, 1994; Shepard, 1994). Assessment should be based on the goals of the program and be used to benefit children (NAEYC & NAECS/SDE, 1991; Shepard, 1994). "The key characteristics of classroom assessment are that it is child centered, classroom centered, and multidimensional" (McAfee & Leong, 1994, p. 3).

Assessment Tools

The purpose of all assessment is to provide teachers with the information to best inform their teaching of individual children (Teale, 1990). Classroom teachers work with resource teachers or skilled psychologists in selecting and administering appropriate assessment tools. These should involve hands-on activities, rather than pencil-and-paper tests (NAEYC & NAECS/SDE, 1991).

> Portfolios, projects, or self-evaluations are used as alternatives to tests and are considered to be more authentic and appropriate.

We must know the purpose of assessment in order to select the most appropriate approach. As the results of the assessment are evaluated, professionals and classroom teachers work together to determine goals for individual children.

Informal assessment. Informal assessments include observations, performance samples, portfolio entries, and other measures of what the child's abilities and disabilities are. The most productive techniques of assessing in early childhood are in individual assessment of children while they are involved in various activities. Teachers can learn the most about what children know, do, and feel by carefully observing them and noting behaviors and comments. The work that they do tells a great story of their development and understanding. Observations and anecdotal records have been traditional forms of informal assessment and are still recommended as a reliable source of information. The more current term, documentation, expands informal assessment from the traditional observation techniques by including technologies such as video- and audio-taping. Thus, documentation may include photographs, drawings, audiotape transcriptions, videotapes, and additional forms of observing and documenting the growth and progress of children (Helm, Beneke, & Steinheimer, 1998).

Formal assessment. The primary purpose of formal assessments is to help teachers to make informed and responsible decisions about materials, grouping students, and what students need to practice (Stallman & Pearson, 1990). It is essential for anyone involved in selecting, administering, and evaluating an assessment to recognize his or her responsibilities and to be accountable. Those involved in any aspect of assessing children must have the training required to participate in the selection, administration, and evaluation of the particular assessment. The person must be familiar with the assessment, what skills and abilities are being assessed, and whether the assessment selected is age appropriate.

Even when formal assessments such as prekindergarten testing, developmental screening, or achievement tests are used, they should be combined with observational or other performance measures to determine appropriate instructional programs for young children. Performance assessment is the process of gathering information by organized observation in order to make a decision about a student (Pierson & Beck, 1993). In performance assessment there is a need for standards for the selection process (as in a portfolio) or for analysis (as in observations or interviews), and performance assessment usually measures what children can *do* or *apply* rather than what they *know* (Pierson & Beck, 1993).

Portfolios are an effective assessment tool to chart progress and show work in various areas. Reflection is the key component in portfolio assessment (Smith, 2000). With modeling, training, and prompting, even young children can be encouraged to look back on their work and to make decisions about which work should be included in the portfolio. In reviewing and studying portfolio assessment, Smith (2000, p. 208) drew these conclusions:

- Preschool children who are given time and who practice reflection will provide meaningful, reflective responses.

- Preschoolers who share their portfolios will teach each other and help one another to expand their reflective abilities.

- Decision making in the classroom encourages and enhances reflective thought.

- Reflective portfolios provide a "meeting place" for parent, teacher, and child to be informed about the preschooler's learning.

Screening and assessment results need to be utilized carefully, with the needs of the individual child being the primary goal. The child's rights must be protected, and teachers and other staff must realize that assessment results are confidential. Results must be interpreted accurately and carefully, and these interpretations must be shared with others working with the child, including the parents, in such a way that they are not misunderstood or misinterpreted. Assessment tools should reflect the diversity of children and be free of biases (NAEYC & NAECS/SDE, 1991).

Even though there have been volumes of literature written suggesting the inappropriate use

We must make it very clear that group-administered standardized achievement tests are not recommended before the third grade (Kamii, 1990). "Individually constructed meanings cannot be measured within the constraints of standardized tests" (Heuwinkel, 1996, p. 30).

of standardized achievement tests for measuring student learning in the early childhood years, the practice still continues. In fact, standardized testing is required for schools to be eligible for such federally funded programs as Chapter One (ACEI, 1995c). "Assessments should be conducted only if they serve a beneficial purpose: to gain services for children with special needs, to inform instruction by building on what students already know, to improve programs, or to provide evidence nationally or in the states about programmatic needs" (Shepard, 1994, p. 209).

Informal assessment.   The focus and trend in early childhood assessment is away from formal assessment (group or individual standardized tests) and toward "alternative" or more informal methods of assessment that are authentic or meaningful (Wiggins, 1992). Such alternative assessment practices as portfolios, individual conferences, and written and verbal explanations of students' work are much more realistic and accurate measurements of children's progress.

Informal, "alternative," or authentic assessment approaches and methods are used when students demonstrate their understanding by writing or making something or by engaging in a performance (McAfee & Leong, 1994; Ybarra & Hollingsworth, 1996). Some authors also refer to this kind of assessment as project-based or performance-based assessment. In these alternative assessments there may be various ways to demonstrate knowledge, and each child's progress is compared to his or her own prior work.

McAfee and Leong (1994, p. 3) suggest that informal assessment

is based on information gained by observing children in a variety of situations; interviewing them; analyzing what they have built, drawn, or written; consulting parents, other teachers, and specialists; studying what children report about themselves and other children; and informal inventories of specific aspects of development, as well as information from appropriate tests.

The following is a suggested informal assessment to be used in whole or in part as a check sheet based on observations of the child and the work that the child does. It is suggested that the assessment *not* be given in the framework of a test. Remember that chronological and developmental age must be taken into consideration. This is a general assessment or inventory and should not be scored. The children should not be judged or placed by the results. The results are used to help the teacher to plan for classroom instruction and learn more about each child's interests, abilities in limited areas, and developmental characteristics. As children are observed and questioned, notes could be taken with specific actions and comments described directly on the assessment sheet. For example, for the item "Knows and recognizes colors," a teacher could write down the colors that the child knows and recognizes. For the item "Cries easily," if the child does cry easily, the teacher could note what frequently causes the child to cry. In other words, the degree to which the child accomplishes the task, or the hows and whys of the behaviors and skills, can be noted, based on careful observation, to make this assessment more meaningful to those who work with the child. Indicating words such as *frequently, occasionally,* or *rarely* could be noted on many of the items.

It is important to use this assessment carefully. It should be used to plan how best to meet the needs of individual children and to help to determine appropriate learning activities. The observations and notes taken should be regarded as confidential information.

Developmental Checklist

- Knows first and last names _____
- Recognizes first and last names in print _____
- Writes first name _____
- Writes last name _____
- Knows address _____
- Knows phone number _____
- Knows how many brothers and sisters he or she has _____
- Has a favorite color _____
- Has a favorite toy _____
- Has favorite kinds of activities _____
- Draws recognizable pictures _____
- Names right hand and left hand _____
- Names some physical characteristics, such as eye color, hair color _____
- Draws a self-portrait _____

Physical and Motor Checklist

- Walks across a balance beam _____
- Hops five times or more on one foot _____
- Balances on either foot _____
- Balances on either foot with eyes blindfolded _____
- Skips _____
- Walks up and down stairs with one foot per step _____
- Jumps using both feet _____
- Throws a ball or bean bag overhand _____
- Kicks a ball _____
- Climbs confidently up and down climbing equipment such as a jungle gym or dome _____
- Catches a ball or bean bag _____
- Dribbles a ball at least three times _____
- Rides wheeled toys confidently _____ What kind? Big wheel _____ Tricycle _____ Bicycle _____
- Easily uses fingers and hands in fingerplays and games _____
- Writes with a pencil _____
- Writes with a crayon or marking pen _____
- Snaps fingers _____
- Uses most cooking utensils, such as knives and peelers _____
- Uses scissors _____
- Has good finger dexterity using manipulative materials and toys such as nuts and bolts, pegs and pegboards, small plastic fit-together units, puzzles, snap beads, etc. _____
- Copies a pattern such as a geometric shape _____

- Traces around shapes such as geometric or animal shapes _____
- Draws various geometric shapes and designs based on chronological age _____
- Ties shoelaces _____
- Fastens snaps _____
- Zips zipper _____
- Builds a tower with cubes _____ How many cubes? _____
- Weaves strips of paper together _____

Social and Emotional Checklist

- Has one best friend _____
- Is accepted by at least five children _____
- Engages in cooperative play _____
- Initiates play activities with other children _____
- Is primarily friendly with other children _____
- Is primarily assertive with other children _____
- Is primarily shy with other children _____
- Is afraid of _____
- Is overly serious _____
- Cries easily _____
- Is bossy with other children _____
- Manipulates other children _____
- Is sensitive to the needs of other children _____
- Has empathy for other children and their problems _____
- Is learning to share _____
- Has self-confidence _____
- Is able to assume some responsibility _____
- Is trustworthy _____
- Usually has good self-control _____

Language and Literacy Checklist

- Is bilingual _____
- Enjoys conversation with others _____
- Initiates conversation with others _____

- Articulates most sounds correctly _____
  Sounds the child does not articulate (list)
  _____
- Speaks and responds in sentences _____
- Average length of sentences _____
- Repeats a five- to six-word sentence with correct word order _____

  (Show 10 picture flashcards, such as of a watch, for the child to label and tell what they are used for.)
- Number labeled correctly _____ Can describe the use or function of how many? _____
- Understands questions and communications from others _____
- Answers questions _____
- Follows simple directions _____
- Participates verbally in songs, fingerplays, stories, and games _____
- Uses all parts of speech (i.e., nouns, pronouns, verbs, adverbs, adjectives) _____
- Listening skills are appropriate for age _____
- Can tell a story or rhyme in sequential order _____
- Likes to use new words _____
- Understands puns or plays on words _____

Cognitive Checklist

- Attempts most tasks or projects _____
- Has adequate attention span to stay on task and complete activities _____
- Is curious _____
- Asks thoughtful questions _____
- Enjoys sensory materials and explorations _____
- Understands and follows given directions _____
- Grasps ideas and concepts quickly _____
- Follows spatial directions such as "Draw a circle above the box" _____
- Recognizes and matches colors _____
- Names colors _____

- Counts by rote up to _____
- Counts by 2s to _____ by 5s to _____
- Recognizes numbers up to _____
- Does addition up to _____
- Does subtraction up to _____
- Understands basic money concepts _____
- Can tell time _____
- Matches basic geometric shapes _____
- Names basic geometric shapes _____
- Recognizes likenesses and differences, and groups things that belong together _____
- Recognizes alphabet letters (upper- and lowercase) _____
- Names alphabet letters (upper- and lowercase) _____
- Knows consonant sounds and can circle pictures representing beginning consonant sounds (e.g., for the *b* sound, can circle pictures such as ball, bear, or button) _____
- Knows vowel sounds and selects correct vowels in words _____
- Makes comparisons _____
- Classifies things according to similarities _____
- Is willing to make predictions _____
- Analyzes a problem or situation _____
- Is able to hypothesize a problem to approach a solution _____

Other informal assessment tools include checklists or matrixes for noting and recording children's development and learning. For example, a card or sheet could be used for each child, and sections for each developmental area might include both large- and small-muscle motor and physical development, cognitive development, language and literacy development, and social-emotional development. In each section there would be space for recording anecdotal notations, observation records, evidence of participation, preference activities, descriptions of specific competencies or knowledge in each area, and other key pieces of information. This information can again be used in planning appropriate learning for

each child and for use during parent–teacher conferences and planning sessions. Documenting children's learning is a powerful tool that benefits the teacher, children, parents, and school (Helm, Beneke, & Steinheimer, 1997).

Later in this chapter, curriculum assessment will be discussed and additional ideas relating to curriculum evaluation will be presented.

PLANNING

Planning the curriculum includes scheduling the entire school day: why the program will be what it is and how it will be carried out. Plans are made, encouraging progression toward objectives. Materials assisting in these plans are prepared and organized.

Adequate time should be allowed in curriculum planning for the children to be able to put on their own coats and backpacks without being hurried.

Rigid Planning versus Flexible Planning

Curriculum planning in the early childhood years does not mean planning a rigid time schedule. "Allowing children to move freely about the classroom, initiating learning experiences in a variety of ways, requires a movement away from rigid scheduling of discrete, subject-driven activities to an integrated, holistic view of curriculum, development, and learning" (Patton & Kokoski, 1996, pp. 39, 40). Too often, programs for early learning are geared to the clock or to a lesson plan, rather than to children. Perhaps the reason young children often become bored, restless, and uninterested in school is not that they are actually tired of school per se, but that they are tired of the daily routines and time schedule. Many routines in early childhood classes waste untold hours, with no real learning taking place. Routines such as greeting, roll taking, and sharing can be changed to foster learning, problem solving, and creativity. The child comes to school knowing that certain things will take place: There will be snack, free play, singing, reading, and a warm, responsive teacher. Knowing that these routines are daily occurrences will provide security, but not knowing exactly how the goals and plans will be carried out or what approaches or strategies will be used in the learning activities will create interest, curiosity, and enthusiasm. This does not mean, however, that the *teacher* does not know how the day will proceed. The order of activities must be formulated, for example, whether the day begins with an activity or free play.

The teacher will need to have a general idea of the time and sequence of activities, but then it is necessary to observe, feel, and determine the needs of the children, allowing for flexibility. For example, free play may be planned for about 30 minutes; but because of the children's involvement and interest, it may be necessary to extend the period to 45 minutes. This, in turn, may make it essential to have another activity shortened or even eliminated during that particular day. Far too often children are rushed from one activity to the next, or an activity is prolonged just because the lesson plan indicates that music is scheduled at 2:00 P.M. Young children need well-planned units of study that are carried out through activities

with objectives, but the amount of time taken by specific activities must be determined by children's interest and involvement (Katz, 1990).

There is great value in a well-structured curriculum of sequential learning plans, but considerable flexibility and skill must be used in following these through. An integrated curriculum does not segment into specific content areas such as math, reading, science, or social studies. Rather, it allows children to learn through relevant and meaningful real-world experiences (Stone, 1995/1996). In an integrated curriculum, children enjoy both the process and content of learning through exploring, discovering, problem solving, inventing, experimenting, imitating, and dramatizing. The teacher who has planned activities, but has built them on a flexible base, is not disturbed when opportunities for taking advantage of teachable moments arise. For example, one day an Angora sheep wandered close to the play yard. The children were fascinated with it and had numerous questions. It was a wise teacher who encouraged the sheep to enter the play yard and allowed the children to smell, romp with, touch, and feed tree blossoms to it. This necessitated eliminating a planned activity, but the advantages were of far greater value than those that would have been obtained through an inflexible time schedule.

Free Play Including Individual Activities

Becoming a master player is a goal worth achieving for young children (Jones, 1997). Every day there should be some time for free play, a time when children individually select areas of involvement. Weather permitting, the children should have daily opportunities for play both inside and outside. Outside, the core of the play will be large-muscle activities: climbing, running, sliding, balancing, jumping, and so on.

Free play should not be a time for teachers to relax and take a break. For children to receive maximum benefit from their play, "Their ideas must be nourished, sustained, and extended by playful adults" (Ward, 1996, p. 24). Guidance from teachers is necessary during free play; they should be nearby to give assistance and encouragement where needed. They should move among the children and engage them in play activities through stimulation and encouragement. Teachers can acknowledge creative and constructive efforts, invite questions, ask thought-provoking questions that extend and expand children's play, and redirect play that needs changing (Crosser, 1992). The teacher helps to create meaning and purposefulness, then moves to another child or group of children. Much learning, teaching, and interacting should go on between children, between individual children and the teacher, and between small groups of children and the teacher.

Young children should have opportunities for computing, exploring, measuring, investigating, constructing, and experimenting. They not only need *many opportunities*, but they also need *adequate time* to do it. *Enough time* refers particularly to large blocks of time, rather than to numerous short periods of inadequate length (Bredekamp & Copple, 1997; NCTM, 1989; Patton & Kokoski, 1996). Children require 30 to 50 minutes of free play or individual exploration in order to become meaningfully involved in an activity (Johnson, Christie, & Yawkey, 1987). Free play should be long enough for children to carry out their play ideas. Research indicates that the length of the play period directly affects the quality and level of play (Christie & Wardle, 1992). To promote both group dramatic and constructive play, it is necessary to provide longer play periods (Christie & Wardle, 1992). It has been suggested that it may be wise to occasionally reduce the number of activities available during free play in order that there might be less distraction and greater opportunity for involvement in particular play activities.

Whole- and Small-Group Activities

In addition to free play (or individual) activities, which may also include centers, the children will participate in small-group and whole-group activities. If all the children are participating at the same time in the same situation and general location, they are engaged in a whole-group activity. A traditional whole-group activity is *community* or *circle time*, when the children sit in a circle and discussions relating to the theme, experiences, music activities, stories, or other activities are presented to the entire group. For small-group activities, the children are divided into groups of three to five.

Many activities are best suited for one of the three approaches: individual, small-group, or whole-group activities. For example, the use of sensory media in the trough is generally best suited to individual play. Other activities, such as finger painting, can be carried out as either individual, small-group, or whole-group activities, depending on the desired objectives, available space, and other planned activities for the day.

Effective transitions to move children from one activity to another must be carefully planned. Children can be "enticed" to move to the next activity (Crosser, 1992, p. 26). Signals such as a designated piano chord, a bell, or a word can signal that it is time to clean up or change activities (Crosser, 1992). Fair time warnings should be given before children are expected to move to the next activity.

Cooperative Learning

Cooperative learning is a versatile approach that can be used in small groups, during free play, or in whole groups. When children are in whole groups, they are divided into pairs or teams to solve a problem, discuss a question, or brainstorm an idea. In cooperative learning activities, children work together in small groups or on teams with a common goal in mind (Johnson, Johnson, Holubec, & Roy, 1986). The cooperative learning strategy is not meant to be used exclusively, but rather should be integrated and used as the teacher feels appropriate. However, research has shown that there are impressive academic and social gains for children who consistently participate in cooperative learning activities (Kagan, 1992). All children, regardless of their backgrounds or abilities, can benefit socially and academically from being in single, inclusive classrooms that incorporate techniques of cooperative learning (Putnam, 1993).

Cooperative learning emphasizes social skills—learning to work together and helping one another. Children learn that no one in the group succeeds until they all succeed; this is positive interdependence (Johnson & Johnson, 1999). Even though the focus appears to be on group behavior, the real purpose is to create stronger individuals. Cooperative learning also encourages children to develop friendships with children who are different from themselves (Kagan, 1992). Additional social skills developed in cooperative learning ex-

Opportunities abound in the curriculum that encourage social interaction and mentoring. The girl is showing this boy how to use the glue stick.

periences include taking turns, self-direction, positive self-esteem, and the ability to take different roles (Kagan, 1992). Cooperative learning encourages peer tutoring, staying on task, and individual accountability, and it promotes interdependence. There is more motivation, enthusiasm, and participation on the part of all children when cooperative learning is incorporated into the curriculum.

Cooperative learning experiences prepare young children today for the democratic world that they will live in tomorrow (Kagan, 1992). Our democratic ideal promotes equal participation by all members; if children have had no experience participating as viable members of a group, they will have difficulty participating as contributing members of society in the future.

Goals of Cooperative Learning

- Build positive interpersonal social skills and habits among students by giving more opportunity for group interaction.

- Give children the opportunity to teach and learn from one another. This builds leadership skills, strengthens self-esteem, and enhances learning.

- Provide experiences that encourage flexibility, cooperation, and problem solving.

- Provide the kind of learning structure that fosters communication skills. In cooperative learning groups, more children have the opportunity to share ideas, exchange information, and talk.

Guidelines for Using Cooperative Learning

- Children need to be shown how to use the cooperative learning strategy, and it must be discussed thoroughly before the children go into their groups.

- The content and objectives of the lesson plan, as well as the developmental level of the children, will determine which particular cooperative learning strategies are used.

- To be an effective member of any group, children need to learn that they will be expected to share ideas (talk), as well as listen to what other group members have to say.

- Cooperative learning can be used during free play as children work together on activities, play with manipulatives, paint at the easel, work on a science project, or participate in any variety of cooperative group activities. The group size may be two, three, four, or more members.

- Cooperative groups can be used to solve a single problem such as a math problem, for more complicated activities, or for a group discussion. Cooperative learning can be used in art, science, language explorations, or virtually any curriculum area. This approach is especially valuable in the language area, because all children can then share, discuss, evaluate, write, act out, plan, play a part, have a turn at the game, listen to another, or otherwise participate in whatever the lesson or activity involves.

- Cooperative learning is different from regular small groups in that the focus is on interactive group behavior, whereby all children must participate and support the group effort.

- After the groups have worked together, it is wise to "debrief" the children. This means that group members decide what went well and what did not go so well. It is a form of evaluation and feedback, as well as an opportunity to bring the activity to an end.

Dividing Children into Groups

- Divide the children into two circles, one inside the other, and have the circles move in opposite directions. When a signal is given, the circles stop and the children facing each other are partners.

- Put numbers, colors, animals, shapes, book titles, or songs in four corners or areas of the room (if you want more than four groups, use more than four areas). Have the children go to the corner or area that designates their favorite number, shape, or whatever category has been chosen.

- Put badges or stickers of different colors, animals, numbers, or even different children on class members. The children go with the group that has the same badge as theirs.

- Cut a picture into three, four, or five parts and give a part of the picture puzzle to each child.

Children are to find the other parts of their picture to form their group (Kagan, 1992).

- Split lines by lining children up, then "folding" the line in half to create a partner for each child. Fold each line again to form groups of four (Curran, 1991).

- Mount a picture of each child on an index card or small piece of cardstock paper. Shuffle the stack of pictures and then draw out three to five per group with the first one being called assuming the role of group leader.

Cooperative Learning Strategies

- *Numbered Heads Together*. Each of the students in a group has a number. For example, four children in a group would be numbered 1 through 4. The teacher asks a question or gives a problem to solve. The children work on it and agree on their team's answer. The teacher calls a number, and the children with that number share their group's answer (Curran, 1991).

- *Think-Pair-Share*. An idea is given for the children to think about. Each child finds or is assigned a partner, and the two discuss the problem together. Then they report back or share what they have learned.

- *Interviews*. Children are assigned to groups of four. Child 1 interviews child 2, and child 3 interviews child 4. Then they reverse so that child 2 interviews child 1 and child 4 interviews child 3. They share what they have learned. This can be used for a review, for end-of-unit feedback, or for focusing on a particular concept.

For additional suggestions regarding strategies used in cooperative learning, we refer you to Kagan (1992), Johnson, Johnson, & Holubec (1994), Johnson et al. (1986), and Curran (1991).

PLANNING UNITS

Teaching young children requires much preparation. The unit must be planned, as well as each day, before the children arrive. Several vital components of planning include the following:

- Choosing a theme or project and the objectives of the entire unit or project.

- Brainstorming activities to teach or support the theme or project (unit plan or web). If you are doing a project, the children will do the brainstorming.

- Determining daily activities, ensuring a balance among various kinds of activities (daily activity plan).

- Deciding on a daily schedule of activities (what will be done first, second, etc., and about how long each activity will last).

- Organizing the lesson plan.

- Preparing materials and resources and planning for each activity.

- Arranging the room's environment. Major room changes may be made each week or less often, and minor room changes can be made daily to accommodate the activities planned.

Every teacher must plan! The more experienced a teacher becomes, the less this planning will be written and the more it will take place in the mind: One teacher may write more on paper, while another relies more on memory. Those with some experience in teaching may be able to think through, instead of writing down, the lesson plan with written objectives; the daily schedule would then serve as the main guide.

A specific part of planning may include planned units in which activities are coordinated to strengthen and reinforce desired concepts or ideas and to meet the developmental needs of individual children. These are organized plans for accomplishing goal-directed teaching. They ensure that the program is in harmony with the needs and abilities of children in early childhood. Children may be included in planning units.

Theme

It is important for us to remember as we plan an integrated early childhood curriculum that "less is more" (Patton & Kokoski, 1996, p. 40). This means that we strive to teach fewer themes or concepts, but to teach them in greater depth. The challenge then comes in going deep rather than wide with regard to curriculum planning. It also means that we plan an in-depth study of a theme, with an open-ended time frame, rather than the traditional theme-of-the-week approach. The curriculum can focus on a topic or theme and at the same time allow for integration of more traditional subject-matter divisions. Using a unit theme, or concept, provides an opportunity for rich and meaningful conceptual development. The unit theme must be selected before further planning can take place. The possibilities for unit themes are infinite and can often be selected on the basis of student interest or suggestion, with the use of textbooks, or by studying the standards and objectives suggested in the state core curriculum. Children at differing stages of development approach a concept from different levels. They first develop an awareness, then explore it, then use inquiry, and finally use the concept or learning (NAEYC & NAECS/SDE, 1991). Thus, any child can benefit and gain something from almost any theme.

A large portion of this text will deal with specific themes and approaches to teaching them. However, a beginning list of possible themes or projects appropriate for children in the early childhood years follows:

Air

Animals: specific categories (farm animals, insects), kinds (bees, dogs), animal houses, animal babies, hibernation

Boxes

Cans

Color

Fire

Flowers

Houses

Magnets

Numbers

Nuts

Paper

People: emotions, self-concept, senses, body parts, family, friends, cultures, professions

Pollution

Rocks

Seeds

Shape

Shoes

Texture

Trains (or other forms of transportation)

Trees

Water (or other resources)

Wheat

Wheels

Many of these suggestions could be narrowed down further to even more specific concepts, projects, or themes. As suggested, the subject of animals could be broken into categories such as farm animals, animal homes, animal products, hibernation, insects, bees, or caterpillars. Teachers, parents, and children can brainstorm for themes and topics appropriate for their classroom (Nunnelley, 1990).

Projects

Project learning is advocated by Chard (1992, 1994) and Wolk (1994) as a constructivist approach to learning that puts the responsibility for decision making, planning, and learning with the child, therefore encouraging more autonomous learning. Distinctive characteristics of Chard's approach include group discussion, fieldwork, some type of representation, investigation, and display or sharing of understanding (Chard, 1994). A project is defined as "an in-depth study of a topic or theme" and may be done individually, in small groups, or as a whole group (Chard, 1994, p. 2). Each project goes through three basic phases: (1) review of the children's present knowledge and interests; (2) giving children new experiences and also opportunities for research; and (3) evaluating, reflecting on, and sharing the project work (Chard, 1994). Some of the topics in this book will be explored either using or adapting Chard's suggested approach.

Unit Plan

A unit plan approach to planning gives a broad overview of possible ideas or the direction that the teaching will go. A unit plan includes numerous possible activities for coordinating and carrying out the unit. It results from brainstorming ideas for experiences in various areas of the curriculum (for example, nutrition or food experiences, science experiences, art activities, field trips, visitors, music experiences, and literary experiences) and results in an integrated curriculum approach. Usually, the unit includes far more activities than could be realistically incorporated into the actual plan. Nevertheless, it provides a rainbow of possibilities and encourages the teacher to plan coordinated activities that support the general theme and meet the needs of the children in the classroom.

Appropriate subjects for unit themes are those that strengthen and broaden the young child's understanding of the world. For instance, a unit plan on seeds geared to 3- to 8-year-old children could include the following suggested activities.

UNIT PLAN ON SEEDS

Lesson plans or projects on seeds can be effectively planned in the fall, when so many plants, particularly weeds and trees, are shedding seeds; or they can be planned in the spring, which is the planting season for flowers, grains, and vegetables. Activities are selected based on the desired goals, the concepts to be taught, the season of the year, and the needs and interests of the children.

Art

- Seed collages
- Seed shakers (used in rhythm activities)
- Finger painting, with seeds added to mixture
- Screen painting with seeds and pods
- Paint with wheat stems, especially bearded wheat
- Paperweight made with potter's clay with seeds pressed in

Field Trips

- Nature walk, to look for seeds
- Home garden or farm, to plant seeds or to watch gardener or farmer planting seeds
- Seed distributor, to see kinds and varieties of seeds and how they are sold
- Grocery store, to look for foods that are seeds (sesame seeds, sunflower seeds, peas, beans, corn)

- Granary, to observe storage of seeds (grains)
- Farm, to observe harvesting of grains or use of seeds (corn, barley, wheat) in feeding some animals

Food

- Chili
- Lima bean soup
- Green bean salad, casserole
- Corn casserole or chowder
- Corn on the cob
- Whole-wheat cereal
- Pea salad or casserole
- Bread sticks sprinkled with sesame seeds
- Seed sprouts (may be used in salad)
- Popcorn
- Food experiences using the seeds of fruits and vegetables that we eat (tomatoes, bananas, beans, peas, corn)
- Some seeds must be cooked before eaten.
- Some seeds can be eaten without being cooked.

Science

- Some seeds need the shell removed before eating.
- Seeds need water, warmth, food, and air to sprout.
- Seeds are different from each other in size, shape, color, and texture.
- Avocado seed supported with toothpicks in a jar of water (observation of growth)
- Seeds sprouted and tasted (alfalfa, wheat, and beans work especially well)
- Planting of seeds
- Study and tasting of seeds that we eat; comparison with inedible seeds
- Study of where the seeds are obtained
- Study of how and why seeds travel
- Comparison of the numbers of seeds produced by various plants

- Study and observation of seedpods
- Observation of the growing stages of seeds: seeds (such as lima beans) are placed between glass slabs or between a plastic or glass jar and a (constantly) wet paper towel lining the jar; may start new seeds every day for 3 to 5 days so that the day-by-day changes can be observed

Music

- Musical chairs, in which a seed package is put on the front of each chair (everyone has a chair). When the music is stopped, directions are given, such as "All the carrot seeds stand up and jump around the circle" or "All the petunia seeds change places."
- Songs about seeds
- Decorated seed shakers used as rhythm-band instruments
- Seedpods such as dried honey-locust pods used as shakers; used to accompany a drum-beat or musical selection
- Creative movements relating to seeds, such as milkweed moving and floating through the air, or the growth and sprouting of seeds
- Creative dramatics involving the care of seeds

Visitors

- Gardener
- Farmer
- Seed distributor
- Grocery store clerk
- Seed nursery worker
- Member of child's family to demonstrate seed planting and care
- Forest ranger

Language and Literacy Development

- Stories about seeds
- Informational or expository texts relating to seeds
- Poetry and choral readings on seeds

- Give seed or package of seeds to each child, who then describes it, tells whether it is edible or inedible, says what it will grow into, how it is cared for, and so on.

- Write, tell, or dictate stories such as "If I were a seed, I would . . . " or "Seeds I like to eat are. . . ."

Webbing or Clustering

The process of webbing, or clustering, is similar to doing a unit plan and, although the end product looks different, it actually has the same result. The approach is to pick a theme, project, or concept and then brainstorm activities and ideas for teaching this concept. In developing engaging and productive themes through curriculum webbing, the following four steps are helpful (Barclay et al., 1995, p. 206):

1. Identify a theme and related subtopics.

2. Brainstorm.

3. Identify desired learning outcomes.

4. Prepare for teaching.

Figure 4–1 is an example of a web on seeds. Throughout the text you will see examples of other webs. Teachers should not find it necessary to do both a unit plan and a web, since they serve basically the same purpose.

Using the project approach to planning a study on seeds, the teacher may brainstorm using his or her own experiences, knowledge, and ideas and then organize these into a topic or concept web. Figure 4–2 is an example of a project web on seeds. It can be noted that the focus of these two webs is the same, but they are approached in a different way. Figure 4–3 illustrates a child's question web. The questions of the child guide the study.

A teacher's own preferences, teaching style, and background will determine whether the unit plan, theme web, or project web is used. In addition, the teacher's philosophy will drive actions. If the teacher desires to be in control of and in charge of the curriculum, more direct methods will be chosen and may begin with unit plans or theme webs to generate ideas. On the other hand, the teacher may begin with ideas, but then seek input from the children based on their interests, ideas, backgrounds, and needs. In the case of the

project approach, the teacher can begin the project or generate some interest in it, but then, with the teacher's guidance and following the web brainstorm, the children work individually or collaboratively on a level that they choose and with experiences that they select (Chard, 1994).

Activity Plan

Using a more teacher-directed approach, once the unit plan or web has been developed, the teacher selects from it the specific experiences to include in teaching. These selections should be made with respect to the goals that the teacher desires to accomplish. Most important, the needs and interests of the children need to be considered. An activity plan, which is a sketch of the activities planned for each day throughout the duration of the unit, is now formulated. It provides the teacher with an overview and enables the unit to be viewed in perspective.

As a teacher moves from a unit plan to an activity plan, care should be taken to balance the day. There should be a balance of kinds of activities (art, music, language and literacy, etc.), as well as types of groups.

In the construction of this activity plan, activities should be included that correlate, reinforce, and support the theme and desired objectives. However, not all activities during the school day need to be, or should be, related to the theme. Too constant exposure to one particular theme results in boredom, lack of interest, and frustration.

Following is an example of a 5-day activity plan on seeds. These experiences have been selected from the array of possibilities listed in the unit plan or from the seed web. The activities are designated as individual, small-group, and whole-group so that a balance of these three kinds of participation can be achieved.

ACTIVITY PLAN ON SEEDS

Day 1

Whole-Group Activity

Science

- How seeds grow

- Plant a lima bean seed.

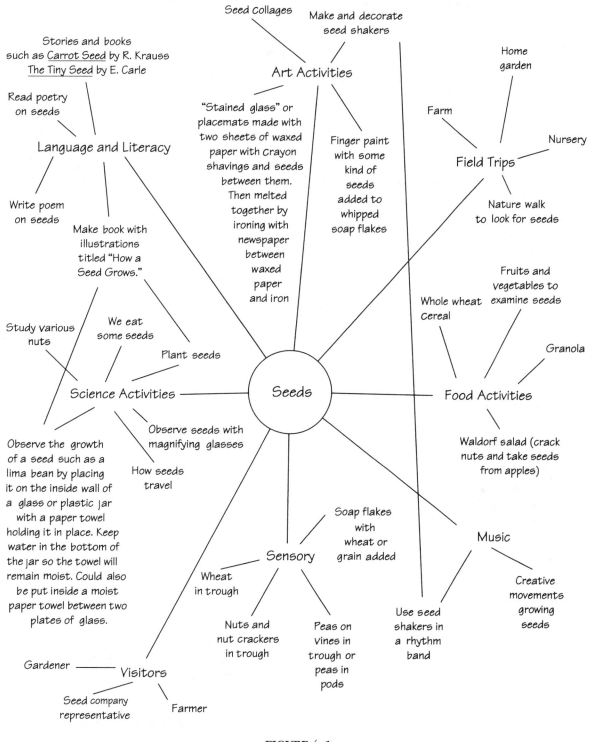

FIGURE 4–1
Web on Seeds

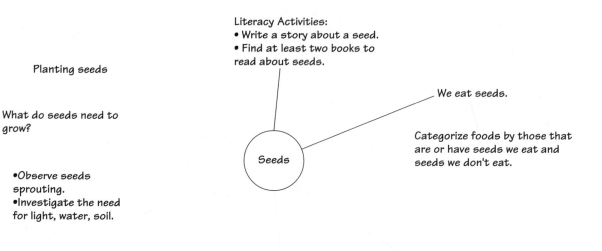

Planting seeds

What do seeds need to grow?

•Observe seeds sprouting.
•Investigate the need for light, water, soil.

Literacy Activities:
• Write a story about a seed.
• Find at least two books to read about seeds.

We eat seeds.

Categorize foods by those that are or have seeds we eat and seeds we don't eat.

Seeds

We can make things with seeds:
• Seed collages
•A seed shaker decorated with seeds

Compare the sizes, shapes and colors of seeds.

FIGURE 4–2
Child's Project Web for Seed Study

Small-Group Activity

Field Trip

• Seed walk

Individual Activities

• Bubble blowing

• Seeds in sensory area

Day 2

Whole-Group Activities

Music

• Rhythm experience using seed pods

Science

• Seeds that travel

Small-Group Activity

Art

• Seed shakers

Individual Activities

• Easel with seed-shaped paper and green paint

Science

• Observe growth of lima bean planted yesterday and plant another bean today.

Day 3

Whole-Group Activity

Visitor

• Musician and playing seed shakers

Small-Group Activity

Art

• Seed collages

Individual Activities

• Paperweight made from potter's clay with seeds pressed in

Science

• Observe and explore foods with seeds.

• Observe growth of bean plant and plant another bean today.

(Once questions are posed by children, they then lead the study and learning.)

How do seeds differ from one another?

How do seeds travel?

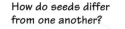

Seeds

Do some plants have more than one seed?

Do we eat seeds?

Does the size of the seed influence the size of the plant?

How do seeds grow into plants? What conditions do they need in order to grow?

FIGURE 4–3
Child's Question Web for Seed Study

Day 4

Whole-Group Activity

Science

- Seeds we eat

Small-Group Activity

Food

- Chili

Individual Activities

- Peanuts and other nuts in the sensory area
- Shape tracing and cutting

Science

- Observe growth of bean plants and plant another bean.

Day 5

Whole-Group Activity

- Photographs on bulletin board to teach positional words and enhance self-esteem

Small-Group Activity

Art

- Finger painting with seeds added

Individual Activities

- Sorting and classifying seeds

Science

- Observe the growth of bean plants and plant another bean.

Table 4–1 is included as another example of an activity plan. This plan lists the developmental

TABLE 4–1
Weekly Activity Plan At-a-Glance

Theme: _____		Date: _____		
Planned activity for:	Monday	Tuesday	Wednesday	Thursday	Friday
Language development					
Cognitive skills					

Creative expression
  Art
  Music
  Dramatic play
  Other					

Emotional development					
Social development					

Physical development
  Gross motor
  Fine motor					

Source: Lisa G. Warner, M.S., Co-Director, Child Development Center, Eastern Kentucky University, Richmond, Kentucky.

areas down the left column so that, as each day's activities are planned, we can see if they are balanced in terms of developmental areas.

Daily Schedule of Activities

The daily schedule of activities is an elaboration of the activity plan and a simplification of the lesson plan. For experienced teachers or students who are at an advanced level, the daily schedule of activities may replace both the activity plan and the lesson plan, even though the objectives must be carefully thought through. The daily schedule of activities specifies the order of activities, approximate length of time, person responsible (if you are working with several teachers), specific responsibilities of individuals, and materials needed. This plan adapts easily to chart form with different columns added, depending on the needs of the program (see Table 4–2). Such assignments as setting up outdoor equipment, cleaning, and greeting

may be included. Routines of the program, such as snacks, may also be added to the chart, showing the teacher assigned to the preparation and the time it is to be presented. When doing a daily schedule of activities plan for a full-day program, include such additional routines as lunch, rest time, and reading and writing workshops. The plans presented adapt easily to either half-day or full-day programs. The number of activities remains basically the same, because longer programs have additional routines of meals, individual play, and quiet periods.

Lesson Plan

When using a direct, teacher-centered approach, after the unit is seen in broad perspective through the activity plan and the specifics defined in the daily schedule of activities, lesson planning takes place. The lesson plan adds the procedures for the activities and reminds the teacher of the goals and objectives to be accomplished. The teacher has

TABLE 4–2
Daily Schedule of Activities

Date:	Unit:	Head Teacher:
	Seeds	Mary

DAY 1

Activity	Approximate Time	Type of Group	Person Responsible	Role of the Teacher	Materials and Resources
Greeting and individual play	45 min.	Individual	Dave	Greet.	
Bubble blowing			Kerry	Guide children as necessary.	Bubbles, blowers, sponges
Seeds in trough			Mary	Encourage discovery and exploration.	Trough and seeds
Field Trip: Seed walk	60 min.	Small group	Everyone will have a group	Encourage questions and discussion on seeds. Encourage each child to collect seeds in a sack.	Name tags color-coded by groups; paper bags for seed collecting
Outside play	30 min.	Individual	Everyone		
Science: How seeds grow. Plant a lima bean seed.	20 min.	Whole group: circle time	Mary	Discuss how seeds grow and describe activity of watching lima beans grow in a jar all week long. Each day prepare new seeds so comparisons can be made.	Jar, wet paper towel, soaked lima beans
Individual play	10–30 min.				

(continued)

TABLE 4-2 (continued)

Date:		Unit:	Seeds	Head Teacher:	Mary
DAY 2					
Activity	Approximate Time	Type of Group	Person Responsible	Role of the Teacher	Materials and Resources
Greeting	15 min.		Kerry	Greet.	
Children directed to rug for seed stories	15 min.	Whole group	Dave	Read stories.	Books: E. Carle, *The tiny seed*. New York: Crowell, 1970; H. Jordan, *How a seed grows*. New York: Crowell, 1960; R. Krauss, *The carrot seed*. New York: Harper & Row, 1954.
Music rhythm: Experience using seedpods; also, several seedpods will be shown and broken open to explore the seeds.	20–30 min.	Whole group	Mary	Discuss seedpods and seeds found within (some are edible and some are not). Dried pods will be available for children to use for music rythm activity.	Seedpods; musical rhythm record, such as Hap Palmer, *Pretend*.
Children could also sing songs and shake pods to rhythm.					
Individual play	30–45 min.	Individual	Everyone		
Science: Observe growth of lima bean planted yesterday and plant another one.			Dave		Lima beans, jar, wet paper towel

Date: **Unit:** Seeds   **Head Teacher:** Mary

DAY 3

Activity	Approximate Time	Type of Group	Person Responsible	Role of the Teacher	Materials and Resources
Greet	15 min.	Individual	Dave	Greet.	
Individual play outside	30 min.	Individual	Everyone	Large parachute will be outside, in addition to regular outside equipment.	Parachute
Art: Seed collages. The children will add water, a small amount at a time, to mix plaster of Paris. Each child will be given a spoonful to smooth out on a paper plate and then encouraged to stick seeds in.	30 min.	Small group	Everyone	Discuss with group of children the seeds collected on the excursion.	Sacks of seeds for children in groups; paper plates, plaster of Paris, aprons, sponge
Individual play inside	45–60 min.	Individual	Everyone		
Science: Observe growth of lima beans already planted and plant another one.	20 min.		Kerry		Lima beans, jar, wet paper towel

(continued)

TABLE 4-2 (continued)

Date:		Unit: Seeds		Head Teacher: Mary	
DAY 4					
Activity	Approximate Time	Type of Group	Person Responsible	Role of the Teacher	Materials and Resources
Greet	15 min.	Individual	Kerry	Greet.	
Food: Chili. Beans will already be soaked, and children will chop onions and add to hamburger. Brown these two. Combine with seasonings and tomatoes in one large pot. Discuss the chili beans as seeds.	30 min.	Small group	Everyone	Discuss the chili beans as seeds and that some seeds are edible. Supervise making chili.	Soaked chili beans, onion, hamburger, tomato, seasonings, electric frying pan, spoons, knives, large pot
Individual play	45–60 min.	Individual	Everyone		
Science: Observe growth of lima beans already planted and plant another one.	20 min.		Dave		Lima beans, jar, wet paper towels

Date: **Unit:** Seeds   **Head Teacher:** Mary

DAY 5

Activity	Approximate Time	Type of Group	Person Responsible	Role of the Teacher	Materials and Resources
Greet	15 min.	Individual	Dave	Greet.	
Individual play	60 min.	Individual	Everyone		
Science: Observe growth of lima beans already planted and plant another one.	20 min.		Kerry		Lima beans, jar, wet paper towels
Sorting and classifying seeds. Muffin tins will be used to sort seeds in many different ways—ways they travel, edible versus non-edible, color, size, shape.			Mary		Muffin tins (or egg cartons), seeds
Art: Finger painting with seeds added	45 min.	Small group	Everyone	Encourage discovery, creativity, and exploration.	Finger paint, butcher paper, sponges, aprons, seeds such as wheat seeds

selected a theme and has determined its benefit and value to the developing child. Through listed objectives, the teacher is able to harmonize the lesson plan's activities with the child's abilities and needs.

If a more child-centered approach is desired, at this stage before the specific activities are planned, input from the children is sought, and their interests determine which activities are selected. Recent research and writing has convinced us that this approach is best for young children (Chard, 1992, 1994; Glasser, 1997; Kohn, 1993a; Levin, 1994; Meier, 1996; Ohanian, 1996). Students are more engaged and interested when they make decisions about their own learning. The webs and plans shared as examples in this book cannot reflect this child-centered focus. All serve as examples, and it will be up to the individual teacher to develop a philosophical, child-centered approach that will result in children making choices and decisions about their own learning activities. The rationale for this approach is that there are convincing benefits, including enjoyment by the children, greater academic achievement, and positive behavior rewards (Kohn, 1993a).

As the lesson planning is viewed in perspective, the teacher should keep in mind some general, overall objectives to be accomplished during the unit. For example, if the unit plan is on seeds, what will be the general objectives and/or concepts to be stressed and taught? What are the various interests of the children and what variety of background knowledge do they have? In addition to theme-related objectives, child-related objectives help to meet the specific needs of the children. For example, a child-oriented objective may be that "the children will be encouraged to put away their own equipment and materials" or that "the children will become more independent in taking off and putting on their own coats." These objectives will be valuable if the children need assistance in either of these two areas.

The goals for a program are general, and the objectives for the unit and lesson are specific. Performance objectives, those that describe an observable, desired behavior, are valuable in measuring and evaluating the unit. Performance objectives usually include such words or phrases as the following: Each child will be able to *say, write, do*, or *complete*. These words deal with concrete, measurable tasks that can be observed and checked for achievement or completion. (Use the verbs suggested in Bloom's Taxonomy on page 82).

The following is a lesson plan on seeds. Keep in mind that as teachers gain experience and insights the amount of writing in lesson plans will diminish. Also, remember that the more that children can make choices and use their own questions regarding what is to be learned and the activities involved, the more powerful and motivated they feel and the more engaged and meaningful their learning is.

LESSON PLAN ON SEEDS
Objectives

Students will:

- Describe concepts associated with seeds, specifically the following:
  1. Seeds come from the fruits of plants.
  2. Seeds are different from one another in color, shape, size, and texture.
  3. Seeds need water to grow. (Warmth, food, and air could also be included.)
  4. We eat some seeds.
  5. Plants grow from seeds.

- Demonstrate basic understanding of some positional words through concrete, repeated experiences with such words and their meanings.

Day 1

Whole-Group Activity

Science—How Seeds Grow

- On this day, and on each of the four following days, put a presoaked lima bean seed between glass and a moist paper towel. (By the end of the unit, the children will be able to see the first five daily stages of growth of the seeds.) Ask the children what seeds need to survive and grow and help them to discover (if not the first day, during subsequent experiences) their need for water, light, air, and soil.

   Teach language labels such as *root, sprout,* and *stem*.

Small-Group Activity

Field Trip—Seed Walk

- In small groups, the children will walk around the area observing plants, trees, and weeds

Planning an appropriate curriculum includes opportunities for children to become independent, which is evident as this boy tries to open up his milk carton.

that are shedding seeds at this time of year. Give a sack to each child for gathering seeds. Ask them to look for differences in seeds, such as texture, shape, size, and color, and clues to how they might travel.

Individual Activities

- Bubble blowing
- Seeds in sensory area

Day 2

Whole-Group Activities

Music—Rhythm Experiences Using Seedpods

- The children will use seedpods to accompany the rhythm of familiar songs and a record with a definite beat. Break open one seedpod and let the children raise questions and observe the seeds inside the pod.

Science—Seeds That Travel

- Raise the question of how a seed goes from one child's house to another child's house. Use a toy town to focus on a demonstration. Then discuss how seeds travel in various ways: burrs cling to animals and people, some seeds fly through the air, some seeds roll.

Small-Group Activity

Art—Seed Shakers

- Juice cans or half-pint milk cartons will be provided in the art center. The children will put some seeds inside and glue seeds on the outside. They can secure the lids with tape.

    Encourage questions and comparisons between seeds.

Individual Activities

Art

- Easel, with seed-shaped paper and green paint

Science

- Observe the growth of the lima bean seed planted yesterday and plant another today.

Day 3

Whole-Group Activity

Visitor—Musician

- The visitor will play various musical instruments for the children. Then show the children how different kinds of seeds can be used to provide music (seed pod shakers, dried gourds, seeds sealed in containers).

Small-Group Activity

Art—Seed Collages

- The children will make seed collages from the seeds that they collected on the field trip the first day. They will make plaster of Paris, put the plaster on a paper plate, and then put the seeds in the soft plaster to harden. (If you do not wish to use plaster of Paris, seeds can be glued on the paper plate or stuck into potter's clay.)

    Encourage questions and observations of various seeds.

Individual Activities

Science

- Observe the growth of the lima beans planted the two previous days and plant another today.

- Display foods with seeds for children to explore, such as watermelon, cantaloupe, tomato, orange, lemon, cucumber, apple, peach, cherry, plum, or others that are in season. Provide plastic, serrated-edged knives and encourage the children to cut the fruits and observe the seeds. Are the seeds edible? Compare sizes, shapes, colors, numbers, textures, and other similarities and differences. Ask the children which of the foods have seeds that we can eat.

Art—Paperweight of Potter's Clay with Seeds Pressed In

- Provide the children with aprons, potter's clay, and a variety of seeds. They will roll the clay into balls, flatten one side, and then push seeds into the clay.

Day 4

Whole-Group Activity

Science—We Eat Some Seeds

- Show the children examples of seeds that we eat, such as peanuts, peas, corn, beans, nuts, squash seeds, cucumber seeds, and potatoes. Show the difference between vegetable seeds that we plant and those that are edible in the vegetable (such as bean or pea seeds). Make comparisons. Show the children examples of some seeds that are not edible only because they have not been cooked (chili beans, lima beans, etc.).

Small-Group Activities

Food—Chili

- The beans will already be soaked and cooking. In small groups, have the children watch and help grind the onion. Then the children will brown the hamburger and onion and add seasonings and tomatoes. These ingredients will be added to one or two large pots and allowed to cook. The children can, on an individual basis, stir and watch the chili as it cooks. Point

out that the beans are actually seeds that are eaten once they have been cooked.

- In small groups, serve chili for the children to eat. While the children are eating, reinforce concepts relating to beans being seeds, how the chili was prepared and mixed, and its nutritional value to our health. Provide opportunity for the children to raise questions and explore concepts that they suggest.

Individual Activities

Science

- Observe the growth of the lima bean seeds and plant another one.

Sensory Area

- Peanuts and edible nuts, with nutcrackers

Shape Tracing and Cutting

- Various shapes, such as toys and cookie cutters, will be available for the children to trace, and scissors will be provided for them to cut out the shapes.

Day 5

Whole-Group Activity

Photographs on Bulletin Board

- Put pictures of the children on the bulletin board, providing an opportunity to use positional words. Each day, rearrange each child's picture so that the pictures vary in position: beside, under, over, or between circles of a particular color. It will now be easy to divide the children into groups. For example, say, "All those who are beside a blue circle go with (teacher's name) group." Review the positional words by having all the children in particular positions stand, hop around the circle, change places, or perform some other movement.

Small-Group Activity

Art—Finger Painting with Seeds Added

- In small groups, have the children finger paint with a mixture to which seeds have been added. When the paint dries, the seeds will stick to the paper. A medium might be whipped soapflakes to which wheat seeds have been added.

Individual Activities

Science

- Observe the growth of the lima bean seeds and plant another one.

Sorting and Classifying Seeds

- Muffin tins will be used to sort seeds by various characteristics, such as the way they travel, color, size, kind, and whether they are edible or inedible.

Multiple Intelligences

Howard Gardner has proposed a theory of multiple intelligences (Table 4–3), and teachers in every grade level, including early childhood teachers, are finding appropriate classroom applications of the theory. A brief overview of the theory will be given and then ideas for applying it in the early childhood curriculum.

Howard Gardner's theory of multiple intelligences challenges the traditional notions of IQ as well as the SAT (Scholastic Aptitude Test). He suggested that intelligence refers to the ability of humans to solve problems or to make something valued in a particular culture (Checkley, 1997). In his book *Frames of Mind* (1983), Gardner proposed that our culture has too narrowly defined intelligence and that there is actually the existence of at least seven basic intelligences. Since that time he has added an additional intelligence and his theory has become ubiquitous and known as the multiple intelligences theory (MI theory). Gardner also suggested that intelligence has more to do with the capacity for solving problems and fashioning products than with the isolated tasks on a standard IQ tests.

TABLE 4–3
Gardner's Categories of Intelligence

	Linguistic Intelligence	Logical–Mathematical Intelligence	Spatial Intelligence	Bodily–Kinesthetic Intelligence	Musical Intelligence	Inter-personal Intelligence	Intra-personal Intelligence	Natural Intelligence
Characteristics and Capabilities	Use words effectively. Ability to manipulate the syntax or structure of language, the phonology of sounds, the semantics of language	Use numbers effectively and reason well. Sensitive to logical patterns and relationships, propositions, functions, and other abstractions.	Perceive the visual–spatial world accurately and perform transformations upon those perceptions. Sensitive to color, line, shape, form, space, and the relationships between these elements.	Proficiency in using one's whole body to express feelings and ideas and facility in using one's hands to transform or produce things. Includes skills such as speed, coordination, balance, dexterity, and flexibility.	Ability to perceive, discriminate, transform, and express musical forms. Sensitive to the rhythm, pitch, melody, and timbre of musical pieces.	Expertise in perceiving and making distinctions in the moods, intentions, motivations, and feelings of other people.	Self-knowledge and the ability to act adaptively on the basis of that knowledge. Has an accurate understanding of oneself; aware of motivations, temperaments, and goals and aspirations. Ability for self-discipline	Ability to understand the natural world and work effectively in it. Allows people to use features of the environment.
Example	Storyteller Politician Poet Journalist Writer	Mathematician Accountant Statistician Scientist Computer programmer	Interior decorator Architect Artist Inventor	Actor, Athlete Dancer Craftsperson Mechanic Surgeon	Musician, Music critic Composer Performer	Counselor, Leader	Psycho-therapist Religious leader	Outdoor guide

Source: Adapted from Armstrong, 1994.

Armstrong (1994, pp. 11, 12) suggests four key points in the MI theory:

1. Each person possesses all eight intelligences. Some people have high levels of functioning in most intelligences, while others are highly developed in one or two intelligences and more modestly or underdeveloped in the other intelligences.

2. Most people can develop each intelligence to an adequate level of competency.

3. Intelligences usually work together in complex ways. Intelligences interact and support one another.

4. There are many ways to be intelligent within each category. There is not a standard set of qualities, characteristics, or attributes that a person must have to be intelligent in a particular area.

Gardner does not advocate a single way to teach and does not believe that there is a blueprint for teaching (Checkley, 1997). However, he does believe that the MI theory, when understood, encourages teachers to take individual differences into account and help all children to use their minds well (Checkley, 1997). In applying the MI model in the classroom, teachers move away from traditional forms of teaching, including lecturing and requiring students to do written work and assignments. Rather, in a MI classroom it looks much like a DAP early childhood classroom. The MI classroom, like the DAP early childhood classroom, includes a variety of presentation methods and activities, including music, art, and creative activities and hands-on experiences in science, nature, drama, and other areas, and gives children opportunities to interact with others in both small and large groups. The MI classroom also gives time to work alone and reflect quietly or even write in one's personal journal. In terms of assessment, Gardner advocates that teachers allow students to demonstrate understanding in a variety of ways (Checkley, 1997).

When teachers apply the MI model to their teaching, it is suggested that they think of the intelligences and how they may appropriately be integrated into a particular unit or lesson. When teachers have the MI theory in mind as they are planning, they think of ways to incorporate the eight intelligences into their plans, and they are sensitive to providing a balance of the eight intelligences in their activities. By doing this, all students can have their strongest intelligences incorporated at least some of the time. Armstrong (1994, p. 58) suggests that once the objective of a unit or lesson is in mind, teachers can ask the following questions to address the eight intelligences:

1. *Logical–Mathematical:* How can I bring in numbers, calculations, logic classification, or critical thinking?

2. *Linguistic:* How can I use the spoken or written word?

3. *Spatial:* How can I use visual aids, visualization, color, art, or metaphor?

4. *Musical:* How can I bring in music or environmental sounds, or set key points in a rhythmic or melodic framework?

5. *Bodily–Kinesthetic:* How can I involve the whole body or use hand-on experiences?

6. *Naturalist:* How can I use the outdoors?

7. *Interpersonal:* How can I engage students in peer sharing, cooperative learning, or large-group simulation?

8. *Intrapersonal:* How can I evoke personal feelings or memories or give students choices?

CURRICULUM ASSESSMENT

Why are we doing what we are doing? How does what we do benefit the learners in our classroom? These are reflective questions that should always be in the forefront of the teacher's mind. A curriculum is planned to meet the needs of the individual children in the group or classroom, using meaningful goals. The organized teaching units or projects provide avenues for the communication of this curriculum. But the desired achievement of the program for young children depends on continual and effective assessment.

Evaluation and assessment are the processes of determining the degree to which children's needs are met and desired objectives are achieved (NAEYC & NAECS/SDE, 1991). This includes assessing the general curriculum, including units or projects as well as activities; the performance of the children; the teacher's role; and determining if the objectives were achieved.

Assessing can be done both formally and informally with written evaluations, check sheets, reports, completed contracts, or anecdotal records and observations. This allows for constant adjustments and redirections in curriculum planning.

Assessing the Curriculum

The curriculum in early childhood needs to be assessed on an ongoing basis to ensure that it is doing what it is supposed to be doing and remains in harmony with children's abilities and needs. In-progress assessment allows any necessary adjustments to be made in the unit or project so that it can be more beneficial for the children. Because children are constantly changing in development, the curriculum, too, must constantly be adjusted to supplement this development. The evaluation or assessment can be made using the following questions as guides:

- *Goals:* Did the project or unit meet the overall goals of the program? What evidence is there to validate this?

- *Objectives:* Did the objectives of the unit, project, or activities match children's needs, abilities, interests, and knowledge?

- *Preparations and procedures:* Were the necessary preparations for the unit, project, or activities considered and completed? Were activities prepared in advance? How else might the procedures have been carried out? Were staff made aware of their assignments and responsibilities? Thoughtfully consider if there were alternative methods, strategies, or procedures that would have been more efficient or appropriate.

- *Activities:* Did the activities support the objectives of the unit? Were the children interested in the activities? Was there motivation to learn? Was interest captured? Did the activities promote learning, competence, enjoyment, engagement, thinking, and success? Were the activities substantive and relevant? Were the children able to make choices and decisions? Were they involved in suggesting and planning the activities? Were the children interested and challenged by the activities? For children who

needed them, were there appropriate extensions? For children who did not understand, were correctives, reteaching, or feedback provided? For children who needed to be challenged, were extensions provided? Were the activities sensitive to the diversity of the children in the classroom? Was there adequate variation in the scheduling of the activities and routines? Was each activity successful or not successful? (Include reasons and analysis of why or why not.) Were there appropriate transitions between activities?

- *Culminating activity(s) to bring closure and provide feedback:* Did the summary or closing action bring closure to the unit or activity and help children to synthesize the planned objectives? (Evidence?) Do you the teacher have a way of knowing if you accomplished what was to be learned? What kinds of changes in the activities and unit would bring about overall improvement?

In evaluating early childhood curriculum, achievement in performance-based objectives can be observed. Examples may be the children's work, comments, or behaviors. This can be combined with the assessment approach in which the teacher evaluates the project, unit, or activities on the basis of the kinds of questions given in the preceding list.

All staff should be involved in ongoing evaluation and should assess each unit or project as it is completed using questions such as those suggested or others that may be appropriate. Evaluations should determine adjustments in the ongoing curriculum and suggest changes that need to be made for improvement. Evaluations should also direct the work with individual children in fostering their positive growth. Feedback from the evaluations can also provide useful information for parents as they have questions about their children and the influence of the curriculum on their learning and growth.

When evaluating, observations should be validated and specific comments and insights shared. Teachers should not just share general statements such as "The activity was very successful." Why? On what basis do you know? Statements such as "The children stayed with the activity for a long time" and "Each child was absorbed in the activity and anxious to participate" are more specific.

To be effective, evaluation must include both negative and positive aspects, or failures and successes, of the activities. For example, if an activity turns out differently from the way it was planned, an objective evaluation may conclude that the activity failed or that it turned out much better than originally planned. Successful and positive evaluations build confidence and ability in the teacher. Failures and negative evaluations show where planning may not have been adequate or follow-through not sufficient. These discoveries, in turn, provide the groundwork for successes in subsequent similar situations.

Assessing Children's Learning and Involvement

The performances or learning outcomes of the children are also part of assessment. Collectively, the group's participation throughout the unit should be assessed. Did the children accomplish the desired objectives? Were there measurable behavior changes when desired? Were the children interested and motivated to participate? Were they actively involved in the experiences, or were activities too difficult or too simple? Individually, the child's performance in the entire classroom program needs constant assessment. Because the teacher keeps abreast of the child's development, objectives can be designed to increase the child's progress. Is the child interested in the program? Is the material too advanced for the child's abilities? Does it provide an adequate challenge? What is the child's relationship with the other children? Is the child socially, physically, and mentally healthy? Does the child have any particular problems that need concentrated guidance and effort? What are the child's strengths?

Figures 4–4 and 4–5 are examples of a checklist and a graph that can be used to evaluate children's participation in various activities. Figure 4–4 is an activity/skill checklist on which the teacher or observer writes down the title of the activity, for example, "Musical Dramatization of 'The Three Bears.'" Then, after each child's name, a + is entered for participation or a − for nonparticipation. There is also space to describe the level of activity and skill development for the individual child. Figure 4–5 is a Specific Skill/Activity Graph for a general curriculum area such as art and is used over a period of time to illustrate the individual child's involvement in various kinds of activities. It graphically illustrates for teachers each child's participation or nonparticipation in classroom activities in particular curriculum areas.

Assessing the Child's Development

Assessment of children's development is imperative. It is a process of continuously appraising and evaluating the children's development in physical, emotional, social, and academic areas. Knowing how the children that you teach are growing and developing is of primary importance in planning what will be taught and how it will be accomplished. Effective assessment must take into consideration laws or generalizations of growth and development, which include the following:

- Each child is an individual and grows in his or her own way.

- A child's self-concept affects how he or she learns.

- The child's total development, not just cognitive functioning, must be the focus of the learning environment.

- Children in the early years learn best through concrete, real experiences by experimenting and discovering.

- The learning experience must take into account the cultural background, needs, interests, and developmental levels of each child in the classroom.

There are different techniques for acquiring and organizing assessment information, such as checklist inventories (like the one described in the Assessing Children's Needs section of this chapter); observation notes; and informal, individually given tests of concepts and skills. Anecdotal records should be kept for each child, with notations of growth, achievements, regressions, and concerns. These can be stored on the computer or they can be a card file, calendar recordings for each child, charts, or in notebooks. Along with observations, actual child dialogue can be recorded as a means of assessing. An especially effective assessment tool is preparing a portfolio of the child's work. Progress in art, writing, math, language, science, and other areas can be assessed through viewing the child's work over time. Also, video-

STAFF: In the space by the individual child's name, place a + if the child participates or a − for nonparticipation. Use the allotted space to describe the level of activity and skill development.

Title of Activity: _____ Date: _____

(Name)

_____ (   ) _____
_____
_____

_____ (   ) _____
_____
_____

_____ (   ) _____
_____
_____

_____ (   ) _____
_____
_____

_____ (   ) _____
_____
_____

_____ (   ) _____
_____
_____

_____ (   ) _____
_____
_____

_____ (   ) _____
_____
_____

_____ (   ) _____
_____
_____

_____ (   ) _____
_____
_____

FIGURE 4–4
Child Development Center Activity/Skill Checklist
Source: Lisa G. Warner, M.S., Co-Director. Child Development Center. Eastern Kentucky University, Richmond, Kentucky.

tapes, photographs, and tape recordings can be used to capture information about the child's growth and provide evaluation information.

Assessment yields important information for the teacher, child, and parents. Through evalua-tion, the teacher can plan learning experiences to match the needs of the child and to challenge the child's abilities. Assessment information is a must at parent conferences to validate the child's achievements and to give the parents some proof

Activity	Finger Paint	Easel Paint	Sawdust Clay	Shape Collages	Straw Paint	Easel Paint	Styrofoam Sculpt.	Shaving Cream	Fabric Collages	Clay
Date	4/3	4/5	4/6	4/7	4/10	4/11	4/14	4/17	4/20	4/21
Name:										
Erin	√	—	—	√	√	√	—	—	√	√

FIGURE 4–5
Specific Skill/Activity Graph
Source: Lisa G. Warner, M.S., Co-Director. Child Development Center. Eastern Kentucky University, Richmond, Kentucky.

of the child's developmental level, as well as learning and progress. Checklists of developmental skills can be sent home for the parents to work on with the child and to give them firsthand information on the child's progress. These checklists can be general and include cognitive skills, motor skills, social developments, and emotional characteristics, or they can focus on specific areas, such as math or reading.

A child's own record keeping can be an assessment tool. One form of record keeping is a journal. It will help the child to understand his or her own progress; it will help the teacher to learn what most interests the child. Journals or diaries also give information on how children feel about themselves and their work. For young children, their early journal entries will be in the form of pictures.

In addition, one can develop assessment rubrics, even for very young children, to help the teacher and parents determine a child's interests and feelings about many different aspects of the school environment. For example, make a list of activities or draw simple pictures of activities, such as looking at books, drawing pictures, playing with toys, singing songs, listening to a story, playing outside, and having individual play inside. Next to each, draw three faces: one smiling, one with a straight mouth or neutral expression, and one frowning. Read each activity on the list and have the children color the face that represents how they feel about that activity.

Evaluating the Teacher

By means of a continuing assessment of the curriculum, units, and children, the role of the teacher automatically receives evaluation. Where changes are needed in the program or activities, the teacher makes the alterations. The teacher continually works to build on the strengths that already exist in the curriculum and children. The teacher should ask the following questions: What is my relationship with the children individually? Collectively? Am I planning the curriculum to meet the abilities and needs of the children? Are my desired objectives being achieved? Am I providing adequate challenge, guidance, and direction to the children? Am I enjoying what I am doing? What changes do I need to make? What are my strengths?

FIELD TRIPS

Because field trips are an integral part of the early childhood curriculum and are not discussed elsewhere in this text, we have included them in this curriculum planning chapter. For field trips to be successful, teachers need to follow important guidelines in both planning and implementing field trips.

Guidelines for Field Trips

Field trips must have a purpose in order to have meaning for children. They are planned as an extension of the children's experiences and to clarify subjects about which the children may have misconceptions or misinformation. They should be planned not just to have fun, provide variety, or take a trip someplace. Field trips should be tied closely to the curriculum; they are often the means by which children make sense and meaning out of what is being taught in the classroom. They need to be kept simple so that they are manageable and developmentally appropriate for young children.

Every school is located in a unique community to explore, and many successful field trips can be planned as walking trips. When planning field trips, consider the type of transportation available. Budgets may provide for buses for a monthly field trip or may prevent the frequent use of buses. Some programs have parent volunteers to provide cars for transportation.

Values and Benefits of Field Trips

When field trips are planned carefully and with purpose, they provide numerous values and benefits.

- Children participate in real experiences with people, places, and things; what is seen, heard, smelled, and felt is most often what is remembered. Also, when experiences are firsthand, the opportunity for knowledge and understanding is enhanced.

This boy is apprehensive as he prepares to leave the school and take his first school bus ride on a field trip.

- Field trips provide excellent opportunities to reinforce and extend concepts and notions.
- Field trips expand children's knowledge of the world about them, including the diversity of people and cultures.

Planning a Field Trip

As plans are made for field trips, careful consideration must be given to a number of important points.

1. *The length of time that the trip will take.* For half-day programs, the actual bus or car ride to the site should take no more than 20 minutes. For full-day programs, no more than 1 hour of riding time each way should be planned. Young children tire too easily to travel farther. If the zoo is a 90-minute ride one way, wait until the children are older and it will be much more effective for them. Third- or fourth-grade children would still be able to enjoy the zoo even though they had a long ride to get there.

2. *The children's safety.* Every effort must be made to ensure the safety of the participants. Whether walking or riding, getting to and from the field trip site must be carefully considered. If the children are riding, drivers should be provided with maps so that they know exactly where to go and the route to be followed. If riding in cars, the children must be required to wear seat belts. Arrange for enough vehicles to comply with this rule. Drivers must be properly licensed, and their vehicles must have appropriate insurance. During the field trip, count the children often. *Never leave a field trip site, or a stop along the way, without making certain that every child is accounted for.*

3. *The ages, attention spans, special needs, and interest levels of the children involved.* Field trips must be carefully evaluated with respect to the children being taken. Particular consideration must be given to children with special needs. For example, if there are children in wheelchairs, the transportation, site access, and restroom facilities must accommodate their needs.

4. *Adult supervision.* Plan for adequate adult supervision based on the number of children going on the field trip. For children ages 2 to 3, there should be one adult for every three to four children; for ages 4 to 6, there should be one adult for every four to five children; for ages 7 to 8, there should be one adult for every five to six children. Supervising adults should be encouraged to ask and answer questions, explain, and extend desired concepts.

5. *Permission.* Permission must be obtained from parents or guardians. Some schools or programs allow for a single written and signed permission to be obtained from parents at the beginning of the year that covers all field trips during the year. The permission should give legal permission for the child to go on field trips, and it should also release the school from liability in case of accident. Parents must be notified of all field trips that the children take and know when and where they are going.

6. *Site visit before the actual field trip.* The teacher should visit the site of the field trip before the children visit. This provides information regarding the required travel time and route and an estimate of the approximate length of the visit. If applicable, the teacher should inform the person on site who will be responsible for the discussion regarding the purpose of the visit, concepts to be taught, the age level of the children, and the amount of time available. The availability and locations of restrooms should be noted.

7. *Need for snacks or lunches.* Preparations for snacks or lunches should be made if warranted by the length of the field trip experience.

8. *Preparation of the children.* Children need to be adequately prepared for and introduced to the field trip. They should be told what to expect and look for, why they are taking the trip, what safety precautions they should follow, and any limits that must be observed. Small groups of children should be assigned to individual adults who will supervise them and with whom they should stay at all times. For safety reasons, children should *not* wear name tags.

Suggestions for Field Trips

The following are suggested field trip ideas. Add other possibilities to this list, especially those unique to your own community.

Community nature center

Zoo

Farm

Neighborhood business, park, home

Pet store or a home with pets

Bus ride

Grocery store

Park

Cemetery

Department store

A parent's place of work

Fire station

Post office

Police department

Library

Nursing home

Shut-in neighbor

Children's museum

Field, park, or open space to fly kites

High school, college, or university music department

Music store

Touch, sound, or smell walk

Train station

Butcher shop or fish market

Treasure hunt

Historical site or monument

Warehouse

Weather bureau

Library

Fish hatchery

Art gallery

Observatory

Bakery

Aquarium

Newspaper printing facility

Field Trip Follow-Up

Field trips are the most successful when the learning is extended with both pre- and postactivities (Patton & Kokoski, 1996). Preactivities could include reading about the topic of interest, looking through magazine pictures, or watching a video. A variety of classroom learning activities could focus on the concept or theme of the field trip. Postactivities might involve writing notes of appreciation, journal entries, art projects with materials gathered while on the field trip, group or individual story writing, and so on.

At a farm, the children are able to learn by touch, smell, sight, and sound about animals and their babies.

Following the field trip, teachers should get feedback to determine comprehension. Use pictures, books and stories, filmstrips and videos, dramatic play, visitors, music, art, and discussions to clarify and enrich the experience, as well as to provide outlets for expressions of feeling. As the children recall their experiences, the alert, observant teacher can evaluate the benefit of the field trip and any misconceptions that need to be clarified or concepts that need reinforcement. Language experience charts can be used to record the children's memories, and over time these can be used to recall trips taken. Depending on the age of the children, letters can be written or pictures drawn as a "thank you" to adults who provided transportation and supervision or to those who guided the children at the field trip site.

VISITORS

Sometimes, rather than taking the children on a field trip, people are willing to visit the center or school. For example, instead of having the children go to the fire station, fire fighters may prefer to bring equipment to the school. Therefore, determine whether it is best to plan for a field trip or a visitor. Inviting visitors into the classroom is less disruptive to the school day and requires less paperwork and concern than field trips. To determine whether a visitor or field trip would be best, teachers should think about the objectives for the experience. A general guideline is that students should be taken on field trips only for the experiences that cannot be duplicated in the classroom.

When visitors come into the classroom, they bring in a portion of the community with them. This allows the children the opportunity to interact with and glean information from someone from the community. The teacher can guide the children in using the information from the visitor to strengthen and add to the concepts and notions that they are working on with their project or unit of study.

When inviting visitors into the classroom, teachers should follow some of the same guidelines outlined for field trips: The visits should have meaning and be tied to the curriculum. The visitors should know precisely the purpose of their visit and what is expected of them. They should be

encouraged to talk on a level that the children can understand. They should be given a specific time limit. Some people should not be invited because they cannot speak on a level that the children understand or lack an understanding of young children and their needs.

Just as the children need to be prepared ahead of time for a field trip, they also need to be prepared beforehand for a visit from someone in the community. Knowing in advance the purpose of the person's visit, they can be encouraged to think of questions to ask the visitor and be reminded of courtesies that should be extended to any classroom guest. The following are suggestions for classroom visitors; for almost any topic, there are a number of community resource people. One of the best resources for visitors is the family members of students. They have jobs that are interesting and hobbies and talents to be shared with the children.

Suggested Classroom Visitors

Person to demonstrate a hobby or skill such as coin collection, bread making, tortilla making, flower arranging, origami, or gardening

Community helpers

Musician

A person to share language, traditions, artifacts, foods, or customs from his or her culture or from one that he or she has visited

Parent to bring an infant

Pet store owner or parent, grandparent, or neighbor with a pet

Angler

Magician

Dancer

Elected official

Baker

Librarian

Medical personnel

Dentist

Banker

This list is just a beginning; a teacher's own thinking and imagination will provide numerous other possibilities. Who visits a classroom and why they visit will, once again, be determined by the objectives and the resources available in the community.

SERVICE LEARNING

The phenomenon of service learning is sweeping our classrooms and schools. There is growing research and evidence that points to school-based service learning as an effective means of influencing children and the needs of the community. Some programs are obtaining grants in order to infuse service learning into the curriculum. However, many classrooms and programs are able to integrate service learning into the curriculum without additional funding. In some communities, service learning is part of district-wide or school-wide projects, but many individual classrooms or programs plan and implement service learning projects that involve substantial hours of service to agencies or programs in the community (Melchior, 2000). Service learning strengthens the bond and often creates a partnership between school and community. Research concludes that the work and effort of students is appreciated and viewed as valuable by community members and agencies (Melchior, 2000).

TECHNOLOGY AND COMPUTERS

Although we once were asking whether we should include the use of computers in our classrooms, we are now asking how we can incorporate the technology into our ever-expanding curriculum! National organizations have given early childhood teachers standards and guidelines for integrating technology into their classrooms. ISTE (International Society for Technology in Education) has created technology standards for all grades including PreK–2 (ISTE, 2000). NAEYC has prepared a position statement on the use of technology in early childhood (NAEYC, 1996c).

We must critically examine the effect of computers in the lives of children and determine how they can be used for the children's benefit. A variety of media and technologies can be incorporated in the early childhood classroom, but what-

---

National Educational Technology Standards for Students PK–2

Prior to completion of grade 2 students will:

1. Use input devices (e.g., mouse, keyboard, remote control) and output devices (e.g., monitor, printer) to successfully operate computers, VCRs, audiotapes, telephones, and other technologies.
2. Use a variety of media and technology resources for directed and independent learning activities.
3. Communicate about technology using developmentally appropriate and accurate terminology.
4. Use developmentally appropriate multimedia resources (e.g., interactive books, educational software, elementary multimedia encyclopedias) to support learning.
5. Work cooperatively and collaboratively with peers, family members, and others when using technology in the classroom.
6. Demonstrate positive social and ethical behaviors when using technology.
7. Practice responsible use of technology systems and software.
8. Create developmentally appropriate multimedia products with support from the teacher, family members, or student partners.
9. Use technology resources (e.g., puzzles, logical thinking programs, writing tools, digital cameras, drawing tools) for problem-solving communication and illustration of thoughts, ideas, and stories.
10. Gather information and communicate with others using telecommunications, with support from teachers, family members, or student partners.

International Society for Technology in Education (ISTE) (2000). *National educational technology standards for students*, p. 15.

---

ever is added must be connected thoughtfully and appropriately in order to get positive results (Rafferty, 1999). Children are attracted to technology and intrinsically motivated to use computers

(Guthrie & Richardson, 1995). Computer "technology is only a means to enhancing students' intellectually appropriate learning" (Gatewood & Conrad, 1997, p. 249). If the children's learning in our classrooms is generally taking place at their desks, listening to the teacher, or doing paperwork, then the addition of computers will not be very beneficial. However, if most of the learning is student centered and actively involves problem solving, open-ended discovery, and critical thinking, then the computer is an asset to the learning and teaching curriculum. Its main purpose is to supplement, not replace, classroom activities such as art, music, blocks, dramatic play, books, writing, and outside play (NAEYC, 1996c). Computers become valuable as they enhance, not substitute for, discovery and exploration through sensory experiences. They offer unlimited opportunities for learning through manipulation, creative problem solving, and self-directed exploration (Clements & Swaminathan, 1995).

Therefore, problem-solving skills must be developed through real-life experiences. "The real test of a pupil's competence is not the mere possession of a skill, but rather performance in a real situation" (Tener, 1995/1996, p. 100). The most important strategy for children using computers in solving problems is for them to create their own solutions. When accomplishing a task on their own, they feel empowered, have increased self-confidence, and develop a keener sense of identity (Bauer, Sheerer, & Dettore, 1997). When computer experiences are supported by concrete activities, children receive the most benefit. Haugland (1995) suggests two ways for teachers to ensure that this occurs: (1) design specific supplemental activities, or (2) integrate the computer experiences into the general curriculum. Technology should be integrated into the curriculum in such a way that it supports instruction, intellectual thinking, and curiosity (Guthrie and Richardson, 1995); in addition, it should prepare students for tools that they will be expected to have mastered as they live and work in the world of tomorrow (Walker & Yekovich, 1999). Children will be the beneficiaries of the enriched learning in the classroom.

Computer effectiveness in the early years of learning can be achieved only when teachers develop competence in computer literacy by understanding how a computer functions and the basic principles of programming. Computer literacy programs should teach teachers to assess the appropriate use of computers in the classroom, locate suitable computer hardware and computer-related materials, and evaluate software for young children (Hyson & Eyman, 1986).

Before we move the discussion to the selection of software, a note of caution: Because some of the children's families will not have computers in their homes, it is important that we take that into consideration as we plan our curriculum. It is also helpful if we determine where parents and children can have access to computers (public libraries; college, high school, or elementary school computer labs; community centers; and so on).

Selecting the computer is not as important as selecting the software (Shade, 1996)! A proliferation of software programs have been developed at a much more rapid pace than we can keep up with. Many make excellent contributions to early childhood education, but even more do not! Frequent in-service training should be helpful in preparing teachers to make wise selections of the software that is available for the classroom. Computer software should not be used to fill empty time or because it happens to be convenient and readily available. We should ask two pertinent questions when evaluating the software programs for our schools: Why is a particular program in the classroom? What does the program teach young children? (Haugland, 1995, p. 99).

Computers should not just entertain; they must support and extend the learning of children (Samaras, 1996). For children to benefit from technology in the classroom, software must be reinforced with concrete activities (Haugland, 1992), be open ended and exploratory, teach about cause-and-effect relationships, emphasize the discovery process (Haugland, 1995), and be developmentally appropriate (Bredekamp & Copple, 1997).

When selecting software for children to use on the computer, consider the four criteria suggested by computer experts Susan Haugland and Dan Shade, in Diffily & Morrison (1996, p. 104):

- Is it age appropriate for the child?

- Is it designed to give the child control?

- Is it easy for the child to understand?

- Is it relatively easy for the child to use alone?

These four questions will aid us in our choice of children's software.

Because of the challenging bombardment of continually changing and advancing technologies and programs, it is difficult for us, as educators, to feel competent in directing the uses of computers in our schools (Gatewood & Conrad, 1997; NAEYC, 1995/1996). In fact, most teachers do not receive adequate training for using technology in the classrooms. Technology training needs to be ongoing and tailored to the needs of individual teachers (Hurst, 1994). As inadequate as we may feel regarding the computer in our curriculum, remember: Good teachers are not those who know the most facts or information, "but rather those who continually incorporate new information in creative ways" (Riel, 1994, p. 465).

Let us consider computer technology as simply another avenue through which all children learn (Snider & Badgett, 1995). Use of the computer, like the use of other media, must be carefully planned to meet the level of understanding of the children in the classroom. Care must also be taken to teach the children how to use the computer. How exciting it is to see the effects of computer exploration on young children when it is carefully integrated into a well-planned early childhood curriculum. Computers offer children opportunities to develop greater control, expand their ways of learning, connect with classrooms all over the world, and access vast amounts of information (Riel, 1994).

The thrill of being on the cutting edge of technology can permeate your entire building or

Sometimes playing is hard work!

center, giving confidence, vision, and life skills to faculty as well as students. It will foster a positive image of your school and engender dynamic, mutually beneficial partnerships with parents, businesses, and other community organizations (Wilson, 1997, p. 251).

Summary

Brandt (2000), thinking futuristically, envisions a structure for curriculum in the new millennium with the following characteristics:

- Has greater depth and less superficial coverage.
- Focuses on problem solving that requires using learning strategies.
- Emphasizes both skills and knowledge of the subjects.
- Provides for students' individual differences.
- Offers a common core to all students.
- Coordinates closely.
- Integrates selectively.
- Emphasizes the learned curriculum.
- Pays greater attention to personal relevance, while drawing on other streams as well.

These characteristics are those that early childhood educators must consider seriously. They might well be a guide for teachers in planning and designing curriculum changes based on the content in this chapter.

The curriculum is everything that takes place in the classroom to meet the needs of the children. This includes the determination of goals and objectives, the needs assessment, and the scheduling of the curriculum, including planning the unit, project, or lesson plan. Continual evaluation should take place regarding the curriculum; the children's learning, involvement, and development; and the teacher. Because the teacher actually does the planning, scheduling, and evaluating, the teacher is the key to their combined success. The cooperative learning strategy is a versatile and valuable approach that encourages children to learn from their peers in a cooperative environment. Field trips, visitors, and service learning activities are valuable elements of the curriculum and often teach and share things with young children that the teacher alone could not do. Early childhood teachers need to become experts at using and incorporating technology into the curriculum. They need to be discerning and wise as they critically select the software for their computer, making sure it is developmentally appropriate and can be used while children work alone at the computer. With commitment, responsibility, and dedication, an exciting and meaningful program can be planned and implemented. When this happens, children not only benefit, they reap great rewards!

Student Learning Activities

1. Visit an early childhood classroom and talk with the teacher about the method or methods of planning used. Compare the approach to those presented in this chapter. Even though the approach will most likely differ from the one in this book, are the basic ingredients and questions (Why? What? How?) a part of the planning? You may wish to visit with several early childhood teachers to discuss and evaluate various approaches to planning.

2. From visits or observations you have previously made in early childhood classrooms or from currently planned visits, evaluate the scheduling. How did the scheduling in the classroom compare to that suggested in this chapter? Were you able to observe some free play during each visit? How do you feel about free play in early childhood classrooms, and what can it accomplish?

3. Select one of the themes suggested in the chapter or one of your own choosing, and complete a unit plan, web, or project according to the format suggested in this chapter. Do not select a theme for which a unit plan or web has already been completed in this book. Follow with preparation of a daily activity plan, daily schedule of activities, lesson plan, project outline, or whatever your instructor suggests.

4. Interview three early childhood teachers and ask them what assessment tools or means they use. How often do they use them? How do they evaluate their program, curriculum, children, and themselves? As they meet in parent–teacher conferences, what do they share with parents as criteria for evaluation? Make comparisons of your findings and draw some conclusions of your own, from your reading and from the interview, as to what you think are the most effective means of assessment and evaluation for early childhood education.

5. If you can find a neighbor or family member who is in the early childhood age range and you have permission from his or her parents, through observation complete the Developmental Checklist and Questionnaire included in this chapter. What did you learn about the child from this?

6. Do some research on cooperative learning and evaluate this strategy using your research, information in the text, and your own feelings. How will you use cooperative learning as an early childhood teacher?

7. Plan three cooperative learning activities on any theme appropriate for early childhood students. Use at least three different strategies. Present at least one of your activities to class members.

8. Study the list of field trips and visitors given in this chapter and add appropriate field trips for your area and community. Is there a particular age

level that is appropriate for each field trip, or could it be adapted to suit any early childhood age level? Think of a project or theme and then brainstorm possible field trips and visitors for your theme.

9. Visit several early childhood classrooms and find out how computers are being used. What kind of software do they have, and does it meet the cri-

teria outlined in this chapter? Ask teachers and children what their favorite software is.

10. Visit a computer store or write to a distributor for a software catalog and become aware of available early childhood software. As you visit classrooms or university technology labs, try out their software. Begin a list of your personal early childhood software favorites.

Suggested Resources

Videos

Assessment for quality learning. The Video Journal of Education.
Cooperative learning and multiple intelligences: Elementary school. The Video Journal of Education.
Focus on thinking. The Video Journal of Education.
How families help children learn. The Video Journal of Education.
How to improve your questioning techniques. Insight Media.

Integrating the curriculum. The Video Journal of Education.
Invitational education. The Video Journal of Education.
Organizing Classrooms. Insight Media.
Performance assessment: Moving beyond the standardized test. Films for the Humanities & Sciences.
Perspectives on assessment and evaluation. Films for the Humanities & Sciences.

Students as multimedia authors. Films for the Humanities and & Sciences.
Teaching to objectives. Insight Media.
Technology and the role of the teacher: How to integrate technology into the classroom. Insight Media.
Using the power of technology to improve student achievement. Insight Media.

Part Two

Personal and Social Development

No matter who children are, what they become, or where they live, they all have a need for people skills. We do not live alone, and people everywhere need to learn to relate initially to themselves and then to others around them. The ability to relate to others depends on one's attitude toward oneself and toward other people. It is never too early to begin building positive feelings and attitudes. The ability to live effectively within the family and later to function capably within the community—neighborhood, classroom, and peer group—hinges on social skills that begin in early childhood.

Developing social skills is not an easy task. It takes knowledge of correct relationship skills, in addition to time, experience, and practice. We must be patient as we provide assistance and guidance to children who struggle to develop positive social and emotional skills. These skills can be taught and learned, but most importantly "caught," as the teacher provides the model. A teacher's own attitude toward the self, children, and adults is one of the most powerful forces in this process. If the teacher likes and enjoys others, particularly children, the message that people are to be liked, respected, and esteemed is received.

A child must recognize early in life the individual responsibility for learning to like and relate to both the self and people in general (Cortés, 1996). The child will also sense that social and emotional patterns, habits, skills, attitudes, and feelings can be improved if one desires to learn more effective ways of relating.

The world is the only limit in creating socioemotional skills studies for children! During the early childhood years, teachers can select units from areas such as sociology, economics, geography, history, and anthropology. Remember: Gear the units and concepts to the level of the children, and provide social studies activities with concrete learning experiences, such as classroom visitors and field trips. Many of these concepts, elementary as they may seem, remain abstract unless they are made concrete through carefully planned learning.

Within selected units in socioemotional skills, additional areas can be integrated, such as economics or history. For example, you may do a unit on a particular community helper such as the farmer and, depending on the ages of the children, discuss various concepts in economics, such as production, distribution, and consumption. A unit on the police officer can include civic concepts that relate to the rights and obligations of responsible citizens.

Historical concepts and perspectives can be taught through a unit titled "People—How They Lived 100 Years Ago." After reading and studying the concepts and ideas for teaching presented in Chapters 5 and 6, you will become aware of other possibilities for units in the social studies area. Along with all the cognitive notions about the self and others, we hope that children are taught, by example as well as concept, that people are important and have feelings, and that all of us need to be sensitive, respectful, and caring about the feelings of others. "As we teach children to see and challenge the contradictions and injustices of our world ... we must ... use their questions, concerns, and insights to support them in becoming strong, critical, caring citizens" (Ramsey, 1995, p.22).

Chapter 5, People and Their Diversities, deals with helping children to relate to others effectively and encouraging them to recognize similarities rather than differences among people. The chapter develops children's concepts of other people and outlines many concepts and ideas for teaching about others. Children are anxious to learn about many people, places, and related subjects in the world around them—family, friends, neighbors, community members, different cultures, and related jobs.

Chapter 5 also discusses developing a basic understanding of children with special needs. Included are discussions of the individualized education program (IEP); public laws regarding the education of individuals with disabilities; special needs in the areas of speech and language; mental retardation; hearing, visual, and physical impairment; emotional, social, and behavioral problems; chronic illness; learning disabilities; and gifted and talented children. Each of the categories of special needs is discussed in terms of particular characteristics, teaching strategies, and available specialists. More and more, we are realizing the benefits of early intervention for children with special needs, and we must tailor our programs and services to meet their individual needs and requirements. A number of authors have reminded us that it is the responsibility of the teacher to adjust the curriculum and the educational system to the developmental needs and levels of the children; children should not be expected to adapt to a system (Bredekamp, 1986; Bredekamp & Copple, 1997; Darling-Hammond, 1997; Elkind, 1996a; Kohn, 1993a).

Chapter 6, Myself and My Family, deals with developing children's self-esteem, helping them to recognize that everyone is unique, worthwhile, and capable, with special characteristics, feelings, talents, and interests. Children must first believe in themselves before they can care about, believe in, and accept other people (Little Soldier, 1990). Thus, the basis of a high-quality program in early childhood is promoting feelings of dignity, self-esteem, and security in the individual child.

Chapter 6 helps us to recognize situations causing stress in children, how they react to stress, and how we can help them to cope with stress. The chapter also discusses the influence of the family. The family plays a paramount role in helping children accept and like themselves, and it contributes greatly to the character education of its members.

In Chapter 7, Myself and My Body, we discuss notions relating to the healthy child, including physical education, nutrition, and general health issues. Each day should provide developmentally appropriate opportunities for motor development and physical fitness. To be physically fit, children must have cardiovascular endurance; muscle strength, endurance, and agility; and body leanness (Poest et al., 1990). Motor development includes locomotor skills, large-muscle activities, and activities that promote physical fitness or the level of healthy functioning of which the body is capable (Poest et al., 1990). These kinds of activities have many values. They encourage children to be physically fit, to develop a positive attitude toward and habit of daily exercise; physical fitness leads to better overall health and well-being. Fitness activities and other physical activities give children an occasion to relieve stress and to be active. Teachers ought to start early to develop children's interest in and routines for keeping physically fit and enjoying their lives. Movement activities and physical

games and activities teach coordination and good sportsmanship, and the skills that they develop have a positive effect on children's social behavior and self-esteem (Poest et al., 1990). In addition, children often do better in perceptual tasks such as reading when they are well coordinated and inclined toward motor and fitness activities.

Included in Chapter 7 is a section on food and nutrition, because, as food is both prepared and eaten, it has an influential effect on the development of the healthy physical self. Nutrition development is often seen as the second part of good fitness, so we have included a discussion on it in this chapter. Teachers of young children should recognize the value of using food activities as part of the curriculum. Not only do children enjoy them, but there are also many social, cognitive, small-muscle, math, science, and other values that can be learned and developed through well-planned food activities, many of them as cooperative learning experiences. Early childhood teachers should select nutritionally sound food activities. In a time when we recognize the strong influence of a balanced diet on health and well-being, it behooves all early childhood teachers to teach basic nutrition principles through the careful selection and addition of high-nutrient food experiences.

Health issues are a primary concern for families and educators. If we begin teaching proper hygiene and other general health issues when children are young, perhaps positive health habits will be learned and practiced.

Chapter 5

People and Their Diversities

Although children are alike in many ways, each is uniquely different from any other: gender, age, ability, ethnicity, socioeconomic status, religion, beliefs, attitudes, values, customs, and culture (Appl, 1998; Marshall, 1998). How children feel about and treat others is influenced by their own regard for themselves, as well as the social skills that they have learned from home, school, and other cultural and community groups (Lucero, 1997). From the earliest years, children need help and guidance in developing positive social values and skills in learning to relate to others effectively. Once again, the teacher provides a model for treating, speaking to, and behaving toward others. Early childhood teachers need patience as they work with children who are often very inexperienced in social behaviors. Teachers should display positive attitudes that serve as models for having friends, learning how to treat others, and understanding their social environment. An antibias attitude is modeled more effectively when the teachers or caregivers are warm, attentive, and responsive to *all* children (Appl, 1998).

A multicultural, antibias approach to learning is a way of looking at the world that challenges our often narrow and distorting views of culture and seeks more thoughtful and inclusive teaching: "multicultural education is not something you do now and then, but something you bring every day to the life of your class" (Hunt, 1999, p. 41). It involves respecting others and their differences.

Spring (1998) suggests four goals of multicultural education:

1. Work to build tolerance of other cultures
2. Abolish racism
3. Teach substance from various cultures
4. Teach and help students to view the world from different cultural perspectives

When young students develop a spirit and attitude of tolerance, an understanding of various cultures, and an ability to understand a different frame of reference, this increases their sensitivity and knowledge and promotes actively working for social justice as they mature (Spring, 1998). Multicultural education "is a movement designed to empower all students to become knowledgeable, caring, and active citizens in a deeply troubled and ethnically polarized nation and world" (Banks, 1993, p. 22).

As concepts about people are taught on a daily basis and in specific units, the focus must be primarily on similarities, as well as promoting a respect for the "richness of difference" (Singer, 1994, p. 287). Recognizing similarities and distinguishing differences are skills learned by preschool-aged children. Learning to identify similarities and respect and accept the nature of differences among peers helps children to realize how much we all actually have in common (Cortés, 1996).

In stressing similarities rather than differences, it becomes evident that all children live in

Appropriate early childhood classrooms include children of various sizes, races, genders, abilities, and developmental levels. These children are all standing on a cement structure while they wait for the school bus to come.

some type of family unit, participate in family activities, play games and enjoy toys, learn songs and stories, celebrate holidays, express similar feelings and emotions, and communicate with one another. By discussing differences, children can see that their specific behaviors are simply one way of doing things, not the only or the best way. Children will then be able to understand and appreciate how people are different.

Accepting and understanding similarities and differences is also very important with respect to children who have special needs, those whose learning and behavioral characteristics differ substantially from others and who require special methods of instruction. A basic understanding of particular categories of exceptionality (their characteristics, possible teaching strategies, and available community specialists) helps teachers in caring for children and planning programs.

Children's orientation to the social world and their initial development of social skills begin in the family unit and with the formation of early friendships. The current social problems and concerns throughout the world make it apparent that there is a need for multicultural learning that must begin at birth and continue throughout the school years. However, the most critical time for shaping positive cultural understanding is during the early childhood years (Swick, Boutte, & VanScoy, 1995/1996). This is the time to start preventing children from developing biases and prejudices as their attitudes, values, and beliefs begin to form. Focusing on how lives are similar, yet sometimes different, helps children to expand their awareness of others, increases their capacity to accept and cooperate with others, and enhances their own positive self-concepts and esteem.

We must be very careful that we do not teach children that others who are different are inferior. Often teachers ignore these differences as if they do not exist, assuming that children will naturally grow up to approach the differences in positive ways.

Derman-Sparks & ABC Task Force (1989) emphasize the need for teachers to confront, rather than ignore, the issues of diversity in their classrooms. When we do not openly discuss concerns, prejudices, racism, and feelings, children resort to physical confrontations and find unacceptable ways to get rid of their anger, intolerance, and frustrations (Lucero, 1997). "Our conspiracy of silence about 'sensitive' issues like race and culture deprives youngsters of the opportunity to develop the vocabulary to express their feelings and ask questions in a positive way" (Lucero, 1997, p. 8). Thus, by opening the lines of communication and talking with and discussing diversity issues, we give children ways of dealing with their feelings and, at the same time, overcoming negative emotions and reactions.

TEACHING AND VALUING DIVERSITY

Developing the Perspective of Diversity

The United States, with a broad range of ethnic and cultural groups, is one of the most diverse countries in the world. Recognizing the value and importance of each individual, while respecting and accepting each other's cultures, is essential to maximum growth and development (Cortés, 1996). "Culture is the fundamental building block of identity. . . . Through cultural learning, children gain a feeling of belonging, a sense of personal history, and security in knowing who they are and where they come from" (Lally, 1995, p. 66). Our individual cultures are shaped by such things as family structures, customs, and rules; educational backgrounds; interpersonal relationships; travel experiences; and religious beliefs (Coleman, 1997). Culture also includes all the subtle aspects of both verbal and nonverbal communication that people use all the time (Sturm, 1997). "Everyone has a language and culture, which are the very essence of who and what people are" (M.P. Anderson, 1996, p. 16). Through activities and discussion, we should respect and develop children's ideas and encourage input from home cultures (Fayden, 1997). A person's ethnicity is his or her connection to the past, and it is one of the keys to the individual sense of self: All people have an eth-

nic heritage! Such aspects as gender, race, class, personality, and ethnicity influence the development of a child's sense of identity, and it is sometimes challenging to develop programs in early childhood education that support the identity of all young children (Korgen, 1998).

As young children begin maturing and acquiring a positive self-concept, they also begin relating to and accepting others. These early years are the time to start influencing children's basic cultural attitudes, values, and beliefs. "Cultural stereotypes arise from incomplete and often distorted conceptions of people and events" (Swick, Boutte, & VanScoy, 1995/1996, p. 75). "We must be continually reminded of the urgency and need for attention to our cultural knowledge, attitudes, and skills" (p. 79). Development and implementation of a diversity perspective is, therefore, imperative. Parents, peers, teachers, and extended families all play a major role in helping children to accept and have pride in their cultural identities (Kich, 1996).

Culturally diverse classrooms are those that foster genuine respect, acceptance, and openness for all children regardless of race, gender, ethnic orientation, or physical ableness (Rogers, 1997). Young children usually begin to notice racial and gender differences during the second year of life (Lucero, 1997; Morrison & Bordere, 2001). During the third year, children begin to learn the names of different colors, and start to apply this knowledge to variations in skin color. Soon they begin to identify with members of a particular race and may wonder why they are a different color than other children or adults.

> Bradie, who attended a culturally rich preschool, had been helping her family work in the garden one sunny weekend. When she returned to class, she showed her suntanned arms to her teacher and announced, "Look, teacher! My skin is just about Spanish!"

Children notice observable characteristics such as skin color, language, and dress (Billman, 1992). How they respond to these differences is, to a great extent, determined by the direct and indirect messages and feelings of those around them. Children who are biased consider others to be inferior because of their differences. Teachers should work to overcome ethnocentrism, the attitude that one's own culture is correct, right, or natural. Accepting and respecting diversity should be a way of life, a value that is lived, felt, and woven into all areas of the classroom and curriculum. This means helping children to value others and express positive feelings and behaviors toward them. It is an active approach to countering attitudes and behaviors that sustain prejudice, ethnocentrism, racism, stereotyping, sexism, discrimination, and oppression. To help us to be culturally sensitive and reflect antibias practices, we must

- Reflect on our own cultural backgrounds and values

- Learn about other cultures that may be different from our own

- Take concrete actions

- Find ways to accommodate values of others while maintaining the integrity of our own (Bromer, 1999).

Teachers and caregivers can learn about other cultures through personal interactions with parents and children, reading books on various cultures, discussions with other teachers and adults, visiting community cultural events, and viewing educational videos (Huntsinger, Huntsinger, Ching, & Lee, 2000).

During the early childhood years, children develop stereotypic attitudes about gender roles, racial and cultural biases, and negative attitudes about having different abilities. Not only are attitudes negatively affected, but experiences become narrow and limited as a result of the stereotyping associated with race, sex, and disabilities. Teachers should, therefore, foster positive attitudes of acceptance and tolerance; children need to come to value differences among one another while recognizing that they have many similarities. The similarities, rather than the differences, ought to be the focus (Cortés, 1996).

> Children can learn very early that, while individuals may view things differently, they still have many common needs, feelings, hopes, and desires; it is this common ground on which we should build.

Teaching diversity means modifying the early childhood environment, including the curriculum and the people involved, so that it is more reflective of the diversity within society. Curriculum activities that emphasize and show respect for various aspects of multiple cultures have a significant, positive influence on all children (Pica, 1997). "Best practices recommend that environment and instructional practices reflect the language and culture of the children they serve" (Duarte & Rafanello, 2001, p. 31). We must ensure that each child achieves maximum development through nurturance, support, and encouragement (Stafford & Green, 1996). Teaching diversity involves helping children to take the perspective of others, to look and see through their hearts, eyes, and minds (Cortés, 1996). Students should recognize that all class members are equally important and deserve equal educational opportunities. We live in a complex, global, diverse society today, and this should be reflected in our schools and neighborhoods. All schools, no matter the diversity of their population, should acquaint students with the broad range of our nation's racial, ethnic, cultural, and religious diversity (Cortés, 1996). "The children and families served in early childhood programs reflect the ethnic, cultural, and linguistic diversity of the nation. The nation's children all deserve an early childhood education that is responsive to their families, communities, and racial, ethnic, and cultural backgrounds" (NAEYC, 1996b, p. 4). The following are two general goals for early childhood education professionals to consider when addressing issues of teaching diversity:

- The profession has an ethical responsibility to understand the role of culture and ethnicity in child development.

- Professionals must develop effective skills to meet the cultural and linguistic needs of families from all cultures. (Sturm, 1997, p. 38).

If we expect children to function cooperatively in this diverse society, we must teach them attitudes, concepts, and skills that will enable them to do so.

A variety of concepts has emerged as the basis for programs and practices relating to the pluralism of our world. Some of these concepts include multicultural education, multiethnic education, ethnic studies, antibias curriculum, and global education. Each has a somewhat different perspective. We have selected the term *diversity* as our approach, both in this text and as we teach young children, for several reasons. First, young children understand the concept of *different* and can expand this understanding to include the word *diversity*. Also, the term *diversity* is positive; and as we teach diversity, our goal is to help children develop positive feelings and attitudes toward others. Diversity among people encompasses differences in gender, social class, religion, race, ethnic group, and physical or mental abilities. Compatible with our approach and focus, we prefer this broad implication of the term *diversity* as it relates to people, and we feel it is the most appropriate term to use with young children.

> Teaching diversity and adopting an antibias approach is not just an idea, fad, or educational movement that will pass with time. It is here to stay—an active process that focuses on the idea that *all* children have a right to learn and to reach their individual potentials.

Teaching diversity enriches the classroom by providing various ways to solve problems and to view people, events, and situations. When children are able to view the world from the perspective of its diversity, their views of reality are broadened (Banks & Banks, 1993).

The following are questions that teachers can consider in evaluating responsiveness to diversity in their classrooms:

- Am I respectful and accepting of each child's gender, race, sex, capabilities, culture, and linguistically diverse background?

- Do the literature, resources, and materials in my classroom reflect the diversities, cultures, and languages of all the children?

- Does the curriculum that I offer celebrate diversity?

- Do I encourage families to maintain their cultures and first languages?

- Do I integrate the various traditions, values, history, interests, games, music, art, languages, and families into my curriculum and program whenever appropriate?

- Do I encourage and provide many opportunities for cooperative learning and interaction with others?

The Teacher

Teaching diversity is a professional and moral responsibility; how teachers think influences their teaching and expectations and, in turn, students' achievement and performance (Ladson-Billings, 1994). Teachers set the stage, and they must begin by evaluating their own culture and eliminating personal biases. It is sometimes difficult for us to set aside our own cultural beliefs, values, and habits as we work with diverse family situations. We learned them when we were young, and they have a strong influence on our behaviors and interactions (Sturm, 1997). We need to acquire knowledge of other races, ethnicities, and cultures so that we do not unknowingly pass on our misunderstandings as stereotypes to the students (Haukoos & Beauvais, 1996/1997).

Teachers may need to change their attitudes and expectations, realizing that differences in lifestyle and language do not mean ignorance. They may need to be more positive toward children from minority groups and those who are different in any way. A genuine desire to know more about other people is absolutely necessary. The following are questions for a teacher to consider when identifying any possible personal, unrecognized biases. Analyzing personal prejudice allows us to make any necessary changes in our own attitude, which, in turn, affects the diversity climate in the classroom.

- Which five students do I like most and feel most comfortable with?

- Which five students do I like least and feel least comfortable with?

- When I need an assistant, do I tend to ask the same few students?

- Do I spend more instructional time with one group of students than others?

- Am I quicker to give prompts, cues, and/or answers to low achievers? (ACEI, 1996b, p. 160-L).

As teachers of young children, there is no way that we can be familiar with all the values, norms, and expectations of all the cultural groups represented in our classrooms. However, a genuine respect and appreciation for the students' cultural backgrounds helps us to interpret their needs, feelings, and behaviors appropriately and respectfully

(Katz & McClellan, 1997). "For the optimal development and learning of all children, educators must *accept* the legitimacy of children's home language, *respect* (hold in high regard) and *value* (esteem, appreciate) the home culture, and *promote* and *encourage* the active involvement and support of all families, including extended and nontraditional family units" (NAEYC, 1996b, p. 5).

Teachers need to affirm their students' diversities, showing and modeling that they value and appreciate differences (Ladson-Billings, 1994). Early childhood teachers need to develop awareness for the feelings of all people and become cognizant of the things that they say and do—some very subtle—that demean, oppress, dehumanize, or exclude others. For example, what we say ("Let's sit 'Indian style'"), what we do (make Indian headbands and decorate them with feathers, or sing "Ten Little Indians"), or what we don't do (we seldom sing Jewish songs or include symbols of their culture) all affect children and their feelings about who they are and the cultures with which they identify. Teachers must set examples of positive actions and attitudes and use teaching approaches and materials that are sensitive to the backgrounds and experiences of all students. We must "be an advocate for our linguistically and culturally diverse children and families by nurturing, celebrating, and challenging them" (Garcia, 1997, p. 42).

Teachers should become reeducated and trained in diversity education (Ladson-Billings, 1994). They must learn about different ethnic and cultural groups' life-styles, patterns, values, and interests. They must be taught *how* to behave toward and communicate with minority children and their parents.

Goals of a Classroom Focused on Diversity

The following are the goals we see as important for teaching diversity in the classroom.

All children must be given opportunities to reach their potential regardless of their gender, social class, religion, race, ethnic group, or physical or mental abilities. Each child is different and has unique behaviors, thoughts, and needs. When we teach children from where they are, according to their needs, and help

them to reach their distinctive potential, we are using developmentally appropriate education and beginning our approach to teaching diversity. In addition, when diversity is taught and practiced within a school, academic achievement improves (Banks & Banks, 1993).

Children's diverse cultural, social, family, and ethnic backgrounds create differences in the ways they think, feel, and behave. It behooves teachers to understand these differences in order to enable them to identify the individual needs of each child.

All children should feel included and valued as worthy members of the class and of society. Our classrooms and centers must become inclusive (Greenberg, 1992), with children developing a sense of dignity and a tolerance for all people. "Inclusion is much more than simply opening up our doors; we must open up our hearts" (Elswood, 1999, p. 66). We must adapt our curriculum, physical space, and interactions if we are to be truly inclusive of all children.

Children should be helped to clarify and feel positive toward their own identity, including their sex, ethnic background, race, and physical abilities. Children need to understand who they are and why they behave, feel, and value things the way that they do. "How prominently race figures in children's perceptions of themselves and others depends, in part, on their majority or minority status in their local community and on the extent and quality of contacts that they have with other racial groups" (Ramsey, 1995, p. 20). An intervention, such as using racially integrated cooperative learning teams, positively affects interracial friendships, helps to decrease racial stereotypes, and increases acceptance of cultural diversities (Ramsey, 1995).

Even though early childhood educators recognize differences in biracial children (children from interracial unions) and their families, the curriculum usually does not adequately address these differences. We must acknowledge this reality and help the children to accept and mesh together this dual parentage as they strive to answer the question "Who am I?" (Morrison & Rodgers, 1996). Until they accept their own differences, they will surely have difficulty accepting the differences in other people.

A modern tradition in multicultural education is cultural pluralism, through which, rather than looking at the assimilation of groups into one American culture, ethnic groups remain intact and are respected for their individuality (Janzen, 1994).

Teachers should help all children to gain greater self-esteem and self-understanding as they view themselves from the perspective of differences and similarities. Early childhood teachers should respect the various backgrounds of the children and make them aware of other cultures in the community. Children can learn to appreciate what they have in common with others, while recognizing characteristics that distinguish them from other children (NAEYC, 1996b). Children need information on their culture and need to develop pride in their heritage. Their family, local community, economic or political level, and particular cultural or ethnic group determine children's expectations and experiences. Educational services must address these diverse backgrounds and allow children to access their social, cultural, and national heritage (Rodd, 1996). This will be followed by greater self-esteem and respect for other people.

Children can learn to take the perspective of children who are different from themselves. Children can develop empathy for many other children, not just those in their own class. They can do this only through positive exposure to and experiences with other children. They must see how they are alike and how they are different and be taught to value the differences. Diversity education that focuses on respect and love for our fellow human beings will be well worth the effort.

The diversity perspective should be integrated into all aspects of the school or program. If, as teachers, we only do "other people" units of study or an occasional multicultural activity, we are not solving the problem. These activities do not allow adequate time for exploring or developing concepts, and they often misrepresent various aspects of a particular culture. Separate units of study also tend to perpetuate stereotypes and emphasize differences. Children become more tolerant of others' diversities when multicultural activities are integrated daily into the curriculum, rather than occasionally presented in isolated units (Boutte, VanScoy, & Hendley, 1996).

When the curriculum includes a particular ethnic group only in a specific unit of study on

The diversity perspective should be integrated into all aspects of the school or program.

that group, children do not learn to view the group as an inherent part of our total society. They view it as being separate, and this separateness is often assumed by children to mean inferiority. One author (Derman-Sparks & ABC Task Force, 1989) refers to this curriculum approach as the "tourist" approach. By this she means that we "tour" a country and provide a sampling of that country—its foods, holidays, and traditions, for instance. We look at "things" from that country. When we do this, we teach on the surface but do not build or teach understanding of other people. All groups have specific attributes that influence their attitudes, values, and behaviors in complex and subtle ways. Sometimes the identifying factors of a culture are so subtle that we may not be aware that we are skimming the surface in our efforts to know more about that culture. Be careful of this tourist approach to multiculturalism (ACEI, 1995a). Another danger of this approach is that we tend to select units on some groups of people and leave others out completely.

If we are really going to solve the problem, the concept of diversity must be infused into our materials, environment, and curriculum, and it must be reflected in staff attitudes and beliefs. Content from diverse groups of people must be integrated into all parts of the curriculum. For example, one Native American teacher said that teachers should mingle Native Americans into all of the curriculum instead of confining them to one unit (Greenberg, 1992). It has been suggested that instead of one-week units "everyday attitudes, discussions, and activities are more respectful and effective" (Billman, 1992, p. 24).

Diversity is not a separate subject that should be added to the curriculum, nor is it the study of isolated facts, cultures, or countries. It is not a specific curriculum or formula, but a critical perspective guided by principles (Lee, Menkart, & Okazawa-Rey, 1998). It is not teaching isolated lessons such as cooking ethnic foods or discussing achievements of African Americans during Black History Month. While these activities have purpose, by themselves they are inadequate. Rather, there need to be both planned and spontaneous integrated learning activities that build positive and reliable concepts about all people. Children need to understand other people's feelings and beliefs and comprehend their daily experiences and ways of life.

Children need to understand the classroom rule that discriminatory or insulting actions, language, or attitudes toward others will not be tolerated. Biased, racist, or other unkind remarks are to be taken seriously by teachers who must validate the feelings of the children who are on the receiving end of these comments (Elswood, 1999). When children know that adults expect particular behaviors, they will seek to live up to these expectations. Our classroom norms must reflect respect and tolerance for all differences in people.

These goals must be tailored to fit your specific needs; however, it is important to recognize the need for some foundation goals that provide direction in teaching diversity. We believe it is also important for you to discuss these goals with the children in your classroom at the beginning of the school year. If children can read, the goals should be posted and reviewed as needed.

GENDER BIAS

It is important that children learn to appreciate the contributions to society that are made by those who have diversities relating to religion, age, culture, race, abilities, and gender. Positive attitudes toward differences develop from the early years and affect behavior throughout children's lives (James & Kormanski, 1999). Between the ages of 3 and 8, children sort out their understanding of gender and what it means. They use external attributes for identifying gender: names, hair styles, hobbies, clothing, and play materials (Wellhousen, 1996b). This is why during the early childhood years it is so important that teachers help children to realize that anatomy, not external attributes, determines gender. We can help them to move from gender role stereotypes to gender fairness. "Children's attitudes and comments should be respected, yet gender bias should always be gently challenged" (Wellhousen, 1996b, p. 83). Overt stereotyping relating to gender bias is not as common as it was 20 years ago, but subtler bias persists, and it hurts both males and females, especially those from minority cultural backgrounds. The ways in which teachers treat students sometimes reflect these biases. Gender bias is found in curriculum materials, in the learning environment, and in teacher expectations and interactions.

Teachers must diligently strive to overcome intentional or unintentional gender bias in classrooms so that *all* their students will feel important, respected, and equal to their peers. Once again, teachers set the stage, and their attitudes either overcome or reinforce biases. Gender bias takes many forms. Several of these are described in the following paragraphs.

Stereotyping

When teachers assign traditional and rigid roles or attributes based on sex, the abilities and potentials of each gender are limited. Stereotyping denies students an understanding of the diversity and variation of genders. Young children need to understand that both boys and girls can do all the activities offered in the educational program. Children who see themselves portrayed only in stereotypic ways may internalize these stereotypes and fail to develop their own unique abilities and interests and their full potential. One common gender stereotype assumes that boys are better in math and science and girls are better in language skills. We expect qualities of caring and sharing in girls and qualities of assertiveness, competitiveness, and critical thinking in boys. Girls are expected to be more courteous and kind than boys. Girls are rewarded for appreciative, dependable, considerate, and dependent behavior, while boys are rewarded for active, curious, and questioning behavior. Interests are stereotyped by expecting boys to prefer carpentry, cars, sports, and science, for example, while we expect girls to be interested in such things as housekeeping, cooking, and quiet activities. Stereotyping is damaging and debilitating to young children and does not promote equity. Make sure children know that discriminatory comments or actions will not be tolerated.

Inequitable Attention

Research shows that, too often, boys are given more attention by the teacher in the classroom (Conroy, 1988). Girls frequently form a quiet background to the active role of boys. Teachers interact more frequently with boys, reward them for their academic work more often, and talk to and question them more often than they do girls. Females are often omitted or included less frequently than males on bulletin boards and in discussions of famous people, books, and displays. One author found that in the Caldecott Medal books, "ten boys are pictured for every girl" (Conroy, 1988, p. 44). Girls are not called on as often as boys, and they are not rewarded as frequently for their academic achievements. Too often females are left out of our culture, creating the impression that the male experience is the norm. Making someone "invisible" is a way of demeaning that person or gender (Sheldon, 1990).

Dividing Students by Gender

By separating boys and girls in classroom procedures such as lining up, forming groups, and organizing sports or recreational activities, teachers promote isolation and division of the sexes. Teachers ought to take measures to ensure mixed grouping. If given experiences and guidance to break down gender barriers, children are able to do so (Zeitlin, 1997). This can be accomplished by mixing genders in activities that frequently separate children by gender: boys form one line, girls form another; girls get their coats on first, then the boys; boys to the science table, girls go to the math table; girls follow (teacher's name), and boys follow (another teacher's name); boys against the girls in kickball; and so on.

Linguistic Bias

Curriculum materials, teacher conversation, and other forms of communication often reflect the discriminatory nature of our language. Masculine terms and pronouns such as forefathers, mankind, or even the generic *he* all exclude women. In addition, masculine labels such as fireman, mailman, or chairman deny the legitimacy of women working in various fields or in different capacities. Other forms of biased language include frequent reference to all doctors, construction workers, or lawyers as "he" or all secretaries or nurses as "she." In conversation and in books, our use of the pronoun *he* when we refer to something or someone whose gender is unknown reinforces the notion that females do not exist or are invisible (Sheldon, 1990). Teachers must carefully monitor what they say and realize the impact of their words on young children. For instance, when reading books that refer to an animal as a "he," sometimes substitute "she."

Behavior Expectations

Too often teachers expect certain kinds of behavior from one sex or the other. For example, boys are expected to behave in a courageous and chivalrous way, swearing is more likely tolerated from them, and more boisterous behavior is acceptable. Girls, on the other hand, are expected to be neat and clean, submissive, gentle, and kind and not to take the lead on any activity. Even duties and chores within the classroom are too often assigned on the basis of sex. Acceptable behavior should be expected from all students, and unacceptable behavior not tolerated from all students. All activities in the early childhood classroom should be available to all children. As both girls and boys hammer nails, construct buildings, shovel dirt, pilot boats, drive road graders, tend babies, cook dinner, sweep floors, paint pictures, kick balls, repair tricycles, sing, dance, follow ants, carve pumpkins, extinguish fires, plant seeds, dress up, and play in the beauty shop, avenues of learning and exploration become limitless.

Teachers should be aware of unintended biases, assess their areas of responsibility, review materials for content and form, evaluate their learning environments, and become aware of their interaction and language patterns with others, particularly young children. The total learning environment must foster integrity, equality, and initiative in all children, both boys and girls, in order to prepare them for sound and vigorous futures. By establishing a nonsexist educational atmosphere, we allow young children to explore freely and identify gradually the roles that they find most comfortable and fulfilling. Because gender bias is often subtle and difficult to recognize, it has been labeled "the hidden bias" (Wellhousen, 1996a, p. 36). Gender-equitable classrooms provide a wide variety of gender-fair experiences that allow for participation and exploration by both boys and girls (Marshall, Robeson, & Keefe, 1999).

Suggestions for Eliminating Gender Bias

- Giving boys and girls equal time and attention [teachers interact with boys more than girls (Sadker & Sadker, 1994); and boys receive more attention because their level of activity is higher (Wellhousen, 1996a)].

- Giving boys and girls equal time to respond or comment (boys are usually allowed more time than girls).

- Making the same rules apply to both boys and girls (girls are frequently reminded to follow the rules, and boys are allowed to call out the answers).

- Giving boys and girls the same opportunities in class competition, organization, and responsibilities (girls often are not assigned tasks that require physical effort).

- Praising both boys and girls for their abilities (girls usually receive more attention for physical appearance and boys for academic successes).

- Challenging boys and girls so that learned helplessness is not encouraged in girls.

- Using nonbiased language and labels (his, her; he, she; firefighter; police officer; chairperson).

- Discouraging play choices and sexist remarks that seem to be divided along gender lines (trucks and blocks for boys, housekeeping for girls; girls do the cooking while boys go to work.)

- Providing bias-free role models (Wellhousen, 1996a).

RELIGIOUS BIAS

There is great diversity in religious preferences in our society today, and children's religious preferences will considerably affect how they behave, the traditions that they share from their homes, and their beliefs, values, and moral standards. Religious beliefs about human events such as birth and death and the very purpose of life all influence what children think, say, and do in the classroom. The degree of religious influence in the school varies from one community to another; however, if a school has a dominant religious group, the perspective of that group may be reflected in the school and its curriculum. A family's religious beliefs will influence what parents expect from the school, the teacher, and the child (Gollnick & Chinn, 1998).

Children are aware of religious diversity early, and they can usually describe their own religious identity by the time they are 5 years of age. By the time they are 9 years old, they know whether someone is religious or nonreligious, and they can tell you what religion some people are by some of the things that they do (Gollnick & Chinn, 1998).

Most parents believe that their children should have religious training at home in order to build character, give security, and promote family unity; however, the majority of families in the United States do not attend weekly church services on a regular basis (Gollnick & Chinn, 1998).

Teachers must be sensitive to the religious beliefs of all of the children in the classroom. Again, the teacher's example of respect and tolerance for different beliefs helps children to build this same regard and consideration for another person's way of life and belief system. Teachers can better understand their students if they know the children's religious identifications. Sometimes religious identity is combined with ethnic identity, as it is for the Russian Jew, the Irish Catholic, and others. A child's membership in two microcultures can help a teacher to better understand the child's behavior and self-concept, and the teacher can then assist other children in gaining the same understanding. Religious perspective affects children's friendships, dress standards, social activities, customs, and dietary habits (Gollnick & Chinn, 1998), and teachers must not tolerate criticism from the children's peers with regard to these obvious differences. Rather, teachers can openly teach and model patience, tolerance, and respect for habits and behaviors that reflect a child's religious beliefs and teachings.

CHILDREN WITH SPECIAL NEEDS

Beyond gender, cultures, and ethnic groups, the concept of recognizing similarities and differences among peers includes children with special needs. Children who have severe disabilities as well as those who are gifted are considered as being exceptional or having special needs. Children with special needs are those who have learning or behavioral characteristics that differ substantially from others and require special methods of instruction. Although children with special needs have differences, they are actually more like other children than unlike them, and they must be treated as individuals, not labeled as members of a particular group (Heward & Orlansky, 1989). We must treat them first as children and then as children with special needs.

A disability becomes a handicap only when the condition limits or stops the person's ability to function normally (Shaver & Curtis, 1981). Vygotsky (1993) and Berk & Winsler (1995) remind us that a child's disability is not as great a problem as how the defect affects the child's participation in activities. We must have an attitude of openness and acceptance and realize that exceptional children are members of our society and can make valuable contributions. Of children who have disabilities, 90 percent have only mild impairments (Heward & Orlansky, 1989). Children with disabilities can be classified into any of 13 categories according to Wolery and Wilbers (1994, pp. 3,4), and many of these children do require specialized attention.

- Deafness
- Dual-sensory impairments
- Hearing impairment
- Mental retardation
- Multiple handicaps
- Orthopedic impairments
- Serious emotional disturbance
- Specific learning disabilities
- Speech (language) impairments
- Visual impairments and blindness
- Traumatic brain injury
- Autism
- Other health impairments

With these individual needs in mind, Congress passed Public Law 94-142 (the Education for All Handicapped Children Act) in 1975. This law mandated that a free and appropriate education be provided for all children aged 5 through 18 years with disabilities in an environment closest to that of a "normal" child. Schools implemented an approach whereby children who need special services are identified and then assessed or evaluated to determine their degree of impairment. Then intervention is planned to best meet their needs. An individualized education program (IEP) is developed with the child's teacher, qualified school personnel, and, most importantly, the child's parents.

An amendment to PL 94-142 has significantly influenced and enhanced early intervention with young children who have special needs. PL 99-457, the Education of the Handicapped Amendments of 1986, did not mandate universal service for children under 5 years of age, but it strengthened incentives for states to serve 3- to 6-year-old children and established a new discretionary program for services to children from birth to 3 years of age. In 1990 the Individuals with Disabilities Education Act (IDEA, 1990) was passed as an amendment to PL 94-142. This legislation replaced the word "handicapped" with "disabled" and expanded services for the disabled. In 1997, amendments to IDEA were passed, which resulted in early childhood educators assuming more responsibility for the education of children with special needs. IEPs are required for all children who receive special education services, and they outline the adjustments that must be made in order for children with disabilities to participate in the appropriate activities provided to children without disabilities (IDEA, 1997). These IEPs, which are reviewed at least annually, identify measurable goals and benchmarks necessary to achieve the following IEP goals:

- Specify behavior or behaviors that the child is to perform

- Describe the conditions under which the desired behavior is to be performed

- State the degree to which the behavior is expected to be performed (IDEA, 1997).

It is often a challenge for teachers to work with the requirements of the IEPs because it is sometimes difficult to write these goals, plan instructional experiences to meet these goals, and document the child's progress toward accomplishment. Creating inclusive environments in developmentally appropriate classrooms for young children suggests a framework of six curriculum areas that are important for all children to achieve:

1. Functioning independently

2. Fulfilling the responsibilities of membership in the classroom community

3. Engaging in classroom learning experiences

4. Establishing satisfying interpersonal relationships

5. Communicating effectively

6. Meeting academic expectations (Edmiaston, Dolezal, Doolittle, Erickson, Merritt, 2000)

By using this framework in defining goals and benchmarks, it becomes easier to embed them within the practices of a developmentally appropriate classroom and curriculum.

"Physical education (is) considered to be so important that lawmakers (have made) it the only curricular area placed in the definition of special education" (Block & Burke, 1999, p. 18). IDEA (1997) mandates that all children with disabilities receive physical education services. It is important that we, as educators and advocates of children, make certain that all children participate in physical education as part of a free and appropriate education (Block & Burke, 1999).

Dealing with Special Needs

It is important for teachers to understand the conditions that children in their classrooms may have. Following are nine general categories of special needs, giving characteristics, possible teaching strategies, and specialists in the community whom teachers may consult. Keep in mind that these are generalizations; not every child with special needs will exhibit the same set of characteristics, but some of the most persistent features are included. Although each child is unique, good strategies can be adapted to meet his or her needs. All children have diverse abilities and needs, regardless of their particular labels or previous experiences, and more can be learned in the company of others who share the same goals and interests than can be accomplished alone (Smith, Miller, & Bredekamp, 1998).

Speech and language impairments

Characteristics.   Many problems can occur in a young child with a speech and/or language deficiency. Knowing the normal development of language and speech sounds will help a teacher to determine whether there is a problem. Some signs include omissions, substitutions, distortions, or additions of speech sounds. Such articulation disorders are common during the early years, but most often disappear after second or third grade. Stuttering is less common, but also more distressing, and may result from anxiety or difficulty with particular sounds. Use of single words and/or gestures, along with difficulty in following directions, is an indication of a developmental problem. An early childhood teacher may also have children in the classroom who are bilingual (learning two languages).

Reaching a child by using his or her first language is also very important. This language is the familiar vehicle of oral communication, and the student needs acceptance and understanding in the use of the language in any program. If a child in an early childhood setting is bilingual, that is, learning and using two languages, someone should be available to communicate with the child in both languages.

Teaching strategies.   There are many things a teacher can do to assist a child in speech and language development. When working with a child who has communication disabilities, be a good listener; use parallel or play-by-play broadcasting during activities; use alternative communications; model good language; encourage specific reasons for language expression (Russell-Fox, 1997). Give simple directions, using phrases or short sentences. When addressing the child, do not talk down or use baby talk. Provide daily oral experiences, such as singing, language activities, or answering questions. Always listen and respond to the child; concentrate on what is said, not on the trouble that the student has in saying it. Avoid finishing a student's sentences or correcting articulation problems in front of peers. Provide good models for the child to listen to. Cooperative and small-group activities give opportunities for children to use language skills in less threatening situations. If problems persist or do not appear to be developmental, refer the child for testing. If the child is bilingual, have an interpreter, seek to understand the culture, and keep the vocabulary as basic as possible. Teach and provide ESL (English as a second language) students with opportunities to teach about their culture and language, and encourage class members to learn words from an ESL student's first language. Unless the culture of the ESL student is understood by the school community that he or she is in, the student will have trouble making steps toward any type of successful integration.

Specialists.   Communication disorder specialists or itinerant migrant education teachers are among the community specialists in the area of speech and language development who can assist or consult with the early childhood teacher.

Mental impairments

Characteristics.   For many years, levels of mental impairments were measured by intelligence testing. Other factors to consider and evaluate when assessing a child's potential in the classroom include the child's developmental gains in motor, language, social, and self-help skills for his or her age; physical difficulties or illnesses; and the length of the child's attention span. Teachers should observe the rate of learning and comprehension of abstract concepts.

Teaching strategies.   If a child is delayed in two or more of the previously mentioned areas, the teacher should refer the child for developmental testing. Adjustments can be made in the classroom that will assist the teacher and child. Low child–staff ratios are necessary to provide the individualized attention that the child will need. Specific learning objectives should be based on an analysis of the child's learning strengths and weaknesses. Tasks that are being taught should be broken into small, logical components, and these should be repeated often and reinforced. The presentation should be consistent and the directions brief and simple. Materials should not insult the student. Skills and concepts should be practical, based on the demands of living. Students with mental impairments must overlearn, repeat, and practice more than children of average intelligence. Children need to experience success; teachers should chart growth.

Specialists.   The following specialists can help in evaluating and programming for children who have mental impairments: psychologist, special education teacher, developmental specialist, communication disorder specialist, occupational therapist, and physical therapist.

Hearing impairments

Characteristics. The following characteristics may indicate a hearing problem: limited communication skills, inability to understand or respond to the speech of others, misbehavior, inattentiveness, watching the speaker's face and lips, turning one ear toward the speaker, and complaints of earaches. If a hearing test has been given, a loss of 20 to 60 decibels (measurement of sound density) is considered hard of hearing, and a loss of 60 decibels or more is considered deaf.

Teaching Strategies. In the classroom, seat a child with a hearing impairment near the source of instruction and where there is good visibility. When working with a child who has hearing disabilities, develop a professional working relationship with the child's parents, speech–language therapist, audiologist, hearing specialist, and other involved care providers; keep the lines of communication open among all people; use visual and tactile aids; get the child's attention (call the child by name) before giving information or beginning an activity; speak normally; and allow adequate time for the child to speak (Russell-Fox, 1997). Articulate clearly, do not exaggerate, and face the child when speaking. If the child is using hearing aids, be familiar with them, check to see whether they are operating, know how to put them in the child's ear, and be prepared to charge the battery. Provide constant language stimulation. The teacher may need to learn some sign language and, if applicable, give the whole class some exposure to sign language.

Specialists. Specialists to be consulted in case of a hearing impairment are the audiologist, communication disorder specialist, and itinerant teacher for students who are hard of hearing. The parents should also be consulted.

Visual impairments

Characteristics. A child who has been diagnosed as having a severe vision problem falls into one of two categories: partially sighted or blind. Children who are partially sighted have a field of vision that is 20/200 (that is, they can see at 20 feet what a normally sighted person can see at 200 feet) or better in the corrected eye, but not greater than 20/70. Children who are blind have a field of vision of 20/200 or less in the corrected better eye. Characteristics of children with visual impairments are excessive blinking; rubbing, crossing, and squinting of the eyes; holding things close or far away; tilting the head when trying to focus; and dizziness or headaches.

Teaching strategies. To adjust materials and activities to meet the needs of a child with a visual impairment, rely on the use of the other senses. When working with a child who has visual impairments, develop a professional working relationship with the child's parents, vision specialist, and other involved care providers; learn about the degree of impairment; orient the child to the layout of the classroom and materials, including any changes; provide tactile, auditory, and manipulative experiences; encourage independence, but be ready to provide physical prompts when helpful (Russell-Fox, 1997). Assign a buddy to help the child orient quickly and develop social interactions. Access and use materials and equipment to help the student who is visually impaired. For readers, make sure that the quality of the print that you expect the child to use is readable.

Specialists. The teacher may consult with the child's ophthalmologist or an itinerant teacher of children with visual impairments to find materials and adjust the program for the child.

Physical impairments

Characteristics. Indications of a physical problem include poor coordination or control of fine or gross motor skills, poor balance, and frustration and discouragement when attempting motor skills. Children with a physical disability may have normal intelligence. Common physical disabilities that can be identified in young children at birth or shortly afterward include cerebral palsy, epilepsy, and spina bifida. In addition to congenital impairments, there are impairments caused by diseases and accidents.

Teaching strategies. When working with a child who has physical special needs, develop a professional working relationship with (and seek suggestions from) the physical and occupational therapists and the parents; arrange environments so that the child can access toys, materials, and equipment; learn the types, uses, and care of adaptive equipment; allow adequate transition time; support and encourage, yet foster independence (Russell-Fox, 1997). One of the major changes necessary when a child with a physical disability is in a regular classroom is acquiring appropriate structures and equipment (for example, ramps, walkers). Learn as much as possible about the physical problems and what limitations they may have on the child. Help the child develop motor, language, speech, and social skills to the fullest potential. Be sensitive to the child's feelings about the disability.

Specialists.   To develop a program that is appropriate for a child with physical problems, the teacher should consult with an occupational therapist, a physical therapist, the child's physician, and the child's parents. In extreme cases, a neurologist should be consulted.

Emotional, social, or behavioral problems

Characteristics.   Children with emotional, social, or behavioral problems may exhibit them to a marked degree in two different ways: passively or aggressively. A passive child may stare for long periods of time; seldom communicate; be withdrawn, afraid, sensitive, or shy; and have poor eye contact. An aggressive or hyperactive child may be overcompetitive, rebellious, easily distracted, disruptive, hostile, assaultive, overly active, impulsive, defiant of authority, inattentive, and restless. These children often have difficulty building positive relationships, staying on task, and being attentive and may experience depression. Children with autism also fit into this category.

Teaching strategies.   A child with behavioral problems may need a change in environment to provide the individualized attention needed to verbalize his or her feelings. Children with these problems need love, patience, and understanding. Communication appears to be a key ingredient. Most of all, they need consistency in expectations and positive reinforcement for appropriate behaviors. Teachers may need to draw information from specialists in the field to assist them in the class. Working with children who have ADHD (attention deficit–hyperactivity disorder) requires a multimodal approach, including behavior management techniques. The most important technique is positive reinforcement, in which the child is provided a rewarding response after a desired behavior is demonstrated. Classroom success may require a range of interventions depending on how the disorder affects the child. The following classroom characteristics that promote success for children with ADD (attention deficit disorder) have been identified:

- Predictability
- Structure and routine (*Harvard Mental Health Letter*, 1995)
- Shorter work periods
- Reduced teacher–pupil ratio
- Individualized instruction (they often need assignments broken into smaller tasks) (*Harvard Mental Health Letter*, 1995)
- Positive reinforcement [Children and Adults with Attention Deficit Disorders (Ch.A.D.D.), 1995a]

The following are teacher characteristics that appear helpful in teaching children diagnosed with ADD:

- Positive academic expectations
- Frequent monitoring and checking of work
- Clarity in giving instructions
- Warmth, patience, and a sense of humor
- Consistency and firmness
- Knowledge of different behavioral interventions
- Willingness to work with a special education teacher (Ch.A.D.D., 1995a)
- Focusing on potential rather than on the disability (Armstrong, 1996b)
- Focusing on strengths and providing the child with a highly stimulating learning environment (Armstrong, 1996a)

Specialists.   Early childhood teachers may need to consult with a psychologist, physician, social worker, counselor, or special education teacher when working with children with emotional, social, or behavioral problems. A comprehensive evaluation is necessary to establish a diagnosis, and a medical exam is imperative (Ch.A.D.D., 1995b).

Note: There are a number of excellent Internet resources for help and suggestions in teaching and working with ADHD or ADD students. The following are examples:

Ch.A.D.D. http://www.chadd.org/

"Attention Deficit Disorder: A Dubious Diagnosis?" From the Merrow Report http://www.pbs.org/merrow

Chronic illness

Characteristics.   Children who are chronically ill generally have a disorder that is always present and that may limit their physical activity. Some examples are asthma, cystic fibrosis, diabetes, tuberculosis, arthritis, muscular dystrophy, and hemophilia. Children who are chronically ill usually have normal intelligence.

Teaching strategies.   When working with a child who has a chronic illness, develop a professional working relationship with the child's parents, physician, school nurse, and other involved care providers; keep the lines of communication open among all people; learn about the child's health needs, diet, and medications; learn what to do in case of an emergency; develop a program plan that may include home visits, phone calls, care packages, activity packets, and so on (Russell-Fox, 1997).

Be aware, if you are the teacher of siblings of a child with a serious illness, that these siblings are often forgotten and lose the needed support from parents and other adults. There is also a disruption in the friendship between the child who is ill and the "forgotten well siblings" (Wallinga & Skeen, 1996, p. 78). It is very possible that the teacher "may be the most important support the healthy child has" (p. 82).

Specialists.   The child's parents, physicians, and the school nurse are the best consultants for teachers when dealing with children who are chronically ill.

Learning disabilities

Characteristics.   The category known as *learning disabilities* has existed for 25 years. It refers to a disorder in one or more basic psychological processes associated with either understanding or using language, reasoning, or math. Some charac-

teristics include motor disinhibition (being unable to refrain from responding), disassociation (responding to the elements of a stimulus rather than to the whole stimulus), figure–ground disturbance (confusing a figure with its background), perseveration (not changing from one task to another), and absence of a well-developed self-concept and body image (Broman, 1989). Other characteristics are poor gross and fine motor skills and lack of established handedness.

Teaching strategies.   Children with learning disabilities often need one-on-one teaching with simple tasks and simple instructions. Proceed slowly, making sure that the child is paying attention. Be sure that the child has mastered skills at one level before proceeding to the next. Frequently, children with learning disabilities seem to have mastered the skills being taught, but they actually need to "overlearn" or receive extra reinforcement and practice in order for the information to be retained (Anderson with Weinhouse, 1997). Increase the amount of time allowed for completing tasks. Provide opportunities for cooperative learning or small-group work, peer tutoring, and learning centers. Provide concrete examples. Use positive reinforcement when a child is learning each task. When working with a child who has learning disabilities, concentrate on the strengths, not the weaknesses of the child; patiently provide for overlearning and practice; use multisensory approaches to experiences; praise progress and successes, and encourage parents to do the same; provide clear, simple directions and transitions (Russell-Fox, 1997). When considering retention, reflect on the following: "Is retention supposed to be a cure for learning disabilities? ... It seems that retaining a child is often just a postponement of a diagnosis and needed assistance" (Anderson with Weinhouse, 1997, p. 29).

Specialists.   Specialists in the area of learning disabilities include psychologists, special education teachers, developmental specialists, and social workers.

Gifted and talented children

Characteristics.   Gifted children are the most underserved group of exceptional children. There is no consensus about what constitutes a gifted child. Children have many individual gifts, and teachers should learn to think of *gifted behavior*, rather than *being gifted*, because giftedness is not an absolute and predetermined condition. It is a set of behaviors that emerges when certain traits interact with one another. Children who are gifted show above-average ability or potential in one or more of the following areas:

1. general intellectual ability,

2. specific academic aptitude,

3. leadership ability,

4. creative or productive thinking,

5. visual and performing arts, and

6. psychomotor ability (Lupkowski & Lupkowski, 1985, p. 10)

Children who are gifted may peak in some areas at particular times, but not necessarily in all cognitive areas. Karnes and Johnson (1989, p. 56) agree that "giftedness comes in many forms. Is the child an unusually creative thinker? Artistic? Musical? Mentally sharp? Good grades and giftedness are not the same thing." However, isolated incidents do not indicate giftedness. Also, gifted children may not necessarily score high on all parts of intelligence tests.

Professionals and those involved in evaluating should look at what children can do instead of what they cannot do. Parent reports and teacher observations should also be used in describing children's strengths, talents, and capabilities. Children who are gifted and talented are creative and observant, ask numerous questions, and learn quickly and easily. They possess a large store of information. They are attentive, have a capacity for seeing relationships and patterns, enjoy problem solving, exhibit an early interest in printed material, and have exceptional memory. They also have in-depth interests, a high energy level, and good reasoning and insight ability (Lupkowski & Lupkowski, 1985). They are sensitive and have high expectations. These children usually have large, accurate vocabularies and use expanded language. It is difficult for children from minority groups, young children, and underachievers to be identified and served by programs for gifted children.

Teaching strategies.   Provide stimulating, challenging, and varied enrichment opportunities to develop knowledge, talents, and work habits. Pro-vide relevant extra assignments or extensions. Build on language skills. Encourage the use of computers. Independence and self-direction need to be encouraged. Involve students in planning their own curriculum. Use delayed, intrinsic, and social reinforcement rather than immediate and concrete rewards. Focus on problem solving and divergent thinking. Older children (5 to 8 years) often need academic acceleration and enrichment (extending the regular curriculum), whereas younger children (3 to 5 years) benefit from individualization, discovery learning, and encouragement of talents.

Specialists.   Itinerant teachers of children who are gifted and talented or psychologists or resource teachers can assist the early childhood teacher in planning activities to enhance the child's program in the regular classroom setting.

Programs for Meeting Special Needs

Although children with special needs are similar in most respects to children without disabilities, they have additional needs, such as environment adjustments and trained specialists (Wolery & Wilbers, 1994). The needs of children who have multiple disabilities (children with more than one of the disabling conditions described previously) must be met according to each child's disabilities and abilities.

Consultants from all areas can provide appropriate programs for the children to achieve their greatest potential. When it is necessary for us to consider referring a child with special needs to a specialist, it may be difficult to approach the subject with the parents. Instead of talking about *treatment* for the child, suggesting the need of an *evaluation* for services tends to help parents to be more receptive (Manning & Schindler, 1997). "While traditional assessments serve the purposes of diagnosis and eligibility, they do not provide the type of information needed to make appropriate intervention decisions regarding functional and developmentally appropriate programming ..." for all children with special needs (Grisham-Brown, 2000, p. 3). Appropriate transdisciplinary activity-based assessments actively involve the family, allow teams to view the whole child, limit the number of people who interact with the child, and result in intervention strategies that are functional and developmentally appropriate (Grisham-Brown, 2000).

After the teacher comes to an understanding of a child's disabling condition, his or her acceptance of that child as a whole child, not just one who has a disability, is critical. The teacher becomes a model in showing acceptance for the child who has a disability for the other children in the classroom. Through the teacher, the other children will come to understand and accept this child. Research suggests that social integration of children, both with and without disabilities, does not occur automatically; it develops only when sensitive teachers structure experiences for social integration (Odom & McEvoy, 1988). "Promotion of specific friendship skills to enhance the social interaction of typical and atypical children requires well-planned teacher strategies and initiatives" (Honig & Wittmer, 1996, p. 65). Children with diabilities often need some direction with prosocial interactions. They need us to help them to learn how to make friends, to enter a play group, and to sustain friendly play (Honig & Thompson, 1994). It may be challenging to include antibias philosophy in developmentally appropriate settings, but educators must foster social interactions among all children (Elswood, 1999). All children can benefit and learn from their relationships with exceptional children. It is the expert teacher who makes the presence of children with special needs an advantage rather than a disadvantage for everyone in the classroom.

A Comprehensive Program for Exceptional Children

1. A teacher knowledgeable in child development who accepts children at their level of development
2. A teacher who understands that children need consistency, a dependable schedule, and gentle but firm limits
3. A curriculum that has a multisensory approach
4. A curriculum that enhances growth in all areas of development
5. A curriculum that provides various hands-on experiences
6. Many opportunities for play

7. A natural, appropriate setting in which learning may be directly applied, with no need for delayed generalization from a highly structured and isolated lesson. (Morgan & York, 1981, p. 20)

A basic understanding of typical child development is necessary if a teacher is to work effectively among children with special needs. This understanding provides the teacher with a guideline to devise developmental instructional activities, a basis to modify the activities to meet the individual needs of the children in the classroom, and a guideline to form realistic expectations for all the children.

With knowledge of typical child development, early childhood teachers can adapt and individualize their programs to meet the needs of the children in their classroom. This individualization process involves breaking down tasks into small steps so that the child can progress successfully, providing appropriate models for the child to follow, maintaining accurate records of the child's progress, and altering the physical makeup of the building and equipment to meet the child's special needs. Consulting with specialists and following through with the programs outlined also assist the teacher in developing individual plans and directions.

Early intervention for young children with disabilities positively affects learning and development, and often reduces the likelihood of more serious problems later (Johnson, 1993). This translates to the need for early childhood special education teachers and staff to be prepared and qualified to implement programs that support the research findings (Garret & Kelley, 2000). "Teachers who are trained in effective early intervention methods and supported by peers, administrators, and parents develop positive attitudes that enable them to meet classroom challenges and recognize the unique potential of each child regardless of ability or disability" (Stafford & Green, 1996, p. 218).

Anderson with Weinhouse (1997, pp. 30, 31) have devised three strategies for helping children with special needs to experience success, which is so crucial to their emotional and educational development: (1) "Never limit your expectations or predetermine the final outcome, (2) Explore all interests and abilities for hidden potential, (3) Include these children in regular education classes and activities whenever possible." Repeated failures lead to more failure.

Children with varying disabilities are frequently mainstreamed into regular classrooms. Mainstreaming means teaching children who are disabled in regular classes for part or all of their school day. To prepare for these children, teachers should learn as much as possible about typical child development, research the disabilities that they will be dealing with, seek help from specialists who work with the children, attend workshops or in-service training sessions, and talk with the children's parents. Teachers need extra skill, flexibility, and tolerance to work effectively with children who have special needs.

"By streamlining the instructional planning process, teachers implementing inclusion may experience less stress, greater confidence, and more success" (Winter, 1997, p. 216). Winter (1997) proposes a practical five-point system (SMART) that helps teachers plan for inclusive education programs:

S   Select curriculum and approaches
M   Match instruction to the child
A   Adapt when necessary
R   Relevant skills targeted
T   Test to inform instruction (assessment)

Mainstreaming can be a positive experience for all children in the classroom. The values of mainstreaming for the typical child are learning to accept differences in people, learning to be a helpful and caring person, and learning how and when to help. Research demonstrates that nondisabled students experience increase in self-esteem, tolerance, and growth in personal moral and ethical principles as a result of the inclusion of children with disabilities (Baker, Wang, & Walberg, 1994/1995; Farlow, 1996; Staub & Peck, 1994/1995). The values of mainstreaming for the child with special needs are the opportunity to choose friends with whom to play, to realize potential skills more fully, and to learn from peers without disabilities (Morgan & York, 1981).

The potentials of special children inherent in heterogeneous groups, including mainstreaming, are greater for language and social development than for academic achievement (Jenkins, Odom, & Speltz, 1989). Educational services should be individually planned to best serve the needs of each child. It is our hope that each child will be evaluated carefully to determine how the school and community can best serve individual special needs. Again, educational services for children with special needs must be individually planned.

Once a child has been placed, ongoing evaluation and observation should be undertaken to determine whether the program is providing optimal education for the child. To determine whether a program or service is effective, the student needs to demonstrate that he or she is progressing successfully (Danielson & Bellamy, 1989).

There are many critics of full inclusion; they propose that it can create inappropriate placement for some disabled children and advocate assessing the child's ability to function in a regular classroom, with necessary support services, as a condition for placement (Shanker, 1994/1995). Others stress the importance of having placement options and suggest that sometimes being placed in a separate setting, rather than the regular classroom, is the best option (Fuchs & Fuchs, 1994/1995; Maloney, 1994/1995). Supporters of full inclusion propose that the development of *all* children is enhanced when children with disabilities are included in regular classrooms. For inclusion to be successful, both teachers and students with disabilities must receive support from parents, peers, extra personnel, special equipment and materials, and related in-service training (ACEI, 1995b). Although including children with special needs in learning environments with their typical peers presents many challenges, the rewards, benefits, and teamwork make it worthwhile (Russell-Fox, 1997)! An effective inclusive classroom community empowers families, provides training and encouragement to teachers, and supports a six-step process for inclusion:

1. Focusing attention on the value of inclusion

2. Involving key stakeholders in the planning

3. Finding and implementing easy successes

4. Identifying long-term service delivery partners in the community

When mother visits the classroom, the child learns that mothers can be teachers too. This provides benefits for the child, the child's mother, and the entire classroom.

5. Promoting ongoing systems support for inclusion

6. Evaluating the impact of change

Successfully incorporating these six steps results in an atmosphere that celebrates diversity in which all children are able to grow, develop, and play together (Olson, Murphy, & Olson, 1999).

In addition, teachers or caregivers should respond to children's curiosity or questions with simple, accurate responses. Disabilities should be introduced to all children through books and materials that depict various disabilities, while still stressing the abilities and similarities among all human beings. All adults should model a sensitivity to all people.

CREATING A DIVERSE CURRICULUM AND CLASSROOM

Bredekamp & Copple (1997) incorporate ideas for meeting the needs of young children who have disabilities, while supporting the importance of providing appropriate activities to support all children with different types of learning experiences (Minzenberg, Laughlin, & Kaczmarek, 1998). The most important goal for early childhood professionals is to provide *every* child with a responsive learning environment (NAEYC, 1996b). Creating a classroom, curriculum, and atmosphere that focus on diversity is challenging. In addition to broadly incorporating the goals stated earlier in the chapter, specific things can be done to create and teach diversity in the classroom.

Derman-Sparks and the ABC Task Force (1989) identified four goals for developing an antibias approach:

• Foster each child's construction of a knowledgeable, confident self-identity

• Foster each child's comfortable, empathetic interaction with diversity among people

• Foster each child's critical thinking about bias

• Foster each child's ability to stand up for herself or himself and for others in the face of bias.

A curriculum program that promotes diversity not only fosters personal identity development in young children, but it also helps them to accept differences and diversities in others. Experiences should include exploring languages, customs, traditions, foods, and cultural activities through play, thematic units, field trips, visitors, stories and books, manipulatives and puzzles, dolls and dramatic play clothing, creative art, and music. Throughout all these activities, we must be sensitive to the racism and prejudice that children of diversity often encounter, and provide support and encouragement to their development of personal identities (Morrison & Bordere, 2001).

The following suggestions are not inclusive; add your own ideas to this list. In addition, each chapter of this text contains specific ideas for including and teaching diversity within the framework of various concepts.

Changing Attitudes and Practices of Teachers

Perhaps most important of all is that teachers do not just add the component of diversity to their curriculum; rather, the entire classroom and curriculum must be revised to reflect a change in attitude and practice that indicates genuine acceptance of all people. Teachers can do much by helping children to rid themselves of the we–they attitude and replace it with the we–us attitude.

Selecting Books, Materials, and Resources

All children need to see images of themselves depicted in early childhood classrooms, but too often children with disabilities are not fairly represented (Favazza, LaRoe, Phillipsen, & Kumar, 2000). Depictions of children with disabilities can be included in photographs, pictures, and posters; materials and equipment; and books and magazines. Studies indicate that when children in the classroom see depictions of various diversities they are more accepting and understanding of children who actually have these differences (Favazza, Phillipsen, & Kumar, 1996; Favazza & Odom, 1997).

Diversity materials need to be consistently available (Derman-Sparks & ABC Task Force, 1989), and teachers must consciously evaluate the

> When all children in classes are depicted in various ways, it sends a message that everyone belongs, that everyone is important, that everyone is accepted. This results in higher self-esteem and more positive personal identities for everyone.

messages that are contained in these materials. "Only when we are deliberately selecting and evaluating can we hope that the messages children receive while in our care are consistent with the philosophy and goals of our programs" (Neugebauer, 1992, p. 160). Teachers should be cautious and careful in selecting materials such as books, pictures, games, and toys that are free of biases and stereotypes. Select materials that show diversity of culture, ethnicity, gender, and racial groups and take the perspective of various minorities. Images of the elderly and people with disabilities should also appear in materials in the environment.

Children's picture books "mirror society and provide children with opportunities to read and discuss information" about the various diversities that they see (James & Kormanski, 1999, p. 32). They provide a natural avenue for opening up communication and fostering environments of respect and understanding. They "allow personal experiences to be revisited many times for reflection and discussion" (Marshall, 1998, p. 195) and help to build bridges and understandings between the known and the unknown. Storybooks can generate attitudes of respect for diversity by talking about differences in people, talking through differences in people, and talking about topics that relate to diversity issues.

We should work to provide all children with the experience of seeing themselves in their books and then learning to care for the others that they see. Children also need to be able to identify with heroes and heroines of their own culture (Harris, 1991). Avoid the practice of tokenism—selecting one book, picture, or doll that includes an ethnic minority. Cook (2001) presents the importance of using stories in early childhood classrooms, and suggests the following five-step process for creating them:

1. Introducing the main character or characters

2. Telling about the problem

3. Talking to a wise person

4. Trying out a new approach

5. Summarizing the lesson

"Stories are the threads that hold together the fabric of our lives . . . and give children with special needs . . . a true sense of empowerment and hope for resolving life's frustrations" (Cook, 2001, p. 67).

Throughout the year, pictures, toys, and books should reflect the diversity of people. The following annotated list includes some of our favorite picture books that give young children a glimpse of other cultures, times, or places. (See Suggested Resources at the end of the chapter for publisher information.)

All the Places to Love, by P. MacLachlan. *Remembrances of an American farm family and feelings of family affection.*

The Always Prayer Shawl, by S. Oberman. *A young Jewish boy and his family leave their home in Czarist Russia during the revolution and journey to a new country. The power of family traditions is captured in this story.*

Aunt Flossie's Hats (and Crab Cakes Later), by E. F. Howard. *The memories of times past that go with Aunt Flossie's hats.*

Boundless Grace, by M. Hoffman. *A young girl seeks to bridge the gap between two families, her own family and her step-family, as well as between two cultures, America and Africa.*

Dear Willie Rudd, by L. M. Gray. *A young girl decides to write a letter of love and apology to her mother and grandmother's African American houseworker prior to Civil Rights.*

The Gift, by A. Brodmann. *A Jewish child ponders what to do with her Hanukkah money and learns that to give from her heart is best of all.*

Grandfather's Journey, by A. Say. *The story of the bridging of two cultures as the author reminisces of his grandfather's life in America and Japan.*

Maria Molina and the Days of the Dead, by K. Krull. *A story of Mexican culture and holiday celebration.*

More than Anything Else, by M. Bradby. *A young African American child's dream to read.*

The Story of Ruby Bridges, by R. Coles. *The story of the first black child to attend an all-white elementary school, the center of a storm of hatred and prejudice.*

Tico and the Golden Wings, by L. Lionni. *A story focused on valuing differences and sharing what we have with others.*

Time to Go, by B. Fiday & D. Fiday. *The economic necessity of a family leaving farm life.*

Uncle Jed's Barbershop, by M. K. Mitchell. *A story of segregation, sharecropping, the Depression, and genuine caring and sharing with others.*

When I Was Young in the Mountains, by C. Rylant. *Children sense the importance of contentment and savoring life's little things in this story capturing life in Appalachia.*

Classroom centers are also valuable resources for supporting an antibias philosophy. They make it easier to

- Meet the needs of a diverse group of children

- Address particular goals and objectives of children with special needs

- Develop varied and interesting activities

- Promote efficient use of time and resources

- Balance the number of structured and unstructured activities

- Coordinate schedules and responsibilities of teachers and staff (Santos, Lingnugaris/Kraft, & Akers (1999)

> Successful centers in the early childhood classroom result when teachers understand the developmental goals, interests, and characteristics of the children; are aware of the environment; and know what materials and personnel resources are available.

Bulletin boards, films and videos, visitors, and field trips should constantly confirm the diversity of our world and present the minority perspective. During the year, invite several visitors from the same culture so that children may capture the variability that exists within a culture (Boutte & McCormick, 1992). Calendars should include dates of ethnic holidays and note outstanding citizens of diverse ethnic origins.

Dolls in the classroom should reflect different ethnic identities, physical abilities, and genders. "Persona" dolls can be used to introduce differences, particularly some of the differences not found among children in the classroom (Derman-Sparks & ABC Task Force, 1989). These dolls have names, and the children personally identify with them through playing, interacting, associating, and listening to stories about their lives. For example, one doll might be named Jenny, and Jenny might be blind and live with her mother and grandmother. Throughout the year, the teacher can build on Jenny's story and help the children to understand not only Jenny, but that her blindness is a way that she is different. Games from other cultures are enjoyed by children and help broaden their perspectives. Music and art from other cultures can be included as a natural part of the early childhood environment.

Dramatic play offers ready opportunities to share clothing and items that reflect such diversities as the different physical abilities, genders, and ages of people.

If available materials are screened and found to be biased or presenting obvious stereotypes, the materials may need to be disregarded or altered. If this is the case, teachers should be honest with the children, pointing out biases and discussing them in ways that children can understand. Teachers can develop or make supplementary materials that help correct some of the misconceptions or biases found in materials.

Exposing Children to the Diversity of Cultures

There are more than 100 ethnic groups in the United States. Teachers cannot include curriculum content about each one, but they can focus on different groups that have a variety of customs, values, and traditions. Children should be acquainted with art, music, literature, and foods from various ethnic groups. Musical instruments, songs, dances, and stories can be presented and taught by people from various cultures. These should not be presented in ways that suggest tokenism, but rather so that children gain the perspective of and feel respect toward

other people. As diversity is integrated into the curriculum, teachers should be mindful that the differences found among people are not to be interpreted as deficiencies or inferiorities. Cultures should not be described in terms of how they deviate from the mainstream culture. Diversity must be recognized as a strength and not considered a weakness (Tiedt & Tiedt, 1986). Young children should understand the value of differences. People have different beliefs, eat many different foods, live in different ways, practice different religions, and have different names—and that is the way it should be!

Visitors with all kinds of talents, skills, and hobbies should be invited into the classroom. Field trips for the same purpose of exposure could be arranged. Borden (1987, p. 23) refers to the *community connection*: "Every school is located in a community. Every community has members who care about the well-being of its children. Every community is filled with people with talents, hobbies, and resources that can enrich the pupils' educational experiences. Reach out! Ask them!"

Focusing on similarities among all people throughout the classroom and the curriculum is a notion that might be referred to as the "common thread idea" and should be integrated, discussed, and felt by all children. We acknowledge the commonality of all people: We are all alike in that we are all people with feelings and hopes, and we are all more alike than different (Wardle, 1990). Yes, we are of different genders, social classes, religions; from a variety of ethnic backgrounds; and have various physical abilities; but we share many similarities.

Accepting Language and Dialect Diversity

Teachers must support language and dialect diversity, including sign language, and even teach words in other languages. If there are bilingual children in the classroom, they should often teach words or phrases relating to topics that are being discussed. Preferably in bilingual classes, children should use their native languages about half of the time, and the teacher should be fluent in the language of the majority of the students from minority groups. If there are no bilingual children in the classroom, the teacher could teach words or phrases from another language. For example, numbers, shapes, colors, units of money or time, the al-

Toys and materials in the classroom must be varied to meet the abilities and interests of all children.

phabet, songs, and fingerplays can all be taught in many languages.

All people speak different dialects, which includes both vocabulary and word pronunciation. Children have the right to their own language, and no dialect should be considered unacceptable.

Using the Daily News as a Springboard for Cultural Awareness and Understanding

As news and current events are discussed, other countries or states can be located on maps and brief dialogues about people in these areas can be included.

Teaching Differences in Occupations and Lifestyles

Children should become familiar with not only the obvious differences among people, but also with the varieties of people's occupations and life-

styles. These varieties can be found in pictures, books, visitors, and field trips. Teachers must connect the classroom with the diversities in the community and neighborhood. Parents and extended family members are great resources; they can share their interests, leisure pursuits, and professions. To overcome sexism, be sure to include women and men doing nontraditional jobs and having hobbies or interests that are nontraditional for a particular sex. This can help children to overcome the biases and stereotypes regarding sex roles and occupations.

Children learn that people have all kinds of jobs. Your challenge as a teacher of young children is to expose them to a variety of jobs. Be careful not to stereotype jobs so that the children develop misconceptions, such as that only boys can be firefighters or police officers. Early childhood teachers should expose children to various kinds of jobs that people do, acquainting them with the necessary tools or machinery involved. As a caution: If you begin discussing the jobs of some of the children's parents, in some way address the jobs of all the parents so that no child is left out.

Visits to or from elderly people and people with different physical abilities help children to overcome stereotypes. Books and stories also help to develop accurate concepts relating to these groups. *Miss Maggie* (Rylant, 1983) is an example of a book that bridges the gap between a young boy and an elderly woman.

Diversity in family life-styles needs to be taught, valued, and accepted. Some families have a single mom or dad; some have a mom who works and a dad at home; some have a dad who works and a mom who is at home; some have both parents who work; some have two moms and two dads (step-parents); some families are headed by grandparents or foster parents; some have interracial parents; some families have members with special needs.

Modifying Curriculum Approaches to Promote and Facilitate Achievement Among Children from Diverse Groups

Teachers can practice a number of strategies to ensure that all students have opportunities for success (Brandt, 1994). Examples include using the language and traditions that children bring to school from their own culture to bridge the gap between what they know and what they need to learn and learning the child's native language well enough to teach some academic content (Ladson-Billings, 1994). Cooperative learning should be used as a strategy. It is a strategy that was discussed previously, but teachers should know that this approach to teaching and learning can promote integration of children from minority groups. As children come to know one another through working together, they naturally develop the respect, tolerance, and sensitivity that we are trying to achieve.

SPECIFIC CURRICULUM ACTIVITIES

Once we have adopted the diversity perspective, many ways of integrating it with our educational goals and implementing it in the classroom become obvious. All aspects of the curriculum should avoid stereotypes and include the diversity approach through experiences and materials that accurately reflect all cultural groups. Activities should be concrete, comprehensible, and linked to experiences in which the children can become involved. These activities will enrich and expand their overall experiences. As teachers, it is important that we make comparisons of similarities and differences among cultures whenever possible, focusing on the ways they are alike.

The following are some activities that can be incorporated into general areas of the basic curriculum. Additional activities are found in this chapter under the heading Activities and Experiences. Also, each chapter in the text includes specific ways of integrating diversity into the teaching of specific concepts.

Communication Skills

Listed here are suggestions for increasing the acceptance and understanding of children's primary languages.

- Listen to records and tapes, and practice singing a variety of songs in different languages.
- Have the children learn many words and phrases in languages other than their native language, and especially in the languages of

children in their class. Use names, foods, greetings, and other appropriate words and phrases.

- Translate children's names into other languages.
- Expose the children to sign language, the fourth most frequently used language in the United States.
- Talk to the children using words from different languages. Ask them whether they can understand the words. How does it make them feel when they are unable to understand the words?
- Have the children share and describe objects that are important to their culture.
- Interview parents and people in your community about their culture, jobs, traditions, beliefs, or other things that will help the children capture a feeling of diversity.
- Share human interest stories from news programs and photographs from the newspaper; locate on a map or globe where the stories take place.
- Have parents, staff members, or community members make tapes reading the children's favorite stories in different languages. These can be enjoyed as a group or with earphones, individually.

Literacy Skills

Stories and poetry have been used for many years to transmit values, traditions, skills, and practices important to various cultures. Listed here are some activities that can point out similarities in language and literacy experiences.

- Use open-ended and problem-solving situations about children from different backgrounds and of different abilities to help to increase sensitivity to others. End with such questions as "How would you feel if . . . ?"
- Have the children observe and discuss pictures from ethnic magazines, calendars, cards, or professional journals so that they can learn about people who are different from themselves. Include a variety of cultures, children or adults doing nontraditional activities for their gender, and children of different physical abilities.

- Provide blank books for the children to dictate and illustrate stories about their families.
- Make a comparison of how alphabets are written in different cultures. Let the children experiment by writing their own.
- During the year, share books, stories, poetry, and folktales that represent the cultures of each child in your class.

Motor and Physical Skills

The following are some activities for increasing awareness that children everywhere develop and enjoy similar motor and physical activities.

- Acquire books, tapes, or records that describe in detail traditional games played by children of different cultures.
- Identify and play such games as hopscotch and tag that may be found in all cultures. Describe specific culture variations.
- Teach the children how to play various card or board games using toys and manipulatives from different cultures.

- Teach authentic dances from other cultures, especially dances that offer cultural insights. Also listen to music and sing songs from that culture.

Creative Arts

Music and art offer many opportunities for providing cultural experiences for young children.

- Frequently listen to music from other countries, even as background music while the children are working or playing.
- Have pieces of art from different cultures displayed in the classroom.
- Invite artists and musicians from different cultures to visit and perform; discuss what feelings or messages they might be trying to portray.
- Have children share music that they listen to in their homes or art that their family appreciates.
- Provide paints or marking pens in such skin colors as brown, black, or peach (Derman-Sparks & A B C Task Force, 1989).

Children of all abilities and developmental levels can participate together in both large and small group activities.

Dramatic Play

The following dramatic play activities offer opportunities to explore various aspects of cultural diversity.

- Provide dress-up clothes and objects from different cultures in the housekeeping area, allowing both sexes to try out a variety of roles. Teachers may need to intervene if they hear stereotypic comments such as, "You can't wear the mail carrier's hat because you are a girl."

- Provide equipment that is used by people with disabilities. Allow the children to explore such things as crutches, wheelchairs, glasses, even a prosthesis.

- Cut from magazines, old sewing pattern books, and other sources pictures of children from various ethnic backgrounds and abilities. Laminate the pictures, mount them to sticks, and use them for telling stories, exploring language, or dramatizing.

Food Activities

Snacks and food activities from various cultures can often be added to the curriculum. Be careful of stereotyping by saying, for example, "This is Mexican food." Instead say, "This is a snack enjoyed by some Mexican Americans." Do not allow children to comment negatively about a food from another culture and do not force any child to eat a particular food (Derman-Sparks & ABC Task Force, 1989). The following are a few examples of food activities:

- Share a particular culture's differences between daily foods and holiday foods.

- Visit ethnic restaurants to capture feelings, smells, and flavors.

- Make a recipe book of families' favorite recipes.

Math Skills

Children can learn about and compare counting systems used by various cultures by participating in some of the following activities:

- Teach the children to count in different languages.

- Study the development of calendar and time systems from different cultures.

- Compare money systems from different cultures. Compare coins and their sizes and values. Convert a dollar into rubles, lira, yen, and marks.

- Compare how numerals are written in various cultures.

Personal and Social Skills

Children's self-concepts grow when they feel that they are an important part of their environment. Some activities that may enhance children's self-concepts as well as build acceptance of diversity follow:

- Names are basic to a person's identity. Explore this concept by asking such questions as these: From where did your name come? Does your surname (last) or first name have an ethnic origin? Who named you? How do you pronounce your full name correctly? Can you say your name in other languages?

- Make a friendship tree by hanging objects from many cultures on the branches of a tree. Have the children identify each object, talk about it, tell whether it has a meaning, and match it with children from that heritage in the class.

- Have the children bring photos of themselves to compile into a book or make a bulletin board in the classroom. Let each child know that he or she is an important part of the class.

- Explore a variety of jobs, in the home and outside of the home, that are nontraditional for either sex.

- Do a bulletin board on the variety of families in the class.

Cultural Comparisons

The study of all cultures should be based on the premise that all people share the same basic needs for food, clothing, and families. Provide activities demonstrating that these and other needs are met in varied ways by different people.

- Use films, videos, and resource people to acquaint children with diverse people.
- Use maps and a globe to show geographic locations.
- Provide dolls from both sexes and various cultures for the children to play with.
- Have children bring in real objects used by their families that may be historical or typical of the child's cultural group (for example, a rice steamer, fish trap, or Krumkake iron).
- Collect ways the families and children recognize special days, seasons, rituals, and holidays. Make a scrapbook or display to share with the class.

PROSOCIAL SKILLS

There are many social skills in which young children learn and develop competence. The skills that we are eager to help children to develop are called *prosocial* skills or behaviors. Most prosocial skills come with experience and maturation. All children need guidance and correct modeling; many are aided by that spirit of self-confidence we call self-esteem. Many prosocial skills depend on the child's attitude; therefore, the teacher's goal in helping the child to develop prosocial behavior is to encourage the development of more positive attitudes among the children. Much of their learning will come with practice.

The following are some of the prosocial skills encouraged by early childhood teachers:

- Following classroom or center rules
- Learning to cope with social conflicts, such as name calling or teasing
- Treating others politely and courteously, and learning to use words such as "please" and "thank you"
- Being able to share the attention of others, including the teacher
- Developing eye-to-eye contact with peers and adults
- Learning to smile at others

- Being helpful and kind to others
- Showing empathy for another's feelings or situation and giving or expressing sympathy to others when they experience difficulties
- Being comfortable talking with others and being a good listener
- Following simple rules of games, taking turns, and cooperating
- Learning to gain attention from friends in positive and constructive ways
- Developing responsible behaviors, such as taking care of one's own possessions
- Learning to compliment, rather than criticize, others
- Showing tolerance for others and their differences
- Sharing and cooperating with others in play situations
- Expressing sorrow when actions or words have hurt another
- Being able to accept the consequences of behavior and actions
- Learning to take the perspective of another person
- Cooperating with others in play and work, including in cooperative group activities

Children learn social skills when teachers give these skills the same attention and focus that they give to academic subjects (Cummings & Haggerty, 1997). Although these skills will be taught and practiced daily, the teacher's modeling, feedback, reinforcement, and caring are critical to learning. For young children it is helpful for teachers to label and identify prosocial and antisocial behaviors and, in addition, to help children to become assertive concerning prosocial matters. Teachers should also model, acknowledge, and encourage understanding and expression of feelings.

Teachers can show pictured scenes of prosocial behaviors such as altruism and ask children to create verbal scenarios. It may be necessary to place a child who is experiencing social problems with another child who is more socially skilled in order to increase the antisocial child's positive peer interactions.

One relevant notion to explore is that people have feelings and that what we do and say can affect these feelings. Occasionally ask, "How would you feel if . . . ?" This question helps to sensitize children to the feelings of others. However, we need to emphasize that individuals are unique and have different feelings, so the same situation or event can result in different responses among various people.

Open-ended stories help to stimulate thinking about how other people feel in particular situations. Reading stories from children's literature also allows opportunities to stop to discuss how children would respond in a similar situation and how they feel about a particular happening. It is our "responsibility to select books of great worth that provide rich metaphors and help children understand themselves and others, books that teach, books that touch the heart. . . . Storytime can nurture a sense of compassion in children" (Smith, 1986, p. 49). Trying to take the place of characters in the story will help children to become more sensitive to the feelings of others in real life.

In addition to sensitizing children to the feelings of others, another social skill that is important to teach young children is conflict resolution. They need specific tools or strategies for dealing with disagreements in positive ways. For example, teachers can teach children that when conflict occurs between individuals they can go through the following steps:

1. Both individuals stop and think.

2. Both take a turn to share what is wrong.

3. Each person listens to the other without interrupting.

4. Each thinks of possible solutions.

5. Choose a solution that both like.

6. Shake hands and smile at one another!

Conflict is unavoidable within classrooms; however, children can learn to change their behavior (Holden, 1997). To foster conflict resolution, teachers need to create environments that look and feel safe (Holden, 1997). This may include peace posters or signs about love, respect, and kindness. One teacher (Holden, 1997, p. 75) uses a class motto that focuses on positive feelings about one another, as well as a rap song that the children repeat every day. The rap song is titled "Hugs Not Slugs" and includes the following words:

> Hugs not slugs is what we say.
>
> We are kind in every way.
>
> We do our best.
>
> We are good.
>
> We solve our problems like we should.
>
> We never fight.
>
> We never bite.
>
> We always share.
>
> We do what's right.
>
> So if you want to join our club,
>
> Just remember,
>
> Hugs Not Slugs!

APPROACH TO TEACHING

Concepts and Ideas for Teaching

1. People are born (all people are babies at one time).

    a. Characteristics and needs of infants.

    b. Differences and likenesses among babies, young children, and adults.

    c. The day of the year on which a person was born is called his or her *birthday*, and it is celebrated each year.

2. People die (all people will die at some time).

3. People do different things at different times.

    a. People generally sleep during the night.

    b. Sometimes people sleep in the daytime.

    c. Children are in school part of the day and at home part of the day.

4. People have different capabilities.

    a. Most can see, touch, hear, taste, and smell.

    b. Some cannot do one or more of these things.

    c. Some are athletic.

    d. Different people have different talents.

5. Different people have the same capabilities.

    a. A barber and a parent can both cut hair.
    b. A teacher and an orchestra member can both play the clarinet.
    c. A sibling and a friend can both play ball.
    d. A parent and a mechanic can both repair cars.

6. People are different sizes.

    a. Babies are smaller, adults bigger.
    b. Not all babies are the same size.
    c. Some people are tall, some short.

7. People are different shapes.
Some people are thin, some fat.

8. People are of different races and nationalities. (Concepts include differences in homes, foods, clothes, and physical characteristics.)

9. People have different thoughts and ideas, and each person's ideas are important.

10. People have various religious beliefs.

11. People have various likes and dislikes.

    a. Some like spinach, some do not.
    b. Some like winter weather, some do not.

12. People have jobs. (Concepts include what these people do; how their jobs help; what equipment, machinery, and materials they use; and that they are important for more than the job that they fill. Be sensitive to children who have a parent or parents who are unemployed.)

    a. Doctor
    b. Mechanic
    c. Musician
    d. Carpenter
    e. Telephone operator
    f. Engineer
    g. Teacher
    h. Secretary
    i. Upholsterer
    j. Salesperson
    k. Gardener
    l. Accountant
    m. Janitor
    n. Photographer
    o. Author
    p. Electrician
    q. Server
    r. Pilot

A diversity perspective acquaints the children with many different occupations and professions.

s. Police officer
t. Jeweler
u. Artist
v. Dentist
w. Clerk
x. Farmer
y. Computer operator
z. Other

13. People change.

  a. Growth and age bring change.(New skills may be learned as a person grows older; sometimes older age curtails activity.)
  b. Makeup, cosmetics, clothes, costumes, jewelry, wigs, and hair styles alter appearance.
  c. Voice changes from infancy through old age; the same voice can sing, talk, and cry.
  d. Exposure to sun may cause suntan or sunburn.
  e. Accidents or injuries result in physical or emotional changes.
  f. People increase in knowledge and learning (following directions, learning to read, walk, tie shoelaces, drive, delay gratification).

14. People eat food.

  a. Kinds of food.
  b. Variations because of the time of day or season of the year.
  c. Likes and dislikes in foods.
  d. Cultural variations.

15. People wear clothes.

  a. Names of particular clothing items; how they are worn.
  b. When specific articles are worn (seasons, professions, occasions).
  c. Sequences of putting on clothing.
  d. Fasteners on clothing.
  e. Care of clothing.

16. People live in homes. (Be sensitive to families who may be homeless.)

  a. Different kinds of homes.
  b. Different building materials used: brick, lumber, rock, adobe, canvas.
  c. Inside and outside of homes.
  d. Separate rooms, furnishings of rooms.

e. Different activities in different rooms.
f. Grounds surrounding homes.

17. People travel.

  a. Places people travel.
    (1) To other homes
    (2) On rides
    (3) To stores
    (4) To church
    (5) For recreation and sports
    (6) To work or business
    (7) To school
  b. Ways people travel.
    (1) Automobile
    (2) Airplane
    (3) Train
    (4) Taxi
    (5) Van
    (6) Bus
    (7) Boat, ship
    (8) Truck
    (9) Motorcycle
    (10) Bicycle, tricycle
    (11) Tractor
    (12) Ice skates, roller skates, roller blades
    (13) Skateboard
    (14) Skis
    (15) On foot
    (16) Wheelchair
    (17) Wagon, cart
    (18) Horse
    (19) Other animals (camels, elephants)
    (20) Snowmobile
    (21) Emergency vehicles (fire truck, ambulance)
  c. Various methods of transportation have particular characteristics and related concepts (make selections appropriate to your specific curriculum plans).
    (1) (Speed and distance (miles per hour, time)
    (2) Size and shape (dimensions, number of passengers, tires)
    (3) Color (owner's choice, no choice, specifically designated)
    (4) Sound (starting, running, stopping, horn or siren, wipers)

(5) Texture (inside, outside)
(6) Smell (fuel, engine, upholstery)
(7) Kind (models, company, use)
(8) Number (passengers, wheels, prices, speed, fuel, tickets)
(9) Shelters (garages, hangars, stations)
(10) Related jobs (mechanic, salesperson, attendant, driver, pilot)
(11) Parts (mechanical, physical)
(12) Purpose and use (recreation, business, education, shopping)

18. People have feelings and emotions.

a. Sadness
b. Anger
c. Fear
d. Happiness
e. Excitement
f. Loneliness

19. People have names.

a. Personal names
(1) Child's own name, first and last
(2) Names of others
(3) Others may have the same name.
b. Gender-related names
(1) Boy-girl
(2) Male-female
(3) Man-woman
(4) Father-mother
(5) Husband-wife
(6) Uncle-aunt
(7) Brother-sister
(8) Grandfather-grandmother
(9) Gentleman-lady
(10) Fellow-gal
c. Other names (may also be roles, and people have more than one name or role).
(1) Relative (cousin, etc.)
(2) Family
(3) People
(4) Person
(5) Child, children
(6) Boss
(7) Neighbor
(8) Friend
(9) Baby
(10) Adult
(11) Teenager, adolescent
(12) Names of professions
(13) Employer, employee
(14) Other

20. People have friends.

a. Friends can be the same sex or the opposite sex.
b. Friends can be the same age or different ages.
c. Friendship takes effort and kindness.

Activities and Experiences

1. Provide hammers, nails, blocks, lumber, canvas, and boxes for building different sizes, shapes, and kinds of houses, businesses, and transportation.

2. Make a neighborhood or community map, including schools, churches, homes, and businesses. Lay this map out flat, and provide small human figures and vehicles for the children to play with.

3. Make a game by cutting out a house or apartment representing the dwelling of each child. Put the child's address on his or her "house." Make cards and letters for each child, and put them in a bag. The children will enjoy playing mail carrier and delivering the mail to the proper homes.

4. Obtain an old camera, or make pretend cameras. Give the children the opportunity of pretending to take each other's picture. They may wish to draw pictures to represent those that they "take."

5. Make a set of flashcards or similar cards with pictures of community helpers. The children could be encouraged to bring pictures of their parents at their jobs or wearing clothing appropriate for those jobs. Another game could be added by collecting pictures of tools or items related to various jobs and having the children sort them. For example, for a hairdresser, use pictures of a comb, brush, scissors, and hair dryer.

6. Interviews with community helpers could be taped on a recorder or video if these persons cannot visit the classroom. Children will be especially proud to hear their parents tell about their jobs.

7. Make up riddles for different jobs or careers and have the children guess the answer to each riddle. For example:"I work with animals. I ride on a tractor. I grow wheat to make bread, and I grow other things that you eat.Who am I?"

8. The children can study briefly the history of their country, state, or community, becoming acquainted with significant people in this history and the part that they played in making the nation, state, or community great. Children can create and illustrate storybooks about their study.

9. Lotto or matching games can be made using pictures or words, depending on the skills of the children.The pictures or names of the community helpers can be matched with tools or items relating to their job. For example, a picture or the words *fire fighter* are matched with such pictures or words as *hydrant, fire engine, fire hat,* or other related tools.

10. Use maps whenever you go on a field trip, helping children to understand that maps give directions and help us to know how to get to a particular destination.

11. The children can interview their parents about their jobs, asking questions about what their jobs are and why, how, and where they are done. Charts or stories can be compiled; plan visits on site or invite parents into the classroom.

12. The children can read or study the classified section of the newspaper where jobs are advertised.They can draw pictures of the persons doing particular jobs and then print the information about the jobs underneath.

13. The children can draw or make a collage of their community and title it "Why (name of community) Is a Good Place to Live." Encourage children to contact community resources and agencies for information brochures that can also supply pictures for collages.

14. The children can tell and/or illustrate stories about their own roots or histories.They can tell about an ancestor, show a pedigree chart, or show family histories, journals, or scrapbooks; they can even invite a grandparent or great-grandparent to visit the class. Some children may have clothing or other antique items to share and discuss with the class.

UNIT PLAN ON PEOPLE

(This could most effectively be broken down into more specific units.)

Field Trips

- Hospital
- Doctor's office
- Grocery store
- Barbershop
- Beauty shop
- Service station
- Fire station
- Police station
- Dentist's office
- Clothing store
- Basketball court
- Landmark buildings or historical sites
- Skating rink
- Another school
- Livestock auction
- Eye doctor's office
- Airport
- Train depot
- Bus station
- Boat dock
- Farm
- Care center
- Court of law
- Museum

Visitors

- Doctor
- Nurse
- Barber
- Hair stylist
- Grocery store clerk
- Grandparent
- Baby
- Mechanic
- Musician
- Train engineer
- Fire fighter
- Dentist
- Clothing store clerk
- Pilot
- Farmer
- Auctioneer
- Garbage truck operator
- Janitor or custodian
- Athlete
- Soldier
- Clown

Music

- Creative movements of various professions, children growing, traveling different ways, dressing up, and so on
- Music from many cultures

Art

- Decoration of handmade musical instrument
- Houses built from large cardboard boxes, poles, canvas, and so on, and decorated
- Boats, trains, cars, wagons built from large cardboard boxes and decorated
- Collage of pictures of people and objects relating to people, cut from catalogs or magazines
- Litter bags

Food (Any Food Activity)

- Common foods, unusual foods
- Foods specific to season
- Foods specific to holiday
- Foods for breakfast, lunch, dinner
- Foods from various cultures

Science

- Study how bricks, canvas, lumber, adobe, or other materials are prepared for use in building; bricks are made of straw and mud and then dried.
- Study germs under a microscope.
- Study effects of aging.
- Study effects of land, water, and air pollution.

Literacy and Diversity Activities

- Make a book titled "Our Families Are Different." All children will have a page to put drawings or photographs of their families and then write or dictate a few sentences about their families.
- Make a book titled "Families Do Different Things." All children will have a page to put drawings, photographs, and sentences that describe things that their families do. They may wish to include parents' or guardians' jobs and hobbies or things that the family does together.
- Make a book or bulletin board titled "How My Family Celebrates Holidays." The children can share through words, pictures, and photographs how they celebrate particular holidays. Be sure to point out the variations that exist even within a particular culture.
- Discuss and/or write about how families worship in a variety of ways. Point out that individuals and families have their own beliefs.
- Make a book on your community titled "Our Neighborhood." Visit, take pictures, and write a few sentences about a variety of neighbors. You may want to visit an elderly person, a person with special needs, or businesses such as the grocery store, service station, restaurant and bank. Put each neighbor or business on a

separate sheet of paper, laminate the sheets, combine them into a book, and allow the children to read it during the year.

- Discuss stereotypes of certain holidays such as Thanksgiving. Share and critique pictures and books. Ask, "How would you feel if you were a Native American and you saw this picture?" (Derman-Sparks & ABC Task Force, 1989).

UNIT PLAN ON AUTOMOBILES

Visitors

- Auto mechanic
- Service station attendant
- New car dealer
- Person from auto body shop who paints cars
- Automobile seat upholsterer
- Parent showing how to care for car, wash car exterior, and change tire
- Police officer with police car
- Taxicab driver
- Chauffeur
- Race car driver
- Older child with model car display

Field Trips

- Auto mechanic shop
- Used car lot
- Car dealership
- Auto seat upholstery shop
- Automatic car wash
- Manual car wash
- Service station
- Junkyard for useless cars
- Self-service gas pump
- Parking lot where numerous cars are parked (shopping center, school parking lot, golf course, etc.); notice colors, sizes, shapes, sounds
- Auto body and paint shop

Science

- Repair of a flat tire
- Discussion of value of keeping car's interior and exterior clean; vacuuming, washing, and drying inside and outside of car
- Demonstration of how wax finish repels water and other agents
- Discussion of parts of auto (depending on ages and understandings of children); allow children to experiment with no-longer-used engine parts (if not greasy)

Food

- Food items commonly eaten in cars: hamburgers, milkshakes, floats, sundaes, french fries, sandwiches, cookies, carrot and celery sticks, candy, ice cream cones

Art

- Tires, windows, doors, or other car-related items pasted on a car shape
- Shapes of cars used for easel painting
- Cardboard-box cars painted and decorated
- Decoration of shakers made from juice cans, then filled with screws, nuts, and bolts from cars

Music

- Musical cars: played the musical chairs, but with decorated cardboard boxes
- Drums made from empty gallon tin cans (both ends cut from can) and rubber from inner tubes; rubber circles cut larger than can ends; rubber circles placed over ends and laced together
- Shakers made from cans and filled with screws, nuts, and bolts of various sizes used in cars
- Creative movements: pretending to be a car going fast or slow, having a flat tire, running out of gas, getting stuck in snow or mud

Webbing provides a visual picture for brainstorming and developing unit plans. See Figures 5–1 and 5–2 for examples of web drawings; refer back to Chapter 4 for a more in-depth description of webbing procedure.

Do any food activity as a cooperative learning experience.

Tell or read story of *A Friend Is Someone Who Likes You.*

Tell or read book *Charlotte's Web* and/or watch video. Discuss characters' friendship traits.

Food

Language and Literacy

Write or dictate letter to a friend.

Do fingerprints and compare similarities and differences among class members.

Each child completes page for booklet titled "How to Be a Friend."

Discuss and share how friends can have similarities and differences.

Science

In cooperative learning groups, make a collage of a picture titled "I Can Have Many Different Friends." Pictures can be cut from magazines and pattern books from fabric stores.

In cooperative learning groups do an activity such as planting a seed.

Art

Friends

Mail a letter to a friend.

Do a picture or simple craft for a friend.

Field Trips

Make a friendship bracelet or necklace to share with a friend.

Visit a dentist at a dental clinic.

Elderly person

Visitors

Make a "pretend" camera using a small jewelry box. "Take" pictures of friends. Put magazine pictures inside. Using a rubber band around the box, the children can "snap" pictures.

Learn a dance for which each child needs a partner.

Music

Librarian to tell about a book that focuses on friends. Example: Tell about friends in *Indian in the Cupboard.*

Police Officer

Teach songs such as "I Have a Friend" that focus on friendships.

Do a rhythm band and focus on sharing instruments.

Suggested Books
(Note: Complete references are provided in "Suggested Resources" at the end of the chapter.)

A Friend Is Someone Who Likes You (Anglund, 1983)   *May I Bring a Friend?* (DeRegniers, 1971)
Indian in the Cupboard (Banks, 1981)   *Best Friends* (Hopkins, 1986)
Do You Want to Be My Friend? (Carle, 1971)   *Best Friends* (Kellogg, 1990)
Will I Have a Friend? (Cohen, 1967)   *Frog and Toad Are Friends* (Lobel, 1970)
Best Friends (Cohen, 1971)   *Charlotte's Web* (White, 1952)

FIGURE 5–1
Project Web for Study of Friends

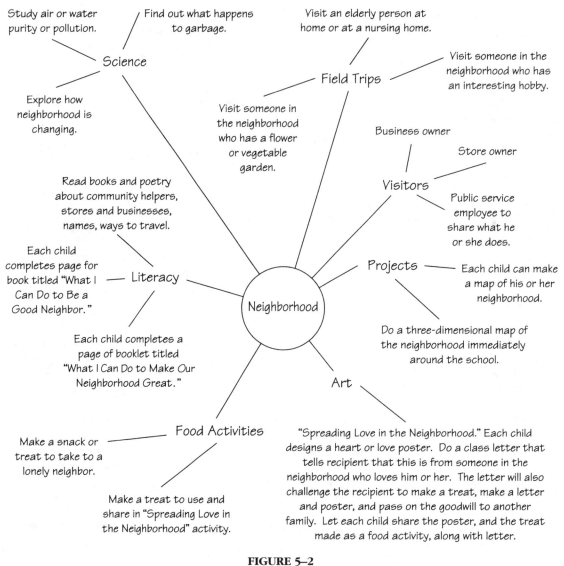

FIGURE 5–2
Project Web for Study of Neighborhoods

Summary

Children need to begin to develop social values and skills in their earliest years, and this social learning should be active as they share different insights of people and culture (Singer, 1994). As children become aware of similarities and differences among people, emphasis should *always* be on the ways that people are more alike than different. This also helps to prevent the development of biases and prejudices.

As teachers strive to incorporate the perspective of diversity, they must successfully foster genuine respect for *all* children, regardless of gender, race, physical abilities, or ethnic orientation. Teachers must also promote attitudes of tolerance and acceptance in order to prevent the acquisition of stereotypes relating to race, gender, or handicaps and other forms of discrimination. Children must be taught positive attitudes, concepts, and skills that enable them to function cooperatively in our diverse society.

It is the professional and moral responsibility of teachers to evaluate their own philosophies regarding diversity, and then demonstrate and model how differences are valued and appreciated. "We need to work with colleagues and communities to expand our own understanding and to reflect on our own teaching practices" (Ramsey, 1995, p. 22).

All children must be given opportunities to reach their potential, encouraged to feel valued as members of society, and taught to understand differences among people. They must be taught that discriminatory actions and attitudes are not acceptable and be helped to feel positive identification with their own gender, race, physical and mental abilities, and ethnic backgrounds.

Teachers must be aware of biases and stereotyping with regard to race, gender, religion, and special needs. Public Laws 94-142 and 99-457 provide direction for identifying and providing educational programs for children who have disabilities. This chapter includes characteristics, teaching strategies, and specialists in such special needs areas as speech and language impairments; mental retardation; hearing, visual, and physical impairments; emotional, social, or behavioral problems; chronic illness; learning disabilities; and gifted and talented children.

In creating a diverse curriculum and classroom, teachers must change their attitudes and practices; carefully select books, materials, and resources; expose children to cultural diversities; focus on similarities among all peoples; accept language and dialect diversity; use the daily news for cultural awareness and understanding; teach differences in occupations and life-styles; and use cooperative learning as a strategy.

Suggestions for incorporating unit plans and lesson plans into the diversified curriculum have been presented, along with the valuable tool of webbing for brainstorming and developing unit or project ideas.

Student Learning Activities

1. Describe yourself in terms of your own culture. Using professional journals or books, find at least two sources that help you to define and understand your own culture. Remember, your culture includes your ethnicity, religion, social class, physical abilities, and gender.

2. Examine and describe some of your own biases. What do you specifically plan to do to overcome these biases?

3. After you have read and studied this chapter, can you think of any additional goals that need to be added to the ones that the authors have presented for developing the perspective of diversity?

4. If you were just setting up a classroom for the first time in your present community, what would be the first five things that you would do to begin to develop a diversity perspective?

5. Suppose that you are preparing a unit on one of the seasons. How might you include the diversity perspective in your teaching?

6. There are many more activities and experiences appropriate for teaching children concepts relating to other people. Think of at least 10 ideas to add to the list in this chapter.

7. Prepare a unit plan, web, or project on one or more of the following: a specific community helper, a type of transportation, homes, similarities among class members, differences among class members. Evaluate your work to see whether you included the diversity perspective.

8. Using one unit plan or web prepared in item 7, prepare a 5-day activity plan following the format shown beginning on page 96.

9. Observe in a classroom of young children and describe how the diversity perspective was woven into the curriculum, environment, and discussions or conversations. What changes would you suggest?

10. Evaluate how you think social skills can best be taught. List five things that you will do as a teacher to encourage the development of prosocial skills in young children.

Suggested Resources

Children's Books

Albert, D. (1991). *Where does the trail lead?* New York: Simon & Schuster.

Aliki (1986). *Corn is maize: The gift of the Indians.* New York: HarperCollins.

Anderson, S. (1996). *A puzzling day in the land of the Pharaohs.* Cambridge, MA: Candlewick.

Anglund, J.W. (1958). *A friend is someone who likes you.* New York: Harcourt, Brace & World.

Ashabranner, B. (1997). *Bark harvest.* North Haven, CT: Linnet.

Aseltine, L., & E. Mueller (1986). *I'm deaf and it's okay.* Niles, IL: Whitman.

Balgerman, L. (1991). *Girders and cranes: A skyscraper is built.* Morton Grove, IL: Whitman.

Banks, L. R. (1981). *Indian in the cupboard.* New York: Doubleday.

Bannerman, H. (1996). *The story of little Babaji.* New York: HarperCollins.

Baylor, B. (1986). *Hawk, I'm your brother.* New York: Macmillan.

Belafonte, H., & L. Burgess (1999). *Island in the sun.* New York: Dial Books for Young Readers.

Bradby, M. (1995). *More than anything else.* New York: Orchard.

Brodmann, A. (1993). *The gift.* New York: Simon & Schuster.

Bunting, E. (1998). *Going home.* New York: Joanne Colter Books, HarperCollins.

Cairo, S. (1985). *Our brother has Down's syndrome.* Buffalo: Firefly.

Cameron, A. (1981). *The stories Julian tells.* New York: Pantheon.

Carle, E. (1971). *Do you want to be my friend?* New York: HarperCollins.

Children's Television Workshop (1980). *Sign language fun.* New York: Random House.

Chocolate, D. (1996). *Kente colors.* New York: Walker.

Chocolate, D. (1996). *My first Kwanzaa book.* Jefferson City, MO: Scholastic.

Christiansen, C. B. (1989). *My mother's house, my father's house.* New York: Atheneum.

Coles, R. (1995). *The story of Ruby Bridges.* New York: Scholastic.

Couric, K. (2000). *The brand new kid.* New York: Doubleday.

Crews, D. (1991). *Big Mama's.* New York: Greenwillow.

Crews, D. (1994). *Freight train.* New York: Greenwillow.

Daly, N. (1996). *Not so fast, Songololo.* New York: Atheneum.

Darling, K. (1996). *Amazon ABC.* New York: Lothrop, Lee & Shepard.

DePaola, T. (1998). *Memo Y Leo (Bill and Pete).* Caracas: Ediciones Ekare.

Dionetti, M. (1991). *Coal mine peaches.* New York: Orchard.

Dorros, A. (1991). *Abuela.* New York: Dutton.

Ehlert, L. (1995). *Mole's hill.* Jefferson City, MO: Scholastic.

Fassler, J. (1983). *My grandpa died today.* New York: Human Sciences Press.

Feelings, M. (1971). *Moja means one.* New York: Dial.

Fiday, B., & D. Fiday (1990). *Time to go.* San Diego, CA: Harcourt Brace Jovanovich.

Fries, C. (2000). *A pig is moving in.* New York: Orchard.

Gavin, J. (1997). *Children just like me: Our favorite stories from around the world.* New York: Dorling-Kindersley.

Gill, S. (1987). *The Alaska Mother Goose and other North Country nursery rhymes.* Homer, AK: Paws IV.

Giovanni, N. (1996). *The genie in the jar.* New York: Henry Holt.

Gray, L. M. (1993). *Dear Willie Rudd.* New York: Simon & Schuster.

Grindley, S. (1998). *A flag for grandma.* New York: DK Publishing.

Hale, I. (1992). *How I found a friend.* New York: Viking.

Hall, D. (1994). *The farm summer 1942.* New York: Dial.

Hartman, W. (1994). *One sun rises: An African wildlife counting book.* New York: Dutton Children's Books.

Heap, S. (1997). *Pequeno cowboy (Cowboy baby).* Madrid: Editorial Kokinos.

Henroid, L. (1982). *Grandma's wheelchair.* Niles, IL: Whitman.

Herold, M. R. (1995). *A very important day.* New York: Morrow.

Hoffman, M. (1991). *Amazing Grace.* New York: Dial.

Hoffman, M. (1995). *Boundless Grace.* New York: Dial.

Hopkins, L. B. (ed.) (1986). *Best friends.* New York: HarperCollins.

Hough, L. (1997). *If somebody lived next door.* New York: Dutton.

Houston, G. (1992). *The year of the perfect Christmas tree.* New York: Philomel.

Howard, E. F. (1991). *Aunt Flossie's hats (and crab cakes later).* New York: Scholastic.

Hoyt-Goldsmith, D. (1990). *Totem pole.* New York: Holiday House.

Hutchins, P. (1993). *My best friend.* New York: Greenwillow.

Igus, T. (1996). *Going back home: An artist returns to the South.* San Francisco: Children's Book Press.

Isadora, R. (1990). *Babies.* New York: Greenwillow.

Isadora, R. (1990). *Friends.* New York: Greenwillow.

Jeffers, S. (1991). *Brother Eagle, Sister Sky.* New York: Dial.

Jimenez, F. (1999). *The circuit: Stories from the life of a migrant child.* Topeka, KS: Econo-Clad.

Johnson, A. (1989). *Tell me a story, Mama.* New York: Orchard.

Johnson, A. (1990). *Do like Kyla.* New York: Orchard.

Joseph, L. (1990). *Coconut kind of day.* New York: Lothrop, Lee & Shepard.

Josse, B. M. (1991). *Mama, do you love me?* San Francisco: Chronicle.

Kellogg, S. (1990). *Best friends*. New York: Dial.

King, M. L., Jr. (1997). *I have a dream*. New York: Scholastic Press.

Krull, K. (1994). *Maria Molina and the days of the dead*. New York: Macmillan.

Kunhardt, E. (1997). *I'm going to be a fire fighter*. Jefferson City, MO: Scholastic.

Kunhardt, E. (1997). *I'm going to be a police officer*. Jefferson City, MO: Scholastic.

Larch, D. W. (1986). *Father Gander nursery rhymes*. Santa Barbara, CA: Advocacy.

Larsen, K. (2000). *The magic kerchief*. New York: Holiday House.

Leventhal, D. (1994). *What is your language?* New York: Dutton.

Levin, J., & W. Lewison. (2001). *What will I be?* New York: Cartwheel.

Lionni, L. (1964). *Tico and the golden wings*. New York: Pantheon.

Locker, T. (1991). *The land of the gray wolf*. New York: Dial.

Macdonald, M. (1992). *Little hippo gets glasses*. New York: Dial.

MacLachlan, P. (1994). *All the places to love*. New York: HarperCollins.

Mandelbaum, P. (1990). *You be me, I'll be you*. New York: Kane/Miller.

Marzollo, J. (1993). *Happy birthday, Martin Luther King*. Jefferson City, MO: Scholastic.

Merriam, E. (1989). *Mommies at work*. New York: Simon & Schuster.

Miller, M. (1990). *Who uses this?* New York: Greenwillow.

Mitchell, M. K. (1993). *Uncle Jed's barbershop*. New York: Simon & Schuster.

Monfried, L. (1990). *The Daddies boat*. New York: Puffin/Penguin USA.

Mora, P. (1996). *Confetti: Poems for children*. New York: Lee & Low.

Morris, A. (1993). *Houses and homes*. Jefferson City, MO: Scholastic.

Morris, A. (1994). *Hats hats hats*. Jefferson City, MO: Scholastic.

Morris, A. (1997). *Light the candle! Bang the drum!* New York: Dutton.

Nomura, T. (1991). *Grandpa's town*. New York: Kane/Miller.

Oberman, S. (1994). *The always prayer shawl*. Honesdale, PA: Boyds Mills Press.

Piper, W. (1980). *The little engine that could*. New York: Platt & Munk.

Porte, B. A. (1991). *Harry gets an uncle*. New York: Greenwillow.

Powers, M. E. (1986). *Our teacher's in a wheelchair*. Niles, IL: Whitman.

Rockwell, A. (1995). *The acorn tree and other folktales*. New York: Greenwillow.

Rockwell, A. (1997). *I fly*. New York: Crown.

Ross, A., & K. Ross (1999). *Jezebel's secret spot*. New York: Dutton.

Ross, L. H. (1991). *Buba Leah and her paper children*. Philadelphia: Jewish Publications Society.

Russo, M. (1992). *Alex is my friend*. New York: Greenwillow.

Rylant, C. (1983). *Miss Maggie*. New York: E. P. Dutton.

Rylant, C. (1982). *When I was young in the mountains*. New York: E. P. Dutton.

Say, A. (1993). *Grandfather's journey*. Boston: Houghton Mifflin.

Scheffler, U. (1994). *The stranger*. New York: North-South.

Scholastic Voyages of Discovery Series (1997). *Bikes, cars, trucks, and trains*. New York: Scholastic.

Sierra, J., & R. Kaminski (1991). *Multiculture folktales: Stories to tell young children*. Phoenix, AZ: Oryx.

Simon, N. (1999). *All kinds of children*. Morton Grove, IL: Whitman.

Soto, G. (1995). *Chato's kitchen*. New York: Putnam.

Stein, S. (1993). *Oh, baby!* New York: Walker.

Stolz, M. (1991). *Go fish*. New York: HarperCollins.

Tabor, N. M. G. (1996). *A taste of the Mexican market (El gusto del mercado Mexicano)*. Watertown, MA: Charlesbridge.

Torre, B. L. (1990). *The luminous pearl*. New York: Orchard.

Tsubakiyama, M. (1999). *Mei-Mei loves the morning*. Morton Grove, IL: Whitman.

Wall, L. M. (1991). *Judge Rabbit and the tree spirit*. San Francisco: Children's Book Press.

Waters, K., & M. Slovenz-Low (1996). *Lion dancer: Ernie Wan's Chinese New Year*. Jefferson City, MO: Scholastic.

Weissman, J. (1981). *All about me: Let's be friends*. Mt. Rainier, MD: Gryphon House.

Welsh-Smith, S. (1988). *Andy: An Alaskan tale*. New York: Cambridge University Press.

White, E. B. (1952). *Charlotte's web*. New York: Harper & Bros.

Wickens, E. (1994). *Anna Day and the O-ring*. Boston: Alyson.

Williams, S. A. (1997). *Working cotton*. Orlando, FL: Voyager Picture Books.

Williams, V. B. (1990). *"More, more, more," said the baby*. New York: Greenwillow.

Wilson, S. (1991). *Garage song*. New York: Simon & Schuster.

Wilson-Max, K. (1997). *The little green tow truck*. New York: Scholastic.

Zhensun, Z. (1991). *A young painter: The life and paintings of Wang Yani—China's extraordinary young artist*. New York: Scholastic.

Resources

Bogdanoff, R. F., & E. T. Dolch (1979). Old games for young children: A link to our heritage. *Young Children 34*: 37–45.

Cooper, T. T., & M. Ratner (1974). *Many lands cooking: An international cookbook for girls and boys*. New York: Crowell with U.S. Committee for UNICEF.

Council on Interracial Books for Children (1966–present). *Interracial books for children: Bulletin*. New York: Author.

Derman-Sparks, L., & ABC Task Force (1989). *Anti-bias curriculum: Tools* for empowering young children. Washington, DC: National Association for the Education of Young Children.

Maehr, J. (n.d.). *The Middle East: An annotated bibliography of literature for children.* Urbana: ERIC/ECE, University of Illinois.

McWhirter, M. (Ed.) (1970). *Games enjoyed by children around the world.* Philadelphia: American Friends Service Committee.

Moll, P. (1991). *Children & books I: African-American story books and activities for all children.* Tampa, FL: Hampton Mae Institute.

Neugebauer, B. (Ed.) (1992). *Alike and different: Exploring our humanity with young children.* Washington, DC: National Association for the Education of Young Children.

Ramirez, G., & J. L. Ramirez (1994). *Multiethnic children's literature.* Albany, NY: Delmar.

UNICEF (n.d.). *Folk toys around the world, and how to make them.* New York: Author.

Vold, E. B. (Ed.) (1992). *Multicultural education in early childhood classrooms.* Washington, DC: NEA.

Tapes and Cassettes

A child's look at ... what it means to be Jewish. Kids' Records.

Fire truck. On *The small singer* (Album 1). Bowmar-Noble.

Food for your body. National Geographic.

Hopping around from place to place. Educational Activities.

I can fly. On *The small singer* (Album 1). Bowmar-Noble.

Lakota/Dakota flute music (played by K. Locke). Featherstone.

The laundry and the bakery story. Scholastic (R7671).

Let's be friends. Tickle Tune Typhoon.

Little lonely sailboat. On *More singing fun* (Album 1). Bowmar-Noble.

The senses. National Geographic.

Songs and rhythms from near and far. Educational Activities.

Your brain. National Geographic.

Your teeth. National Geographic.

Pictures

Cherokee alphabet card. Cherokee, NC: Cherokee Pub.

Children around the world. The Child's World.

Children in America. The Child's World.

Communities provide resources. Society for Visual Education.

Communities provide services. Society for Visual Education.

Dairy helpers. Society for Visual Education.

Fire department helpers. Society for Visual Education.

Going places by air. The Child's World.

Going places by land. The Child's World.

Going places by water. The Child's World.

Home and community helpers. David C. Cook.

Hospital helpers. Society for Visual Education.

My community. David C. Cook.

People who come to my home. The Child's World.

Police department helpers. Society for Visual Education.

Postal helpers. Society for Visual Education.

Supermarket helpers. Society for Visual Education.

Transportation. David C. Cook.

What is a community? Society for Visual Education.

Also available: Several sets on ethnic groups and children around the world. David C. Cook.

Videos for Teachers and Children

About us: The dignity of children. Guilford Press Video.

Appreciating diversity. Insight Media.

Assessing ADHD in the schools. Guilford Press Video.

Autism and applied behavioral analysis. Films for the Humanities & Sciences.

Autism: A world apart. Films for the Humanities & Sciences.

Bear in the big blue house. Jim Henson Company.

The big space shuttle. Little Mammoth Media.

Celebrating our differences series: Race, Religion, and Language. National Geographic.

Classroom interventions for ADHD. Guilford Press Video.

Color-blind: Fighting racism in schools. Films for the Humanities & Sciences.

Coping with attention deficit disorder in children. Films for the Humanities & Sciences.

Cultural bias in education. Films for the Humanities & Sciences.

Dealing with diversity in the classroom. Insight Media.

Diversity issues in the classroom. Insight Media.

Dyslexia in the primary classroom. Films for the Humanities & Sciences.

Empowering people with disabilities through technology. Films for the Humanities & Sciences.

Enough already! Roseberry Entertainment.

Families of the world series: Mexico, Japan, Egypt, Central America, Israel, Australia. National Geographic.

Farming. National Geographic

The gifted child. Films for the Humanities & Sciences.

Hello! From around the world. Ernst Interactive Media (EIM), video series.

Learning disabled: Special education schools. Films for the Humanities & Sciences.

Me and You Series (includes *Express yourself, I can help, too, I can make friends, Playing fair,* and *I can take care of myself*). National Geographic.

Respecting diversity in the classroom. Films for the Humanities & Sciences.

Sam and the lucky money. Weston Woods.

Sing me a story (with Rabbi Joe Black). Sounds Write Productions.

Special needs students in regular classrooms? Sean's Story. Films for the Humanities & Sciences.

Teaching the academically diverse classroom (episode #22) (1993). NEA (video).

Tell me who I am: The journey begins. Positive Communications.

Understanding attention deficit hyperactivity disorder. Films for the Humanities & Sciences.

Understanding learning disabilities. Films for the Humanities & Sciences.

Unequal education. Films for the Humanities & Sciences.

Valuing diversity: Multicultural communication. Insight Media.

Your Town Series (includes *Communications, The fire station, The hospital, The library, The police station, The post office, Public works, Recreation, Schools, Transportation*). National Geographic.

Computer Software

The Human Body (CD-ROM kit). National Geographic.

People behind the holidays (CD-ROM kit). National Geographic.

Chapter 6

Myself and My Family

In educating the whole student, we must bring together "mind and heart in the classroom" (Goleman, 1995, p. xiv). The socioemotional development of the person is a process involving feelings and thinking. To be able to relate to and work effectively with others, one must first be able to relate positively to oneself. Unfortunately, some people care so little about themselves that they are unable to care for others. Children come to the classroom with various backgrounds, values, and points of view regarding themselves and their family. They must be accepted as they are and encouraged to like themselves. Indeed, children need concrete experiences, moments, and ideas directed toward building positive feelings and attitudes about themselves.

The basis of a high-quality program in early childhood is promoting feelings of self-esteem and dignity in each child. As caregivers, we are better able to help children to develop positive feelings about themselves if we understand some basic generalizations and suggestions regarding building children's self-esteem. Katz (1995) presents six necessities that every child must have for healthy development:

1. **A sense of safety.** "The young child has to have a deep sense of safety . . . psychological safety, which we usually speak of in terms of feeling secure, that is, the subjective feeling of being strongly connected and deeply attached to one or more others. Experiencing oneself as attached, connected—or safe—comes not just from being loved, but from *feeling* loved, *feeling* wanted, *feeling* significant. . . . The emphasis is more on *feeling* loved and wanted than on *being* loved and wanted" (p. 4).

   Children need to feel loved because of who they are, not what they do. Such children's qualities as kindness, helpfulness, flexibility, and willingness to help must be encouraged and appreciated more than their accomplishments. This results in feelings of personal empowerment, confidence, and success (Wald, 2000)! Safety grows out of being able to trust people to respond warmly, honestly, intensely, and sincerely. A secure early childhood environment is predictable, accepting, and responsive (Hyson, 1994).

2. **Optimum self-esteem.** Self-esteem is nurtured during the developing years by significant adults, siblings, and other children. We must be sensitive to the various criteria of self-esteem that children bring with them, formed from families, neighborhoods, ethnic groups, peer groups, and community, and not downgrade or undermine it, even though it might not be something with which we agree.

3. **Feeling that life is worth living.** Whether children are at home, in child-care centers, or

in schools, they should be able to experience their lives as worth living, real, authentic, and satisfying.

4. **Help with making sense of experience.** "[O]ur major responsibility is to help the young child improve, extend, refine, develop, and deepen their own understandings or constructions of their own worlds" (p. 6).

5. **Authoritative adults.** Young children need adults who accept their own authority that has come from having greater experience, knowledge, and wisdom. These adults must set and maintain limits, while being warm, supportive, and encouraging. Children must also be treated with respect, even when adults may disagree with the opinions, feelings, ideas, and wishes of the children.

6. **Desirable role models.** Children need association with older children and adults who exemplify the personal qualities that we want children to acquire.

The Seven Irreducible Needs of Children

1. Ongoing nurturing relationships
2. Physical protection, safety, and regulation
3. Experiences tailored to individual differences
4. Developmentally appropriate experiences (DAP)
5. Limit setting, structure, and expectations
6. Stable, supportive communities, and cultural continuity
7. Protecting the future

Greenberg, 2001, 8.

It is also important that we recognize situations causing stress, how children react to stress, and how they can be helped to cope with stress. When we help children to develop resiliency, we fortify them for a lifetime!

Children's families are very much a part of how they feel about themselves; and even though family structures and makeup might vary, still the family's role in facilitating character education is paramount.

Feelings of insecurity that may result when a child enters the early childhood classroom for the first time, are soon dissolved as the new environment becomes familiar and friendly.

A HEALTHY SELF-ESTEEM

One's attitude toward oneself is usually referred to as *self-esteem*. Children's self-esteem affects their actions, behavior, learning, and playing and how they relate to others. Self-esteem is a feeling or attitude of personal worth, and it determines the extent to which each child believes himself or herself to be capable, attractive, worthy, responsible, important, and lovable. Self-esteem is enhanced when children feel competent and display the traits that are valued by their particular cultures.

A person with healthy self-esteem:

• Accepts the self and limitations, while trusting the self to cope with most situations that occur.

• Accepts and assumes responsibility.

- Is proud of successes and accomplishments, but does not have to use them in proving the self to others.

- Approaches new challenges, assignments, and experiences with enthusiasm.

- Has a broad range of emotions and feelings, but the general attitude and feelings focus on the positive.

- Is able to feel control of his or her personal life.

- Recognizes that an innate sense of self-esteem determines how he or she feels and acts.

A person with unhealthy self-esteem:

- Avoids situations or experiences in which he or she may not be successful.

- Feels incompetent, unsuccessful, untalented, unloved, and powerless.

- Blames others for anything that goes wrong.

- Tears down or views negatively any strengths or talents that he or she may have.

- Easily gives in to pressure from others.

- May have problems with drug and alcohol abuse, depression, hostility, or making friends.

Generalizations Regarding Self-Esteem

What you think of me
I will think of me.
What you think of me
I will be.

(Bakley, 1997, p. 21)

From significant research and study of self-esteem, we not only can describe what it looks like and doesn't look like in a person, but we can also understand the impact and implications of self-esteem on the individual.

- Our behavior matches our self-image. Much of children's behavior, both positive and negative, is influenced by the way that they view themselves, that is, their self-image.

- The significant people in children's lives have a great influence on how children see themselves. Children tend to view themselves as they think others see them.

- A child cannot grow in confidence and self-esteem without positive feelings, without being praised for appropriate behavior, accomplishments, and successes. Warm and loving approval from others is essential to the development of positive self-esteem.

- Children with healthy self-esteem are poised, confident, and pleasant to be with. Their social skills are generally good. They are less influenced by peers and tend to make better decisions.

- Whenever an act results in a feeling of satisfaction, this act is likely to be repeated. Within each child, there is an innate need for attention, preferably positive; but if there is no attention for positive behavior, children soon become conditioned to misbehaving in order to receive attention, even if it is negative attention.

- Self-esteem affects the relationships, actions, interactions, and play of children. It influences stability, integrity, and creativity. Creative activities involve risk, and being able to take a risk requires self-confidence. Therefore, to be able to respond creatively, one must be able to trust that those one likes and loves will accept one through both failures and successes. Also, a child who is overly concerned with success, approval, and acceptance will not venture a risk, but will find security in assuming that it is better not to try at all than to try and fail.

- What we are and how we feel about the child has more effect than anything we do. Feelings are modeled—caught, not taught.

- Children with low self-esteem feel isolated, unloved, and defenseless. They often feel powerless to attain goals that they desire in life and are often withdrawn and passive about life and experiences.

- Children with low self-esteem are more influenced by the negative experiences in their lives and allow these experiences to control their feelings and perceptions of the environment.

- Because we cannot give away what we do not possess, because we cannot teach what we have neither learned nor understood, because we cannot build with materials we have not obtained, we cannot strengthen children with more positive self-esteem until we first find the courage, insight, wisdom, and determination to strengthen and build our own self-esteem. Thus, the stronger and richer the teacher's own self-esteem, the more successful she or he will be in creating like attitudes and concepts in the children being taught.

- Children and parents need to learn that "I can" is more important than IQ. Self-confidence can often compensate for deficits in other areas.

Positive self-images are developed as children learn more about themselves and have numerous successes resulting in increased confidence and a sense of self-worth. This, in turn, tends to give children the feeling that they are important to others and contributors to society. At the same time, children also develop feelings of the importance of and need for others. Children, in fact, cannot accept others until they accept themselves. Esteem for others begins with esteem for, and acceptance of, oneself. Teachers need to help children to find themselves.

Leslie and Megan were playing hide-and-go-seek and had hidden from Kyle and Curtis. When Kyle and Curtis became frightened because they could not find Leslie and Megan, the four children decided to play hide-and-go-seek all together at the same time. They covered their eyes and counted "One, two, . . . nine, ten." Then Megan instructed, "Come on, let's go find ourselves!"

Suggestions for Building Children's Self-Esteem

Knowing the significance of self-esteem, teachers need guidelines for fostering and facilitating children's self-esteem.

Here are some general suggestions for strengthening children's self-esteem:

- Be honest, sincere, and consistent in expressing feelings.
- Value the children's work and efforts (Marshall, 1989).

- Accept each child for himself or herself. This means not only accepting but searching for individual differences. As you assist children in discovering and accepting their strengths and limitations, help them to capitalize on strengths and work with limitations that can be changed (Klein, 2000).

- Do whatever is possible to help children to overcome any physical problems, but also help them accept those things that cannot be changed.

- Encourage academic achievement. Knowledge and understanding are forerunners to feelings of worth.

- Praise children for specific efforts and accomplishments. The effort is often more important than the product or outcome. Encourage the development of a wide range of skills and competencies (Klein, 2000).

- Encourage children to help, build, and support others. They can learn to respect others who excel in different areas (Klein, 2000). This results in positive feelings of joy and internal satisfaction, in addition to healthy social skill development. There seems to be a close relationship between early social adjustment in the peer group and later adult adjustment.

- Independence breeds self-esteem; allow children to do things for themselves. Children gain confidence in themselves as they accomplish new developmental tasks and acquire the ability to have some control. Giving children responsibilities and trusting them to complete these tasks helps build capabilities and self-confidence. Children learn to make competent decisions by being allowed to make decisions and accept responsibility for them.

- Smile and be cheerful, happy, and courteous and focus on the positive with children. These attitudes must be genuine and come from within; remember, your attitude is the key.

- Your actions must convey the worth and value of the children. Little acts of kindness, individual attention, and positive deeds become very important. For example, a short note or phone call expressing a positive feeling or congratulations for a new accomplishment can make a child feel valuable and accepted.

- Your words make a difference. Children perceive themselves as competent or the opposite by what teachers say and the tone in which they say it. Words or phrases such as "Congratulations," "I'm proud of you," "I'm sorry," "Excuse me," and "Thank you" should be included frequently in conversations with children. Phrases either build up or tear down, depending on how they are worded. For instance, put the "problem" on the item or action, rather than directing it toward the child. Say "That water fountain is too high," rather than "You are too short to reach the water fountain"; "That shoe is too hard to tie," rather than "You are too little to tie your shoe"; "That water is too deep," rather than "You're too young to go in the water."

- Listen to the child in order to understand the child. Pose questions to children that will help you to understand their self-concept, questions such as "Tell me something about yourself" and "What do you like about yourself?"

- Invite the child to sit by or interact with you.

- Provide support groups in the classroom (for resolving conflicts, for addressing personal problems and concerns in their lives, and so on).

well-being is an indicator or predictor of academic success, and five dimensions of this well-being appear to be significant: self awareness, handling or coping with emotions, motivation for moving toward goals, empathy, and social skills (Pool, 1997).

Being able to develop independence results in feelings of pride and confidence, as demonstrated when this girl was able to put her jacket and backpack on by herself.

Children's emotional well-being largely hinges on how well they accept themselves. Psychotherapists have found that the most common denominator of mental health problems is a deficiency of self-esteem. Regardless of the symptoms, most children with such problems suffer feelings of self-doubt, inadequacy, guilt, and helplessness. In their efforts to defend themselves against self-esteem deficiency, they may develop problems in behavior, motivation, and even physical health. Teachers working with young children need to do everything that they can to inculcate in each child feelings of importance and self-respect. Emotional

Teachers should help children to understand that this basic psychological need for self-respect is, to a degree, determined by their own attitudes toward themselves and their choice of values and goals. In other words, it is not totally up to parents and teachers to build this feeling; children must add their share of the building blocks—they need to find themselves. "The bottom line is that children need to feel good about themselves" (Wolfson-Steinberg, 2000, p. 38).

Concern is voiced in the current literature that well-intentioned school programs are creating a self-oriented self-esteem (McMillan, Singh, & Simonetta, 1994). When children see themselves as the center of the universe, it can be psychologically damaging and, in addition, it is difficult for them to care for others when they care first and foremost for themselves (McMillan, Singh, & Simonetta, 1994). Healthy self-esteem comes from accomplishment and academic achievement; our challenge is to help students to become absorbed with learning, rather than focused on performance (Kohn, 1994). "There is nothing that will improve a student's self-esteem better than academic success" (Butler, 1997, p. 30). Positive self-esteem is most powerful and has the greatest impact when it is competency based or comes from one's genuine, earned achievements, rather than from a constant barrage of gold stars, blue ribbons, stamps that say "Great job," and other forms of extrinsic rewards (Butler, 1997; McGerald & Nidds, 1996; Owens, 1997). "If we subscribe to the simplistic panacea that we are to constantly give positive affirmation, it can be a barrier to academic achievement" (McGerald & Nidds, 1996, p. 55). The key for development of self-esteem then is to develop strong inner self-esteem that comes from within and is based on children's "effectiveness in mastering their environment" (Owens, 1997, p. 48). The following points are offered as suggestions for teachers in helping children to develop strong inner or intrinsic self-esteem:

1. Help your students to understand that they control their own academic destinies.

2. Help your students to understand that their actions have logical consequences.

3. Help your students to see that their efforts count.

4. Give your students encouragement rather than praise.

5. Do away with fear tactics, negative comments, and labels, and encourage parents to do the same.

6. Let your students know that you believe in them.

7. Identify your students' strengths and build on them. (Owens, 1997, p. 52)

An integrated music program is an excellent way to enhance language development, creative expression, knowledge of musical concepts, a sense of collaboration, and self-esteem. It is important to select a variety of music that helps children feel successful, includes movement activities, uses musical terms to enhance development of concepts, and uses children's names (Warner, 1999). Names are the first words most children write and are an important aspect of identity and self-esteem (Green, 1998).

Each Child Is Unique

Most of the foundation concepts presented in this chapter show that children in many ways are alike—and in many ways are not alike. Remember to stress their similarities more than their differences. From the suggested teaching approaches, children will gain insight into their feelings, names, roles, families, friends, abilities, foods, homes, clothes, travels, and many other characteristics. Children must sense that they are unique and special.

I Have Feelings

I have feelings and you do too,
I'd like to share a few with you.
Sometimes I'm happy and sometimes I'm sad,
Sometimes I'm scared, and sometimes mad.
The most important feeling, you see,
Is that I'm proud of being me.

Refrain

I feel just right in the skin I wear,
There's no one like me anywhere.
I feel just right in the skin I wear,
There's no one like me anywhere.

No one sees the things I see,
Behind my eyes is only me.
And no one knows where my feelings begin
For there's only me inside my skin.
No one does what I can do,
I'll be me, and you be you.

(Refrain)

It's a wonderful thing how everyone owns
Just enough skin to cover his bones.
My dad's would be too big to fit,
I'd be all wrinkled inside of it.
Baby sister's would be much too small,
It wouldn't cover me up at all.

(Refrain).

STRESS IN CHILDREN AND DEVELOPING RESILIENCY

One precursor of self-esteem deficiency is stress in young children. Stress results when we cannot cope with either external or internal demands (Marion, 1995). Internal sources of concern or stressors may include hunger, pain, illness, fatigue, shyness, and emotions. External sources or stressors may include abuse, divorce, separation from family, illness, hospitalization, exposure to conflict, social conflicts, negative discipline, excessive high achievement expectations, a death, violence, blended family, a catastrophe, and so on (Jewett, 1997). Stress can be acute or chronic. Acute stress is sudden and intense and then gradually diminishes. Chronic stress, which has a more serious effect on children, is continual or ongoing. Honig (1986, p. 52) lists several aspects of stress in young children: "A stressor, how a child perceives that stressor, the coping resources a child has, the support systems available internally and externally for the child, and the child's skill in making coping or adjusting responses when stressed." Such stressors may include situations, events, or people and are not necessarily good or bad; they are just particular demands. "Multiple stressors can interact with one another, and their effects can be cumulative" (Jewett, 1997, p. 172). Variables associated with different kinds of stress in children's lives include prematurity, age, sex, intellectual capacity, neurological strength, living environment, socioeconomic status, family events or situations, and parenting practices (Honig, 1986). Even if we could avoid all stress, which we cannot, we would deprive children of valuable life-coping skills. Stress is produced by the very process of living. Many events in our lives over which we have little or no control create stress. One of the great stressors in the lives of young children is hurrying them: from one location to another, to get ready, to do well on work or assignments, to grow up. To counteract this, we can either decrease our demands or increase our support.

Often the cause of the stress response in children is not the actual situation or person, but the child's attitude toward that particular situation or person. For example, stress in young children can be created by fears of unreal things such as monsters or witches. It is often a difficult task for young children to make a distinction between reality and fantasy. Children misconstrue situations, events, or conversations to mean something that they do not mean. This results in worry, anxiety, concern, and stress. Children also experience personal fears and concerns that result in stress. Separation itself is not always stressful and harmful to children, but too much separation too soon is a major source of stress. When children become surrounded with fears, anxieties, quarreling, complaining, bickering, and other potentially anxious situations, they can experience emotional overload.

School often creates many stressors for children, and emotionally stressful classroom environments are counterproductive because they can reduce children's ability to learn (Sylvester, 1994). Geiger (1993) reports that more than 160,000 students each year miss school because they fear aggression there. Extremely demanding and developmentally inappropriate classroom practices and demands may also cause stress. There is competition for grades, high expectations, demand for excellence, and social concerns. At every educational level, there is a feeling that we must master certain concepts at this particular level; that is, we must get through this material by a specific time. On the other hand, school can stress some children if they find it dull, boring, and unchallenging. Children in this situation become fatigued, inattentive, uninterested, and stressed. Adults suffering job burnout, especially when their work is meaningless and repetitive, react with the same symptoms.

Violence and Conflict Resolution

Television and movies can create stress by giving children more information than they can understand and information that is too complex. This results in a discrepancy between the amount of information that children have and the amount that they can process (Elkind, 1988). Of particular concern is the influence of violence in the lives of children. When children witness violence, their sense of security and predictability is threatened. "Terror is the primary element of emotional trauma" (Jackson, 1997, p. 70). Violence results in children believing that there is no safe place, that

Developing and maintaining friendships allows children to increase social skills and learn to solve problems.

Children who are exposed to violence often exhibit symptoms of posttraumatic stress disorder:

- Frequent nightmares
- Dramatizing the event during play
- Reactions to reminders of the event
- Withdrawing or becoming passive
- Regression of acquired developmental skills
- Increased irritability and emotional outbursts
- Night walking
- Increased aggression and hostility
- Decreased concentration

(Zero to Three, 1994)

Additional negative effects of violence on the development and behavior of children, specifically related to violence in the media:

- Mistrust and fearfulness behavior toward others
- Desensitization and callousness toward violence and suffering of others
- Children seek violent heroes as role models
- Provides justification for personal use of violence
- Increases appetite for viewing more and more violence
- Disrespectful behavior toward others seems acceptable

American Medical Association, 1996

"their protectors can no longer protect them." These feelings not only influence their emotional development, but also negatively affect all relationships! When children witness violence or learn in detail about violent incidents, it can be almost as traumatic to them as when they are victimized themselves (Jackson, 1997)!

"Much of what media culture teaches children is not what the adults who care about them would choose for them to learn. It also is not what child development theory and research tell us is what children need" (Levin, 1998, p. 16). How children think affects how they interpret their experiences. They are not able to fully distinguish between fantasy and reality; they focus on the concrete, dramatic aspects of the situation; they are unable to make logical and appropriate cause-and-effect connections; and they concentrate on only one aspect of the situation at a time.

"Violent behavior is, in large part, learned early in life . . . and habits of aggression and violence can be prevented if addressed when children are young" (Anderson, 2001, p. 61). Young children can be taught skills that not only help them develop nonviolent behaviors, but also equip them to form nurturing and caring relationships throughout their lives. Loving, consistent, and reliable care are of utmost importance in helping children to feel the emotional and physical safety that is conducive to their growth, learning, and development. The following daily experiences will assist children in acquiring these attitudes: providing a safe environment, building and fostering supportive relationships, promoting emotional and social competence, providing positive interactions with others, strengthening interactive skills, demonstrating positive role modeling, and fostering problem solving (Anderson, 2001; Jackson, 1997). In our daily interactions with young children, we must be aware of the words and language that we use, careful of our tone of voice, cautious of our own actions, positive in our approach to guidance, sensitive to the feelings and relationships of others, and mindful of the importance of creating a safe harmonious learning environment in our classrooms. We can make a difference!

Children need to use peaceful conflict resolutions to counteract the violent conflict approaches that they may learn from the media or from personal experiences in their lives. When children encounter conflicts with one another, it is important that we empower them with the skills to use problem solving as an opportunity for learning (Eaton, 1997). If we consider that conflicts among young children are a natural part of life, we can also recognize that valuable lessons can be learned through these conflicts. When we intervene too early in these conflicts, we prevent children from learning valuable interpersonal skills and problem-solving techniques (DaRos & Kovach, 1998). Even though we may desire to resolve the conflicts ourselves, it is important for us to observe and allow time for children to find their own solutions, providing any needed guidance and support for their efforts and accomplishments. Stomfay-Stitz (1998) discusses the importance of books in helping children to learn to resolve problems. Books show that, although conflicts may be a part of daily life, they can still be resolved in peaceful ways.

A "Fussbuster program" (Gillespie & Chick, 2001, p. 194) was developed to assist young children in a Head Start classroom to resolve conflicts. The plan has valuable application to all who are involved with early childhood education. A "peace table" was designated, which was used only for the "Fussbuster program." Whenever a conflict occurred, the involved children and a mutual friend chosen by them immediately moved to the Peace Table. The teachers and children made up a list of

---

Key Elements of Peaceful Conflict Resolutions

- See the problem from both sides
- Come up with possible solutions
- Find a solution that everyone agrees to try
- Try out the solution and see if it works
- Evaluate how the solution worked
- Use what is learned for solving future conflicts

Levin, 1998

---

rules and procedures that were to be followed. In the children's own words, they included:

1. "No hitting; keep hands and feet to self.
2. Talk things over.
3. One person (talking) at a time.
4. Take a helper—a Fussbuster.
5. Stay until the problem is solved.
6. Shake hands at the end.
7. You get your spot back (where you were playing)."

A sense of teamwork and ownership resulted as students developed the rules and procedures, chose Fussbusters, and were chosen as Fussbusters. The number of conflicts in the classroom dramatically decreased. The results supported the philosophy that young children, with proper training and modeling, can take control of their conflicts and find peaceful solutions to problems.

Children's Reactions to Stress

Considering individual differences among children, remember that what may cause stress in one child will not necessarily cause stress in another. Children respond to stress in various ways. Zegans (1982) explains that children's reaction to stress comes in four different stages: (1) event causes alarm, (2) child tries to make some meaning out of the event, (3) child searches for coping strategies, and (4) child implements one or more identified strategies. Children have different coping abilities, as do adults, so what causes one child to fall apart may make another child stronger. The child's reaction relates in part to the notion of accumulation: In one child, stress and anxiety build up faster than the natural adaptation process can handle; another child naturally adapts to the stress. How children respond and react to stress is an individual matter. However, we do know that children who are aggressive or who have been rejected find it more difficult to cope with stress (Hardy, Power, & Jaedicke, 1993). There are also some children who keep all the stress and symptoms of stress inside, learning to cover up.

Proneness to injury or accidents

Tiredness

Depression

Nervousness, tenseness

Forgetfulness

Difficulty sleeping and staying awake

Uncommon personality or behavior patterns

Picking at scabs or sores

Frequent physical, verbal, and/or emotional outbursts

Signs That Suggest That Children May Be Experiencing Undue Stress

Crying, fussing

Reverting to less mature behaviors

Nervous habits such as twisting or pulling hair; sighing deeply; nailbiting; thumbsucking; tapping feet, fingers, or pencils

Increased irritability, sometimes to the point of tantrums

Lethargy or withdrawal from activities

Distractibility

Daydreaming

Outbursts of anger

Sweating palms

Dry throat

Ulcers

Subtle reactions, such as a strained look about the eyes, tightened mouth, or furrowed brow

Excessive energy, restlessness, or aggression

Inability to stay on the task or concentrate

Nausea, eating disorders

Aches: head, stomach, neck, back, muscle

Pounding heart

Susceptibility to colds, illness

Difficulty in breathing, asthma

Helping Children to Cope with Stress

There is much literature on helping children cope with stress. Stress management helps children to develop coping skills, interpret events, and reassure themselves that they *can* cope (Jewett, 1997). "Crisis proofing" helps children to learn about stress-producing events before they actually occur and helps them to evaluate an event when it happens (Hendrick, 1998). Encouraging children to solve their own problems also increases their ability to cope with stress. It is imperative that they see the adults around them model appropriate and successful coping strategies. Our attitudes of confidence, love, acceptance, and understanding help children to get through stressful times (Diffily & Morrison, 1996).

When we allow children to determine the direction of learning and exploring, they become problem solvers and negotiators, planners, and thinkers. After a classroom pet rabbit died, the students, through the guidance and support of the teacher, initiated the resulting discussion and projects. The following unspoken messages were sent to each of the classroom children throughout the experience:

- "I trust you.
- You are big.
- Your decisions are meaningful.
- You are valuable.
- Help is available.
- Questions are good.

Sometimes situations arise in the classroom that result in feelings of insecurity and sadness.

- Death is another part of life.
- Grownups cry.
- People have different ideas, and that's OK.
- Feelings are important.
- Talking and discussion helps you understand.
- Writing is powerful.
- You can learn from everybody (not just teachers)." (Sandstrom, 1999, p. 15).

Respect conveys and fosters esteem. The atmosphere and feeling tone surrounding the child are vital. Listen to children and encourage them to communicate. Talking about the "worst thing that could happen" or asking them to "tell me what is worrying you" helps children to express such feelings openly. Care for the child. With loving guidance, the child can be emotionally equipped to face whatever life brings. Understand and accept (and sometimes encourage) crying and tears. "Crying seems to be a healing mechanism, a natural re-

> ### Additional Suggestions for Helping Children to Cope with Stress
>
> Reading
>
> Lying down, resting, taking a nap
>
> Listening to music, playing music, singing, whistling, humming
>
> Daydreaming, mental imagery, positive self-talk
>
> Breathing deeper and slower
>
> Laughter and humor
>
> Slowing the pace down
>
> Appropriate video games, computer activities, movies, television
>
> Physical contact: hugging, touching, holding
>
> Pets: playing, watching, petting
>
> Constructing or building
>
> Eating, chewing gum or soft candy
>
> Swinging (playground, lawn, hammock)
>
> Warm bath
>
> Art activities and materials
>
> Speaking quietly or softly to the child
>
> Physical activity
>
> Playing with a friend
>
> Consistency, routines, schedules, limits
>
> Honesty, openness from others
>
> Talking, drawing, or writing about concerns

pair kit that every person has. It allows people to cope with stress" (Solter, 1992, p. 66).

Training in physical and mental relaxation or self-induced relaxation skills tends to reduce stress and its effects on children (Margolis, 1987). For example, one technique is meditation; the teacher's primary function is to provide a quiet, comfortable environment for relaxation and meditation (Margolis, 1987). Another technique is progressive muscle relaxation, because one cannot be simultaneously relaxed and stressed and because mental relaxation is a natural consequence of physical relaxation. By tensing and relaxing muscle groups, children can learn to relax muscles when necessary (Margolis, 1987). Another technique, visual imagery, encourages children to imagine a peaceful and happy scene or experience. Or they can imagine a warm ball of liquid gold that starts at the top of their head and slowly flows down their whole body. This visual imagery can be turned into creative brainstorming as children imagine similar kinds of things while both their minds and bodies relax.

Another way of teaching children to deal with stress is to encourage children to use positive, rather than negative, self-talk. Train them to think that "I can" instead of "I can't." Have them brainstorm positive self-talk, that is, positive attitudes and ideas that they think about themselves. Help them to clarify their values by asking, "Is it worth worrying about right now?" or "Will my worrying about it solve it?" Manning et al. (1996) and Sang (1994) suggest the use of "worry doctors" as part of a team to both support adults working with children in stressful situations and helping children themselves to handle stress.

Help children to develop a sense of humor and enjoy laughing. During the early childhood years, they enjoy telling riddles and "knock–knock" jokes; they can learn that it is fun and relaxing to laugh at and enjoy a good joke. One clinical and consulting psychologist calls himself the "world's one and only joyologist" and explains that his favorite motto is "If it's not fun, I don't want to do it." Steve Wilson tells us that "teachers who encourage laughter in their classes have children who learn quickly, retain more, and have fewer classroom problems." He continues by reminding us that "we demonstrate through our behavior and our own freedom of speech how to minimize tensions with a joke; how to loosen uptight, closed-in thinking systems with good-natured joking" (Chenfeld, 1990, pp. 56, 59). "A sense of humor allows children to cope with sources of conflict and distress" in their lives (Diffily & Morrison, 1996, p. 86).

Children should be encouraged to eat a healthy diet with foods from the basic food groups. They should be surrounded with adults who model relaxed living. The curriculum and feeling tone in the classroom should model happy, peaceful living. This atmosphere will not only affect the children's feelings in a positive way, but it can also influence their attitudes toward and treatment of others in the classroom. In psychologi-

cally safe school environments, children are able to develop personal meaningful social relationships. Children are able to form positive self-images as problem solvers, learners, friends, and family members (Novick, 1998). Faith that things will work out can "be sustained, even under adverse circumstances, if children encounter people who give meaning to their lives and a reason for commitment and caring" (Werner, 1984, p. 72).

Wadlington and Partridge (1998) remind us of the importance of stress management for teachers. They suggest the following ways for teachers and other adults working with children to reduce their own stress:

- Look at the big picture, the long-range goals.
- Form support groups with other teachers.
- Provide mentors for new teachers or teachers in transition.
- Contract with a teaching buddy.
- Make your needs and constraints known.
- Be a lifelong learner.
- Enhance the profession's reputation and build self-esteem.
- Cultivate realistic expectations.
- Be a positive role model.
- Take time to relax.

Fostering Resiliency in Children

Resiliency is the "capability to cope effectively with vulnerabilities" (Werner & Smith, 1982, p. 4). It is the ability to recover from stress and adversity and adapt successfully (Henderson & Milstein, 1996; Weinreb, 1997). "The capacity to bounce back requires the ability to see the difficulty as a problem that can be worked on, overcome, changed, endured or resolved in some way" (Novick, 1998, p. 201). This ability develops over time and is greatly influenced by the individual child's behavior and personality, family attributes, and social environment (Garmezy, 1985). If early childhood professionals become familiar with the factors influencing resiliency, they will be able to positively affect the lives of the young children for whom they care.

Resiliency is directly related to a child's self-esteem and general attitude toward life. Children who are resilient usually have hope, a positive outlook, and good self-esteem. They are independent, confident, communicative, friendly, responsive, social, cheerful, and competent. We need to not only recognize but also verbalize our respect and appreciation for children, for their talents, abilities, good qualities, and helpfulness. Such character traits as caring, helping, sharing, and being successful, competent, and sympathetic that we see children demonstrate should not go unnoticed! These same traits tend to be apparent in children who are more resilient. To prepare resilient youth for uncertainty, teachers should foster feelings of competence, belonging, usefulness, and optimism (Sagor, 1996). When children participate in classroom decision making, peer tutoring, problem solving, room arranging, or theme and project selection, they become more confident and resilient.

Also, to build resiliency in children requires care and support from significant adults, high expectations, and the opportunity for meaningful participation (Henderson & Milstein, 1996). Children need to be guided through self-directed understanding and need help in managing negative emotions such as anger or stress (Oehlberg, 1996).

Families have particular traits that help support and promote resilience in children: close bonds with immediate and/or extended family members, school involvement, bias-free attitudes of acceptance and equality, firm and consistent rules, positive discipline, and appropriate supervision (Weinreb, 1997). As we model these strategies in our classrooms, it strengthens the families and helps children learn coping techniques through observation. Positive experiences in the schools, neighborhoods, and communities provide additional resilient influences outside the home atmosphere. Because of space, economics, work schedules, and time, many activities such as music, sports, and drama are not available in the home, but are readily accessible in the religious, educational, and community environments.

"Perhaps the single most important intervention . . . is you" (Weinreb, 1997, p. 17). Because teachers can be mentors, models, examples, providers, and supporters, individually we can have a positive effect on children. It is important that the attitudes that we spread to the children convey "I understand. I am here for you. I will help you. I care about you. You are important to me." As the children realize this through our associations and interactions, we help them to work with the stressors in their lives now and fortify them with confidence and abilities to handle the problems that they encounter in the future. Bakley (1997, p. 21) confirms that "A child loved by us at two will reflect that love at seven. A child encouraged by us at age three will show confidence at age seven. A child affirmed by us at four will demonstrate self-esteem at seven." Sometimes our influence is readily apparent in a short time, but at other times we may not be aware of it until many years later; it is possible that we may never know that the "life we touched" became more resilient because of our caring.

CHARACTER EDUCATION

Moral or character education is "the training of heart and mind toward good" (Bennett, 1993, p. 11). In the wake of a deteriorating social fabric in today's world, schools have sought to take rather comprehensive approaches to character education, with teachers expected to model, teach, and encourage moral values (Lickona, 1993). *Character* involves possessing and demonstrating such qualities as self-control, honesty, courage, equality, compassion, integrity, self-discipline, industriousness, responsibility, empathy, and patriotism (Berreth & Berman, 1997; Lickona, 1993). Most everyone recognizes that there is a core of values, often tied to our democratic beliefs, and that children do not innately possess these characteristics; for them to develop these qualities, they need to have examples of right and wrong taught and modeled (Bennett, 1993). This does not merely refer to the traditional religious reference, but to the spark of fire in each person, the very essence of uniqueness (Turner, 2000). Moral education involves understanding and practicing the do's and don'ts of relating to others (Bennett, 1993). Children must develop clear values that help them to grow up being fair and considerate of others. To accomplish this, they must learn to express and understand their own feelings and those of other people (Eaton, 1997). "We grow morally as a consequence of learning how to be with others, how to behave in this world, a learning prompted by taking to heart what we have seen and heard" (Coles, 1997, p. 5).

In a poll addressing family values in the United States, the following were identified as the 10 most important character traits: being responsible, providing emotional support, showing respect for others, having a happy marriage, having faith in God, living up to potential, following a moral code, earning a good living, helping the community, and being free (Massachusetts Mutual Insurance Company, 1991). Since the family is the first unit of society to which the child is introduced, it has paramount responsibility for encouraging character education of young children; however, more and more our schools have included character education as a significant aspect on the educational agenda.

Teachers and parents can assist young children in developing a lifelong prosocial attitude and a pattern of caring behavior by

- Accepting that children are unique
- Modeling caring and helping behavior
- Encouraging empathy
- Monitoring amount and types of television and computer activities
- Providing warm, nurturing relationships with children

- Promoting internal motivation, feelings of sympathy, and a desire to do what is right (Wyckoff, 2000).

Our schools serve as a resource for developing and fostering positive character traits in children. An effective K–12 character education program helps to make our schools more caring, reduces negative student behavior, improves academic performance, and prepares youth to be productive and responsible citizens (The Character Education Partnership, Inc., 1996). These same character education program goals are also appropriate for the earlier childhood years. According to the Character Education Partnership of Alexandria, Virginia (a consortium of educational groups), about one in five schools uses character programs, ranging from an occasional assembly to actual curriculum content (Glazer, 1996). The two underlying character skills that are prerequisites for character development are empathy and self-discipline (Berreth & Berman, 1997). Empathy allows children to understand the perspective of others, and self-discipline is the ability to take action or defer gratification in order to commit to a set of values or goals (Berreth & Berman, 1997). Recent research supports

Being able to demonstrate feelings of caring for others is an important part of developing friendships.

the century-old child-guidance approach of helping infants, toddlers, and older young children to develop self-discipline and self-regulation. For many years, specialists in child development, psychoanalytic theory and research, clinical child psychology, and early childhood education have encouraged parents and teachers to

- Meet the needs of young children
- Develop trusting, warm relationships with young children
- Give young children opportunities for making sensible choices
- Have children assist in conflict resolution and problem solving
- Create predictable routines
- Model responsible behavior
- Expect age-appropriate responsible behavior
- Show appreciation for responsible behavior (Bronson, 2000)

Along with teaching democratic and civil values, our young people need to be taught to think for themselves and to make responsible decisions (Berreth & Berman, 1997). As children develop positive character traits and internalize them as worthwhile values, their ability to function and behave as responsible, valuable citizens rapidly expands. *Values* represent standards or principles of worth. Human values are the core of our democracy and are "recognized by all civilized people and taught by all enlightened creeds" (Lickona, 1993, p. 8). Many values are explicitly taught or implicitly caught within both the family unit and classroom. They are taught in a democratic classroom environment through curriculum topics, conflict resolution, and modeling; in cooperative learning activities; and with continual practice (Berreth & Berman, 1997; Lickona, 1993). Through example and specific curriculum activities, teachers and families attempt to teach responsible behavior and strive to help children to acquire a sound set of values with which to make decisions. We teach them what character traits are and why they "deserve both admiration and allegiance" (W. J. Bennett, 1995, p. 6). Children learn fair play, justice, and morality from how they are treated by their families, teachers, and peers. To interact co-

operatively, get along well with others, and develop close social relationships, children must be able to understand the feelings and intentions of others, often referred to as the development of social understanding. We can facilitate this learning in young children by encouraging pretend play and talking to them about minds and mental states through storybooks or real-life encounters (Lillard & Curenton, 1999).

The foundation for strong values rests in empowering children with the following principles. The child must:

1. Develop self-esteem and courage to defend his or her convictions, values, and beliefs
2. Have the self-motivation to set and accomplish individual goals
3. Be tolerant of and show respect for *all* other people regardless of their gender, race, social class, or abilities
4. Have the ability to judge right from wrong as defined by laws and to make moral judgments
5. Be honest with self and others
6. Do his or her best and act responsibly

We must provide educational activities that allow students the opportunity of experiencing and internalizing desired values. There is growing popularity in schools for service learning or community service projects to assist others, gain personal growth, and internalize positive values (Howard, 1993; Raywid, 1993; Silcox & Leek, 1997). However, it appears that positive character traits are best fostered in a social environment of caring and respect. As educators of young children, we have both the opportunity and responsibility to nurture their spirits during the years when their interests, values, and attitudes are taking root. Spiritual nurturing is not programmed into the curriculum routine at a particular time on a particular day. It must be present in our philosophies and approaches to teaching, classroom environments, and day-to-day interactions with each other (Wolf, 2000). "Thoughtful spiritual nurturing may be the most longlasting and satisfying gift you can give" to the young children in our care (Wolf, 2000, p. 36).

APPROACH TO TEACHING

Concepts and Ideas for Teaching

1. I am a person, and I have a name.
2. I have a body.
   a. Body parts
   b. How and why to care for various parts (hair, teeth, nails)
3. I have different physical characteristics.
   a. Freckles
   b. Glasses, contacts
   c. Brown eyes
   d. Red hair
   e. Braces worn on teeth
   f. Braces worn on leg(s)
4. I am growing.
   a. I weigh more than I did a year ago.
   b. I am taller than I was a year ago.
   c. I was once a baby.
5. I am sometimes sick.
   a. Colds
   b. Diseases
   c. Headaches
6. I have strengths, talents, and capabilities, but I also have some weaknesses.
   a. What are my talents?
   b. What are my strengths?
   c. What are my weaknesses?
7. I have some goals for myself. I would like to be . . . .
8. I have a particular race and nationality.
9. I have feelings, and they are always acceptable, but I must learn to express them in acceptable ways.
10. I have unique thoughts and ideas that are important.
11. I live in a neighborhood.
12. I live in a city (on a farm, in a small town), in a state that is part of a nation that is part of the world.
13. I have favorite
    a. Songs
    b. Colors
    c. Seasons
    d. Friends
    e. Things I like to do
    f. Television programs
    g. Movies or videos
    h. Holidays
    i. Foods
    j. Things to collect
    k. Subjects in school
14. When I grow up, I want to be . . . .
15. I have a family.
    a. My family takes care of me.
    b. I learn many things from my family.
16. My family is unique.
    a. I may have one or two parents.
    b. I may have brothers and sisters.
    c. I may have a grandmother and grandfather.
    d. I may have cousins, uncles, aunts.
    e. I may have a foster family.
    f. My family lives in a house, apartment, shelter.
17. I have fun with my family.
    a. We play together.
    b. We go places together.
    c. We work together.
18. My family sometimes changes.
    a. Divorce
    b. Death
    c. Parent remarriage
    d. Illness, disease
    e. Move to a different home, city
    f. Job changes
    g. New baby
    h. Adoption
19. I depend on many people and need the help of many people.
20. There are many elderly people in my community; I can serve and help them.

Activities and Experiences

1. Take photographs of individual children, especially in action shots. Photograph the entire child, not just the head. These photographs can be used to build the self-concept and can be displayed on the child's locker or desk.

2. Take or collect photographs of children with their families. These can be used to discuss family characteristics, diversity, similarities, and differences. Remember: Always stress how families and individual children are more alike than different.

3. Provide mirrors for the children to use—on the tables for use during free play and on the walls in various locations. Every classroom should have a full-length mirror.

4. From magazines, children can cut out pictures that they like or that remind them of themselves and/or their families.

5. Draw body images of the children. The children lie on a sheet of butcher paper while a teacher (or another child, if older) draws around the body shape. After being decorated, the images are displayed around the room so that the size and shape variations of the children can easily be observed. As a variation, the children can cut body parts from magazines or newspapers for collaging onto the drawing.

6. Create songs (words and music), with the children initiating ideas. These songs should become an important part of daily singing times.

7. Make hand or foot prints in plaster. They can be compared with those of other children in the classroom and also with the hands and feet of parents or other family members.

8. Do posters and sheets titled "All About Me" or "This Is Me." Include such topics as "My Favorite Things to Do," "My Family," "A Picture of Me," "Physical Characteristics," and so on. These could be put together into a booklet.

9. Set up areas for makeup and cosmetic exploration, as well as for dressing in clothes representing various roles.

10. Put articles of clothing in a sack or box (gloves, boots, sweater, hat, sandals, swimsuit, etc.). As one child reaches in and pulls out an article, the other children say when and where it would be worn appropriately.

11. Provide charts, models, and pictures of the human body; include bones, muscles, and so on.

12. Weigh and measure each child who wishes to be weighed and measured. Repeat this activity often so that comparisons can be made.

13. Make a neighborhood or community map, including the area and house where each child lives, if possible. Lay this map out flat, and provide small "people" and cars for the children to play with.

14. Have children complete open-ended sentences relating to their feelings. For example:

    a. I wish . . .
    b. The best thing I can do . . . .
    c. I feel proud when . . . .
    d. I feel angry when . . . .
    e. I am happy when . . . .
    f. When I get big, I'm going to . . . .
    g. I get scared when . . . .
    h. I like it when my family . . . .
    i. I wish my family would . . . .

15. Collect cartoons or pictures that depict emotional qualities, and have the children write comments or captions for them.

16. Have each child decorate an envelope with "Love Notes" written on the outside. The envelope can be left at school or taken home so that other children or family members can write or draw pictures of what they like about the child.

17. Make "I Can Do" cards with pictures or drawings of tasks and skills that the majority of the children in your class can do. As the cards are held up, the children do the skill or pretend to do it.

18. Make a puzzle of each child's name, using both first and last names. Example:

19. Collect many songs, stories, poems, and fingerplays that help to increase each child's self-esteem by focusing on the child's name or other personal characteristics, such as physical size or inherited traits.

20. Make "Guess Who" riddles describing individual children. Suggest clues that reflect the child's positive characteristics.

21. Make job or "To Do" charts. Assist children in individualizing these charts to their own responsibilities and activities. It is satisfying for children to see their accomplishments on paper as they mark off daily tasks. (See Figure 6–1.)

FIGURE 6–1
Sample "To Do" Chart

22. Use the following selection for role playing, creative dramatics, memorization, program presentations, ideas for visitors and field trips, development of literacy skills through reading and listening enjoyment, and so on:

When I Grow Up

I can't decide just what to do
When I get big someday.
There are so many different things—
It's really hard to say.

I know I can be more than one,
More than two or three;
But what to be when I grow up?
I'll have to wait and see!

Maybe I will drive a bus,
A taxi, or tow truck;
And when the snow gets very deep,
I'll help you get unstuck.

Maybe I will put out fires,
Or save a frightened cat.
I'll ride upon the fire truck
And wear a fire hat.

I could become a dentist, too,
And care for people's teeth.
I'd clean the ones in front, behind,
Above, and then beneath.

I could be a custodian
And make the buildings shine.
They would ask, "Whose careful work?"
I'd proudly answer, "Mine!"

Maybe I'll take care of hives,
And learn about the bees.
When I serve honey sandwiches,
They'll say, "Another, please!"

Maybe I will take a pen
And write a reading book
'Bout how to plant, or how to fix,
Or how to jog or cook.

Maybe I'll a plumber be,
And hear the people say:
"The pipes won't drain, the faucet drips.
Please help me right away!"

Maybe I will sell new cars
To folks who trade their old.

They'll say, "I think I'll take this one."
And I will answer, "Sold!"

I could engineer a train,
And speed along the track.
As people pass and wave at me,
I will wave right back.

Maybe I will gather trash,
And empty garbage, too.
I'll keep clean the city streets,
The playground, and the zoo.

I could be a magician with a
Traveling magic show.
They'd ask me how it works, I'd say:
"That's just for me to know!"

Maybe I could sell new shoes—
Check fit at toe and heel.
I'd say, "Now walk around a bit,
And see how those two feel."

Maybe I will fix up cars,
And keep them good as new.
They'll ask me, "How long will it take?"
"I'll call you when I'm through."

Maybe I'll help students learn—
A teacher then to choose.
I'd work with 4's, or 8's, or 12's,
16's, or 22's.

Maybe I'll make people laugh,
And be a circus clown.
I'll show them that a frown is just
A smile turned upside-down.

I'll likely be a grandparent
With tales about "Back when . . ."
After I am through, they'll say:
"Please tell that one again."

I could become a baker, and make
Cookies every day.
They'd ask me which kind was the best.
"Chocolate chip," I'd say.

You see, there are so many things
That I could grow to be;
But what I'll be when I get big—
I'll have to wait and see.

Reprinted by permission from Loa T. Jenkins.

Occasionally it is important that you have some time by yourself just to think.

23. Help children to make character decisions about what is right and what is wrong. The following situations readily lend themselves to cooperative learning in smaller groups:

   a. You are in a store and see something that you really want to have. But in your pocket is only enough money to buy milk for your family. What would you do?

   b. You are supposed to take an object starting with the letter B to school, and you have forgotten to bring one from home. Your friend sitting next to you has a rubber ball in his coat pocket. What would you do?

   c. You are shopping with a friend, and your friend takes a candy bar without paying for it. You are the only one who saw this happen. What would you do?

   d. You are on the school playground, and a child is teasing and hurting another child. What would you do?

   e. You are with a group of friends, and several begin saying negative and mean things about another friend who is not present. What should you do?

24. Seat the group in a circle. As each person's name is said, a positive adjective that begins with the same letter as the person's name is added: Friendly Frank, Happy Heidi, Jolly Justin.

UNIT PLAN ON MYSELF

Field Trips

- Dance studio or ballroom where children can see themselves move in front of large mirrors
- Own homes, playgrounds, or yards
- Doctor's office
- Dentist's office
- Beauty shop
- Beauty college (children could have their hair done)
- Eye doctor's office
- Hospital nursery

Visitors

- Dentist
- Doctor
- Nurse
- Barber
- Beautician
- Parent(s)
- Grandparent(s)
- Sibling(s)
- Person to perform and involve the children in mime

Music

- Children make and decorate their own musical instruments and then accompany familiar songs, as well as songs that they have created themselves
- Body sounds to accompany the songs in rhythm (snapping fingers, clicking tongue, clapping hands, etc.)
- Music to skip, jump, hop, run, exercise, relax, and listen to
- Teaching sessions in which children learn to play musical instruments (depending on the ages of the children, these may be rhythm sticks, drums, autoharps, harmonicas, etc.)
- Songs (music and words) created from children's own ideas
- Songs and creative movement about feelings

Art

- Decoration of handmade musical instruments
- Body images: trace around children's bodies while they are lying on paper; the children paint and decorate
- Shapes of eyes, noses, mouths, ears, and so on, cut out paper by the teacher or the children and pasted onto a face-shaped base by the children
- Foot or hand prints set in plaster, dried, and then colored

- Self-portraits
- "Me Posters" (can be collaged or drawn)

Food

- Any food activity that allows and encourages children to develop skills and make something themselves
- Favorite snacks or foods

Science

- Health-care activities that help children to understand and learn good health habits
- Looking at germs from their hands under a microscope
- Studies relating to growth: bones, hair, healing, fingernails
- Magnifying glass for a closer look at eyes, teeth, freckles, fingers, pores, hair, nose, tongue, scars, and so on

Literacy Development

- Any stories that the children write themselves about their experiences, feelings, families, and selves (these can be dictated if the children do not have handwriting skills)
- Stories or thoughts that are the children's own ideas

Note: For a project web on families, see Figure 6–2.

Summary

As infants discover early the existence of their bodies, they also begin to become aware of others around them. Through the development of positive self-images, children are able to accept and value other people. Children must be able to relate positively to themselves before they can relate effectively and successfully with others. The family provides the child's first social interactions, and it has a significant role in helping the child establish a positive self-image and healthy, realistic expectations. At the same time, teachers and caregivers need to accept children as they are and from these acceptances provide a caring, supportive, high-quality program designed to help the children to progress in their continuing quest for self-esteem. Teachers should focus on helping children develop inner strength and self-esteem based on what they learn and accomplish.

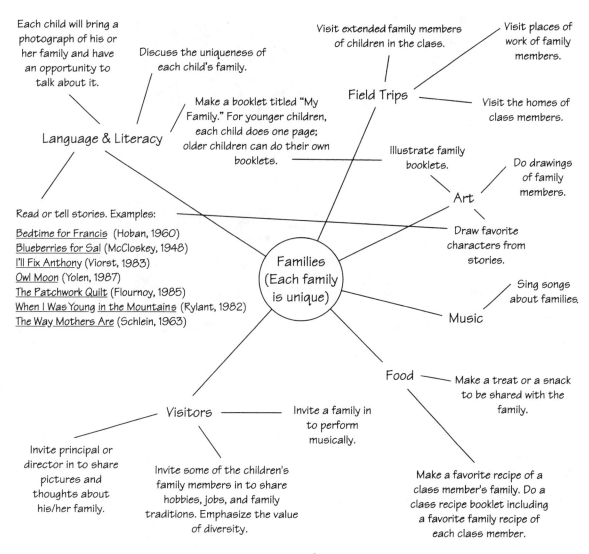

Each child will bring a photograph of his or her family and have an opportunity to talk about it.

Discuss the uniqueness of each child's family.

Make a booklet titled "My Family." For younger children, each child does one page; older children can do their own booklets.

Language & Literacy

Read or tell stories. Examples:

Bedtime for Francis (Hoban, 1960)
Blueberries for Sal (McCloskey, 1948)
I'll Fix Anthony (Viorst, 1983)
Owl Moon (Yolen, 1987)
The Patchwork Quilt (Flournoy, 1985)
When I Was Young in the Mountains (Rylant, 1982)
The Way Mothers Are (Schlein, 1963)

Visit extended family members of children in the class.

Visit places of work of family members.

Field Trips

Visit the homes of class members.

Illustrate family booklets.

Do drawings of family members.

Art

Draw favorite characters from stories.

Families (Each family is unique)

Sing songs about families.

Music

Food

Make a treat or a snack to be shared with the family.

Visitors

Invite a family in to perform musically.

Invite principal or director in to share pictures and thoughts about his/her family.

Invite some of the children's family members in to share hobbies, jobs, and family traditions. Emphasize the value of diversity.

Make a favorite recipe of a class member's family. Do a class recipe booklet including a favorite family recipe of each class member.

FIGURE 6–2
Project Web on Families

In our effort to understand the influences of stress in the lives of children, it is helpful to recognize situations causing stress, how children react to stress, how they can cope with stress, and how to help them become more resilient. We must understand the effects of violence on young children and empower them with the skills for solving conflicts peacefully. We also have a great responsibility to help children to learn and develop values and positive character traits, that is, to provide character education. Our values are the traits that we deem to be worthwhile; they determine our behaviors and goals throughout our lives. Children learn most from the examples of the significant adults in their lives. It is therefore important for teachers and caregivers to exemplify the character traits that they desire children to acquire!

Friends do not always have to be other people.

This chapter includes important basic principles in the development of self-concept, along with suggestions of techniques for building self-esteem in children. A teacher's own self-acceptance and attitude are of utmost importance when seeking to assist young children in developing self-concepts that will destine them for success.

Student Learning Activities

1. Prepare a unit or project plan on one of the following: My Family, My Friends, or some other concept relating to the self. For your web, unit, or project plan, include a section titled "Literacy" and include stories, poems, and other appropriate activities.

2. Using your plan prepared for item 1, prepare a 5-day activity plan using the format shown beginning on page 96. If you have chosen a project plan, invite the children to develop personal or group projects with their own ideas.

3. Observe in a classroom of young children and describe how the teacher enhances individual children's feelings of self-worth.

4. Prepare a list of teacher-made learning materials that you would like to make that focus on teaching children concepts related to the self.

5. Prepare and make at least two of the materials that you listed in item 4.

6. The text discusses stress in children. Using the lists given as possibilities, add ideas that are applicable to your own life: What situations cause you stress? How do you react to stress? How can you cope with stress more effectively?

7. Study children's books relating to "myself and my family." Select one to share with the class. How would you present this story to an early childhood class? Why do you like this book? Is it free of sexism and racism?

8. Listen to television or radio newscasts, or read newspaper articles relating to violence. How can you minimize the negative effects of these types of information on young children?

Suggested Resources

Children's Books

Adedjouma, D. (1996). *The palm of my heart*. New York: Lee & Low Books.

Anderson, S. (1996). *A puzzling day in the land of the Pharaohs*. Cambridge, MA: Candlewick.

Anholt, C., & L. Anholt (1992). *All about you*. New York: Viking.

Anholt, L. (1999). *Summerhouse*. New York: DK Publishing.

Baer, E. (1996). *This is the way we go to school*. Jefferson City, MO: Scholastic.

Bailey, D. (1994) *Grandpa*. Buffalo, NY: Firefly Books.

Bailey, L. (1999). *When Addie was scared*. Buffalo, NY: Kids Can Press.

Bourgeois, P., & B. Clark (2000). *Franklin goes to the hospital*. Toronto, Canada: Kids Can Press.

Brown, M. W. (1958). *The dead bird*. New York: William R. Scott.

Brown, R. (1997). *Cry baby*. New York: Dutton Children's Books.

Buckley, H. E. (1959). *Grandfather and I*. New York: Lothrop, Lee & Shepard.

Carlson, N. (1994). *How to lose all your friends*. New York: Puffin/Penguin.

Cannon, J. (1996). *Stellaluna*. New York: HarBrace.

Cheltenham Elementary School Kindergartners (1995). *We are all alike . . . We are all different*. Jefferson City, MO: Scholastic.

Church, K. (1991). *My brother John*. New York: Tambourine.

Clarke, G. (1990). *Eddie and Teddy*. New York: Lothrop, Lee & Shepard.

Cohn, J. (1987). *I had a friend named Peter*. New York: Morrow.

Cosby, B. (1997). *The meanest thing to say*. New York: Scholastic.

Couric, K. (2000). *The brand new kid*. New York: Doubleday.

Couzyn, J. (1990). *Bad day*. New York: Dutton.

Cowell, C. (2000). *What shall we do with the boo-hoo baby?* New York: Scholastic Press.

Dijis, C. (1990). *Are you my daddy? A pop-up book*. New York: Simon & Schuster.

Dijis, C. (1990). *Are you my mommy? A pop-up book*. New York: Simon & Schuster.

DiSalvo-Ryan (1999). *A dog like Jack*. New York: Holiday House.

Dutton, C. (1990). *Not in here, Dad!* New York: Barrons.

Esbensen, B. J. (1999). *Jumping day*. Honesdale, PA: Boyds Mills Press.

Farber, N. (1997). *The boy who longed for a lift*. Scranton, PA: A Laura Geringer Book, HarperCollins.

Fassler, J. (1983). *My Grandpa died today*. New York: Science Press.

Fernandes, E. (1999). *A difficult day*. Buffalo, NY: Kids Can Press.

Flournoy, S. (1985). *The patchwork quilt*. New York: Dial.

French, V., & A. Ayliffe (1997). *Oh no, Anna!* Atlanta, GA: Peachtree.

Garland, S. (1992). *Billy and Belle*. New York: Viking Penguin.

Green, M. (1961). *Everybody has a house and everybody eats*. Reading, MA: Addison-Wesley.

Greenfield, E. (1991). *First pink light*. New York: Black Butterfly.

Hamm, D. J. (1991). *Laney's lost mommy*. Morton Grove, IL: Whitman.

Hausherr, R. (1996). *Celebrating families*. Jefferson City, MO: Scholastic.

Heap, S. (1997). *Pequeno Cowboy (Cowboy Baby)*. Madrid: Editorial Kokinos.

Herron, C. (1997). *Nappy hair*. New York: Knopf.

Hines, A. G. (1985). *All about myself*. New York: Clarion.

Hoban, L. (1985). *Arthur's loose tooth*. New York: Harper & Row.

Hoban, R. (1960). *Bedtime for Francis*. New York: HarperCollins.

Isadora, R. (1990). *Babies*. New York: Greenwillow.

Isadora, R. (1990). *Friends*. New York: Greenwillow.

Kachenmeister, C. (1995). *On Monday when it rained*. Jefferson City, MO: Scholastic.

Kay, V. (1999). *Gold fever*. New York: Putnam's.

Keller, H. (1991). *Horace*. New York: Morrow.

Kesselman, W. (1985). *Emma*. New York: HarperCollins.

Kingman, L. (1990). *Catch the baby!* New York: Viking.

Konigslow, A. W. (1998). *En el bano (Toilet tales)*. Caracas: Ediciones Ekare.

Krause, U. (1989). *Nora and the great bear*. New York: Dial.

Krauss, R. (1971). *Leo the late bloomer*. New York: Windmill.

Kurtz, J. (1990). *I'm calling Molly*. Niles, IL: Whitman.

Lawrence, M. (1999). *Baby loves*. New York: DK Publishing.

Leonard, M. (1988). *What I like series: Going to bed, getting dressed, eating, taking a bath*. New York: Bantam.

Lionni, L. (1973). *Swimmy*. New York: Knopf.

Lionni, L. (1986). *It's mine! A fable*. New York: Knopf.

Lurie, A. (1999). *The black geese: A Baby Yaga story from Russia*. New York: DK Publishing.

MacDonald, A. (1999). *The pig in a wig*. Atlanta, GA: Peachtree.

Mandelbaum, P. (1990). *You be me, I'll be you*. New York: Kane/Miller.

Mayer, M. (1983). *All by myself*. New York: Western.

Mayer, M. (1983). *When I get bigger*. New York: Western.

McCloskey, R. (1948). *Blueberries for Sal*. New York: Viking.

Miles, M. (1972). *Annie and the old one*. Boston: Little, Brown.

Munsch, R. (1999). *Ribbon rescue*. New York: Scholastic.

Naylor, P. R. (1999). *Sweet strawberries*. New York: Atheneum Books for Young Readers.

Nemiroff, M. A., & J. Annunziata (1990). *A child's first book about play therapy*. Washington, DC: American Psychological Association.

Patterson, B. (1992). *In my house*. New York: Holt.

Patterson, B. (1992). *In my yard*. New York: Holt.

Patterson, B. (1992). *My clothes*. New York: Holt.

Patterson, B. (1992). *My toys*. New York: Holt.

Poydar, N. (1999). *First day, horay!* New York: Holiday House.

Rice, M., & C. Rice (1987). *All about me*. New York: Doubleday.

Ricklen, N. (1992). *My first day at school*. Hauppauge, NY: Barron's.

Ringgold, F. (1991). *Tar Beach*. New York: Crown.

Rogers, F. (1985). *Going to day care*. New York: Putnam.

Rogers, F. (1991). *So much to think about*. Pittsburgh, PA: Family Communications.

Rogers, J. (1999). *Tiptoe into kindergarten*. New York: Cartwheel.

Ross, A., & K. Ross (1999). *Jezebel's secret spot*. New York: Dutton Children's Books.

Schachner, J. (1999). *The grannyman*. New York: Dutton Children's Books.

Scheidl, G. M. (1999). *Tommy's new sister*. New York: North-South Books.

Schlein, M. (1963). *The way mothers are*. Chicago: Whitman.

Sendak, M. (1963). *Where the wild things are*. New York: Harper & Row.

Senisi, E. B. (1997). *Brothers & sisters*. Jefferson City, MO: Scholastic.

Seuss, Dr. (1968). *Horton hatches the egg*. New York: Random House.

Skorpen, L. (1999). *We were tired of living in a house*. New York: Putnam's.

Spelman, C. (2000). *When I feel angry*. Morton Grove, IL: Whitman.

Steig, W. (1969). *Sylvester and the magic pebble*. New York: Simon & Schuster.

Torre, B. L. (1990). *The luminous pearl*. New York: Orchard.

Trafuri, N. (1998). *I love you, little one*. New York: Scholastic Press.

Tucker, S. (1991). *At home*. New York: Simon & Schuster.

Tucker, S. (1991). *Going out*. New York: Simon & Schuster.

Tucker, S. (1991). *My clothes*. New York: Simon & Schuster.

Tucker, S. (1991). *My toys*. New York: Simon & Schuster.

Udry, J. M. (1969). *Let's be enemies*. New York: Harper & Brothers.

Vagin, V. (1998). *The enormous carrot*. New York: Scholastic Press.

Viorst, J. (1972). *Alexander and the terrible, horrible, no good, very bad day*. New York: Atheneum.

Viorst, J. (1983). *I'll fix Anthony*. New York: Atheneum.

Weedn, F. (1999). *Flavia and the dream maker*. San Rafael, CA: Cedco Publishing.

Wellington, M. (1989). *All my little ducklings*. New York: Dutton.

Wells, R. (1997). *Bunny cakes*. New York: Dial.

Wild, M. (2000). *Tom goes to kindergarten*. Morton Grove, IL: Whitman.

Williams, B. (1974). *Albert's toothache*. New York: Dutton.

Yashima, T. (1955). *Crow boy*. New York: Viking.

Yolen, J. (1987). *Owl moon*. New York: Putnam.

Zolotow, C. (1972). *William's doll*. New York: Harper & Row.

Zolotow, C. (1984). *I know a lady*. New York: Greenwillow.

Character Education Book Sets

Each Character Development Book Set includes three paperbacks, a discussion and activity guide with take-home reproducibles, and a carrying bag. The sets cover the following five character development areas: cooperation, honesty, friendship, fairness, and respect for others. For example, the set on honesty contains: *Jamaica's Find, Too Many Tamales*, and *The Tale of Peter Rabbit*. Jefferson City, MO: Scholastic.

Tapes and Cassettes

Be my friend. On *Getting to know myself*. Hap Palmer Record Library (AR543 or AC543).

Brush away. On *Learning basic skills through music* (vol. 1). Hap Palmer Record Library (AR526 or AC526).

Cover your mouth. On *Learning basic skills through music* (vol. 1). Hap Palmer Record Library.

The downtown story. Scholastic Book Services (R7670).

Everybody cries sometimes. Educational Activities (AR561 or AC561).

Everybody is somebody. On *It's a happy feeling*. Cheviot (T-305).

Everyone has feelings. Scholastic Book Services (R7567).

Exercise every day. On *Learning basic skills through music* (vol. 1). Hap Palmer Record Library (AR526 or AC526).

Feelings. On *Getting to know myself*. Hap Palmer Record Library (AR543 or AC543).

The frog's party. A Gentle Wind.

Fun and fitness for primary children. Bowmar-Noble (B2057).

Helping and sharing. David C. Cook.

Hopping around from place to place (vols. 1 and 2). Educational Activities.

I've got a reason to sing. Cheviot (T-307).

Keep the germs away. On *Learning basic skills through music* (vol. 1). Hap Palmer Record Library (AR526 or AC526).

Left and right. On *Getting to know myself*. Hap Palmer Record Library (AR543 or AC543).

Lullabies from 'round the world. Cheviot.

Rainy day dances, rainy day songs. Educational Activities (AR570 or AC570).

Sing around the world. Miss Jackie.

Take a bath. On *Learning basic skills through music* (vol. 1). Hap Palmer Record Library (AR526 or AC526).

What are you wearing? On *Learning basic skills through music* (vol. 1). Hap Palmer Record Library (AR514 or AC514).

Won't you be my friend? Educational Activities (AR544 or AC544).

You can do it. On *Ooo we're having fun*. Cheviot (T-306).

Pictures

Developing my values. The Child's World.

Disney safety study prints (series). Walt Disney.

Guidance. The Child's World.

Health and cleanliness. David C. Cook.

Health and personal care. The Child's World.

Learning about careers. David C. Cook.

Learning about values. David C. Cook.

The many moods of Mother Goose. The Child's World.

Moods and emotions. The Child's World.

Moods and emotions. David C. Cook.

The rural environment. Scholastic Book Services.

Safety. David C. Cook.

Social development. David C. Cook.

Understanding my needs. The Child's World.

Videos

The adventures of Elmer and friends. Featherwind Productions.

Character education: Application in the K–6 classroom. Insight Media.

Character education: Restoring respect and responsibility in our schools. Insight Media.

Communicating during conflict. Insight Media.

Dr. Seuss's my many colored days. Minnesota Orchestra Visual Entertainment (MOVE), Notes Alive! Series.

Emotional development of children. Films for the Humanities & Sciences.

Emotional intelligence: The key to social skills. Films for the Humanities & Sciences.

Everyday self-esteem (in a series titled *Everyday Character Development*). Insight Media.

Express yourself. National Geographic.

I can help, too. National Geographic.

I can make friends. National Geographic.

I can take care of myself. National Geographic.

Include us! TiffHill Productions.

Integrating character education into the curriculum. Insight Media.

Introduction to conflict resolution. Insight Media.

Mama, Do You Love Me? Sony, Doors of Wonder series.

Me and my world. National Geographic.

On the day you were born. Minnesota Orchestra Visual Entertainment (MOVE), Notes Alive! Series.

Playing fair. National Geographic.

Senses: How we know. National Geographic.

Share with us. Warner Brothers Family Entertainment, The Big Bag series.

Ten things every child needs. Dreaming Big Publishing.

Veggie Tales series. www.bigidea.com

Wilbur teaches the parts of the body. EKA Productions, Wilbur series.

Chapter 7

Myself and My Body

An effective wellness program for young children must be developmentally and chronologically appropriate and involve the integration of the body, mind, and spirit (Huettig & Connor, 1999). The healthy development of the child includes a variety of components, including physical and motor development; spiritual, emotional, social, and intellectual health; nutrition fitness and good eating habits; and attention to general health and safety issues. "Establishing early patterns of healthy lifestyles is important to enhancing physical and psychological well-being for a lifetime" (Werner, Timms, & Almond, 1996, p. 49). Blair & Morrow (1997) report that physical inactivity is a major public health problem of people in the United States. In addition, more than half of American children are overweight and regularly inactive (Miller, 1999). "Physical inactivity is the second largest health risk factor in the United States" (Human Kinetics, 2001, p. 29). Evidence suggests that hardening of the arteries is even showing up in 5-year-old children (Leibler, 1999). Because children are less physically active than ever before, early childhood educators must recognize the importance of including regular physical activity in the curriculum. Ernest L. Boyer, late president of the Carnegie Foundation for the Advancement of Teaching, stressed the connection between students' physical and emotional needs and their ability to learn (Marx & Wooley, 1998). The American Academy of Pediatrics (AAP) recommends that children in the early childhood years should be involved in some form of age- and developmentally appropriate physical activity (Leibler, 1999). Recent research on brain-based learning and brain-compatible learning suggest that movement activities are essential to learning, (Jensen, 2000b). Especially in early childhood, more activity meaningfully applied will make significant contributions to the learning process.

The goal of units, activities, and projects relating to the children's health should be for them to learn notions relating to good health, gain competencies that will guide their choices and behavior, get exercise, and have fun. As educators we must examine more carefully the role of exercise in the lives of children. Teaching about and participating in activities relating to healthy development should be integrated throughout the curriculum. For example, as children participate in food activities, snacks, or meals, they can learn about good nutrition. Many opportunities throughout the day should be provided for fitness and physical and motor activities. Also, many locomotor and fitness activities can easily be combined with creative movement and music activities or with fingerplays. However, often teachers become passive and lack thought or planning when it comes to physical education. "Many parents and teachers think the needs of the mind should take precedence over those of the body—as if the two can be separated! Thus these adults allocate little time to physical activity at school (and even at home)" (Pica, 1997, p. 5). Teachers believe that adding an activity here or there or making sure the children get to play outside is enough. It is dur-

A variety of climbing equipment encourages physical fitness and endurance in young children.

ing the early years that children's brain development is expanding so rapidly; but without proper environmental experiences and movement, the brain will be limited in its ability to develop properly. Physical fitness is an important element of brain development (Leppo, Davis, & Crim, 2000). We cannot ignore the physical and emotional health of our students and expect them to be able to concentrate on learning (Marx & Wooley, 1998).

"No knowledge is more crucial than knowledge about health. Without it, no other life goal can be successfully achieved." (Ernest L. Boyer in Marx & Wooley, 1998, p. 304)

Children's physical, social, emotional, spiritual, and intellectual life is a crucial part of the curriculum! Programs should be designed to represent a developmental sequence and can be integrated or stand as independent experiences, but they should

provide a challenge for young children and allow them to progress developmentally in physical and motor aspects (Payne & Rink, 1997). Nutrition notions can be a part of the curriculum in a variety of ways. Concepts relating to healthy eating can be taught using the Daily Food Guide Pyramid, as well as when preparing and eating foods and snacks.

PHYSICAL FITNESS

"Play is the primary way children develop physically" (Stone, 1995, p. 49) and provides many opportunities for development of both fine- and gross-motor skills. Physical activity has many short- and long-term benefits for physical, emotional, and social well-being (Payne & Rink, 1997). For children to have adequate physical exercise, they must have a minimum of 30 minutes of "huff and puff" activity where the heart beat is above 140 beats per minute (Huettig & Connor, 1999; Werner, Timms, & Almond, 1996). This does not necessarily mean that it must be completed all at one time; it could be one 30-minute, two 15-minute, three 10-minute, or five 6-minute segments. "Regular, vigorous physical activity in a supportive environment will in turn develop into a long-term habit of activity for optimal fitness, a process that has positive health effects into adulthood" (Miller, 1999, p. 58). All young children should have daily instruction in movement concepts and motor-skill themes (Council on Physical Education for Children, 1994).

Benefits of Being Physically Fit

- Weight control
- Decreased blood pressure
- Improved concentration, attention, and retention
- Decreased disruptive behavior
- Reduced risk of diabetes and heart disease
- Healthy bones, joints, and muscles
- Better overall health
- Decreased anxiety, depression, and stress
- Increased energy, endurance, and strength
- More positive self-esteem

Similar to other content areas, the National Association for Sports and Physical Education (NASPE, 1995) has outlined the following seven national standards for physical education:

1. Demonstrates competency in many and proficiency in a few movement forms.
2. Applies movement concepts and principles to the learning and development of motor skills.
3. Exhibits a physically active life-style.
4. Achieves and maintains a health-enhancing level of physical fitness.
5. Demonstrates responsible personal and social behavior in physical activity settings.
6. Demonstrates understanding and respect for differences among people in physical activity settings.
7. Understands that physical activity provides opportunities for enjoyment, self-expression, and social interaction.

The four movement concepts are

1. Body (body parts and shapes)
2. Space (moving body through space)
3. Effort (moving body with various efforts and speeds)
4. Relationship (body in relationship to other people or objects)

The three motor-skill themes are

1. Locomotor (moving feet)
2. Manipulative (sending and receiving objects)
3. Stability (moving around an axis)

(Staley & Portman, 2000)

Movement and motion are basic to the needs of young children, in developing their bodies and also in developing the whole child (Benelli & Yongue, 1995). Pica (1997, p. 11) adds, "After all, if we truly educate the whole child, we must first recognize children as thinking, feeling, moving human beings." Much of the physical fitness activity in early childhood will be in the area of movement, since children are acquiring competence in fundamental locomotor movements such as walking, running, skipping, climbing, throwing, and kicking. From "2 through 7 years, the child's gross movement abilities begin to expand dramatically" (Payne & Rink, 1997, p. 155). Movement can be added to any classroom without any special equipment; all we need is our bodies, imaginations, and the willingness to try (Rodger, 1996). In most areas of the curriculum, teachers will be able to find opportunities for children to participate in movement experiences and, as they do, children can be creative and also use problem-solving adeptness (Payne & Rink, 1997). Hannaford (1995, p. 16) asks, "We have spent years and resources struggling to teach people to learn, and yet the standardized achievement test scores go down and illiteracy rises. Could it be that one of the key elements we've been missing is simply movement?" "In the happiest of ways, movement gives children another medium through which to understand the world and communicate their ideas" (Rodger, 1996, p. 6). The development of movement skills (locomotion, gross- and fine-motor manipulation, and stability) requires plenty of opportunities for practice, positive reinforcement and encouragement, and quality instruction (Gallahue, 1995). Consider the following suggestions by Werner, Timms, & Almond (1996) and Gallahue (1996) for creating a positive movement environment for early childhood:

- Allow for individual choices and decisions
- Create simple and appropriate fitness activities
- Provide demonstrations and modeling
- Keep directions and instructions simple
- Provide variety
- Allow adequate time for practice and participation
- Encourage more active play
- Focus on the process, not the product
- Eliminate competition
- Be patient
- Allow and encourage creativity

The pattern for fundamental movements is predictable, and the items in the Physical and Motor Checklist in Chapter 4 will help you in determining the child's current state of physical and motor competence.

Fitness, Motor, and Movement Guidelines

1. To develop their large muscles adequately, young children need teacher or adult guidance in physical activities, not just the opportunity to play on large-muscle equipment. This is facilitated by planning motor and physical activities and centers.

2. Physical and motor activities should be rewarding and positive experiences. Children should soon sense that moving and exercising make them feel more energetic and strong.

3. Teachers should emphasize fitness, not competition. Competition must be avoided by early childhood teachers. Competitive pressures result in decreased self-esteem and quality of learning and increased rivalry, anger, withdrawal, and sense of inadequacy. A child should be taught early to compete with himself or herself, to try to improve and do better.

4. Teachers should observe carefully so that children do not overdo. Gear your guidance and expectations to the needs and abilities of individual children.

5. Teachers should provide positive models for the children by participating in physical and motor games and activities whenever appropriate.

The optimum environment must be

- Physically and emotionally safe
- Free of teasing, humiliation, stress, intimidation, comparison, competition, failure, and rejection
- Full of acceptance, encouragement, creativity, success, support, discovery, enjoyment, and fun

---

FUNDAMENTAL PHYSICAL MOVEMENTS

Locomotor Movements

Developing and exploring locomotor movements is an important aspect of physical fitness. These movements adapt readily to music and rhythm activities. Some of the basic locomotor movements include walking, climbing, marching, running, hopping, jumping, skipping, galloping, rolling, crawling, leaping, sliding, and trotting. The most basic of these movements, and the one to begin with, is walking. Rhythmically, this movement has a basic, steady-beat pattern that can be slower or faster. Background stimulus for locomotor movements can be provided by a drumbeat or other instrument beat, a musical recording, a song, or an accompaniment on a tuned instrument such as a piano. As children develop skill in each of the locomotor movements, they should be given the opportunity and encouragement to use them in a variety of ways and to find different ways of exploring the movement. For example, the following are some ways to explore walking; many of these same suggestions could be applied to other basic locomotor movements.

Fast	With eyes closed
Slow	On hands and feet
Heavily	Like . . . (a tin soldier, etc.)
Lightly	Happily, sadly, etc.
Low	In the wind
In the middle	In the cold
High	In the snow
With toes in	When it is hot
With toes out	Barefoot
On heels	in the sand
On tiptoe	on the grass
On the outside of the foot	on pebbles
	on hot pavement
Backward	in cold water
Sideways	In the dark
Diagonally	Following your hand as you walk
In big steps	
In short steps	Leading with your
Stamping	ear
Skating	eye
With knees out	elbow
With knees high	shoulder
Lazily	

Long steps	When going someplace
Tiny steps	special
In slow motion	When going someplace
In the rain	you do not care to go

Further examples of exploring different loco-motor movements might be variations of running. Children could run lightly or heavily, stop suddenly, or change directions. Bells and triangles could be used to evoke lighter running and drums and tam-bourines for more vigorous action. Marching is an of-ten used locomotor movement in early childhood classrooms. However, the goal there is usually to keep time to music, to keep in step, or to stay in the circle. We propose that the goal should not always be to keep time or to keep in step. Children should not always have to be in a line or circle; they can learn to march in different directions without interfering with others. Explore variations with marching.

Axial Movements

There are other types of movements, often re-ferred to as *nonlocomotor, axial* movements. They include the following (suggestions for stimu-lating these kinds of movements are given):

1. Swinging and swaying

    a. Swing arms like the pendulum of a clock, from side to side.
    b. Swing arms over and around, as though winding yourself up.
    c. Swing arms and body back and forth, as though getting ready to take off in flight or rocking in a chair.
    d. Swing and sway any part of your body like a monkey.
    e. Make some part of your body move like a railroad signal.
    f. Make some part of your body move like trees and leaves moving in the wind.
    g. Make some part of your body move like windshield wipers.

2. Bending and stretching

    a. How many different parts of your body can you bend? How many parts can you stretch? In how many different directions?
    b. Bend yourself small and then stretch your-self tall.
    c. How many ways can you stretch your face?
    d. Can you stretch some part of you like a rubber band, and what happens when you pop?
    e. Pretend you are walking on stilts.
    f. Stretch, move, and bend your body through the stages of a sneeze.
    g. Move your body as though you were reaching for something on the highest shelf in your home.
    h. Pretend to be an inchworm.

3. Pushing and pulling

    a. Pretend that you are pushing a wagon.
    b. How many ways can you pretend to be pushing and pulling a piano?
    c. Pretend you are digging and hoeing weeds in the garden.
    d. Show me how you would move to work the oars of a boat.
    e. Pretend that you are swimming. How about pretending that you are rescuing someone who is drowning?

4. Rising and falling

    a. Pretend to be a jack-in-the-box.
    b. Show me how you would move if you were the sun rising and then setting.
    c. Pretend to be an airplane taking off in flight and then landing.
    d. Pretend to be a seed growing into a flower, and then a petal on that flower falling and blowing away.
    e. Pretend to be a ball bouncing up and down. Do you always bounce to the same height?

5. Twisting and turning

    a. How would you move if you were a top?
    b. Pretend that you are using a Hula-Hoop.
    c. Show me how you would move if you were an ice skater making a turn.
    d. Pretend that you are a lid being screwed onto a jar.

6. Shaking

    a. Shake like Santa Claus.
    b. Pretend to be some jelly.
    c. Show me how you would move if you were being washed in a washing machine.
    d. Shake as though you were a milkshake being mixed.

Using Locomotor and Axial Movements

There are many ways to teach and use both loco-motor and nonlocomotor movements. By exploring and getting children involved in these kinds of movements, you will enhance their coordination, give them experience with movement, provide opportunities for creative problem solving, and encourage physical activity and development. The following are further suggestions for accomplishing these goals:

- Many songs offer opportunities for locomotor and nonlocomotor movements. For example, use "I Went to Visit a Friend One Day," "Rig-a-Jig Jig," or an adaptation of such songs as "If You're Happy and You Know It" or "Mary Had a Little Lamb" (the lamb could walk, run, or skip to school with Mary).
- Use a follow-the-leader approach.
- Suggest movements that resemble those of animals.
- Suggest ways to "cross the river" or go across the room.
- Use nursery rhymes to stimulate movements.
- Suggest ways to go around a dowel or other stick.
- Use records to stimulate ideas for movement.
- Lay foot patterns out on the floor for fundamental locomotor movements.
- Draw shapes in the air using different parts of the body (include shapes, letters, and numbers, making them different sizes).
- Jump into the middle of a space and find various ways to move to get out.

Once children have explored locomotor and nonlocomotor movements, they are ready for what we often refer to as *creative movements.* Having had the basics of movement, they are ready to create more on their own and use more freedom. Much of what we have suggested with both locomotor and nonlocomotor movements leads to creative movements, and the two categories become difficult to separate.

Fitness and Motor Activities

Large-motor activities. Examples of these are walking, running, galloping, skipping, jogging, balancing, hopping, jumping, sliding, and climbing. Throwing and catching can include beanbag tosses, ball-throwing and -catching games and skills, or ring tosses. Other ball-handling skills include kicking, bouncing, dribbling, and rolling. Riding wheeled equipment is also a good large-motor activity. Balancing skills include walking a beam, stretching, bending, swinging, and twisting. Opportunities to run, walk, or jog should be provided daily to increase cardiovascular fitness.

Small-motor activities. These include zipping, lacing, twisting, pouring, cutting, inserting pegs, pounding nails, tracing, and writing. Such activities enhance small-motor skill.

Stunts or self-testing activities. *Note:* These must be adapted to the developmental physical and motor abilities of the children in your group. Many are more appropriate for 6- to 8-year-old children. Many can be done to music.

- *Frog jump.* The children assume a squat position with hands on the floor. They move forward with a springy jump, extending their legs and landing first on hands and then on feet.
- *No arms.* The children lie flat on their backs and fold their arms. The object is to get to a standing position without unfolding the arms.
- *Crab walk.* The children clutch their ankles with their hands and walk forward step by step.
- *Seesaw.* Two children sit on the floor facing one another with their feet together. They clasp hands and, as one leans forward, the other pulls back as far as she or he can. They seesaw back and forth.
- *Toe touch.* The children stand with their feet apart. They touch the right toe with the left hand and then alternate.
- *Back to back.* The children are in pairs, standing back to back. They try to sit down and then stand back up while keeping their backs together.
- *Partner pull-up.* The children are in pairs, sitting on the ground, facing one another, knees

Being active physically is important for both emotional and physical health.

bent, feet flat on the ground, toes touching. With hands grasped, they try to pull each other up, then try to sit back down.

- *Jumping jacks*
- *Forward roll*
- *Backward roll*

PHYSICAL GAMES

During early childhood, games are played much differently than they are when children are school age. We need to consider our traditional games of Duck, Duck, Goose; Red Rover, Red Rover; Charlie, Charlie, Butcher Boy; The Farmer in the Dell; I Have a Little Doggie; Drop the Handkerchief, and so on. Just because they are traditional does not mean they are educational! They may be fun for some, but are they fun for all? "Is the focus on physical activity, movement concepts, skill themes, success, and positive self-esteem, or are we really playing games of waiting, rejection, competition, failure, and humiliation" (Staley & Portman, 2000, p. 67)?

Guidelines for Effectively Playing Physical Games

1. Select games on the basis of the developmental characteristics of the children.
2. Keep the games simple, with few rules. The older the children are, the more rules that can be added.
3. Make sure that games are noncompetitive. Children cannot tolerate losing before 5 or 6 years of age. Focus on skill development, having fun, and encouraging a sense of fair play.
4. Make sure that the children experience accomplishment.
5. When selecting "It," be impartial. For example, draw from a set of class cards that includes each child's name.
6. When the game has reached its peak of interest, change activities.
7. Be aware of the physical abilities of all children. Plan how you will include children with physical disabilities.
8. Do not match boys against girls.

9. Make sure that all children are allowed to participate, but do not force children to take part.
10. Explain how to play the game and then demonstrate how to play.

Examples of Active Games

The following are some games that are appropriate for early childhood. Some are more suitable for younger children; most are more suitable for 5- to 8-year-olds. Some can be adapted to meet the needs of a particular age or group of children. Only a few suggestions are included here. Many other acceptable physical games can be found in game books available at your local library or in bookstores.

Hot Potato. Children sit or stand in a circle. The ball, rolled on the floor, is a "hot potato" and must be pushed or kicked away when it comes near.

Jump Ball. Players are in a circle, with "It" in the center of the circle. Players roll the ball, trying to touch "It," who jumps over the ball. If the ball touches "It," she or he changes places with the last child who rolled the ball.

Piglet. All players except Piglet form pairs in a circle. When Piglet says "face to face," the partners face each other. When Piglet says "back to back" or "side to side" or "toe to toe," the direction must be followed. If Piglet says "Piglet," everyone tries to find a new partner. The person left without a partner becomes Piglet.

Find the Leader. Players are in a circle. "It" is sent from the room, and a leader is designated. After returning to the room, "It" has so many guesses to identify the leader. The leader changes the activity, and the players must copy the leader. If the leader is guessed, he or she becomes "It."

Cooperative Musical Chairs. Musical chairs can be played the traditional way, or supply a chair for everyone, or share a chair with a partner. Leave no pair or partners out.

Freeze Tag. All children are "It" and can freeze other players by touching them and yelling

"Freeze!" Players that are frozen must freeze in the positions that they are in when touched. When everyone but one person is frozen, that person says "Unfreeze" and the game begins again.

Railroad Cars. Players are in pairs, one behind the other, and each places his or her hands on the waist of the child in front. Put some train music on, and the children try to add other cars onto their train.

Smile If You Love Me. Children are in a circle (if the group is large, make each circle about six to eight children). "It" goes to a player and says, "Smile if you love me." "It" can make faces, sounds, or movements as he or she tries to make the other child smile. If "It" makes the player smile, that child becomes an "It." Make certain every child has an opportunity to be "IT."

Run Home. The players stand in a single circle facing the center. "It" walks around the outside and then holds up a beanbag between two players. These two players run around the outside of the circle in opposite directions, each aiming to get back first and grab the beanbag. The one getting it may go and hold it up between two other players.

Who Has Gone? The children move about in the room. When a chord on the piano is played, or another signal is given, all children sit down and hide their eyes. The leader touches one who quietly disappears. Then all look up and discover who is gone.

Other games of skill include those that require small-muscle coordination such as passing a Lifesaver around a group of four to six children using a small wooden dowel or a straw. Other examples include beanbag or ball tosses, ring tosses, or coin drops (a coin is dropped into a soda bottle).

Outdoor Activities

Outdoor activities are an integral part of the early childhood curriculum. Weather permitting, children should spend some time outdoors each day. The equipment on the playground should be inviting, challenging, durable, and safe. The playground must be fenced and provide built-in limits. Adults must always supervise children's play while they are outdoors. Some of the general areas for play include climbing equipment, sand, a playhouse, a paved area for riding toys, a shaded area for opportunity to get out of the sun, a developmentally appropriate basketball hoop, and additional equipment such as Hula-Hoops, balls, and riding toys. Also, many programs have garden plots that are planted and cared for by the children during the spring and summer and harvested in the fall.

Outdoor explorations offer opportunities not available inside the classroom.

> To plant a single pumpkin seed in the garden and watch it grow, to dig in the earth and uncover one very wiggly redworm, to gaze at a spider on a tree branch as it spins an intricate web, to catch snowflakes on the tongue, to watch a hummingbird sip nectar from the crimson phlox, to catch a flashing firefly in a jelly jar—a whole wide world is waiting for young children just outside the door (Hillman, 1995, p. 57).

Outdoor climbing equipment also helps children develop social competence as friendships are developed and maintained.

GENERAL HEALTH AND SAFETY ISSUES

As a part of the total well-being of the child, attention needs to be given to general health issues. "Early health education can begin children on a lifelong process of learning about themselves and their relationships to others and to the world around them" (Hendricks & Smith, 1995, p. 79). The most effective method for children to learn about health, nutrition, and safety is through direct experience rather than admonitions (NAEYC, 1996a). Health education should be included in the daily classroom activities and routines, with the support of adult modeling and direct teaching; it cannot be adequately addressed in occasional themes or units (Hendricks & Smith, 1995). Integrating health education in the early childhood curriculum will include routine health practices, incidental learning (teaching moments), and planned activities. Teachers must also model the importance of health through personal example by frequently washing hands (Newman, 1997), brushing teeth, exercising, and so on. "Health education works best in the framework of a healthy environment and healthy adult behavior" (Kendrick, Kaufmann, & Messenger, 1995, p. 11). Many health concepts appear to be common sense, but for many children they are not habits that they have learned at home. Gentle reminders and encouragement need to be shared and positive reinforcement given when appropriate behaviors are demonstrated.

Health Education Curriculum

An appropriate health education curriculum should include the 10 topics proposed by the Association for the Advancement of Health Education in 1990 (page numbers following topics refer to Hendricks and Smith, 1995):

1. **Personal health.** "To help children establish positive health habits and begin to understand that they are responsible for their own health" (p. 70).

2. **Emotional and mental health.** "To help each child develop a positive self-concept and the ability to identify and express his or her own emotions" (p. 72).

3. **Family life.** "Young children should be aware that many different family structures

exist and be comfortable with their own family structure; and recognize that, as a family member, they have certain rights, privileges, and responsibilities" (p. 73).

4. **Nutrition.** "To foster awareness of different types of foods and to promote exploration and inquiry into food choices" (p. 73).

5. **Disease prevention and control.** To encourage "the practice of personal cleanliness and hygiene" (p. 74).

6. **Injury prevention.** "To help children develop skills in injury prevention and safety" (p. 75).

7. **Community health.** To help children "become familiar and comfortable with health keepers," and "to continue toward commnity-wide health" (p. 75).

8. **Substance use and abuse.** "To help children make informed decisions about *all* substance abuse, including tobacco, alcohol, over-the-counter and prescription medicines, and other drug use and abuse" (p. 77).

9. **Consumer health.** To help children "understand that the purpose of advertisements is to sell products," and to help them "see how advertisements promote both health- and non-health-promoting products" (p. 78).

10. **Environmental health.** To help children "recognize that their behavior directly affects their environment" (p. 78).

The following are some of the concepts to present, depending on specific needs, to your group of children:

- My hands need to be washed often with soap. The Mayo Clinic suggests the following times when handwashing is needed: before eating, preparing food, or setting the table; and after using the bathroom, playing with animals, coughing or sneezing into hands or a tissue, handling money, handling trash, or playing outdoors (Frye, 1993). Washing our hands is the most simple way to avoid infection (Frye, 1993).

- I must have immunizations to prevent diseases.

- If I am ill, I need to stay home so that I do not spread my illness to others. When I sneeze or cough, I need to cover my mouth and nose. After I use a tissue, I must throw it away in the garbage.

- I must brush my teeth every day, at least in the morning and before I go to bed.

Regular brushing of teeth helps to maintain health and prevent disease.

- I must take a bath often and keep my clothing clean and my hair brushed.

- I must go to bed early every night and get a good night's rest.

- I must eat healthy foods.

- I must get adequate physical exercise.

Additional things that staff can do to promote good health and safety include the following (*Pre-K Today*, 1990c, Aug./Sept.; *Pre-K Today*, 1990a, Nov./Dec.):

- Take time to clean and disinfect toilet areas and surfaces.

- Open windows to let in fresh air.

- Make sure permanent health records and emergency cards are up to date for each child.

- Arrange for appropriate sick-child care for the child who comes to school ill or becomes ill during the school day.

The safety of the school, classroom, and playground also needs to be assessed continually. Close supervision is often the best measure for accident prevention. Other considerations include keeping the walking areas free of toys, cords, spills, or loose flooring. Toys should constantly be evaluated for safety, and any with sharp edges, toxic finishes, or small parts should be removed. All cleaning supplies, poisons, and other toxic materials should be out of the reach of children.

Safety in schools is also achieved through establishing civic values, initiating a standard and expectation of cooperation, and teaching conflict resolution (Johnson et al., 1997). In addition, peacemaker conflict resolution includes the following processes: role playing, negotiating, and mediation (Johnson et al., 1997).

Fire safety particularly needs to be addressed with both children and staff. Make sure that your building meets all fire codes. Fire extinguishers and smoke alarms need to be checked regularly to make sure that they are in working order. Go over fire-safety procedures and a fire drill with the staff and children at least monthly. With chil-

Children should learn about health and safety issues in the early childhood classroom. This girl is making a semaphore or stop light for a classroom game involving safety.

dren, use these additional guidelines (*Pre-K Today*, 1990b, Oct.):

- Discuss fire hazards such as the dangers of playing with fire or matches.

- Acquaint children with firefighters and what their roles are, and let them hear an actual fire alarm. Visit the fire station. Teach them exactly what they are to do in case of fire or when they hear the alarm sound.

- Role play the "Stop, Drop, and Roll" drill often.

The health and safety thread needs to be woven into the daily activities of the classroom in early childhood programs. It can be taught during specific units or lessons, but these are aspects of the program that need to be lived and attended to daily.

NUTRITION AND FOOD EXPERIENCES

A significant aspect of personal and social development, especially the healthy development of self, is related to good nutrition. Children who have adequate rest and nutritious, balanced diets are better prepared to learn and are able to handle the stresses in their lives (Marx & Wooley, 1998). During the early childhood years, teachers can have an important impact on fostering good nutrition and healthy eating habits.

Seven Do's for Fostering Good Nutritional Attitudes

1. Modeling appropriate behavior
2. Being positive and using pleasant facial expressions when presenting a new food
3. Eating what the children eat, and eating with them
4. Encouraging, not forcing, children to taste new foods
5. Helping make eating experiences pleasant
6. Remembering that a new food may have to be introduced repeatedly to children before they accept it
7. Not letting one experience limit the opportunity for variety in the children's diet

From Bomba, Oakley, & Knight, 1996.

To grow up healthy, with vitality and energy, children need adequate nutrition. Their early experiences of preparing, tasting, and eating nutritious foods can have an impact on their long-term eating preferences and habits. According to Jungers (1996), most young children know little about the basic food groups and have never tasted many foods with a high nutritional value.

For developmentally appropriate practices relating to the nutrition of young children, only healthy foods should be provided, and eating should be considered a happy and social time (Bredekamp & Copple, 1997). Children generally have a natural curiosity about and interest in food activities. From the time that they are born, food is vital to nurturing; it brings security, comfort, and love. To help children make proper food choices, a wide variety of wholesome foods should be available. In accomplishing these goals, food should neither be used for reward nor withheld as punishment (Bredekamp, 1997).

Being involved in food activities is an important way of teaching good nutrition to young children. In selecting a food experience, one of the first questions that a teacher should ask is, "Will the food be nutritious?" Traditionally, early childhood classrooms have prepared cookies, candies, ice cream, and other foods that provide little nutritional value or have a low nutrient density. Most preschool programs provide a time for snack and opportunity for occasional food activities, and careful judgment must be used with both. To judge whether a food should be served as a snack, we must determine whether the food is part of the basic food groups and is nutritious. Acceptable snacks can be chosen from each food group. These are also excellent criteria for any other food prepared or served in the early childhood education classroom.

Nutrition Education

Nutrition education is most successful in the early childhood years when health-promoting concepts and behaviors are more easily learned. Young children who have participated in nutrition-education programs

- Report eating more desirable foods and nutrients
- Express more positive attitudes toward eating fruits and vegetables
- Are able to apply nutrition-education behavior in the classroom (McDonald, Burns, & Esserman, 1981)

For healthy development of the self, nutrition must be of primary concern to early childhood teachers and can be integrated into many curriculum areas. Nutrition units, as well as food activities, should be planned carefully to teach nutrition concepts specifically and directly to children. Listed at the end of this chapter are many excellent curriculum guides on nutrition for preschool and primary-grade children. As a nation, we are becoming more concerned about this important aspect of health and well-being. Articles, books, programs, school units, extension programs, and White House conferences all have served to alert and educate us. Councils such as the national or state Dairy Councils® are an excellent resource for nutrition information and teaching materials. Nutrition activities should encourage children to explore the limitless potential for learning by providing open-ended experiences that allow them to extend their understanding beyond any specifically outlined objectives. Children should

- Be able to eat in a matter-of-fact way sufficient quantities of the foods that are given to them, just as they take care of other daily needs

- Be able to manage the feeding process independently and without unnecessary dawdling or hurried eating

- Be willing to try new foods in small portions the first time these foods are served and try them again and again until they are at least willing to eat a bite or two when served (Fuhr & Barclay, 1998, p. 75)

It is easier to learn to like new foods during the earlier childhood years than it is in later years (Nahikian-Nelms & Mogharrehan, 1994). Children are also very receptive during these early years to understanding the basics involved in nutrition and the importance it plays in our lives (Swadener, 1995).

Although we choose food and nutrition activities with objectives that we desire to achieve, numerous other learnings occur as children are (and should be) allowed to explore in an attempt to answer the questions How? Why? What if? How come? and I wonder.

Many early childhood programs, such as day care or Head Start, serve complete meals. The subject of nutrition provides many learning opportunities, and it must not be viewed as only preparing, serving, and cleaning-up food activities. The potential for nutrition education in the early childhood program is limitless!

It is more difficult today to remain aware of nutritional values because of prepackaging, vending machines, and fast-food restaurants. We subtly teach children that sweets are the best kinds of food when we make comments such as "Eat your salad and meatloaf, and then you can have your cake and ice cream."

It is imperative that both children and parents be well educated in nutrition. It would be beneficial to plan parent meetings and workshops to educate parents on good nutrition. Children are building bodies that are to last them a lifetime, and both children and parents must know that the food that they eat has a direct relationship to the quality of their health. They must be informed of the interaction between early eating choices and habits and the development of diet-related diseases later in life. Nutritionally healthy eating habits are acquired early in life. The goal of nutrition education should be that children eat a well-balanced, nutritional diet that contains a variety of foods and that teaches children to make wise food choices. Eating habits that condition children to consume processed foods or foods high in sugar, salt, and fat are physically detrimental and instill in children a taste for foods that are unhealthy.

People in the United States each consume about 100 pounds of sugar annually. Sugar-laden foods provide empty calories and dull the appetite, leaving children uninterested in nutritious foods. In addition, overconsumption of sugar causes dental caries. Caregivers must try to reduce children's sugar consumption by avoiding high-sugar foods, selecting alternative natural sources of sweetness, and finding ways to celebrate special events other than with sugary foods (Rogers & Morris, 1986). Sugar substitutes or artificial sweeteners should not be ingredients in the diets of young children unless specified by a physician. More than a decade ago the surgeon general of the United States issued a report titled "Healthy People," in which he urged Americans to eat a diet lower in cholesterol, saturated fat, sugar, and salt.

Values of Food Experiences

Families today are eating fewer meals together, and they are eating more fast foods and snack foods. All family members need to be taught to eat a well-balanced diet and select nutritional foods. As teachers, we send many messages about food and nutrition to young children in the ways that we use specific foods for room decorations and teaching materials. Frequently, we display more desserts than fruits, vegetables, or grains.

The sensory experiences in food activities offer the greatest learning value. In addition, children enjoy working with and manipulating food—mixing, measuring, pouring, stirring, and eating. Food experiences provide natural means for exploring and developing basic concepts such as size, shape, number, color, measurement, weight, smell, taste, sound, touch, texture, flavor, preservation, and temperature change. Food activities provide opportunities for increasing language skills and labels. Teachers can teach what a particular food is, where it comes from, what it looks like, and how it compares to familiar and unfamiliar foods. Children can describe and label foods, equipment being used, and what is being done with the food (grating, mashing, kneading, stirring, beating, pouring, spreading, grinding, or peeling). Food experiences offer opportunities for teaching safety concepts and proper use of utensils, such as knives, forks, beaters, and peelers. If a stove, hot plate, or frying pan is being used for cooking, children can be taught safety concepts related to fire and heat. Cleanliness must also be stressed: children should be encouraged to wash their hands before any food activity and to help to clean up.

The value of snack time's contribution to the development of healthy social–emotional growth in young children is often overlooked. "It is an intimate, comforting break in which children gain physical and emotional nourishment" (Murray, 2000, p. 43). It also encourages the growth of cognitive learning as valuable preschool concepts are practiced. So that children are not required to wait unnecessarily, food should be ready before they are called to meals or snacks (Bredekamp & Copple, 1997), unless the preparation of the food involves the children. Especially for toddlers, bowls, spoons, and cups should be easy to handle. Children also benefit from working cooperatively as a team while interpreting directions in the recipe, following sequences, and keeping time. Social values include learning table manners, sharing, and developing appropriate eating habits. The children's self-images are enhanced as they set the table, prepare the food, eat their own product, and then clean up.

Many local health departments do not allow homemade food items to be brought into the classroom. Dahl (1998) suggests that parents bring recipes and ingredients into the classroom and make or bake the food with the children. If you do not have access to kitchen facilities, consider acquiring a small refrigerator, convection oven, and electric frying pan (Dahl, 1998).

Cooking provides an excellent way to integrate curriculum learning in the classroom. It can involve:

- Reading, writing, and drawing
- Math and problem solving
- Science
- Multicultural activities
- Creativity
- Social skills
- Independence
- Language and communication
- Following directions

Working with recipes provides young children with foundational understandings of measuring and fraction concepts: They can best learn the concept of one-half by measuring

$\frac{1}{2}$ cup water,

$\frac{1}{2}$ teaspoon vanilla,

$\frac{1}{2}$ apple,

and so on. Also, working with food recipes exposes children to concepts relating to various units of measure. Collecting and sampling recipes from diverse cultures helps children to develop an awareness of and respect for people of many cultures and backgrounds. This is also an excellent way to encourage parental involvement.

Murray (2000) suggests the use of place mats during snack time and food activities that have been decorated with the child's name and photo. These place mats help to:

- Define "personal spaces"
- Provide visual cues to assist in organization
- Focus child's attention

- Facilitate matching, comparison, and contrast skills
- Contribute to feelings of belonging and sense of self
- Increase fine-motor development skills
- Encourage understanding of one-to-one correspondence

Food and Nutrition Concepts

Many of the following food and nutrition concepts can be incorporated as objectives for food experiences, meals, and snacks. A teacher's understanding of these concepts makes classroom food activities more interesting and educational.

1. Nutrition is the process by which we assimilate or absorb food.

2. Food helps us live, grow, acquire energy, and stay healthy.

3. There are many varieties of foods.

4. Foods vary in shape, color, size, flavor, texture, smell, and sound.

5. The quality of food is influenced by how it is grown, processed, stored, and prepared.

6. Animals and plants are sources of foods.

7. Foods can be prepared for eating in various ways: raw, cooked (fried, boiled, steamed, baked), canned, frozen, or dried.

8. Food selection and eating are influenced by many factors:

   a. society
   b. culture
   c. economy
   d. preparation
   e. cleanliness
   f. manners
   g. appearance
   h. season
   i. traditions
   j. availability
   k. cost
   l. individual and family habits
   m. preferences
   n. mass media
   o. celebrations
   p. atmosphere or environment
   q. weather
   r. taste
   s. person's age
   t. health

9. Foods may be classified into various categories.

   a. breads
   b. cereal, seeds, grains
   c. dried beans, peas, lentils
   d. eggs
   e. fruits
   f. meat
   g. milk and cheese
   h. nuts
   i. pastas
   j. vegetables

10. A healthy diet includes foods selected from each of the categories in item 9.

Many children believe that foods originate in the supermarket, vending machine, or restaurant. Children need to know where foods come from and have opportunities to help in preparing wholesome foods. Children's diets often include large quantities of soda pop, potato chips, french fries, candy, and other sweets such as cookies, cakes, jams, and jellies. These may be termed *junk foods*; nutritionists label them *foods with low nutrient density*, which means that they have few nutrients in relation to their calories. These kinds of foods are not appropriate for preschool children because they lead to poor nutrition habits and obesity, and they take the place of more important foods. Teachers of young children should be aware of opportunities to help children to learn to select and enjoy nutrient-dense foods, those with a high ratio of nutrients to calories. Examples are fruits, vegetables, dairy products, and meats. Children can learn that certain foods aid and support good health, while others do not. The key to adequate nutrition is variety, which means that many different foods are needed in order for the body to develop and grow normally.

The primary focus in this text is on nutritious food activities for use with young children. White flour is often replaced by whole-grain or wheat flour; sugar content in the recipes is reduced or completely eliminated; flavored gelatins are replaced by unflavored gelatin and fruit juices in most cases.

The food guide pyramid, developed in 1992, illustrates a balanced diet that includes greater amounts of bread, cereal, rice, and pasta; medium amounts of vegetables and fruit; lesser amounts of dairy products, meat, poultry, fish, beans, eggs, and nuts; and least amounts of fats, oils, and sweets. Even young children can learn to follow the Daily Food Guide Pyramid (National Dairy Councils®; see Fig. 7–1) in order to ensure a well-balanced diet. This pyramid was developed by the U.S. Department of Agriculture to provide a guide to eating for good health. The five major groups that form the pyramid are described here.

Grain Group (Bread, Cereal, Rice, and Pasta)

- Six to eleven servings daily.
- Select only whole-grain and enriched or fortified products, but include *some* whole-grain bread or cereals for sure!

- Includes all products made with whole grains or enriched flour or meal: bread, biscuits, muffins, waffles, pancakes, cooked or ready-to-eat cereal, cornmeal, flour, grits, macaroni, spaghetti, noodles, rice, rolled oats, barley, and bulgur.

Vegetable Group

- Three to five servings daily.
- Frequently include deep yellow or dark green vegetables (for vitamin A).
- Include other vegetables, such as potatoes.

Fruit Group

- Two to four servings daily.
- Include one citrus fruit or other fruit that is a good source of vitamin C.
- Frequently include unpeeled fruits and those with edible seeds such as berries (for fiber).

Helping children learn about the foods in the Food Guide Pyramid will encourage them to eat healthy foods and also to taste unfamiliar fruits and vegetables.

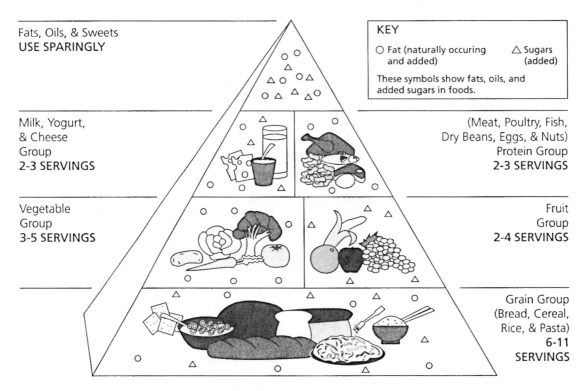

Fats, Oils, & Sweets
USE SPARINGLY

KEY
○ Fat (naturally occuring and added)   △ Sugars (added)
These symbols show fats, oils, and added sugars in foods.

Milk, Yogurt, & Cheese Group
2-3 SERVINGS

(Meat, Poultry, Fish, Dry Beans, Eggs, & Nuts) Protein Group
2-3 SERVINGS

Vegetable Group
3-5 SERVINGS

Fruit Group
2-4 SERVINGS

Grain Group (Bread, Cereal, Rice, & Pasta)
6-11 SERVINGS

HOW TO USE THE FOOD GUIDE PYRAMID

What counts as one serving?

The amount you eat may be more than one serving. For example, a normal dinner portion of spaghetti would count as two or three servings. Most serving sizes for children are slightly less.

Breads, Cereals, Rice and Pasta
1 slice of bread, dinner roll or biscuit
1/2 cup of cooked rice or pasta
1/2 cup of cooked cereal
1 ounce of ready-to-eat cereal
1/2 of a bagel, english muffin, hamburger or hot dog roll

Milk, Yogurt and Cheese
1 cup of milk or yogurt
1 & 1/2 to 2 ounces of cheese
2 cups of cottage cheese

Vegetables
1/2 cup of chopped raw or cooked vegetables
1 cup of leafy raw vegetables
3/4 cup of vegetable juice

Meat, Poultry, Fish, Dry Beans, Eggs and Nuts
1 ounce of cooked lean meat, poultry or fish
1/2 cup of cooked dry beans, peas or lentils
1 egg
2 tablespoons of peanut butter

Fruits
1 "fist size" piece of fruit or melon wedge
3/4 cup of juice
1/2 cup of canned fruit
1/4 cup of dried fruit

Fats, Oils and Sweets
This includes foods such as salad dressings, cream, butter, margarine, sugars, soft drinks, candies, sweet desserts and alcoholic beverages. Remember that fats, oils and sugars are in all food groups.

FIGURE 7–1
The Food Guide Pyramid

Milk Group (including Yogurt and Cheese)

- Two to three servings daily.
- Children aged 2 to 7 should have 2 to 3 cups of milk per day.
- Includes milk in any form: whole, skim, low-fat, evaporated, buttermilk, and nonfat dry milk; also yogurt, ice cream, and ice milk; and cheese, including cottage cheese.

Protein Group (Meat, Poultry, Fish, Dried Beans, Eggs, and Nuts)

- Two to three servings daily.
- Includes beef, veal, lamb, poultry, pork, fish, shellfish, dry beans or peas, soybeans, lentils, eggs, seeds, nuts, peanuts, and peanut butter.

Most other foods fit into a sixth, or "others" category of fats, oils, and sweets. This is not a food group, and foods in this category should be used sparingly. This area includes such foods as butter, margarine, mayonnaise, candy, sugar, jams, jellies, and unenriched, refined bakery products. These kinds of foods provide calories, but relatively low levels of vitamins, minerals, and protein compared to the number of calories.

Food Activities

Food experiences planned in the classroom must be well organized and explicitly planned, and adequate time must be allowed for completion. If the food activity takes place in small cooperative groups, care should be taken to explain the procedures and methods to the teachers working with these groups, and each group should have its own copy of the recipe. If the activity takes place in a large group, the recipe could be written on the chalkboard or an experience chart. The teacher should discuss the recipe, ingredients, and procedures with the children before they begin.

Tasting experiences can easily be set up in a classroom as an interest center for use during free play, or they can be group activities. Children can taste several different foods, such as familiar foods, unfamiliar foods, different foods with similar fla-vors, or different forms of such foods as potatoes or tomatoes.

Children can also be introduced to new and interesting foods. It may be wise to begin with sensory experiences other than tasting. For example, the children may be encouraged to smell, feel, listen to, and look at a new food before tasting it. New foods can also be compared with familiar foods. For example, lima beans or kidney beans can be compared to familiar beans, Brussels sprouts to cabbage, an avocado to a pear, a lime to a lemon, a kiwi to a strawberry. It should also be remembered that, when first introducing children to a new food or unfamiliar recipe, very small servings should be given. The family style of serving, in which the children serve themselves, is preferred.

Another food activity consists of acquainting children with the origins of foods. Many children assume that milk, for example, comes from the store or the milk delivery person, rather than from the cow. This activity provides an opportunity for teaching categorization games. Children can sort picture cards into categories, such as plant products or animal products. Even more specifically, cards could be sorted into underground plant products, tree products, vine products, cow products, and so on. Also, picture or flash cards can be used simply for naming the food item. Pictures can be found in magazines or discarded workbooks, or stickers can be purchased from stationery stores.

Foods and food activities can be integrated into every aspect of the curriculum in early childhood. "Cooking activities in the classroom lend themselves to a whole realm of marvelous learning opportunities for children" (Klefstad, 1995, p. 32), including language arts–reading readiness, math, science, fine-motor skills, art, health, music, and social studies (L. Bennett, 1995; Klefstad, 1995). Most learning is through the senses, and since food appeals to all senses, it is a powerful learning tool. In physical development, there is opportunity for both small- and large-muscle coordination. In mathematics or number work, there are experiences for counting, classifying, and measuring. In science, possibilities abound for using the process skills in food activities—questioning, observing, interpreting, categorizing, and solving problems. There are opportunities for studying and discovering the nature and origin of foods, the changes that they make from seed to maturity, and their physical properties. In terms of social studies, children can study cultural aspects of foods and become acquainted with other people and the foods common to their culture, ethnic group, or region. For example, baking and studying about breads from many cultures and countries is an excellent activity for children of all ages (L. Bennett, 1995) and exemplifies a common food staple among various people all over the world.

Opportunities for language and literacy development are limitless: learning new words, reading directions and labels, following recipes, questioning, and naming and labeling foods are just some of the language activities inherent in food activities. There are also possibilities for art and creative expression. Many food projects, such as salads or sculptures, are creative processes in themselves. With foods such as a pineapple slice, a lettuce leaf, one-half of a banana, and a maraschino cherry, there is no limit to creative ideas (for example a candlestick or a tree). In music, children can do creative movements to interpret the growth of plants and changes made in preparing in foods. Empty food containers are useful as shakers or music instruments. In addition, every food activity provides practice in socialization as children learn patience, sharing, respect for one another, and cooperation.

Food Activity Guidelines

Foods, whether approached as a general area or as specific food items, make excellent choices for unit themes. The following ideas for activities have been grouped into basic food groups, although this approach to teaching is not the only possibility. For example, a unit may be presented on dairy products, the cow, milk, or the person who delivers milk. These suggestions for activities could fit into a variety of units. A food activity can be included in a unit as an unrelated activity; therefore, many of the suggestions given here could be utilized in any unit to support food activities.

Considerations for Integrating Food Activities into the Curriculum

1. Plan and organize all cooking activities. Generally, the younger the child, the more simple the project, perhaps one or two steps.

Practice making the food activity yourself before doing it with the children.
2. Make sure that all foods, utensils, and other items necessary for cooking are ready and assembled.
3. Plan adequate time for the food activity, remembering that children take longer to prepare foods than adults. Allow enough time to question, taste, touch, smell, discover, and compare. Utilize each step in the food activity as a learning experience.
4. Show the children a copy of the recipe so that they know that specific directions must be followed. Write the recipe on a large chart or on individual cards for small groups. Draw pictures or use children's recipe books with directions in picture form. Review the recipe before starting the activity.
5. Adhere to rules of cleanliness: wash hands before beginning, wipe up spills as you go, and involve the children in cleaning the area at the end of the activity.
6. Follow all safety rules appropriate for the particular food activity. Demonstrate proper use of utensils and supervise their use. Caution about the dangers of hot items and electric appliances.
7. Provide for unlimited learning by allowing the children to explore the questions of How? Why? What if? How come? and I wonder.

APPROACH TO TEACHING

Fruits and Vegetables

Fruits and vegetables can be approached either in general units or in units featuring specific fruit or vegetable concepts. The children should first be made aware of the foods growing in the local surroundings, and units can easily take advantage of particular growing seasons.

In general or specific units on fruits or vegetables, some of the following concepts could be incorporated:

• Where and how the food grows: on a tree, underground, on a vine, in a pod, on a bush; singly or in bunches

When children assist in the preparation and serving of nutritious foods, they are more likely to make choices independently to eat healthy foods.

- Growing climate and season
- Number, size, and location of seeds
- How to tell when the food is ripe
- Various forms and preparations of the food: fresh or cooked; mashed, sliced, cubed, shredded, crushed, juiced, or chunked
- Varieties or kinds of the food (apples: Jonathan, Roman Beauty, Delicious; beans: kidney, green, lima, pinto)
- Sizes
- Colors (ripe compared to unripe; variations in different kinds)
- Parts to be eaten (skin, seeds, leaves, pulp)
- Methods of storage and preservation (freeze, can, dehydrate)

See Figure 7–2 for a project web on beans. There are actually foods from two different food groups in this project, green beans from the vegetable group and dried beans from the protein group. This can be explained during the project.

 **UNIT PLAN ON FRUITS OR VEGETABLES (GENERAL OR SPECIFIC)**

Note: Some of the listed activities may be related to specific fruits or vegetables. Make appropriate selections to suit your plans. Also see Figure 7–3 for a web on apples.

Field Trips

- Processing plant or cannery
- Orchard, garden, grove, farm, before, during, and after harvest
- Food stand
- Grocery store
- Sorting shed
- Ride on pickup wagon during harvest
- Fruit and vegetable picking

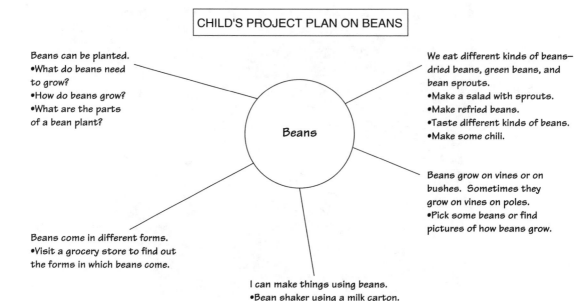

FIGURE 7–2
Child's Project Plan on Beans

- Truck loading freight for store
- Bakery
- Ice cream store
- Nursery or greenhouse

Visitors

- Orchard, garden, grove, farm owner
- Person demonstrating food storage and preservation
- Grocer
- Fruit or vegetable picker
- Food stand salesperson
- Employee of cannery or processing plant
- Baker
- Ice cream maker, to demonstrate the use of fruits in ice cream
- Employee of nursery or greenhouse
- Home economist from county extension service

Food

- Making jam, jelly
- Making juice
- Blending fruits or vegetables into drinks or shakes
- Peeling, slicing, grating, mashing foods
- Fruit or vegetable salad
- Fruit or vegetable pies, pastries, or turnovers
- Fruit or vegetable leather
- Sherbet or ice cream
- Gelatin salad
- Cobbler, strudel, or crisp
- Baked vegetables or fruits
- Fruit cocktail
- Stew
- Soup
- Casserole
- Fruit or vegetable cake, cookies

- Fruits and vegetables used with dips, cheese fondues, white sauces
- Breads

Science

- Observation of food during the decaying process
- Tasting familiar and unfamiliar foods
- Observation of wormy food
- Where food grows: trees, vines, or shrubs; above, under, or on the ground; in gardens, orchards, or farms
- Edible parts: peelings, seeds, flesh, stem, root, flower
- Number of seeds: many, few, one
- Size of seeds
- Number of sections
- Kinds of food that taste the same
- Kinds of food that taste different
- Sizes of food
- Textures of food
- Noise made during chewing: loud or soft
- Seed or plant in classroom, cared for by children
- Observation of various types of one specific food
- Smells of vegetables and fruits
- Climates and seasons of food
- Preservation of food
- Seeds sprouted for tasting or use with other foods
- Method of teaching how plants obtain water: piece of celery is cut in half lengthwise, but not all the way up; each half is put in glasses of different-colored water; within a short time, the leaves at the top of the stalk will be the same color as the water, with the veins of the stalk also filled with colored water

Art

- Pieces of food traced on paper
- Food shapes cut from paper

- Pictures of food cut from magazines
- Seed collages
- Collages made from food pictures
- Shakers made from empty food containers
- Paintings or printings on food shapes
- Food sculpture: pieces of vegetables and/or fruits attached to a base with toothpicks (prepared for eating later)
- Food puppets: drawn or outlined; then decorated or given faces; then cut out and mounted on tongue depressors, dowels, or sticks

Music

- Shakers made with seeds on inside and outside, shaken while singing and marching; shaken loudly, softly, quickly, slowly, like an elephant walks, like a kitten creeps
- Musical chairs: pieces of fruits or vegetables placed on chairs for children to identify when they sit down
- Creative movement: children pretending to be various fruits or vegetables being planted, picked, harvested, falling to the ground
- Singing of expandable songs in which fruit or vegetable names can be included

Language and Literacy

- Booklets made by class or individuals on "Fruits (or Vegetables) I (or We) Like"
- Fruits and vegetables cut from magazines and made into a booklet with children's descriptions of them

Additional Activities

- Unusual fruit or vegetable presented for tasting and for exploring with a magnifying glass
- Trough or tubs filled with soil, then foods planted; root vegetables or bush fruits placed in the soil just as they grow
- Trough filled with pea, potato, bean vines (vegetables to be eaten)

See Figure 7–3 for a project web on apples.

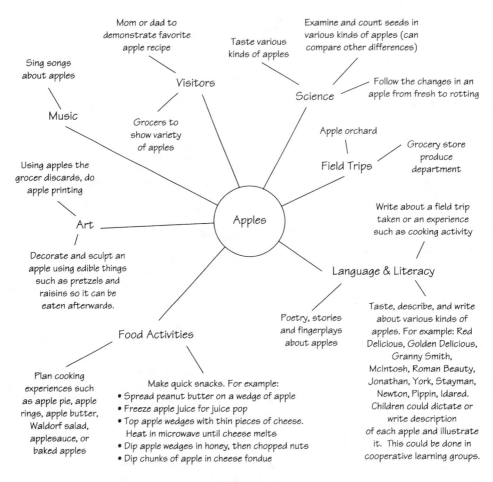

FIGURE 7–3
Project Web on Apples

Grain, Rice, and Pasta Products

Cereals, like the other food groups, can be approached in many ways as units. Units might be presented on wheat, breads, macaroni, rice, or oats. When any of these units are taught, some of the following ideas could be incorporated as teaching concepts or goals:

- Where and how the grain grows
- How it looks when it is ready to harvest
- How the seeds of some of the grains (for example, wheat) can be used:

eaten raw, sprouted, or in food preparation.

- Number of forms in which the cereal or grain can be eaten.

Perhaps one of the most stimulating units features wheat, including experiences with raw wheat, cooked whole-wheat cereal, and wheat ground into whole-wheat flour to be used in many different food activities.

The following is a suggested unit plan for bread; for a unit plan on wheat and flour, see Chapter 11.

UNIT PLAN ON BREAD

Art

- Sculptured bread dough: worked and molded, then baked and eaten
- Sculpture made with different kinds of breads: small cubes or pieces of rye bread, sweet bread, sourdough, and so on, may be combined with chunked fruits and/or vegetables (prepare to be eaten later); Styrofoam base could be used

Food

- Open-faced sandwiches made in different shapes: cookie cutters used to cut shapes of bread; spreads or toppings added
- Toast or cinnamon toast (no sugar)
- French toast
- Rolls: any kind, in any shape
- Bread: pumpkin, zucchini, onion, honey, raisin, or garlic
- Dilly bread, made with cottage cheese and onions
- Muffins
- Biscuits
- Blueberry muffins, rolls, bread
- Scones, made from bread dough or sweet bread dough
- Eggs in a ring: cut hole in center of a slice of bread, butter both sides, put in frying pan, break egg into center of bread; turn when white begins to look firm
- Canned refrigerator biscuit recipes (listed at the end of this chapter)

Field Trips

- Bakery
- Cafeteria or other restaurant where breads are prepared
- Child's home where a parent is baking bread

- Zoo or other place where animals are fed bread or bread crumbs
- Grocery store: kinds, shapes of bread; bread products

Visitors

- Baker
- Parent: rolls made in interesting and unusual shapes
- Home economist or community nutritionist
- Bread deliverer: delivery truck brought, if possible; children encouraged to climb in and observe many kinds and forms of bread

Music

- Songs relating to bread

Science

- Discussion of grains used to make breads (wheat emphasized)
- Kinds of bread and their different tastes; tasting activities
- Observation of process of grinding wheat into flour
- Comparison of taste, texture, and smell of raw versus cooked bread: dough form compared to baked form
- Comparison of size of bread before and after baking: combine

  $\frac{1}{4}$ cup sugar,

  two packages dry yeast, and

  $\frac{1}{2}$ cup warm water;

  put mixture into pop bottle with balloon over neck of bottle; mixture causes air to expand in the bottle, just as it does in the bread; balloon inflates
- Animals that eat breads and/or bread crumbs (birds, insects); ant farm, with a focus on observing the ants as they carry bread crumbs

Language and Literacy

- "Little Red Riding Hood": story adapted so that the children will not be frightened; used as object story by focusing on the different breads that filled her basket; sampling of such breads

- Make booklet of different kinds of breads. 🔡

Dairy Products

Milk can be used in such foods as baked custard, yogurt, and soups such as cream of potato. Cream can be used in foods such as ice cream, or whipped cream can be used in desserts, in salads, and as a topping on gingerbread or other cakes.

Butter made by the children and then spread on bread or crackers can be made in several ways. Approximately one-half pint of whipping cream should be left out to warm to room temperature and then put into a container with a tight lid. As the children shake the container, the cream separates and becomes butter. Yellow food coloring and salt may then be added and the buttermilk drained off. To allow each child to make butter, a small amount of room-temperature cream can be put into a baby food jar and shaken until butter forms. How delighted the child will be to take the butter home and share it with the family (if it lasts that long)! From this activity the children will learn that butter comes from cream, which is a product of the cow.

Sour cream and plain yogurt are used in making dips, fruit salads, and stroganoff and as a topping on baked potatoes. Cottage cheese is used plain, as well as in making salads, dilly bread, chip dips, lasagna, and other dishes. Many recipes for casseroles, desserts, sandwiches, dips, tacos, and so on, use other cheese. The children can learn that cheese comes in many different forms, such as spreads, cream cheese, bricks, curds, melted, or grated.

🔡 *UNIT PLAN ON DAIRY PRODUCTS*

Art

- Cheese sculpturing: more economical if used in combination with additional foods, such as fruits and vegetables (then eaten)
- Collages made with magazine pictures of dairy products: additional media such as yarn and paper scraps can be added for variety

- Decoration of milk cartons to be used as litter containers, planters, or puppets
- Musical shakers made with milk cartons, cream cartons, cottage cheese containers; decorated with glue and collage items, or by dipping paper scraps, tissue paper, and other materials into liquid starch and then putting them on the carton

Science

- Milk separating
- Butter made from cream
- Milk curdling
- Discussion of the need for milk in the diets of both animal and human babies; actual experience of seeing babies drinking milk

Music

- Creative dramatics: exploring such movements as milking a cow or dramatizing a cow chewing its cud, swatting flies with its tail
- Rhythm shakers: milk cartons (half-pint size easiest to handle) or cottage cheese cartons partially filled with rice, beans, wheat, or other grains

Field Trips

- Dairy farm
- Cheese factory
- Creamery
- Dairy
- Grocery store
- Milk depot

Visitors

- Dairy farmer
- Grocer
- Ice-cream shop proprietor: may discuss flavors, colors, ingredients
- Person who delivers milk (and the milk truck, if possible)
- Person to make a food product in class using milk

Food

- Any of the activities presented and discussed previously
- Any food activity featuring dairy products
- Tasting different forms of milk (skim milk, buttermilk, evaporated milk, condensed milk, cream)
- Tasting and using different kinds of cheeses
- Making butter
- Making ice cream

Language and Literacy

- Experience charts relating to trips, visitors, movies, and other activities
- Poetry and story writing
- Movie, *The Cow:* opportunities for sensory experiences with young children; speaking or writing about experiences in the film
- Stories and poems about cows, dairies, and persons who deliver milk

Protein Products

Meat units most often tie in with animal units in which meat is the product of the animal. For example, a unit on beef cows could elaborate on different forms of beef: hamburger, steaks, roasts, wieners, liver, stew meat, and others. In a unit such as this, it is not necessary to have food experiences with each form of beef. The children synthesize the concept of beef and its different forms by observing pictures of these different meat cuts and by visiting a butcher shop or meat market to see various meat cuts.

Additional meat units could include pigs (bacon, sausage, wieners, pork chops, pork roast), poultry (turkey, chicken, eggs), and fish (tuna, salmon, halibut, trout, shrimp, cod, turbot). A general area of meat could be approached as a unit, with subcategories such as those just listed (beef, pork, fish, poultry, etc.).

Whatever approach is chosen in developing units of study on meat, teaching should include both the origins and methods of preparation for the various meats. The taste of the meat changes as the method of preparation is varied: For example, the taste of chicken varies according to whether it is fried, put in a salad, baked, and so on.

The following unit plans present each of the basic meat categories. Again, these categories can be combined and activities selected for teaching a general unit on meat. These suggested activities could also be applied to other meats, such as wild game or sheep.

Note: Foods such as cheese, bacon, eggs, and fried foods are high in cholesterol and should be used in moderation.

UNIT PLAN ON BEEF COWS AND BEEF PRODUCTS

Art

- Paper-sack cow puppets
- Pictures of cows painted or drawn
- Print with designs similar to cattle brands

Music

- Creative movements or dramatics: dramatizing an auction or a roundup, lassoing a cow or calf, branding
- "Galloping" music: children pretending to lasso or herd cattle

Food

- Hamburger

  Foil dinners

  Spaghetti

  Pizza

  Casseroles

  Meatloaf

  Patties: baked, fried, or broiled

  Tacos

  Lasagna

  Unusual foreign foods

- Wieners

  Pizza

  Casseroles

Broiled, boiled, or fried

Sliced with cheese in the center and broiled or microwaved

• Stew

• Soups made from beef soup bone, hamburger, or stew meat

• Chili

• Beef pie or shepherd's pie made from leftover roast or stew meat

Field Trips

• Livestock auction

• Grocery store

• Farm to observe beef cattle

• Butcher shop to see beef carcass and meat cuts

• Child's home, where parent will show meat cuts in freezer and/or cook a beef cut such as a roast

Visitors

• Leather tanner or tooler

• Parent to cook some beef cut

• Butcher

• Rancher

• Cowboy or cowgirl

Science

• Comparing size of meat before and after cooking (meat shrinkage)

• Preservation of beef: frozen, canned, dried; discussion of what happens when not properly preserved

• Observing the processing of meats such as hamburger or wieners: grinding, seasoning, and others

• Observing a carcass

• Uses and preparation of leather

• Tasting different forms of beef: jerky, liver, steaks, roasts, and others

• Diet of beef cow: hay and silage in winter, grass in summer

• Calves: appearance after birth, diet, growth changes

Language and Literacy

• Stories and poems relating to cows

• Creative story and poetry writing

• Films, filmstrips relating to cows

• Class or individual booklet titled "I Like Beef"

UNIT PLAN ON POULTRY AND POULTRY PRODUCTS

Art

• Paper-sack chicken puppets

• Painting with chicken feathers

• Collages made with chicken feathers

• Eggshell collages: colored with egg coloring or food coloring mixed in alcohol or water; may be combined with media such as chicken feathers, cut straws, or paper scraps

• Chicken wings made to wear on the children's arms: attach with string and decorate with feathers, paper scraps, and other objects; beak made out of paper (could be used for creative movement)

Music

• Creative movements or dramatics: dramatizing chickens and their movements; a chick pecking its way out of the shell, learning to stand and walk, drinking water, eating

Food

• Eggs

Eggnog (commercial or cooked)

Baked, fried, broiled, scrambled, poached

French toast

Custard

Bakery products using eggs as ingredients

Desserts using eggs

Omelets

• Chicken

Croquettes

Baked, fried, broiled

Casserole

Salad

Sandwiches

Ground chicken used as chicken spread

Chicken and dumplings

Chicken pie

Chicken soup

Stir fry

Field Trips

- Poultry farm
- Grocery store: observation of chicken in meat section, eggs in dairy section, and canned chicken
- Hatchery
- Place where egg candling and sorting can be seen
- Child's home: parent to show poultry cuts in freezer, cook poultry cuts such as chicken, make chicken casserole or salad
- Restaurant selling or specializing in chicken

Visitors

- Parent to prepare chicken product: possibly an unusual product such as an omelet, cooked eggnog, or chicken croquettes
- Poultry farmer
- Someone to demonstrate egg candling
- Butcher

Science

- Parts of eggs: shell, yolk, white
- Process of beating eggs or egg whites: become foamy as air is beaten in
- Eggs used as thickening
- Various kinds of eggs: brown, white; chicken, turkey, swan, duck, bird
- Hatching of chicks in an incubator: watching as they peck out of the shell and then grow to be mature hens and roosters

- Candling of eggs
- Preservation of eggs: refrigerated, frozen, dried
- Food eaten by chickens

Language and Literacy

- Stories and poems relating to chickens
- Creative story writing: "Chicken Is Good"

Activities and Experiences

1. Prepare a "Basic Five" snack. Using the Food Guide Pyramid (available from your state Dairy Councils®), prepare a snack plate of small, bite-sized pieces of food. As the children use toothpicks to taste each snack, they should identify the corresponding food group. Make sure that at least one food from each food group is included. The following are examples:

   a. Fruits: fruit pieces such as apple, orange, banana
   b. Vegetables: vegetable pieces such as carrots, celery, cauliflower
   c. Bread and cereal: small crackers or pieces of bread (preferably whole grain)
   d. Milk and cheese: small pieces of cheese
   e. Protein group: hard-cooked egg slices, small pieces of meats, such as wieners, cooked ham, or beef

2. Name-a-food game: The teacher tosses a ball or beanbag to a child. When the teacher names a food group, such as milk and cheese, the child must name a food within the food group. Or, if the teacher names a food, the child must name the food group to which it belongs.

3. Sort the foods: Pictures of different foods are pasted on heavy paper or cardboard. The children then name the foods and sort them into the five basic food groups. Or foods can be sorted into two groups: foods that are good for us and foods that are not good for us. (Some seed companies will provide teachers with empty seed packets. The fruit and vegetable packets make excellent pictures for this food group.)

4. Teach the following fingerplay:

> What do we need to grow on? and
> What do we need to go on?
> From head to feet,
> The food we eat
> Is what we go
> And grow on.

5. Favorite food song: Sing to the tune of "Skip to My Lou":

> We have to eat so we might as well eat
> Some food we think is a special treat.
> ————'s my choice. It can't be beat,
> So serve it every Sunday.
> (Second time) So serve it every Monday.
> (and so on through the week)

Assign cooperative groups each a day of the week. When the verse of that day is sung, the group names a favorite food to fill in the blank.

6. Discuss the relationship between food and exercise and the value of exercise. Food gives us energy to run, play, and exercise. We must eat right to have the energy that we need to play, run, and exercise.

> You can't feel fit
> If you just sit.
> Skip and jump and run!
> Play some ball,
> And stretch up tall.
> Exercise is fun.

7. Talk about the different parts of plants that are eaten as vegetables. Let the children taste a sample of each part. For example: leaf (lettuce, spinach); root (carrot, parsnip); flower (cauliflower); stalk or stem (celery); seeds (peas, corn).

8. Obtain a catalog from a nursery or seed distributor and cut out pictures of fruits. Have the children name each fruit and discuss individual characteristics, such as one large seed, skin that is peeled, skin that is eaten, or color. Have tasting samples of some of the unusual fruits, such as dates, fresh pineapple, cranberries, or other fruits of the season that the children may taste less frequently.

9. Fishing for foods: Make fishing poles out of dowels, string, and magnets. Cut food pictures from magazines and catalogs; then attach paper clips. Let the children fish for the foods, and as each food is "caught" its name and/or food group should be mentioned.

10. Food riddles: Make up riddles about foods. For example: "I am a fruit. I am yellow. I have a skin you peel off. I am long and thin and delicious to eat. What am I?" (banana). Break up into cooperative learning groups and have each group make up a riddle.

11. Play "Which One Does Not Belong?" Have a group of three to four pictures. For younger children, three may be foods and one not a food. They need to find the one that does not belong. For older children, have three in one food group and the fourth in another food group, or have three good foods and one food that is not nutritious.

Playing games with balls, both inside and outside the classroom, improves physical fitness and increases confidence.

12. Food sequence: Find or make pictures of the growing or processing stages of a particular food. For example, several pictures could be used in the sequence of wheat to bread. The children put the pictures in the proper sequence.

13. Make a scrapbook of foods grouped into the five food groups. This could be done in five cooperative learning groups with each group assigned a food group.

14. Compare raw and cooked vegetables. For example, compare raw to cooked broccoli or raw to cooked cauliflower.

15. Put different foods, one or a few at a time, into a "feely" box and have the children identify the food by feeling it. If possible, have them tell which food group it belongs to.

16. Have children identify the sources of food: for example, plant, animal, or, even more specifically, milk, potato.

17. Divide the children into cooperative learning groups, using the strategy (see Chapter 4) Numbered Heads Together. Give each group an unfamiliar fruit such as a pomegranate, kiwi, mango, papaya, pineapple, raspberry, or whatever you can find in season and available. Each group will sample the fruit and then prepare a description using descriptive words. Call out a number, and that child in each group will be spokesperson to describe the fruit for the rest of the class.

Summary

Physical education and motor experiences in early childhood must be developmentally appropriate. The physical and motor needs of young children are different from those of elementary-aged children, but can be planned as part of their play experiences as well as integrated into curriculum areas. In all physical fitness activities and games, children enjoy the opportunity of participating, being active, and having fun. Competition is not a necessary ingredient for success in the activities and games. Physical fitness is great play for young children. Through play, children are able to develop understandings in socialization, values and ethics, sense of right and wrong, stress management and relaxation, creativity and curiosity, and occupations and vocations (Huettig & Connor, 1999).

Society as a whole is becoming more aware of the importance of nutrition in maintaining physical and psychological health. This is especially important in the early childhood years, when habits and patterns are being learned and internalized.

Food activities with young children should largely include fruits, vegetables, and grains, with less fat, cholesterol, refined sugar, and salt. Children, by becoming aware of the Food Guide Pyramid ("Basic Five"), are better able to make individual selections that help to ensure a well-balanced diet. Food activities can contribute to learning in every aspect of the curriculum: math, music, social studies, language and literacy, cultural diversity, creative arts, science, and others. When we, as teachers, incorporate sound nutritional concepts into our various teaching experiences, not only will young children benefit now, but the positive influence will be evidenced for years to come. Remember, *learn* to select good, nutritious foods. The foods children eat affect their growth, behavior, and health. Good food habits must be learned; they are not instinctive. As young children participate in a variety of wellness activities, they develop habits that will help ensure their physical, spiritual, emotional, social, and intellectual health throughout their entire life!

Student Learning Activities

1. Select two physical games for any early childhood age and prepare a game sheet with directions. Teach class members one of your games.

2. Begin a file of fitness activities and games appropriate for early childhood. You may wish to group them by categories or ages.

3. Select three unit topics and describe how you would integrate physical–motor activities into the unit.

4. Describe three movement experiences and the locomotor skills involved in your experiences.

5. Interview at least three early childhood teachers and determine how physical and motor development are included in their program. Evaluate the effectiveness of their program.

6. Observe in a classroom to determine what evidence there is of students practicing good health habits. Interview the teacher to determine what she or he does to ensure the children's health and safety needs.

7. Using the Food Guide Pyramid and suggestions from this chapter, plan one snack time and one meal per day for children for a 5-day period.

8. Using the Food Guide Pyramid, plan two days of meals (three meals each day) for children. These meals should be balanced, nutritious, and inviting.

9. Have a group of children try out at least one of the food experiences from each of the five food groups in the recipe section of Appendix B. Evaluate the experiences. Would you use this recipe again? Would you organize the experience in the same way the next time? If not, what changes would you make?

10. Plan an appropriate food experience for children for each of the five food groups.

11. Implement at least one of the food experiences that you have planned with children in item 10. Evaluate the experience. Was it appropriate? Was it organized in the most efficient way? Would you offer the same experience again? If so, would you make any changes?

12. Try out at least two of the food-related activities suggested in this chapter. Where materials are suggested, prepare them. Evaluate each experience.

13. Select a food theme and prepare a project, unit plan, or web on it.

14. Prepare a lesson plan on a food theme. Try to include at least one food experience during the week. Use the unit and lesson plans in this chapter as a guide.

Suggested Resources

Physical and Health Education Guides

American Academy of Pediatrics (prepared by Early Childhood Education Linkage System) (1997). *Model child care health policies—revised 1997*. Washington, DC: National Association for the Education of Young Children.

Ballinger, E. (1996). *The learning gym: Fun-to-do activities for success at school*. San Diego, CA: The Brain Store.

Council on Physical Education for Children (1992). *Developmentally appropriate physical education practices for children*. Reston, VA: American Alliance for Health, Physical Education, Recreation, and Dance.

Council on Physical Education for Children (1994). *Developmentally appropriate movement programs for young children ages 3–5*. Reston, VA: American Alliance for Health, Physical Education, Recreation, and Dance.

Early Childhood Committee of the Pennsylvania Chapter of the American Academy of Pediatrics (1997). *Preparing for illness: A joint responsibility for parents and caregivers—revised 1997*. Washington, DC: National Association for the Education of Young Children.

Hannaford, C. (1995). *Smart moves*. San Diego, CA: The Brain Store.

Jensen, E. (2000). *Learning with the body in mind*. San Diego, CA: The Brain Store.

Kaiser, B., & J. S. Rasminsky (n.d.). *HIV/AIDS and child care: Fact book and facilitator's guide*. Washington, DC: National Association for the Education of Young Children.

Kendrick, A. S., R. Kaufmann, & K. P. Messenger (eds.) (1995). *Healthy young children: A manual for programs*. Washington, DC: National Association for the Education of Young Children.

National Association for Sports and Physical Education (1992). *Outcomes of quality physical education programs*. Reston, VA: American Alliance for Health, Physical Education, Recreation, and Dance.

National Association for Sports and Physical Education (1995).

Moving into the future: National standards for physical education—A guide to content and assessment. St. Louis, MO: Mosby.

Silberg, J. (2000). *125 Brain games for toddlers and twos: Simple games to promote early brain development*. San Diego, CA: The Brain Store.

Sugar, S. (1998). *Games that teach*. San Diego, CA: The Brain Store.

Cookbooks

Avis, J., & K. Ward (1990). *Just for kids*. West Monroe, LA: Avis and Ward.

Baxter, K. M. (1989). *Come and get it: A natural foods cookbook for children*. Ann Arbor, MI: Children First.

Berman, C., & J. Fromer (1991). *Meals without squeals: Child care nutrition guide and cookbook*. Menlo Park, CA: Bull.

Betty Crocker's new boys' and girls' cookbook (1992). Upper Saddle River, NJ: Prentice Hall.

Cheney, S. (1990). *Breadtime stories: A cookbook for bakers and browsers*. Berkeley, CA: Ten Speed.

Christenberry, M. A., & B. Stevens (1985). *Can Piaget cook?* Atlanta, GA: Humanics.

Domke, L. (1991). *Kids cook too!* Rock Hill, SC: Carolina Consultants Network.

Dunkle, J. L., & M. S. Edwards (1992). *The (no leftovers) child care cookbook: Kid-tested recipes and menus for center and home-based programs*. St. Paul, MN: Readleaf.

Faris, D. (ed.) (1987). *Favorite foods for pre-school*. Dallas, TX: Stone Canyon.

Herick, N. (1990). *Natural, nutritious recipes for children*. Birmingham, AL: EBSCO.

Jello desserts kids' stuff recipes (n.d.). Order from General Foods Corp., Kids' Stuff, P.O. Box 4157, Kankakee, IL 60901.

Johnson, B. (1990). *Cup cooking: Individual child-portion picture recipes*. Rainier, MD: Gryphon House.

Kendrick, A. S., R. Kaufmann, & K. Messenger (eds.) (1991). *Healthy young children: A manual for programs*. Washington, DC: National Association for the Education of Young Children.

Moore, C. E., M. Kerr, & J. Shulman (1990). *Young chef's nutrition guide and cookbook*. Hauppauge, NY: Barron.

National Cancer Institute (1997). *Take the 5 a Day challenge.* The 5 a Day Toolkit is an activity-driven curriculum designed to provide teachers with a creative resource for teaching students the significance of eating more fruits and vegetables. The program is available through your state department of health.

Olmsted, C. (1990). *Alphabet cooking cards*. Carthage, IL: Fearon.

Robins, D. (1994). *The kids around the world cookbook*. New York: Kingfisher.

Robson, D. (1991). *Cooking: Hands-on projects*. New York: Watts.

Sledge, S. (1988). *Guess what I made? Recipes for children around the world*. Birmingham, AL: Women's Mission Union.

Stephens, F. (1991). *Baking projects for children: Fun foods to make with children from 4–10*. Nazareth, PA: Murdoch.

U.S. Department of Agriculture, Food & Nutrition Services (1994). *Quantity recipes for child care centers*. FNS-86. Washington, DC: Author.

Wilms, B. (1984). *Crunchy bananas and other great recipes kids can cook*. Layton, UT: Gibbs Smith.

Children's Books

Appelt, K. (1996). *Watermelon day*. New York: Henry Holt.

Bell, S. (1990). *Gingerbread man*. New York: Western.

Brink, C. R. (1995). *Goody O'Grumpity*. New York: North-South.

Brown, M. W. (1959). *Nibble, nibble*. Reading, MA: Addison-Wesley.

Brown, M. W. (1974). *Stone soup*. New York: Scribner's.

Carle, E. (1969). *Very hungry caterpillar*. New York: Philomel.

Carle, E. (1970). *Pancakes, pancakes*. New York: Knopf.

Carle, E. (1997). *From head to toe*. New York: HarperCollins.

DePaola, T. (1978). *The popcorn book*. New York: Holiday House.

Dooley, N. (1991). *Everyone cooks rice*. Minneapolis, MN: Carolrhonda.

Gershator, D., & P. Gershator (1995). *Bread is for eating*. New York: Henry Holt.

Gibbons, G. (2000). *Apples*. New York: Holiday House.

Green, M. (1961). *Everybody has a house and everybody eats*. Reading, MA: Addison-Wesley.

Greenaway, K. (1886). *A–Apple pie*. London: F. Warne.

Hader, B. (1990). *Little red hen*. New York: Smithmark.

Hoban, R. (1964). *Bread and jam for Frances*. New York: Harper & Row.

Krauss, R. (1971). *The carrot seed*. New York: Scholastic.

McCloskey, R. (1946). *Blueberries for Sal*. New York: Viking.

Neitzel, S. (1997). *We're making breakfast for mother*. New York: Greenwillow.

Nelson, N. (1996). *Looking into my body*. Westport, CT: Reader's Digest Young Families.

Numeroff, L. J. (1985). *If you give a moose a muffin*. New York: HarperCollins.

Potter, B. (1903). *The tales of Peter Rabbit*. London: F. Warne.

Sawyer, R. (1953). *Journey cake ho!* New York: Viking.

Sendak, M. (1962). *Chicken soup with rice*. New York: Harper & Row.

Seuss, Dr. (1960). *Green eggs and ham*. New York: Beginner.

Showers, P. (1997). *Sleep is for everyone*. New York: HarperCollins.

Slangerup, Erik J. (2000). *Dirt Boy*. Morton Grove, IL: Albert Whitman.

Swain, R. F. (1999). *Bedtime!* New York: Holiday House.

Tolstoy, A. (1968). *The great big enormous turnip*. New York: Franklin Watts.

Tudor, T. (1962). *Pumpkin moonshine*. New York: Henry Z. Walck.

Weiks, S. (1996). *Noodles*. New York: Harper-Festival.

Tapes and Cassettes

Exercise everyday. *On Learning basic skills through music* (vol. 1). Hap Palmer Record Library (AR526 or AC526).

Fun and fitness for primary children. Bowmar-Noble (B2057).

Kinds of food. On *Learning basic skills through music—vocabulary*. Hap Palmer Record Library (AR521 or AC521).

Your body—How to use food and stay healthy (9). Society for Visual Education.

Pictures, Posters, and Pamphlets

Common fruits. Society for Visual Education.

Daily Food Guide Pyramid handout. National Dairy Council.

Eat the five food group way. National Dairy Council.

Food and nutrition. David C. Cook.

Food models: For early childhood educators. National Dairy Council.

For your good health. David C. Cook.

Fruits and vegetables. Scholastic Book Services.

Keeping healthy: Parents, teachers, and children (brochure). National Association for the Education of Young Children.

Keeping physically fit. The Child's World.

Merrily we roll along (brochure). National Association for the Education of Young Children.

Playgrounds: Safe and sound (brochure). National Association for the Education of Young Children.

Rx for keeping healthy in group programs (poster). National Association for the Education of Young Children.

Videos

How apples grow. National Apple Institute.

The new food pyramid. National Geographic.

Teeth: The better to eat with. National Geographic.

Your Body Series (series includes Circulatory and Respiratory Systems, Muscular and Skeletal Systems, Digestive System, etc.; this series is more appropriate for third grade and intermediate grades). National Geographic

Software

The human body. National Geographic (CD-ROM kit).

The Senses. Sunburst.

Part Three

Cognitive and Literacy Development

From a child's cognitive and literacy growth, he or she is able to construct meaning and build understanding. Language, critical thinking, and science encompass virtually every aspect of the early childhood curriculum. Although creative and aesthetic topics, social studies, and other topics are not included in this part of the text, this should not imply that these areas are not related to cognitive and language development—they are! There is not an area of the curriculum that does not involve cognitive and language competence. However, in this part we will be focusing primarily on literacy and science mastery.

To enhance cognitive and language development, teachers should value inquiry and thoughtfulness. The following unfinished phrases will serve as springboards to deeper thinking for children and are especially appropriate for literacy and science explorations:

What if . . .

I wonder why . . .

Were you surprised that . . .

Did you notice . . .

Did you think about . . .

Did it remind you of . . .

What do you think happened . . .

Can you think of another way to approach . . .

Is there another alternative . . .

How would you feel if . . .

These kinds of questions and inquiries encourage students to question, ponder, analyze, grapple, look for relationships, look below the surface, and think. Children should learn to explain, add to, and validate their responses and answers.

One approach for encouraging children to think is to have them become the teacher. When children explain an idea to someone else, they synthesize that idea into their own thinking more thoroughly. They should be encouraged to observe, question, find out, and then share what they have learned with others.

Thinking—seeking for understanding and meaning—should be the center of all we do with young children. Critical thinking should not be a tacked-on lesson or exercise, but should be part of an integrated approach to the entire curriculum. Teachers should create an environment that stimulates thinking and inquiring.

Literacy learning is a process that begins at birth with language that allows the child to translate raw experiences into meaningful symbols that can be used for both communicating and thinking (Gambrell & Mazzoni, 1999). Literacy involves the speaking, listening, writing, and reading skills. These skills develop concurrently and are interrelated (Gambrell & Mozzoni, 1999). The foundation of literacy is language development. Because the development of language skills begins in infancy

and relies heavily on experiences, children exhibit great differences in their language acquisition and growth. These differences are individual, normal, and acceptable. Chapter 8 covers the development of early language, literacy, listening and speaking, reading and writing, and poetry. The approach is a balanced literacy approach. Included are suggested activities for increasing skills and facilitating development in speaking, listening, reading, and writing. Also included are guidelines and methods for selecting, preparing, presenting, and evaluating stories. Language and literacy should be active ingredients in all curriculum activities and experiences, rather than separate elements assigned to be taught at specific times. Research indicates that "outstanding primary-level literacy classrooms are characterized by intense, sustained literacy experiences and are filled with high-quality reading, writing, and skills instruction" (Gambrell & Mazzoni, 1999, p. 97).

The remaining chapters of this part deal with science in the early childhood curriculum. Science in the early childhood years should be taught in very concrete terms, using exploring, manipulating, questioning, comparing, and other process skills. Science explorations happen in almost every unit and occur spontaneously nearly every day. Taking advantage of questions and incidental learning opportunities allows for limitless science and critical thinking skill development. Teachers of the young must seek to help children think in scientific ways, to foster thought processes that encourage children to utilize scientific ways and methods. The questions that teachers ask, the comments that they make, and their approaches to problem solving can do much to help children to incorporate scientific thinking. "Adults facilitate children's engagement with materials and activities and extend the child's learning by asking questions or making suggestions that stimulate children's thinking" (Bredekamp, 1986, p. 10). Explanations should not be too involved, intricate, or mysterious. Teachers must communicate simple and honest facts that are appropriate for the child's level of understanding and interest.

Selected science activities must take into consideration the experiences and interests, ages, and special needs of the children. To be developmentally appropriate, these materials and experiences should be concrete, real, and relevant to the lives of young children, while allowing learning to take place through active exploration and interaction with adults, other children, and materials. As children develop understanding and skills, then, teachers should increase the difficulty, complexity, and challenge of the activities (Bredekamp, 1986).

We should encourage children in their science education to learn the value of keeping records. Teachers can do the writing for young children who have not yet acquired writing skills; when children are able to write, they should write their own observations and keep their own records. Just as scientists are record keepers and record information such as how much, where, when it happens, and what makes it happen, so must we teach young scientists the importance of recording the information that they have observed (Beaty, 1992).

A key to a developmentally appropriate science curriculum is to properly match science content to the child's cognitive abilities; when the proper match does not occur, this can lead to frustrations and misconceptions (Lind, 1997). The themes, activities, projects, concepts, and activities suggested in these chapters focus on hands-on, experience-based learning and encourage children to foster perplexity, curiosity, and inquiry as they seek answers and understanding. Much of children's cognitive growth in early childhood is stimulated by their "wanting to know," by their insatiable curiosity about their world, and by their interest in solving problems and answering questions. Many of their inquiries relate to science notions or math problems.

Because science themes, projects, and activities are so broad, we have included three chapters on science-related topics. Chapter 9 focuses on Physical Science and also contains general science guidelines, including the value of science in the curriculum and how to teach it effectively. Specifically, Chapter 9 also includes teaching color, fire, light and shadows, magnets, weight and balance, and additional science activities and concepts. Chapter 10 centers on Earth Science and includes concepts of air, rocks, and water. It also includes temperature, weather, and seasons. Chapter 11 focuses on Life Science and incorporates plant and animal concepts and themes, in addition to concepts relating to the senses.

Chapter 12 includes math and problem solving, size, and shape. The key to a successful math program in early childhood is that it be developmentally appropriate. Growth and learning in mathematics are facilitated by providing opportunities, activities, and materials that foster mathematical thinking and awareness (Geist, 2001). All children are ready for problem-solving activities, but at differing levels. Their environment is full of problem-solving options, such as patterns, ordinal numbers, weight, measurement, and time, to name only a few. However, all their experiences need to be integrated in order that the child might develop and learn as a whole, instead of in fragmented, inappropriate ways.

Chapter 8

Language and Literacy Development

Literacy, or learning to read and write, is critical to the child's success both in school and in life, and all children have a right to quality reading instruction [International Reading Association (IRA), 2000; International Reading Association (IRA) and the National Association for the Education of Young Children (NAEYC), 1998]. In literacy development, as in other areas, the teacher's challenge is to match best practices to the ways that children think, know, and understand.

Literacy activities are best provided in the context of meaningful, authentic activities (Novick, 1999/2000).

Early childhood teachers facilitate children as they develop competence in language and literacy, including knowledge about sounds, letters, words, and sentences. Development of these competencies begins early, even before the child enters school; they are shaped by instruction and do not emerge spontaneously (Bodrova, Leong, & Paynter, 1999; D'Arcangelo, 1999). Literacy learning can be interwoven into the preschool curriculum, with adults taking the role of modeling, optimizing children's play, and enriching the environment with literacy materials and experiences (Nel, 2000).

Morrow and Smith (1990, p. 2) summarize insights that have emerged from research that have prompted a new perspective of early childhood literacy:

1. Literacy development begins long before children start formal instruction in school.
2. School personnel should recognize the knowledge about literacy that children bring to school with them and build early reading and writing experiences on this existing knowledge.
3. Literacy involves the concurrent and interrelated development of oral language, reading, and writing.
4. Learning is promoted when literacy is based on functional experiences in which there is a need to read and write.
5. Learning is promoted in social settings as children interact with adults and peers during literacy activities.
6. Although children's learning about literacy can be described in terms of generalized stages, children can pass through these stages in a variety of ways and at different ages.
7. Adults serve as models for literacy behavior by demonstrating the use of books and print themselves.

It is important that parents begin talking to and reading to children from infancy on.

Children's early experiences will begin with language, and when we stimulate young children's linguistic awareness with books, rhyming activities, storytelling, singing, and games, this early stimulation will influence the child's ability to read and write (Arnqvist, 2000). Children "learn what language *is* through what language *does*" (Novick, 1999/2000, p. 70). Through language, we are able to exchange and understand communicated thoughts and feelings. Language functions in many ways for the child, and it may well be the most significant feature of the child's early learning. Through assessing and considering the complexities of learning language, it is imperative that activities and experiences involving language and literacy be developmentally appropriate. By the time most children reach 5 years of age, they have a large vocabulary, speak in sentences, and are often able to use proper syntax or grammar (Burns & Broman, 1983). Table 8–1 gives a brief overview of normal language development.

Language is the instrument of thought, personal expression, and social communication. "Language is a powerful tool that allows (children) to organize and express their views and questions about the world and to communicate with other people" (NAEYC, 1996a, p. 75). Language gives children power to deal with a friend, to solve a conflict, to express a feeling (Novick, 1999/2000). Children's power to grasp, enter into, and reflect on their experiences depends largely on their facility in using verbal symbols. Thus, language is the device through which raw experiences are translated into meaningful symbols that can be dealt with coherently and used for both thinking and communicating. As experience is broadened and deepened, language acquires meaning and further growth and learning become possible. Also, it is through language that we are able to express our own thoughts and emotions and share vicariously in those of others. Language competence is also important in concept formation, school performance, and problem solving.

To develop proficiency in organizing, classifying, categorizing, and understanding concepts, the child must have a wide range of appropriate vocabulary. A certain level of attainment in language acquisition is essential in order for the child to begin formal education successfully. Literacy development is growth in communications skills,

TABLE 8–1
Normal Language Development

By the Age of	Development Activity
1 year	Imitates sounds Between 9 and 18 months, begins to use words intentionally to communicate Responds to many words that are a part of experience
2 years	Puts several words together in a phrase or short sentence (telegraphic language) Can recognize and name many familiar objects and pictures Has a vocabulary of about 30 words
3 years	Uses words to express needs Uses pronouns as well as nouns and verbs in speech Identifies the action in a picture Rapid increase in vocabulary—may average 50 new words a month
4 years	Loves to talk Verbalizes experiences by putting many sentences together Recites songs, poems, and stories Uses words to identify colors, numbers, and letters Sentences grow longer Likes to make up new words Likes rhyming
5 years	Generally has few articulation problems Talks freely and often interrupts others Sentences are long, involving five to six words Describes artwork Learns plurals Enjoys silly language
6 years	Asks the meanings of words Describes the meanings of words Makes few grammatical errors Talks much like an adult Is interested in new words
7 years	Speaks very well May still be mastering some sounds or learning to articulate the following sounds: *s, z, r,* *th, wh*

including initial speaking and listening and then writing and reading. The IRA and NAEYC collaborated on a position statement to give teachers and parents an understanding of the goals of literacy instruction and to enable them to assess children's progress toward these goals. Being aware of the continuum of reading and writing development enables teachers to set goals for individual children and then adapt instructional strategies for children whose learning and development are either advanced or lag (IRA & NAEYC, 1998). Their position statement suggests the following in brief:*

---

*(Note: The suggestions given here are not meant to be exhaustive. In addition, students at any grade level will function at a variety of phases. Adapted from IRA & NAEYC (1998). View the complete continuum at http://www.naeyc.org/resources/position_statements.)

Phase 1: *Awareness and Exploration* (goals for preschool). In this phase children explore their own environment and build foundations for preparing to read and write. They do this by listening to read-alouds, attempting to read and write, participating in literacy games, and identifying some letters and making letter–sound matches.

Phase 2: *Experimental Reading and Writing* (goals for kindergarten). During this phase young children develop basic concepts of print and begin to experiment with reading and writing. They do this by listening to read-alouds, using language in a variety of ways, recognizing letters and letter–sound matches, becoming aware of rhyming and beginning sounds, writing letters, and matching spoken words with written ones.

Phase 3: *Early Reading and Writing* (goals for first grade). During the first-grade phase young children begin to read and write. They read and retell stories, use a variety of strategies to aid comprehension, recognize many words by sight, and begin to use punctuation and capitalization.

Phase 4: *Transitional Reading and Writing* (goals for second grade). In this phase children read and write more fluently. They use a variety of strategies for comprehension and word identification. They increase their sight vocabulary. They write using a variety of topics.

Phase 5: *Independent and Productive Reading and Writing* (goals for third grade). This is a phase for extension and refining of reading and writing skills. Children in this phase can read fluently, utilizing a variety of strategies for comprehension and word identification. They can critically examine texts and structures. They can utilize all aspects of the writing process, including revising and editing.

Organizations such as IRA and NAEYC are committed to the goal of facilitating children in learning to read well enough by the end of their third-grade year "that they can read to learn in all curriculum areas" (IRA & NAEYC, 1998, p. 2). However, a number of authors have encouraged the use of information or expository texts with emergent readers (Dreher, 2000; Guillaume, 1998). This most recent proposition is that young children learn to read and read to learn at the same time. One way we can facilitate this is by focusing more attention on informational text and comprehension of text.

DEVELOPMENT OF EARLY LANGUAGE

Since the foundation of literacy is language development, early childhood teachers must be aware of the development of language, as well as the factors that influence its development. Children make the language of their family and neighborhood their own language as they imitate the accents, usage, structure, and colloquialisms of the people around them. Verbal imitation begins in the first year of life. Babies imitate rhythms and patterns of pitch and stress, and they begin to be aware of differences in word order and intonation. Children learn to pronounce words primarily through imitation. When children produce sounds, responding adults usually repeat actual words that closely approximate these sounds, which provides auditory reinforcement. As they practice these sounds, correct or incorrect speech forms are reinforced through feedback. Careful observation of language progression determines that children's speech is actually a systematic reduction of adult speech, with function words that carry little information being omitted. For example, an adult might ask: "Do you want some more milk?" The toddler will often respond with "More milk." The fact that children learn the language of their environment reinforces the importance of imitation.

Vocalizations that normally occur in the first year of life are the forerunners of language. These vocalizations must be reinforced or rewarded by certain kinds of responses from others if they are to persist and develop into language. The more reinforcement given, the better this is for young children. Problems with language are often rooted in the early stages of language development, when imitation of a model is relevant. Sometimes the linguistic patterns learned from model imitation are both limited and wrong by the standards of the school that the children will attend. Adults need to provide exemplary imitation standards and shape children's language behavior through differential reinforcement.

The child's language does not proceed from word to concept to experience, but from action or experience to concept to words. Piaget (1955) asserted that infants do think and that thought develops before children are even capable of speech. When babies first begin to speak, they have learned that words are symbols for things or feelings. The Russian cognitive psychologist Vygotsky (1962) believed that it was children's language that made them capable of thought. From the Vygotskian perspective, cognitive development depends much more on the people in the child's world than on the physical environment. Therefore, for Vygotsky the importance of language in cognitive development is critical. Young children draw language meaning from the context in which it is used. In other words, children may not initially understand the meaning of a word, but they understand what the person using the word means.

Motor and mental readiness are prerequisites for children to begin verbalizing or using oral language. Association of word meanings depends on memory and reasoning. Children begin using oral language by blending real words in a stream of jargon, but the jargon quickly disappears and is replaced by one-word utterances. Initially, a sentence or phrase is combined and understood as one unit, for example, "awgone" instead of "all gone."

Oral language continues with the combination of words into utterances—two at a time, then three, and so forth. Whether the child is uttering a stream of jargon or a four-word sentence, others extend the child's language by filling in missing prepositions, conjunctions, verbs, and other parts of speech that reflect the way that the language is used in the child's environment.

Children progress in language just as they do in other developmental areas—at their own rates and in their own individual ways. Some are very talkative and engage in rather extensive language play or private speech, according to Vygotsky (1962). Others appear reticent in using oral language, and these differences are normal. Environmental experiences and maturation vary among children, so it is difficult, if not impossible, to provide a definite age sequence or time line for the development of language and literacy (Whitmore & Goodman, 1995).

Before their second birthday, most children are forming sentences of two or more words. Although the grammar of these sentences is not identical to that of the adult model, we can usually translate the child's sentence by adding function words and inflectional affixes. Although there is no syntax in children's early utterances, nouns, verbs, and interjections are the most common classes of words used. These reflect vocal stress, frequency in adult speech, or semantic importance.

Semantics

Children's development in semantics, or the meanings of words, is directly related to the experiences and interactions that they have. Children can program sentences that they have never heard before, but they cannot use a word they have not heard or read. Background knowledge (schema) and vocabulary are essential for successful comprehension. The more experiences children have, whether in the context of language, real experiences, or vicarious experiences such as books and other media, the more they expand their language meanings and vocabulary. A rich variety of well-planned experiences that involves labeling and drawing meaning helps children to expand their language and become more literate. However, an experience without attached language does not develop understanding. The following example illustrates the importance of labeling children's experiences. Four-year-old Amy was given one-half of a grapefruit. When asked, "What is this?" Amy confidently replied, "It is vitamin C." Amy's association with grapefruit may have included the instruction "Here, eat your vitamin C." Therefore, the experience with grapefruit lacked real meaning because an incorrect label had been attached to it.

It is imperative that adults constantly share, converse, interact, extend, and exchange language as children have experiences at the zoo, grocery store, park, school, home, in the car, in the classroom, or in any setting. A word with no meaning is an empty sound, not a word. The meanings of a word for a particular individual depend on previous associations with it, and the more limited the experience, the more limited the resulting language and meanings.

A child's early utterances are often global or generalized, and a sound may represent several different objects or persons. As children continue hearing the verbal contexts of words and have a rich variety of labeled experiences, they increase their knowledge of meanings. For example, *dog* may refer to all animals. As vocabulary and experiences increase, the child is able to narrow the range and to organize, classify, and categorize words and their meanings. The child discovers not only that everything has a name, but also that "this is the name for that." As experiences are made meaningful through word attachments, these words are stored in the brain and used to understand later experiences and communications.

Syntax

Syntax is the set of rules for creating or understanding a sentence. As children first begin to use words, they display no evidence of systematic grammar; yet, by about 4 years of age, most observers agree that the fundamentals have been learned. Training in the use of word sequence to relate and unify cognition is important. Since the sentence is the smallest complete unit of thought, sentence structure is a key to the logic of thinking. Symbols and sounds need to be put together correctly to make words that are understandable; then the words must be placed in a particular order to make a sentence that conveys meaning. Children's ability to form complete sentences is also an index of their growth in thinking and cognitive understanding.

Children learn syntax by first imitating sentences or phrases or by extracting their meaningful parts. Expansion is another process in the acquisition of grammar. Adults often expand what the child has said. If the child states, "Me drink water," the adult will often expand the phrase with a complete sentence such as "You want a drink of water." In effect, the adult is saying, "Is this what you mean?" as well as expanding the child's phrase to a complete sentence. However, these two processes alone teach no more than the sum total of sentences that speakers have either modeled for a child to imitate or built up from a child's reductions. The child's linguistic competence extends beyond this. All children are able to understand and construct sentences that they have never heard but that are, nevertheless, well formed. Somehow, then, children process the speech to which they are exposed in order to derive from it latent rule structures or innate abilities to think and form

sentences on their own. Thus, children are intuitively able to master the rules of language and make inductive generalizations that go beyond what they hear. As children grow, they gain increased facility with syntactic structures, leading us to believe that maturation is a variable in syntax growth.

Variables in Early Childhood Language Acquisition

Language Acquisition Variables
Maturation
Experiences
Amount and quality of verbal interaction provided
Relationship to and rapport with language model
Motivation for acquiring language
Television habits
Language-rich environment
Bilingual–bicultural learner

A significant variable in language acquisition is whether the child is a bilingual–bicultural learner. Many teachers recognize the need to support a child's native language and give enrichment in the second language, which is English. This philosophy is referred to as additive because it recognizes the need to *add* new language skills, but not to replace the child's existing language skills. A child's language will reflect who that child is, for one's language is a reflection of the his or her culture. (Chesebro, Berko, Hopson, Cooper, and Hodges, 1995).

Teachers need to value and preserve children's native language and culture, build on students' existing language competencies, and also recognize that second-language acquisition follows the same stages as native-language development (NAEYC, 1996b; Soto, 1991). Instructional strategies in literacy for second-language learners will likely need to be in their primary language (Snow, Burns, & Griffin, 1998). As teachers encourage oral communication among ESL (English as a second language) learners, it is recommended that children be taught the differences between their native language or dialect and the standard elements of conversational as well as formal speech, for example, English, and then be helped to identify the various contexts in which each style is appropriate or inappropriate (Chesebro et al., 1995). Williams (2001) suggests that learning activities for ESL students be context rich and that teachers work to build background knowledge and schema by using pictures, real objects, demonstrations, and graphic organizers to clarify. It is also recommended that teachers and parents work together to help children to strengthen their native language and culture, while gaining the skills needed to participate in the shared language and culture of the school arena (NAEYC, 1996b).

LITERACY DEVELOPMENT

Children seek to become literate for both survival and pleasure. To teach in developmentally appropriate ways, teachers should understand the continuum of reading and writing development, as well as each child's individual and cultural variations (IRA and NAEYC, 1998). In addition, a developmentally appropriate environment for developing literacy in early childhood includes play, games, manipulative materials, dramatic play, and physical and motor play (Fields & Spangler, 1995). Children need opportunities to use language in both the spoken and the written form. Children should frequently see a written copy of what they are hearing or what is spoken to them (Bear, Invernizzi, Templeton, & Johnston, 2000). Even when they are not yet able to read, seeing the written images helps them to make connections between what is heard and the written symbols. Bodrova, Leong, & Paynter (1999, p. 45) suggest for preschool and kindergarten children using a "scaffolded writing" approach in which the teacher "takes dictation" by drawing lines representing words that the child dictates for a message or story. The child will then fill in as many words or as much of each word as he or she can.

We can always find ways to create a print-rich environment regardless of what activities or materials we are using, and the print must make sense (Adams, 1990). Print-rich environments provide opportunities for students to see and use written language for a variety of purposes, and teachers can draw children's attention to the words and specific letters (IRA & NAEYC, 1998). Children frequently see printed words in their environment; they learn, whether they read or not, that things have spoken and written labels.

> Children who are successful readers in school have had written language as a dominant part of their daily activities.

Because of literacy artifacts such as wallpaper with alphabet letters and print, nursery pictures, picture books with print, stickers with print, cereal boxes, mail and letters, signs, newspapers, and many other things with print, children learn very early that print corresponds to oral language and represents ideas that can be read. Teachers can prepare a "logo chart" from newspaper ads, food labels, and other sources. These logo words (environmental print) that are common in advertising can be used in literacy skill lessons. For example, a logo chart could be used for teaching long or short vowel sounds, diagraphs, or such skills as plural possessives. Just spending a few minutes to read some of the logos is also a valuable strategy, because they make connections between school and the real world (Rule, 2001). In addition, encouraging reading of environmental print helps children to recognize that reading helps us to survive and reading is everywhere.

> **Reading Is Everywhere That We Look and Helps Us in Many Ways**
>
> Some of the places that we use reading include the following:
>
> Mileage on roads
>
> States on license plates, and the cities and states on road signs
>
> Signs about animals at zoos and in parks
>
> Plaques on statues and at museums
>
> Information on a ticket or pass
>
> Washing instructions on clothing

Messages on doors or outside buildings

Directions on signs such as speed limit, waiting area, one way, and no smoking

Dosage on drugs

Contents on labels and nutrition information

Menus at restaurants

Prices on items at stores

Children learn that the symbols called *words* convey meaning and tell something. Even though most preschool children cannot actually read, they have a great deal of competency and knowledge related to the functions and nature of print (Fields & Spangler, 1995). Some early childhood concepts of print include the following:

Text is meaningful; we are able to read the words which are formed by the letters

Reading goes from left to right and top to bottom

Punctuation marks help to create meaning

Books have front and back covers, a title page, an author, and sometimes an illustrator

A storybook or narrative has a beginning, a middle, and an ending

Informational or nonfiction text informs about people, places, or things

For children who come into early childhood classrooms without a feeling for and background in literacy, teachers need to provide a nurturing atmosphere of literacy—exposure to books (narrative and information), print, reading, and writing. One way to provide a positive literacy atmosphere is to organize literacy learning centers to motivate early readers and writers (Hill, 2000a; Morrow, 1997). Instruction using appropriate techniques to present new concepts and skills that are slightly ahead of what a child can do independently provides developmentally appropriate early childhood literacy instruction (Bodrova, Leong, & Paynter, 1999).

BALANCED LITERACY APPROACH

Literacy development includes listening, speaking, reading, and writing. The interrelationships among these components should be obvious, since they all involve words. In listening, ideas are received through words; in speaking and writing, ideas are expressed through words; and in reading, ideas are communicated through printed words. Children learn to

listen by listening

speak by speaking

read by reading

write by writing

listen by speaking, reading, and writing

speak by listening, reading, and writing

read by writing, listening, and speaking

write by reading, listening, and speaking

Figure 8–1 shows the interactive relationships among listening, speaking, reading, and writing.

In a balanced literacy program, teachers provide developmentally appropriate literacy activities. They balance structured or explicit instruction with more informal opportunities for extending practice in listening, speaking, reading, and writing. They balance whole-group and small-group instructions according to the needs of the learners. Teachers in a balanced literacy program must also balance instruction that focuses on learning words and the strategies for decoding with instructions

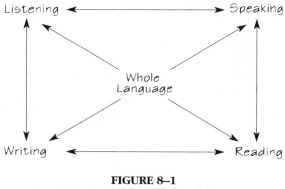

FIGURE 8–1
Language Interrelationships

that build comprehension and thoughtfulness (McGee & Richgels, 2000).

We are opposed in early childhood to the isolated skill-and-drill tasks and worksheets that fill so much time and are termed the literacy curriculum component. More can and should be done in these early years to engage children in capturing the literacy vision. All children benefit from developmentally appropriate literacy activities. However, those children who come to programs and classrooms with limited literacy experience and proficiency particularly reap great value from activities such as reading stories aloud, sharing big books, working on a word wall, seeing the environment filled with meaningful print, and writing for the purpose of enhancing emergent reading abilities (Taylor & Heibert, 1994). In a balanced program, literacy should be integrated into every part of the early childhood curriculum. Music, science, art, food activities, social studies, math, and any other kind of experience should provide opportunities for emerging literacy.

In the past decade heated debates have occurred about whether young children should receive whole-language or phonics instruction. We propose, along with many other experts in the field, an approach that incorporates both approaches. Many refer to this as the balanced or integrated approach to literacy. With the balanced approach, teachers create a literate environment and then use the best tools available to teach the components of literacy. For example, some tools include the language experience approach (LEA), in which children dictate to the teacher their thoughts and ideas; the sight- or whole-word approach, in which children see the representation of the whole word and begin to read it; or phonics, in which children learn the letter sound in order to facilitate sounding out the words as they read. They learn word identification skills, develop vocabulary in a variety of ways, and always work on comprehension. USOE Cooperative Research Program in First-Grade Reading Instruction found that "the approaches that included both systematic phonics and considerable emphasis on connected reading and meaning surpassed the basal-alone approaches on virtually all outcome measures" (Adams, 1990, p. 9). This same study found that the single best predictor of students' achievement in reading at the end of the first-

grade year was their ability at the *first* of the year to recognize and name upper- and lowercase letters (Adams, 1990). Understanding the alphabetic principle, the notion that spoken language is made up of sounds and that these sounds can be formed into written letters, makes both reading and writing achievement easier for young children (Hill, 2000b).

Components of the Balanced Literacy Approach

High-quality children's literature.   In early childhood classrooms, substantive literature is imperative and often is used to integrate the curriculum. Good literature is a model for accuracy and correctness in language usage and grammar. Meaningful literature can raise awareness of such values as empathy, generosity, and kindness and may be the impetus to move students to "compassionate action" (Miller, 2001, p. 381). Using literature as a basis for language in the early childhood classroom develops readers instead of just developing a set of skills; in addition, literature makes learning engaging and enjoyable. Enhance language and literacy opportunities for young children by increasing the volume and quality of children's experiences with high-quality books at an early age (Neuman & Celano, 2001).

A variety of kinds of texts is included in a balanced literacy program to arouse children's interest and motivation (Dreher, 2000). A basal reading series, which is a published reading series with stories and activities on increasingly difficult reading levels, may be selected by programs or school districts for all early childhood classrooms. The leveled texts, like the basals, are arranged into levels of text difficulty. Some programs, such as Reading Recovery, use leveled texts and for a particular grade may have 12 to 16 levels of text difficulty. Some districts and programs have developed their own lists of leveled texts, and publishers will often level texts according to their difficulty. In addition, balanced literacy programs should have a collection of authentic or quality literature, including fiction and nonfiction or informational texts. Providing children with opportunities to hear and read both narrative and information text appears to improve reading motivation and also reading achievement (Dreher, 2000). "Providing such a balance enables children to engage in reading for learning as they simultaneously learn to read" (Dreher, 2000, p. 73). The daily read-alouds should also include information books.

There is a plethora of choices of children's picture books, but not all are substantive and provide the meaningful literature that children need. Teachers need to be wise in their selection of books for their classrooms and use criteria and good judgment to ensure quality literature. Hefflin and Barksdale-Ladd (2001) suggest the following general characteristics of high-quality primary-grade picture books:

- Memorable, well-portrayed *characters*
- A clear and understandable *plot* with an easy-to-follow sequence of events
- Well-crafted *language* that is concrete, vivid, and reflects the mood of the story
- A worthy and truthful *theme*
- Quality *illustrations* that enrich the story

The balanced or integrated literacy approach saturates the environment with wonderful books—about characters with which children can identify; about both familiar and unfamiliar animals, places, and events; and about experiences that encourage children to think, laugh, cry, or feel sad. "Humor helps children to grow cognitively as they act on what is seen and heard and resolve what is not understood in the spirit of fun. Literature that encourages or enables children to engage in such activity facilitates cognitive growth" (Zeece, 1995, p. 93). Suggested children's books involving humor include *Dog Breath: The Horrible Trouble with Hally Tosis* (Pilkey, 1994); *Frogs in Clogs* (Samton, 1995); *A Goodnight Opus* (Breathed, 1993); *Making Friends with Frankenstein* (McNaughton, 1994); *Prowlpuss* (Wilson, 1995); *Sheep Take a Hike* (Shaw, 1994); *Six Thick Thumbs: A Tongue-Twisting Tale* (Charney, 1994); *That Pesky Toaster* (Hillman, 1995); *The Three Little Wolves and the Big Bad Pig* (Trivizas, 1993); *Two Cool Cows* (Speek, 1995); and *Yo, Hungry Wolf!* (Vozar, 1993). (See Suggested Resources at the end of this chapter for complete references.)

Young children enjoy hearing the same stories or books over and over, about children their own age, animals, adventures with familiar things, humor,

and the alphabet; they enjoy rhymes, the ridiculous, silly, fantastic, factual, and nonsensical. They enjoy their own creations, beginning reading books, poetry, and books with new words (Bronson, 1995).

Genres of Early Childhood Literature

Informational or nonfiction books: Provide realistic and authentic information about people, places, animals, plants, weather, and other real things in our world

Traditional tales and stories: Handed down from one generation to the next and within cultures

Multicultural books: Allow the reader an accurate glimpse of another culture

Fantasy: Amusing, pretend, or fantastic stories

Folktales: A traditional tale with good prevailing over evil

Fables: Tales about animals with an explicit moral

Myths: Created to explain natural incidents

Historical fiction: May include fictional characters, but the setting accurately reflects the time period in which the story is set

Biographies and autobiographies: Accurate stories about the lives of real people

Poetry: Usually anthologies or collections of poems; poetry appeals to the senses and includes imagery and rhythm, and may include rhyme.

Songbooks: Collections of songs

Student-authored works: Collections of writings from individuals and groups of class members

The literature selected must be developmentally appropriate (Neuman & Celano, 2001; Neuman, Copple, & Bredekamp, 2000). For example, picture books should be provided for toddlers, with pictures that depict various ages, ethnic groups, and disabilities in positive ways (Bredekamp, 1986). Song picture books promote language growth by "building on familiarity and enjoyment, providing repetition and predictability, expanding vocabulary and knowledge of story structures, promoting critical thinking and problem solving, and fostering creative expression and language play" (Jalongo & Ribblett, 1997, p. 16). They unite literacy development with music in an interesting way, provide a way for children to express their thoughts, stimulate the imagination, and teach literacy skills (Jalongo & Ribblett, 1997). Wordless books should include both the concept type, which works well for children at the labeling stage, and the story type, which can lead children to constructing their own stories (Raines & Isbell, 1988). Alphabet books use the sequence of the alphabet to present a story, teach the letters, or organize information around a topic such as the circus. As children develop good reading skills, they should be guided toward making responsible choices and judgments in selecting reading materials. Certainly, not all children's literature is high quality. Providing children with reading lists appropriate to their reading level, including Caldecott and Newbery Award books, is helpful in guiding them to excellent choices.

Good literature can also be used as a springboard for a study of a topic or an understanding of a concept, as well as a basis for integrating curriculum. Books are memorable and often raise awareness and inculcate understanding. For example, as a springboard to a class service-learning project, a teacher might read *The Gift* (Brodmann, 1993), the story of a young girl deciding what to do with her Hanukkah money. The listeners or readers understand the true meaning of giving as the child's journey is enjoyed. The story provides a foundation for service learning, and children will come up with many ideas for service projects and sharing with others following this story of giving.

Another book that can serve as a means to integrate curriculum is *Sarah, Plain and Tall* (MacLachlan, 1985). This is a Newbery Medal-winning tale of life on the prairie frontier, so the story can help young children to better understand a part of history as well as a different culture. In the story, Sarah, homesick for her native Maine, tries to "bring some sea" to the prairie. She has brought some shells, stones, a snail, and a picture to remind her of her native home. An activity for young children that could emerge from this story is for each child or a group of children to do a sense box that would include souvenirs, pictures, or other items from a different place. Another activity would be to compare Sarah's time with the present by making contrasts. A food activity might be preparing and eating something from the prairie days such as biscuits or scones. "Classrooms that support literature-based curriculum practices are assuring active learning as well as affecting the learner's sense of story, influencing reading and writing skills, and providing a context for literacy learning" (Sorensen, 1991, p. 31).

Language experience approach as a part of balanced literacy.   In the language experience approach (LEA), children write and read about their experiences (Stauffer, 1970). When they go on a field trip, for example, they return and write about it. Younger children dictate to the teacher; older children write their own stories, poems, ideas, or summaries. When you write down the actual words that a child says when making storybooks, it helps them to recognize that "print is 'talk' written down" (Diffily & Morrison, 1996, p. 58). Perhaps each child could draw a picture following the field trip and write or dictate to the teacher a description of the picture. These words could be compiled into a class book so that the experience can be enjoyed, as well as reinforced, in the future.

Another approach is to have the class participate together in writing an experience chart. The teacher initially begins with a statement such as "We had an exciting time at Mr. James's farm. Tell me about our trip, and I will write about our experience." The children are invited to participate as they dictate to the teacher where they went, what they did, what they liked, what they did not like, and any other individual perceptions and feelings. The language experience approach can also be used in writing a thank-you letter following a field trip or a meeting with a visitor. The children dictate to the teacher what to say, including their individual reactions. Experiences such as these are termed holistic because they incorporate all the components of literacy development.

Prior to the field trip, in addition to the discussion and other preparations (which include speaking and listening), the children could write a note home or take one written by the teacher that tells of the forthcoming field trip and activities. Also, directions for getting to the field trip destination could be written down and followed as the trip is made. Children then learn that we communicate with people by speaking, writing, listening, and reading. They also learn that their own thoughts can be both written and read, whether they do the writing and reading themselves or someone else does it for them.

Throughout the planning and carrying out of the field trip, the children listen for the purpose of gaining meaning and understanding. In addition, they are able to use oral language before, during, and after the field trip as they ask questions, participate in discussions, comment, make inferences, answer questions, and use other forms of oral language. Following the trip, they write about the experience by making an experience chart, individual or class book, or thank-you note. Afterward, they read, sometimes many times, what they have written.

The described environment and experiences focus on the values and meanings of literacy. In balanced or integrated literacy, all components of literacy are woven in a natural way throughout the curriculum.

Reading and writing aloud as part of the balanced literacy approach.   The balanced literacy approach encourages teachers to read aloud to children at least once a day from high-quality children's literature (Campbell, 2001; McKean, 2000/2001).

Read-alouds are the basis and foundation of literacy learning, as well as a springboard for activities such as role plays, reader's theater, shared readings, music, and art (Campbell, 2001).

Children are never too old or too young to be read to. "When we take the time to read aloud and converse with our children, they learn to value language—as well as our company" (Diffily & Morrison, 1996, p. 47). The most important exercise for building the knowledge and competence eventually needed for reading appears to be reading aloud to children (Adams, 1990). Trelease (1995) adamantly reminds us that we read aloud to children for the same reasons that we talk to them: reassurance, entertainment, information, and inspiration. Children who have stories read and told to them are more likely to become good story

writers (Hayes, 1990). Reading to children fosters reading development, increases reading comprehension, develops listening comprehension skills, cultivates appreciation of literature, and expands oral language abilities (Cecil, 1999). For younger children, this is more often done individually or in small groups; whole groups are often used with older children. However, this does not mean that whole groups of very young children do not enjoy having teachers read to them. On the contrary, they do; but the stories need to be shorter and should not be continued from one day to another.

Children in first and second grades still enjoy having teachers read from picture books in small groups, but they also begin to enjoy books that are not completed in one sitting, but are carried over from day to day, such as *Charlotte's Web* (White, 1952); *The Indian in the Cupboard* (Banks, 1981) or its sequels, *The Return of the Indian* (1986) and *The Secret of the Indian* (1989); *The Cricket in Times Square* (Selden, 1960); *James and the Giant Peach* (Dahl, 1961); *The Hundred Dresses* (Estes, 1944); *Little House in the Big Woods* (Wilder, 1932) and others in the series; and *Sarah, Plain and Tall* (MacLachlan, 1985). (See Suggested Resources at the end of this chapter for complete references.) In addition to reading aloud to young children, it is also important to write aloud to model for young children how to write. As the teacher writes she or he comments outloud on the thought processes going on during the writing process.

Guided reading and writing as a part of a balanced literacy approach.   Using this strategy in the literacy program gives support to readers who need help. In guided reading the teacher or a peer guides students through the text, which they read silently and then discuss (Fountas & Pinnell, 1996). The teacher or peer leader might encourage students to make predictions, give background information to help students to construct meaning, ask questions, and give appropriate prompts. During guided reading the teacher might stop and give a mini lesson on a phonics concept, word-identification skill, vocabulary concept, or any reading strategy that might benefit the children in the group. In guided writing the teacher or peer guides the students through their own writing by prompting and asking questions to support them.

Cooperative reading and writing as a part of a balanced literacy approach.   This approach is modeled after the principles of cooperative learning. Pairs of students take turns reading aloud text to one another or they might read silently to a particular point and then stop and discuss their reading with one another. One approach to cooperative reading is called discussion circles. After students have finished reading a book or story, they get together in small cooperative groups to discuss the book. They may talk about what they liked or didn't like about the book, if they have experienced something similar to the characters in the story, or new and interesting words in the story. Cooperative writing allows partners to work together on a writing piece. This might be modeled after the LEA approach.

Shared reading and writing as a part of a balanced literacy approach.   Text in this approach is shared by the teacher with students. The teacher reads aloud the book, story, poem, or song, and students are invited to join in the reading when they feel comfortable. They respond to the text through art, writing, music, drama, and other activities (Slaughter, 1993). Shared reading gives young readers support in real reading. The "big book" concept used frequently in early childhood classrooms models the shared reading concept. Shared writing is similar to the LEA approach in which a group works together on a writing piece and actually goes through the writing process.

Literature circles.   In small groups, children read and discuss books that they self-select or wish to read. Books that foster thinking and discussion require careful selection (Harvey & Goudvis, 2000). During discussion the children share personal responses, explore interpretations, reflect on their feelings about the story or characters in the story, and raise thoughtful questions of their peers (Daniels, 1994). Making connections between home and school in literature response groups prompts dynamic discussion among group members (Bond, 2001).

Independent reading and writing as part of a balanced literacy approach.   As soon as children are able to read or write on their own, they should have time to do so by themselves. This type of reading and writing requires no support from others in the student's ability to read the text or write text. Many children in early childhood can read and write and should be given the opportunity to do so independently. For example, journals provide a means by which students can respond in writing or, for children not ready to write, by drawing pictures.

Literacy lesson as a part of a balanced literacy approach.   A format for developing a literacy lesson in early childhood is fairly simple. Once the piece of literature has been selected, there are three parts to the literacy lesson:

1. *Introducing the literature.* Background knowledge and prior knowledge must be activated. This may also include discussion of key vocabulary words. In addition, children must be given a purpose for the reading.

2. *Reading and responding to the literature.* The literature can be read in a variety of ways including reading aloud, shared reading, and others. During this part of the lesson, students reflect on the meaning of the literature and summarize what is meant through discussion, questions, applications, and prompts.

3. *Extending the literature.* In this part of the literacy lesson, teacher and students are encouraged to go beyond, to invite a guest to the class or to take a field trip to extend the piece of literature. The children do something with the literature: write about it, dramatize it, or sing songs about it. Or they may do an art or craft that extends or relates to the piece of literature.

Early Childhood Literacy Lesson: The Very Hungry Caterpillar

Objectives

Students will:

- Learn about the life cycle of a butterfly

- Discuss and chart the different types of food and categorize them into healthy or nonhealthy snacks

- Participate in a listening activity

- Create a class book and write what they would eat if they were the caterpillars
- Participate in the "Caterpillar Song"

Materials Needed

- Copy of the book *The Very Hungry Caterpillar* by Eric Carle
- Copy of the poem "Caterpillar" (author unknown)
- K–W–L (Know-Want-Learn) chart
- Flash cards of the physical changes that a caterpillar goes through
- Sock, with eyes and all colors of felt to make the different shapes of food
- Food cards of the foods that the hungry caterpillar eats
- Enough $8\frac{1}{2}$ by 11 inch pieces of cardstock for each class member to have one
- Hole punch, yarn, crayons, and pencils
- Copy of the "Caterpillar Song"

Introducing the Literature

1. To introduce the book, first ask the children to think back to when they were on summer vacation and imagine a summer day. Ask them, "Did you ever chase a butterfly?" Then ask, "Where do you think butterflies come from?" Pause and wait for the students to respond with a caterpillar as their answer.
2. Begin by reading the poem called "Caterpillar."

   A fuzzy, wuzzy caterpillar
   On a summer day
   Wriggled and wriggled and wriggled
   On his way.

   He lifted up his head
   To get a better view
   He wanted some nice green
   Leaves to chew.

   He wriggled and he wriggled
   From his toes to his head
   And he crawled about until
   He found a comfy bed.

   He curled up tight
   In a warm little wrap

   And settled himself
   For a nice long nap.

   He slept until
   One day he awoke
   And broke from his shell.

   He stretched and stretched
   And he found he had wings!
   He turned into a butterfly
   Such a pretty colored thing.

   On how happily
   He flew away
   And he flew and he flew
   In the sun all day!

3. Discuss what the children know about caterpillars by using a K–W–L chart. (What do you know about caterpillars, what do you want to know, and what did you learn about them?) List on the chart the children's responses to the first two parts of the chart. Use prompts such as "What do caterpillars eat?" to guide their thinking if needed. Be sure to write down what they want to know about caterpillars.
4. Following the K–W–L chart, use the flash cards to teach and discuss the physical changes that the caterpillar goes through during the life cycle.
5. To introduce the book *The Very Hungry Caterpillar*, do a walk-through of the book. Begin by pointing out the cover of the book, the back of the book, the title, and the author. Then quickly flip through each page, predicting what might happen in the story. Make sure that you open the discussion to the class so that children are able to voice their predictions. After the predictions, begin reading the story.

Reading and Responding to the Literature

1. While reading the story, use a green sock puppet and food made out of felt to dramatize the story.
2. While you read the story, stop at various places in the book and ask questions, point out special details, and talk about new words. For example:
   - What kind of egg do you think is on the leaf?
   - Why do you think the caterpillar is so hungry?

- What do you think he will eat?
- Do you know what kind of food an apple is? A pear? A plum? A strawberry? An orange? And so on.
- Are these healthy snacks?
- When you get to the salami, pause and ask, what do you think might happen if he eats all of this food?
- Why did the caterpillar make a cocoon? What is a cocoon?

3. After reading the last page to the class, ask the children to share some ways that they have changed from the previous year to this year. Go back and discuss how much food the caterpillar ate by having the children count all the different food items throughout the story.

4. Next the class will participate and join in while you reread the story. Before you begin, distribute the food cards and explain each card to the children so that they are aware of what picture they have. While rereading the story, have the children stand up when you read their particular picture in the story. This promotes listening and being involved during the story.

Extending the Literature

1. Have the children return to their tables or desks and ask questions such as:
   - What part of the story did you like best?
   - What are your feelings about the story?
   - What kinds of food did the caterpillar eat? (Based on their prior knowledge, you might discuss categories of foods or the Food Pyramid.)
   - What kinds of healthy foods do you like to eat?

2. Finish the K–W–L chart by discussing what they have learned about caterpillars.

3. Give the students an $8\frac{1}{2}$ by 11 inch sheet of cardstock with the sentence: If I was the Very Hungry Caterpillar, I would eat ———. Have children finish the sentence and then illustrate a caterpillar and what food they chose for it to eat. Support those who need help with their writing. When the class is finished, punch holes down the left side of the cardstock sheets and tie them together with yarn. When completed, the children will have a class book to look at and read throughout the year.

4. Teach the song "Caterpillar." (The tune of the song is to "I'm a Little Teapot.") Allow opportunity for the children to sing in groups in front of the class.

I'm a hungry caterpillar walking slowly (slowly walk two fingers from right hand up your left arm)

Looking for something (place hand above eyes searching for something)

To fill my belly (rub belly)

When I go to sleep (close eyes, tilt head, and rest on folded hands)

I make a little cocoon (cup hands together)

Pop! I'll be a butterfly soon (throw open hands, link thumbs, and make flapping movement)

5. Make a fruit salad using the same fruits that are mentioned in the book: apples, pears, plums, strawberries, and oranges.

Encouraging Literacy Development

We suggest the following general ways to encourage literacy development:

1. Recognize that the teacher is the key to effective instruction in reading. Use the literacy time as well as the free-play period to provide a prime time for teachers to interact with children on a one-to-one basis or in small groups to teach literacy concepts and skills. One-on-one interactions support oral language development and provide foundation for later literacy learning (IRA & NAEYC, 1998). As children play with manipulative toys, work with blocks, enjoy books, play in the dramatic play area, use sensory materials, or use any of the areas provided during free play, teachers should encourage them to talk and listen to one another. Also, teachers and caregivers should talk with, listen to, and read to children. One kinder-

garten teacher always puts paper and marking pens in the dramatic area, and children learn to label the things there. For example, during a unit on the farm, the dramatic area had a number of things, including the barn and rubber animals. Some of the child-made signs read: "One hors fur seele," "The tractr," and "R Farm." Early experiences with writing build confidence in the belief that they can author and write. Often teachers use free-play time as a break period for themselves; they do not realize the valuable opportunity for individual and small-group speaking, listening, and reading so beautifully provided in free play. Discussions with children can address the project with which they are involved, or they can be unrelated and address their home, hobbies, or other interests.

2. Provide many opportunities for talking, and then be sure to listen. Provide a model for listening. Do not talk too much—the voice that goes on and on is often tuned out. If you do not listen to children, how can you expect children to listen to others? Let the children know that you are listening to them by being attentive and focusing your eyes on them. Find time to listen to each child every day.

3. Inquire of children often, and provide for stimulating inquiry. (*Inquiry* refers here to the use of questions.) Two practices that stifle inquiry are emphasis on exact answers and emphasis on competition. Teachers should ask questions that require thoughtful responses; they should also encourage and respect the questions that children ask. Unusual questions and answers lead to deeper thinking; deeper thinking requires greater communicative ability; and greater communicative ability means language growth. Use thought-provoking questions often.

4. Acknowledge, accept, and celebrate individual language diversity in children (Soto, 1991; NAEYC, 1996b). However, teachers must be diagnosticians. Thus, they must determine literacy deficiencies and then select the procedures that they will use in trying to overcome these deficiencies. They evaluate where the children are in their literacy development and how they can be stimulated

and challenged to progress further. Teachers also determine individual needs for literacy instruction.

5. Keep in mind the factors influencing the development of language, and therefore strive to be high-quality models—speaking distinctly, calmly, pleasantly, and with well-chosen words. Teachers should also give and encourage language feedback and provide new experiences.

6. Use the sentence as the basic unit of speech, and teach children to speak likewise, in complete thoughts or sentences. When we speak in sentences, we express complete and meaningful thoughts. This instruction is also excellent for emergent reading, since books are written in complete sentence form.

7. Establish a comfortable, relaxed atmosphere that stimulates children to talk freely with others.

8. Use strategies and provide experiences that develop phonemic awareness (that is, songs, fingerplays, games, poems, and stories with phonemic patterns such as rhyme and alliteration). Phonemic awareness is the attentiveness in children that spoken language consists of a sequence of phonemes or the small units of speech that make a difference in our communication and that exist independently of meaning (Cecil, 1999; Cunningham, 2000; Wasik, 2001; Yopp, 1995; Yopp and Yopp, 2000).

9. Recognize that grammatical errors, particularly verb and pronoun problems, are typical in the early childhood years. Rather than putting too much emphasis on exactness of speech, repeat the sentence to the child, using correct grammar so that the proper form is heard. Thus, the child will not feel a sense of failure, but will nevertheless be made aware of correct usage.

10. Use specific words that will help to expand the children's vocabularies as well as teach the meanings of words. Too often we speak in general terms such as "Put the book over there," as opposed to "Put the blue book on the middle bookshelf."

11. Verbalize what children are doing. Paint word pictures for them about whatever activity they are involved in, for example, "I see Amy climbing very high on the jungle gym."

12. Help children to draw meaning from listening, speaking, reading, and writing experiences with literacy. For example, when someone speaks, it may be necessary to rephrase or ask, "Is this what you mean?" When a visitor comes or when the class goes on a field trip, it may be helpful to rephrase some of the conversation in order for the children to draw meaning from and understand what is communicated. Rephrasing may also be necessary as selections of children's literature are read and shared. Sometimes it is only necessary to define the meaning of one word in order for the context and ideas to be understood. Our goal in literacy development is to encourage children not only to speak, listen, read, and write, but also to do so with meaning and with understanding of what has been spoken, heard, written, or read.

13. Create a print-rich environment (IRA & NAEYC, 1998). The classroom environment should include print in areas besides the book or story area. Research indicates that opportunities to engage with print during the early years may provide a prevention of reading difficulties (Snow, Burns, & Griffin, 1998). Even before children read, they should see words and print in their environment—word lists, word walls, phrases, charts, signs, labels, calendars, recipes, and so on. Label and read the items seen and used in the classroom. For example, during science or food activities, ingredient labels can be read to the children. When children are away from the classroom, labels on signs, doorways, billboards, and other areas can be read and pointed out. Take advantage of opportunities for using notes, charts, or written instructions, even when the children themselves cannot read. For example, the recipe should be available during a cooking experience so that the teacher can read the instructions and the children understand that the recipe communicates what to do. On a

field trip, the children can follow a map of instructions that tells them how to get to their destination, as well as what to look for when they get there. As children begin reading, the written word should permeate the classroom, and written instructions for activities should be given to them to follow.

14. The importance, value, and rewards of daily reading aloud, meaningful stories, and information texts to children of *all* ages cannot be overemphasized (IRA & NAEYC, 1998; McKean, 2000/2001). These daily readings aloud will be one of the best parts of the day, and children will have cherished memories of the stories that they hear (Trelease, 1995). Choose books suited to the experiences and needs of children in your classroom (Wolter, 1992). Big Books (enlarged textbooks or children's oversized books) have become valuable tools for enhancing children's enjoyment and understanding of literature. Provide sufficient time for questions, discussion, and response to the literature (McKean, 2000/2001). Big books can be obtained commercially or prepared by the teacher or individual children. In one kindergarten class, for example, after the children had listened to the song "What a Wonderful World," they each illustrated a phrase or word in the song and then put it together as a Big Book. In addition, interest centers for listening should be encouraged. Earphones can be attached to a tape recorder, and children can listen to commercially prepared stories. Cassettes of teachers reading favorite stories can be enjoyed over and over again by the children, either individually or in a small group.

15. Encourage children to write their own books and stories, which are placed in the story or literacy area to be read and enjoyed again and again. Book writing is more purposeful and meaningful than doing worksheets (Fields & Spangler, 1995). Children's self-directed writings demonstrate how much they know and can do. If children are able to write, they can be encouraged to write and illustrate their own stories. If they do not write, they can illustrate their

stories (pretend or real experiences) and dictate them to a teacher or caregiver. Children in early childhood classes will enjoy making calendar books. For each day of a particular month, cut a sheet of paper approximately 4 by 5 inches. Put the numeral representing the day at the top of the paper, and then put the papers on a bulletin board in the correct order and placement representing that month. After each day, have a child in the class draw a picture on the paper representing that day and perhaps something that happened at home, at school, or with the weather. Children who are able to write can write about what was drawn. Children who do not write should dictate something about the picture to the teacher. At the end of the month, take the numbered pictures down and put them in order. Add a cover sheet with the name of the month and then staple or bind the pages together. Add this "book" to the book center for the children to enjoy reading again and again. They will especially enjoy "reading" the pages that they have created.

Literature, books, and stories can often be a springboard for a class, group, or individual book. For example, the book *Fortunately* (Charlip, 1964) adapts easily to having the class do their own "fortunately-unfortunately" episodes. Or, after reading *All the Places to Love* (MacLachlan, 1994), the children can write about the places that they love. *The Jolly Postman or Other People's Letters* (Ahlberg & Ahlberg, 1986) will serve as a great prompt for letter writing. (See the Suggested Resources for complete references.) Almost any story can serve to launch a writing activity. How proud children are when they realize that they can author stories or pages worthy of being bound as well as read and reread!

16. Involve parents with their children learning to read. Give them support, training, and encouragement in developing the skills and competencies to provide a literate environment for their children and to participate in many literacy-building activities and experiences with them.

LISTENING AND SPEAKING

Listening

"We hear with our ears, but we listen with our minds" (Garman & Garman, 1992, p. 5) and "with our hearts" (Jalongo, 1995, p. 18). Listening is a skill that needs to be taught deliberately in the early childhood years. "When teachers build children's listening skills, they are making an important contribution that will serve the child well, not only during early childhood but also throughout life" (Jalongo, 1995, p. 26). Modeling active listening by teachers promotes active listening in students. Remember: Listening is active, not passive (Jalongo, 1995). It is a serious mistake to ignore the need for instruction in listening. "Children do not need to listen *more*, they need to listen *better*" (Winn, 1988, p. 144).

Listening skills include *auditory perception*, the ability to perceive and understand what is heard; *auditory discrimination*, the ability to

Developing listening skills is a necessary part of learning to read and write.

make fine discriminations among sounds; *auditory memory*, the ability to remember the sequence of sounds within words and sentences; *auditory association*, the ability to associate sounds or words with experiences, objects, ideas, or feelings; and *rhyming skills*, the ability to recognize and reproduce words that rhyme.

Speaking

"Children learn to speak by being immersed in a verbal atmosphere, a rich broth of words, gestures, and expressions" (Freidberg, 1989, p. 13). Speaking or oral communication influences, and is influenced by, every other aspect of development. Most children in the early childhood years have the ability to speak, but their oral language skills need enhancement and refining. Teachers must respect and accept the language of the child and provide an exemplary role model for good listening. In other words, encourage oral language by being a good listener!

Activities for Listening and Speaking

The following are some suggested activities for listening and speaking, with a focus on helping children to acquire literacy. Remember, good listening skills influence reading abilities, and good speaking skills influence writing abilities.

1. Plan question periods in which questions are given and answers brainstormed and shared. The questions might be thought-provoking realistic questions, or they might be thought-provoking nonsense questions. For example:

    What new machine might you invent?

    What would you do if you could only walk backward?

    What would you do to red to make it more beautiful?

    What would you do if you woke up one morning to a backyard full of elephants?

    What would be your one wish?

    What would you purchase if you could purchase anything in the whole world?

    If you could make a contribution to the world, what would it be?

    What would you like instead of school?

    What would you give feathers to make them softer?

    What is your greatest hope?

    What changes would you like to make in yourself?

    What if everyone had a long neck like a giraffe?

    Once the children catch on to this type of questioning, they will enjoy making up questions. Perhaps this activity could be done in cooperative learning groups, using Think–Pair–Share as a strategy (see Chapter 4). Remember that all questions and answers are correct and acceptable.

2. Simple question–answer games can be played, in which the children sit in a circle while questions are asked. Then a ball or beanbag is thrown to a child, who answers the question in a complete sentence. This same child asks another question in complete-sentence form, and the beanbag or ball is tossed to another child for answering.

3. A sack of objects can be used for discussion and language development. The children can learn about and discuss the objects; then directions will be given, in complete sentences, about what will be done with the objects. The teacher or a child might say, "Put the green block on top of Jenny's head," or "Put the gerbil food underneath Stephanie's chair," or "Put the box on the floor and hop over it three times." This game not only teaches new words, or labels, but also develops prepositional understandings.

4. Divide the children into smaller groups and give a picture to each group for discussion. The pictures could be snapshots that the children brought from home, which would encourage children to talk as their pictures are shown to the group.

5. Show-and-tell, or sharing time, is enjoyable if it is not presented too often. In one preschool class, the children are assigned a particular day during one week when they can bring something from home and tell about it. Each day during the set-aside time,

five chairs are placed in front of the class, and five proud children bring their sacks holding the secret of the item that they are anxious to tell the class about. In another class, the teacher uses a large duffle bag and calls it the "mystery bag." Each day, one child brings something to show or tell about and places it in the mystery bag. The class can guess what is in the bag; if they have trouble guessing correctly, the child who brought the object can give clues. The child who guesses what is in the mystery bag is allowed to take the bag home that day if he or she has not had a turn for a while.

6. Rhyming couplets can be shared with children; the last word of the couplet, which rhymes with the word at the end of the first line, can be left off so that the children can guess what the word is. This activity can also be used with poems that rhyme, with the second word in a rhyming sequence left out for the children to guess. Younger children can listen to the couplet and tell the two words that rhyme. Children could work in cooperative learning groups on these activities.

7. Give three or four words in sequence, all but one of them beginning with the same consonant sound, and then ask the children to listen for the one that is not the same (for example, *tomato, trunk, egg, tumble*).

8. After a story with a definite sequence of events, have the children recall the events in the order in which they occurred. They could also prepare a reading flow chart by drawing pictures of the story in the order in which events occurred, and then the teacher could write a sentence or phrase for each picture.

9. Make use of sequence stories in workbooks or cartoons. The various parts of the story can be glued to wooden blocks, plywood, or poster paper to make sequence puzzles. The children must find the correct sequence and then tell the story. Older children might wish to write a sentence or phrase under each picture.

10. Make surprise boxes by wrapping them up and having the children guess what might be inside. Then unwrap them and have the children describe the object or objects and how they are used.

11. Have the children draw pictures representing specific experiences and then discuss the pictures. Instead of drawing the pictures, they can be asked to think of the experience and then relate it to the group. For example, they might be asked to share the most embarrassing experience, the saddest experience, the funniest experience, the most frightening experience, or the most exciting experience that they have ever had. An alternative would be to have children bring snapshots from home from experiences that they have had and describe them orally. Also, the experiences could be written down as the child tells them.

12. As stories or poems are read or told, words or phrases can be left out, and the children can guess what the missing words might be.

13. A group of rhyming words can be shared (for younger children, three words are enough), including one word that does not rhyme. The children listen and then tell which word does not rhyme.

14. Give rhyming riddles for the children to guess. Examples: "I rhyme with *damp*. I sit on a table. What am I?" "I rhyme with *chose*, and I am on your face. What am I?"

15. Have each child pick an object out of a sack and describe the object.

16. Children form inside–outside cooperative learning circles and face their partners. The teacher gives a word and the outside-circle person thinks of a synonym for it for his or her partner; then the inside-circle person gives a word that rhymes with it. The activity can progress in this way with the teacher giving new words to explore. Other ideas: The children could give a word that begins or ends with the same sound and use the word in a sentence, or give a word that is an antonym. The teacher adapts the way that the word is approached to the developmental needs of the children.

Throughout the day, there will be many opportunities to develop listening and speaking skills in young children. Be alert to these opportunities and cognizant of their importance. Also remember that children's attempts to express themselves and share their ideas are more important than perfect language usage. Do not drill on perfect grammar or articulation. Let children learn to enjoy listening and speaking.

READING AND WRITING

Reading and writing are the other two main ingredients of literacy in early childhood. The more children see us read, the more inclined they are to want to read; the more children see us write the more inclined they are to want to write. The process of emergent literacy or learning to read and write is an ongoing process that begins "as children become aware of the relationship of print and meaning" (Raines & Canady, 1990, p. 3). Before children learn about letter sounds and names, they must have numerous developmentally appropriate opportunities to observe the values and usefulness of reading and writing (Bredekamp, 1986). If a teacher believes (and teaches accordingly) that children will be successful readers and writers, generally the children *will* be successful readers and writers (Mills & Clyde, 1991).

Reading and writing are connected. "Reading and writing curriculum for young children should be integrated, connected, whole, and meaningful and should focus on developing thematic and interdisciplinary studies" (Reutzel, 1997, p. 226). Reutzel describes some assumptions noted by Hall (1987) relating to the young child's emergent literacy:

- Reading and writing are closely related.
- The process of learning to read and write is social and influenced by the child's search for meaning.
- Even without formal instruction, most preschool children know a lot about printed language.
- The process of becoming literate is developmental.
- Children need to read authentic literature.
- Children write for personal reasons.

Reading

Often when parents are selecting a preschool for their children, one of the first questions they ask is "Do you teach reading?" The knowledgable preschool teacher, aware of the importance and directions of the early years, should enthusiastically respond with "Yes, emergent reading." Many of the study areas presented in this book are specific emergent reading concepts (for example, shape, sound, and color). Before children have reading facility, they need to have had numerous experiences to sharpen their visual and aural perception. Before children can become readers, they learn about reading—why people read and what they read. They are aware that their environment is full of print. This is called *print awareness*. Reading involves the ability to differentiate similarities and differences in visual patterns, forms, and sounds. However, "children do not learn to read in order to make sense of print. They strive to make sense of print and as a consequence learn to read" (Smith, 1985, p. 120). Raines & Canady (1990, p. 5) also take this constructivist perspective when they point out that the reading process is no longer considered a word-by-word decoding process designed to unlock the meaning embedded in the print. Balanced literacy teachers view reading as a process of constructing meaning from interacting with the print and relating the information to what one already knows.

The ability to read is a slow and gradual process that emerges through regular engagement with print (Adams, 1990). Print awareness, letter familiarity, and phonemic awareness can all be developed through classroom instruction in the preschool, kindergarten, and first grade (Adams, 1990). According to a number of researchers, phonemic awareness plays a significant role in the teaching of reading, is a foundation for reading success, and is a predictor of early reading acquisition (Adams, 1990; International Reading Association and the National Association for the Education of Young Children, 1998; Snow, Burns, & Griffin, 1998; Wasik, 2001; Yopp, 1995; Yopp & Yopp, 2000). Phonemic awareness is the awareness of the sound structure or sequence of our language, and activities that promote both the recognition and manipulation of sounds in words foster phonemic awareness (Wasik, 2001; Yopp &

Yopp, 2000). Developmentally appropriate activities for teaching phonemic awareness include songs, chants, nursery rhymes, fingerplays, and word-sound games that focus on rhyme, syllable units, onset and rime, and phonemes (Cooper, 2000; Wasik, 2001; Yopp & Yopp, 2000). Phonemic awareness is stimulated by providing a language-rich environment and through a variety of experiences throughout the day.

Phonemic Awareness

The following categories are used to instruct and assess children in phonemic awareness:

- Phonemic isolation or onset (word beginnings). Example: What is the first sound you hear in *fish*?

- Phonemic identity. Example: What sound do these words have that are the same? (*bat, bee, boys*)

- Phoneme categorization. Example: Which word begins with a different sound? (*cat, come, map, cape*)

- Phoneme blending or the ability to put together an onset (beginning sound) and the rime (sound that follows the onset). Example: Put together these sounds and tell me the word you make. (/p/ig/) or (/tr/—/ee/)

- Phoneme segmentation. Example: How many sounds to you hear in *dog*?

- Phoneme deletion. Example: What is *spoon* without the *p*?

- Phoneme manipulation or the ability to manipulate beginning, middle, and ending phonemes. Example: Change the word *take* by changing the first sound or change the word *cap* by changing the middle *a* to a different vowel.

- Rhyme. Example: Think of a word that rhymes with *lamp* (*damp, stamp*, etc.).

Children must also reach a certain cognitive maturity and readiness resulting in their desire to read. There are "two kinds of children: those who love to read and those who think they don't"

(Fadiman, 1984, p. xviii). Fadiman (p. xix) refers to Fitzhugh's *Harriet the Spy* (New York: Harper & Row, 1964), where "Harriet sits down to read. 'How I love to read,' she thought. 'The whole world gets bigger.' As for those who think they don't like to read, well, they're making a mistake, just as all of us do when we try to judge ourselves."

Like any other skill, learning to read takes time, patience, desire, and readiness. One of the most important ingredients in children's emergent reading is whether they have been read to. Basically, children learn to read by being read to. "Every time a child climbs on someone's lap to hear a story, literacy learning takes place" (Collins & Schaeffer, 1997, p. 68). Children who have enjoyed picture, alphabet, nursery rhyme, and storybooks from early infancy will have a greater desire to read because they know that reading opens new doors, provides information, and is enjoyable. Some ask how old young children should be when parents start reading to them. Our answer is, early infancy. From the earliest days, infants develop listening skills and learn how books look and feel, how to turn pages, how to be careful with books, and that words and pictures have meaning. Not only is it important that children have access to books, but they must have some books of their own. We advocate reading to very young children and suggest giving children as much as they are ready for as early as they are ready for it. In addition to reading to children, speaking clearly, distinctly, and with a broad and ever-expanding vocabulary will also foster emergent reading.

Reading is a communicative art involving both recognizing and understanding words. Children cannot read with understanding and comprehension something that they do not have background knowledge about. As we speak to and communicate with children, we should endeavor to expand their vocabulary to include both word pronunciation and definition. A child who reads a word but attaches no meaning to it is not reading with comprehension. Learning the meaning of words evolves through experiences with them. The more experiences that children have and the more these experiences are labeled with words, the more effective their reading experiences become. During emergent reading stages, stories about the children's experiences should be written on chart paper and read aloud often. When children begin writing, they can write and read about their own experiences. Other related skills prerequisite to fluent reading include large- and small-muscle development, social and emotional maturity, and intellectual and language experiences.

Teachers can do much in the early childhood years to prepare children for reading. Ideally, effective early learning activities are combined with the teacher's understanding attitude, resulting in the development of positive attitudes toward reading. The ability to read is important in academic success.

Components of the Reading Process for the Emergent Reader

1. Growing vocabulary and concept development
2. Recognize, name, and match the letters of the alphabet, both upper- and lowercase
3. Associate sounds with letter(s)
4. Attend to, identify, and manipulate sound segments of speech (phonological awareness)
5. Recognize some basic sight words
6. See a connection between speech and print
7. See a relationship between letters and words
8. See a relationship between words and sentences
9. Know that we read from left to right, top to bottom

Adapted from Bear, Invernizzi, Templeton, & Johnston, 2000; Johnson, 1983.

Before recognizing and naming letters of the alphabet, children must be familiar with letter shapes. The alphabetic principle is that sounds of the spoken code are represented by letters of the written code (Griffith & Leavell, 1995/1996). It is important for children to be familiar with letters and to recognize that these letters are related to reading (Wasik, 2001). We believe that it is difficult to teach letter shapes and functions without teaching the names of the letters. Usually, among the first letters that children are able to recognize and name are those in their own name. In teaching letter recognition, make children aware that 11 of the letters have basically the same shape in both

As these boys work together, they are able to practice putting the alphabet letters in the correct order.

upper- and lowercase (*Cc, Kk, Oo, Pp, Ss, Uu, Vv, Ww, Xx, Yy, Zz*). Seven of the letters are similar in upper- and lowercase (*Bb, Hh, Ii, Jj, Mm, Nn,* and *Tt*). Differences between upper- and lowercase are greatest in the other eight letters (*Aa, Dd, Ee, Ff, Gg, Ll, Qq, Rr*). Adams (1990, p. 126) points out that letter recognition is extremely important in the development of word recognition. "For children with little letter knowledge on entry to school, current learning theory suggests it is unwise to try to teach both uppercase and lowercase forms of all twenty-six letters at once. For children who do not know letter names on school entry, special care should be taken to avoid confusion of names and sounds."

As children begin to recognize words, they discover that letters have sounds. Initially, children learn the characteristic sound of each letter. Eventually, they learn that some of the letters, such as the vowels, have more than one sound. Children learn alphabet recognition in context or as they interact with materials relating to their written language (books, chalk, chalkboards, paper, pens, markers, etc.).

Children can be encouraged to develop and strengthen reading skills. To become readers in the sense that they seek out and enjoy reading, children should develop skill in drawing meaning from the printed word, which gives purpose to reading.

When using phonics, many words are not sounded out. Some words may be best attacked using the sight-word strategy. Children are often faster and smoother readers when they build up a repertoire of sight words; otherwise, they tend to try to sound out each word, sound by sound.

Phonics is a strategy using the sounds that letters represent and the resulting sounds made as they are combined with other letters. Once children are able to sound out words, they also begin to spell words. Spelling, in fact, is practice for phonics strategies. However, the same words that are difficult to sound out using phonics are also difficult to spell. For example, if you ask a young child to spell *wait*, a word unknown as a sight word to this child, the child would probably apply some beginning phonics to the problem and spell it *w-a-t-e*.

Reading is a vital part of literacy development. It is our hope that teachers sense their responsibility in helping children acquire both the ability and the desire to read. We believe that too much emphasis in early childhood classrooms is put on dittos and worksheets. "Children have a right to learn to read from people rather than procedures and programs" (Reutzel & Cooter, 1992, p. 22). We suggest that dittos and worksheets make reading a task and create a feeling of drudgery and boredom for many children. In too many early childhood classrooms, the focus for literacy development is copying material off the board—boardwork. This task has little or no regard for comprehension and meaning and does not promote literacy.

There are many ways of preparing teacher-made learning materials that focus on reading competency and give children practice and experience without the drudgery of worksheet after worksheet. For example, lotto games could be adapted to a word game in which the children classify words as a person, place, or thing. To explain further, a number of words (such as *girl, park, baby, ball, hammer, store, pen*, or *man*) can be written in boxes drawn on poster paper or card stock paper. A number of cover category cards would individually read *person, place*, and *thing*. The children then match these cover cards on top of each word. This activity not only helps children to classify, but also facilitates drawing meaning from words.

An additional suggestion for reading games involves making flowers. On a flower center (or circle), write a word ending, such as *er* or *est*. With a paper fastener, attach petals to the flower center. On each petal, write a word such as *fast, slow, bright*, or *light*. As the petals are rotated around the center, new words are formed. A variation could have *ing* or *ed* as center suffixes, with words such as *work, talk, jump*, and *walk* as petal words. This same concept can be used with two wheels made from card stock or tagboard attached in the center with a paper fastener. The inside wheel could have consonant sounds, blends, root words, or prefixes. The outside wheel could have suffixes or word endings.

Another example is to cut word cards out of heavy stock or use precut 3 by 5 inch index cards. Fold the right side of the card under about 1 inch from the edge. Now write a word that uses the "silent *e*" rule on each of the cards. For example, words such as *cape, tape*, or *care* can be used. Write each word on the card in such a way that the *e* can be folded under. The children then read the word both without and with the silent *e* on the end.

Ideas for teacher-made games are limitless and only confined by your own imagination and creativity. When you recognize that a child needs help on a particular skill or strategy, make a game or activity for him or her to work with, rather than giving the child a ditto worksheet to complete.

Additional Strategies for Teaching Early Childhood Reading and Writing

A variety of strategies support the teaching of literacy in early childhood. We suggest some of the approaches used successfully and supported in the research.

Word Wall and Word Banks. Word walls are bulletin boards or places on the wall for words that children are learning to decode and recognize; they serve as a visual scaffold to temporarily assist children in their independent reading and writing (Brabham & Villaume, 2001; Cunningham, 2000; Tompkins, 1997). They may be words from particular categories or themes, such as weather words or words that begin with the letter *b*. They may be words that cause children to stumble such as *because, brought, eight, neighbor, the,* or *have*. Word walls help learners to remember the words that they are learning and then make them readily available for reading and spelling. For emergent readers, teachers could write the words on small cards and put them in a pocket chart so that they could be used at a child's desk or to match words to objects and pictures. A word bank is similar to the word wall except it is an individual file of words that the student is interested in learning. These may be in a book, card file, or individual chart. Word walls and other similar strategies must be interactive, and the children must *do* something with them; they are not classroom adornment (Cunningham, 2000; Pinnell & Fountas, 1998).

Author's Chair. A chair in the classroom that is designated as the author's chair. When students have finished a writing project, they sit in the author's chair to share their work with class members. After a student has shared his or her writing aloud, students are invited to make comments and ask questions about the writing.

Reader's Theater. A dramatic, interpretative production of a story using the dialogue of the characters in the story. It motivates children, develops fluency, and builds comprehension through the repeated reading of text (Larkin, 2001). Children can use script directly from books or they can create their own scripts. Students assume various roles and then read the character's lines in the script. No constumes or props are required, and a narrator may guide the audience through the story.

Choral Reading. Poems, songs, or stories are read aloud by students. They may read the entire script together, or they can divide it and read sections in small groups or assign sections or lines to individuals.

Graphic Organizers. Graphic organizers are visual displays of information for structured overviews used for prereading, during-reading, and postreading tasks (Dunston, 1992; Griffin, Simmons, & Kameenui, 1991; Merkley & Jefferies, 2000/2001). Graphic organizers such as webbing can be used to demonstrate learning (Bromley, 1996) or to prompt writing (Sidelnick & Svoboda, 2000). A variety of graphic organizers can be used in reading to help students focus on or organize information.

- The K–W–L strategy, developed by Ogle (1986) for the purpose of activating students' prior knowledge and then helping them to determine their purpose for reading informational text, can be put on a chart with three columns. The first column is what I know (K), the second what I want to learn (W), and the third is what I learned and still need to learn (L).
- Another example of a graphic organizer is the Venn diagram. This graphic organizer encourages learners to compare and contrast similarities and differences. For ex-

ample, the Venn diagram includes two overlapping circles. In the middle of the overlapped circles you may put the similarities or common properties of two characters or places. In the two portions of each circle left, put the ways that each of the two characters is different or their individual properties.

- Semantic maps help children to see relationships in a particular topic. For example, in teaching the concept of seeds, this would be represented by a circle in the middle with lines with arrows and words written on the lines that represent the various relationships. For example, several lines might give examples of seeds, others might say *are, are used for, have* (Cooper, 2000).
- Word maps (Schwartz and Raphael, 1985) are graphic organizers that increase students understanding of words. They include information for *What is it? What is it like?* and *What are some examples?*

Writing

Handwriting.
Another ingredient in the language and literacy program is handwriting, which should be an integral part of the oral and written language program. There is a connection between listening, talking, reading, and writing. Diffily & Morrison (1996) suggest at least six different stages of writing: drawing, scribbling, invented letters, random letters, invented spelling, and common spelling. Matthew was drawing circle-type shapes on the fogged-up car window. "I'm writing in cursive," he proudly announced. "What does it say?" asked his father. "Oh, I don't know. I can only write in cursive, I can't read in cursive!" answered Matthew.

Lamme (1982, p. 109) lists six skill areas that are prerequisites for handwriting: small-muscle development, eye–hand coordination, holding a writing tool, basic strokes, letter perception, and orientation to printed language. We suggest that children need many experiences with tools such as paper, paints, pens, markers, chalk, brushes, pencils, and crayons to develop abilities not only

This boy, who is learning to hold the crayon correctly, is "drawing" his name on his picture before he hangs it up.

in handling and using these tools, but also in making refined strokes. Adding envelopes and stamps encourages note "writing" to family, teachers, and friends. As children begin to understand symbols and expand their awareness that these symbols have meaning, alphabet letters begin to appear in their artwork (Dyson, 1990). Children should be able to copy simple shapes, differentiating likenesses and differences in both the shapes and sizes of objects and letters. Just as with reading, children must display a keen interest in learning to write and a desire to do so. For example, children who are ready for writing activities often try to write or copy letters, words, and even sentences.

Alphabet letters may be abstract to the child and should be kept in units or words. Teaching them apart from the words would make them developmentally difficult for young beginners to learn. Because many children develop writing skills at home, parents should be aware of when children might begin writing, aware of specific signs indicating readiness for writing instruction, and knowledgeable of how to teach correct skills.

Before children begin to write and use the alphabet letters in writing activities, they should have many experiences using alphabet and sight-word manipulative toys. For example, matching games with upper- and lowercase alphabet letters can be made by the teacher. Alphabet cards, either teacher made or purchased, can be used for various alphabet games and activities.

Learning to form, remember, and read letters is a difficult and slow process, and each letter offers a unique challenge. Teachers must allow for mistakes, reversals, and incorrectly formed letters. It is challenging for children to maintain uniform size and stay within the lines. Writing takes much practice before it becomes natural, attractive, and neat. Teachers must be patient, allow plenty of time, praise positive efforts, and avoid pushing children who are not ready for the experience. Early experiences can be tracing activities; next experiences should be words, followed by short sentences and then short stories.

> Writing is thinking made manifest.

Writing or composing. "Just as readers use print to construct meaning, writers also use print to construct meaning. Young writers select a thought to be expressed and choose words and whatever print symbols they know, to convey that thought" (Raines & Canady, 1990, p. 6). Preschool children may simply draw a picture to convey their story (Fields & DeGayner, 2000). Children learning to write need patient, supportive, accepting, and appreciative adults who realize that errors are a part of the learning process. Teachers should provide many opportunities for creative writing or composing, beginning with those experiences for which children dictate their ideas, stories, or poems to the teacher. When children begin their first composition efforts, there should be no focus on the form of the writing, spelling, or punctuation. These mechanics can come later. Spelling, punctuation, neatness, and accuracy can be worked on once the child has had many experiences in writing for the sake of communicating an idea. When children invent spellings for words, it helps us to assess their level of understanding concepts and principles regarding the written word. Invented spellings are based on the sound of a word, rather than on sound–letter correspondence (Chapman, 1996; Griffith & Leavell, 1995/1996). As children invent their own spellings to represent the sounds of words, they are actually developing their abilities to use phonics (Diffily & Morrison, 1996)! The initial focus in composing should be on the idea and the effort that the children make. Drill and practice writing are not appropriate for early childhood writing experiences.

Emergent writers can use a modified writing process during the writer' workshop. The writer's workshop is a way of organizing some class time to do writing on a topic of the student's own choosing.

> The writing process (Calkins, 1994) involves the following components:
>
> 1. Prewriting (brainstorm the topic and generate ideas prior to writing)
> 2. Drafting (first attempt at writing the piece or story)
> 3. Conferencing (reflect and share writing with another for suggestions and changes)

4. Revising (making suggested changes)
5. Editing (attend to mechanics and refine the piece of writing)
6. Publishing (share the piece with others)

Teachers must be very flexible and cautious with emergent writers in using the writing process. It may be used only occasionally with those children ready for part or all of the process (Morrow, 2001). Many kindergarten children, for example, may not get past the drafting stage because of their developmental phase. As children increase in their writing competency, additional steps of the writing process can be added. Some emergent writers, with excellent writing competency, will, over a period of time, reach the publishing stage with some of their work.

One of the most successfully used writing experiences in early childhood is journal writing. Children learn that here is an opportunity to express their thoughts and feelings and not have to worry about mechanics. "Children write to record things, to manage their lives, and to share their feelings and truths for much the same reasons adults do. . . . Journals are places where we share the story of our lives" (Reutzel, 1997, p. 245). Fields and Spangler (1995) advocate the teacher responding specifically to children's journal entries with comments that relate to the child's writing. At the end of the year, teachers and parents enjoy the sequence of activities and feelings expressed by the children, while seeing progress in the children's abilities to compose and write. Reutzel (1997) suggests the following guidelines for engaging children in journal writing:

• Set aside time daily to write or draw something in their journal.

• Each child should have a bound book for his or her writing.

• To start, tell children that writing or drawing is a way of recording or saving what you think or say, and tell them that they can begin by drawing and dictating or labeling their drawing.

• The teacher can suggest topics for children who have a difficult time getting started or thinking of something about which to write.

In addition to journal writing, other writing activities are appropriate for the emergent writer. For example, children can draw pictures of a field trip or a family vacation and then write about each picture and put them into a book. They write a story for a roller movie by drawing the pictures and then writing about each picture. After completing the pictures and words, they can then put the long piece of paper on rollers and the rollers into a box. Another writing activity for young writers is to do their own flip-chart story and then read it from the author's chair. Almost any experience in the classroom or outside the classroom can be a prompt for a story. In early childhood, simple, self-authored books become texts for independent reading (Bradley & Pottle, 2001).

Writing can also be prompted in functional ways when children write birthday or other greeting cards to classmates, friends, or family members (Morrow, 2001). Notes to parents also offer opportunity for writing. Pen pals and other letter writing experiences can be easily fostered, and using e-mail to correspond is another writing prompt.

When children are routinely involved in the writing process, their reading ability grows rapidly: readers become better writers and writers become better readers (Cecil, 1999; Reutzel & Cooter, 1992). There is an interconnectedness between reading and writing and the idea that "What I can say, I can write (or someone can write for me) and what I can write, I can read" is recognized early (Sampson, Sampson, & Allen, 1995, p. 33).

Generalizations for Effective Writing Experiences and Activities

1. Children should write every day.
2. Include a writing center in the classroom with writing and publishing materials.
3. Teachers should model effective writing behavior and share their own narrative stories with children.
4. Children's writing should grow out of real experiences.
5. Writing should be integrated throughout the curriculum.
6. Young writers should be given opportunities to share their work with others.

7. Expose emergent writers to aspects of punctuation as they are ready.
8. Invented spelling should be accepted.
9. Give meaningful feedback through teacher–student conferencing and peer review of the child's writing to encourage progress (Bradley & Pottle, 2001).
10. Respect the children as writers, recognizing that there is a range of differences in every classroom (Bradley & Pottle, 2001).

Activities for Reading and Writing

Some of the first reading experiences that teachers should provide for young children will be those that children have composed or "authored" themselves. Very early, children should learn that what they have spoken that has been written down could be read by someone. Therefore, as the children describe an experience, a picture that they have drawn, or their feeling about an idea, the teacher can write down their exact words, which can then be read back to the children. Class books can be made by giving the children an idea, having them illustrate it, and then dictating to an adult their description, which the adult writes on the illustration. Pages can then be put together, with each child "authoring" a page. These books will become favorites to read again and again. Examples of class books are "Our Favorite Animals," "Zoo Animals We Like," "Favorite Dinosaurs," "Vacations We Have Taken," and ideas that tie into themes being explored. Teachers should model and share their own personal writing. They should use picture books as models of good writing and the kinds of experiences and thoughts about which authors can write (McElveen & Dierking, 2000/2001). For example, books such as *Alexander and the Terrible, Horrible, No-good, Very Bad Day* (Viorst, Atheneum, New York, 1972) or *When I Was Young in the Mountains* (Rylant, Dutton, New York, 1982) are the kinds of picture books that prompt students to discover their own personal experiences and thoughts to write about.

Many of the activities listed under Speaking and Listening Activities can be adapted for reading and writing. Instead of listening, the children read; instead of speaking, they write. Simply adapt the activities to the developmental abilities and levels of the children in your class.

There are a number of ways, beyond the early experiences just described, to help children who are ready for writing. To encourage children who are ready for more advanced writing experiences, you may wish to use one of the following approaches:

1. Show them how to build a web. For example, perhaps they will write about a summer vacation. The name of the vacation would be the center circle, and circles around that might be things that they did each day. One circle might be the beach, one an amusement park, one a visit to the zoo, and another a visit to Aunt Mary's. For each of these, ask children to describe what happened or what they remember about the experience, and then write these ideas around each circle, connecting them to the center circle. When they finish their web, each circle can represent a paragraph that they can write about.

2. A second approach is to give them steps to writing or the writing process. For example, you can teach them to think about their ideas and what they might write about and then brainstorm or organize these ideas and even number the order that the ideas should be in. Next they should read what they wrote and make changes if they desire.

The following are some additional writing and reading activities that can be used in early childhood. Remember, just because children do not have handwriting skills does not mean that they cannot write. Instead, they can speak or dictate as an adult writes down word for word what they say.

1. Use open-ended proverbs. Each child is given an open-ended proverb to finish by writing or dictating and then illustrate. The children fold their paper in half. On the left side, they write the part of the proverb assigned, and on the right side, they finish it. Or the first part of the proverb can be written at the top of the paper and the children write or dictate the ending at the bottom of the page and then illustrate it in the middle of the paper. Examples of open-ended proverbs include the following:

Don't count your chickens . . .

He who is too greedy . . .

Think twice before . . .

Borrowed feathers . . .

Kindness works better . . .

You can't tell a book . . .

One good turn deserves . . .

The apple doesn't fall . . .

Half a loaf is . . .

Do unto others as . . .

Think before . . .

Biggest is . . .

Slow and steady . . .

A soft answer . . .

What goes up . . .

An ounce of prevention is worth . . .

Spare the rod and . . .

Silence is . . .

The following are some examples of how first-grade children completed some proverbs:

If you can't stand the heat . . . go in the snow.

A penny saved is . . . money in my bank.

The grass is always greener . . . on the ground.

Everything comes to him who . . . reads and makes money.

Money is the root of all . . . trees.

Early to bed and early to rise makes . . . me cry.

If at first you don't succeed . . . wait until you're stronger.

All that glitters . . . isn't the stars.

You can't teach an old dog . . . to read.

2. Show the children a picture and have them dictate or write about it. Calendars, magazines, and photographs are sources for pictures.

3. Have the children create an ABC of pretend monsters. Each child selects a letter of the alphabet, imagines a monster, and then writes or dictates a description of that monster. For example, *A* might be an "Atarox", a 17-foot-long garbage-eater that loves "rox" (rocks) for dessert. The children would illustrate their monsters on their pages.

4. Have the children bring a favorite possession from home in a paper bag. On the outside of the bag, write at least five words that describe it without telling what it is. Class members guess what is in the bag.

5. Give each cooperative learning group a different hat. Each group will write five words to describe the hat and then write who would use the hat.

6. Give each cooperative learning group five words and have them write a synonym for each word. Examples include the following:

scream–yell	cent–penny
fast–speedy	little–small
glad–happy	leap–jump
pal–friend	share–divide
large–big	start–begin
hurry–rush ·	smell–sniff
town–city	smile–grin
skinny–thin	angry–mad
scared–afraid	save–keep
close–shut	stop–quit

This activity can be done with rhyming words, words that start with the same sound, antonyms, or other language activities.

7. Give the children open-ended similes to complete in the same way as the proverbs in activity 1. Examples include the following:

As quiet as . . .	As busy as . . .
As sly as . . .	As slow as . . .
As slippery as . . .	As free as . . .
As wise as . . .	As red as . . .
As silly as . . .	As hungry as . . .

8. Give the children story starters to complete. These can be done individually or in cooperative learning groups. Examples include the following:

I make the most unusual sundae! First I take . . .

I have an unexpected houseguest in the bottom drawer . . .

While working in my lab late one night . . .

I opened the door and . . .

I know how to make a lizard laugh . . .

My mom says, "Don't . . ."

9. Have the children write recipes or directions for their favorite dishes.

10. After reading a story, have the children orally describe or write about their favorite character.

11. After reading a story or book, have the children describe a present that they would give to the main character or a character of their choosing.

12. Pick an item that will change over time, and once every few days have the children use 5 to 10 words to describe it. Items might include a seed that will sprout, a flower, a glass of milk, a carved pumpkin, or a slice of bread in a moist wrapper.

13. Assign each cooperative learning group a different topic or word and have them brainstorm and write as many ideas as they can for each spoke on the wheel shown in Figure 8–2. Topics might include insects, books, a yo-yo, homes, cages, umbrellas, spaceships, water, red, weekends, or spring, or they might relate to a theme being studied.

14. Set up a "mailbox" in the room and have the children write letters to a character such as Barnaby Bear or Lassie. When a child "mails" a letter, he or she should always receive a reply. Perhaps a volunteer parent could be assigned to answer each letter during the year.

15. As a class, name a stuffed animal such as a bear. Each night one child will take the stuffed animal (the friend) home along with a binder with blank paper and stories about the friend written previously by classmates. The children are directed to take their friend with them to whatever activities they partici-

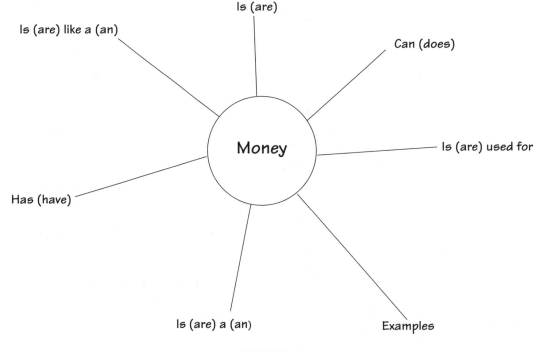

FIGURE 8–2
Topic Wheel to Stimulate Ideas

pate in and then at the end of the day make an entry into the binder about what they did with their friend. When the child comes to school the next morning, he or she sits in the author's chair and along with the friend and reads his or her entry in the binder.

16. Take advantage of the link between artwork and writing. When children draw or paint something and then describe their work, teachers can write on the children's papers what they dictate about their drawing or painting.

17. Have writing materials in a specific area and use the computer as a writing center. Teach young children how to use the word processor on the computer for story writing (Fields & Spangler, 1995). The writing center should have plenty of paper, pencils, and pens. It might also include envelopes, stamps, tape, staplers, paper clips, erasers, and anything else to encourage writing.

18. Hold a consonant scavenger hunt. Throughout the classroom, put objects and pictures of objects whose names begin with consonant sounds that the children have learned. Assign each child or pair of children a different consonant and have them search the room to find three items or pictures that begin with the sound of their consonant. After sharing their sound and the objects found to match it, they can return them and trade consonants and do the scavenger hunt again (*Learning*, 1994a).

19. To make a game for working on compound words, use cardstock paper or 5 by 8 inch index cards and write the first part of each compound word on the left side of the card and the second part on the right side. Laminate the cards and then cut them in half in a zigzag pattern so they become a puzzle. As children read them and match the correct pieces together, they will practice reading compound words (*Learning*, 1994a).

20. Have individuals or groups of children make reading flow charts from a story, fingerplay, or poem that they have read. A flow chart shows pictures and words in the order of the events as they occurred in the story or

phenomenon being described. They can also cut up newspaper cartoons, order them, and write new words for them. For younger children, cartoons can be cut up and used as an activity, ordering them from beginning to end.

21. Following the reading of a favorite story, the children can make their own class Big Book of the story by having individual children illustrate each page and then author the words for their illustration (depending on their developmental level, they can either write the words or dictate them). When they are finished, they can put the pages together to be enjoyed in the reading center.

22. The daily news process can be used to benefit children's reading and writing. The children share events that are important in their lives. It can be written by the entire group or by small groups of students. This is motivating for children, because they enjoy reading about themselves, their friends, and the experiences of their classmates (Wiencek, 2001).

Reading and writing should both be significant parts of the early childhood curriculum; they often are integrated together. Writing is thinking made manifest, and young children need to sense early that their thoughts can be put on paper and shared with others. Too often writing is left out of the curriculum, and then we wonder why older children lack writing skills.

Other Activities in Language Arts

Several other areas of literacy are vital to early childhood education and therefore need specific discussion. Stories, poetry, and fingerplays are all activities that involve listening, speaking, reading, or writing. It is hoped that toward the end of the early childhood years, children will be given many opportunities and much stimulus for writing their own stories and poems.

Children's literature. Shared stories assist children in organizing their thoughts and expressing emotions (Booth & Barton, 2000). Stories capture the attention of children and adults and give enjoyment and relaxation. In addition, stories provide information, teach new words and concepts, are often remembered more easily than general information, and encourage an appreciation for literature. A story, although a vicarious experience, can often teach a concept or give information that otherwise might be difficult to learn.

Stories can be used to teach social skills and values; children learn from the "friends" that they identify with in stories. Stories offer opportunities for children to enjoy the world of pretend, encourage appreciation of beauty and various cultures (Harris, 1991), and help children to learn to follow a sequence of events. Try telling a story and then retelling it using the "What happens next?" approach. Begin the story and then allow the children to relate the sequences and events. Well-chosen and well-told stories will also provide appropriate patterns of speech and foster language skills. Reading aloud satisfies emotional needs as the listeners enjoy physical closeness with the reader, and it facilitates development of social skills through pictures, content, and learning appropriate behavior during the reading experiences (Conlon, 1992, p. 15). Children learn early to value stories, and they learn that the printed word is the key that opens the door to the world. Once children see storytelling modeled, they can become the storyteller; this fosters sharing their own culture and helps to build a sense of community and inclusion in the classroom (Gillard, 1995). Often when children are restless or when the teacher is in need of an immediate activity, a well-told story is the best solution. For this reason, teachers of young children should know many stories and use a variety of storytelling techniques, such as felt boards, puppets, origami, photographs, music, chalk talks, and flip charts (Morrow, 1997). What a teacher needs most to tell a story effectively to young children is a love of stories and enthusiasm for telling them.

Guidelines for Selecting Stories. The various ages of children should be remembered when stories are selected. The following guidelines include additional criteria for selecting books and stories. Just because a story has been published does not mean that it is appropriate for young children.

1. For *3- and 4-year-olds,* avoid stories with a strong fear element. For this reason, some of the fairy tales should be avoided until children can better separate fact from fantasy. The stories should be short; if a story is told from a book, there should be few printed words in relation to the number of pictures. Choose stories with a simple, linear plot, as well as stories with repetition; children will enjoy chanting or saying the repetition after they have heard it several times. Stories should be realistic. Children prefer stories about animals, children, and other people.

For *5- and 6-year-olds,* stories can be more complicated, and they can distinguish fact from fantasy. These children like adventure and nonsense stories and those with surprise endings.

The *7- and 8-year-olds* like legends, folk literature, animal stories, fiction, science stories, stories that relate to their hobbies and other interests, and adventure stories. They enjoy longer stories and can be read to without having to see pictures; however, they still prefer hearing a story more than reading one themselves.

Fingerplays, nursery rhymes, and fairy tales all encourage the development of socialization, listening, talking, reading, and writing skills.

2. Select books and stories geared to the children's age levels, interests, levels of understanding, and attention span.

3. For younger children, a book or story that is being read should include illustrations that are colorful, attractive, clear, and appropriate. (However, remember that you can tell a story with no visual aids or pictures and still be effective.)

4. Select a well-balanced diet of books and stories to tell and have available for the children. Have samples of many categories, including those of various cultures, genders, and ethnic origins.

5. The books and stories that children especially enjoy will be repeated and retold often (Wolter, 1992). However, books that are selected for use in individual play should be rotated so that not too many are available at one time. Public libraries loan books to classrooms for this purpose.

6. The theme or main point of selected books should have value and importance. Books and stories used should have memory value; in other words, the children will remember good stories and books.

7. The characters in stories and books should be strong, having worthy character traits. Avoid stories that stereotype people and cultures.

8. Plots should be fresh and well paced.

9. Stories should be short and simple.

Guidelines for Preparing Stories. Once the story is selected, it must be prepared and presented. Unfortunately, many teachers do not adequately prepare stories before reading or telling them. If stories are read, we suggest preparing ahead of time so that you are acquainted with the story and its message.

Preparing to Tell a Story

1. Careful preparation is needed to create a vivid experience for children (Wolter, 1992). Allow adequate time before presentation to learn the story thoroughly.

2. Outline in your mind the sequence of the story events; recall the characters, their names, and where they fit into the sequence of events.

3. Practice telling the story, but do not try to memorize the author's exact words.

4. If visual aids will accompany the story, practice using them.

5. Practice appropriate gestures.

6. Make a note of words or references that the children might not understand so that you can give explanations before the story begins; then the story can continue without interruptions.

Methods of Presenting Stories. Remember, a story can be told while using your own body and facial expressions as the visual aids.

1. *Flip chart.* Illustrations or pictures representing the story are put on heavy paper and attached with large rings. Words for each page are printed on the back of the following page so that they are easily read, and then the page is flipped around. The children can view the illustrations while the teacher retains eye-to-eye contact during the presentation.

2. *Single object or picture.* A doll, animal figure, or puppet for single focus.

3. *Flannel-board story.* Use medium-weight Pellon® colored with marking pens or crayons. Often the figures can be traced from picture books or coloring books. A small piece of masking tape with a number on the back of each figure helps to order the sequence of each figure in the story.

4. *Record or record book*

5. *Tape-recorded story.* Presented with or without pictures

6. *Demonstration*

7. *Dramatization.* During or following the presentation

8. *Film, filmstrip, slides*

9. *Movie-box story.* Put story illustrations on a long piece of butcher paper, and then roll the paper on rollers or dowels. Show each

illustration as it is unrolled and viewed in a box with a hole cut in it, resembling a television screen.

10. *Chalk-talk story.* Use simple chalkboard illustrations to accompany a story.

11. *Child involvement.* Give each child a picture or object to hold during a particular part of the story, or give each child a part in the story.

12. *Overhead transparencies*

Guidelines for Presenting Stories. Stories can be read to children, but they are much more effective and meaningful when told. "Oral storytelling is a tradition even richer in its way than written storytelling—because it's something almost all of us can do," claims Richard Stone, a storyteller from Orlando, Florida (McLeod, 1997, p. 269). Storytelling is an interactive experience involving the story itself, the storyteller, and the audience (Turner & Oaks, 1997). Susan Klein was telling a story when the lights went out in the school auditorium. She continued, saying to the 200 high-school students, "I don't need the light if you don't. The pictures are all in your head" (McLeod, 1997, p. 271).

Suggested Guidelines for Presenting Stories

1. Make sure that all the children are comfortable and are able to see the storyteller; if visual aids are used, all children should be able to see them.
2. Generally, the smaller the group listening to the stories, the more effective the experience (Miller, 1990). Teachers can effectively group children by their developmental abilities, including their listening ability and their experience level (Wolter, 1992).
3. Use eye-to-eye contact in telling stories.
4. Keep a natural voice that is conversational and clear and that reaches all the children. Change the pitch and tempo of your voice to add interest.
5. Use gestures that are spontaneous and natural; use appropriate facial expressions. "Relax and allow your face to mirror your words and inner feelings" (Sherman, 1979, p. 26).
6. Relax and enjoy the story yourself. Keep it full of life, as well as simple and direct. Live the characters—feel their joys and sorrows, their laughter and struggles.
7. Draw on your own experience to add richness and meaning to the story.
8. Do not hesitate to ask an occasional question or give an explanation, but do not lose the flow and feeling of the story.
9. Younger children especially enjoy having their names in stories so that they become the characters in the story.

Guidelines for Evaluating Stories. Once the story has been told, the teacher should evaluate whether the desired goals and objectives were reached.

1. Did I tell the story instead of reading it?
2. Did the story maintain high interest throughout?
3. Did I clearly make the point intended?
4. Was eye-to-eye contact maintained?
5. Were my facial expressions suitable to the actions of the story?
6. Was my voice natural, enthusiastic, and appropriate in tone and pitch?
7. Were my gestures natural and spontaneous?
8. Were visual aids appropriate and easy to use?
9. Did the children listen to and enjoy the story?

Teachers should constantly acquaint themselves with the best in children's literature, both old and new. It is also suggested that each early childhood teacher have an anthology of children's literature available. Good literature can be the means of integrating many activities and planning projects around a single book. As an example, see Figure 8–3 for a web constructed around the story *The Jolly Postman or Other People's Letters* (Ahlberg & Ahlberg, Little Brown, Boston, 1986).

Poetry. "Poetry paints verbal pictures for children, tells them stories, and expresses emotions that they are feeling" (Diffily & Morrison, 1996,

On an outline of a mailbox, each child can decorate his or her personal box with a pen or collage materials.

Children use felt-tipped pens to make drawings, and then each child mails his or hers to a grandparent or relative.

Mail drop box

Food Activities

Field Trips

Art

Post office

Make and mail a treat to a child who has moved from the area or a class member's grandparent. Or, collect and prepare a box of treats and supplies such as toiletries to send to an area where they have suffered a natural disaster. Take it to the post office and mail it.

Songs about mail carriers. Example: "What Do You Want To Be When You Grow Up?"

Jolly Postman

Music

In cooperative learning groups, children come up with three reasons they would like to be a mail carrier.

Mail carrier

Visitors

Discuss with the children the label "postman." What is wrong with it? Discuss other sexist labels and brainstorm better choices. Make a chart titled "Use this instead of this."

Language & Literacy

Children write letters and then mail them. (Could write to a family member so they could see them received.) (If children do not write, letter can be dictated.)

Female mail carrier

Post office worker

Make a class booklet. On each page it will say: "A mail carrier experiences. . . ." Each child completes the sentence and then illustrates it.

FIGURE 8–3
Project Web on a Storybook

p. 49). Poetry stirs imagination and creative thinking. Through poetry, children become more keenly aware of sensory impressions. They find enjoyment and satisfaction in these impressions as they are expressed through the imagery of poetry. "Poetry can capture children's hearts and emotions, but only if it is nurtured through positive and satisfying experiences" (Buchoff, 1995, p. 151). Chil-

dren also delight in the sound and rhythm of language as it is expressed. Poetry sings, and it is rich, warm, and definite.

Poetry allows children to experience various emotions, feelings, and moods; become familiar with creative language; expand concept and language development; model desirable behaviors; and increase attention spans. Young children enjoy writing their own impressions in the form of poetry, especially when they learn that poetry does not require lines that rhyme.

Many types of poems are appropriate for children in the early childhood years. Children throughout time have loved Mother Goose and other nursery rhymes, perhaps because of the variety of subject matter, the surprise quality found in many, the rhyme, the musical movement, the repetition, and the short, easy-to-remember actions. Jump rope rhymes, also a form of poetry, are "part of an oral tradition that links communication and play . . . and expose(s) children to the arresting qualities of rhyme, rhythm, and humor" (Buchoff, 1995, p. 149). As children get older, they generally tend to show less interest in poetry. However, their enjoyment increases with the inclusion of humor, rhythm, and rhyme (Cullinan & Galda, 1994). Once children's enthusiasm for poetry is rekindled through rhymes and chants, then gradually add other types of poetry: ballads, free-form verse, haiku, limericks, and narrative poems (Buchoff, 1995). Since they are easily memorized, after just a few readings children will be saying them with you, and should be encouraged to do so. Young children also enjoy nonsense verse or poetry, ballad and story poems, poems based on fact, and those that are make-believe or fanciful. There are poems about nearly everything experienced in our world. If a poem cannot be found relating to a subject or concept, one can surely be written!

Poetry should not be read or presented in a singsong pattern, but with directness and sincerity. It should appeal to the emotions and flow with the right meter or rhythm. Most poems need not be explained, but read and enjoyed for the sake of the poem and its appeal to the individual child. Many of the suggestions presented in this chapter regarding stories are also appropriate for poetry. Poetry can be presented with pictures (or a single picture), puppets, objects, recordings, flannelboard illustrations, slides, overhead transparencies, or other visual aids.

In addition, many poems lend themselves to dramatization; even short nursery rhymes can be dramatized and put into action. For groups of children who are beginning to read, their favorite poems can be put on charts so that they can follow along as the poem is read. Children enjoy illustrating the poems that they hear.

Poems lend themselves to choral readings. The older the children, the more sophisticated the choral readings can be. Even young children can repeat their favorite poems and rhymes in choral speaking or reading. To begin choral speaking or reading, you will want to say the poem in unison first. Younger children can be divided into separate or solo parts from the group. For older children, there are other alternatives; for example, the children could be divided by voice pitch into groups of high, medium, and low voices or soft, medium, and heavy voices. When dividing a poem into choral speaking parts by voice pitch, have the high or soft voices take the delicate or lighter lines. Usually, these are the lines that ask questions. The low voices should take the lines that suggest mystery, gloom, or solemnity or that answer questions. The medium voices carry the narrative, give explanations, or introduce characters. When teaching choral speaking, be careful not to drill, and remember that it should be enjoyable and therapeutic.

Fingerplays also increase fine motor skills and facilitate the young child's ability to listen to and follow directions

Choral speaking also improves speaking ability by helping children to create a crisp, vigorous speech.

Fingerplays. When children learn action songs and fingerplays, they learn about number, shape, color, size, order and sequence, and names of body parts; they also learn muscle control and manual dexterity, rhythm of music and speech, new words, to follow directions, to be attentive, listening skills, predictability, and auditory discrimination (Diffily & Morrison, 1996). Fingerplays and chants are especially suited for younger children, and very often they are repeated in unison as a type of choral speaking. Fingerplays are short poems accompanied with finger motions; thus they are also a type of dramatization. They are useful attention getters and rest exercises. Whenever you prefer, change dramatizations, finger motions, or words to fit the developmental level, desired objectives, and enjoyment of the children. To extend the opportunities for literacy development, have the children illustrate each part of the fingerplay and then put them together as a book to be read!

Fingerplay Examples

Five Little Monkeys

Five little monkeys jumping on the bed.
One fell off and broke his head!
Mama called the doctor, and the doctor said,
"No more monkeys jumping on the bed."

(Continue with four little monkeys, three little monkeys, etc., until:)

No little monkeys jumping on the bed.
They all fell off and broke their heads!

Frogs

Five little frogs standing in a row.

(Hold up five fingers.)

This little frog stubbed his toe;

(Point to each finger in turn.)

This little frog cried, "Oh, no!"
This little frog laughed and was glad;
This little frog cried and was sad;
This little frog did what he should—
He ran for the doctor as fast as he could.

My Senses

I have two eyes to see with,
I have two feet to run.
I have two hands to feel with,
And a nose, I have but one.
I have two ears to hear with,
And a tongue to say good-day,
And two red cheeks for you to kiss.
So I will run away!

Summary

Young children should sense that "language is a tool for exploring, discovering, discussing, and learning across the curriculum" (Reutzel, 1997). We advocate an environment rich in opportunities for speaking and listening and also rich in print, where children see adults reading and writing and where they are given opportunities to make sense out of print and to express their thoughts both orally and in print.

Teachers should make certain that practice in reading and writing is purposeful and that children see writing as a way to communicate meaningfully. Literacy should be integrated into every part of the curriculum, and young children should have many opportunities daily for writing and reading, even if that means reading and writing to or *with* the child rather than *by* the child on his or her journey toward independent work (Reutzel, 1997). Make certain that you provide many writing tools: pencils, pens, markers, chalk, and crayons.

The primary factors influencing the development of language appear to be (1) the child's innate ability to learn language, (2) the quality of the model or the early stimulation and variety provided by the model, and (3) the ability of caregivers to expand or extend the child's language.

Oral language can be encouraged in early childhood by conversing, discussing, clarifying, reporting, explaining, reacting, dramatizing, storytelling, fingerplays, poems, and rhymes.

Young children should have many opportunities to read for enjoyment from excellent literature: narrative and information. Children's experiences provide a frame of reference for them to draw on in order to make sense of what is read to them or what they read themselves. In addition, they need help if they are in reading trouble, ample materials for reading and writing, and much time to read and be read to.

The balanced literacy approach takes children from where they are, accepts what they do or do not bring with them, accommodates differences, and then builds on each child's language competencies and guides the child toward becoming literate and finding joy, meaning, and pleasure in literacy. Children need to view others around them as being literate; and then, as maturation, readiness, and experiences allow, children need to be given many opportunities to talk, read, and write so that they view themselves as literate. Early childhood teachers can stimulate the child's interest in literacy and facilitate the child's efforts to become literate.

Student Learning Activities

1. Study the language development of a child 3 to 8 years of age and compare it to the chart of Normal Language Development (Table 8–1). What similarities do you find? What differences do you find? You may wish to make comparisons with another child of approximately the same age.

2. You have learned that there is much variation in language development in young children. From your own experiences, describe situations in which variation in language has been obvious. Then try to determine some of the factors influencing the language development of a particular child.

3. As a teacher of young children, how can you be influential in helping young children to expand, refine, and enhance their language development?

4. Observe in an early childhood classroom with a focus on literacy development. What is the approach of this particular teacher to teaching literacy? What literacy components did you observe? Describe the activities that you observed, and identify the ways that each activity contributed to the development of literacy. For example, did the activity enhance listening or speaking skills? Did the activity teach new words? Were the activities appropriate, or can you think of ways to achieve the desired objectives and goals in a more appropriate way? Did the classroom integrate literacy development into all areas of the curriculum?

5. Plan, implement, and evaluate at least two activities to encourage listening skills in young children.

6. Plan, implement, and evaluate at least two activities to encourage speaking skills in young children.

7. Plan, implement, and evaluate at least two activities to encourage emergent reading skills in young children.

8. Plan, implement, and evaluate at least two activities to encourage emergent writing skills in young children.

9. Select a meaningful picture book and then plan, implement, and evaluate a literacy lesson using the format described in this chapter.

10. Based on the criteria given in this chapter for selecting appropriate stories, begin a story file with at least five excellent, culturally diverse stories for children 3 to 8 years of age. Make a card for each story. On the card, include the title of the story, author, illustrator, publisher, copyright date, age level that the story is appropriate for, and a brief summary of the story.

11. Based on the guidelines for selecting, preparing, and presenting stories, select a story appropriate for preschool, kindergarten, first-, or second-grade children and then prepare and present it. Afterward, use the questions suggested in this chapter as a guide for evaluating your story presentation.

12. Prepare two stories using two different methods of presentation suggested in this chapter. For example, prepare a flannel-board story and a flip-chart story.

13. Begin a poetry file representing many varied cultures for use with children 3 to 8 years of age. Include on your file card the title, author, citation of the source of the poem, and the poem.

14. Begin a collection of appropriate culturally diverse pictures to accompany poems. Mount the pictures neatly and make them durable. Attach or write the poem on the back.

15. Memorize at least three fingerplays and teach them to children. Use cooperative learning strategies to teach at least one.

Suggested Resources

The list of suggested resources for language and literacy development could be limitless, because there are so many excellent pictures, books, records, tapes, multimedia kits, films, filmstrips, videos, and computer software that could be used to stimulate speaking, listening, reading, and writing. Only a few of our favorites have been selected as examples here. Be selective in the kinds of resources that you choose to stimulate literary development in young children.

Resources for Children's Literature

Cullinan, B. E. (1987). *Children's literature in the reading program*. Newark, DE: International Reading Association.

Cullinan, B. E. (1992). *Read to me: Raising kids who love to read*. New York: Scholastic.

Hurst, C. O. (1997). *Once upon a time . . .*. DeSoto, TX: McGraw-Hill Learning Materials.

Hurst, C. O. (1997). *Picture book guide for first and second grade*. DeSoto, TX: McGraw-Hill Learning Materials.

Hurst, C. O. (1997). *Picture book guide for pre-kindergarten and kindergarten*. DeSoto, TX: McGraw-Hill Learning Materials.

Lipson, E. G. (1988). *Parent's guide to the best books for children*. New York: Times.

Norton, D. (1995). *Through the eyes of a child: An introduction to children's literature* (4th ed.). Upper Saddle River, NJ: Merrill/Prentice Hall.

Trelease, J. (1989). *The new read-aloud handbook*. New York: Penguin.

Children's Books

Abolafia, Y. (1991). *Fox tale*. New York: Greenwillow.

Ackerman, K. (1988). *Song and dance man*. New York: Knopf.

Ahlberg, J., & A. Ahlberg (1986). *The jolly postman or other people's letters*. Boston: Little, Brown.

Ahlberg, J., & A. Ahlberg (1990). *Peek-a-boo!* New York: Viking.

Anglund, J. W. (1977). *In a pumpkin shell*. New York: Harcourt Brace Jovanovich.

Anglund, J. W. (1977). *Nibble nibble mousekin: A tale of Hansel and Gretel*. New York: Harcourt Brace Jovanovich.

Banks, L. R. (1981). *The Indian in the cupboard*. New York: Doubleday.

Banks, L. R. (1986). *The return of the Indian*. New York: Doubleday.

Banks, L. R. (1989). *The secret of the Indian*. New York: Doubleday.

Bradby, M. (1995). *More than anything else*. New York: Orchard.

Breathed, B. (1993). *A goodnight opus*. Boston: Little, Brown.

Brett, J. (1995). *Armadillo rodeo*. New York: Scholastic.

Brodmann, A. (1993). *The gift*. New York. Simon & Schuster.

Brown, M. W. (1947). *Goodnight moon*. New York: Harper.

Brown, M. W. (1972). *The runaway bunny*. San Diego, CA: Harcourt Brace Jovanovich.

Buehner, C. (1995). *It's a spoon, not a shovel*. New York: Dial.

Bunting, E. (1995). *Dandelions*. San Diego, CA: Harcourt, Brace.

Burton, A. (1991). *Where does the trail lead?* New York: Simon & Schuster.

Burton, R. (1994). *My best shoes*. New York: Tambourine.

Butler, D. (1991). *Higgledy piggledy hobbledy hoy*. New York: Greenwillow.

Butler, S. (1991). *Henny, Penny*. New York: Tambourine.

Cameron, A. (1986). *More stories Julian tells*. New York: Knopf.

Carle, E. (1985). *The very busy spider*. New York: Philomel.

Charlip, R. (1964). *Fortunately*. New York: Macmillan.

Charney, S. (1994). *Six thick thumbs: A tongue-twisting tale*. New York: Troll.

Coles, R. (1995). *The story of Ruby Bridges*. New York: Scholastic.

Dahl, R. (1961). *James and the giant peach*. New York: Knopf.

dePaola, T. (1986). *Tomie dePaola's famous nursery tales*. New York: Putnam.

Ernst, L. C. (1996). *The letters are lost*. New York: Viking.

Estes, E. (1944). *The hundred dresses*. New York: Harcourt Brace Jovanovich.

Fiday, B., & D. Fiday (1990). *Time to go*. San Diego, CA: Harcourt Brace Jovanovich.

Fitzhugh, L. (1964). *Harriet the spy*. New York: Harper & Row.

Gahnnon, G. (1996). *Tomorrow's alphabet*. New York: Greenwillow.

Gifford, H. (1991). *Red fox*. New York: Dial.

Gray, L. M. (1993). *Dear Willie Rudd*. New York: Simon & Schuster.

Guarino, D. (1989). *Is your mama a llama?* New York: Scholastic.

Hillman, B. (1995). *That pesky toaster*. New York: Hyperion Books for Children.

Hoopes, L. (1996). *The unbeatable bread*. New York: Dial.

Hughes, S. (1988). *Out and about*. New York: Lothrop, Lee & Shepard.

Hughes, S. (1994). *The sweet and sour animal book*. New York: Oxford University Press.

Hurwitz, J. (1991). *"E" is for Elisa*. New York: Morrow.

Kalan, R. (1979). *Blue sea*. New York: Greenwillow.

Kellogg, S. (1976). *Much bigger than Martin*. New York: Dial.

Kimmel, E. A. (retold by) (1991). *Baba Yaga: A Russian folktale*. New York: Holiday House.

Koss, A. G. (1991). *City critters around the world*. Los Angeles: Price Stern Sloan.

Lear, E. (1991). *The owl and the pussycat*. New York: Lothrop, Lee & Shepard.

Leventhal, D. (1994). *What is your language?* New York: Dutton.

Lionni, L. (1973). *Swimmy*. New York: Pinwheel.

Livingston, M. C. (1986). *Sea songs*. New York: Holiday House.

MacLachlan, P. (1985). *Sarah, plain and tall*. New York: Harper & Row.

MacLachlan, P. (1994). *All the places to love*. New York: HarperCollins.

Mahurin, T. (1995). *Jeremy Kooloo*. New York: Dutton.

Martin, B. (1983). *Brown bear, brown bear, what do you see?* New York: Holt.

Martin, B., & J. Archambault (1989). *Chicka chicka boom boom*. New York: Simon & Schuster.

Martin, J. (1991). *Carrot/parrot*. New York: Simon & Schuster.

Mayer, M. (1968). *There's a nightmare in my closet*. New York: Dial.

Mayer, M. (1987). *There's an alligator under my bed*. New York: Dial.

McDonald, M. (1992). *Whoo-oo is it?* New York: Orchard.

McIlwain, J. (1995). *The Dorling Kindersley children's illustrated dictionary*. New York: Dorling Kindersley.

McNaughton, C. (1994). *Making friends with Frankenstein*. Cambridge, MA: Candlewick.

Miller, M. (1991). *Whose shoe?* New York: Greenwillow.

Mitchell, M. K. (1993). *Uncle Jed's barbershop*. New York: Simon & Schuster.

Morrissey, D. (1994). *Ship of dreams*. New York: Abrams.

Neitzel, S. (1995). *The bag I'm taking to Grandma's*. New York: Greenwillow.

Nelson, N. (1994). *Writing and numbers: Non-verbal communication series*. New York: Thomson Learning.

Nikola-Lisa, W. (1991). *Night is coming*. New York: Dutton.

O'Neill, M. (1961). *Hailstones and halibut bones*. Garden City, NY: Doubleday.

Pilkey, D. (1994). *Dog breath: The horrible trouble with Hally Tosis*. New York: Blue Sky.

Piper, W. (1930). *The little engine that could*. New York: Grosset & Dunlap.

Potter, B. (1902). *Peter Rabbit* (series). New York: Frederick Warne.

Prelutsky, J. (1990). *Something big has been here*. New York: Greenwillow.

Raffi (1995). *Raffi's top 10 songs to read*. New York: Crown.

Rosen, M. (1995). *The best of Michael Rosen*. Berkeley, CA: Wetland.

Rylant, C. (1982). *When I was young in the mountains*. New York: Dutton.

Rylant, C. (1983). *Miss Maggie*. New York: Dutton.

Samton, S. W. (1995). *Frogs in clogs*. New York: Crown.

Scarry, R. (1976). *Early words*. New York: Random House.

Scheer, J., & M. Bileck (1964). *Rain makes applesauce*. New York: Holiday House.

Scieszka, J., & L. Smith (1992). *The stinky cheese man and other fairly stupid tales*. New York: Viking.

Selden, G. (1960). *Cricket in Times Square*. New York: Farrar.

Sendak, M. (1963). *Where the wild things are*. New York: Harper & Row.

Shannon, G. (1995). *April showers*. New York: Greenwillow.

Shaw, N. (1991). *Sheep in a shop*. Boston: Houghton Mifflin.

Shaw, N. (1994). *Sheep take a hike*. New York: Houghton Mifflin.

Sierra, J., & R. Kaminski (1991). *Multicultural folktales: Stories to tell young children*. Phoenix, AZ: Oryx.

Sieveking, A. (1990). *What's inside?* New York: Dial.

Speek, T. (1995). *Two cool cows*. New York: Putnam.

Stewig, J. W. (retold by) (1991). *Stone soup*. New York: Holiday House.

Tolhurst, M. (1990). *Somebody and the three bears*. New York: Orchard.

Trapini, I. (1995). *Oh, where, oh, where has my little dog gone?* Boston: Whispering Coyote.

Travizas, E. (1993). *The three little wolves and the big bad pig*. New York: Margaret K. McElderry.

Van Allsburg, C. (1985). *The polar express*. New York: Houghton Mifflin.

VanLean, N. (1995). *In a circle long ago: A treasury of native lore from North America*. New York: Apple Soup.

VanLean, N. (1995). *Mama rocks, Papa sings*. New York: Random House.

Vaughan, M. K. (1995). *Tingo tango mango tree*. Morristown, NJ: Silver Burdett.

Viorst, J. (1972). *Alexander and the terrible, horrible, no good, very bad day*. New York: Atheneum.

Vozar, D. (1993). *Yo, hungry wolf!* New York: Bantam Doubleday Dell Books for Young Readers.

White, E. B. (1952). *Charlotte's web*. New York: Harper & Bros.

Wilder, L. I. (1932). *Little house in the big woods*. New York: Harper & Row.

Wilder, L. I. (1994). *My first Little House books: Dance at Grandpa's*. New York: HarperCollins.

Williams, M. (1985). *The velveteen rabbit*. New York: Knopf.

Wilson, G. (1995). *Prowlpuss*. Cambridge, MA: Candlewick.

Wilson, S. (1991). *Garage song*. New York: Simon & Schuster.

Winter, J. (1984). *Hush little baby*. New York: Pantheon.

Children's ABC Books

Anglund, J. W. (1960). *A Mother Goose ABC*. New York: Harcourt, Brace & World.

Anno, M. (1975). *Anno's alphabet: Adventure in imagination*. New York: Crowell.

Auerbach, S. (1986). *The alphabet tree*. Mt. Desert, ME: Windswept House.

Base, G. (1987). *Animalia*. New York: Abrams.

Bayer, J. (1984). *A—My name is Alice*. New York: Dial.

Bender, R. (1996). *The A to Z beastly jamboree*. New York: Lodestar.

Berg, C. 1991. *D is for dolphin*. Santa Fe, NM: Windom.

Cleaver, E. (1985). *ABC*. New York: Macmillan.

Crews, D. (1984). *We read: A to Z*. New York: Greenwillow.

Darling, K. (1996). *Amazon ABC*. New York: Lothrop, Lee & Shepard.

Fain, K. (1996). *Handsigns: A sign language alphabet*. San Francisco: Chronicle.

Feelings, M. (1974). *Jambo means hello: Swahili alphabet book*. New York: Dial.

Fujikawa, G. (1974). *Gyo Fujikawa's A to Z picture book*. New York: Grosset & Dunlap.

Gag, W. (1933). *ABC bunny*. New York: Putnam.

Garten, J. (1964). *The alphabet tale*. New York: Random House.

Greenaway, K. (1886). *A—Apple pie*. New York: Frederick Warne.

Grimes, N. (1995). *C is for city*. New York: Lorthrop, Lee & Shepard.

Hague, K. (1984). *Alphabears: An ABC book*. New York: Holt, Rinehart & Winston.

Hepworth, C. (1992). *Antics*. New York: Putnam.

Hyman, T. S. (1980). *A little alphabet*. Boston: Little, Brown.

Johnson, S. (1995). *Alphabet city*. New York: Viking.

Jordan, M., & T. Jordan (1996). *Amazon alphabet*. New York: Viking.

Lionni, L. (1968). *The alphabet tree*. New York: Pantheon.

Lobel, A. (1990). *Alison's zinnia*. New York: Greenwillow.

Lobel, A. (1994). *Away from home*. New York: Greenwillow.

Lobel, A., & A. Lobel (1981). *On Market Street*. New York: Greenwillow.

MacDonald, S. (1986). *Alphabatics*. New York: Bradbury.

McPhail, D. (1997). *Animals A to Z*. Jefferson City, MO: Scholastic.

Miller, E. (1972). *Mousekin's ABC*. Upper Saddle River, NJ: Prentice Hall.

Miller, J. (1987). *Farm alphabet book*. Jefferson City, MO: Scholastic.

Mullins, P. (1994). *V is for vanishing: An alphabet of endangered animals*. New York: HarperCollins.

Musgrove, M. (1976). *Ashanti to Zulu: African traditions*. New York: Dial.

Phillips, T. (1989). *Day care ABC*. Niles, IL: Whitman.

Rotner, S. (1996). *Action alphabet*. New York: Atheneum.

Sendak, M. (1962). *Alligators all around*. New York: HarperCollins.

Shannon, G. (1996). *Tomorrow's alphabet*. New York: Greenwillow.

Shaw, E. (1997). *Grandmother's alphabet: Grandma can be anything from A to Z*. Duluth, MN: Pfeifer–Hamilton.

Updike, J. (1995). *A helpful alphabet of friendly objects*. New York: Knopf.

Van Allsburg, C. (1987). *The Z was zapped*. Boston: Houghton Mifflin.

Walker, J. (1995). *Ridiculous rhymes from A to Z*. New York: Henry Holt.

Well, R. (1992). *A to Zen*. New York: Simon Schuster.

Wildsmith, B. (1970). *ABC*. New York: Pantheon.

Children's Poetry, Rhyme, and Chant Books

Anglund, J. W. (1980). *Almost a rainbow: A book of poems*. New York: Random House.

Baldwin, R. M. (1972). *One hundred nineteenth-century rhyming alphabets in English*. Carbondale: Southern Illinois University.

Boardman, B., & D. Boardman (1993). *Red hot peppers: The skookum book of jump rope games, rhymes, and fancy footwork*. Seattle, WA: Sasquatch.

Cole, J. (1989). *Anna banana: 101 jump rope rhymes*. New York: Morrow.

Cole, J., & S. Calmenson (1990). *Miss Mary Mack and other children's street rhymes*. New York: Morrow.

Colgin, M. L. (comp.) (1982). *Chants for children*. Manlius, NY: Colgin.

de Angeli, M. (1979). *Marguerite de Angeli's book of nursery and Mother Goose rhymes*. Garden City, NY: Doubleday.

Delmar, G. (1983). *Children's counting-out rhymes, fingerplays, jump-rope and bounce ball chants and other rhymes*. Jefferson, NC: McFarland.

dePaola, T. (1985). *Tomie dePaola's Mother Goose*. New York: Putnam.

DeRegniers, B. (1976). *A bunch of poems and verses*. Boston: Houghton Mifflin.

DeRegniers, B., E. Moore, & M. M. White (1969).*Poems children will sit still for*. New York: Scholastic.

Dodson, F. (1978). *I wish I had a computer that makes waffles.... Teaching your children with modern nursery rhymes*. LaJolla, CA: Oak Tree.

Dunn, S.(1987).*Butterscotch dreams*. Markham, Ont.: Pembroke.

Dunn, S.(1990). *Crackers & crumbs: Chants for whole language*. Portsmouth, NH: Heinemann.

Edwards, P. (1996). *Some smug slug*. New York: HarperCollins.

Frank, J.(1968).*Poems to read to the very young*. New York: Random House.

Frank, J. (1982). *More poems to read to the very young*. New York: Random House.

Geismer, B., & A. Suter (1945). *Very young verses*. Boston: Houghton Mifflin.

Greenaway, K. (ill.) (1882). *Kate Greenaway's Mother Goose, or, the old nursery rhymes*. New York: Frederick Warne.

Hague, M.(1984).*Mother Goose:A collection of classic nursery rhymes*. New York:Holt,Rinehart & Winston.

Hearn, M. P. (1981). *A day in verse: Breakfast, books, and dreams*. New York: Frederick Warne.

Hopkins, L. B. (1995). *Good rhymes, good times*. New York: HarperCollins.

Hughes, S. (1995).*Rhymes for Annie Rose*. New York: Lothrop, Lee & Shepard.

Jaramillo, N. P.(1994).*Grandmother's nursery rhymes (Las nans de Abuelita)*. New York: Holt.

Langstaff, C., & J. Langstaff (1973). *Shimmy shimmy coke-a-pop: A collection of city children's street games and rhymes*. Garden City, NY: Doubleday.

Larrick, N. (1983). *When the dark comes dancing:A bedtime poetry book*. New York: Putnam.

McMillan, B. (1994). *Puffins climb, penguins rhyme*. New York: Gulliver Books, Harcourt, Brace.

Milne, A.A. (1961). *Now we are six*. New York: Dutton.

Milne, A. A. (1961). *When we were very young*. New York: Dutton.

Prelutsky, J. (1977).*The snopp on the sidewalk and other poems*. New York: Greenwillow.

Prelutsky, J. (1982). *The baby uggs are hatching*. New York: Greenwillow.

Prelutsky, J. (1983). *The Random House book of poetry*. New York: Random House.

Prelutsky, J. (1983). *Zoo doings: Animal poems*. New York: Greenwillow.

Prelutsky, J. (1984). *The new kid on the block*. New York: Greenwillow.

Prelutsky,J.(1991).*For laughing out loud: Poems to tickle your funnybone*. New York: Knopf.

Schwartz, A. (1992). *And the green grass grew all around*. New York: HarperCollins.

Silverstein, S. (1974). *Where the sidewalk ends: Poems and drawings*. New York: Harper & Row.

Silverstein, S. (1981). *A light in the attic*. New York: Harper & Row.

Sutherland, Z. (1990). *The Orchard book of nursery rhymes*. New York: Orchard.

Tompert, A. (1984). *Nothing sticks like a shadow*. Boston: Houghton Mifflin.

Tudor,T. (1944).*Mother Goose*. New York: Henry Z.Walck.

Wayman,J.(1988).*Don't burn down the birthday cake*. Houston, TX: Heartstone.

Wildsmith, B. (1970). *Mother Goose*. New York: Pantheon.

Withers, C. (1988). *A rocket in my pocket: The rhymes and chants of young Americans*. New York: Henry Holt.

Wright, B. F. (ill.) (1961). *The real Mother Goose*. Chicago: Rand–McNally.

Yolen,J.(1992).*Street rhymes around the world*.Honesdale,PA:Wordsong.

Tapes, Cassettes, and CDs

Many kinds of recordings can be used to stimulate language development. Frequently, records can enhance listening skills. Children can listen to records to learn songs and sing along, they can be encouraged to listen for rhythms or beat patterns of rhythm records, and they will be anxious to listen to many story records. Thus, specific suggestions will not be given, but teachers are encouraged to find new approaches to using records, tapes, CDs and cassettes in order to stimulate the language development of young children.

Pictures

The Child's World. A variety of subjects organized into sets. Resource booklets giving additional activities and language experiences accompany the sets. Examples are *The many moods of Mother Goose* (8 pictures) and *Moods and emotions* (8 pictures).

David C. Cook. Many sets to select from; suggested activities accompany each picture. Examples are *Nursery rhymes* (30627) and *Storyland* (68510).

Society for Visual Education. A variety of subjects organized into sets. Information for discussions, activities, questions, and other language activities appear on the backs of the pictures. Sets deal with science themes, seasons and holidays, community helpers, and children around the world.

Multimedia Kits

Beginning auditory reading skills with Winnie-the-Pooh.Walt Disney.
Beginning visual reading skills with Winnie-the-Pooh.Walt Disney.

Creative dramatics. The Child's World.
Early world of learning (preschool– K). World Book Educational Products.
Let's talk with Winnie-the-Pooh. Walt Disney.
Sing consonants with Winnie-the-Pooh. Walt Disney.
Sing short vowels with Winnie-the-Pooh. Walt Disney.
Tales of Jiminy Cricket. Walt Disney.
Walt Disney read-along libraries 1, 2, 3, 4. Walt Disney.
Welcome to reading. World Book Educational Products.

Teaching Videos

Beginning to Read and Write. Films for the Humanities & Sciences.
Classroom Management. Heineman.
Doing What Comes Naturally: Childhood Language Acquisition. Films for the Humanities & Sciences.
Guided Reading. Heineman.
Language Development. Films for the Humanities & Sciences.
Teaching Beginning Readers and Writers. Films for the Humanities & Sciences.
What Is Whole Language? Films for the Humanities & Sciences.

Computer Software

A to Zap. Sunburst.
Bailey's Book House. Riverdeep Interactive Learning.

Beginning Writing Skills. Sunburst.
Broderbund's Living Books. *Grandma and Me.* Broderbund Software.
Broderbund's Living Books. *Little Monster.* Broderbund Software.
Broderbund's Living Books. *The Ruff's Bone*: Broderbund Software.
Broderbund's Living Books. *Tortoise and Hare.* Broderbund Software.
Consonant Blends and Digraphs (designed by *Tenth Planet*©). Sunburst.
Creepy Cave (designed by Learning Resources©). Sunburst.
Every Child a Reader (designed by *Stepping Stones Software*). Sunburst.
First Phonics (designed by *Stepping Stones Software*). Sunburst.
Kidtalk. First Byte.
Let's Go Read! 1: An Island Adventure (PreK–K). Riverdeep Interactive Learning.
Letter Sounds (designed by *Tenth Planet*©). Sunburst.
The Letterbugs Get Ready to Read. Sunburst.
Max's Attic: Long & Short Vowels (designed by Learning Resources©). Sunburst.
Paint, Write and Play. The Learning Co.
Python Path: Phonics Word Families (designed by Learning Resources©). Sunburst.
Read, Write & Type. The Learning Co.
Reader Rabbit and friends: Let's start learning (preschool–K). The Learning Co.

Reader Rabbit 1 (K–1). The Learning Co.
Reader Rabbit 2 (1–3). The Learning Co.
Reading Blaster (K–2). Sunburst.
Reading Blaster (1–3). Sunburst.
Reading Who? Reading You! Something Phonics, Something New! (designed by *Stepping Stones Software*). Sunburst.
Roots, Prefixes, and Suffixes (designed by *Tenth Planet*©). Sunburst.
The Semantic Mapper. Teacher Support Software.
Snapdragon (1994). The Learning Co.
Stanley's Sticker Stories. Riverdeep Interactive Learning.
Storybook Weaver. The Learning Co.
Sunbuddy Writer. Sunburst.
Sunken Treasure Adventure: Beginning Blends (designed by Learning Resources©). Sunburst.
Super Story Tree. Scholastic.
Talking Text Writer. Scholastic.
Vowel Patterns (designed by *Tenth Planet*©). Sunburst.
Vowels: Short and Long (designed by *Tenth Planet*©). Sunburst.
Why Do We Have to? World Book Educational Products.
Word Parts (designed by *Tenth Planet*©). Sunburst.
Words Around Me (PreK–3rd grade). Riverdeep Interactive Learning.
The Writing Adventure. Developmental Learning Materials.
Writing with Picture Books. Sunburst.

Chapter 9

Physical Science Experiences

The child is the focus and center of the science curriculum. From a constructivist perspective, the individual child should be viewed as an explorer making his or her own discoveries and constructing knowledge and understanding (Lind, 1997). Constructivist teaching is "based on the notion that humans are constructors of their own knowledge, rather than reproducers of someone else's knowledge" (Zahorik, 1995, p. 8). This focus on the individual child can be seen in the first three goals recommended by the National Center for Improving Science Education (1990, p. 9). They are to:

- develop each child's innate curiosity about the world;
- broaden each child's procedural and thinking skills for investigating the world, solving problems, and making decisions; and
- increase each child's knowledge of the natural world.

In 1995, after nearly 5 years of development, the National Research Council (1996) completed the National Science Education Standards. These standards suggest criteria for judging quality in

- Scientific knowledge of students
- Excellence in teaching
- Professional development for teachers
- Assessment procedures
- Programs to support effective science teaching

These standards are of particular importance to teachers in early childhood education in two specific areas: science content and teaching science—or what should we teach and how should we teach it? (Rakow & Bell, 1998). These questions will be addressed throughout Chapters 9, 10, and 11. The standards suggest that the goal of science education should be science literacy, rather than acquisition of specific content-related vocabulary (Owens, 1999). It should promote wonder, inquiry, and understanding (Rakow & Bell, 1998).

Science for young children is not so much a body of facts and information as it is a process of doing and thinking. It is also a system for "organizing and reporting discoveries" (Lind, 1997, p. 75). Children have a natural curiosity about the environment in which they live, and this curiosity is the driving force behind problem solving (Lind, 1997). "A young child's natural curiosity and willingness to explore new things make the preschool years the perfect time for beginning the science curriculum" (Diffily & Morrison, 1996, p. 75). This natural curiosity, enjoyment, and desire in young children provide the motivation for them to explore, ask

---

Chapters 9, 10, and 11 address numerous ideas, concepts, and activities relating to the physical, earth, and life sciences. The introductory section of this chapter discusses science in general and is relevant to the next two chapters as well.

questions, and seek answers (Stone & Glascott, 1997/1998). Their questions reflect their interest in everything about them—nature, people, animals, plants, and so on. "Do snakes crawl backward?" "What does an earthworm eat?" "Do trees have birthdays?" "Why do magnets pick up pins?" These endless questions often open up avenues into the realm of science. As we answer questions through exploring, providing experiments and materials, and problem solving, we are supplying answers and encouraging the child's continued curiosity. It has been found that "problem solving and reflective thinking play an important role in children's learning of science in school" (Lind, 1997, p. 89). This great emotion of curiosity and its importance in learning was discussed by Rachel Carson (1956, pp. 42–43) over 45 years ago.

> If I had influence with the good fairy who is supposed to preside over the christening of all children, I should ask that her gift to each child in the world be a sense of wonder so indestructible that it would last throughout life, as an unfailing antidote against the boredom and disenchantments of later years, the sterile preoccupation with things that are artificial, the alienation from the sources of our strength.

Although reasons for science instruction are usually stated in terms of cognitive objectives, Stone & Glascott (1997/1998), remind teachers of the importance of also including the affective (or emotional) side of science. This involves three important areas for consideration:

- Affective environment (risk free, enjoyable, not bound by time limits, allows choices)
- Affective teacher (model excitement, enjoyment, and desire to know; value and support children's explorations)
- Affective child (experiences autonomy, self-confidence, self-esteem, success, freedom to explore)

Teachers of young children must "promote the affective [emotional] side of science or risk strangling the scientific process" (Stone & Glascott, 1997/1998, p. 102).

THE TEACHER

The responsibility of teachers is to facilitate, not direct, the scientific explorations of children. Kupetz & Twiest (2000, p. 60) remind us to "teach less and

Discovering for yourself what happens when you mix colors together is much more exciting than being told what will happen.

share more." The outcomes of too many science activities are controlled by the teacher, rather than by the children (Moscovici & Nelson, 1998).

> When children's natural inquiry and curiosity drive the outcomes of science experiences, understanding is expanded, motivation is maintained, and retention is increased.

The teacher's interest and curiosity will often kindle the child's interest in exploring and finding out. Children's curiosity naturally leads them to experiment and learn about science in their environment. When the teacher's behavior demonstrates a sense of interest, wonder, and curiosity, it is modeled by the children. Answered questions add to children's reserves of knowledge and increase their interest in, awareness of, and understanding of the world in which they are living (Lind, 1997). However, it is best to allow them to discover the answers themselves through exploring, reading, listening, questioning, observing, and other process skills. Skilled early childhood education teachers "understand that direct exploration of materials and meaningful phenomena is the cornerstone of science for young children" (NAEYC, 1996a, p. 83).

> To teach science effectively, it is suggested that teachers:
>
> - Allow time, because children need time when they are engaged in exploring and discovering.
> - Know something, because the teacher's knowledge is what sparks and directs the children's learning.
> - Be open to their own lack of knowledge, but demonstrate their excitement in learning.
> - Value and expect children's questions, as well as their interpretation of and perspective on teacher queries.
> - Demonstrate for children how to record observations, because writing down what

> is observed and remembered enhances learning.
> - Provide materials and supplies for science explorations.
>
> Perry & Rivkin, 1992.

"Because . . . children learn best by working with concrete materials, employing all their senses and discussing their ideas, early childhood teachers help children do science rather than only read about it" (NAEYC, 1996a, p. 84). "Active, hands-on, student-centered inquiry should be at the core of good science education" (Lind, 1997, p. 75).

DAILY SCIENCE EXPERIENCES

> Science is, and should be, a natural part of a child's daily experiences. It is not a separate subject to be reserved for specific experiences in the curriculum; it is present everywhere in the world around the children, and they are anxious to explore it, discover answers, and build new understandings.

Keep science integrated into the entire curriculum, that is, where it naturally is, in math, history, health, literacy, and so on. Do not treat it as a segregated topic to be explored every so often in only designated themes or set time schedules. Take advantage of the unplanned experiences, and select planned activities from the children's daily experiences. Many science activities are planned and prepared for ahead of time. However, take time with the children to notice and enjoy everyday opportunities for experiencing the wonders of science: fluffy clouds, lacy spider webs, soft breezes, the daytime moon, flower shoots, migrating insects, rain shower puddles, drifting snowflakes, darting fireflies, crisp leaves, snake skins, singing birds, and so on. When materials for exploring the physical world are included in the daily learning environment, when we ask open-ended questions, and when children record their experiences, we are helping them to experience physical science. Creative thinking, problem solving, decision making, cooperative learning, social interactions, verbal skills, and self-confidence are all enhanced through "sciencing." "Experiences in the out-of-doors tend to be rich in opportunities for nurturing growth in all of the developmental domains, including adaptive, aesthetic, cognitive, communication, sensorimotor, and socioemotional" (Wilson, 1995b, p. 4).

VALUES OF SCIENCE ACTIVITIES

Science should not emphasize teaching children facts, but should involve them in the process of understanding their world through observing, manipulating, problem solving, and engagement with science activities and materials—in short *doing*. Kilmer and Hofman (1995, p. 44) prefer to use the term "*sciencing*, which conveys the child's active involvement in learning about science and points out the emphasis on process. Sciencing is a 'hands-on, brains-on' undertaking." The benefits of science for young children include the promotion of intellectual growth, greater potential for success in school, and opportunities for the development of positive self-image. Sciencing can occur in any place at any time (Kilmer & Hofman, 1995) and should be integrated with other parts of the curriculum (Lind, 1997).

Process skills provide the framework for science education in early childhood, and children should be encouraged to develop them as they participate in science experiences. Examples of process skills include

- Analyzing
- Classifying
- Communicating
- Comparing
- Computing
- Counting
- Creating
- Defining
- Experimenting
- Explaining
- Hypothesizing
- Inferring
- Investigating
- Measuring
- Observing
- Organizing
- Predicting
- Recording
- Verifying

These skills are important in the cognitive, reasoning, and thinking processes. Process skills are, in fact, thinking skills; these skills will affect every area of learning and can be particularly encouraged and developed in science activities.

Teachers should pay careful attention to the skills just listed and should write direct objectives for science activities and other appropriate experiences that will assist in the development of these skills. Skillful, careful, and wise teaching is essential for children to be taught to observe, compare, create, communicate, analyze, and hypothesize. The kinds of comments, questions, and approaches to planned activities, as well as the activities themselves, make a difference in whether these process or thinking skills are developed. Teachers should constantly be aware of children's individual development in science and try to stretch their abilities by expanding process skills and teaching higher-level process skills as children are ready for them.

To elaborate further on the process skills that will be particularly utilized in early childhood: In *observing*, children are taught to use all their senses to learn about things and experiences. In *comparing*, children compare likenesses and differences among objects and ideas. In *classifying*, children are asked to group or sort by categories, to find something that does not belong, and to be able to name the group or say how the members of a group are alike. *Communicating* is using words orally and, for children in the later early childhood years, writing to explain or describe an event or happening. In *measuring*, children are involved in using standard or nonstandard units of measure; in either case, the children give a quantitative description. This may involve time, distance, volume, temperature, weight, or numbers. When children *infer* something, they observe and add meaning to their observation. When they *predict*, they guess what they expect will happen. When they *record* information, they either dictate or write down what they observe.

However, sciencing is more than these processes alone. Science experiences in early childhood should help children to form scientific concepts. Science activities that build on children's natural curiosity help them to learn about physical properties and stimulate problem-solving skills (Marxen, 1995). For this to be accomplished, such activities should meet the four criteria suggested by Kamii and DeVries (1993):

- Children must be responsible for producing the movement by their own action.

- Children must be able to vary their action.

- Children must be able to observe the object's reaction.

- The object's reaction must be immediate.

Science, then, enables children to better understand their world. By understanding their environment, some of their fears are alleviated, they are more comfortable with nature, and they have an increasing awareness of the events, people, and materials surrounding them. Sciencing is of value because it creates high interest and is fun, exciting, and enjoyable. Through science studies, particularly open-ended or discovery activities, children develop methods of thinking that include problem solving, inquiry, reasoning, and rationalizing.

Science activities encourage children to observe, explore, inquire, and make generalizations, and they provide opportunities to use and develop sensory capacities—to see, hear, taste, smell, and touch. The children will learn to use skills that scientists use: inferring, observing, interpreting, classifying, and drawing conclusions. In addition, they will gain scientific knowledge. Abruscato (1992, p. 3) reminds us that "it is curiosity, the drive to make sense out of something in our surroundings, that causes children to reach out, touch, and wonder and it is curiosity that moves scientists to do the very same things."

Children and scientific researchers have one thing in common—they are both scientists at play! (Ross, 2000)

TEACHING METHODS

To be most effective in stimulating learning, the teacher should (1) encourage the child's curiosity and (2) provide learning experiences that extend children's daily activities (Harlan, 1996).

Two strategies that warrant consideration when addressing the ways that we approach children and science learning are the *K-W-L* (Ogle, 1986) and the *learning spiral* (Hobbs, Dever, & Tadlock, 1995). The K-W-L strategy encourages children to pursue their sense of wonder by sharing what they *know* (K) about a subject, determining what they *want* (W) to know about the subject, and then sharing what they have *learned* (L). The learning spiral suggests that we create developmentally appropriate practice in early child classrooms through *engaging, investigating, sharing*, and *assessing*. Both of these strategies support learning throughout all areas of the integrated curriculum. The primary objective is to create a learning environment that encourages children to use their developing skills in helping them to understand their physical and social surroundings (Dever & Hobbs, 1998).

Since concepts are built slowly from numerous activities and facts, teachers should plan many related science experiences to reinforce a single idea. Science activities become less meaningful to children if they are offered as isolated events. Random experiences are not sufficient to allow children to link important ideas together and fit them into other meaningful situations. Science notions and concepts should also be built on what the child already knows. Therefore, teachers need to inventory what the children know, understand, and are familiar with and then add concepts that are new and unfamiliar.

As science activities are approached, it is hoped that teachers will see the value of some experiences that are structured; that is, the answers or conclusions are predetermined, and only one conclusion is correct. (For example, if a plant has neither water nor light, it will die.) However, many of the activities should have an open-ended or discovery approach; that is, there is no single correct answer, but rather many possibilities or hypotheses. (For example, while exploring with water, ask the children, "How many different ways can you think of that we use water?") Both types of activities are valuable and encourage the kind of thinking that we are endeavoring to develop in young children.

Some science activities suggested in this book are of the more structured type in which a conclusion can be made as a result of the experience. Examples include the salt–chemical garden, as well as experiences involving changes in properties such as texture, size, and shape. However, even with these kinds of experiences, it is hoped that the teacher will still take advantage of the discovery approach and not be too hasty in giving the answers or conclusions. Allow the children to discover them. *Caution*: Do not smother a child's interest and curiosity with too many facts and instructions (Harlan, 1996).

There are also experiences that lead children to question and explore, but the conclusions must remain open ended. For example, one may ask, "How many hairs do I have on my head?" This problem may lead to a study of hair and the average number of hairs that a person may have, but it is doubtful that the child will be able to obtain a specific conclusion or answer, nor can the teacher supply that answer! Children should not be discouraged by unanswerable questions and problems. They should be reminded that thousands of scientists are working today to discover the answers to many unanswered questions—what kinds of life may exist in outer space, what are the causes and cures for cancer, and many others.

One of the most exciting ways to teach science is by taking advantage of spontaneous learning experiences. Teachers need to be aware of opportunities for daily science experiences, such as those with animals, plants, numbers, nutrition, creative art, music, social studies, and numerous others. The child may ask a question that could lead to an entire unit of study. A child may ask where a butterfly sleeps. This could result in a unit on butterflies, insects, or sleeping habits of animals. Children learn by doing, by becoming in-

volved. This theory is supported by Helm & Katz (2001), who believe that children's inquiry and learning are encouraged when they become actively involved in projects.

Take advantage of the daily happenings and of the materials often brought into class. A child bringing in an icicle could stimulate a unit of study on the forms of water, especially focusing on ice and how it is formed and used. Illustrations from the authors' own experiences include the day a cement mixer poured a cement platform in the children's playground. A science experience emerged relating to the ingredients of cement and the mixing, pouring, and setting of cement. Another activity occurred when people entered the classroom to fix a broken radiator. The children were invited to gather around and watch as the radiator was repaired. The experience included a discussion of heat and its source. As steam escaped, it was discussed as a form of water, and the tools needed to repair it were named while the children observed them in use.

Another approach to teaching science is the use of a science center or science interest table. This area, like other areas of the room, can be used continually or just occasionally. Materials can be put out for the children to explore, or science activities can take place on an individual basis in these areas. The materials used and activities selected need to be simple. For example, some modeling clay and toothpicks can be placed beside a tub of water. The children are challenged to work with and model the clay in such a way as to make cargo ships, with the toothpicks becoming cargo. In this subtle way, concepts of sinking, floating, and displacement can be learned. The materials and experiences are simple and easy to obtain and set up. If a science theme has been selected as a unit of study, the science center or table can serve as reinforcement and review.

Science should be integrated throughout various aspects of the curriculum. As food activities are being carried out, there are many opportunities for exploring and including scientific concepts. What will happen to the butter when the electric pan is turned on? What will happen to the dry ingredients when the milk is added? What is happening to the cream as it is being whipped? Is something being added? Is it getting larger or smaller? Will it weigh the same before and after it is whipped?

Music activities also offer opportunities for exploration of science. Experiment with sound and the changes in sounds as the size of the strings of instruments changes. Explore the parts of instruments and how they work. Additional science opportunities can be found in the realm of art. What happens to media such as glue and papier-mâché as they dry? The secondary colors are often successfully taught through exploring and combining different colors of paints. Individual activities during free play, such as the sensory table or trough, blocks, easel painting, books, and manipulative materials, all offer opportunities for critical thinking and science exploration. Outdoor play offers limitless experiences in science concepts.

Field trips and visitors, by providing the first-hand experiences so valuable for scientific learning, offer natural ways for teaching science. Field trips frequently require no resource persons other than the teacher; however, if field trip resource persons or classroom visitors are involved, they should be well informed about the concepts that you are teaching and should be given specific instructions regarding age-appropriate discussions or experiences.

Many activities in science lend themselves to record keeping, thereby enhancing measuring, observing, and recording skills. For example, when sprouting a bean seed in a glass jar between a wet towel and the jar, the children can record how many days it takes for their seed to sprout (see Figure 9–1). On a daily basis, the children can record the weather with symbols on a calendar, and then at the end of the month they can compute how many days of sunshine, rain, clouds, or snow there were that particular month. Still another example is observing the incubation period of eggs and recording how many days it takes for the eggs to hatch (see Figure 9–1).

The safety of the children should be of primary concern in planning science activities. As well as eliminating fears, science offers the opportunity to teach the use of caution. The teacher must model intelligent caution while encouraging exploration and investigation. The teacher should always know and understand what is going on and help children to understand where and why precautions are necessary. Never assign children a task or let them participate in an activity for which they are not developmentally ready. However, as they become ready for new tasks and adventures that involve safety factors, supervise them closely and carefully as they are learning. Give them rules that are necessary for their own health and safety, as well as those of their classmates.

Science activities can be planned on an individual, small-group, or whole-group basis. In small groups, cooperative learning works well as the children use experimentation and discovery to reach possible solutions. Often, when a science experience is explained and demonstrated to a whole group, it readily adapts to follow-up either individually or in small groups. This enables the children to try out the materials while the experience is clarified, explained, and reinforced.

As with other concepts, once a science concept has been taught, the teacher needs to receive feedback from the children to determine whether the ideas and information have been properly synthesized and understood.

Science is important. It is a way of life. It brings children into closer touch with themselves and the world that they live in. Children enjoy science; they love to discover, explore, and find out!

Some Do's and Don'ts

- **Do** have actual materials for children to explore. Whenever exploring the natural world, make certain there are ample supplies of containers, magnifying glasses, paper and pencils, and crayons.

- **Do** use the water trough or similar container for science materials and equipment. For example, fill the trough with soil, often including some earthworms and/or other insects. Put the balance scales in the trough with boxes, blocks, or other toys, or even with sensory media such as sand or wheat. Put egg cartons, eyedroppers, and colored water in the trough for color-mixing experiences.

- **Do** frequently provide sciencing tools such as magnifying glasses, thermometers, magnets, and scales. Include them with the sensory media, at the science table or corner, or outdoors. When children are constructing, touching, etching, coloring, and exploring in the outdoors, they are better able to make connections with their natural environment as they extend

Susan

How many days for the seed to sprout?

1	2	3	4	5
N	N	N	N	Y

N = No
Y = Yes

How many days before the chicks hatch?

N = No
Y = Yes

1	2	3	4	5	6	7	8	9	10	11
N	N	N	N	N	N	N	N	N	N	N
12	13	14	15	16	17	18	19	20	21	22
N	N	N	N	N	N	N	N	N	Y	

FIGURE 9–1
Sample Charts for Recording Observations

beyond the limitations imposed by classroom boundaries (Patton & Kokoski, 1996).

- **Do** develop an interested, curious, and enthusiastic attitude toward science yourself. The children will have some inherent interest in and enthusiasm for science, but they will also catch much of the teacher's spirit.

- **Do** relate science activities and units to the children's environment and their daily experiences. For example, it may not be wise to do a whole unit on the walrus unless the children are familiar with it. However, such a unit would provide an excellent study in some locations. There are so many possibilities for units and activities for children in these early childhood years that relate to *their* world, *their* weather, the plants in *their* locality, the animals in *their* environment, and there will be adequate time

later for learning about the world beyond their surroundings (Rivkin, 1992).

- **Do** perform experiments and activities ahead of time to have confidence in what is being done. The success of many experiments depends on the specific ways that they are carried out. Previous tryouts provide knowledge and assurance in the performance of the experiment.

- **Do** remember to use open-ended questions such as

  What do you think . . . ?

  What can you do with . . . ?

  Can you . . . ?

  What would happen if . . . ?

  How else . . . ?

Learning how levers work is easier when experimenting with scissors and tools while using play dough.

Do you think . . . ?

Why do you think . . . ?

These questions have no wrong answers and allow for unlimited and expandable possibilities.

- **Do** scale ideas and concepts down to the child's level of understanding. During activities, ask questions frequently to determine whether the information being taught is also being understood. So often with science explorations, it is erroneously assumed that the child already knows some of the basic concepts.

- **Don't** make science activities magic; make them a part of the real world and help children to see the cause-and-effect relationship. Magnets are not magic; they are tools of science. Thunder and lightning are not magical or unidentified happenings; they are acts of nature that have a cause and an effect.

- **Don't** be afraid to say "I don't know." But do attempt to help children to find the answers to their questions. Seek answers through books,

materials, computer software sources, and knowledgable persons. Remember, too, that some questions cannot be answered, even with study. When questions are asked that cannot be answered, tell the child that no one knows the answer to that question. However, if the situation can be explored, encourage the child's curiosity and self-discovery.

- **Don't** let children use equipment, materials, or substances that are dangerous. For example, when doing experiments involving fire, the teacher should perform the activity. However, this does not mean that children should not be taught how these materials are used and the caution necessary in handling them.

- **Don't** just teach scientific facts; assist children in learning to think, discover, and solve problems.

TEACHING ABOUT COLOR

Children delight in learning colors, and the world opens new doors for them as color concepts are mastered. The environment is full of colors; color is a concept that children live with daily. They see, feel, use, and respond to colors. Usually, when we teach young children about colors, we rely mostly on the visual aspects, even though we know that children learn best through multisensory discovery, experimentation, and investigation (Elkind, 1987a; Holt, 1989; Katz & Chard, 1989; Malaguzzi, 1993; Rinaldi, 1993; Staley, 1997). A color, such as purple, is not understood as purple until it is compared in relationship to other colors. As children learn that purple looks different from the other colors, they can also realize that purple *tastes* and *smells* different. With the multisensory approach, children discover that "purple smells like grapes and purple tastes like grapes, too" (Staley, 1997, p. 242).

Infants are quick to notice brightly colored objects and patterns in their surroundings. Using color names is one way that a child can describe his or her world. In addition, a child uses them for classification and seriation as he or she orders them from lightest to darkest.

Being aware of various properties of color enables us to understand better how color concepts can be approached in the early childhood curriculum. These properties include name (or hue), intensity or saturation (brightness or dullness), pure (primary) or mixed (secondary), and value (lightness or darkness).

Color Concepts and Labels

Color often is used as a clue in identifying and describing objects before other concepts, such as size, shape, and number, are used. When becoming interested in color, the child first recognizes what color is and will describe items in terms of color. However, frequently the color label is wrong; it takes time to learn correct color labels. When beginning to learn colors, the child is unable to label or name the colors, and yet is able to recognize that a particular item is the same color as another item. In effect, the child is able to *match* colors. Comments such as the following may be heard: "My shoes are licorice color" or "I want to wear the lemon shirt" or "I'll use the book that's fire-engine color."

One day as Creighton entered the classroom, the teacher asked him if he remembered the color of his eyes. When his expression indicated

This boy is explaining how he used both tempera paints and crayons to produce the unusual color patterns on a paper plate.

that he had forgotten, and since there was no mirror close by, the teacher gave him a clue by saying, "They're the same color as my eyes." As he looked at the teacher's eyes, he responded excitedly, saying, "Them there eyes are root beer!" The teacher recognized that, although he did not yet know the label brown, Creighton knew that his eyes and hers were the same color as root beer, surely the beginning of understanding the color brown.

Thus, the child should not be assumed to be wrong if, in the process of naming colors of familiar items, nontraditional names such as *chocolate brown, fire-engine red, lemon yellow*, and *lime green* are used. When a child uses such a label, the teacher might suggest that is one name for the color and then also say the traditional name.

Brady announced to his teacher, "Today I wore my coat with flag colors!" as he hung up his red, white, and blue jacket. A teacher asked a child to examine his plaid shirt and tell her any of the colors in the shirt. He responded with a quick "My shirt is rainbow-colored," and he was indeed correct.

Before young children are taught the labels of colors, they can be given many experiences in matching and sorting colors. A deck of cards can be sorted by color, or construction paper can be cut into squares, circles, or other shapes and then sorted into piles of similar colors.

Even before children label colors, they have the ability to point to a particular color when asked to find it. For example, on a particular page of a story being read, if there are several animals of different colors, the teacher might say, "Point to the animal that is yellow." Or, while eating, say, "Find something that is red." As long as this game is not overused, children will continue to enjoy playing it.

While learning a specific color (for example, yellow), the child may readily identify objects that are yellow, while not yet being sure which ones are not yellow. The child who knows that apples, tomatoes, and stop signs are red may then ask whether a banana is also red. Or the child may know what green *is*, but not yet know what green *is not*.

Once children begin to identify colors by their names or labels, there should be many opportunities for using colors. One way is to give children color choices. For example, when crayons or papers are distributed, the children can be asked what color they chose. Since they often have a favorite color, when feasible, allow them to select items on the basis of their color preferences. Most children prefer lighter and brighter colors to darker and duller colors.

Teaching Color Concepts

Since the world is saturated with colors, there are numerous opportunities for encouraging children's awareness of the world of color. When experimenting with color, use all kinds of media: water, watercolors, oil paints, colored shaving cream, fingerpaints, tempera; hands, feet, brushes, eyedroppers, sponges, spray bottles, toy balls, squirt guns; leaves, sticks, canvas, sidewalks, paper, fabric, wood, and so on. There is no "right" way to experience color (Demarest, 1996). Color should be used often in everyday conversations with children. The teacher can comment on the color of the sky, trees, flowers, clothing the child is wearing,

eyes, hair, or the book being carried. Questions such as "What else is this color?" or "This is the same color as what?" should be used often for problem solving relating to color.

To avoid confusion when teaching color, it is important to remember that color is an attribute, not an object. Grammatically, color names are both nouns and adjectives, but when they are taught as adjectives, children understand them more easily. In other words, use the name of both the color and the object being described. For example, of a seashell, say "That is an orange seashell" or "That seashell is orange in color," rather than "That is orange." As a lesson plan on color is being prepared, the teacher should be well aware of the needs and abilities of the particular group of children before deciding on an approach.

Several alternatives are available, depending on the developmental level of the children in terms of their color understandings. For children who have little understanding of color, begin the experiences with color by focusing on what color is. Then spend perhaps one or two days or even a week on each of the primary and secondary colors. This approach will provide a sure understanding and knowledge of these six basic colors. Along with each color, the various shades could also be taught. For example, as blue is being studied, also teach dark blue, navy blue, light blue, turquoise blue, and so on. Another approach is to begin with the primary colors and then advance to the secondary colors. While learning secondary colors, the children discover that they are made by combining the primary colors. After the study of the primary and secondary colors, the children then go back to shades of colors. Since they have learned that the secondary colors are made by combining colors, it is exciting to learn how shades of a particular color are made by adding white paint to make it lighter, by adding black paint to make it darker, or by adding another color to change the shade. Color mixing provides other opportunities for young children to explore.

Psychological Influences of Color

The psychological influences of color should be included in discussions about color. Colors are symbolic and often influence feelings. People react differently to colors for cultural reasons, and different cultures attach various meanings to color. For example, to the Irish, green is lucky; to the Chinese, red means good luck or happiness. Colors can affect some people's moods and create particular memories. Colors in the environment can influence behavior, reactions, and morale; but usually colors are *associated with* particular behaviors; they are not the *reason* for the behaviors. However, adults who are working with children should select the colors that are to be part of the children's surroundings carefully. For children, color is a way of describing and communicating the details of something or explaining a mood.

Concepts and Ideas for Teaching

1. Colors have names, and these names are used to describe objects.

2. Most objects have a color.

3. Some objects do not have a color.
   a. Water
   b. Clear plastic
   c. Clear glass

4. Many items are similar in color.
   a. Red: apple, cherry, tomato, berries, items of red clothing, hair
   b. Green: plants, vegetables, books, sweaters
   c. Yellow: lemon, sun, yellow butterfly, corn on the cob

5. The same items may vary in color.
   a. Cars: red, black, green, and so on. The same model and kind will come in various colors.
   b. People: red, white, black, brown
   c. Eyes: blue, black, green, brown, hazel
   d. Apples: yellow, green, red, brown

6. Single items may vary in shades of the same color.
   a. Trees: shades of green
   b. Fabric: shades of any color
   c. Paint: shades of any color

7. Single items may have various colors.
   a. Fabrics: plaids, stripes, others
   b. Trees: In the fall, a tree may have leaves of many colors.
   c. Pictures or paintings

8. Color may be modified or changed.
   a. Combining: When two or more colors are combined, the color will be changed and a new one made, or the shade of the original color will be different. Working with colored water or paints offers many possibilities for exploring, making new colors by combining colors. The child should learn that the secondary colors (green, orange, and purple) are made by combining the primary colors (red, yellow, and blue). Red and yellow make orange, red and blue make purple, and yellow and blue make green. When combining these colors, start with the lighter of the two colors and then add the darker color. (It is easier to make colors darker than lighter.) The child who has learned these combinations can easily understand that every other color is made by combining the primary colors in various ways.
   b. Adding: In food, art, and science activities, colors can be changed by adding ingredients. For example, when making gingerbread, the original ingredients of sugar, eggs, and shortening will change color when the molasses is added.
   c. Heat, cooking, or the sun: Exposure to the sun or the process of heating or cooking will often change the color of an item. Meats change, when cooked, from red to brown; bakery items such as gingerbread or chocolate cake often become lighter in color. Toast, waffles, or pancakes become darker, as will anything that burns. Roasted marshmallows or hot dogs become darker. Exposure to the sun often fades or lightens items, but people become tanned or sunburned.
   d. Freezing or cooling: Most items become lighter when frozen. When comparing the changes in color before and after freezing, make sure to have examples of the item both before and after the freezing process.
   e. Drying: The colors of fruits or other foods will change as they are dried. The colors of some art media may change as drying occurs.

f. Aging: Food in various stages shows changes in color. Physical characteristics of people may change color during the aging process, and the skin, hair, and eye colors of babies often change in a short period of time.

g. Natural changes: Weather changes, such as frost, freezing, rain, and sun, can result in changes in color. It is exciting to teach the changes of the autumn leaves resulting from cooler temperatures.

h. Camouflage: Some animals will change color to camouflage, disguise, or hide themselves. Examples are the snowshoe rabbit and the chameleon.

9. Colors may be symbolic.

a. Seasons: green for spring and summer; yellow, orange, and brown for fall

b. Holidays: red and green for Christmas; orange and black for Halloween

c. People: red, black, white, yellow

d. Clothing: particular shades and colors are worn more typically during certain seasons; black clothing signifies mourning

e. Feelings: moods described in terms of color—blue for depressed, red for angry, or yellow for cheerful

f. Safety: red meaning stop, green meaning go, yellow meaning caution

g. Danger: red

h. Sickness: yellow, red (flushed), white (pale), green

i. Injury: black-and-blue or red

j. School colors

k. Patriotism: red, white, and blue for the United States, or patriotic colors representing other native countries of students

l. Foods: perceived alteration of taste when food is not the expected color (it is assumed that the taste *is* altered)

Activities and Experiences

1. Let the children observe and have opportunities for mixing colors, especially the primary colors into the secondary colors. The following media and methods are possibilities:

a. *Food coloring:* Use either a quart jar or gallon jar filled with water, and put enough drops of yellow in it to make it a deep yellow color; mix well. Then add a few drops of red and watch as the yellow water changes to orange; mix well. Repeat this experience with other colors. For a similar experience, use baby food jars, clear glasses, or plastic containers with water colored with the primary colors in them. In additional containers, mix the secondary colors. (Always begin with the lighter of the two colors when mixing.) Or use white Styrofoam egg cartons and cut the tops off. In each carton, in one of the holes put some red-colored water, in another blue, and in another yellow. Let the children use eyedroppers or spoons to mix new colors in the empty holes.

b. Mix instant powdered milk with water, enough to fill a pie tin or similar shallow container one-third to one-half full. Have the children drop in a row of four or five drops of red food coloring and a row of four or five drops of yellow, and continue with two or three more rows of different colors. Next, have them drop one or two drops of liquid dish detergent in the middle, and watch the colors blend into a rainbow.

c. *Finger paint:* Begin with white paint and sprinkle dry powdered paint on it. After that color is mixed in, sprinkle a second color on it for another change. Or start with a particular color of finger paint and add a second color of finger paint to it.

d. *Paint:* Provide opportunities for mixing colors at the easel or in other areas. Also provide for mixing shades of colors and for mixing more than two colors.

e. *Cellophane:* Collect three Styrofoam meat or pastry trays, and cut the centers out so that they resemble frames. Staple sheets of cellophane, in the primary colors, to each of these frames, producing a red frame, a yellow frame, and a blue frame. When these frames are put on top of one another and held against white paper or up to the light, the secondary colors are seen. For a similar activity in color mixing, drop small amounts of colored water (the three primary colors) between two pieces of acetate and then put the acetate on an overhead projector. Press on the acetate in different areas to make the colors mix together. Also using an overhead projector, once again show color mixing by using pieces of colored cellophane.

2. Once the children have discussed how colors often reflect particular moods, ask them to describe their day in terms of a color. Older children could be encouraged to write stories, describing everything in the story in terms of colors.

3. For older children, read the book *Hailstones and Halibut Bones* (O'Neill, Doubleday, Garden City, NY, 1990); then discuss or write additional similes and metaphors for each of the colors.

4. As each of the colors is studied, ask the children to wear clothing of that color.

5. Use the plastic rings that are six-pack can holders and cut them apart into separate rings. Thread a piece of yarn through the top of each, and then let the children glue pieces of colored cellophane on each one. They will enjoy hanging them as mobiles, hanging them at the window, or putting them on top of one another to form different colors.

6. From colored paper, cut patterns that have the same shape but different colors. To make them more durable, laminate or cover them with clear adhesive paper. Spread them on the floor and tape them down. Cut smaller corresponding shapes and colors, and give one to each child. Put on music and have the children march, slide, skip, and so on, to the music; when it stops, each child must find and stand on a shape the same color as the one being held. As an alternative, instead of giving each child a color, give verbal directions. For example, say "Donna, please stand on an orange circle." Another approach would be to use a drum or another instrument to create a particular rhythm, rather than using a record or tape. With a little innovative thinking, this activity could be approached in many different ways. The game Twister could also be used.

7. Have the children sort colored items: buttons, paper shapes, marbles, colored macaroni, pieces of fabric. You can make a color-sorting tray from a white Styrofoam egg carton. Use felt-tip pens or acrylic paints to make each of the 12 holes a different color. Now provide small shapes of colored paper, colored beads, or colored buttons for the children to sort according to the various colors.

8. Have the children play color lotto. Use paint chips from a paint store or colored construction or poster paper. Cut two squares (or other shapes) the same size of each color. On a base of poster paper or cardboard, paste the desired number of colors: for older children, 8 to 12 colors, or shades of the same color; for younger children, 4 to 8 colors. Cover with clear adhesive paper or laminate; then cover duplicates individually to be matched to the corresponding color on the larger base.

9. Make a color wheel of wood or heavy cardboard. The colors can be felt pieces or paper (colored with felt-tip pens) glued to the base. Now put corresponding colors on clip-type clothespins, using felt or colored pens, one color per clothespin. The clothespins are clipped to the corresponding colors of the color wheel. Older children may use shades of a single color, but younger children should use distinct colors.

10. Fill a glass or container partly full of water. Drop a single drop of food coloring into the water and stir. Add another drop and stir, continuing this procedure so that the children can see how the same color can be changed from light to dark. Let the children follow up with the same experiment. For a similar experience, instead of using the same container of water, use different or separate containers, such as clear medicine bottles. To each container successively, add one or two more drops of coloring than to the previous one. Then order the containers from lightest to darkest.

11. Sing songs that create awareness of the colors that children are wearing and the colors in their environment.

12. Show outlines of objects such as fruits, vegetables, flowers, trees, and the sun. Do not show them colored. Have the children name the color or colors of the object.

13. Name a color and have the children respond with names of objects of that color.

14. Make up color riddles and have the children guess the color being described. For example, "I am the color of strawberries, cherries, and fire engines. What color am I?" Have older children make up the riddles and share them with one another. The riddles could be written and illustrated for a book. One page could have the riddle and the next page could have the answer, either written or drawn.

15. Obtain paint chip samples from paint or hardware stores. Cover them with clear adhesive-backed paper or laminate them. Cut them up into separate chips and put each series of a single shade into a container or envelope. Children can then order them from lightest to darkest.

16. Have a color day when the majority of activities focus on one color. If the children are alerted to this event, they can even be encouraged to wear clothing of that color.

17. Dye hard-boiled eggs. Use Easter egg dye or food coloring. You may wish to give the children the opportunity to mix colors or have them dip the egg into one color and then into another to discover the effect.

18. Make fishing poles of sticks or dowels (15 to 18 inches long). Attach screw eyes to one end of each for threading string. On the end of the string, attach a small magnet. Now let the children fish for fish of various colors that have been cut from colored paper and have paper clips attached. Encourage the children to name the color of each fish that they catch.

19. For older children who are ready to expand their color vocabulary, make word cards of the following color words and help the children to sort them into color piles. Find examples of each, if possible; paint chips would be a good source.

a. Red: scarlet, coral, terra cotta, crimson, vermilion, Castilian red, ruby, cherry, fire-engine red, calypso red, poppy

b. Green: shamrock, sea green, hunter green, olive green, chartreuse, avocado, army green, celery green, apple green, Kelly green, emerald, jade, verdant green, viridian green, grass green, cactus green, khaki green, pea green

c. Brown: chocolate, caramel brown, hazel, mahogany, maple brown, dirt brown, sepia, olive brown, tan

d. Yellow: mustard, lemon, saffron, chamois, blonde, canary yellow, sunshine yellow, citron yellow, buff, amber, sallow, primrose, tawny, gold

e. Purple: violet, lavender, orchid, amethyst, grape, lilac, burgundy, damson

f. Orange: carrot, peach, pumpkin, coral, mandarin orange, tangerine orange, copper, rust

g. Blue: indigo, royal, navy, cobalt, turquoise, sky blue, robin's-egg blue, baby blue, teal blue, azure, sapphire blue, midnight blue, peacock blue

20. Make chromatograms (color patterns). Using water-based (not permanent) markers, make drawings or lines on paper towels. Put one edge of the paper towels into water, and watch what happens as the water rises up the paper to the dry marker patterns. The water loosens the pigments from the paper and carries them up the towel. Heavy pigments don't travel as far as the lightweight ones, so the colors separate (ACEI, 1997).

UNIT PLAN ON COLOR

Field Trips

- Color walk

- Art gallery

- Art department of college or other school

- Paint store
- Fabric store
- Flower shop
- Grocery store
- Nursery or greenhouse in the spring

Art

- Mosaic of dyed rice, macaroni, or other media
- Finger painting
- Painting with tempera paint or watercolors
- Collages with colored cellophane
- Mixing primary colors of clay or play dough to make secondary colors
- String painting
- Melted crayon pictures
- Blot painting
- Clay sculptures or modeling (use primary colors)
- Colored macaroni strung for necklaces or bracelets
- Collages using items that come in various colors: toothpicks, marshmallows, cereal

Music

- "Color Song" or "Color Parade" (Hap Palmer)
- Songs that incorporate colors of the children's clothing, colors in their environment, favorite colors
- Musical Chairs, with colors on the backs of each chair. After the children each have a chair, give instructions for each color. For example, say, "All who have red on their chair stand up and hop in a circle." (Do not eliminate children in this game, as with any game with younger children.)
- In small groups, make shakers that are of different colors, or give groups of children baby food jars with objects of different colors or colored water in them. Say "All those with (name a color) shakers play on the next song (or on the chorus)."

- Creative movements with colors. Play some classical music; have the children decide what color the music represents and then move like that color or something representing that color.

Food

- Almost any food activity can be planned with a focus on color or color mixing.
- Make gelatin: Use flavored gelatin, or begin with one of the three primary colors, lemon, for example. After the hot water is added and the gelatin dissolved, use ice cubes that have been deeply colored another primary color. For example, if blue ice cubes are added to lemon gelatin, green gelatin will result.
- Make a white cake and, before it is baked, marble it with drops of food coloring.
- Make cakes, cookies, or breads and add food coloring to change the color.
- Make fruit salad in small groups and have each group whip the cream and add food coloring, or use plain yogurt with color added to it, so that each group has salad of a different color.
- Make an apple salad, using green, yellow, and red apples.
- Make any meat dish in which the children cook the meat first so that the change in color can be observed.
- Make colored popcorn.

Visitors

- Paint dealer or distributor
- Artist to mix paints and paint picture
- Animals of various colors, perhaps with their babies to see whether they are the same colors (for example, a baby and adult mouse)
- A mother with her baby and a suitcase filled with clothing of different colors for the baby to wear
- A parent or other visitor to make snow cones, with children selecting the desired color and flavor
- A clown to put on different colors of face makeup

Science

- Chemical garden, made with food coloring of different colors on top (see Chapter 11 for directions)

- Coloring or dying carnations, Queen Anne's lace, or celery by putting in glasses with food coloring or ink in water

- Any experience showing how particular animals use color camouflage

- Any experience in color mixing and color changing

- Color changes of autumn leaves

- Color changes resulting from aging, ripening, or molding

Literacy

- Write or dictate stories on favorite colors. Story springboards might be "My Favorite Color Is . . ." or "I Like (color) Because . . . ."

- Make a book for each color studied; the title of the book could be that color. Children could cut pictures from magazines or draw their own pictures of things that are that color.

- Encourage children to write or tell color similes and metaphors.

When fire fighters bring their firetruck to school, children are able to learn about fires and safety firsthand. Firetrucks look a lot larger when you are standing next to them!

TEACHING ABOUT FIRE

Fire is an interesting part of the child's world, since it stimulates curiosity, but it is often not approached with necessary caution. Therefore, along with teaching young children about fire, its dangers must be emphasized and, if not already acquired, a certain caution toward it must be taught.

A unit on fire may be planned in conjunction with learning about fire fighters. Often a unit of study focuses on the fire fighter as a community helper, but never brings in concepts related to fire. We suggest that many concepts relating to fire be taught to young children so that they know that fire has many uses, but that it is dangerous and is not to be played with.

On one occasion when Smokey Bear visited the classroom of 3- to 5-year-olds, his role had been previously discussed, that he is a symbol of fire safety and is not actually a live bear. It was also explained that there was a real bear named Smokey Bear living in Washington, DC. However, excitement ran high when Smokey walked in with the forest ranger; heartbeats stepped up, eyes widened, breathing increased, and one child exclaimed: "It's the real Smokey Bear. I thought I would never get to meet you." Even when Smokey Bear removed his head and an actual person's head emerged, the reality of Smokey Bear still remained in the minds of those 3- to 5-year-olds.

Concepts and Ideas for Teaching

1. Fire has many uses: heating, lighting, cooking, and burning of waste material.
2. Fire needs air (oxygen) and fuel (wood, paper, or other flammable material) to burn.

3. Fire can be ignited in many ways: striking rocks together, using matches or heat, focusing light on one spot for some time, combustion.
4. There are several ways to extinguish a fire: dousing with water or salt; smothering with dirt or a blanket; using a fire extinguisher.
5. People have different feelings toward fire. We may be frightened if our lives or homes are in danger because of a fire; we may experience pain if our bodies are burned with fire; we may feel warm and safe if we are gathered around the fireplace when it is cold and stormy outside; we may feel excitement and warmth as we are gathered around a campfire cooking our dinner and singing campfire songs; or we may feel relief and security when the power goes off and the candles are found and lighted.

Activities and Experiences

1. Demonstrate that fire needs air (see activity 7 in the section Teaching about Air in Chapter 10).
2. Demonstrate ways to put out a fire; role play.
3. Demonstrate first aid in treating a burn: If it is not severe, put it under cold water and then treat it with ointment.
4. Demonstrate how to build a fire outdoors and then how to put it out.

UNIT PLAN ON FIRE AND THE FIRE FIGHTER

Art

- Collages of flammable and nonflammable materials
- Melted crayon pictures: take care with the iron so that no fire will start and no one is burned.

Food

- Hot dogs roasted over a fire
- Marshmallows roasted over a fire
- Any food cooked over a fire

- Foil dinners baked on coals
- Fondue

Field Trips

- Fire station
- Home or school on fire-safety inspection
- Picnic at a park, canyon, or picnic site; fire built in designated safe place; hot dogs cooked, marshmallows roasted; fire put out carefully

Visitors

- Fire fighter
- Smokey Bear
- Scout to show how to start a fire and how to put it out properly

Science

- Necessity of air in building a fire or keeping it going
- Ways to start or build a fire
- Ways to put out a fire

Literacy

- Stories and poems about fires and fire fighters
- Story of Smokey Bear
- Open-ended story: "I like fire because . . ."

Music and Dramatic Play

- Dramatization of putting out a fire
- Dramatization of sitting around a campfire cooking food and singing songs

TEACHING ABOUT LIGHT AND SHADOWS

The question posed to a group of preschoolers, "What would you do if you had no light?" resulted in some interesting comments and answers. One child said, "I would get a blind man's dog," and another said, "God would help me." Another replied, "I would light a candle." "But a candle is one source of light," the teacher replied. "Then I would get a flashlight," the child responded quickly. "And that is another source of light," the teacher told him. "Then I guess I would just have to sit," concluded the child. It is difficult for children to imagine a world without light, and it is interesting for them to begin to understand the several sources of light. In every situation in which people are without natural light and there is a power failure preventing the use of electricity, there are still sources of light, such as flashlights and fire.

Shadows, an aspect of light, are so fascinating that even babies find them interesting. Very young children may find shadows frightening, but as preschool children learn the cause of shadows, their fears are alleviated, and they delight not only in watching them but in making them. "Young children think of a shadow as an object or substance and that light is the agent that causes the object to form or that allows people to see the shadow, even when it is dark" (Lind, 1997, p. 81). What child, at the conclusion of a movie when the projector is still casting light on the screen, does not try to make hand and finger shadows on the screen?

An activity children enjoy is to hang a sheet in front of a light. Have some of the children perform shadow dances, shadow dramatics, or shadow games behind the sheet (but in front of the light), so that the other children can watch the shadows on the sheet. After a story, one teacher decided to have the children dramatize it by means of shadow dramatics. There was awe, fascination, and excitement as the children in the audience watched the shadows of the performing children as the story was dramatized. Children also enjoy guessing who other children are by their shadows. One young boy said, "I know that is Stacy, because the shadow has pigtails!"

Concepts and Ideas for Teaching

1. Light is either natural (sunlight) or artificial (flashlights, lanterns).
2. Plants need light and will grow toward the light.
3. Light has many uses.

   a. Used by people

      (1) Lamps: used by people to see in the dark

      (2) Lighthouses: used to warn ships and boats of nearness to land

      (3) Freeway and street lights, lighted airport runways, traffic lights, headlights, lighted signs: used with forms of transportation to light the way and let people know where they are going

      (4) Light or fire at a campsite: used for warmth and cooking, and to discourage wild animals

      (5) Natural sunlight: used for warmth and also as a source of telling time

   b. Used by animals

      (1) To see in the dark

      (2) For warmth

      (3) To determine the approximate time

   c. Used by plants: warmth and sunlight needed by most plants to grow

4. Shadows are produced when an object passes in front of light; shadows result from the interruption of light. If the object making the shadow is removed, the shadow also disappears.

   a. Relation of object's shape to its shadow

   b. Relation of the size and shape of a shadow to a change in the location of the object and the position of the light source

---

Activities and Experiences

1. Collect as many sources of light as possible: flashlights, lanterns, candles, matches, lighters, and so on.

2. Try growing a plant in a closet or room where there is no light.

3. Watch a plant "follow" the sun or light.

4. Show pictures or slides of the uses of light.

5. Show, discuss, and demonstrate the effect of sunlight on photographic paper, ice, cold water, colored construction paper, fabric.

6. Explore shadows.

   a. On a sunny day, divide the children into pairs to trace each other's shadows.

b. Play shadow tag, with the one who is "It" trying to step on another person's shadow.

c. Make a sundial: tie string around the end of a dowel; put the other end of the dowel in some sand or soil next to cement; and extend the string on the end of dowel across the cement and secure with tape. Throughout the day, draw a line on the cement with a piece of chalk where the shadow is being cast.

d. Use an overhead projector for making shadows of objects, letters, numbers; encourage the children to make hand and finger shadows.

7. Give a pair of children an ordinary flashlight battery, a piece of wire, and a flashlight lamp and have them figure out how to make the lamp glow.

Note: See Lesson Plan on Light and Shadows in Appendix A.

TEACHING ABOUT MAGNETS

"I've never seen a pin jump before," exclaimed one excited child as magnets were introduced. Another child said, "I didn't know pins were alive," as she observed the magnets attracting the pins. Magnets are fascinating for children to explore. Simply showing the children magnets and telling them what they can do takes away the excitement; children need opportunities to experiment and discover for themselves what magnets are and can do. Ideally, each child should have a magnet; however, magnets can be put on a science table for use in individual exploring.

The children need many objects to use for experimenting with the magnets so that they can determine what kinds of materials the magnets attract. A container of common objects such as a cork, scrap of material, pencil, eraser, paper clip, scissors, tack, coin, soap, washer, pin, needle, fastener, and tape provides continued motivation for exploration. The objects in the box could be sorted into two groups: those attracted by the magnet and those not attracted by the magnet. (A dog's two-sided food dish works very well for this sorting or classifying activity.) After adequate experi-

mentation, the children will be able to see some similarities in the objects that the magnet attracts.

During a sorting activity, one child replied, "All the things that the magnet picked up are silver. Magnets must pick up silver things." True, many iron and steel objects are silver in color, but this concept was not accurate. Then the teacher said, "Let's test your idea to see whether it is correct." The teacher selected some silver paper, aluminum foil, a piece of aluminum, a nickel coin, a silver button, and silver fabric. After trying to pick up each of these objects with the magnet, the child concluded that magnets do not necessarily pick up items that are silver in color. The teacher took the opportunity to explain that the objects attracted by the magnet were made of iron and steel. Also, even though an object of iron or steel may be too large for the magnet to pick up, the pull or attraction can still be felt.

It is sometimes difficult to present an entire unit on magnets; therefore, they are presented here as a science concept, with several supporting ideas and activities. Perhaps an experience with magnets could be presented each day for a week or two or incorporated as a science activity within another unit of study. Magnets make a great project!

Concepts and Ideas for Teaching

1. Magnets attract objects made of iron and/or nickel and/or steel. (Although it is not necessary to teach the components of magnets to young children, they are actually made from rock called *magnetite*, which does attract iron and steel. Magnetite is also called *lodestone*.)

2. Magnets come in many shapes, sizes, and strengths; some have stronger magnetism than others.

3. Stronger magnets will attract through paper, glass, cardboard, wood, and water.

4. Magnetism can be transferred. It is possible to magnetize such objects as iron nails, paper clips, needles, and knitting needles by stroking them 30 to 50 times in one direction with a magnet. However, as the children will discover, these homemade magnets do not retain their magnetism for very long.

5. Opposite or unlike poles attract (the north pole attracts the south pole), whereas like poles repel each other.
6. A compass needle is a magnet, always pulling to the north. When a magnetized needle is floated in water, it acts as a compass and points north.
7. All magnets have a north pole and a south pole, and magnets are strongest at their poles.

Activities and Experiences

1. Collect magnets of different sizes, shapes, and strengths. Also collect objects that use magnets, such as clips for holding notes to bulletin boards or refrigerators, toys using magnets, and potholders with magnets attached.

2. Compare the strengths of magnets by counting or comparing the number of pins or paper clips that each magnet can pick up by "hooking" them one to another until the magnet can no longer hold another pin or paper clip. Order the magnets from strongest to weakest. In this experience, the children can discover that the strength of a magnet is not necessarily determined by its size.

3. Have the children put a piece of paper between their magnet and paper clip to see whether the magnet still attracts. During this activity, children will discover that magnetism works through glass, cardboard, wood, fabric, and other materials. Fill a glass bowl with water and drop the paper clip into it. The children will learn that the magnet will attract the paper clip through the glass and the water.

4. Suspend a bar magnet from a thread or string tied to its center; in a few minutes, the magnet will align itself with Earth's magnetic field and point north and south. It becomes a simple compass. Notice that as some types of metal are brought close to the magnet there will be an attraction and the compass will not work.

5. Put iron filings on glass, a paper plate, or cardboard. Put a magnet underneath and let the children discover what happens as the magnet is moved around. Sprinkle the iron filings over a glass slab and touch a magnet under-neath the glass. Now put this slab on an overhead projector so that the iron filings designs can be enlarged on the wall or screen.

6. Make small fishing poles from $\frac{1}{4}$ by 12 inch dowels and attach small magnets to them with fishing line. The children fish from a box containing assorted items: iron and steel, as well as objects that will not be attracted by the magnet. Fish are cut from paper, and paper clips are attached to them so that they can be caught. If desired, basic concepts such as color, number, and shape can be put on the fish to enable the children to tell about their catch. Larger poles can also be made from dowels or sticks, and a dramatic-play fishing area can be built in one area of the room. Use large-unit blocks for the rocks surrounding the fishing pond or lake; the children sit on these rocks and proceed to fish.

7. Place a horseshoe or bar magnet on a table and cover it with a white piece of paper. As iron filings are sprinkled onto the paper, they will align themselves with the magnetic field. If you put two bar magnets with like and then unlike poles next to each other, the iron filings will show the interaction of the magnetic fields.

Note: After a period of time, magnets may lose their force. They can be remagnetized in high school or university physics or electronics departments. Also, you can rejuvenate a weak magnet by pulling it lengthwise across the pole of a powerful magnet (Hardy & Tolman, 1993). To preserve their magnetism when the magnets are not in use, attach the iron keeper over the poles of a horseshoe or bar magnet, do not store the magnets with the north and south poles together, and do not store magnets in metal boxes. Remember, magnets can be damaging to electronic products (Hardy & Tolman, 1993).

TEACHING ABOUT WEIGHT AND BALANCE

Weight and balance are difficult but exciting concepts to explore with young children. Like many of the other concepts that have been discussed, these must be explored through concrete experiences. Children usually judge the weight of an object by its size. As a result, children often misjudge the weight of an object and how much strength they need to pick it up. Also, an understanding of weight is necessary before we can comprehend the meaning of balance.

The children were learning about weight, and a scale was included in one of the centers. Melissa watched as some of the children stood on the scale and were weighed. Soon she said to the teacher, "Pound me next!"

A discussion of the relationship between gravity and weight will depend on the age and understanding of the children. Weight is the result of gravity, and gravity is stronger closer to the center of Earth. Therefore, the farther away an object is from Earth's center, the lighter in weight it is. An object at sea level will weigh slightly more than the same object on a high mountain.

After several attempts, this girl is able to maintain her balance and walk successfully along the raised beam.

The same principle accounts for the pressure felt on the ears when we rapidly change altitude. The air is heavier near the surface of Earth, and changing altitude alters the pressure (or weight) of air on the ears.

Older children will be able to understand the effect that gravity has on an object, as well as the air pressure on ears. Younger children will understand weight in terms of heaviness.

Weight is the heaviness or lightness of an object as it is weighed on a scale by use of a standard of measure. The terms *heavy* and *light*, commonly used in defining weight, are relative, or comparative. We must have two objects to compare before being able to determine that one object is heavier or lighter than the other. It is impossible, technically, to state that a single object is heavy unless it has been determined that an amount greater than so many pounds is heavy. We must also consider to whom an object would seem heavy. What is heavy to a child is very different from what is heavy to a teen-ager or adult. What is heavy to a dock worker, a farmer, a furniture mover, or someone with great strength is very different from what is heavy to someone with little physical strength.

An object is *balanced* when stability has been achieved by an even distribution of weight on each side of a fulcrum, or point of support. A *fulcrum* provides the point of balance between two objects. It is not necessarily located at a central point between these objects, however. When objects are balanced, their weight or number is equalized on both sides. Thus, two objects of unequal weight can be balanced by either (1) moving the fulcrum or (2) moving the two objects in such a way that the lighter of the two is farther from the fulcrum on one side and the heavier is closer to the fulcrum on the other side. If objects are of equal weight, such as identical blocks or chips, two or more can be put on one side, closer to the fulcrum, and one on the other side, farther from the fulcrum, thus equalizing the weight on both sides. This discovery is exciting to children; it can be achieved in another way by having children of different weights balance on a seesaw.

Children acquire the concept of balance by balancing themselves. They may try to balance on one foot with their eyes open and then with their eyes closed. They may then change feet and try the same activity again. Soon they begin to recognize the state of stability of objects in balance.

Daily Experiences with Weight and Balance

It is important to remember that daily experiences are valuable in developing an awareness of weight and balance. Riddles are easily used in teaching weight and balance. For example, say "I weigh the same as a pound of hot dogs, and you use me on toast in the morning. What am I?" The answer is a pound of butter or margarine. Or one may say: "You use me in cakes and cookies and on your cereal, and I weigh the same as 5 pounds of flour. What am I?" The answer is 5 pounds of sugar. Guessing games are especially adaptable with weight and balance. Display objects of different weights and ask which ones weigh the same, which one weighs the most, and which one weighs the least. Which toy is heaviest? Which of these two books weighs more? Can you find at least three objects in our room that weigh more than 5 pounds each? Can you balance the balance board or the balance scales with sand on one side and blocks on the other side? A balance scale is an excellent piece of equipment to include in the water trough with small, dry media; it gives children an opportunity for practical exploration of both weight and balance. Similes and metaphors also can be used with weight. For example, the phrases "as heavy as ___" and "as light as ___" could be completed with the children's own ideas of heavy and light objects. Exploratory questions asking what makes an object heavier or lighter could also be used frequently.

As young children begin to have experiences with weight, they need many opportunities to compare weights by using their own muscles. They should have practice in determining *equivalents*, weights that are the same. Scales or balance scales can be used for these activities. Experiment with directive questions, such as "How many pennies are the same weight as 20 buttons?" or "How many little rocks weigh the same as two pencils?" Children also need activities requiring balance: using their bodies as the means of balance or using equipment such as a seesaw or the balance scales to achieve a balanced state.

Many opportunities to become familiar with weight vocabulary should be provided. As children have many exposures to words and their meanings, the words soon become possessions and are active parts of the children's vocabularies. The following are examples of weight words:

> heavy, light
>
> heavier, lighter
>
> heaviest, lightest
>
> ponderous
>
> weighty

Children must also relate weight to the standard units of weight measurement. They must therefore understand that weight is measured in ounces, pounds, and tons. Eventually, they will need to know what these terms mean and how they relate to one another, for example, 16 ounces in a pound or 2,000 pounds in a ton. Children should also be exposed to the standard units of weight measurement in the metric system: grams, milligrams, kilograms, and so on. Simplify the prefixes for the metric units as follows: $1,000 = $ kilo-; $100 = $ hecto-; $10 = $ deka-; $\frac{1}{10} = $ deci-; $\frac{1}{100} = $ centi-; and $\frac{1}{1,000} = $ milli -. Ounces can be compared with grams and pounds with kilograms. In addition, inches can be compared with centimeters, feet with decimeters, yards with meters, miles with kilometers, and degrees Fahrenheit with degrees Celsius.

Children often relate weight to themselves and their own body weight. A child may know that she weighs 42 pounds, but not know exactly what that means. It would be interesting, then, for the children to find other things that weigh 42 pounds: How many large-unit blocks would it take to weigh 42 pounds? How many books could weigh 42 pounds? What could you pack in a suitcase to make it weigh 42 pounds? Probably anything the child can lift is "light," and anything that cannot be lifted is "heavy."

Concepts and Ideas for Teaching

1. Gravity determines weight and depends on an object's distance from the center of Earth. The farther from Earth's center, the less the weight. Weight is the force with

which a body is attracted toward Earth by gravitation.

  a. A parent weighing 180 pounds on the seacoast would weigh less on a mountaintop and only 30 pounds on the moon.
  b. The higher in the sky that an airplane flies, the less it weighs.

2. Anything that takes up space has weight; even items having seemingly no weight still have weight that can be measured on a fine scale.

  a. Feather
  b. Scrap of paper
  c. Penny
  d. Small piece of candy

3. Weight is measured through the use of instruments called scales.

4. Weight can change.

  a. Additions

    (1) People gaining weight by adding pounds
    (2) Air added to an inner tube
    (3) Water added to a dry sponge
    (4) Balloon inflated

  b. Subtractions

    (1) Release of air from a balloon
    (2) Drying out a wet sponge
    (3) Removal of a baby's clothes (making the total weight less)

  c. Physical growth and aging

    (1) Children generally gaining weight as they grow
    (2) Older people often losing weight as they become very old
    (3) Old, shriveled apples weighing less than young, firm apples

5. A change in weight may result in an alteration of appearance.

  a. Either adding or subtracting many pounds from a person
  b. An inflated balloon compared to a deflated balloon

6. Changing the form or rearranging the structure of an item will not change its weight.

  a. A pound of butter weighs the same when melted.
  b. A tower of 10 blocks weighs the same as these 10 blocks in a pile.
  c. An amount of water weighs the same when it is frozen into a solid as when it is a liquid.

7. Weight is not determined by size, shape, age, or equal amounts. Some items may look heavy but are light; and some items may look light but are heavy.

  a. A pound of nails is not equal in volume to a pound of feathers.
  b. A large Styrofoam container, such as that used to hold a tape recorder, weighs less than a smaller cardboard container, such as a jewelry box.
  c. Older people do not necessarily weigh more than younger people.
  d. Gifts of various shapes do not vary in weight merely because of their variation in shape.

8. Different items may have the same weight.

  a. An 11-year-old child may weigh about the same as a bale of hay.
  b. A 10-pound bag of sugar may weigh the same as a child's dog.
  c. A pound of butter weighs the same as a pound of bacon.

9. Many items are sold and packaged in 1-pound units of measure.

  a. Bacon
  b. Butter
  c. Rice
  d. Cereal
  e. Meat
  f. Candy
  g. Nuts
  h. Nails
  i. Plaster
  j. Salt

10. The same items may vary in weight.

  a. Apples
  b. People
  c. Boxes
  d. Rocks

    e. Marbles
    f. Automobiles
11. Air has weight.
12. Weight experiences may involve making comparisons between the weights of two or more objects, in addition to ordering items from lightest to heaviest.
13. Balance is not necessarily achieved by supporting an object or a group of objects in the middle, but by obtaining stability through an even distribution of weight on either side of a fulcrum, or vertical axis.
14. Materials do not have to be of the same kind, substance, or amount to be balanced.
    a. A roll of cellophane tape balanced on one side of the balance board, with a wooden block on the other side (heavier object moved closer to the fulcrum to achieve balance)
    b. Wheat on one side of the balance scale, rice on the other
    c. Two wooden blocks balanced against one wooden block

Activities and Experiences

Experiments with Weight Comparisons

1. Have the children place wrapped packages of different sizes and shapes in order, from lightest to heaviest.

2. Visit a pumpkin patch, or collect as many pumpkins as you can find. Weigh and measure them, and order them from lightest to heaviest. (Use other seasonal items such as potatoes or apples or other objects such as shoes, blocks, and so on.)

3. Have the children match duplicate weights of items—even when the items are not the same or the items are not the same size, shape, or equal in amount.
    a. Boxes of different sizes filled with various items and then wrapped (or use paper sacks)
    b. Balance scales used to match items of same weight
        (1) Scales or pans in the same position on either side of the fulcrum
        (2) Children try to choose items of similar weight and verify the weights by using a scale
        (3) If possible, a scale measuring both pounds and ounces showing actual weights
    c. Different amounts of various items: feathers, candies, nails, bolts, wheat, balloons, dry cereal. These are weighed by children to determine how much of an item is required to equal a pound

4. Have the children close their eyes and determine, by lifting various objects, which are heavier.

5. Ask the children to examine groups or pairs of objects and decide by observation which are heavier. Have them follow up by lifting the objects or weighing them to determine whether their selections are correct.

6. Have the children keep a record of their own weight and record the changes. The children can then find things that weigh less than they do, things that weigh more, and things that weigh the same.
    a. Number of large-unit blocks equaling their own weight
    b. Comparison of weights
        (1) Children weighed on scales
        (2) Children weighed holding an item such as a book, a pound of butter, or some blocks

7. Introduce the children to units of measure by introducing them to scales. Focus first on scales that weigh in pounds, and give them many experiences with pounds. Then introduce the concept of ounces (a unit for measuring less than a pound), and let the children measure items on an ounce scale (for example, a diet scale). After this exposure, introduce older children to a unit of measure that is less than an ounce, a gram, and try to locate a scale sensitive enough to weigh grams. In addition, older children may be exposed to the unit of measure representing 2,000 pounds, a ton. Many heavy items are weighed in tons. A weigh station or trucking corporation is a possible place to see items being weighed in tons.

8. Use the balance scales with sensory media such as wheat, rice, or buttons to enable the

children to explore the concepts of balance and weight. Various kinds of items can be used with the balance scales for making weight comparisons, as well as for balancing items of equal weight and for distributing weight in order to make the scales in balance.

9. Perform experiments to show that air has weight. (See Chapter 10 for additional experiments with air.) For example, select two balloons that are exactly the same (put them on the balance scales). Measure two lengths of string that are exactly the same kind and length (about 10 inches). Tie the strings to the deflated balloons. Suspend a yardstick with a string in the middle, or balance it on the spine of a book, using the book as a fulcrum. Tie a string with a balloon attached to each end of the yardstick in the same location. Whether the yardstick or a balance scale is used, the balloons should balance evenly. Now remove one of the balloons and blow air into it. Tie it back on in the same place on the yardstick. It will be obvious that the balloon containing air has more weight because the yardstick or balance scales will tip lower on the side with the inflated balloon.

Experiments with Sinking and Floating

1. Put a number of different objects (feathers, corks, small wooden sticks, hairpins, pebbles, coins) near a bowl, basin, or trough of water. Let the children predict which objects will sink and which will float. Have a box for the objects that sink and a box for those that float.

2. Give each child an equal amount of oil-based clay (a ball about 1 inch in diameter). Ask the children to see whether the clay will float in water. Challenge them to see whether they can change its shape in such a way that it will float. If the children are not successful, show them how to press the clay flat and then mold the edges up to make a little boat. (This can also be done with pieces of aluminum foil.)

Experiments with Balance

1. From a school physics laboratory, obtain an analytical balance scale that is sensitive to weights of less than an ounce. Then have the children experiment with balancing such objects as feathers, scraps of paper, toothpicks,

hairpins, needles, and thumbtacks. They can also determine which is the heaviest of the objects that they are using for the experiment. Working with this balance scale is the same as working with the larger balance scale, except that objects of lighter weight can be balanced.

2. Put two children of different weights on a seesaw and challenge them to find a way to make it balance. The heavier child will be closer to the fulcrum, and the lighter one will be farther away.

3. Provide a balance board made from plywood about $\frac{1}{2}$ by $2\frac{1}{2}$ by 24 inches. The fulcrum can be made with a block of wood measuring $\frac{1}{2}$ by $\frac{1}{2}$ by 3 inches. Starting at the middle and working toward the ends, mark off the board at 1-inch intervals, and draw a line across the board at each mark. Label the center mark 0, and begin labeling the marks on either side 1, 2, 3, and so on. Now give the child six or eight 1-inch blocks (made by the teacher or commercially). Many experiments with balancing can be performed with these simple materials. One of the best ways to begin is to let the children experiment with balancing the materials without giving any directions. After the children have balanced the board on the fulcrum, some of the following activities will provide reinforcement (see Figure 9–2):

a. One block placed on each side of the fulcrum after balancing the board on the fulcrum: children determine whether each block must be placed at the same distance from the fulcrum to make the board balance

b. Two blocks placed on each side of the fulcrum: children discover ways to position the blocks and still have the board balance (continue this with three blocks, four blocks, and so on)

c. Two sets of unequal numbers of blocks used to balance the board on the fulcrum

   (1) One block placed on one side and two blocks on the other side of the fulcrum; one block on one side and three on the other; many more variations

   (2) The principle discovered here, that one or two blocks placed farther from the fulcrum can balance several blocks

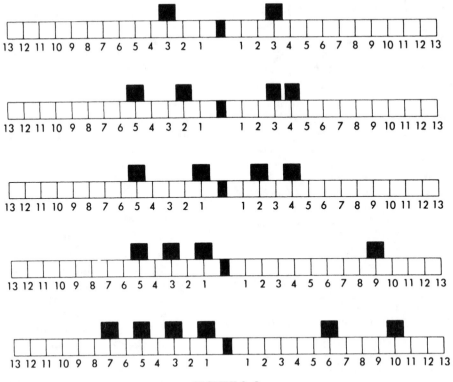

FIGURE 9–2

closer to the fulcrum, can be taken a
step further with older children; for example, show them that blocks placed
on positions 1, 3, and 5 on one side balance one block placed on position 9
on the other side, since $1 + 3 + 5 = 9$.

  d. Fulcrum moved by the children so that it
      is not at the midpoint (perhaps under po-
      sition 1 or 2 on either side). The children
      determine whether and how balance can
      be achieved.

UNIT PLAN ON WEIGHT AND BALANCE

Art

• Wrapped packages of various weights decorated with paint or collage materials, then used
  for balancing or weighing

• Decorated music shakers: empty juice cans,
  milk cartons, or boxes filled with items of
  varying weight such as rice, rocks, and sand

• Papier-mâché molded around an inflated balloon; let dry, then pop the balloon, and paint or
  decorate ball as desired. Use to compare differences in weight.

Food

• Any food experience dealing with items sold
  in 1-pound quantities (bacon, rice, meat, butter, bread, etc.)

• Making a cake and weighing it in various
  stages: cake mix first, then weight change by
  adding water and eggs, and then again by
  putting it in baking pan

• Spaghetti or macaroni, which has changed
  weight from lighter when dry to heavier after
  being cooked in water

Visitors

- Person from school physics department: various scales brought to the classroom
- Doctor or nurse: use of scales
- Grocery clerk with items in 1-pound packages
- Employee from state department of weights and measures
- Parent with bathroom scales

Music

- Decorated music shakers to use with selected records
- Musical boxes (instead of musical chairs) of different sizes, shapes, and weights. (As music stops, children lift box that they are sitting on; then, when game is finished, see if they have been able to determine which box was lightest and which box was heaviest.)
- Creative movements: pretending to carry a heavy rock; pretending to toss a light rock into the air; pretending to be a balloon being filled with air and suddenly bursting

Science

- Deflated inner tube weighed, then inflated one weighed
- Deflated balloon weighed, then inflated one weighed
- Dry sponge weighed, soaked with water, weighed, allowed to dry, weighed again
- Seesaw set up for comparison of children's and teachers' weights; also for comparative weighing of various objects in the room
- Wrapped packages matched by weight
- Pound of butter weighed in cube form, then after melting
- Rice, wheat, or spaghetti weighed, soaked in water, then weighed again

Field Trips

- Physics department in a school: observation of scales and their uses
- Doctor's office: use of scales with people

- Medical supply store: observation of various scales and their uses
- Weigh station or trucking corporation: use of scales with vehicles
- Grain elevator: use of scales with crops and produce
- Grocery store: scales at checkout stand, meat scales, and scales in produce department
- Livestock auction yards: use of scales with animals
- Beach or sandy hills: different-sized containers for filling and weighing amounts of sand
- Post office: observation of weighing of packages

Literacy

- Write and illustrate a story. "___ Is One Pound."
- Write and illustrate a story using the comparisons "___ Is Heavier Than ___" and "___ Is Lighter Than ___."

PHYSICAL SCIENCE EXPERIMENTS UNRELATED TO SPECIFIC UNITS

Scientific explanations are presented simply in many of the experiences suggested in this chapter. Older children can understand and be introduced to scientific explanations in more detail. Younger children will find the demonstrations themselves adequate. Many experiments help children to understand about ecology and being sensitive to preserving Earth and its environment.

Vinegar and baking soda. To a small amount of vinegar ($\frac{1}{4}$ cup), add 1 teaspoon baking soda. Watch, hear, and feel what happens. [Carbon dioxide gas (bubbles) is formed when vinegar and baking soda are mixed together.]

Buoyancy of raisins or alfalfa seeds in carbonated soda or in soda and vinegar solution. Add 3 tablespoons of vinegar and 2 teaspoons of baking soda to 1 cup of water. Add 1 teaspoon of alfalfa seeds or other tiny seeds; observe as the seeds rise to the surface of the water and then sink to the bottom of the container. Carbon dioxide bubbles pick the seeds up and carry them to the surface. When the bubbles pop, the seeds return to the bottom, where they are surrounded again by bubbles and are carried to the surface. As an alternative, drop raisins, whole or part, into a cup half filled with carbonated soda. Count how many times a raisin surfaces and sinks in a given time period, such as 3 minutes.

Another variation. Fill a cup half full of vinegar. Add 1 tablespoon of soda. After fizzing is through, add 1 to 2 grapes. Carbon dioxide bubbles will adhere to the grapes, and the grapes will rise to the top of the liquid. As the bubbles are released into the air, the grapes sink back down. The process then is repeated. *Note*: Compare what happens when grapes are put in a cup of plain water. (*Basic concept*: Gases can be produced that help objects to float.) (ACEI, 1996a).

Blowing up a balloon. Pour 1 inch of vinegar into a pop bottle. Put 1 or 2 teaspoons of baking soda inside a balloon and affix the balloon opening to the open top of the bottle. Then allow the soda and vinegar to mix together. The balloon will slowly inflate.

Crystals. Unique crystals can be grown with ordinary table salt or alum. Heat some water, and then dissolve as much salt as possible in the water. The solution will then be saturated. Pour the solution into an old open pie pan (the disposable aluminum kind works well; since the solution may be corrosive to some metals). Then place it in a corner of the room where it will not be disturbed. As the water starts to evaporate, small crystals will be observed forming. If these crystals are viewed through a microscope, they will show a crystal shape unique to that particular salt. Also note that the slower the water evaporates, the larger the crystals will grow.

Chemical garden. Combine the following ingredients: 2 tablespoons ammonia, $\frac{1}{4}$ cup bluing, $\frac{1}{4}$ cup salt, $\frac{1}{4}$ cup water. (Caution the children against smelling the ammonia, except at a safe distance.) Pour the mixture over coal, bricks, charcoal, or similar materials. Drops of food coloring may be added on top. In a few hours, salt-crystal formations will begin to appear. Use glass containers for this experiment, since the chemical may corrode aluminum. The chemical growth that occurs is made up of salt formations created when the liquid evaporates. The growth can be continued if more of the chemical ingredients are added or if 1 or 2 teaspoons of ammonia are added.

Floating an egg and pencil. Partly fill two containers, one with fresh water and one with salt water (4 tablespoons salt to 1 cup water). Let the children try floating the egg in each container. Try a hard-boiled egg. Now place a pencil in the water with the lead end up and the eraser end down. What happens to the pencil in the fresh water? What happens in the salt water? Do the items float in the salt water or the fresh water?

Rainbow. On a sunny day, stand a mirror in a bowl filled with water. Set the bowl near a wall. Now turn the mirror to reflect (and refract) the sun's rays onto the wall. This exhibits the colors of the spectrum. What colors are seen?

Mirror images. Hinge together two mirrors with tape. Stand the hinged mirror on its edge. Place bits of colored paper in the mirror angle. Observe the different patterns in the double reflection. Try using a penny instead of the colored paper bits. How many pennies can you see? Open and close the mirror and observe as the number of pennies reflected in the mirror changes.

A–Z science fair. Hold an A–Z science fair during school, after school, or in the evening, with parents and other classroom students being invited to attend. The teacher and children collaborate and think of a science experiment, activity, demonstration, or concept to represent each letter of the alphabet. Each child selects a letter of the alphabet or a science idea to be presented during the science fair. Flags or labels identify each letter, enabling participants to progress from activity A through activity Z, observing, trying out, manipulating, and inferring with each one. The following is a list of possible general concepts or ideas to represent each letter in the alphabet. These are only suggestions; there are numerous other possibilities.

A	Air	Q	Quarts (measuring liquids)
B	Bubbles	R	Rainbows
C	Crystal garden	S	Sounds
D	Degrees (Celsius and Fahrenheit)	T	Tasting
E	Electric current	U	Unhatched eggs
F	Floating and sinking	V	Violin strings
G	Gravity	W	Water
H	Hive	X	Xylophone sounds
I	Ice	Y	Yards (measuring)
J	Jack (observe and try spinning a jack)	Z	Zucchini (observe differences between zucchini and cucumber)
K	Keys (which key fits the padlock)		
L	Light and shadows		
M	Magnets		
N	Nests		
O	Owl facts		
P	Plants		

Following the science fair, write a book about the experience. Let each page represent a letter, with a picture drawn by the child and then a sentence or two in the child's words about that experiment or activity.

Summary

Because children are naturally curious about their environment, science is frequently a part of their exploration, play, questioning, and experimentation. Science can teach patience, inquiry, respect for evidence, self-reliance, and open-mindedness. Many science activities are preplanned into the curriculum, but often science-related experiences result from natural, spontaneous environmental stimulation. As children gain more knowledge in the areas of science, they become more able to understand their world. As they become more familiar with Earth, they also should learn that they can make a difference in protecting our environment, that the quality of air, soil, and water is determined by human treatment and care. They become more aware of, and comfortable with, nature, people, events, and the materials surrounding them.

Valuable science activities for children include hearing, tasting, smelling, touching, inferring, observing, interpreting, classifying, drawing conclusions, solving problems, inquiring, reasoning, rationalizing, exploring, generalizing, comparing, creating, verifying, analyzing, predicting, and hypothesizing. Possibly no other single area of the curriculum involves as many process skills that are so important to the development of understanding and thinking in young children. Young children have a natural curiosity about their world and how it works; they constantly wonder, explore, examine, describe, manipulate, compare, and question things relating to the natural environment. They should be encouraged to observe carefully, note similarities and differences, make predictions, test their predictions, ask questions, and interact with one another and the teacher. They should be constantly encouraged to think and talk about what they are doing and seeing. Career choices in the sciences are often fostered from early interests and experiences (NAEYC, 1996a).

Student Learning Activities

1. From your reading and study of this chapter, develop criteria for science activities and units for children. For example, science activities and units should provide opportunities for firsthand or real experiences.

2. From your study of this chapter, write down at least five of the process skills that science helps to develop in young children. For each skill that you listed, suggest one science activity that would specifically give children practice in developing

this skill. For example, to develop the skill of inferring, a good activity would be to pass around a gift-wrapped box containing several objects, such as paper clips and pennies. Have the children guess or infer what might be inside the box.

3. Make a list of science equipment and materials that you would begin collecting for science kits. Examples might be rocks, seed collections, thermometer, magnifying glass, tape measure, and others. Pick an area, such as magnets, and develop a science kit. Time will be provided in class to share your kits.

4. Plan and make at least one science material or piece of equipment.

5. Visit an early childhood classroom and observe science-related materials, books, visual aids, software, centers, or activities. Interview the teacher about his or her science curriculum. What role do you feel science plays in this classroom and what would you change?

6. Interview and visit with children ages 3 to 8 about concepts relating to weight. Ask them how much they weigh. Ask the children to make weight comparisons of objects in the environment. How do concept understandings of weight vary between the older and younger children that you interview? Study some of the references listed for this chapter. From your study, write down three additional science activities.

7. Obtain, study, and evaluate at least three of the children's books suggested as references for this chapter. What science concepts does the book teach? How would you use the book with children? How effective would the book be in teaching a science concept to children?

8. Plan and carry out with children at least three science activities.

9. Select a science theme and prepare a unit plan or web for it. Invite a child to do a project plan for a topic such as fire or water.

10. From the unit plan or web prepared for activity 9, complete an activity plan on the science theme that you have selected.

11. From your work in activities 9 and 10, prepare a lesson plan on a science theme.

Suggested Resources

Science Resources

Note: These resources will also provide many suggestions for the next two chapters: Chapter 10, Earth Science Experiences, and Chapter 11, Life Science Experiences.

Althouse, R. (1988). *Investigating science experiences with young children*. New York: Teachers College Press.

Brown, S. (1981). *Bubbles, rainbows, and worms: Science experiments for preschool children*. Mt. Rainier, MD: Gryphon House.

Busch, P.O. (1995). *Backyard safaris: Fifty-two year-round science adventures*. New York: Aladdin.

Butzow, G. M., & J.W. Butzow (1989). *Science through children's literature*. Englewood, CO: Teacher Ideas Press.

Chaille, C., & L. Britain (1991). *The young child a scientist: A constructivist approach to early childhood science education*. New York: HarperCollins.

Claycomb, P. (1991). *Love the Earth: Exploring environmental activities for young children*. Livonia, MI: Partner.

Cleaver, J. (1992). *Doing children's museums: A guide to 262 hands-on museums*. Charlotte, VT: Williamson.

Cohen, R., & B. P. Tunick (1993). *Snail trails and tadpole tails: Nature education for young children*. St. Paul: Redleaf.

Cornell, J. (1979). *Sharing nature with children*. Nevada City, CA: Ananda.

Cornell, J. (1989). *Sharing the job of nature*. Nevada City, CA: Dawn.

Edom, H. (1992). *Science activities*. Tulsa, OK: Educational Development.

Gallas, K. (1995). *Talking their way into science: Hearing children's questions and theories, responding with curriculum*. New York: Teachers College Press.

Harlan, J. (1996). *Science experiences for the early childhood years* (6th ed.). Upper Saddle River, NJ: Merrill/Prentice Hall.

Holt, B. G. (1989). *Science with young children* (rev. ed.). Washington, DC: National Association for the Education of Young Children.

Kamii, C., & R. Devries (1978). *Physical knowledge in preschool education: Implications of Piaget's theory*. Upper Saddle River, NJ: Prentice Hall.

Katz, A. (1986). *Naturewatch: Exploring nature with your children*. Reading, MA: Addison–Wesley.

Lingelbach, J. (1986). *Hands-on nature*. Woodstock, VT: Vermont Institute of Natural Science.

McIntyre, M. (1984). *Early childhood and science*. Arlington, VA: National Science Teachers Association.

National Science Resources Center/ Smithsonian Institution/National Academy of Sciences (1988). *Science for children: Resources for teachers.* Washington, DC: National Academy Press.

Neuberger, B. (1989). *The wonder of it: Exploring how the world works.* Redmond, WA: Exchange Press.

Neuman, D. B. (1992). *Experiences in science for young children.* Prospect Heights, IL: Waveland.

Neuman, D. B. (1993). *Experiencing elementary science.* Belmont, CA: Wadsworth.

Richards, R. (1989). *An early start to nature.* New York: Simon & Schuster.

Rockwell, R. E., E. A. Sherwood, & R. W. Williams (1986). *Hug-a-tree: And other things to do outdoors with young children.* Mt. Rainier, MD: Gryphon House.

Roth, C., C. Cervoni, T. Weilnitz, & E. Arms (1988). *Beyond the classroom: Exploration of schoolground and backyard.* Lincoln, MA: Massachusetts Audubon Society.

Sherwood, E. A., R. W. Williams, & R. E. Rockwell (1990). *More mudpies to magnets.* Mt. Ranier, MD: Gryphon House.

Taylor, B. J. (1993). *Science everywhere: Opportunities for very young children.* San Diego, CA: Harcourt Brace Jovanovich.

Ticotsky, A. (1985). *Who says you can't teach science.* Glenview, IL: Good Year Books, Scott Foresman.

Williams, R. W., R. E. Rockwell, & E. A. Sherwood (1987). *Mudpies to magnets.* Mt. Ranier, MD: Gryphon House.

Wilson, R. (1993). *Fostering a sense of wonder during the early childhood years.* Columbus, OH: Greyden.

Your big back yard. Available from the National Wildlife Federation, 1400 Sixteenth St., NW, Washington, DC 20036-2266. (Phone: 1-800-432-6564)

Periodicals

Chickadee: The Canadian Magazine for Children. Young Naturalist Foundation, 56 The Esplanade, Suite 304, Toronto, Ont., M5E 1A7.

Child Life. P.O. Box 10681, Des Moines, IA 50381.

Children's Playmate Magazine. Children's Better Health Institute, P.O. Box 567, Indianapolis, IN 46206.

National Geographic News. P.O. Box 2330, Washington, DC 20009.

Ranger Rick's Nature Magazine. National Wildlife Federation, 1412 16th St., NW, Washington, DC 20036.

Scholastic Let's Find Out. Scholastic Magazines, 1290 Wall St., W, Lyndhurst, NJ 07071.

Science Weekly. P.O. Box 70154, Washington, DC 20088.

Scienceland, Inc. 501 5th Ave., Suite 2102, New York, NY 10017.

Sesame Street. Children's Television Workshop, P.O. Box 2896, Boulder, CO 80322.

3 2 1 Contact. P.O. Box 2933, Boulder, CO 80322.

World. National Geographic Society, P.O. Box 2895, Washington, DC 20077-9960.

Your Big Back Yard. National Wildlife Federation, 1412 16th St., NW, Washington, DC 20036.

Children's Books*

Asch, F. (1985). *Bear shadow.* New York: Simon & Schuster.

Asch, F. (1985). *Skyfire.* New York: Simon & Schuster/Young Readers.

Asch, F. (1994). *The earth and I.* New York: Harcourt.

Bang, M. (1996). *Yellow ball.* New York: Morrow.

Bragg, R. G. (1992). *Colors of the day.* Saxonville, MA: Picture Book Studio.

Bulla, C. (1994). *What makes a shadow?* New York: HarperCollins.

Carle, E. (1991). *The tiny seed.* Saxonville, MA: Picture Book Studio.

Crisp, M. (2000). *Black and white.* Flagstaff, AZ: Rising Moon.

Davis, K., & W. Oldfield (1990). *My mirror.* Garden City, NY: Doubleday.

Edom, H. (1992). *Science with light and mirrors.* Tulsa, OK: Educational Development.

Edom, H. (1992). *Science with magnets.* Tulsa, OK: Educational Development.

Ehlert, L. (1988). *Planting a rainbow.* San Diego, CA: Harcourt Brace Jovanovich,.

Ehlert, L. (1989). *Color zoo.* New York: HarperCollins.

Ehlert, L. (1990). *Color farm.* New York: HarperCollins.

Ehlert, L. (1991). *Red leaf, yellow leaf.* New York: Harcourt Brace.

Fleming, D. (1996). *Where once there was a wood.* New York: Henry Holt.

Groening, M., & M. Groening. (1991). *Maggie Simpson's book of colors and shapes.* New York: HarperCollins.

Hiscock, B. (1991). *The big tree.* New York: Atheneum.

Hoban, T. (1990). *Shadows and reflections.* New York: Greenwillow.

Hoban, T. (1995). *Colors everywhere.* New York: Greenwillow.

Hubband, P. (1996). *My crayons talk.* New York: Henry Holt.

Jeffers, S. (1991). *Brother Eagle, Sister Sky: A message from Chief Seattle.* New York: Dial.

Knowlton, J. (1985). *Maps and globes.* New York: Harper & Row.

Livingston, M. C., & L. E. Fisher (1986). *Earth songs.* New York: Holiday House.

Locker, T. (1991). *The land of Gray Wolf.* New York: Dial.

Martin, B. (1967). *Brown bear, brown bear, what do you see?* New York: Holt, Rinehart & Winston.

Marzollo, J. (1996). *I am fire.* Jefferson City, MO: Scholastic.

---

*See also lists of children's books in other text chapters.

Olaleye, I.O. (2000). *In the rainfield: Who is the greatest?* New York: Blue Sky Press.

Patent, D. H. (1990). *Yellowstone fires: Flames and rebirth.* New York: Holiday House.

Paul, A. W. (1992). *Shadows are about.* New York: Scholastic.

Pendziwol, J. (1999). *No dragons for tea: Fire safety for kids (and dragons).* Buffalo, NY: Kids Can Press Ltd.

Pinkney, A., & B. Pinkney (1997). *Pretty brown face.* New York: Red Wagon Books/Harcourt Brace.

Repchuk, C. (1997). *The snow tree.* New York: Dutton.

Steig, W. (1969). *Sylvester and the magic pebble.* New York: Windmill.

Taylor, B. (1992). *Over the rainbow! The science of color and light.* New York: Random House.

Vagin, V. (1998). *The enormous carrot.* New York: Scholastic Press.

Verdet, J. P. (1995). *Earth, sky, and beyond: A journey through space.* New York: Dutton (U.S. edition).

Webb, A. (1988). *Talk about light.* New York: Franklin Watts.

West, D. (1992). *Why is the sky blue: And answers to all of the questions you always wanted to ask.* New York: Barron's.

Wilkes, A. (1991). *My first green book.* New York: Knopf.

Williams, J. (1992). *Simple science projects with color and light.* Milwaukee, WI: Gareth Stevens.

Woolfitt, G. (1992). *Blue.* Minneapolis, MN: Carolrhoda.

Woolfitt, G. (1992). *Green.* Minneapolis, MN: Carolrhoda.

Woolfitt, G. (1992). *Red.* Minneapolis, MN: Carolrhoda.

Woolfitt, G. (1992). *Yellow.* Minneapolis, MN: Carolrhoda.

Pictures

Colors and shapes. The Child's World (Panorama)

The desert. The Child's World.

Earth movements. The Child's World.

Ecosystems. David C. Cook.

Important minerals. Society for Visual Education.

Learning about energy. David C. Cook.

Learning about nature. David C. Cook.

Polar regions. The Child's World.

Safety. David C. Cook.

Science themes no. 1. David C. Cook.

Science themes no. 2. David C. Cook.

The sea. The Child's World.

Volcanoes. The Child's World.

Multimedia Kits

Exploring the solar system and beyond. National Geographic.

Let's explore space. National Geographic.

Our earth. National Geographic.

Weilbacher, M. *The magnetism exploration kit.* Philadelphia: Running Press.

Videos

Me and my world. National Geographic.

Computer Software

Millie & Bailey Preschool and Kindergarten. Redmond, WA: Riverdeep.

Sammy's science house. Redmond, WA: Riverdeep.

School house science. Torrance, CA: Davidson.

Science blaster Jr. Torrance, CA: Davidson.

Thinkin' science. Redmond, WA: Riverdeep.

Thinkin' things: Collection 1. Redmond, WA: Riverdeep.

Thinkin' things: Collection 2. Redmond, WA: Riverdeep.

Thinkin' things: Collection 3. Redmond, WA: Riverdeep.

Travel the world with Timmy. Redmond, WA: Edmark.

Chapter 10

Earth Science Experiences

This chapter presents ideas, concepts, and activities relating to the environment, air, water, rocks, temperature, weather, and seasons. Again, science is best learned through hands-on exploration and experiences. It is virtually impossible to designate science only as a subject to be occasionally taught as a unit or theme. It should be child centered and activity oriented; it should provide children with a varied environment to explore at their own pace and according to their individual cognitive abilities. Both girls and boys should be encouraged in science activities and inquiry (Rivkin, 1992). Science should interest the children in the world in which they live.

Kupetz and Twiest (2000) suggest that children today have less exposure to the world of nature than did children of the past. They propose the following reasons why children are not as interested in exploring their natural outdoor environments:

- Safety concerns (dangerous or unsafe materials or environments)

- Organized activities (team and individual sports, music lessons, clubs)

- Travel (more traveling among family members, vacations, more time spent in transportation)

- Technology (computers, television)

Refer to the introduction to Chapter 9, Physical Science Experiences, for a more detailed discussion of the sciences in general.

> Science is a part of everyday life, so it must be a part of the everyday curriculum!

TEACHING ABOUT ENVIRONMENTAL CONCEPTS

"Environmental education for young children is about wonder, and curiosity, enjoyment of our world, and caring for one's natural surroundings" (Kupetz & Twiest, 2000, p. 61). Early childhood programs should be both developmentally and environmentally appropriate, with the latter reflecting care, concern, and responsibility for our natural environment. "(Environmental concern) must become a way of life . . ." (Wilson, 1995a, p. 107), not just an occasional holiday, celebration, unit, lesson, or activity.

Demonstration (modeling) and active involvement are both needed for children to understand the importance of protecting and preserving our natural environment. Teachers, share your own respect and appreciation for *all* living things, and children will learn the same (Ross, 2000). Children learn today how to become responsible environmentalists of the future (Wilson, 1995a). "Respect for life, preservation of resources, and care for our planet are cultivated in the early childhood years" (Humphreys, 2000, p. 20). "Three- and four-year-old children . . . are the perfect age to learn habits that will become part of their lives" (Shantal, 1998, p. 71). Children can begin early to learn the need to protect our environment and that they can make a difference. They can learn that there are many natural beauties on our planet to be enjoyed, appreciated, and protected by all people. They can learn that the quality of the soil, air, and water is determined by human treatment and care. Some of Earth's problems are the following:

- *Air pollution.* This is caused by combustion and burning fuel. Factories, woodburning stoves, and cars all emit harmful pollutants into our air.

- *Water pollution.* People allow waste into our water supplies or spill chemicals or oil into our rivers and lakes.

- *Soil erosion.* We farm soil so much that it becomes poor, and we cut down trees and clear away land for cities and buildings, leading to erosion.

- *Solid waste.* We throw away tons of garbage each year, and Earth is running out of space to put this huge amount of garbage. The average resident in the United States throws away 4.3 pounds of waste each day (ACEI, 1996c, p. 228-I). Children can learn that preventing waste is much easier than trying to get rid of it. Tips for doing that include using:

> Both sides of writing and drawing paper
>
> Reusable loose-leaf binders, book covers, and bookmarks
>
> Refillable pencils and pens
>
> Reusable lunch bags and food containers
>
> Swap boxes for exchanging no-longer-needed items from home
>
> Scrap boxes for reusable paper
>
> Fewer handouts
>
> Discarded items for creative arts projects
>
> Food wastes for compost piles
>
> Washable plates, utensils, cups
>
> Equipment that does not need batteries (ACEI, 1996c)

The study of the environment for young children must provide for interactions with nature.

Concepts and Ideas for Teaching

Remember: One child *can* make a difference! Teach the children what they and others can do to save Earth, protect our environment, and be environmentally responsible.

1. "Foster close observation of the natural world" (Wilson, 1995a, p. 107). Children learn the interdependency of living things and that the natural world is interesting and always changing. When children collect materials from the outdoors (wood, leaves, seeds, etc.), these should be returned to the natural environment, if possible, after study is complete. Teach the children to "find, examine, and return" (Humphreys, 2000, p. 18).

2. "Avoid harming plants and animals when playing outdoors" (Wilson, 1995a, p. 107). All living things should be treated with respect and care. Help children to be aware of this and not to disturb nests, trees and bushes, animals and insects, flowers, and so on. When animals or insects are kept for study, try to return them to their natural habitat whenever possible.

3. "Reduce, reuse, and recycle" (Wilson, 1995a, p. 107). Children can learn and teach their families about excessive packaging; conserving water, energy, paper, food, and other resources; repairing and reusing containers, clothing, and other materials; and recycling paper, tin, plastic, aluminum, clothing, and glass.

4. Stop wasting water. Turn off the water while brushing teeth, and do not let the water run to waste outside in yards and on playgrounds. Keep cold water in the refrigerator for drinking so that it does not have to run from the faucet each time to get cold. Take a shower instead of a bath.

5. Encourage families to buy products that are biodegradable, that is, they rot or decompose when discarded. "Avoid the use of disposable cups, plates, napkins, and so on, as much as possible, while still maintaining health standards" (Wilson, 1995a, p. 108). Learn to conserve such things as paper. For example, school lunches can be brought in

lunch boxes instead of paper bags, and bags, sacks, and other consumables can be reused.

6. "Avoid any types of littering and, where safe, clean up areas that have been littered by others" (Wilson, 1995a, p. 108). Children can check the playground every day for any garbage or litter that can be gathered up and disposed of properly. *Note*: Any dangerous trash (broken glass, sharp metal) should be handled by an adult. Always put trash in a trash can.

7. Pick only what they plant themselves, and leave other things in nature for all to enjoy. Involving children in growing some of their own food not only minimizes food packaging, but it teaches children about nutrition, food sources, and the environmental needs of plants.

8. Make a compost pile. Besides making one outside, individual compost piles can be made in individual cups. Allow a few days of decomposition and then plant a seed (bean) and care for it as it grows.

9. Care for toys and other possessions so that they do not need to be replaced and can be passed on to others.

10. Turn the lights off when leaving a room, turn appliances off when not in use, and turn the thermostat down in winter and up in the summer to conserve fuel.

11. "Encourage parent involvement in environmentally responsible practices" (Wilson, 1995a, p. 109).

Young children are busy people. Because they enjoy touching, poking, digging, patting, hearing, shaking, smelling, and pouring, "they are excellent candidates for nature education experiences" (Wilson, 1995b, p. 4). Experiences with trees, parks, flowers, and their community all help children to acquire an appreciation for and commitment to our world and its environment. Teachers should build environmental awareness in young children; and the best approach to support environmental and nature themes and concepts is to provide hands-on activities. For example, children can adopt a tree by naming it, studying and learning everything they can about their kind of tree, watering it, having a picnic under it, enjoying its shade, observing it during different seasons, seeing how animals use it, and making sure it is free of insect or other problems that could be treated. Teachers have an important role in helping young children to cultivate an attitude and sense of caring, understanding, and appreciation for their natural environment.

Wilson (1995b, pp. 6–9) provides suggestions for helping children to experience nature:

- "Forget about trying to name everything found in nature."
- "Focus on the beauty and wonder of nature."
- "Introduce nature-related materials into the different learning centers."
- "Share pro-nature books with children."
- "Go outdoors as often as possible."
- "Model interest in and caring for the natural environment."

Take the children out into the natural environment, and "forget the fancy environmental curriculum" (Fenton, 1996, p. 8). Fenton's rule of "outside and unarmed" (p. 8) generally only uses teaching materials that can be found outdoors. "Climbing big rocks, mucking in puddles, whacking sticks on trees, collecting acorns and pinecones, looking for life under logs, and wallowing in the snow are all perfect, and frequent, opportunities for learning natural science" (Fenton, 1996, p. 10).

Whenever we want children to learn about something, we should provide the materials, space, and time for them to actively use their hands, noses, ears, eyes, and mouths. "Then step back and watch" (Diffily & Morrison, 1996, p. 5). Science is best understood when children are allowed to "mess around in the physical world" (p. 75).

Activities and Experiences

1. Do a nature-based scavenger hunt. The collected items could be put in an exhibit and later returned to their natural environments (Diffily & Morrison, 1996).

2. Make a nature scrapbook with drawings, magazine pictures, photos, stickers, and children's summaries (Diffily & Morrison, 1996).

3. As children gain basic science understandings regarding geography and its relationship to their environment, it is well to begin encouraging them to observe the physical features around them (playground, garden, zoo,

sandbox, grass, stream, houses, parks, hills). Then talk about how things came to look the way that they do. Photos, drawings, and blocks then tell the story of the things that the children see. As the objects are arranged according to the way that they are observed, beginning map-making geography skills are formed (Maxim, 1997).

4. Have a "class-repair" day when a fix-it person comes to the school and helps the children to find items that need fixing or do not work (broken toys, wobbly tables and chairs, dripping faucets, broken shelves or cabinets, torn books, burned-out light bulbs, loose door knobs, and so on). If the item cannot be repaired, determine if it can be recycled.

5. Make a trash collage or sculpture. Provide each child with a sack and go for a trash-collecting walk in a schoolyard, park, or other location. The trash that the children gather can be recycled into an art project. They could also bring some discarded items from home to use.

6. Set up a recycling center in the classroom, lunchroom, or school. Have three collection containers: paper, plastic, and aluminum.

7. When crayons are in pieces and no longer used for coloring, melt them for making candles, place mats, or other items.

TEACHING ABOUT AIR

Young children soon learn that air is all around us, is real, and takes up space. Air can also be touched and felt, as we feel the blowing wind, the cold and hot temperatures of the seasons, our breath, or the air from a compressor or pump. An exploratory science activity taking place in the preschool classroom is described in the following example: The teacher had given the children small boxes of various sizes wrapped as gifts. They were told to explore the boxes in any way that they wished (except opening them) and to try to discover what might be inside them. One young boy said, "I know for sure one thing that is inside." The teacher, wondering how he could "know for sure," asked, "What do you think might be inside?" He confidently answered, "I don't just think, I know for sure air is inside!"

Manipulating materials to make a balloon inflate makes it easier to understand the concept of air expansion.

Once children learn the concept that air is all around us, they can "know for sure" that air is in a wrapped package, even though it is not known what else is actually contained in the mystery box.

Air concepts could be taught as a separate unit or as individual activities supporting other themes. There are numerous supportive curriculum activities relating to air.

Concepts and Ideas for Teaching

1. Air is part of Earth and is all around us.
2. Air takes up space.
3. Animals, people, and plants need air for survival.
4. Fire needs air to burn.
5. Air has weight.
6. Air has force.
7. Air moves.
8. There is air in dirt.
9. There is air in water.
10. Bubbles are formed with air. If you are blowing bubbles, the air comes from inside your body.
11. Air expands when heated, and warm air rises.
12. Air helps many items to float on water.
13. Air has many uses.
14. Air can be hot or cold.
15. Air can make noise.
16. The quality of air is affected by humans.

Activities and Experiences

1. Have the children hold their hands close to their mouths and noses to feel the air as it is exhaled. Also, have them put their hands on their chests to feel their chests (lungs) expand and contract as air is inhaled and exhaled.

2. Obtain a flexible cardboard box no smaller than a gelatin box and no larger than a cereal box. Cut a hole in one end and wrap the box with paper, making sure to wrap around the hole but not cover it. Above the hole, glue tiny tissue-paper streamers so that they hang across the hole. Pass the box around so that all the children can shake it or feel it. Then ask them, "What is inside the box?" Un-

less the children have had a previous discussion on air, they will probably reply that the box is empty. When the box comes back to you, squeeze the box in the center and ask the children, "If nothing is in the box, what is making the tissue paper move?" The conclusion should be drawn that there is air in the box; when the box is squeezed, some of the air is forced out through the hole, making the tissue paper move.

3. Place a tissue in the bottom of a glass. Invert the glass in a large glass bowl that has been filled with water. Ask the children why the tissue does not get wet. If they do not know, explain that the glass is full of air and that air takes up space. When the tissue stays dry, it is because the glass is full of air and there is no room for water to enter. If the glass is tipped to the side, air bubbles will escape and water will take the place of the air, allowing the tissue to get wet.

4. Fill a glass or jar half full of dry soil or dirt. With the children gathered very close around the jar, pour water onto the soil. Ask the children what they see and hear. They should be able to both see and hear air bubbles come up out of the soil. Explain that there is air in dirt, and water that is poured onto the soil and seeps down into it takes the place of the air and forces the air to the surface.

5. Fill a clear glass container with water. Allow it to stand for a brief period of time. Soon air bubbles will begin to form against the edge of the container. The air from the water has formed the air bubbles.

6. Fill a trough, tub, or sink with water. Obtain a small plastic container with a lid, such as an empty detergent bottle. Put the lid on and place the container on the water. Ask the children whether it will float or sink. It will float because of the upward force (buoyancy) of the water and because the container is light, being full of air. Take the lid off and fill the plastic container with water. Will it still float? A similar activity can be carried out in a larger body or pool of water. Show the children a deflated inner tube. Will it float or sink? Now inflate it with air and see what happens. Air helps things to float.

7. To demonstrate that fire needs air, obtain three pie plates or saucers and put identical small candles on each (you may need to melt a little wax to hold the candle in place). Select three glass jars of varying sizes (pint, quart, and gallon jars work well). Light one of the candles, and then put a jar over the candle. Ask the children to observe what happens. When the candle goes out, ask the children if they know why the candle went out. Now perform the same demonstration while using the other two candles and jars. Put the jars on the candles at exactly the same time. Why does the candle under the smallest jar go out first? Explain that fire needs air to burn or that air has oxygen in it, and once the oxygen in the jar is used up, the fire goes out; it cannot burn without the oxygen. This same experiment can be demonstrated at Halloween time with two jack-o'-lanterns, one carved and one only hollowed out. Put candles in both. Light both candles and replace the lids. Ask why one candle stays lighted and one goes out. Explain that the jack-o'-lantern with the carved face allows air inside, but the other one is sealed and does not allow air inside. Thus, when the fire has used up all the air on the inside, the flame goes out because it needs air (oxygen) to burn.

8. Discuss what would happen if people, animals, and plants did not have air. Put a glass jar over a plant and observe what happens in a few days. Make sure that the plant still has water and sunlight. The plant will die without adequate air. Do all plants need air? (Not all, mold will grow in an air-tight jar.)

9. Put a balloon on the edge of a table or desk. Put a book on top of the balloon and then blow the balloon up. The air in the balloon will force the book up.

10. Even on a day that is not windy, go outside and observe the trees and other plant life. They will be moving slightly because of moving air. Blow some soap bubbles and watch them float on the air. Turn on a fan or vacuum and observe as the air moves items.

11. Give the children a container of water and a straw. While blowing, they will see and hear the bubbles created when the air inside them blows through the straw and makes the bubbles in the water. Once the children have mastered blowing (and not sucking), add a small amount of detergent to water in a bowl, cup, or other container. Give them a straw and let them blow bubbles. Keep sponges close by to absorb water.

12. Make kites and pinwheels. Explain that it is both the construction of the objects and the moving air that make them fly or move.

13. Blow soap bubbles outside and explain that air from inside the child fills the bubbles, whereas the air outside makes the bubbles move; the more wind (moving air) there is, the faster and farther the bubbles will move. A good solution for bubble blowing can be made from either 8 ounces liquid detergent and 1 ounce glycerin or from 8 ounces liquid detergent and $\frac{1}{4}$ cup sugar. Blower wands can be made by bending and twisting wire coat hangers or other heavy wire such as pipe cleaners.

14. Challenge the children to invent new bubble machines. Each child could bring something from home to use to blow bubbles. In addition, if the children are blowing bubbles outside, food coloring can be added to the bubble solution and a large piece of butcher paper put on the fence or building so that the blown bubbles make a bubble mural. The children's names can be put on their own spots, and the mural can be cut up so that the children can take their own parts home. The children can measure and see which bubble is the largest. In addition, the children can autograph their bubbles on the mural.

15. For activities to teach that air has weight, see Chapter 9.

UNIT PLAN ON AIR

Art

- Hummers decorated to be used as rhythm instruments

- Straw painting
- Inflated balloons decorated with paper scraps, felt scraps, rickrack, gummed stars, or other objects; perhaps they could be decorated as human heads
- Pinwheels
- Paper airplanes (to make and fly)
- Fans (to make)
- Miniature parachutes made from different materials
- Bubble-blow liquid tempra paint onto paper at the easel

Visitors

- Someone to play a wind instrument
- Someone to demonstrate household machines and how they utilize air
- Fire fighter to show how a fire can be smothered (with the air taken away)
- Parent to help to fly kites

Field Trips

- Dentist's office: use of air in the equipment (air hose)
- Service station
- High school, junior high, or college music department
- Pet store: observation of fish and how they breathe air through the gills
- Place where there are machines that use air: vacuum, hair dryer, clothes dryer, appliances, fans

Food

- Food activity featuring whipped cream: air beaten into cream
- Food activity featuring meringue: air beaten into egg whites
- Homemade ice cream
- Homemade root beer

Science

- Any of the activities mentioned in this chapter
- Pictures or slides of animals and plants: discussion of how they need air
- Pictures or slides of machines that use air
- Observation of what happens on a windy day when you open a milkweed pod
- Exploration of bubble

Literacy

- Use the language experience approach to write about the uses of air.
- Write or tell about things that fly.
- Study and write about keeping the air clean.

Physical–Motor

- Play with a large parachute. Develop simple games to use with it.

Music

- Creative movements interpreting bubbles or kite flying: faster music as air moves more rapidly or the weather becomes more windy
- Use of hummers, with discussion of how the air vibrating on the waxed paper makes the sound (see Chapter 13 for directions on making hummers.)

TEACHING ABOUT ROCKS

"Teacher, I have something really, really valuable for you in my sack. I was going to give it to my mom, but I have given her one before, so I decided to give it to you." As the first-grade teacher opened the brown paper bag, she found a rock with fool's gold on it! The child proceeded to tell her of the value of gold and, therefore, of this rock's value. Rocks are of interest to young children and are readily available. Early in life, children become aware of the many variations; rocks come in different sizes, shapes, colors, textures, and weights. Children enjoy classifying rocks in many of these ways. Probably one of the first ways of classifying is by kind, even though specific names may not be known.

The children learn that rocks are made up of minerals and are unique because of the variations and characteristics of these minerals.

Concepts and Ideas for Teaching

1. There are many kinds of rocks.
2. Most rocks are made up of minerals or smaller particles, and they are formed in different ways.
3. Rocks have different hardness values. Some rocks can be broken more easily than others. (Mineralogists and geologists use the Mohs scale of hardness to classify rocks according to relative hardness from 1 to 10; 10 is the hardest, and the diamond has a hardness value of 10.)
4. Rocks have different uses, depending on their hardness (hard and long-lasting rocks may be used for buildings), beauty (many are used for jewelry), or other qualities.
5. Some rocks may be used for writing and drawing on other rocks.
6. The inside of a rock often differs from the outside.
7. Rock fossils are specific kinds of rock. During the rock's formation many years ago, a plant or animal became embedded in the rock and left its imprint.
8. A person who collects, cuts, and polishes rocks as a hobby or profession is called a *lapidary*.
9. Rocks cannot burn.
10. Small or fine rocks are called *gravel* and are used in making cement or concrete. *Sand* consists of extremely fine rocks.
11. Water changes rocks, making most rocks smooth.

Activities and Experiences

1. Collect rocks to sort and classify by general groups such as igneous (formed from cooling lava; examples: pumice and obsidian); sedimentary (formed from rocks, sand, and stones that are compacted by pressure; examples: sandstone, limestone, and shale); and metamorphic rock (formed when igneous or sedimentary rocks are completely changed through pressure and heat; examples: limestone becomes marble, shale becomes slate, sandstone becomes quartzite).
2. Collect rocks to sort and classify by specific kind of physical characteristics, such as color, shape, or size.
3. Collect rocks from bodies of water, streams, creeks, and other locations, and note their smoothness.
4. Make "fossils" from clay, and then let the clay harden.
5. Visit a lapidary shop, or invite a lapidary or jeweler to visit the classroom to explain the hobby.
6. Visit a gravel pit and notice the different sizes of gravel.
7. Visit a construction site and watch concrete being poured.
8. Visit a geological museum.
9. Obtain the Mohs scale of hardness and classify rocks (minerals) by hardness. Determine whether they can be scratched with a fingernail, penny, or nail or by other means.
10. Crack rocks open to examine them on the inside. Make sure that safety precautions are taken for protecting the eyes.
11. Invite a geologist to visit your classroom.
12. Collect geodes for children to observe.
13. Investigate how weathering changes rocks.
14. Have each child bring a rock from home or the playground. The children will write or dictate descriptions of the rocks. They can weigh them, measure them, and describe their physical characteristics. They can draw illustrations of their rocks and then put the pages into a class booklet.
15. Order rocks by weight from lightest to heaviest.

TEACHING ABOUT WATER

Water! Both children and adults have a natural attraction to water. Not only does it provide such a ready source for problem-solving and critical-

thinking skills, it also allows for emotional catharsis. It is relaxing, comforting, soothing, pleasing,
rhythmic, and calming. "Water comforts, fascinates
and instructs" (Rivkin, 1995, p. 41). Even though it
is one of the substances most familiar to children,
they never tire of exploring it. We have found that
even unusual media such as rock salt and Styrofoam
packing material placed in a trough do not capture
as much attention as water—ordinary water! Water
play not only seems to interest all children, but it
also holds and maintains their attention for longer
periods of time than do many other media. When
playing with water, children refine social skills,
discover cause-and-effect relationships, increase
sciencing knowledge, expand problem-solving capabilities, improve eye–hand coordination, and
fine-tune small-motor development (Planje, 1997).

Ordinary water is exciting, but adding new dimensions to water or changing its form adds further interest. New concepts can be learned as
various changes are made in the water. In addition
to using ordinary water as a sensory medium, the
following ideas are suggested: adding food coloring, adding detergent to make bubbles (perhaps
adding some straws to go with the bubbles), and
adding ice to the water. On the other hand, it
would be possible to begin with another medium,
such as sand, and then let the children add water
to it in the trough. These suggestions are only a
few of the ways to utilize water in exploring and
discovering.

Matthew wiped across his mouth with the
back of his hand and announced: "I just had a drink
of water so I wouldn't waste all that thirst!"

Although water is a substance with which the
children have daily contact, many concepts can be
taught relating to it. The children can, of course,
learn that it is a liquid and therefore can be poured.
It can be compared to other liquids, or it can be
pointed out that water is the base of many liquids,
such as punch or reconstituted orange juice.

Like other science areas, water can be used as
an independent experience or it can be developed and expanded into a unit. The following is a
discussion of some of the possible units relating
to water: characteristics of water, forms of water,
uses of water by people, the water cycle, and general uses of water. Never underestimate the values
of water, sand, and mud in the early childhood
curriculum!

**Water can be used for many more things than
just washing hands—it is also fun to play in!**

Concepts and Ideas for Teaching

1. Characteristics of water. (Teachers should
   not attempt to investigate the components
   of water with young children.)

   a. Has weight.
   b. Is a liquid.
   c. Is colorless, but can be colored by add-
      ing substances (food coloring, gelatin,
      ink, bluing).
   d. Takes the shape of the container into
      which it is poured.
   e. Natural taste is changed with the addi-
      tion of chemicals used in purifying.
   f. Temperature is changed by heating and
      cooling.
   g. Evaporates (goes into the air).

2. There are different forms of water.

   a. Liquid (as previously explained)

b. Ice: water in frozen form

c. Steam: water that has changed to a gas or vapor

3. Water has many uses.

a. People: drinking for survival; washing and cleansing of self, clothes, home, food; watering crops, gardens, and all plants in the surroundings; cooking; ice for preserving and cooling foods; steam for cleaning; ironing; removing wallpaper, stamps, or other items glued to surfaces; in generators and in steam turbines

b. Animals: survival; habitat

c. Plants: survival; habitat

4. There is a water cycle. Water in the air condenses into clouds and comes to the ground in various forms: rain, snow, and so on. It then collects in lakes, ponds, and seas. From there, rivers and streams carry it to reservoirs and storage tanks. After purification, it is carried through underground pipes into homes, schools, buildings, and other places. Children may also be interested to learn that water collects underground, so a well can be dug to pump the water from the ground. Children could observe the water pipes in a home under construction or in a home where the water pipes are easily viewed.

5. Many forms of recreation utilize water.

a. Fishing

b. Boating

c. Swimming

d. Water skiing

e. Surfing

6. Water is involved in many professions.

a. Fire fighting, for extinguishing fires

b. Fishing

c. Sailing: protecting the seas

d. Plumbing: repairing water pipes and water systems

e. Water quality engineer

f. Life guarding

g. Freighting to other countries

h. Research of oceans and seas and animals that live there

7. Some objects sink in water, and some objects float.

8. Some materials dissolve in water, and some do not.

9. Some items absorb water, and some do not.

10. Humans affect the quality of water.

11. The surface of Earth is mostly water (400 billion billion gallons), and most of Earth's water is in the oceans (97%) and therefore is salt water. About half of our fresh water is in ice caps and glaciers, so we must conserve and protect the available fresh water.

12. People use more and more water all the time. The average person uses 125 gallons of water each day. That is too much; we need to conserve.

Activities and Experiences

1. Observe the forms and cycles of water by first discussing ice cubes and how they are formed. Then put them in an electric frying pan with the temperature on low. Observe as the ice cubes change first to water and then to steam as the water boils. Hold an aluminum pie plate above the steam to collect some of the moisture, and then observe the drops of water on the pie plate.

2. Bring into the classroom animals that live in water: fish, tadpoles, and other aquatic life.

3. Allow the children to discover what kinds of objects float and what kinds of objects sink in water. Provide a container of water and a box of materials (paper clips, marbles, cork, sticks, beads, rocks, sponges) for experimenting with sinking and floating. The children will discover that heavier items sink and lighter items float. However, through experimentation, they can also discover that items that sink are not always heavier than those that float. Begin with two equal-sized balls of oil-based clay. Ask the children if they think the clay balls will sink or float; then let them see that the balls will sink. Shape one of the balls of clay into a boat so that it will float. As an alternative, provide each child with a container of water, or have the children gather around a trough of water. Give each child a ball of the oil-based clay and

ask whether they can do something to it so that it will float and not sink. If oil-based clay is not available, aluminum foil can be used. Ships do not sink for the same reason that this small clay boat does not sink. The boat is larger than the ball and pushes aside, or displaces, more water than the ball. The amount of water displaced by the boat weighs more than the boat itself. The water pushes the boat up until the weight of the boat and its cargo equals the weight of the displaced water.

4. Children will also enjoy decorating boats that have been cut from foam core, attaching and winding up a propeller with an elastic, and then racing the boats in wallpaper trays partially filled with water.

5. Put an empty, capped detergent bottle in a bowl or tub of water. It should float. Put a small amount of water in it, and it should still float. As more water is added, it sinks lower and lower, because an object will float if it is lighter in weight than the amount of water that would take up an equal amount of space. This same experiment can be performed with smaller plastic bottles. For younger children, a simple explanation might be that some objects are too heavy to float, or some objects are not porous enough (do not have enough air in them), or some objects need to be shaped like a boat in order to float.

6. Allow children to experiment with substances that dissolve in water and substances that do not. Compare sand, salt, marbles, an antacid tablet, flour, tapioca, soda, sugar, gelatin, and powdered drink mix.

7. Give children two ice cubes each. Have them sprinkle rock salt on one ice cube and then press the ice cubes together. The children should be able to see that the salt melts the ice. Try the same experiment with small rocks and note the difference.

8. Build a terrarium and observe the rain cycle. (See Chapter 11 for directions for making a terrarium.)

9. Fill a large glass or plastic container partly full of water and mark the water level. Put

the container in the freezer, or outside if the temperature is below freezing. After the water freezes, determine whether the ice line is above or below the water line. The children should discover that when water freezes it expands. Allow the container of ice to melt back into a liquid. Compare ice and water lines again.

10. Fill two clear glass containers with water and mark the water levels. Leave the lid on one of the containers; leave the other container uncovered. Each day, observe and mark the water level in the uncovered bottle. Frequently compare the current water levels in both containers. Include the word *evaporation* often in the discussion.

11. Have the children take turns lifting different containers of water. They can lift a glass of water, but what about a pitcher or large bucket of water? Can they lift the pitcher or bucket without the water in it? Water has weight.

12. Compare the weight of a dry sponge with the weight of a wet sponge. Compare the weight of clothes that are dry with the weight of clothes that are damp and those that are wet.

13. With water tables, basins, or tubs, provide opportunities for pouring and measuring. Provide a variety of containers of various sizes for the children to play with, along with funnels and measuring cups. Encourage exploration of the concepts of more or less, substance, volume, and weight. Also provide small plastic bags to demonstrate that water has no definite shape, but takes the shape of the container that it is in.

14. Water play in a water table or basin can interest children for long periods of time. Other materials that can be included with the water on various occasions are sponges, straws, strainers, eggbeaters, medicine droppers, syringes (without needles, of course), a rubber bulb with a perforated nozzle, a hollow rubber ball with a hole in it, and rubber or plastic tubing.

15. Place an ordinary drinking glass in a dish and fill it carefully with water. As it is filled,

carefully pour more water into the glass; the water will bulge above the edge of the glass and form a convex shape. This is because of surface tension. To show the effect of detergents on water, a drop of liquid detergent placed in the water will cause it to flow over the edge of the glass.

UNIT PLAN ON WATER

Field Trips

- Water laboratory
- Creeks, rivers, streams
- Fire station
- Fire hydrant
- Ice pond
- Place selling bricks of ice and dry ice
- Car wash
- Frozen-food locker plant
- Gymnasium: water fountain, swimming pool, shower room, steam room
- Pet store or place where children can observe an aquarium

Art

- Painting with water (this works best outside on a fence or sidewalk)
- Watercolor painting
- Easel painting
- Paper-sack fish
- Mixing paint
- Papier-mâché
- Plaster of Paris molds
- Soap-flake finger painting
- Salt–flour clay

Music

- Moving like water: locations, stages, sounds
- Sounds of water used for rhythms

- Rhythm sticks: tapping out rhythm of falling rain, thunder, and so on
- Containers with varying amounts of water; containers tapped with metal rod

Visitors

- Someone who will bathe a baby in the classroom
- Animals that need water (fish)
- Person to cook with water
- Custodian: water vacuum
- Forest ranger
- Fire fighter
- Parent to wash car

Food

- Boiled vegetables
- Cooked rice, macaroni: absorbing water
- Liquid for leavening
- Drinks
- Ice used for cooling
- Snow cones
- Homemade vegetable soup
- Gelatins
- Drink made from powdered mix
- Homemade ice cream

Science

- Floating objects
- Terrarium: rain cycle
- Stages and forms of water
- Items that absorb water and those that do not
- Items that dissolve in water and those that do not
- Uses of steam
- Uses of water in cleaning
- Animals that live and survive in water
- Overhead projector: colors mixed together in water
- Homemade ice cream: how salt changes the temperature of ice

Literacy

- Write or tell "I like water because . . . . "

- Write or tell "Water is . . . . "

- Read and recite poems about water.

- Read stories relating to water, such as *Fish Is Fish* (Lionni, 1970).

Additional Activities

- Water, ice, snow in trough

- Blowing bubbles

- Painting with water and brushes (outside)

- Role playing with fire-fighter's clothes, hats, fire trucks

Note: A lesson plan on water can be found in Appendix A.

TEACHING ABOUT TEMPERATURE, WEATHER, AND SEASONS

"There's so much more to weather-and-children than the daily weather chart" (Huffman, 1996, p. 34)! Weather so easily integrates with science, math, literacy, and other parts of the curriculum.

> Because weather has such an influence on children, there is always available subject matter: rain, rainbows, prisms, clouds, precipitation, storms, temperatures, snow, hail, ice, sun, air, wind, barometers, thermometers, hygrometers, and so on. Weather and the changing seasons influence what we wear, what we do, where we go, how we get there, and how we feel.

The concepts of temperature, weather, and seasons are related to one another because each influences the others. For example, the season often determines the weather for a particular locale. The temperature influences every aspect of weather and often determines the exact type of weather that is experienced. At the same time, the temperature is usually influenced by the time or season of the year. Thus, none of these concepts can be discussed without involving at least one of the others.

Children and adults are greatly influenced by temperature, weather, and seasons. Activities, feelings, moods, and choices of games, recreation, foods, and clothes are often determined by the temperature, weather, or season. Everyone is interested in the weather report, for it often determines what we can and cannot do and where we can and cannot go. People listen to the weather report to decide whether windows should be washed, cars polished, or picnics planned. The weather report helps to determine whether it will be a good day for skiing, the fruit trees in blossom will be damaged by frost, or a planned trip can still be made. It is amazing to realize the extent to which our lives are controlled by the weather, the temperature, and the seasons.

Expanding children's awareness of weather and how it affects our lives enhances problem-solving

This girl has decided it is too warm to have her jacket zipped up. Besides, "My mother said I didn't have to zip my jacket!"

skills, observation abilities, potentials for predicting outcomes, and vocabulary building (Newman, 1995b). Consider sounds, smells, and colors involved with weather and seasons. In teaching units relating to temperature, weather, and seasons, remember that young children should be exposed first to concepts regarding the seasons and kinds of weather that they actually experience. For example, it may not be practical to have units on snow and/or winter for children in Florida. Also, it is best to teach the kinds of weather and specific seasons at the time when the children are most apt to experience these particular conditions.

As with other concepts, the child may be able to group together pictures and objects relating to a season, but may not be able to label this season. Thus, a good approach to introducing and teaching a particular season or aspect of weather is to give the children the experience of classifying or grouping together objects and/or pictures of that season or aspect of weather. For example, the teacher may introduce winter by telling the children that they are going to talk about a time of year when the weather is very cold, when snowstorms are typical, and when the trees are usually bare. The label of the season, *winter*, is introduced. Then the teacher shows season pictures and objects, such as a snow shovel, a snowshoe, a swimming suit, a hoe, a rake, tire chains, a window scraper, and a flyswatter and asks the children to select those that are appropriate for the season being studied.

Another teaching approach involves helping the children to learn that the seasons always follow the same sequence. Thus, winter always follows fall, spring follows winter, summer follows spring, and fall follows summer, or whatever sequence is appropriate for your own region. In addition, children could draw pictures of scenes or objects, such as trees, in each season; then these pictures (or pictures provided by the teacher) could be arranged in sequence. It is interesting to teach the seasonal changes of animals: the snowshoe rabbit, monarch butterfly, and frog.

Since nature always foretells a coming season with signs, daily experiences outside offer the opportunity for spontaneous learning experiences. A sensitive teacher points to the buds on the tree and asks the children what season the buds signal. Or, as the children discover and explore the icicle hanging from the roof outside, the wise teacher re-

lates it to temperature and season. The teacher may also ask such thoughtful questions as "What will happen to the icicle or to your snowman if the sun comes out and it gets very warm?"

Lesson plans relating to the concepts of temperature, weather, and season can be approached in a variety of ways. For example, it is possible to plan a unit on a particular season, with discussion of the most typical weather and temperatures accompanying this season. Thus emerge units on fall, wind, and cooler temperatures; spring, wind, rain, sunshine, and warmer temperatures; and summer, sun, and hot temperatures. On the other hand, each subject could be treated alone and approached as a separate unit. For example, during the fall season a unit could be done on fall, with perhaps a follow-up unit on wind. Temperature could be included in one or both of the units as it relates to the main subject. A separate unit on temperature could also be linked to the current season and a visit by the weather forecaster with weather instruments, such as the thermometer.

Weather, seasons, and temperature are a part of the world in which children live; children are curious and interested and have a desire to learn more about them. Gear your units to the uniqueness of your own area and to the individual situations of the children in your classroom. Thus, depending on the seasons that the children in your locality experience, at least two and as many as eight or nine units could be developed from just these three concepts.

Concepts and Ideas for Teaching

1. Each day we experience a particular season, a particular kind (or kinds) of weather, and temperatures ranging from the high to the low for the day.
2. We live in a particular area where we experience certain seasons, certain kinds of weather, and a temperature variation.
3. The area where we live determines the characteristic temperature range that we experience, and this determines the climate in which we live. Thus, we live in a (warm, cool, cold, humid, dry, seasonal, constant, or changing) climate. (The children should describe the characteristics of their climate.)

4. Some animals are characteristic of our area because of the characteristic climate, temperature, weather conditions, or seasons of our area. (Describe animals of your own area.)
5. Some plants are characteristic of our area because of the characteristic climate, temperature, weather conditions, or seasons of our area. (Describe characteristic plants in your own area.)
6. A thermometer is an instrument used for measuring the temperature. The measured temperature goes up when the weather is warmer and down when it is cooler.
7. There are different kinds of thermometers.

   a. Thermometers for measuring the air inside and outside
   b. Thermometers for measuring body temperatures, especially during illness
   c. Thermometers for use in cooking, such as for meat and candy

8. When the temperature of some items changes, the items either expand (get larger) or contract (get smaller).

   a. Water expands during freezing.
   b. Metal expands during heating.
   c. Breads, cakes, cookies, and other foods that are baked expand in a hot oven because of the effect that high temperature has on their ingredients.
   d. Some types of meats get smaller when they are heated or cooked.

9. People, animals, and plants make changes in varying seasons, kinds of weather, and temperatures.

   a. Observation of a tree during each season
   b. Observation of what particular animals (bears, frogs, insects, birds, monarch butterflies) do during specific seasons or kinds of weather, or when the temperature changes

10. We are influenced in many ways by the weather, season, or temperature.

    a. How we feel
    b. What we do
    c. What games and sports we participate in
    d. How we dress
    e. What foods we eat
    f. How our bodies react to temperature changes, perspiring in excessive heat or getting goose bumps and shivering in cold weather

11. The length of the day varies with the season; in the Northern Hemisphere, the days are shorter in winter and longer in summer.
12. There are many different kinds of clouds. We can often determine the approaching weather by the clouds.
13. Clouds have many different shapes and sizes, often resemble different objects, and may change shape rapidly.

Concepts and Ideas for Teaching Seasons

1. Each season has its own particular characteristics.
2. Each season has sensory characteristics.

   a. Sounds
   b. Sights
   c. Smells
   d. Feels (or feelings)
   e. Tastes

3. For each season, people make particular preparations involving their cars, homes, clothing, and outside grounds.
4. For each season, animals often make particular preparations or changes.
5. For each season, many plants make changes.
6. Each season has jobs, inside and outside the home, directly related to it.
7. Each season has characteristic kinds of recreation and activities.
8. Each season has characteristic foods.
9. Each season has holidays that always fall within its boundaries.

In the following material, each season will be treated separately in terms of the preceding teaching ideas. The suggestions presented here are not meant to be inclusive; you may wish to contribute ideas more appropriate to your own locality. Encourage the children to brainstorm their own ideas as a season is being studied.

Winter

1. Winter has its own particular characteristics: cold, wet, quiet, white and gray, sleepy, snowy. It is an indoor season for some and an outdoor season for others.

2. Winter has characteristic sensory qualities.

   a. Sounds: quiet, furnaces turning on, sleet hitting the windowpane, wind, cars stuck on icy roads, snowplows, children playing in the snow or sledding, snowmobiles, and road graders

   b. Sights: snow figures, snow, snowplows, warm and heavy clothing, boots, hats, frost on windows, chains for tires, icicles, bare trees, footprints in the snow

   c. Smells: crisp air, woolly clothing, wet clothing, soups, stews, Christmas smells, fire, homemade bread, furnace smells, pine

   d. Feels: cold, toasty warm, tingly fingers and toes, wool, fur, blankets, fire, snow, ice, wet clothing

   e. Tastes: soup, snow, icicles, hot bread, chili, turkey, hot chocolate; Hanukkah, Christmas, New Year's Day, and Valentine's Day tastes and foods

3. People prepare their cars, homes, clothing, and yards for winter.

   a. Cars: antifreeze, chains, snow tires, ice scrapers

   b. Clothing: purchased or taken out of storage; items such as boots, coats, hats, gloves, and scarves located and checked for fit and condition

   c. Homes: furnaces checked (if not previously done in the fall), windows sealed or shut tightly, air conditioners covered or stored away, chimneys cleaned

   d. Yards and grounds: lawn furniture and gardening equipment stored, snow shovels purchased or taken out of storage, feed for animals obtained, shrubs tied up, coarse salt purchased for icy walks

4. Animals prepare for winter in a variety of ways. Some animals hibernate; some grow thick, warm coats of fur; farm animals are usually provided with shelter; some animals, such as birds, migrate during the fall in preparation for winter; some animals store nuts, seeds, or other food; some animals change color to blend with the environment.

5. Plants prepare for winter in a variety of ways. Some trees are bare and dormant during the winter; flowers often are nonexistent in the winter, unless they are grown in greenhouses; bulbs of such flowers as tulips and daffodils are dormant underneath the ground; shrubs survive if the temperatures do not fall too low.

6. Jobs related to winter include shoveling the snow from the walks and driveways, feeding farm animals that in other seasons are on the range or graze in the pasture, operating snowplows or sanders, cleaning off snow-covered or icy car windows, and keeping the furnace in good working order. In addition, professional jobs include furnace repair, ski patrol, operation of ski resorts, and

This boy is searching in his backpack for some elusive mittens.

the sale of snowmobiles or other winter recreation equipment.

7. Recreational activities characteristic of winter include playing in the snow, building snow figures, snowball fights, hockey games, basketball games, skiing, snowshoeing, sledding, and ice skating.

8. Foods characteristic of winter include soups, chili, hot breads, Christmas foods, Valentine cookies, traditional New Year's foods, oranges, and grapefruit.

9. Holidays of winter include Hanukkah, Christmas, New Year's Day, Martin Luther King, Jr., Day, Valentine's Day, Groundhog Day, President's Day, and St. Patrick's Day.

(Note: When approaching holiday celebrations, be sensitive to the various family cultures and beliefs.)

Spring

1. Spring has its own particular characteristics: warmer; sometimes wet and sometimes windy, and with more storms (tornadoes and thunderstorms), but mostly sunny and dry; active; alive; colorful; busy; home and grounds cleanup; gardening and planting; green; new growth; birds; snow melting; flowers blooming; people wearing pastel colors.

2. There are many sensory characteristics of spring.

   a. Sounds: voices of children playing outside, roller skates, roller blades, skateboards, songbirds, wind, rain, bees, lawnmowers, motorcycles, cleanup crews using machinery to pick up and clean up trash

   b. Sights: kites, mud puddles, grass growing, newborn animals, new growth, flowers, people doing home and yard cleanup, children playing outdoors, snow melting

   c. Smells: rain, earth and soil, newly cut grass, fresh paint, washed and cleaned homes (spring cleaning), flowers, fertilizer, fresh-air smells

   d. Feels: chilly temperatures in morning and evening, warmer days; energetic; the feel of grass, earth, and soil (pulling weeds and cleaning flower gardens)

   e. Tastes: flavored ice pops, wiener roasts, ice cream, fresh vegetable salads, fresh strawberry pie and shortcake

3. People prepare their cars, homes, clothing, and yards for spring in numerous ways.

   a. Cars: snow tires and chains removed, air conditioning checked

   b. Clothing: winter clothing put away, spring and summer clothing brought out of storage or purchased, boots and raincoats kept close by

   c. Home: inside spring cleaning, such as washing walls, cupboards, windows, floors, drawers, and closets, as well as sorting household items and throwing some of them away; outside spring cleaning, such as cleaning out flower beds, planting flowers, trimming shrubs and trees, raking and fertilizing grass, painting or fixing up the outside of the home, storing snow shovels and equipment, and bringing gardening equipment and lawn and patio furniture out of storage

4. What animals do in the spring: Many animals come out of hibernation, birds return, baby animals are born, animals may begin to lose fur coats, many livestock and farm animals are taken to the range for the late spring and summer months, sheep are shorn, and birds build nests.

5. What plants do in the spring: Plants that have been dormant during the winter come alive with buds, flowers, and leaves. Pussy willows are in season. Bulbs that have been dormant now poke up through the ground in the form of daffodils, tulips, and other early flowers. Some indoor plants are taken outdoors once the possibility of frost is over. Buds are seen on trees. Fruit trees blossom. Flowers, shrubs, and vegetable gardens are planted. Farmers plant vegetables, grains, and feed for their animals.

6. Jobs related to spring include those of city cleanup crews, gardeners, construction workers, farmers, professional carpet and rug cleaners, and nursery and seed people.

7. Recreational activities characteristic of spring include sandbox play, tricycle and bicycle riding, roller skating, roller blading, skateboarding, baseball, golf, fishing, tennis, outdoor neighborhood games, and picnics.

8. Foods characteristic of spring include strawberries and fresh strawberry desserts, asparagus, avocados, fresh vegetable salads, Easter candy and hard-boiled Easter eggs, and picnic foods.

9. Holidays of spring include April Fool's Day, Passover, Good Friday, Easter, Arbor Day, Mother's Day, and sometimes Father's Day, Memorial Day, and May Day.

Summer

1. Summer has its own particular characteristics: hot, humid, lazy, sunny, dry, green, active, busy, vacations, flowers, gardens beginning to produce, lightweight and little clothing, sweating, visits from vacationing friends and relatives, usually no school.

2. Summer has many sensory characteristics.

   a. Sounds: lawnmowers, motorcycles, water splashing, hiking, parades, fire engines, birds, crickets, children playing outside, bees, water sprinklers, sounds that often seem louder because windows are open

   b. Sights: campers, boats, trailers; people wearing less clothing and people on vacation; fishing, camping, and hiking gear; gardens, flowers, and leaves on trees; parades, sunburned skin; green; people and animals sweating; sprinklers, fans, and air conditioners; sunglasses; swimming suits

   c. Smells: chlorine, beaches, flowers, sunburn ointment, earth, perspiration of people and animals, fresh fish, campfires, fresh fruit and vegetables, freshly cut hay, outdoor barbecues, hot asphalt, overheated cars, bug spray

   d. Feels: going barefoot on grass, sand, or hot pavement; mosquito and other insect bites; bee stings; being sweaty, hot, and sticky; cool drinks and ice; a refreshing swim

   e. Tastes: lemonade and other cold drinks, fresh fruits, melons, fresh vegetables, picnic foods, roasted hot dogs and marshmallows, potato salad, barbecued foods or charcoal-cooked meats, ice-cream cones, fresh fish

3. People work in their yards and on their homes and wear cooler clothing in summer. They also take vacations.

   a. Clothing: swimsuits, shorts, and lightweight clothing for hot summer weather; sweaters or light jackets for cool evenings in the canyon or park; shoes often not worn, especially by children

   b. Homes: yards and gardens watered often; flowers in bloom; harvest season in late summer; lawns cut often; bugs and weeds sprayed or treated; home repair; screens put on windows

   c. Recreational activities and vacations: canyons, parks, beaches, and other places outdoors; a day spent away from home relaxing and having fun, or a vacation lasting for several days or weeks

4. Animals are seen in abundance in the summer, including those that are not seen in other seasons. Fish jump from lakes and ponds, insects buzz or move about everywhere (mosquitoes can be a nuisance), bats and fireflies may be seen at night, and crickets may be heard. Livestock are seen grazing in the fields and on the ranges, other farm animals are seen away from their winter shelters, and pets often rove freely about the neighborhood.

5. Plants are usually at the peak of their growth in the summer. Farmers are busy keeping their crops of vegetables and grains irrigated and weeded. Yards and gardens are beautiful with flowers, green trees, and green lawns. Fruit trees bear fruit, and vegetable gardens are productive. In late summer the farmers harvest crops: grains, vegetables, and other plantings.

6. Jobs related to summer include city cleanup operations, gardening, construction work, farming, baseball umpiring, life guarding, ice cream sales, home-and-garden sales, and the harvesting of crops as a temporary job.

7. Recreational activities characteristic of summer include especially the outdoor activities. Vacations are often taken, and many activities are planned on vacations. The following summer activities are enjoyed by many: picnics,

hiking, fishing, baseball, water skiing, sailing, swimming, tennis, golf, camping, boating, volleyball, tricycle and bicycle riding, roller skating, running through sprinklers, outdoor neighborhood games, and sandbox play.

8. Foods characteristic of summer include fresh fruits; melons, especially watermelon; hot dogs; hamburgers; lemonade and other cold drinks; ice cream; milkshakes and sodas; fresh vegetables; tomatoes; tossed green salads; picnic foods; barbecued foods such as steaks, hamburgers, and shish kebabs; and corn on the cob.

9. Holidays of summer include Father's Day (sometimes), Independence Day, and Labor Day.

Fall

1. Fall has its own particular characteristics: cooler days, quietness, colors (especially red, yellow, orange, rust, brown), harvest, school, new clothing, wind, the first frost, raking leaves, yard and garden cleanup in preparation for winter, warm days and cool nights, shorter days, dry leaves, first snowfall.

2. Fall has numerous sensory characteristics.

   a. Sounds: slower chirp of crickets, back-to-school sounds of children, farm machinery sounds as harvesting is done, rain and wind sounds, blowing and crunching of dry leaves as children play in them, football activities

   b. Sights: colorful leaves, harvest, wheat, raking and playing in leaves, falling leaves, apples, pumpkins, school buses, trees becoming bare, countertops and storage areas filled with freshly canned fruits and vegetables, children in jackets and sweaters

   c. Smells: dry leaves, wet leaves, smoke, home canning, harvest smells, carameled apples, cinnamon, chili, brisk cool nights, cut hay

   d. Feels: chilly nights, sometimes warm and sometimes cool days, dry leaves as they are played in and raked up

   e. Tastes: cider, pumpkin pie, cranberries, squash, apples, turkey, chili, doughnuts, stew, hot soup, carameled apples

3. People prepare their cars, homes, clothing, and yards for fall.

   a. Cars: snow tires, chains, antifreeze
   b. Clothing: new purchases for school or last year's garments brought out of storage and checked for fit and good repair; warmer clothing substituted for summer's lightweight clothing; sweaters, jackets, and other outerwear
   c. Home: screens taken off and windows shut tightly; air conditioners covered or put into storage; furnaces checked and/or cleaned and new filters installed
   d. Yards and gardens: leaves raked; bulbs such as tulips planted; shrubs trimmed and tied; flower beds cleaned up; yard tools put into storage and hoses put away; outside water shut off so that pipes do not freeze; fall harvesting of farm crops and foods

4. Some animals, such as bears and snakes, go into hibernation in late fall; other animals grow thick, warm coats of fur. Livestock are brought down from summer ranges; birds migrate; other animals store nuts and other foods; and some animals change color as a camouflage for winter. The caterpillar forms a pupa case (chrysalis) from which it emerges as a butterfly.

5. Leaves turn color and fall from the trees. Many trees, plants, and weeds bear seeds, and plants may dry or die. Some plants, like chrysanthemums, bloom in the fall. The first frost often kills many plants.

6. Jobs related to fall include raking leaves and yard and garden cleanup. Many jobs are associated with the harvest season. Farmers and farmhands are especially busy; in homes there is fruit and vegetable canning, and the busy season arrives for turkey farmers.

7. Recreational activities characteristic of fall include football, volleyball, soccer, playing in the leaves, and hunting.

8. Foods characteristic of fall include turkey, apples, carameled apples, apple cider, pumpkin pie, squash, Halloween candy, doughnuts, and cranberries.

9. Holidays of fall include Rosh Hashanah, Yom Kippur, Columbus Day, Halloween, Veterans Day, and Thanksgiving.

Concepts and Ideas for Teaching Weather

1. The particular kind of weather, how it is caused, and where it comes from
2. What this type of weather does, what its uses are, and what its positive and negative aspects are
3. The various ways in which each kind of weather is manifested
4. Each kind of weather has sensory characteristics.

   a. Sounds
   b. Sights
   c. Smells
   d. Feels
   c. Tastes

5. Each kind of weather makes us feel different inside, depending on our feelings toward that kind of weather.
6. Each kind of weather makes us dress differently.
7. Each kind of weather makes us do different things.
8. We participate in different games and activities in different places, depending on the kind of weather.
9. We go to different places in different kinds of weather.
10. The different kinds of weather are often related to other aspects or kinds of weather.

In the following material, each main aspect of weather (snow, rain, wind, and sun) is treated separately in terms of the foregoing ideas. The suggestions are not meant to be inclusive. You may have to contribute ideas that are more appropriate to your own locality. Encourage the children to brainstorm and to share the resulting ideas as the various kinds of weather are being studied and explored. Other types of weather can also be approached with these same questions.

Snow

1. Snow begins as frozen water vapor that forms around microscopic particles afloat in the air. When this water vapor freezes, transparent ice crystals are formed. As more water

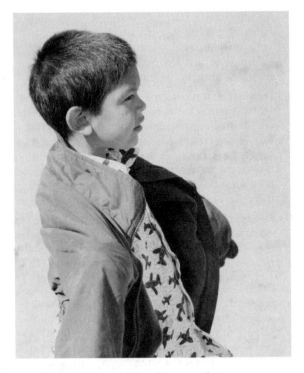

Deciding whether it is cold enough to wear a jacket or coat is not always easy.

vapor condenses around these ice crystals, they become heavy enough to fall out of their clouds. Air currents then toss them about in the atmosphere, causing them to collide and to break into tiny chips of ice that form more ice crystals. The crystals clump together on their trip down to the earth, forming snowflakes. The crystals in a snowflake are always in the form of a six-pointed star (hexagon). (*Note:* Select parts of this explanation that are suitable to your children's understandings.)

2. Snow falls in the colder climates and often blankets the earth during the winter months, especially in the mountains. Snow has many uses. Most of our water comes from snow, because when it melts it builds up the watersheds or melts into the lakes and reservoirs from which the streams and rivers flow to bring water to people. Snow is also used in many winter sports activities. Children play in snow and use it to build

things such as snow figures. Snow also serves as insulation for plants and animals.

3. Snow comes in different forms. It comes as a blizzard, sleet, hail, large flakes, or small flakes. It can be wet or dry (powder).

4. Snow has many sensory characteristics.

   a. Sounds: quiet, light; when snow falls against the windowpane, it may make a soft, tapping sound; sleet and hail are louder when they fall.
   b. Sights: white, sparkling; each snowflake is small and fragile and quickly melts when touching a surface warmer than itself.
   c. Smells: damp, wet; there is no other characteristic smell for snow.
   d. Feels: cold, wet, icy; snow can cause stinging or numbness, especially in the fingers and toes.
   e. Tastes: wet, tasteless, like ice or ice water; children find clean, white snow inviting to taste because it looks good to eat.

5. Snow creates different feelings in different people. The first snow of the season is welcomed by most people, especially children. However, usually the last snow of the season is not welcomed and creates negative feelings because most people are ready and eager for spring. Teachers must remember that feelings toward snow depend on whether snow is a favorite kind of weather or not. Children should be allowed to explore and share their feelings toward snow.

6. Snow makes us dress in warm clothing: woolens, furs, boots, mittens, heavy coats, hats, sweaters, long socks.

7. Snow makes us do different things. When it snows, we play inside more often than we do in other seasons. We often do not travel very far or take vacations (some people vacation in warmer climates to get away from the snow and cold). We also build snow figures, play in the snow, go sledding, and participate in other winter sports.

8. We participate in different games and activities in different places when there is snow. We play many inside games, but we also play games and participate in snow activities: Fox and Geese, ice skating, sledding, skiing, building snow figures, having snowball fights, building snow structures, snowmobiling, and snowshoeing. Many of these activities take place in our neighborhoods and backyards, but others occur in winter resorts in the canyons or mountains.

9. We go different places when it snows. Usually we stay home, but we may go to resorts or mountain areas to participate in winter sports or travel to warmer climates.

10. Other kinds of weather influence snow. Sun melts snow; wind creates blizzards and snowdrifts; rain melts the snow; if the temperature goes down after a snowmelt in the wintertime, it can create icy conditions.

Rain

1. Rain begins as moisture or water that has evaporated from the ground and from bodies of water. This water vapor collects (condenses) into rain clouds and then falls to the earth in the form of rain. Once again moisture from the ground and plants evaporates and forms vapor in the air, and the rain cycle continues. (*Note:* Use only those parts of the explanation that are appropriate for your children's understanding and levels of comprehension.)

2. Rain is useful in many ways. Heavy rainstorms, like snow, help build up the watersheds. Rain waters gardens and grass, helps farmers to irrigate crops if it comes at the right time, clears dust and smog from the air, and helps plants to grow. The water from rain is also used by people for washing, bathing, and drinking, as well as by plants and animals. Rainstorms may also bring rainbows, and their beauty is enjoyed by all, especially children. Rainstorms may cause damage and may occasionally have negative influences. They can be accompanied by thunder and lightning, and the lightning can cause fires, especially forest fires, which are damaging and dangerous. Heavy rainstorms can also cause flooding.

3. Rain has different forms. It can come in a torrent, a drizzle, a mist, light rainfall, heavy

rainfall, a thunderstorm, large drops, and small drops.

4. Rain has various sensory characteristics.

    a. Sounds: cars on highway, rain on roof or windowpane, thunder and lightning, windshield wipers
    b. Sights: rainbows, lightning, gray and dark, blurry, fresh and green after a rainstorm
    c. Smells: fresh, wet, musty, moist
    d. Feels: wet, clean, fresh, humid, cool
    e. Tastes: drops of water on the tongue have no taste.

5. Rain creates different feelings in different people. On a rainy day, the following conversation between two children was overheard:

    > Dennis: *I surely like rainy days-they are my favorite kind!*
    >
    > Sam: *They aren't your favorite kind-they are ugly, and they are the worst.*
    >
    > Dennis: *They aren't ugly, and they are my favorite day. I love them because they are wet!*

    Rain does indeed create different feelings in both children and adults. Some people enjoy it, and some do not like it at all. For some, it creates feelings of enthusiasm, exhilaration, and delight; for others, it stirs feelings of depression, sadness, and laziness. Our reactions and feelings toward rain may depend on the plans for the day or how long it has been since the last rainfall. For example, if a picnic is planned with family or friends, rain could bring disappointment or disgust. On the other hand, after many long days of hot, dry weather, a rainfall is refreshing and welcome. Farmers also have different reactions to rainfall. It may be desperately needed and hoped for; on the other hand, if farmers are just ready to plant or if the hay has just been cut or baled, rain is not a welcome sight. If rain has been falling for several days, it can often bring disgust or depression, especially to adults. A major city in the Northwest that experiences much rainfall year round is known to have one of the highest suicide rates in the United States. Many psychologists attribute this phenomenon to the fact that so many days are gray, cloudy, and rainy. Thus,

several factors determine our reactions to rain. As children discuss their feelings, it might be well to give them actual situations to explore. For example, ask "How would rain make you feel if it came on the day we were planning our field trip to the zoo?"

6. Rain makes us dress in special clothing. We wear boots and raincoats and carry umbrellas.

7. Rain makes us do different things. When it rains, we probably play inside more often. However, after a spring or summer rainstorm, we may especially enjoy playing in the sandbox or in puddles, or sailing boats down small streams caused by the rain.

8. We engage in different games and activities in different places when it rains. We play more inside games and activities and are often in a hurry to come out of a rainstorm. Immediately after a rainstorm, children like to play in the sandbox because the wet sand makes such good mud pies and molds so readily. They also like to sail boats and other objects in the streams created by rainstorms. Teachers often like to plan musical games and other inside activities for rainy days.

9. We go to different places when it rains. Usually, we stay home, and rainstorms often cause us to seek cover if we are enjoying outdoor recreational activities such as a picnic, hiking, or boating.

10. Other kinds of weather influence rain. Sunshine during or after a rainstorm creates a rainbow. A rainstorm on a hot day may create steam from the pavement or rooftops. Wind combined with rain often creates torrents or other miserable conditions. Wind can often blow away a potential rainstorm. Warm temperatures turn spring snowstorms into rain showers. Or cold temperatures can turn rain into sleet or freezing rain.

Wind

1. Wind is the result of moving air currents, caused when hot air rises and cold air takes its place.

2. Wind is good for flying kites, drying clothes or other items, moving storms or other kinds

of air masses, making windmills work, and moving sailboats. It is not good for neat hair-styles; keeping dust in place; or freshly painted houses, garages, fences, or other out-side structures. Most animals do not like wind. People who wear contact lenses do not like wind because it causes irritation to the eyes. Wind can also cause damage to the environment by contributing to soil erosion or causing other environmental problems. A farmer who has just planted a field does not like wind because of the soil erosion.

3. Wind has different forms, such as gusts, windstorms, hurricanes, dust storms, gentle winds or breezes, high winds, and tornadoes.

4. Wind has numerous sensory characteristics.
   a. Sounds: whistling, fluttering, gusting, rap-ping, whining, blowing, wailing; may be frightening or pleasant
   b. Sights: hair blowing, trees swaying, shrubs and flowers moving, branches blown down, people holding their hats on and moving in a hurry, women hold-ing their skirts and dresses down, chil-dren flying kites
   c. Smells: dusty; may blow in unusual odors from nearby swamps, farms, industrial plants, lakes, or other areas; may bring the smell of a potential rainstorm
   d. Feels: gritty, dusty, cool, stifling, gentle, strong, cold, pleasant, irritating, welcome, unwelcome
   e. Tastes: sand that has blown into the mouth

5. Wind creates different feelings in different people. Again, the feelings generated by the wind depend on what has been planned for the day and whether the wind interrupts the plans and is unwelcome or welcome in terms of the day's activities. Children may en-joy spring winds because they can fly their kites. A cool breeze on a hot summer day or evening may be just the thing needed to cool off. Strong winds are most often un-pleasant and unwelcome, at least to adults. During the winter, wind combined with al-ready cold temperatures will create a chill factor that will make the temperature seem even lower and make the weather more un-pleasant. Gentle, light winds in summer are often welcome, but heavy, strong winds stir up too much dust in the air. On days when it is extremely windy, children often come into the classroom just like gusts of wind, and the emotional climate in the classroom on these days is often high.

6. Wind makes us dress in heavier clothing. In the spring or fall, we may need only a jacket or sweater. In the winter, if it is windy, we may need to put on extra-heavy clothing and coats.

7. Wind makes us do different things. We have to hold on to things we are carrying and hold down other things. If it is windy, we are often in a hurry to arrive at our destination or to go inside.

8. We engage in different games and activities in different places in the wind. We sail boats, enjoy windmills, and fly kites when it is windy. Children also seem to enjoy running outdoors when it is windy—almost as if they were chasing the wind or the wind were chasing them!

9. We go to different places when it is windy. Usually, we stay inside and enjoy inside activities. However, windy weather is also the time for flying kites and sailing boats, as well as enjoying windmills and pinwheels.

10. Other kinds of weather influence wind, and wind influences other kinds of weather. Wind may blow a storm in or blow one away. If wind occurs with a snowstorm or rainstorm, we have a blizzard or a gusting rainstorm. During dry weather or in dry places, wind creates dust storms.

Sun

1. The sun is a star in our galaxy. It is a source of light, heat, and energy. It does not turn off at the end of the day or on cloudy days. At the end of our day, it is making light and day for people on another part of Earth. On cloudy days the sun is still shining, but the clouds are in front of it so that we do not benefit as much from the rays of sunshine or from the sun's heat. Every day has a sunrise and sunset for most people; however, there

are places on the earth (such as the North Pole and South Pole) where, during particular times of the year, because of the position of the sun, children do not see the sun for many days or the sun does not go down for many days, and there is no sunrise or sunset.

2. The position of the sun, or the position of Earth in relation to the sun, makes or changes the seasons. The sun produces light, heat, and energy, which are necessary for plant growth. The warmth of the sun creates good outdoor play conditions so that children and adults enjoy being outdoors. In the middle of summer, the sun can create so much heat and the temperature can get so high that it is uncomfortable to be in direct sunlight for long. In some places it is necessary to have homes, schools, and other buildings air conditioned because of the high temperatures. When the sun is very warm, it can melt such objects as crayons and objects made of wax. It can also fade colors, particularly in draperies, cars, or furniture, that are constantly exposed to the rays of the sun. It can make crops dry up, particularly on unirrigated farms, if rainfall is not adequate; it can wilt flowers and burn grass if they are not watered. It can cause painful and dangerous sunburns.

3. The sun has different effects, usually depending on the particular locality and the season of the year. It can feel slightly warm or extremely hot. In the winter when the sun shines, its rays are welcome and may create some warmth through a windowpane, but outside the temperature may be too cold for the sunshine to feel warm at all. Two of the beauties of nature are sunrise and sunset; they seem to have particular beauty and great variety of color in the summer.

4. The sun has various sensory characteristics.

   a. Sounds and tastes: no characteristic ones
   b. Sights: bright, yellow, orange, beautiful and colorful sunrises and sunsets, shadows, reflections of sunlight, glaring
   c. Smells: hot asphalt or tar, dry soil, melted wax or plastic, hot car seats, hot rubber (created by the warmth of the sun's rays)
   d. Feels: warm, hot, sunburn, perspiration, lazy, dry, sticky

5. The sun creates different feelings in different people. Most often the sun is a welcome aspect of weather. Children enjoy the sunshine because it means that they can play outside more often. During the winter, sunshine usually means that there will be no snow or rain; thus, even though temperatures may be cold, children can often play outside. In the springtime everyone is anxious to see warm, sunny days because outside work and play are then possible. The sun also brings growth to trees, shrubs, flowers, and other kinds of plants. To farmers, the springtime sun means that the soil and land will begin to thaw and dry out enough for the ground to be worked and planted and for crops to grow. The summer sun means that many outdoor activities and games can be enjoyed. We plan many outdoor experiences in the summer, and the sun is welcome because it creates warmth and dryness. The fall sun casts more light on the bright colors of nature and makes them even more beautiful. For most people, the sunshine brings happy feelings. However, during the middle of summer, when the sun brings high temperatures, we may feel lazy, sweaty, and lacking in energy.

6. The warmer the sunshine, the lighter we dress. We wear less clothing and lighter-weight clothing when the sunshine is very warm. We wear sunsuits, shorts, sleeveless shirts and blouses, and sundresses. We also wear sandals, and we do not need to wear sweaters and coats.

7. The sun allows us to do different things. We go on vacation. We play outside, run through sprinklers, and go swimming, wading, and on picnics. We play in the summer more than at any other time of the year. We enjoy projects such as lemonade stands, neighborhood plays, and hobbies of every kind. We go bicycle riding and play with outdoor equipment.

8. We participate in different games and activities in different places in the sunshine. We play outside, games and activities of every kind. We play in the sandbox, ride bicycles and tricycles, and play with other wheel toys outside. We play many neighbor-

hood games, such as hopscotch. We ride skateboards and roller skates. We enjoy games and activities in the parks and other recreation areas and use equipment such as slides and swings.

9. We visit different places when the days are sunny, including recreation areas, parks, amusement parks, the zoo, the canyons, and mountains. Activities enjoyed at such places include picnics, wiener roasts, campouts, hikes, and boating. Visits to relatives and friends are more frequent, and families often plan outings and family reunions on sunny, warm days. Swimming is a favorite sport on sunny days.

10. Other kinds of weather influence the sun, and the sun influences other kinds of weather. Clouds may prevent the rays of the sun from reaching Earth, creating an overcast day. The wind may decrease the sun's warmth, lowering the temperature. The sun influences almost every other aspect of weather. It may melt the snow, shorten a rainstorm, and dry up puddles and mud.

Shadows are an interesting additional aspect of sunshine. They are created when objects pass in front of light; thus objects that pass in front of the sun create shadows. Clouds are actually objects that pass in front of the sun and cast shade on Earth. In addition, the movement of the sun during the day will create different shadows. For example, a tree, building, home, fence, or other object will cast shadows in different positions as the sun moves during the day. When the day is very hot, people move to the shade (places where shadows are cast) to escape the heat. When the day is cold, people like to move into the light of the sunshine to warm up. (See Chapter 9 for additional ideas on light and shadows.)

One additional concept is that day and night are caused by the movement of Earth around the sun. One child, in a discussion of day and night, said that it was the moon that made it dark. The teacher explained that it was not the moon, but the sun setting, that brought nighttime. It is also the sunrise that brings the beginning of day. Children can also understand that the length of daylight and nighttime will vary with the season.

Activities and Experiences

Very few specific activities and experiences are included here, since many of them are listed in unit plans (particularly the science sections) and other places in this chapter.

1. Plant a garden indoors or outdoors.

2. Plant bulbs in the fall and observe their growth in the spring.

3. Discuss the thermometer and frequently check the temperature. Help the children to understand that the temperature goes up when it gets warmer and goes down when it gets colder. Chart the temperature on a graph at the same time each day for a month and observe any changes. The high and low temperatures each day could be graphed the same way.

4. Observe carefully the effects of temperature on a growing plant.

5. Have the children cut pictures that represent hot or cold items from old magazines. These are then collaged onto a poster that has been divided in half: hot items on one half and cold items on the other.

6. Visit a greenhouse and measure temperature variations in different areas of the greenhouse.

7. Visit a grocery store and measure and compare temperature variations in different food areas: shelves, frozen food case, refrigerated case, storage areas, and so on.

8. Fill a few containers with different temperatures of water and arrange them in order from hottest to coldest. Record the various temperatures in both Fahrenheit and Celsius (centigrade).

9. Make sets of sequence pictures to be ordered by season. One set might be of a tree pictured in fall, winter, spring, and summer. Another set might be of a child dressed for the four seasons.

10. Collect picture cards of things representative of various seasons: clothing, weather, trees in various seasons, tools, jobs, and others. Let the children categorize them by season. A similar set of sorting cards could be made to represent various kinds of weather.

11. Brainstorm with the children what they like best and least about each season. Write their ideas down, and have them illustrated and put into a booklet.

12. Make a season scrapbook with a section for each season. Include pictures of jobs, recreation, weather, and many other aspects of the season. Write ideas for each page in a sentence or two.

13. Play a Guess What? game for any aspect of weather or a particular season. Example: "Guess what I like to do in the summer."

14. Interview each child to determine favorite seasons and kinds of weather. Chart or graph the results.

15. Hold a watercolor watch. Assign each child a quiet place by a window or on the grass or sidewalk and a suggested weather word, such as *rain, sun, wind*, or *snow* (depending on the current weather conditions). Supply the child with watercolors, crayons, markers, colored pencils, pens, chalk, or pencil. During a period of about 15 minutes, the child draws or tells what is observed (adapted from Charron & Jones, 1992).

16. Make a weather-related scrapbook with drawings, magazine pictures, photos, stickers, and children's summaries (Diffily & Morrison, 1996).

From the foregoing material, many ideas for approaching lesson plans should emerge. However, we also include the following unit plans to give additional ideas for organizing activities for lesson plans. We have combined a season with the kinds of weather associated with that season. The units need not be combined, but they often fit together.

UNIT PLAN ON SUMMER AND SUN

Field Trips

- Beach or swimming pool for wading or swimming
- Picnic
- Backyard garden
- Canyon or park
- Zoo
- Outdoor walk to observe summer and sun characteristics
- Planetarium
- Aviary
- Farm
- Early morning sunrise breakfast or outing

Art

- Blot painting with white paint to portray clouds on gray or blue paper that represents the sky
- Flower pictures made with cupcake holders
- Flowers made out of nut cups, using pipe cleaners for stems; stems placed in clay base in paper cup
- Sponge painting of sunrise or sunset
- Fans made and decorated
- Collage of summer objects: sand, shells, rocks, pebbles, grass
- Rock painting
- Paper-plate hats decorated for a summer parade
- Paint with water outside

Science

- Study and observation of shadows
- Study, observation, and growing of seeds and plants
- Study of the life cycle of the frog
- Fire prevention
- Flowers
- Clouds
- Sunlight and its effect on growing plants

Music

- Shadow dancing behind screen or sheet
- Creative movements relating to summer activities: fishing, swimming, throwing a Frisbee, and others

- Creative movements interpreting a sprinkler, fountain, waterfall
- Creative movements representing the sun rising or setting
- Creative movements interpreting the growth of a seed into a plant, the wilting of a plant in the summer's heat or sunshine, and how it perks up when it is watered
- Creative movements interpreting animals seen in summer: birds, butterflies, insects, life cycle of a frog, fish, and others
- Marching parade with or without rhythm instruments

Food

- Homemade ice cream or frozen yogurt
- Marshmallows and hot dogs cooked over a grill on the playground or at a park
- Fresh fruits in salads and other forms
- "S'mores"—two graham crackers, piece of chocolate bar, marshmallow toasted by the child; "sandwich" put together while marshmallow is warm
- Sandwiches and other picnic snacks, even if the picnic is outside the classroom on the grass or at a nearby home or park
- Potato salad
- Making jams and jellies
- Fruits dried in the sunshine and eaten a day or two later
- Flavored ice pops, slush, or other frozen treats
- Gelatin squares

Visitors

- Person from a nursery
- Lifeguard
- Farmer
- Gardener
- Florist or flower arranger
- Person who enjoys fishing
- Golfer

- Ornithologist
- Entomologist
- People to share vacation experiences
- Carhop
- Ice-cream vendor

Language and Literacy

- Slides and/or pictures of summer scenes, with children discussing them, individually or in small groups
- Objects or pictures of food, recreational equipment, clothing, and so on, relating to all seasons; items are passed out to all the children, with each child who has something relating to summer telling about it
- Sharing of vacation experiences
- Sharing of a favorite summer activity, food, place to visit, and so on
- Stories, written or told, of most memorable summer vacation or experience
- Writing and illustrating booklets on "Why I Like Summer," "What I Like to Do in the Summer," "Summer Is . . . ," or "What I Did This Past Summer"

UNIT PLAN ON WIND

This unit could easily be related to the concept of air.

Field Trips

- Outdoor walk on windy day to observe characteristics of wind
- Kite flying or watching others fly kites
- Airport
- Dam on nearby lake to watch a sailboat
- Weather station or television station to watch the weather forecast
- University or high school band class where children can see and hear wind instruments
- Music store that sells wind instruments

Art

- Kites made by children
- Straw painting or blow painting
- Hummers made to use in musical activity
- Balloons decorated with papier-mâché; or powdered paints

Science

- Study and observation of effects of wind: soil erosion, wearing away of rocks, sand dunes
- Observation of a weather vane to determine wind direction
- Study of the effects of strong windstorms such as hurricanes and tornadoes
- Study and discussion of positive and negative aspects of wind

Music

- Hummer band (see discussion of hummers in Chapter 9)
- Creative movements interpreting leaves blowing in the wind, people moving in the wind, kites blowing in the wind, trees moving in the wind, feathers moving in the wind, clothes drying in a breeze
- Visitors with wind instruments: children allowed to try to play instruments; visitors asked to play their instruments while children play their hummers

Food

- Hot soup: children allowed to blow on it to cool it
- Hot chocolate
- Food activities related to air: egg whites or whipping cream beaten as a part of a food activity, with emphasis on how air is beaten into it and the concept that wind is also moving air

Visitors

- Musician to play wind instrument or harmonica
- Parent to fly kites on playground

- Weather forecaster
- Pilot to tell about watching the wind direction and speed when flying
- Forest ranger to discuss the effects and influences of wind in the forest and mountains

Language and Literacy

- Pictures or slides of different kinds of weather, with children identifying those that depict wind
- Stories about wind, written or told
- Poems about wind, written or told
- Variety of articles of clothing, with children determining which articles should be worn on windy days
- Booklet written and illustrated on wind, including why the children do and do not like it

UNIT PLAN ON RAIN

Field Trips

- Lake, pond, stream, or river
- Reservoir
- Fish hatchery
- Water laboratory
- Home where the family has a terrarium or rain garden
- Water tower

Art

- Painting or collage of rainy scenes
- Children mixing their own paint so that they see the water base; painting with watercolors
- Paintings of rainbows
- Screen spatter painting: screen mounted on a frame (or use an old window screen), which is then placed several inches above and parallel to the tabletop; paintbrush dipped into paint and passed over the screen to give a spatter effect on the paper below; alternatively, shadow

pictures made by placing an object or shape cutout (or cookie cutter) on the paper and spattering paint around it

Science

- Study and observation of the rain cycle: evaporation and condensation
- Building and observation of a rain garden or terrarium
- Study of rainbows
- Study and observation of what rain does to plants
- Study and observation of a prism

Music

- Creative movements interpreting falling rain, plants, or flowers: how they wilt before a rainstorm, droop during the storm, and perk up after the storm
- Rain dance by children (perhaps after a visit from a Native American who performs a rain dance)
- Rhythm interpretations of rain: hitting a windowpane, falling slowly or very rapidly

Food

- Rainy-day foods such as soup or chili
- Hot chocolate

- Foods with a water base, such as root beer or lemonade
- Foods dissolved in water, such as gelatins or powdered drinks
- Foods cooked in water, such as vegetables, macaroni, or rice

Visitors

- Weather forecaster
- A visitor to explain and build a rain garden or terrarium
- Farmer
- Forest ranger

Language and Literacy

- Stories about rain, written or told
- Poems about rain, written or told
- Shared rainy-day experiences
- Pictures or slides of different kinds of weather, with the children identifying those that depict rain
- Variety of articles of clothing, with the children determining which articles of clothing should be worn on rainy days
- Writing and illustrating booklets titled "I Like Rain Because . . . " or "Rain"

Summary

This chapter has dealt with the widely varied subjects of the environment, air, water, rocks, temperature, weather, and seasons. As children become more familiar with Earth, they also should learn that they can make a difference in protecting our environment, that the quality of air, soil, and water is determined by human treatment and care. They become more aware of and comfortable with nature, people, events, and the materials surrounding them. Since the concepts of temperature, weather, and seasons are so closely related to each other, a discussion of one of them usually involves at least one of the others. All people are greatly influenced by temperature, weather, and seasons. These factors affect clothing, food, activities, games, recreation, feelings, and moods. Many people prefer one season over another because of the kinds of activities that are characteristic of that season. Not all people, however, react the same way to weather variations. For example, a particular temperature could make one person feel cold, another feel hot, and another feel just right. Weather, seasons, and temperature are natural parts of the world in which we live. The spontaneous curiosity and interest of children in their environment makes related learning both enjoyable and rewarding.

Young children's natural curiosity about their environment make the early years an excellent time to instill positive attitudes and practices regarding the world in which they live.

Student Learning Activities

1. Visit an early childhood classroom and observe science-related materials, books, visual aids, software, centers, or activities. Interview the teacher about his or her science curriculum. What role do you feel that science plays in this classroom and what would you change?

2. Using one of the science unit plans or a science topic of a child's own choosing, discuss with a young child his or her ideas about plans for study with this theme. Invite the child to propose a project plan for this study. Evaluate results.

3. Write a paragraph or two on your attitudes about temperature, weather, and seasons. How might your own attitudes about the season, temperature, or weather influence the children in your classroom?

4. Interview a preschool, kindergarten, or first- or second-grade teacher. Find out this teacher's attitudes toward temperature, weather, and the seasons. Ask the teacher whether and how these attitudes affect the children. In addition, find out how the teacher includes temperature, weather, and seasons in the curriculum. Are units planned relating to any of these topics? How do the children respond?

5. Begin a picture collection for weather and seasons. Mount the pictures appropriately.

6. Begin a collection of children's poems relating to air, rocks, water, weather and seasons, and other aspects of the environment.

7. Write down your most and least favorite season or aspect of weather. Have a group of children ages 3 to 8 brainstorm and share their most and least favorite seasons or types of weather.

8. With a group of children, implement at least one of the activities and experiences related to a science concept suggested in this chapter. The group of children may be a classroom group or a gathering of relatives or neighborhood children. Evaluate your experience.

9. Think of additional ideas for two of the unit plans in this chapter.

10. Prepare an activity plan or web for one of the science concepts in this chapter.

11. Visit a children's library or media center and see whether you can discover books, pictures, recordings, or media relating to science themes in this chapter.

Suggested Resources

Science Resources

See additional science resources listed at the end of Chapter 9, Physical Science Experiments, and those relating to nutrition at the end of Chapter 7.

Caduto, M. J., & J. Bruchac (1988). *Keepers of the earth: Native American stories with environmental activities for children*. Golden, CO: Fulcrum.

Claycomb, P. (1991). *Love the earth: Exploring environmental activities for young children*. Livonia, MI: Partner.

Herman, M. L., J. F. Passineau, A. L. Schimpf, & P. Treurer (1991). *Teaching kids to love the earth*. Duluth, MI: Pfeifer-Hamilton.

Katz, A. (1986). *Naturewatch: Exploring nature with your children*. Reading, MA: Addison–Wesley.

Lingelbach, J. (1986). *Hands-on nature*. Woodstock, VT: Vermont Institute of Natural Science.

Children's Books

Adoff, A. (1997). *In for winter, out for spring*. New York: Harcourt Brace.

Allen, M. N. (1995). *Changes*. New York: Aladdin.

Asch, F. (1994). *The Earth and I.* New York: Harcourt.

Asch, F. (1997). *Water.* Jefferson City, MO: Scholastic.

Blades, A. (1989). *Winter, spring, summer, fall.* New York: Lothrop, Lee & Shepard.

Booth, D. (1990). *Voices in the wind: Poems for all seasons.* New York: Morrow.

Brink, C. R. (1995). *Goody O'Grumpity.* New York: North-South.

Brown, M. W. (1947). *Goodnight, moon.* New York: HarperCollins.

Bunting, E. (1996). *Market day.* New York: Joanna Colter.

Burningham, J. (1996). *Cloudland.* New York: Crown.

Canizares, S., & B. Chessen (1998). *Storms.* New York: Scholastic.

Canizares, S., & B. Chessen (1998). *Wind.* New York: Scholastic.

Canizares, S., & D. Moreton (1998). *Sun.* New York: Scholastic.

Chanko, P., & D. Moreton (1998). *Weather.* New York: Scholastic.

Chapman, C. (1994). *Snow on snow on snow.* New York: Dial.

Demarest, C. L. (1997). *Spring.* New York: Red Wagon/Harcourt Brace.

Demarest, C. L. (1997). *Summer.* New York: Red Wagon/Harcourt Brace.

Eagle, K. (1994). *It's raining, it's pouring.* Boston: Whispering Coyote.

Edom, H. (1992). *Science with water.* Tulsa, OK: Educational Development.

Ehlert, L. (1988). *Planting a rainbow.* San Diego, CA: Harcourt Brace Jovanovich.

Engvick, W. (ed.) (1985). *Lullabies and night songs.* New York: Harper & Row.

Evans, L. (1995). *Rain song.* Boston: Houghton Mifflin.

Evans, L. (1997). *Snow dance.* Boston: Houghton Mifflin.

Fazio, B. L. (1996). *Grandfather's story.* Seattle, WA: Sasquatch Books.

Fife, D. H. (1996). *The empty lot.* San Francisco: Sierra Club.

Fuchs, D. M. (1995). *A bear for all seasons.* New York: Henry Holt.

Garland, S. (1995). *The summer sands.* New York: Harcourt Brace.

George, L. B. (1995). *In the snow: Who's been here?* New York: Greenwillow.

Gibbons, G. (1990). *Weather words and what they mean.* New York: Holiday House.

Harshman, M. (1995). *The storm.* New York: Cobblehill.

Hesse, K. (1999). *Come on, rain!* New York: Scholastic Press.

Hest, A. (1995). *In the rain with baby duck.* Cambridge, MA: Candlewick.

Highwater, J. (1995). *Songs for the seasons.* New York: Lothrop, Lee & Shepard.

Hines, A. G. (1994). *What Joe saw.* New York: Greenwillow.

Hirschi, R. (1996). *Spring.* New York: Puffin.

Horton, B. S. (1992). *What comes in spring?* New York: Knopf.

Hughes, S. (1985). *Bathwater's hot.* New York: Lothrop, Lee & Shepard.

Keats, E. J. (1962). *The snowy day.* New York: Viking.

Laser, M. (1997). *The rain.* New York: Simon & Schuster.

Leslie, C. W. (1991). *Nature all year long.* New York: Greenwillow.

Lindberg, R. (1997). *North country spring.* New York: Houghton Mifflin.

London, J. (1997). *Puddles.* New York: Viking.

Maas, R. (1997). *When autumn comes.* New York: Scholastic.

Maas, R. (1997). *When spring comes.* New York: Scholastic.

Maas, R. (1997). *When winter comes.* New York: Scholastic.

Manning, M. (1997). *Nature watch.* New York: Kingfisher.

Marzollo, J. (1996). *I am water.* Jefferson City, MO: Scholastic.

Nikola-Lisa, W. (1991). *Night is coming.* New York: Dutton.

Oliver, S. (1990). *My first look at seasons.* New York: Random House.

Omerod, J. (1981). *Sunshine.* New York: Lothrop, Lee & Shepard.

Omerod, J. (1982). *Moonlight.* New York: Viking.

O'Neill, M. (1990). *Hailstones and halibut bones.* Garden City, NY: Doubleday.

Repchuk, C. (1997). *The snow tree.* New York: Dutton.

Riser, L. (1995). *Night thunder and the queen of the wild horses.* New York: Greenwillow.

Ross, T. (1995). *Bedtime.* New York: Red Wagon/Harcourt Brace.

Ross, T. (1995). *Weather.* New York: Red Wagon/Harcourt Brace.

Serfozo, M. (1997). *Rain talk.* New York: Scholastic.

Siddals, M. M. (1997). *Tell me a season.* New York: Clarion.

Simon, N. (1991). *Mama cat's year.* Morton Grove, IL: Whitman.

Spier, P. (1982). *Rain.* Garden City, NY: Doubleday.

Steig, W. (1969). *Sylvester and the magic pebble.* New York: Windmill.

Suen, A. (1997). *Man on the moon.* New York: Viking.

Szilagyi, M. (1985). *Thunderstorm.* New York: Bradbury.

Tafuri, N. (1997). *What the sun sees, what the moon sees.* New York: Greenwillow.

Tafuri, N. (1999). *Snowy flowy blowy: A twelve months rhyme.* New York: Scholastic.

Taylor, B. (1992). *Over the rainbow! The science of color and light.* New York: Random House.

Tresselt, A. (1969). *White snow, bright snow.* New York: Lothrop, Lee & Shepard.

Tudor, T. (1977). *A time to keep: The Tasha Tudor book of holidays.* New York: Random House.

Tyers, J. (1996). *When it is night, when it is day.* New York: Houghton Mifflin.

Watts, B. (1997). *Harvey Hare postman extraordinaire.* New York: North-South Books.

Whitby, J. (1984). *Emma and grandpa (1) (January, February, March).* Essex, England: Longman.

Whitby, J. (1984). *Emma and grandpa (2) (April, May, June).* Essex, England: Longman.

Whitby, J. (1984). *Emma and grandpa (3) (July, August, September).* Essex, England: Longman.

Whitby, J. (1984). *Emma and grandpa (4) (October, November, December).* Essex, England: Longman.

Wildsmith, B. (1980). *Seasons*. New York: Oxford University Press.

Wildsmith, B. (1984). *The north wind and the sun*. New York: Oxford University Press.

Zolotow, C. (1983). *Summer is . . . .* New York: HarperCollins.

Zolotow, C. (1995). *When the wind stops*. New York: HarperCollins.

Pictures

Astronomy. The Child's World.

Common rock and rock-forming minerals. Society for Visual Education.

The desert. The Child's World.

Earth movements. The Child's World.

Ecology: The pollution problem. David C. Cook.

Ecosystems. David C. Cook.

Erosion. The Child's World.

Fall and winter holidays. Society for Visual Education.

Familiar cloud forms. Society for Visual Education.

Glaciers. The Child's World.

Holidays. David C. Cook.

In the fall. Society for Visual Education.

In the spring. Society for Visual Education.

In the summer. Society for Visual Education.

In the winter. Society for Visual Education.

Land forms of running water. Society for Visual Education.

Learning about energy. David C. Cook.

Learning about nature. David C. Cook.

Learning about weather. David C. Cook.

Polar regions. The Child's World.

The sea. The Child's World.

Seasons. David C. Cook.

Seasons and holidays: Fall. Society for Visual Education.

Seasons and holidays: Spring. Society for Visual Education.

Seasons and holidays: Summer. Society for Visual Education.

Spring and summer holidays. Society for Visual Education.

Take a walk in fall. The Child's World. (Sequence chart)

Take a walk in spring. The Child's World. (Sequence chart)

Take a walk in summer. The Child's World. (Sequence chart)

Take a walk in winter. The Child's World. (Sequence chart)

Volcanoes. The Child's World.

Weather phenomena. The Child's World.

Tapes and Cassettes

Fall is here. The Child's World.

Holiday songs and rhymes. Hap Palmer Record Library (AR538 or AC538).

Holidays. David C. Cook.

Magic monsters around the year. On *The magic monster mix*. The Child's World.

More singing fun (1). Bowman-Noble.

Rain is falling. On *The rainy day record*. Bowman-Noble.

Seasons and weather. David C. Cook (DC-24190).

Singing fun. Bowman-Noble.

The small singer (2). Bowman-Noble.

Spring is here. The Child's World.

Summer is here. The Child's World.

Time and time again. Educational Activities (AR87 or AC87).

The weather. On *Ooo we're having fun*. Cheviot (T-306).

Winter is here. The Child's World.

Videos

Autumn. National Geographic.

Reflecting on the moon. National Geographic.

Solid, liquid, gas. National Geographic.

Spring. National Geographic.

Summer. National Geographic.

Winter. National Geographic.

Multimedia Kits

A tree for all seasons (Big book and kit). National Geographic.

Captain conservation: All about recycling. National Geographic.

Captain conservation: All about water. National Geographic.

Exploring the solar system and beyond (CD ROM kit). National Geographic.

Our Earth (CD-ROM kit). National Geographic.

Seasons (CD-ROM kit). National Geographic.

The sun, the moon. National Geographic.

A tree through the seasons. National Geographic.

What happens in autumn? National Geographic.

What happens in spring? National Geographic.

What happens in summer? National Geographic.

What happens in winter? National Geographic.

Why does it rain? National Geographic.

Computer Software

Learn about astronomy. Sunburst.

Learn about weather. Sunburst.

Sammy's science house. Riverdeep.

Science blaster Jr. Davidson.

Thinkin' science. Riverdeep.

Chapter 11

Life Science Experiences

This chapter addresses teaching concepts included in the sensory-related, animal, and plant aspects of life science. Frequently, teachers rely too heavily on the sense of sight, or the visual process, rather than encouraging expansion and use of the other four senses. As children develop perception and the ability to distinguish differences in what they see, hear, taste, smell, and touch, they learn more quickly because all five senses are "tuned in" instead of only one or two. Exploring nature effectively with young children must involve all the senses: hearing, seeing, smelling, tasting, and touching (Humphreys, 2000).

Children are naturally curious as they use their senses to explore the world. They try to touch, poke, pinch, taste, lick, chew, smell, watch, listen to, or examine objects, people, and situations in great detail (Beaty, 1992). This is how they learn! We need to encourage children to maintain their sensory tools and use them to explore their world and answer their questions. "Our world is a huge hands-on museum, a well-stocked laboratory, a fascinating never-ending field trip. . . ." (Ziemer, 1987, pp. 44–45). Infants respond to sounds, tastes, smells, and touch very early in life.

As children learn to use their senses with precision, they become more aware of their environment and use these senses to build and determine concepts.

Included in the sensory-related discussion are smell and taste, texture (touch), and sound (hearing). Sight is not included since it is the primary sense most people use in learning, and it is used in every activity.

The outdoor playground can help children to develop respect, appreciation, and understanding for the natural environment. Playgrounds provide the perfect setting for children to become aware of protecting and preserving plants and animals in nature (Wilson, Kilmer, & Knauerhase, 1996).

Environmental education is critical! Animals and plants are living parts of the natural world. Many concepts can be gleaned from studies of animals and plants: size, shape, number, color, texture, weight, smell, sound, nutrition, appreciation and respect for life and environment, conservation, and so on.

Most children have limited experiences with animals and plants in their surroundings. More of the acquired knowledge they do have comes from schoolbooks and television than from direct experience (Rivkin, 1995). We must increase direct-experience learning! "Positive interactions with the world of nature during the early childhood years [are] strongly recommended as a way of both preventing the development of negative attitudes and feelings about nature and establishing lifelong habits of conservation" (Wilson, Kilmer, & Knauerhase, 1996, p. 57). Share your own respect and appreciation for all living things, and children will learn the same. When exploring nature with children, it is wise to model the philosophy of "find, examine, and return" (Humphreys, 2000, p. 18).

What possibilities for teaching lie within the realm of animals in the child's environment! It is impossible to imagine going through a year of study at any level of early childhood without some units and experiences with animals. Young children have sensitivity to and seek an understanding of animals. Specific concepts relating to individual animals or to categories and classes of animals emerge as a result of animal studies. For example, children will become aware of the physical characteristics of the animals, where they live, what they eat, the uses of the animals, and how they reproduce and care for their young. Children will also enjoy making comparisons among animals as they become acquainted with the characteristics of the animal categories.

There are additional values and by-products of animal experiences and studies. Children learn how to care for animals properly: how to hold them (if they can be held), how and what to feed them, and how to care for and clean their surroundings. Young children gain feelings of importance as they feed the classroom animals and provide for their care. Many children are afraid of animals, but through experiences with these animals, the fears can often be lessened or overcome. Children can become aware of our tremendous reliance on animals as sources of food and clothing, while at the same time becoming aware of animals that are either a potential danger or a nuisance.

> Through utilizing the senses while studying plants and animals, children become more aware of our reliance on plants and animals as sources for food, clothing, and shelter.

Children enjoy caring for and nurturing plants through their growing stages. There is particular excitement for young children the day that they discover that their little seed, carefully planted, watered, sunned, and cared for, is pushing its way through the soil and taking its first peek at the world! In addition to the satisfaction of planting seeds and caring for plants, there are many opportunities for learning about plant life and teaching

concepts through studies of seeds and plants. Concepts specific to individual plants or to categories or classes of plants will emerge as a result of plant studies. For example, children will become aware of the characteristics of plants, what plants need in order to grow, and the uses of plants. Children will also learn by making comparisons among plants by comparing sizes, colors, rates of growth, seasons of growth, and other factors. For example, as you observe a tall tree with young children, ask "I wonder . . ." open-ended questions. We do not need to know all the answers, because we are encouraging curiosity, rather than just teaching facts.

Children should have opportunities for exploring plants in the classroom environment. With so many varieties of plants, teachers need to select those appropriate for the climate and season. Rubber plants and geraniums are especially hardy, and children enjoy watching geraniums bloom and observing the color of the blossoms. When there are plants in the classroom, the children should be allowed to care for them: water them, put them in sunlight, give them plant food, and assume many other responsibilities in nurturing or caring for plants. A number of plants are poisonous and should be avoided. Examples include English ivy, philodendron, laurel, and dieffenbachia. Before purchasing plants for your classroom or center, check with your local nursery to make sure that the plants are nontoxic. The specific varieties of plants that are in your environment, both inside and outside, should be named often.

Ideally, children should have a garden space outdoors where they can plant and care for vegetables and/or flowers. Children become more aware of their environment as well as learning what plants need to grow. When children are involved in growing some of their own food, they learn about nutrition, food sources, environmental needs of plants, and cutting down on excessive packaging (Wilson, 1995b). As children plan a garden, select and plant the seeds, and then tend and harvest the produce, they understand the natural process of growth and are introduced to an area of science that can have lifelong influence. They realize the relationship of plant growth to other plants, animals and insects, humans, water, soil, sun, weather, and temperature (Clemens, 1996). "When we provide gardening experiences for children, we help them to discover themselves as well as the natural world" (p. 27).

Through studies of plants, children become aware of our reliance on plants as sources of food, clothing, and shelter, as well as for aesthetic beauty in both indoor and outdoor surroundings. However, children can also learn that many plants, such as noxious weeds and poisonous plants, may be a nuisance or harmful to humans.

TEACHING SENSORY-RELATED CONCEPTS

Smell and Taste

Through the two important senses of smell and taste many new ideas are learned. These two concepts may be incorporated into a unit on the senses, taught together, or taught as separate unit themes.

Even though taste and smell are separate senses, they are closely related, and one greatly influences the other. Often a child may dislike a food because of its smell, not because of its actual taste. Chewing a food while the nose is being held diminishes the taste of the food. Likewise, nasal congestion from a cold results in a decrease in the sense of taste.

The teacher's own sense of taste may be enhanced (so that children can be made more aware of their sense of taste) by a review of the location of the taste buds for the four basic tastes. The salt taste buds are located on the tip and sides of the tongue; sweet is on the tip of the tongue; bitter and sour are on the sides of the tongue and on the palate.

Too often in learning activities, children are not encouraged to use their senses of smell and taste. They hear a teacher say "Look at it. What do you see?" But there are times when it is better to say "Smell it (or taste it). Now what do you know about it?" Children should be given the opportunity to taste and smell during food experiences, as well as after the product is finished.

A child relies on previous experiences when learning through smell and taste. In a study by Hirsch (1992), adults were asked about smells that made them feel nostalgic. Most of the responses of adults born between 1920 and 1950 involved natural smells such as flowers, cut grass, baking bread and other foods, manure, soap, pine, cinnamon, and fresh air. However, most of the nostalgic smells for adults born during the 1960s and 1970s

Discriminating between actual and plastic foods requires much experimenting. Plastic tomatoes do not taste as good as they look!

were from manufactured sources such as fabric softener, disinfectant, marijuana, hair spray, nail polish, and scented magic markers. Consider the implications regarding our natural environment and how children's knowledge and understanding of science may be affected by their exposure to and experiences with nature.

When learning textures, the child can use other senses in addition to touch: taste, hearing, and sight. However, smells or tastes cannot be seen, felt, or heard unless the child has had previous experience with the items being smelled or tasted. For example, if a child who had never had experiences with a lemon was asked to describe its smell or taste, the child could not rely on touch or sound for clues; the child would have to taste or smell the lemon. Also, the way a child describes a taste or smell will depend on his or her experience with it. The child must have experience in hearing and using the word *sour*, for example, and must know the meaning of this word (the concept) before he or she can describe the smell or taste of a lemon.

Children understand that they learn about some things and identify them by smelling and/or tasting them. A good experience for assisting in this understanding is to paint the outside of a bottle so that the children cannot see the contents (or use a small brown glass bottle) and fill it with root beer, orange juice, or other liquid. The children then taste this liquid, and the teacher asks them whether they would like to learn what they have tasted. The teacher can follow this experience with ways in which the children could learn what the bottle contains—by smelling or tasting the contents. In this case, it would probably be better to have each child smell the liquid to discover what it is. Teachers need to approach this activity with one specific safety precaution: teach children *never* to taste the contents of bottles or other containers unless they have been told and are certain that the contents are edible and something that they should taste. They must understand that this practice can be very dangerous.

Also, if the children are smelling cleaning agents, gasoline, or other such fluids, mark the containers with the poison sign or a large red × so that the children know that these containers are for smelling only. They are not to be left unattended, and they should be taken from the room when the smelling is completed. Other health precautions to consider are sanitation and cleanliness when participating in all tasting activities.

Children should be encouraged to rely more often on their senses of smell and taste. Smells and tastes are frequently tuned out of daily experiences. One meaningful activity is to have children write down or discuss all the smells and/or tastes that they have experienced during a particular day. They might do a follow-up exercise in which they make it a point to be aware of smell and taste. In teaching smell and taste, exploratory questions can be asked. For example, you might ask "What else smells like _____?" or "What else tastes like _____?"

Smell

Approach to Teaching.   A broad base for understanding smell can be built by increasing the child's vocabulary. Many opportunities for describing smells and using smell words should be provided, and new smell words should be introduced, along with their meanings. Whenever a smell word is learned, opportunities for smelling items described by the word should be provided. For example, learning the word *bitter* will have no meaning unless something bitter is smelled (or tasted), and it would be better if several bitter items were smelled. The following is an incomplete list of possible words describing smells; various objects representing these smells are easily accessible for meaning and reinforcement.

sour	lemony	strong
dusty	pleasant	burned
moldy	salty	smoky
rancid	rusty	fishy
sweet	bitter	fresh
dirty	offensive	clean
new	crisp	delicious
piney	sharp	

After experiences with these words, exciting brainstorming or creative writing sessions may evolve. Children can discuss or write about items, foods, or experiences related to the words. For example, they may think, talk, or write about an experience or memory related to anything that smells smoky. Simple poetry can evolve from smell words.

Smells can be divided into categories and unit themes can be developed on the sense of smell or on one or more of these "smell" categories. Each day the teacher can introduce a different category of smells, providing examples of smells relating to this category through experiences. For example, if the teacher chooses a unit on cleaning smells, a visit to a motel can be planned whereby the children meet the motel cleaning personnel, learn about the job, and smell some of the solvents and materials used for cleaning. Another experience during this unit might be a visit by the school custodian, in which cleaning materials are shared with the children. A salesperson who sells cleaning aids might also visit. The children could participate in a food experience, including the cleanup, with emphasis on smelling the cleaning aids. It is easy to see how exciting it would be to correlate a unit with the theme of cleaning smells.

The following is an incomplete list of some of the categories of smells:

inside	hospital	cleaning
outside	food	kitchen
animal	holiday	store
automobile	nature	school
seasonal	bakery	cosmetic

Concepts and Ideas for Teaching

1. Some smells give messages or direct behavior.

   a. Smoke: leads people to discover what is burning and to take necessary action.
   b. Favorite foods: may create hunger for a particular food, especially if a person is already hungry.
   c. Medicine: indicates when someone is ill, has a cold, or is sucking a cough drop, which in turn points to sore throats, colds, coughs, and so on.
   d. Food smells: often strong and distinct enough to signal what is cooking.
   e. Fire or matches: may tell us that children are playing with matches or warn us of danger.
   f. Unfamiliar smells: may make a person curious about the source.
   g. Undesirable smells: may remind a person of previous experiences and sometimes even cause nausea.

2. The same items do not always smell the same.

   a. People: perfume, soap, foods, culture, and other factors
   b. Automobiles: age, care, places parked, and so on
   c. Flowers: tulips, roses, violets, and others
   d. Perfumes: kind, type of container, age, and other factors

3. Items that look the same do not always smell the same.

   a. Potato flakes and soap flakes
   b. Strawberry gelatin and cherry gelatin
   c. Root beer extract and vanilla extract

4. Different items may have the same smell.

   a. Campfire smoke and cigarette smoke
   b. Vinegar taffy and liquid vinegar
   c. Various items with a lemon smell: lotion, cleaning solvents, shampoo

5. Not all things have a smell.

   a. Dish
   b. Wall
   c. Most water
   d. Some fabrics
   e. Glass

6. Smell may be changed or modified.

   a. Cooking: foods in various stages of the cooking process, such as meat before and after cooking; bakery products before and after baking; any food product before and after burning; or bread before and after being toasted
   b. Aging: a tomato that is fresh and one that is old and spoiled; a freshly cracked nut and one that is becoming rancid because of age; new perfume and older perfume that is partially evaporated
   c. Temperature: frozen items, which lose their smell or develop distinct or stronger odors; melted butter; melted plastics
   d. Drying: fruits, paste, glue, paints, which usually acquire a less distinct smell in the drying process
   e. Additions: modification of smells in food experiences, science experiences, and art activities by adding or combining ingredients

Activities and Experiences

1. The children can smell items and group them into categories, or the teacher can name a smell and the children tell which category or categories it fits into.

2. Colored bottles or containers with the outsides painted or taped can be used to identify the contents by smell. Care should be taken to select mostly substances with which the children have had previous experience. If the substance is not edible, caution the children against tasting it.

3. To help the children differentiate by smell items that look alike, the teacher can select combinations of the following items within each category. Bottles or containers can be coded for older children; they can write down the number code of the bottle and its contents. Children must be cautioned that these items are to smell, *not* to taste.

1-A	Alcohol
1-B	Polish remover
1-C	Water
1-D	White vinegar
1-E	Clear carbonated drink
2-A	Perfume
2-B	Vanilla
2-C	Cider vinegar
2-D	Root beer extract
2-E	Steak sauce
2-F	Dark flavorings
3-A	White glue
3-B	School paste
3-C	Lotion
3-D	Cold cream
3-E	Thick dairy cream
4-A	Glycerin
4-B	Liquid detergent
4-C	Rubber cement
4-D	Honey
4-E	Baby oil
4-F	Some shampoos
5-A	Molasses
5-B	Maple syrup
5-C	Dark corn syrup
6-A	Soap flakes
6-B	Potato flakes

Familiar and unfamiliar smells can be explored when cotton balls in bottles are saturated with various liquids and powders.

6-C	Onion flakes
6-D	Oatmeal
7-A	Salt
7-B	Sugar
7-C	Garlic salt
7-D	Onion salt
7-E	Celery salt
7-F	Sand
8-A	Powdered sugar
8-B	Cornstarch
8-C	Flour
8-D	Baby powder
8-E	Soda
8-F	Baking powder
9-A	Cinnamon
9-B	Chili powder
9-C	Cloves
10-A	Oregano
10-B	Parsley flakes

4. Once the children have identified an ingredient by its smell, they can then use descriptive words for it. Similes can also stimulate creativity: "It smells as salty as a soda cracker" or "It smells like a soda cracker."

5. For a "smell" walk or field trip, the children could walk around their own classroom, building, or neighborhood searching for smells.

6. Make up a "smell" story, with the children smelling actual smells at various intervals.

7. Put sensory materials in a trough, large tub, or other similar container for exploring and smelling. Items could include mud, flour, lemonade, barley, and wheat.

8. Discuss with the children how their sense of smell can protect them from danger.

9. Brainstorm with the children their favorite or most pleasant smells and their least favorite or most offensive or unpleasant smells. These can be dictated or written into a booklet or chart.

10. Demonstrate the interrelationship of taste and smell. Have the children, while blind-folded, taste a piece of apple and at the same time hold a piece of cut onion near their nose. Some children may believe that they taste an onion.

11. Fill various saltshakers with different flavors of red gelatin, sprinkle gelatin on the children's hands, and have them determine the flavor by the smell. Follow this with tasting. (*Remember:* Have the children wash their hands prior to this activity.)

UNIT PLAN ON SMELL

Field Trips

- Outside walk
- Bakery
- Meat market
- Paint store
- Cosmetic representative's home
- Drugstore or department store where a cosmetic counter could be visited
- Pet store
- Farm
- Hospital
- Flower shop
- Pharmacy

Art

- Collages with scented papers
- Collages made out of foodstuffs that have particular odors (use those discarded because of age)
- Finger painting with soap flakes and/or whipped cream (no longer edible): comparison of smells of the two; alternatively, finger painting with creams that look like soap flakes but smell different
- Lemon halves dipped into tempera paint for lemon printing: the combination of lemon juice and paint releases an offensive odor (use lemons that are no longer edible)

Music

- Various media put into opaque bottles or other nontransparent containers to be used for rhythm shakers after an experience in smelling. The teacher says, "All those with cinnamon smell in their bottle, shake or play with me on the next song."

- Creative expressions and movements, dramatically portrayed as to how you would respond or move if you were smelling ammonia and other suggested smells

Food

- Any food activity, planned with a focus on smell
- Pickles
- Root beer or milkshakes
- Vanilla ice cream, made and then flavored with peppermint or other flavoring
- Gelatin: different groups of children making different flavors and guessing individual flavors through their sense of smell
- Bread or other bakery products: smelled during the mixing process and then during the baking process

Visitors

- Cosmetics representative
- Salesperson for cleaning supplies
- Paint dealer or distributor
- Father, to bring in shaving creams and lotions
- Mother, to bring in various cosmetics
- Custodian, to bring in cleaning solvents and other cleaning agents
- Animals
- Parent, to conduct a demonstration on smells of foods

Science

- Salt garden (see Chapter 9 for directions)
- Smelling of bread each day as it progresses toward the moldy stage
- Smelling of changes in any item as it is changed or modified

- Smelling and identifying substances in opaque bottles or other containers

Language and Literacy

- The children write or dictate and illustrate booklets such as "Smells I Like" or "Smells I Don't Like."

- Write down a category of smells such as "Strong Smells" or "Summer Smells" and have the children write or brainstorm specific ideas.

Taste

Approach to Teaching. To build a broad base for understanding taste, begin with building vocabulary and an understanding of taste words. Many opportunities for describing tastes and using taste words should be provided; new taste words should be introduced and the meaning behind them taught. Whenever a taste word is introduced, the children should have an opportunity to taste an item that the word describes. For example, the word *sour* will have no meaning unless a child tastes something sour. It is best to provide several items that are sour tasting, such as a lemon, a grapefruit, or powdered drink mix. The following is an incomplete list of possible words describing tastes; various objects representing these tastes are easily accessible for meaning and reinforcement.

salty	tart	moldy	pleasant
soapy	sticky	bitter	hot
sour	puckery	strong	burned
sweet	lemony	juicy	offensive
spicy	unpleasant	fishy	

After experiences with these words, exciting brainstorming or creative sessions can evolve. The children can discuss or write about items, foods, or experiences related to the words. For example, they might think about, write about, or discuss everything that they can remember that tastes fishy and the experiences that they have had in tasting items that are fishy.

   Tastes can be divided into categories. Unit themes can be developed on taste or on one or more of these categories. Each day a different category of tastes could be introduced, with examples of tastes fitting into this category being provided through experiences. The following is an incomplete list of categories of tastes:

inside	fruit	bakery	holiday
outside	vegetable	sweet	seasonal
spicy	fish	bitter	bland

Concepts and Ideas for Teaching

1. Tastes may affect behavior or reactions.

   a. Lemons or chokecherries: may make mouths pucker.
   b. Salty or sweet foods: often create cravings or a desire for more, or create thirst.
   c. Bitter foods or other substances: may make one want to spit out what is being tasted.

2. The same items do not always taste the same.

   a. Apples: some might be sour, others sweet.
   b. Cakes: come in many flavors.
   c. Gum: comes in many different flavors.

3. Different items may have the same taste or flavor.

   a. Lemon-flavored items: ice cream, cakes, cookies, pie, pudding, gelatin
   b. Cherry-flavored items: lollipops, gelatin, cakes, soda pop

4. Items that look the same do not always taste the same.

   a. Salt and sugar
   b. Cinnamon, cloves, nutmeg
   c. Olive juice, prune juice, root beer

5. Tastes may be changed or modified.

   a. Cooking: foods in various stages of the cooking process, such as vegetables before and after cooking; bakery products before and after baking; overcooked foods, which may have been wet or juicy, but after overcooking have a dry or even burned taste
   b. Aging: change in the taste of foods, such as fresh bread to stale, moldy, or rancid; a fresh green-yellow banana to brown and overripe
   c. Temperature: freezing or melting of foods, which will often change the taste as well as the texture

   d. Drying: apricots, cherries, apples, jerky
   e. Additions: adding or combining ingredients, such as adding even a drop of flavoring to a bowl of frosting, causing the flavor or taste to change

This little girl is trying a new food for the first time. She does not like it, but is not sure what to do about it.

Activities and Experiences

1. Have a blindfolded child taste various foods and then guess their flavor or identity.

2. Have a blindfolded child sample various items and then group them into taste categories, or name a taste and have the child fit it into a category or categories.

3. Have the children make a taste book. For example, at the top of a large piece of poster paper write the word salty. The children can then go through magazines and cut out

pictures of salty foods or tastes for this page. The word descriptions should be included.

4. Have a child poke a toothpick into an opaque bottle or other container, withdraw the toothpick, and try to guess the contents (a food item) by tasting the flavor on the toothpick.

5. Have the children identify a food or ingredient by its taste and then think of descriptive words for the taste. Similes and metaphors can be used for creative thinking and brainstorming. These can be written down and used later for a poem.

6. Tell a "taste" story, and at various intervals in the story have the children sample actual flavors.

7. Put sensory materials into a trough, large tub, or similar container, and encourage the children to taste them. Items used might include flour, wheat, gelatin, cornmeal, cooked or uncooked rice, and cooked or uncooked macaroni.

8. Encourage the children to list tastes they like and do not like. Develop an experience chart that includes the children's likes and dislikes.

9. Have the children play tasting games, such as the identification of the various tastes in a prepared dish of blended ingredients, to increase the children's awareness of their sense of taste.

10. Brainstorm with the children the following: sweet tastes, sour tastes, bitter tastes, and salty tastes.

11. Let the children grow plants with characteristic flavorings, such as mint, onion, chives, sage, or parsley. Have the children taste these plants.

12. Prepare a food activity, but leave out the spice or seasoning. For example, make two custards, one with nutmeg and one without. Have the children taste the difference.

13. Prepare puddings that look alike but taste different: lemon, coconut, pineapple, vanilla. Have the children identify and compare the tastes.

UNIT PLAN ON TASTE

Field Trips

- Restaurant
- Picnic
- Cookout
- Canyon or park: roasting marshmallows
- Grocery store
- Child's or teacher's home: tasting or cooking activity
- Factory where food is made or packaged

Art

- Finger painting with whipped cream: tasting it before and after it turns into butter
- Vegetable printing (use vegetables that are no longer edible)

Music

- Creative movements: children pretend to milk a cow; to pull a carrot, peel it, grate it, and eat it; to eat something sweet, salty, bitter, or sour

Food

- Any food activity planned with a focus on taste: children are encouraged to taste the ingredients
- Gelatin: different groups making different flavors of red gelatin, for example, with children guessing the various flavors by taste alone
- Cooking of unusual foods
- Cooking of common foods in unusual ways

Visitors

- Nutritionist
- Baker
- Butcher
- Parent: cooking or food demonstration featuring some aspect of taste, such as talking about the tastes of various nuts; making something

using various spices, with the children tasting the spices beforehand

- Grocer

Science

- Pineapple juice colored red or green: will not change the flavor
- Children blindfolded and asked to guess various flavors by the taste or to describe the taste
- Various activities in which the children can learn that tastes can be modified by such processes as aging, adding, or melting

Language and Literacy

- The children write or dictate and then illustrate booklets such as "Tastes I Like" or "Favorite Tastes."
- The children or teacher write down a category of tastes, such as "sweet" or "salty," and the children write or brainstorm specific examples. Illustrations can be made and pages collected into a booklet.

Texture (Touch)

Approach to Teaching. Texture is an identifying quality. It is the way we describe substances or things in our environment when they are touched. Children are fascinated with different textures. It is important for children not only to identify things by the way they feel, but also to use descriptive words in explaining how things feel when touched.

Assisting children in learning about texture requires that the teacher's own awareness of touch first be increased. Teachers need to acquaint or reacquaint themselves with touch sensations that they experience but do not notice.

After the teacher's own awareness of touch has been increased, the children are more likely to be made aware of the various common and uncommon textures in their environment. Becoming more cognizant of familiar textures automatically also makes us more aware of unfamiliar or uncommon textures.

Children need to know that the word *texture* refers to the surface feeling of an item. The words *feel* and *feeling* have various meanings that may need to be clarified so that the children can understand the relationship of feeling to texture. The children's first response to *feel* or *feeling* is likely to be in terms of happy, sad, tired, or other emotion-depicting words.

Texture words are usually adjectives, but often they are used in such a way that children may understand them as nouns. For example, when pointing to a brick, the teacher may say, "This is rough." It would be clearer to say, "The brick is rough" or "That is a rough brick." The child, having had no experience with bricks, may refer to the next brick seen as a "rough." It is important, then, that texture words be clearly used as adjectives.

The child can be encouraged to use many senses when exploring and building concepts related to texture. The sense of touch should be the main sense used in learning texture, even though many teachers point to an object and say "Look, how does it feel?" Eyes are not always able to tell how objects feel; we must have had experiences in feeling or touching honey, pine needles, sheep's wool, or some kinds of plants in order to be familiar with their textures. Although textures can be described through seeing, perhaps even hearing, it is much more valuable to feel and then describe them. Even then, they are difficult to explain.

The way a child describes a particular texture will be based on previous experiences with this texture. The child who has never had experience with a wiry, stiff texture would have difficulty in describing the raw wool of sheep. Again, feeling a texture is one thing, but describing it is another. Knowing how grass feels is much easier, even for adults, than describing it in a way that can be understood by others; how much more difficult the task becomes with children, whose experiences are more limited.

To build a broad base for understanding textures, it is wise to begin by building the child's texture vocabulary. Many opportunities for describing textures and using texture words should be provided, and new texture words should be introduced and taught. Whenever a texture word is

The wool on this sheep does not feel very soft!

introduced, the child should have an opportunity to feel a texture that the word describes. For example, if the word *bumpy* is being learned, it will have no meaning unless the child feels what bumpy is, that is, unless the word takes on a meaning. The following is an incomplete list of words describing texture; various objects representing these feelings are easily accessible for meaning and reinforcement.

coarse	crunchy	prickly
rough	sticky	wiry
slimy	spongy	grainy
slick	gritty	sharp
smooth	sandy	wet
stringy	velvety	furry
hard	bumpy	dry
soft	fuzzy	slippery
crinkly	hairy	waxy

When teaching texture, begin with familiar textures and then progress to more difficult or unfamiliar ones. Children draw from previous learning experiences to build new concepts, and experiences with familiar textures will help them to understand and categorize the feelings of unfamiliar textures.

Textures can easily be narrowed down to specific categories, including words already mentioned as texture descriptions: animal textures, human textures, fabric textures, nature textures, food textures, and so on.

Concepts and Ideas for Teaching

1. Most things have a texture.
2. Single items may vary in texture.
   a. Trees: leaves, bark, limbs, buds, others
   b. Cars: tires, seats, carpet, fenders, steering wheel, and other parts
   c. Insides and outsides of items: suitcase, sandpaper, fabric, corrugated cardboard, leaf, bark, banana, orange, and so on
3. Different items may have the same texture.
   a. Glass and ice
   b. Mirror and metal
   c. Brick and cement
4. Texture may be modified.
   a. Heat: items that become stiff or even "set up"; items that dissolve or become liquid;

items that become hard, smooth, thick, or lumpy; foods, which offer many possibilities for changes in texture; items such as wood, plastic, and paper, which also change texture

b. Cold or freezing: hardening of most items; making ice cubes and discussing changes in the texture of the water as it freezes and then melts

c. Drying: change in the texture of wet clothes, fruits, paste, glue, and finger paint

d. Sanding: change of a rough surface or edge to a smooth surface

e. Additions: in food experiences, science experiences, and art activities, texture changed by adding additional ingredients

f. Pressure: application of pressure to a rough surface, creating a smooth surface (such as wet cement), or creating a rougher one

g. Aging: food in various stages showing changes in texture from hard to soft or from soft to hard; skin texture of an elderly person changed from childhood skin texture

h. Chewing: food items changing texture in the chewing process

i. Beating or whipping: whipping cream or egg whites showing changes in texture through the whipping and beating process

j. Natural changes: weather changes such as frost, wind, freezing, and erosion creating changes in texture

Activities and Experiences

1. Give each child an envelope containing items with textures that match those found on the pictures that will be shown. As each picture is shown and a particular texture is described, the child selects an item with the matching texture. For example, show a picture of a cat having a tongue made of sandpaper. Tell the child, "Put your hand in your envelope and find something that feels just like this cat's tongue." The child will need to feel the cat's tongue and be encouraged to describe how the tongue feels.

2. A texture book can be made by giving each child a piece of poster paper (all will be given the same size) and a piece exhibiting some kind of texture. The texture is pasted on the paper and then described in terms of how it feels or what else feels similar. The exact words, phrases, and sentences are recorded on the page, either by the child or the teacher, depending on the child's age level and ability. The pages can be put together with rings so that the children can enjoy their own book.

3. Place handprint shapes of various textures around the room at the children's level. When they match their hands on top of the shapes, encourage them to describe the textures that they feel.

4. Pass around materials of various textures (paper, wood, fabric), and when music or drumbeats stop, have the child describe the texture being held.

5. Pass around sacks or put them on a table or rug. Have each child put a hand inside a sack and then describe the texture and item without using visual clues.

6. Use texture collages to teach textures. Have a manila envelope with the ends stapled or sealed and one side cut open. After items of various textures have been put into the envelope, a child puts a hand into the envelope and then describes the texture of one item. The item may then be pasted on the front of the envelope. Many kinds of texture collages may be made by using items of various textures for background surfaces.

7. Put sensory materials into a trough, large tub, or similar container. Examples might be sand, soapy water, rock salt, and mud, all substances that can be used to introduce new texture words and concepts.

8. Invite a person who is blind to the classroom and have the person describe the importance of touch in the life of someone who is blind. If possible, have this person demonstrate reading Braille through using the sense of touch.

9. Have the children bring, describe, and write descriptions of items that they like to touch. Have them collect or describe items

that they do not like to touch and write the descriptions.

10. Encourage the children to brainstorm words that describe textures (suggestions were given earlier in this section). Now encourage them to find objects or items representing these textures. This makes an exciting interest center.

11. Let the children feel cornstarch and describe the texture. Now add some cold water and mix it to about the consistency of white glue. Give the children about $\frac{1}{2}$ teaspoon on the palm of their hand and let them experiment. Can they roll it into a ball? What does it feel like? Tell them to leave it on the palm of their hand without working it. What happens? How does it feel now?

12. Help the children to differentiate between how things can feel and how they can feel (emotionally) by making a list of each. The following are examples of each.

How Things Can Feel

scratchy	hot	wet
bumpy	velvety	greasy
crinkly	slivery	silky
ripply	waxy	oily
fuzzy	sticky	mushy
cold	rubbery	glassy
prickly	rough	gooey
slimy	grainy	gritty
slithery	oozy	pliable
slippery	sandy	hard

How I Can Feel (Inside)

empathetic	lucky	fearful
angry	rejected	sorry
in pain	sad	eager
depressed	hurt	pleased
delighted	joyous	happy
courageous	defensive	lonesome
fortunate	carefree	cautious
loved	sensitive	strong
excited	sympathetic	resentful

13. Put some foods with varying textures in a bag and have the children identify the textures that they feel, such as waxy, hard, bumpy, sticky, prickly, seedy, or moist. Also, they can try to identify the foods. Now take these same foods, adding additional ones if desired, and have the children taste them and describe the "eating" textures (the inside texture). Are they the same as or different from the "feeling" textures (the outside texture)?

UNIT PLAN ON TEXTURE

Art

- Melted crayon pictures
- Mud pies
- Collage items of different textures: a variety of textures to be pasted, as well as a variety of background textures
- Seed collages: seeds of different textures
- Fabric collages: fabrics of different textures
- Texture smearing
- Collage of items found on a texture walk
- Cotton swabs used for painting on different grains of sandpaper
- Finger painting with sawdust, sand, or other media added

Visitors

- Person who is blind
- Carpenter
- Butcher
- Skin diver
- Sculptor
- Cake decorator
- Person from fabric store
- Grocer
- Baker
- Upholsterer
- Two persons with different skin and/or hair textures

Food

- Hamburgers: comparison of textures before and after cooking
- Smooth and chunky peanut butter

- Candied apples
- Gelatin: quick-setting with ice cubes, to see changes as the mixture thickens
- Sponge cake
- Angel food cake
- Soups
- Root beer floats
- Cream puffs or popovers
- Apples: apple cider, applesauce, chopped in salad, apple strudel
- Potatoes prepared in various ways (raw, mashed, hash browns, fried, baked)

Music

- Creative movements that depict textures: interpreting butter melting; an ice cube freezing and then melting; a person walking on sand or rocks, walking barefoot, walking or skating on slippery, cold ice
- Texture band with such items as sandpaper blocks, different textured sticks; washboards, vegetable graters, pots and pans, corrugated cardboard, and sticks or spoons used for striking
- Shakers or containers partially filled with media of various textures: sand, water, macaroni, sawdust, and so on

Field Trips

- Sawmill
- Furniture store
- Dairy
- Zoo
- Farm
- Bakery
- Lumberyard
- Park
- Fabric store
- Greenhouse
- Upholstery shop
- Carpet store

- "Texture" walk
- Hat store
- Gravel pit

Science

- Two ice cubes with rock salt rubbed or pressed between them: change in texture of ice cubes
- Chemical garden (see Chapter 9 for recipe)
- Any experiment or experience in which there is a change in texture beforehand and afterward
- Making Styrofoam: two chemicals, purchased where Styrofoam or boats are made, are mixed together to create an immediate reaction that results in Styrofoam.
- Freezing of various substances
- Clay or play dough mixed by children
- Melting of butter, ice, and other substances
- Observation of mold growing during the aging and spoiling process of a substance such as bread

Language and Literacy

- Make texture booklets by having the children describe textures and write down their own words.
- Encourage the children to dictate and/or write similes for textures such as "as soft as . . ." or "as sticky as . . . ."

Sound (Hearing)

Approach to Teaching. Auditory discrimination is the ability to differentiate sounds, including likenesses and differences in tone, rhythm, volume, or the source of sound. Hearing is one of the five senses, and when we teach children to listen carefully, we are teaching auditory discrimination.

Children learn much about their world by listening. Infants, unable to respond to many stimuli, do obviously respond to sounds around them, both familiar and unfamiliar. Perhaps children can be helped to sharpen their awareness of sound when a teacher's own awareness of sound is refined. Considering individual differences also, it must be remembered that people do not respond to sounds in the same way. Even though some adults have lost their sensitivity to pitch (which describes whether a sound is a low, middle, or high tone), young children are extremely sensitive to pitch; in fact, a very high sound can actually cause pain. By discovering that sound occurs when something vibrates, children will often overcome fears relating to sounds, especially unfamiliar ones.

New emphasis on hearing and sound can be made by assisting children to learn by listening. For example, when children are taken across a street, they are told: "Stop and look. Do you see any cars coming?" They might also be told: "Stop and listen. Do you hear any cars coming?" A brainstorming session could be the children's responses to the question "What have you heard today?" or "What sounds do you hear right now?" In addition to this exercise, sounds could be selected and then described without using the sound word itself. Riddles could be made in which a child describes and gives clues to a sound, while the other children guess what sound is being described. Older children should be able to write these clues as riddles. For example, "This is a loud, piercing, sharp, continuous sound. It varies regularly from high to low and back. What sound is it?" (siren).

In teaching the concept of sound, or the skill of auditory perception or discrimination, teachers should give children daily experience in careful listening, in developing awareness to sound, and in describing sounds. Motivating questions should often be asked, such as "What might that sound be?" or "What else has the same sound?" or "How would you describe that sound?" Creative thinking and stimulating brainstorming emerge from explorations with similes and metaphors relating to sounds. For example, the children could describe sounds that are "as soft as _____," "as loud as," or "as shrill as _____." Adults have trite phrases such as "as quiet as a mouse," but children will come up with new ideas such as "as quiet as cutting thread," "as quiet as a snowflake hitting my nose," or "as quiet as my mother kissing me goodnight."

As teachers begin providing experiences with sounds, it is wise to start with the familiar before going on to the unfamiliar. Many adults find it difficult to identify specific sounds on the basis of hearing alone. They often use their sense of sight, along with listening, even for identifying familiar sounds. Less familiar sounds are much more difficult to recognize, not only for adults but especially for the less experienced child.

Another skill is auditory memory, the ability to remember and recall sounds. Often achievement tests for children as young as 4 or 5 years test for auditory memory. A good way to teach younger children this skill is to clap rhythm patterns and have the children clap the exact rhythms back to you. Older children can repeat concept sequences in the exact order; these can be objects, names, colors, numbers, or any variety of items.

Concepts and Ideas for Teaching

1. There are different categories of sounds. For example:

   a. Cleaning
   b. Holidays or other special days
   c. Seasonal
   d. Home
   e. Country and farm
   f. Musical
   g. Machines or automobiles
   h. Animals
   i. Nature and weather: water, wind, thunder, leaves, fire, rain
   j. Cooking
   k. Human

      (1) External: hopping, eating, chewing, scratching, snapping fingers
      (2) Internal: stomach growling, swallowing, hiccupping, burping

2. Sounds have different qualities and thus can be described in different ways, for example:

Light	Noisy
Heavy	Pleasant
Soft	Fearful
Loud	Comforting
Happy	Silly
Angry	Frightening
Sad	Exciting

3. We learn from sounds; they give us information and motivate our behavior.

   a. Hungry baby crying
   b. Something boiling over
   c. Time of day: the clock chiming; children outside playing, indicating that school is over and it is late afternoon
   d. School dismissal: school bell
   e. Someone at the door or waiting outside: doorbell, knock, honking horn
   f. People outside: walking sounds, vocal sounds, laughing
   g. Activity of parent: pounding nails, washing windows, preparing dinner, running sewing machine
   h. Feelings of animals or people: whining, growling, laughing, crying
   i. Emotional quality of such things as movies, homes, music, television

4. The same sounds can influence or affect people differently.

   a. Alarm clock: pleasant if it rings on the morning of a long-awaited vacation, but unpleasant on a morning when you want to stay in bed
   b. Telephone: unpleasant in the middle of the night, but pleasant when a call is expected from someone special

5. We can hear things we do not see.

   a. Wind
   b. Jet breaking the sound barrier
   c. Stomach growling
   d. Cat purring
   e. Furnace clicking on
   f. Voices in another room

6. Some things are so soft that they cannot be heard.

   a. Snowflakes falling
   b. Feathers falling
   c. Eyes blinking
   d. Worms crawling
   e. Butterflies flying
   f. Foods baking

7. Some sounds are alike.

   a. Thunder and fireworks
   b. Dog barking and seal barking

   c. Telephone and alarm clock
   d. Hair dryer and vacuum cleaner

8. The same items sometimes make different sounds.

   a. Child
   b. Musical instrument
   c. Dog
   d. Cars

9. Sound travels both long and short distances.

   a. Through systems of communication such as the telephone, telegraph, radio, television, and satellite
   b. By walkie-talkie: on tightly stretched wire or string
   c. Through a tabletop: a child with an ear placed on the table can easily hear sounds made on the underside at the opposite end of the table.
   d. Through vibrations: a rather abstract concept for young children, but can be introduced by feeling a tuning fork, striking a tuning fork and then putting it in water, or feeling musical instruments that have definite vibrating qualities.

Activities and Experiences

1. Tape-record sounds and have the children determine what the sounds are. The sounds selected should be familiar ones and should be heard long enough on the tape so that the children can hear them adequately. Some sounds should be made twice: for example, a squeaky door. The following are kinds of sounds that can be used with this activity:

   a. Liquid boiling
   b. Food frying
   c. Batter being stirred
   d. Carrot being peeled
   e. Doorbell ringing
   f. Oven timer buzzing
   g. Water running
   h. Toilet flushing
   i. Car starting, windshield wipers working, seat belts being fastened, gears being shifted

j. Traffic moving

k. Dog barking, other familiar animal sounds

l. Telephone ringing

   There are commercial records or tapes of these and other sounds; check your library's audio department.

2. The preceding activity could be modified if the teacher performs the task that makes the sound. The teacher could make the sound behind a screen; if the children cannot guess the sound, it can be made in front of the screen so that the children can watch the task being performed and listen to the accompanying sound.

3. Have the children listen to a particular sound and then suggest several adjectives or descriptive words for the sound.

4. Encourage the children to tell stories containing numerous sounds. This activity is especially effective at Halloween time.

5. Set out pairs of containers, such as empty film containers, that the children cannot see through. Put equal amounts of media in pairs so that when children shake matching pairs, they hear the same sounds. Media or items might include wheat, rice, beans, sugar, paper clips, beads, sand, or seeds. With older children, more pairs can be included.

6. Allow the children to feel and/or see things that vibrate, such as a rubber band stretched between two nails and plucked or a radio, timer, music box, or simple machine that vibrates as it runs. Ask the children what they feel and hear.

7. Assign the children to cooperative learning groups, and give each group a small, wrapped, jewelry-sized box. Each box could contain a small, rubber ball; a flat object such as a coin, paper clip, or washer; a marble; and a nail, screw, or similar item. Have each group try to discover what the four items are in the box by listening carefully as they shake and tap the box at their ears. Each box could have the same items, or they could each have different items. After they have guessed and explored, have the children open the box and see what is in it. If just the lids of the boxes are wrapped in wrapping paper, the boxes can be tied and used again without having to be rewrapped each time.

8. Have the children compare loud and soft sounds. Ask, "Can the same sound be either loud or soft? How about a whistle or pounding with a hammer—can they be either loud or soft?" Tap softly on a wooden table and describe the sound. Then have the children put one ear to the table and cover their other ear. Now tap the table again. Ask, "Was the sound loud with the ear close to the table?"

9. Play a pretend sound game. Have a child pretend to be something that makes a particular sound (without making the sound). As the children guess what the child is, instead of saying the name of the object, they should try to make the sound of the object. This game can be played with a focus on particular categories, such as machines, animals, or weather.

10. Obtain a set of six or eight bottles of the same size and shape. Fill them with water to various levels. Have the children strike each bottle with a spoon and compare the sounds; order the bottles from lowest to highest sounds; and blow across the tops of the bottles to compare the sounds (if the tops are narrow).

11. Have the children strike various lengths of conduit pipe or the various-sized strikers on a child's xylophone and compare the sounds.

12. Have some children try to describe particular sounds with words (without imitating the sound). Then have the other children try to guess what the sound is. For example, they might try to describe a typewriter sound, a toilet flushing, boiling water, or a siren.

13. Have the children brainstorm and/or describe their favorite or happiest sounds and their most frightening or unpleasant sounds. Write their responses on a chart or collect them in an illustrated booklet.

14. Tape-record each child's voice. Let the children listen to the recordings and discuss the differences.

15. Make a simple telephone system using two tin cans or paper cups and string, wire, or thread. Punch two small holes in the bottom

of each can (cup) and fasten the ends of the wire (string) to the can. Stretch the system out and have a child at each end of the wire with the can. The system functions best when the wire is tight; it should not be allowed to touch anything between the cans. The wire can be several yards long. As a child talks into the can, the sound waves travel from that can along the wire to the other can, where the sound is reproduced.

UNIT PLAN ON SOUND AND PITCH

Visitors

- Person to play musical instrument: one instrument making many sounds; many instruments making the same sound
- Ensemble from portion of band or orchestra
- Custodian to bring in materials, equipment, and supplies that make various sounds
- Vocalist
- Baby: comparison of baby's sounds with the sounds that the children in the classroom make; listening to sounds made by the baby's equipment and toys
- Parent to bring in materials or equipment relating to job, hobby, or home activities: electric shaver, power tools, hammer and nails, and so on; pitch of parent's voice compared to that of children's own voices also noted
- Tap dancer
- Garbage collector with truck
- Pet store owner or anyone with animals that make sounds
- Plumber
- Mechanic
- Native American dancer
- Piano tuner

Field Trips

- Farm
- School where music room, band, or orchestra could be visited
- Pet shop
- Zoo
- Service station or automobile repair garage
- Outside walk to listen to sounds of nature in the everyday environment
- Bird refuge
- Factory: machine sounds
- Office
- Music store
- Sawmill
- Fire station
- Construction or building site
- Barbershop
- Cafeteria: cooking sounds

Science

- String and cans to make walkie-talkie
- Dry-cell circuit: hooked up to make a buzzing sound or ring a bell
- Lengths and widths of strings on musical instruments (and bottles of water at various levels): variation of the pitch of the sound made when they are plucked or struck
- Experiments with a tuning fork
- Experiences with sounds traveling or vibrating
- Activities with elastics

Food

- Popcorn
- Rice crispy squares
- Grilled or broiled hamburgers or other foods
- Boiled vegetables or other foods
- Chopped foods
- Shredded foods such as cabbage for making coleslaw
- Homemade root beer

Art

- Decorated sound shakers
- Other instruments made and decorated: tambourines, hummers, drums

Music

- Making any kind of musical instrument for musical band or orchestra

- Shakers made by groups of children, with each group using a different medium; for a music activity using the shakers, the first verse of a song to be accompanied by one group whose shakers have a particular sound, and the chorus accompanied by another group whose shakers have another sound; alternatively, various parts of a record accompanied by individual groups

Literacy

- At Halloween, write or dictate and illustrate a booklet titled "Spooky Sounds."

- Develop a chart or booklet, with or without illustrations, titled "Sounds We Like—Sounds We Don't Like." Have each child do a page for "Sounds We Like" and a page for "Sounds We Don't Like." The pages can be illustrated and then described with a written or dictated sentence.

TEACHING ABOUT ANIMALS

Animals make excellent visitors to the classroom, where children observe, investigate, learn about, and care for them.

> A genuine concern for . . . creatures and their habitats can promote great fulfillment in one's individual life and a sense of caring for other people (Wilson, 1995b, p. 7).

Cassidy had missed a couple of days of school because she had the flu. During the time she was gone, the classroom had acquired a hamster. Cassidy explained to the teacher, "If him gets sick, him will have to puke!"

Categories of animals appropriate for indoor interest centers include pets, some farm animals, fish, birds, and insects. Through studying about insects, curiosity replaces fear and squeamishness, and concern for their safety and protection replaces the urge to squash them (Jaelitza, 1996).

"We . . . can remember the wonder of our world when we allow children to pursue their investigations without our being too preoccupied with concerns for order and cleanliness or the touching of small crawling and wriggling creatures" (Tomich, 1996, p. 28). Some traditional favorites are tadpoles and frogs, turtles, gerbils, hamsters, guinea pigs, goldfish, caterpillars and butterflies, chicks that hatch, rabbits, and hermit crabs. Children also enjoy ant farms, bug cages, and bird feeders. Individually made bird feeders can be taken home, where they further extend children's interest and understanding through continued observation and feeding of the birds.

The world of animals is a big world indeed, and many units of study can develop from this single category. There are numerous forms of animal life, ranging in size from animals so small that they cannot be seen without the aid of a microscope to those that are much larger than humans.

Many of the concepts, projects, and units developed may result from the children's inquiries about particular animals or categories of animals or because the children have brought pets or other animals into the classroom. Children will especially enjoy doing a project study on a pet that is their own.

A well-planned animal unit or project should include, if possible, a field trip to visit the animals being studied, a visitor who will bring animals into the classroom, or animals that can stay in the classroom for study and observation. Remember the importance of the firsthand sensory experience. It is difficult to imagine a unit on eggs and chickens without including a visit to a poultry farm; having eggs incubated and hatched right in the classroom; or having chicks, hens, or roosters in the classroom for study and firsthand observation. Even when there are actual animals for classroom observation, misconceptions may occur.

Lyn had been watching the incubator as the chickens hatched from eggs. When only one more egg remained to hatch, Lyn inquired, "But when is the mother going to come out?"

After the experience of having a live angora sheep on the playground, the children discussed it and compared it to pictures of sheep with which they were more familiar. However, one child told his mother as she was picking him up from school that day, "We had a real live buffalo come to our class today."

After several days' experiences with guinea pigs, one child commented, "Baby pigs are guinea pigs." Another child stated that "baby pigs are skinny pigs."

As animal units, projects, and experiences are planned, do not be afraid to develop units around the most common animals. For example, many new concepts can be taught and many ideas reinforced and clarified through units on dogs, fish, or cows. Many children are familiar with these animals and may even have some for pets; however, new concepts can be built on those already understood, and broader meanings can be obtained. Children can also be introduced to generally less familiar animals, such as tadpoles, guinea pigs, and lizards.

Categorization games will help children to distinguish animals from other groups, such as toys, foods, furniture, people, and plants. Even more specifically, animal picture cards can be sorted into categories, such as insects, farm animals, circus animals, pets, animals that live in water, birds, and animals that live underground; many additional categories could be developed as well. A set of animal pictures or flash cards can also be used for naming the animals. Pictures can be found in such places as magazines, stickers purchased from stationery stores, or discarded workbooks. Whether approached in general areas or in specific projects or units, animals make excellent choices for study.

The following is a list of suggested animal unit themes. It is not meant to be inclusive, since the ideas and themes are almost endless, limited only by the teacher's own creative thinking and planning. Also, a unit need not necessarily emerge from each theme; it is possible to use one of the suggested themes for a science experience. For example, a teacher might not wish to do a whole unit on the life cycle of tadpole to frog, but it would provide an excellent experience for the science center or as a single science activity.

Note: The general theme is in boldface, and the subthemes listed may be included in the general unit of study or may stand alone as a project or unit of study.

Farm animals

Cows

Pigs

Rabbits

Horses

Ducks

Chicks, hens, roosters

Sheep

Goats

Turkeys

Zoo animals

Elephants

Monkeys

Lions

Tigers

Seals

Penguins

Bears

Jungle animals
Circus animals
Desert animals
Ocean animals

Fish

Shellfish

Mammals (whales and dolphins)

Pets (domestic animals)

Birds

Dogs

Cats

Hamsters

Guinea pigs

Gerbils

Fish

Turtles

Insects

Bees

Ants

Butterflies

Flies

Bugs and bottles make great companions when one is learning about insects and nature.

Worm

Birds (perhaps specific birds common to the locale)

Tadpoles and frogs (life cycle)

Animal babies

Animal homes

Hibernation

Animals that live in trees

Animals that live underground

Animals that lived long ago

The following animals are suggested for classroom observation:

Hamsters	Worms
Guinea pigs	Insects of various kinds
Gerbils	Turtles
Fish	Mice
Snails	Lizards
Rabbits	Chickens
Ant (farm)	Birds

Concepts and Ideas for Teaching

1. Animals have various kinds of physical characteristics.

   a. Various body parts that often serve important purposes

      Wings: how many?
      Legs: how many?
      Claws
      Shell
      Eyes
      Tail
      Mouth
      Feet
         (study footprints)
      Nose
      Arms
      Beak
      Antennae
      Lungs
      Gills
      Backbone
         (or no backbone)
      Other

   b. Various body coverings that have characteristic textures and serve different purposes.

Fur	Shell
Skin	Hair
Feathers	Scales

2. Animals move in various ways, some in only one way and others in several ways.

   a. Walk
   b. Swim
   c. Fly
   d. Crawl
   e. Have wings and do or do not use them for flying
   f. Use a fin or tail for moving

3. Animals live in various places or environments and in various kinds of homes.

   a. Trees
   b. Desert
   c. Jungle
   d. Farm
   e. Zoo
   f. On the land

g. Underneath the ground
h. Near garbage
i. In cold climates
j. In water but not on land
k. In water but also on land
l. Change in habitat in particular seasons

4. Animals eat various kinds of things.

   a. Plants
   b. Insects
   c. Nuts
   d. Other animals
   e. Garbage
   f. Wood

5. Animals reproduce and care for their young in various ways.

   a. Give birth to live young
   b. Lay eggs: with hard shells or without shells
   c. Abandon young after giving birth
   d. Feed milk to young (mammals)
   e. Keep young nearby to nurture and care for
   f. Usually have multiple offspring
   g. Usually have single offspring
   h. Provide the food for the offspring

6. Animal babies have different characteristics in relation to their parents. Animals go through life cycles while changing and growing.

   a. May or may not look like the parent
   b. Sometimes have identifying names
   c. May eat different things or the same things as the parent
   d. May or may not move in the same way as the parent
   e. May or may not sound the same as the parent
   f. Change as they grow

7. Animals may make characteristic sounds; the sounds may have a particular purpose.

8. Some animals are extinct, and we learn about them from fossils.

   a. Dinosaurs: the largest land animals that ever lived on the earth
   b. Mammoths
   c. Saber-toothed tigers

9. Some animals are make-believe, such as dragons.

10. Many animals are useful to humans.

    a. Animals that provide food for humans: cows, chickens, pigs, turkeys, deer, fish
    b. Animals that provide clothing or apparel for humans: sheep; animals that provide furs; silkworms; animals that provide leather for making shoes, purses, wallets
    c. Animals that are friends or pets to humans
    d. Animals that eat other animals that are harmful or a nuisance to humans: snakes eat mice, cats eat mice, birds eat insects such as grasshoppers
    e. Animals that eat plants that are harmful or a nuisance to humans: livestock eat mustard weed, which is harmful to humans
    f. Animals that provide humans with entertainment and recreation

       (1) Animals that are hunted for sporting purposes, as well as meat: deer, elk, fish, rabbits, pheasants, ducks, geese
       (2) Zoo and circus animals, which are always enjoyable to observe

    g. Animals that work for humans

       (1) In some parts of the world, animals provide transportation: horses, donkeys, camels, dogs
       (2) Dogs that help to herd sheep and cattle
       (3) Dogs that are trained as seeing-eye dogs for people who are blind
       (4) Dogs that are used in detective work or serve as guards
       (5) Cattle, mules, and horses, which do farm work

11. Many animals are harmful to humans.

    a. Animals that are dangerous if they are threatened by humans
    b. Animals whose bites are poisonous: coral snake, black widow spiders
    c. Animals whose bites may cause disease, such as rabies or malaria

12. Many animals are a nuisance to humans. Some animals eat plants or animals that are

important to humans (insects such as wee-vils eat wheat and other grains); coyotes eat sheep and chickens; bears eat sheep.

13. Some animals may be useful, while also being either harmful or a nuisance to humans. Range cattle are useful, but be-cause of trampling and overgrazing, the possibility of erosion increases.

14. Animals adapt in various ways to seasonal changes.

    a. Animals that hibernate: fish, frogs, bears, snakes
    b. Animals that migrate: birds, geese
    c. Animals that acquire a heavier fur or covering: cows, horses, sheep, dogs

15. Animals respond to temperature in vari-ous ways.

    a. Dogs and other animals that pant to cool themselves
    b. Pigs, which shunt their blood away from the skin surface in cold weather, but are more susceptible to death in hot weather
    c. Bees, which cluster together in masses to keep warm in cold weather

Activities and Experiences

1. The most beneficial kinds of activities and ex-periences with animals are firsthand. Take field trips to places where animals are found or bring animals to the classroom. When animals are in the classroom, children need to be told exactly what they can and cannot do with them and, if the animals can be handled, how to do that kindly, gently, and properly. The safety of both the children and the animals should be considered. Teachers should check their program or school policies to see whether there are any restrictions or regula-tions that need to be observed. When the ani-mals are in the classroom, the children should have the opportunity to feed them and care for their needs. In this way, the children learn that all animals need food, but that they do not all eat the same kinds of foods. The children also learn that all animals need water and air.

A favorite observation activity with ani-mals is observing the life cycles of particular animals such as the frog (tadpole to frog), monarch butterfly (caterpillar to chrysalis to butterfly), or chicken (egg to chick). When-ever possible, return animals to their natural environment.

2. Make a bug cage. Obtain two large lids (at least 3 inches in diameter) of exactly the same size or use two small cake pans. Obtain a piece of heavy, stiff screen about 8 to 10 inches in length and wide enough to fit in-side the circumference of the lids or pans plus several inches for overlap. Roll the screen to fit inside the lids or pans exactly, and then, with string or yarn, "sew" around the overlap to hold the screen securely in the roll that will fit inside the lids or pans. Now mix a small amount of plaster of Paris and pour it into one of the lids or pans. Then immediately put one end of the roll of screen into that lid or pan. Hold it until the plaster of Paris dries. A twig or stick may be stuck into the plaster of Paris before it sets so that there will be something for the bugs to crawl on. When bugs are caught in the cage, simply put the other lid or pan on the top of the roll.

3. Collect pictures of many kinds of animals and glue them to cards. They can be sorted into such categories as farm or zoo animals, animals that fly or that do not fly, animals that provide food for humans, and so on. Pass these cards out to the children. Give a char-acteristic of animals and have the children raise their card (or cards) of animals that have that characteristic. For example, say "Hold up your animal(s) if it eats other ani-mals" or "Hold up your animal(s) if it lives in the jungle."

4. Concentrate on a specific animal or group of animals, and provide as many firsthand expe-riences as possible with this animal or group and the characteristics involved.

5. Make animal scrapbooks. Collect as much in-formation or as many pictures as possible for each animal in the scrapbook. The scrapbook could relate to a particular group of animals,

The children in preschool were able to observe the stages from a caterpillar to a butterfly. This butterfly would crawl around on the floor, furniture, and children!

such as pets, or it could be for animals in general. Encourage literacy by writing something about each animal.

6. Present animal riddles. Either the teacher or the children can give the clues for a particular animal. The children guess what animal answers the riddle. These can be written in an animal riddle book, with additional riddles added during the year.

7. Use animal stick puppets for dramatizations, for demonstrating animal sounds and other characteristics, or for categorizing by characteristics.

8. Make plaster molds of animal footprints by mixing plaster of Paris (it sets up quickly, so mix it just as you are preparing to make the mold) and putting a cardboard rim around the footprint. (The cardboard rim could be the rim of a small box such as a jewelry box. Cut several sizes out beforehand.) Place the rim around the footprint and pour plaster into the impression. When dry, remove the plaster and return it to the classroom to classify and label it. Put a picture and the name of the animal next to the footprint cast.

9. Make written or dictated observations of animals that the children see or visit. For example, after visiting a zoo or farm, each child could dictate or write about one animal that he or she has carefully observed. The children could illustrate their observations and these could be put together into a class booklet. First- and second-grade children could add research to their observation report. If the animal is in the classroom, a language experience chart could be recorded on observations made of the animal each day.

10. Following an experience with an animal, have the children help to make a web to review what has been learned. For an example, see Figure 11–1.

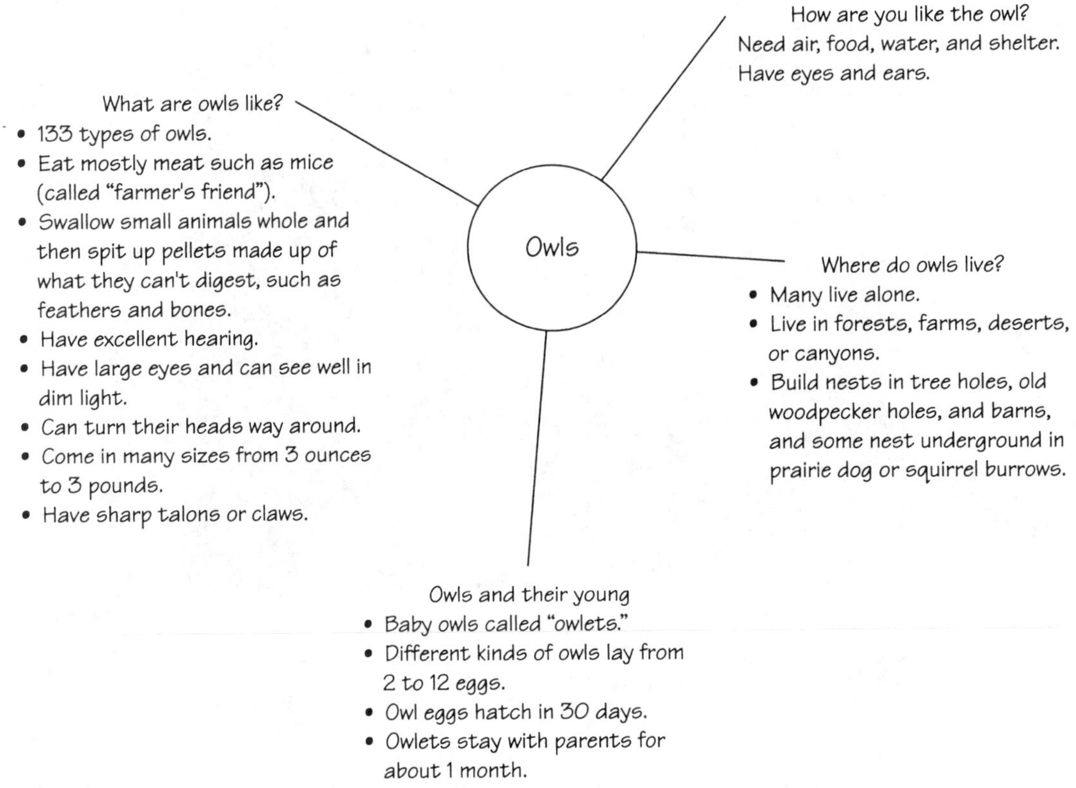

How are you like the owl?
Need air, food, water, and shelter.
Have eyes and ears.

What are owls like?
- 133 types of owls.
- Eat mostly meat such as mice (called "farmer's friend").
- Swallow small animals whole and then spit up pellets made up of what they can't digest, such as feathers and bones.
- Have excellent hearing.
- Have large eyes and can see well in dim light.
- Can turn their heads way around.
- Come in many sizes from 3 ounces to 3 pounds.
- Have sharp talons or claws.

Owls

Where do owls live?
- Many live alone.
- Live in forests, farms, deserts, or canyons.
- Build nests in tree holes, old woodpecker holes, and barns, and some nest underground in prairie dog or squirrel burrows.

Owls and their young
- Baby owls called "owlets."
- Different kinds of owls lay from 2 to 12 eggs.
- Owl eggs hatch in 30 days.
- Owlets stay with parents for about 1 month.

FIGURE 11–1
Sample Web: What Has Been Learned About Owls

11. Compare one animal to another or one group of animals to another group of animals.

    a. Similarities
    b. Differences

12. Have the children compare an animal or group of animals to themselves.

    a. Similarities
    b. Differences

Unit and Project Plans on Animals

Many different unit, project, and lesson plans could be done on animals or concepts relating to animals; the following serve only as examples, and they should spark your imagination and creative planning for other units and lesson plans relating to animals, such as those on hibernation, baby animals, or animal homes.

The following are unit and lesson plans on some animal themes. Whenever possible, select unit and lesson plans that will provide experiences with actual animals. Again, be aware that they can be either general (such as zoo or farm animals) or specific (such as cows, bees, frogs, or animal babies) and that they make great projects for children to plan.

UNIT PLAN ON FARM ANIMALS

Art

- Farm mobiles

- Farm animal collages

- Salt or oil-based clay farm animals

- Finger paint, with media such as oats or wheat: food for farm animals
- Farm animal sack puppets

Field Trips

- Farm
- Grocery store, to look for products from farm animals
- Butcher shop

Visitors

- Farmer
- Someone to bring in a pet that is a farm animal
- Storyteller to tell a farm animal story
- Grocer to bring in farm animal products
- Parent to cook a farm animal product

Food

- Milkshakes
- Eggs prepared any way
- Ice cream
- Bacon and tomato sandwiches
- Hamburgers or hamburger used in any way
- Chicken prepared in any way
- Turkey prepared in any way
- Jerky or salami pizza
- Various preparations of pork, lamb, or fish

Science

- Animal corner with live farm animals, eggs incubating, baby farm animals
- What farm animals eat
- Physical characteristics of some farm animals
- Farm animal babies: what they look like, what they are called, how they are cared for, what they eat
- What happens to farm animals in summer and in winter
- Small samples of food products provided by farm animals

Music

- Creative movements dealing with farm animals
- Paper cups decorated and used as rhythm accompaniment to songs about animals walking or running
- Familiar fairy tales sung and dramatized

Language and Literacy

- Poetry and stories relating to farm animals
- Tape of farm animal sounds; identification of the animals by the children
- Puppets or felt figures of farm animals made by the children; stories dramatized about farm animals; stories made up using animal figures
- Dramatized nursery rhymes, poems, and fairy tales relating to farm animals
- Open-ended stories, with children telling the endings
- Display of pictures of farm animals (Say "I went to the farm and saw a _____"; let the child select a picture and talk about that animal.)
- Slides of farm animals, with discussion about them
- Writing or telling and illustrating stories about favorite farm animals

UNIT PLAN ON BEES

Art

- Bee mobiles: bees and beehive painted or colored; holes punched in hive, and bees hung all around it with string
- Bees made with Styrofoam base and materials such as pipe cleaners
- Bees made and decorated, using toilet-paper roll as base

Field Trips

- Bee farm
- Honey distributor

- Flower garden where bees are collecting nectar to make honey
- Library

Visitors

- Parent or grandparent to make something using honey: honey candy, honey butter
- Beekeeper: description of job, telling how the hive is smoked in order to obtain honey; demonstration of a beekeeping outfit or uniform, including veil, gloves, and clips around trousers to prevent bees from getting inside pants; equipment used, including smoker machine, bee brush, knife for opening hives, and beehive frames
- Someone to show honeycomb

Food

- Honey butter
- Honey candy or cookies
- Muffins with honey butter (see recipe)
- Honey bread (see recipe)

Recipe for Muffins and Honey Butter

2 cups baking mix   1 cup milk
$\frac{1}{4}$ cup sugar $\frac{1}{4}$ cup oil
1 egg

Mix baking mix and sugar. Add beaten egg to milk and oil; then add this liquid to the dry ingredients. Stir until moistened; the batter will be lumpy. Fill greased muffin tins two-thirds full. Bake at 400°F for about 20 minutes. Serve with a mixture of butter and honey.

Recipe for Honey Bread

$1\frac{1}{2}$ cups honey $1\frac{1}{2}$ tsp salt
$1\frac{1}{2}$ cups milk $\frac{1}{3}$ cup oil
$\frac{3}{4}$ cup sugar   2 eggs
$3\frac{3}{4}$ cups flour   2 tsp vanilla
$1\frac{1}{2}$ tsp soda

Bring honey, milk, and sugar to a boil and cool the mixture. Mix dry ingredients together; add oil, eggs, and vanilla. Add cooled liquid mixture and beat for 2 minutes. Put in greased loaf pans. Bake at 325°F for about 1 hour.

Science

- Science corner or table with pictures of bees, beehives, and beekeepers doing their jobs; display of objects such as honeycomb, equipment beekeeper uses, bee eggs, bees, and bee products
- Science discussions, experiments, and observations focusing on the following topics: members of the bee family (queen, workers, and drones and their various functions within the hive); making of honey; characteristics of bees; honeycomb (six-sided wall cells in the hive that bees use for storing food and as a place for hatching young bees); collecting nectar from flowers to make honey; bees' role in pollinating flowers and trees (use pictures and any visual material available)
- Discussion of first-aid treatment for bee stings; discussion of why bees sting people and animals

Music

- Creative movements and dramatics relating to bees: hatching from eggs, flying, moving about in the hive, searching for nectar in flowers
- Songs and records relating to bees

Language and Literacy

- Stories and poems relating to bees
- Making bee puppets or flannel-board figures, with the children telling stories or dramatizing them
- Slides of bees, with discussion and storytelling
- Films and filmstrips relating to bees
- Tape of bee sounds; discussion
- Story writing about bees

UNIT PLAN ON BIRDS

Art

- Finger painting, with birdseed added
- Feather painting
- Feather collages
- Decoration of eggs (made from plastic colored eggs)

- Bird collages or bird stickers from stationery store
- Birdseed collages
- Decorate birdseed shakers with birdseed and/or other materials
- Use of the outline or form of birds on large sheets of butcher paper; children paint and/or make collages with them
- Bird puppets

Food

- Any food activities using poultry products: chicken, turkey, or eggs

Field Trips

- Pet store
- Bird refuge
- Walk to observe birds and look for birds' nests
- Museum or university ornithology department to observe stuffed birds
- Poultry farm
- Aviary
- Home where pet birds may be observed

Visitors

- Pet store owner
- Ornithologist
- Bird watcher
- Child or other member of family who can bring a pet bird
- Storyteller to tell stories about birds
- Parent to cook a poultry product
- Person who knows birdcalls; demonstration
- Someone who owns a talking bird such as a parrot

Science

- Science discussions, experiments, and observations focusing on the following topics: kinds of birds, sizes of birds, characteristics of birds (such as having feathers and having been hatched from eggs), colors of birds, birds that migrate, birds common to the locale, bird food
- Study of bird eggs: sizes, colors, and so on
- Study of bird's nests: sizes, materials used in construction, matching of specific birds with their characteristic nests
- Bird feeders; a simple one is a pinecone, with flour and water mixed into a thick paste and stuffed into the pinecone, which is then rolled in birdseed and hung in a tree with a piece of string
- Slides of birds; discussion
- Tape recording of bird sounds from the library or made by teacher

Music

- Musical games about birds
- Songs about birds
- Creative dramatics relating to birds: hatching from the egg, drying feathers, swimming, flying, hunting for worms
- Records lending themselves to dramatization of bird characteristics and actions

Language and Literacy

- Pictures of birds; discussion and storytelling
- Stories and poetry about birds
- Puppets or flannel-board figures, with children dramatizing or telling stories
- Display of pictures of birds with a discussion beginning "I saw a bird that . . . ," with individual children selecting a picture and telling about this bird by finishing the statement. These accounts could be written and collected into a book.
- Dramatization of stories, poems, and songs relating to birds

UNIT PLAN ON FISH

Art

- Fish made from a small brown-paper sack stuffed with newspaper, tied with string on the open end so that it resembles a fishtail, then painted or decorated

- Fish drawn by each child and put on an overhead or opaque projector for enlarging (older children can trace their own) and then painted or decorated (makes a creative bulletin board)
- Fish made and decorated and then put behind blue cellophane paper to create the illusion of a fishpond or aquarium
- Seafood collage made by cutting types of fish that we eat and fish products from newspaper grocery advertisements

Visitors

- Parent to cook fish by any method
- Parent to bring in fishing gear and demonstrate its use, perhaps cooking fish as well
- Fish and game officer
- Person from a hatchery, cannery, or restaurant
- Grocer to bring in several varieties of fish, perhaps allowing the children to taste some
- Someone to bring in slides of fishing trips
- Someone to bring in pet fish

Music

- Creative dramatics or movements representing fishing or moving like fish
- Shakers made from tuna fish or shrimp cans; can be decorated with seashells

Field Trips

- Fish hatchery
- Fish cannery
- Sporting goods store or department store to see fishing gear and supplies, such as salmon eggs and fishing flies
- Pet store with several varieties of fish
- Fish market, to see various cuts of fish and to notice fish odors
- Restaurant that serves fish
- Grocery store

Food

- Fish burgers
- Baked, fried, broiled fish
- Casseroles
- Fish patties: salmon, tuna
- Fish salads: tuna, shrimp
- Sandwiches
- Fish and chips
- Chowder

Science

- Kinds of fish and where they live
- Parts of fish: scales, fins, gills, and so on
- What fish eat
- How fish breathe
- Hibernation of some fish
- Spawning habits of some fish
- Aquarium placed in classroom
- Tasting and comparing of various kinds of fish
- Fish placed in a trough or large container for observation and touching
- Characteristics of a specific kind of fish, such as salmon

Language and Literacy

- Slides, pictures, stories, poetry, songs, films relating to fish
- Teacher-made puppets or flannel-board fish characters for children to dramatize or tell stories about
- Stories about fish: tell or illustrate
- Book, *Swimmy* (L. Lionni, Pantheon, New York, 1968)

UNIT PLAN ON PETS

For this unit it is suggested that one particular pet be chosen for each day's focus, with concepts relating to that pet brought into the discussion. The children should be able to handle the pets, feed them, and care for them. Baby pets will also add interest for the children.

Art

- Decoration of rocks to resemble a desired pet, using felt scraps, hobby-store eyes, beans, fabric scraps, and other media
- Sock pets: child's sock decorated with felt scraps, yarn, and other fabrics
- Sack-puppet pets
- Pet collages: pictures of pets cut from magazines or animal pet stickers purchased from stationery stores
- Salt dough or salt clay pets
- Collages using dry foods for pets, such as birdseed

Field Trips

- Pet store
- Home where pets can be observed
- Zoo
- Animal hospital

Visitors

- Pet store owner
- Family member of student to share family pet
- Storyteller to tell pet stories
- Veterinarian
- Zookeeper

Food

- Sandwiches cut with pet-animal cookie cutters
- Green salad, with discussion of pets that enjoy vegetables: sesame seeds sprinkled on salad, followed by discussion of which pets enjoy eating seeds
- Bread dough shaped into a favorite pet

Science

- Science discussion, experiments, and observations focusing on the following topics: kinds of

pets; sizes of pets; characteristics such as footprints, colors, sounds, diet, sleeping habits
- Care and needs of particular pets
- Pet babies: appearance, care required, diet

Music

- Songs about pets
- Creative dramatics relating to pets: how they move, what they do during the day, how they respond to friends, how they respond to enemies

Language and Literacy

- Slides of pets; discussion
- Pets or pictures of current or former pets brought by the children; sharing and discussion
- Puppet or flannel-board figures; dramatization or storytelling by the children; discussion of particular pets by the children
- Tape recording of pet sounds, with the children naming the pet and discussing the sounds that it makes and why
- Stories and poetry about pets
- Game in which individual children select a particular pet and then describe it so that other children can guess which pet has been described
- Game in which a child leaves the room, class members select a particular pet, and then the child returns and tries to discover which pet was selected by asking yes or no questions
- Children illustrate a favorite pet and then dictate or write something about this pet. Children's stories are made into a class booklet.

PROJECT PLAN ON DINOSAURS

For a project plan on dinosaurs, see Figure 11–2.

TEACHING ABOUT PLANTS

As units of study relating to plants are selected, the teacher should utilize the appropriate seasons and climates and select for study the plants that are most common to the children's surroundings and

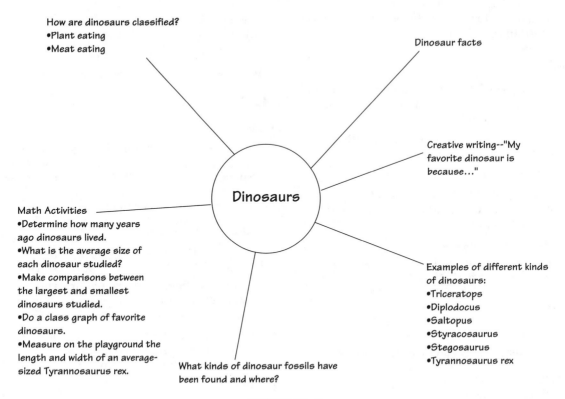

How are dinosaurs classified?
•Plant eating
•Meat eating

Dinosaur facts

Creative writing--"My
favorite dinosaur is
because..."

Dinosaurs

Math Activities
•Determine how many years
ago dinosaurs lived.
•What is the average size of
each dinosaur studied?
•Make comparisons between
the largest and smallest
dinosaurs studied.
•Do a class graph of favorite
dinosaurs.
•Measure on the playground the
length and width of an average-
sized Tyrannosaurus rex.

What kinds of dinosaur fossils have
been found and where?

Examples of different kinds
of dinosaurs:
•Triceratops
•Diplodocus
•Saltopus
•Styracosaurus
•Stegosaurus
•Tyrannosaurus rex

FIGURE 11–2
Child's Project Plan for Dinosaur Study

locality. Where possible, give the children actual experiences with plants.

Plants could be approached as a general theme or unit. However, specific areas such as seeds, vegetables, fruits, trees, wheat, or flowers also provide appropriate units of study. Categorization games help children to distinguish plants from other groups, such as animals, people, or toys. Even more specifically, plant picture cards could be sorted into categories, such as vegetables, fruits, flowers, and trees. The cards could also be used as flash cards for naming the specific plants. Pictures of plants can be found in magazines, stickers purchased from stationery stores, discarded workbooks, or seed packets.

The following is a list of suggested plant unit themes. It is not meant to be inclusive, since ideas and themes are limited only by the teacher's own creative thinking and planning. Furthermore, a unit need not necessarily result from each idea or theme; for example, a suggested theme could be

used for a science experience supporting any unrelated unit of study.

Plants	Fruits (also specific)
Seeds	Vegetables (also specific)
Nuts	Plants as food for humans
Wheat	Plants that grow in water
Trees	Flowers
Wood	Berries

After a plant unit such as pumpkins is presented, the children can help complete a web such as the one illustrated in Figure 11-3.

Concepts and Ideas for Teaching

1. Most plants need air, light, water, and food in order to grow.

2. We eat different parts of plants.

   a. Roots (turnips, carrots, radishes, parsnips, onions)

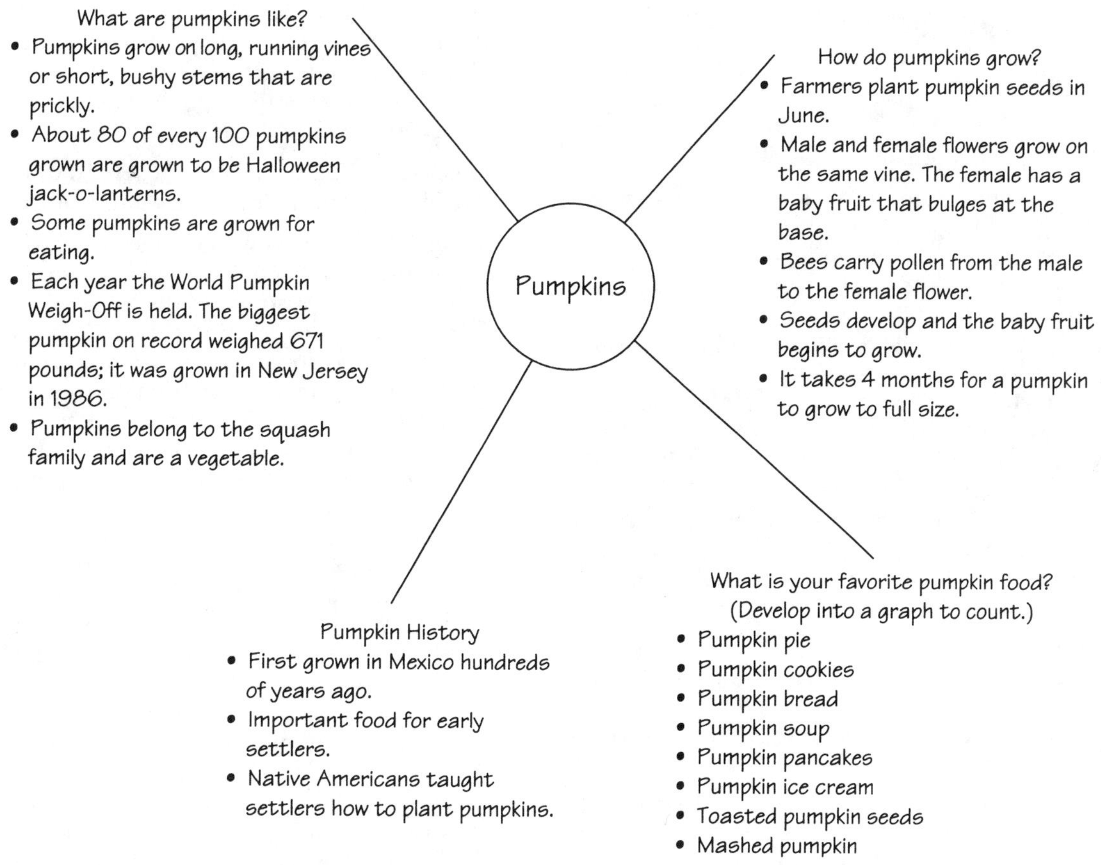

What are pumpkins like?
- Pumpkins grow on long, running vines or short, bushy stems that are prickly.
- About 80 of every 100 pumpkins grown are grown to be Halloween jack-o-lanterns.
- Some pumpkins are grown for eating.
- Each year the World Pumpkin Weigh-Off is held. The biggest pumpkin on record weighed 671 pounds; it was grown in New Jersey in 1986.
- Pumpkins belong to the squash family and are a vegetable.

Pumpkins

How do pumpkins grow?
- Farmers plant pumpkin seeds in June.
- Male and female flowers grow on the same vine. The female has a baby fruit that bulges at the base.
- Bees carry pollen from the male to the female flower.
- Seeds develop and the baby fruit begins to grow.
- It takes 4 months for a pumpkin to grow to full size.

Pumpkin History
- First grown in Mexico hundreds of years ago.
- Important food for early settlers.
- Native Americans taught settlers how to plant pumpkins.

What is your favorite pumpkin food?
(Develop into a graph to count.)
- Pumpkin pie
- Pumpkin cookies
- Pumpkin bread
- Pumpkin soup
- Pumpkin pancakes
- Pumpkin ice cream
- Toasted pumpkin seeds
- Mashed pumpkin

FIGURE 11–3
Sample Web: What We Learned About Pumpkins

b. Leaves (cabbage, lettuce, spinach, chard, beet greens)

c. Stems or stalks (asparagus, celery, broccoli)

d. Skins (tomatoes, apples, carrots)

e. Seeds (nuts, peas, beans, potatoes)

3. Plants vary in color, size, texture, shape, and weight.

4. Plants may change in appearance as they progress through various stages of growth and as they are affected by temperature, weather, and season.

5. Some plants can grow only in particular seasons and climates.

6. Plants have various characteristics.

a. Roots
b. Stems or stalks
c. Flowers
d. Leaves
e. Seeds
f. Skins

7. There are many kinds of plants.

a. Trees
b. Flowering plants
c. Foliage plants
d. Vegetables
e. Grains

f. Vines
g. Mosses
h. Molds
i. Other fungi

8. Plants have many uses.

a. Some plants provide food for humans (vegetables, fruits, grains).
b. Trees provide products such as wood, paper, poles, gum, drugs, paint, waxes, and dyes.
c. Some plants provide clothing (cotton, linen).
d. Many plants provide beauty (trees, houseplants, flowers).
e. Some plants provide shade, shelter, and protection for humans and animals (trees and large plants such as shrubs and bushes).
f. Some plants provide homes for animals (trees, shrubs, foliage).
g. Many plants are food for animals.

9. Some plants are harmful to humans (poisonous, such as poison ivy).
10. Some plants are a nuisance to humans (for example, weeds).
11. Some plants grow on land and some grow in water; some grow in light and some in shade.
12. Most plants grow from seed, although there are variations. Some plants grow from bulbs, some grow in particular circumstances without seeds (moss and mold), some grow from cuttings (geraniums), and some grow from suckers or runners.
13. Seeds differ in color, shape, size, and texture.
14. We eat some types of seeds. (After being shown examples of edible seeds, Christian exclaimed, "Real people doesn't eat seeds!")

Activities and Experiences

1. Observe and discuss characteristic parts of different plants.

a. Apple tree
b. Geranium
c. Broccoli
d. Wheat

2. Have a tasting experience in which the children taste different parts of plants. Ask the children to name and give examples of edible parts of plants. (Refer to teaching concept 2 for ideas.)

3. Observe the growing cycle of several different plants from their beginning to maturity.

a. Observe the day-by-day stages of a growing seed such as a lima bean seed. Line the inside of a straight-sided jar with a paper towel or blotting paper. Keep water or a soaked sponge in the bottom so that the towel remains wet. Each day put a soaked lima bean seed between the jar and the wet paper. Do this each day for about 5 days so that the changes on each of the 5 days can be observed. Record observations in writing and in drawings or photographs, and put them together in a book to read and reread about the experience. When the seeds are well sprouted, plant them in soil and continue to watch their growth until they bear beans.
b. Observe the growth of an orange tree from its beginning as a seedling. Record observations in pictures and writing.
c. Observe the growth of a flower. Record observations in pictures and writing.
d. Observe the growth of bread mold. Record observations in pictures and writing.
e. Observe the growth of grass seed by having each child plant some in an egg shell filled with potting soil.

4. Plant some bean seeds. When the bean plant begins to grow, each day cut a strip of paper the length of the plant. Over a period of time, compare the lengths of the strips of paper in order to study the growth of the plant. Maintain the bean plants until the plants flower and reproduce seeds. Count the leaves on the plant as it is growing. When a pod appears, cut it and count the seeds.

5. Observe and record the day-by-day growth of various seeds; compare the ways that they are different and the ways that they are alike.

6. Have the class adopt a tree in the neighborhood or schoolyard and observe the tree's

changes throughout the year. The class could measure the tree's diameter, examine its bark, observe the leaves during the different seasons, and keep a year-long book or record describing its growth and changes. Photographs of the tree could be taken at different times during the year and then individually mounted for use as a sequencing material or in a book.

7. Observe how plants absorb water and food. Put a fresh stalk of celery under water; trim the end off and cut it up the center while the stalk is still under water. Cut it almost the entire length of the stem but not quite all the way. Fill two glasses with water and put food coloring of different colors in each (red and blue work well). Put half of the celery in one glass of colored water and the other half in the other glass. Within hours, the veins going up the stem of the celery and the leaves on the top of the stalk will assume the color of the water in the glasses. You can also put a white carnation or Queen Anne's lace (a common wildflower) in the colored water, and the petals will change color.

8. To enable the children to see what happens when a plant does not receive one of the necessary ingredients for growth, perform the following experiment: Obtain five similar plants, such as bean plants or flowers. Give one plant all the necessary ingredients except air; another, everything except light (put it in a dark room or closet); another, everything except water; another, everything except soil (food). Provide all the necessary ingredients to the fifth plant. Observe how long each plant grows and lives. Record observations.

9. Put different plants or parts of plants in a paper bag. Have a child describe one of the items, and ask the other children to guess the name or part of the plant from the description given.

10. Compare the sizes of plants, such as a radish plant and a tree or one kind of bean plant and another.

11. Put plant pictures on cards and have the children sort the plants into categories, which might include the following:

    a. Plants that we eat or do not eat
    b. Fruits; vegetables; trees; foliage; flowers
    c. Plants that grow above the ground or below the ground or in water

12. Collect leaves and make comparisons. Classify and label those of the same variety. Either use them for creative art activities or return them to their natural environment.

13. Study and observe plants that do not grow from seeds: plants that grow from bulbs and plants that grow in particular media, such as moss and mold. Allow the children to look at the plants through a magnifying glass. Do forced-bulb planting indoors.

14. To teach the children that stems grow upward and roots grow downward, obtain a clear glass or plastic jar and secure a piece of fine gauze over the top with an elastic band or a string. On top of the gauze, sprinkle seeds such as wheat kernels and then fill the container with water. Make sure that on the first few days the container is filled to the top and that the seeds remain wet enough to sprout. Be sure to put the container in a dish or pie plate, since the gauze absorbs the water. Within a few days the seeds will sprout, with the roots growing downward (because of gravity; this is called *geotropism*) and the stems growing upward.

15. Locate a tree stump that is fairly old and demonstrate to the children how to count the rings to learn the age of the tree.

Unit Plans on Plants

The following are examples of unit plans on various aspects of plants, from general to more specific categories. (For unit plans on seeds, see Chapter 4, and on fruits and vegetables, see Chapter 7.)

UNIT PLAN ON PLANTS (GENERAL)

Art

- Plant collages: seeds, dried flowers, leaves, sticks, or others parts, in plaster of Paris, play dough, or other medium

- Screen painting with parts of plants
- Painting with flowers, leaves, or grains instead of brushes
- Seeds added to finger paint
- Melted crayon and parts of plants (seeds, leaves, flowers) between waxed-paper sheets
- Flowers made out of nut cups, egg cartons, or cupcake holders; attached to a pipe cleaner, put in clay base, and arranged in paper-cup vase
- Flowers and leaves cut from wallpaper or fabric to glue on a paper or cardboard base
- Shakers decorated with plant parts

Field Trips

- Home garden
- Nature walk, with emphasis on looking for plants
- Greenhouse
- Plant nursery
- Flower shop
- Houseplants in home
- Botany department at a college or high school

Visitors

- Florist
- Person owning houseplants
- Member of one child's family to show seeds that they will plant in a home garden and to discuss the care of plants at home
- Person to build a terrarium
- Person to bring in a pet or animal that eats plants

Food

- Any food experience using plants, such as fruits, vegetables, seeds, or nuts

Science

- Growth cycle of plants
- Needs of plants: air, sun, water, food

- Uses of plants
- Harmful plants
- Nuisance plants
- Types of plants
- Places where plants grow
- Parts of plants
- Observe the growth of mold, and study it under a microscope. What objects grow mold?
- Sweet potato supported with toothpicks in a jar of water; observation of growth
- Pineapple planted by twisting the top off a fresh pineapple and then planting it in wet sand
- Carrot tops grown by cutting them $\frac{1}{4}$ to $\frac{1}{2}$ inch down and then putting them in water

Music

- Songs about plants and seeds
- Seed shakers made and used as rhythm instruments; seedpods and gourds used as rhythm instruments
- Creative movements and dramatics relating to growth of plant from seed to mature plant; plants wilting because of lack of water and then being revived; plants following the sun, moving in the wind; seeds traveling and sprouting
- Dramatization of care of plants
- Dramatization of musical story: growth of plant

Language and Literacy

- Stories about plants
- Poetry
- Slides of plants; discussion
- Different kinds of plants brought by children from their homes; discussion
- Game in which individual children select a particular plant and describe it to the other children; guessing which plant is being described

- Children's own stories based on experiences in planting, growing, and caring for plants or gardens

- Take pictures of various garden plants, such as carrots or peas, and then have the children dictate or write a story about each; assemble the stories into a booklet.

UNIT PLAN ON TREES

The children should understand that trees are a kind of plant and that they start from small seeds. The products of trees, as well as other uses, should be among the concepts studied during this unit. The children should also be exposed to the wide variety of trees. The activities selected will be determined by the goals and objectives desired for the particular unit. A unit on trees would be appropriate around Arbor Day. Children could each do a project on a kind of tree of their choosing.

Art

- Tree product collages using paper and wood products
- Pinecone mice
- Wood collages using wood shavings, sawdust, and wood scraps
- Sawdust painting
- Paper collages
- Tree trunk drawn or pasted on paper, with children using sponge painting or hand prints from finger paint to paint the leaves
- Nutshell animals
- Four-season paintings or drawings of trees
- Shakers
- Texture smears with leaf rubbings, wood products, or other parts of trees such as twigs
- Leaf collages
- Pinecone printing

Field Trips

- Nature walk to observe trees
- National or state forest
- Lumberyard
- Carpenter shop
- Home under construction
- Sawmill
- Hobby shop or woodworking shop
- Store where wooden things (furniture, for example) are sold
- Christmas tree farm
- Grocery store to observe edible tree products such as nuts and fruits
- Tree nurseries
- Visit to tree(s) in which the children can see animal homes, such as birds' nests
- Visit to a site where trees are being planted
- High school or university industrial arts shop
- Museum to see wood sculptures
- Divide the children into pairs. One child in the pair is blindfolded and taken to a tree. The child can hug the tree, feel it, and explore it. The child returns to the starting position, removes the blindfold, and then finds the tree that was explored.

Food (see also Chapter 7)

- Fruit salads, desserts, or juices made from fruits of trees
- Foods that have nuts as an ingredient, such as cakes, cookies, candy
- Dried fruits

Visitors

- Forest ranger or urban forester
- Forest-fire fighter
- City fire fighter
- Carpenter
- Wood carver
- Logger
- Owner of a tree nursery
- Grocery store employee

Science

- Examination of circles in tree trunks to determine age of tree
- Discussion of tree products
- Tree planted and cared for
- Discussion and study of tree parts
- Observation of how wood burns
- Tasting of foods that are products of trees: fruits, nuts, pine gum
- Observation of process of making a tree product such as paper
- Observation of selected tree over a period of time, preferably a year (keep a record in writing and with pictures)

Music

- Creative movements relating to trees growing, moving in the wind, heavily laden with snow, leaves falling
- Use wooden rhythm sticks or wooden blocks as rhythm instruments
- Musical Chairs in which pictures of different kinds of trees or tree products are placed on the front of the chairs. Play music and have the children do locomotor rhythms. When the music stops, for example, give directions such as "All pine trees stand and hop to this music" or "All weeping willow trees stand and skate to this music." A variation of this is to tape the pictures of the trees or tree products securely to the floor. Have each child stand on one when the music stops and then proceed with the game as suggested.
- Wooden drums
- Shakers with seeds from trees
- Instruments made from wood
- Drumsticks

Language and Literacy

- Stories about trees written by the children or other authors
- Poetry

- Pictures of trees, and children brainstorming words that come to their minds as they see each tree
- Slides of trees; discussion of characteristics, season, feelings relating to each tree
- Cinquain poetry for trees
- Prepare a book, with each child doing one page. On this page, the child is to draw a picture of a favorite tree and dictate to the teacher or write why he or she likes this tree.
- Have children finish the sentence "The best thing about a tree is . . . " or "I like trees because . . . ." The children could write or dictate their answers and then illustrate them. These pages could be put together into a book to be enjoyed over and over again.

Related Activities

- Rope swing in a tree
- Hammering
- Sawing
- Container with wood chips, sawdust, toothpicks, wooden spoons, bark, leaves

UNIT PLAN ON WHEAT AND FLOUR

Art

- Finger painting with flour paste
- Finger painting with wheat kernels added
- Shakers: cans filled with wheat kernels, then decorated with tissue paper, kernels of wheat, or parts of the wheat shaft, and glued with flour paste
- Collages: wheat, parts of the shaft, wheat cereals
- Clay made from flour
- Papier-mâché
- Painting with wheat shaft
- Vase or pencil container made by molding clay around a 6-ounce can and sticking small bits of wheat shaft, kernels of wheat, or other collage items into the soft clay

Field Trips

- Bakery
- Flour mill
- Wheat field
- Granary, wheat silo, or grain bin
- Home to see how wheat is stored
- Home or bakery to see wheat grinder and observe how it grinds wheat into flour
- Cereal company

Food (see bread unit plan in Chapter 7)

- Cooked wheat cereal, whole or cracked
- Sprouted wheat salad
- Chewing of wheat into gum
- Any food activity utilizing flour: cakes, cookies, breads, muffins, biscuits, pancakes
- Dry wheat cereals eaten as cereals or used in recipes

Science

- Sprouting of wheat
- Grinding of wheat (blender may be used)
- Observation of growing plant (see activity 14, page 375)
- Wheat in stages of the growing process
- Equipment farmer uses to plant, harvest, and store wheat

- Kinds of wheat
- Separating of wheat from chaff (shaft rubbed between hands; chaff blown off)

Music

- Shakers used in shaker band or rhythm activity
- Musical dramatization of the story "The Little Red Hen"
- Wheat shafts used to play drums

Visitors

- Farmer showing kinds of wheat
- Baker
- Parent making bread
- Person grinding wheat with stone
- Botanist showing how wheat grows
- Nutritionist

Language and Literacy

- Story such as "The Little Red Hen"
- Poems
- Create own stories, for example, "How We Use Wheat"

Note: A lesson plan on wheat and flour can be found in Appendix A.

Summary

This chapter has dealt with the subjects of animals, plants, and sensory-related concepts. Although smell (olfactory) and taste (gustatory) perceptions involve separate senses, they are closely related and influence each other. Texture is the way that the touch of an object can be described. It is important that children be able not only to identify items by feel, but also to use appropriate descriptive words. As children have experiences in listening, they also develop the skill of auditory discrimination. The ability to distinguish sound and pitch is an important aspect of reading readiness. Even very young infants respond to smell, taste, touch, and sound. As we increase our own sensory awareness, we become better able to make children more cognizant of using their senses for learning. Experiences with familiar smells, tastes, textures, sights, and sounds should be presented before unfamiliar ones, allowing children opportunities to solidify concepts and continue building new understandings on already established foundations. These sensory skills readily adapt to combined units, separate units, or incorporation into other areas of study.

Teaching units about animals provide numerous possibilities for explorations and experiences regarding various animal-related concepts. Young children generally have a natural curiosity about animals and their characteristics. An environmental curriculum that includes animals abounds with opportunities for studying size, shape, number, color, texture, categorization, weight, smell, sound, and food, along with the physical characteristics, habitats, uses, and habits of animals. By studying animals, children are able to lessen or overcome fears while gaining insight into and understanding of the proper care of animals. Most of all, children can appreciate animals and sense the dependence of humans on them.

Plants are a natural, living part of the children's environment both inside and outside the classroom. Regardless of the locality, climate, and season, there are numerous possibilities for plant studies and experiences. At most times of the year,

in most areas of the world, there is some kind of vegetation in some stage of development. Young children are generally curious and eager to broaden their understanding of their surroundings, particularly of growing plants. This is especially evidenced by their excitement over the discovery that a newly planted and cared for seed has begun to grow. Related concepts such as size, number, color, texture, categorization, shape, characteristics, needs, and uses of various plants can be explored.

When children study about animals and plants, they can learn to not disturb trees, bushes, rocks, logs, and streams which are homes to creatures that live in the outdoors. Animals and plants that live in the wild should be returned to their environments whenever possible; they do not belong to the finders (Wilson, 1995b).

Student Learning Activities

1. Visit with a preschool, kindergarten, or first- or second-grade teacher. Find out whether projects, units, or activities relating to animals and plants are included in the teacher's programs. (Note the units or experiences included in the curriculum.) Ask the teacher to relate to you the children's (and the teacher's) feelings about animal and plant units and experiences in the classroom. Does the teacher ever have live animals in the classroom? Discuss with the teacher any other ideas and questions relating to animals and plants as a part of the curriculum. Following your interview, describe what you learned and your reactions.

2. Visit a classroom where there is a live animal, or bring a live animal into class. What are the children's reactions? Ask the children questions about the animal. Do you see any reinforcement relating to the animal, such as pictures, books, or other materials?

3. Visit a children's library and evaluate at least four of the books in the Suggested Resources. Evaluate and describe each of the four books. How would you use them with children? What concepts relating to animals or plants are taught in the books? Add four additional books of your own choosing to the Suggested Resources.

4. Study the unit plans on animals and plants included in this chapter. Then prepare a unit plan, project, or web on an animal, category of animals, topic relating to animals, or plant. From this plan, prepare a 5-day activity plan. Balance your days with a variety of activities that are not theme related.

5. Plan and implement with a group of children at least one of the activities on animals, one on plants, and one on sensory concepts suggested in this chapter or added by you. Evaluate your experience. The group of children may be a classroom group or a small group of relatives or neighborhood children between the ages of 3 and 8 years.

6. Many records, tapes, and CDs include songs about the senses, animals, and plants. Visit a library or early childhood classroom and listen to at least three recordings relating to animals. Evaluate each recording. Would the recording teach accurate facts about the animal or is it a "pretend" song? How would you use the recording with children?

7. Write down your most and least favorite tastes and smells. Have a group of children ages 3 to 8 brainstorm and share their most and least favorite tastes and smells.

8. Make yourself aware of the smells and sounds around you on a particular day. List the many smells or sounds that you become aware of. Which of these alerted you to danger? Made you aware of something important? Taught you something? Created certain feelings or emotions?

9. Prepare a demonstration or experience for young children to show that texture changes.

10. Make a sounds tape. Record a variety of sounds and play them back to children to see if they can identify them.

Suggested Resources

See additional science resources at the end of Chapters 7, 9, and 10. There are so many books, songs, pictures, films, filmstrips, and videos about animals and plants that teachers should check available resources for additional suggestions. Whenever a unit or project is done on a category or specific kind of animal or plant, check the Internet, multimedia computer encyclopedias, or the computer listing at the library under the desired subject heading. Space limits the list provided here to only a few of the possible suggestions in this category. Four excellent resources include (1) *Science and Children*, a journal of the Natural Science Teachers Association that provides in each issue a column on the care of a specific living organism; (2) National Geographic Society, 17th and M Streets, NW, Washington, DC 20036; (3) National Audubon Society, Rt. 4, Box 171, Sharon, CT 06069; and (4) National Wildlife Federation, 1400 16th Street, NW, Washington, DC 20036.

Children's Books and Magazines

Alcantara, R. (1998). *Perro y gato [Dog and cat]*. Barcelona, Spain: La Galera.

Aliki (1995). *Tabby*. New York: HarperCollins.

Aliki (1997). *A visit to the zoo*. New York: HarperCollins.

Arnold, C. (1999). *Sleepytime for zoo animals*. Minneapolis, MN: Carolrhoda.

Aylesworth, J. (1999). *Aunt Pitty Patty's Piggy*. New York: Scholastic.

Barton, B. (1990). *Bones, bones, dinosaur bones*. New York: Harper-Collins.

Bornstein, R. L. (1995). *Rabbit's good news*. New York: Clarion.

Brandt, K. (1985). *Sound*. Mahwah, NJ: Troll.

Breslow, S., & S. Blakemore (1990). *I really want a dog*. New York: Dutton.

Broutin, A. (1999). *Baldomero va a la escuela [Baldomero goes to school]*. Barcelona, Spain: Editorial Corimbo.

Brown, M. W. (1977). *The runaway bunny*. New York: HarperCollins.

Brown, M. W. (1982). *Home for a bunny*. New York: Western.

Brown, R. (1996). *Toad*. New York: Dutton.

Buchholz, Q. (1998). *Duerme bien, pequeno oso [Sleep well, little bear]*. Salamanca, Spain: Loguez Ediciones.

Carle, E. (1986). *My first book of touch*. New York: HarperCollins.

Carle, E. (1986). *The very hungry caterpillar*. New York: Putnam.

Carle, E. (1987). *The tiny seed*. Natick, MA: Picture Book Studio.

Cole, J. (1999). *The magic school bus explores the senses*. New York: Scholastic Press.

DePaola, T. (1997). *Mice squeak, we speak*. New York: Putnam.

Eastman, P. D. (1960). *Are you my mother?* New York: Random House.

Fisher, R. M. (1982). Animals in winter. In *Books for young explorers* (Set 9). Washington, DC: National Geographic.

Flack, M. (1986). *Ask Mr. Bear*. New York: Macmillan.

Gag, W. (1952). *Millions of cats*. New York: Putnam.

Greenaway, T. (1996). *The hairy scary spider*. New York: DK Publishing.

Greenaway, T. (1996). *The horrible horned toad*. New York: DK Publishing.

Greenaway, T. (1996). *The wicked droning wasp*. New York: DK Publishing.

Inkpen, M. (1997). *Juega al escondite con el cerdito Wibbly [Everyone hide from Wibbly Pig]*. Barcelona, Spain: Timun Mas.

Kitamura, S. (1997). *Ardilla tiene hambre [Squirrel is hungry]*. Madrid, Spain: Grupo Anaya.

Kitamura, S. (1997). *Gato tiene sueno [Cat is sleepy]*. Madrid, Spain: Grupo Anaya.

Kitamura, S. (1997). *Pato esta sucio [Duck is dirty]*. Madrid, Spain: Grupo Anaya.

Krauss, R. (1945). *The carrot seed*. New York: HarperCollins.

Lemieux, M. (1988). *Pat the bunny*. New York: Western.

Lemieux, M. (1985). *What's that noise?* New York: Morrow.

Lionni, L. (1968). *Swimmy*. New York: Pantheon.

Lionni, L. (1970). *Fish is fish*. New York: Pantheon.

Martin, B., Jr. (1983). *Brown bear, brown bear, what do you see?* New York: Henry Holt.

McMillan, B. (1994). *Puffin climb, penguins rhyme*. New York: Gulliver/Harcourt, Brace & Co.

National Geographic Society (1980). Life in the woods. In *Wonders of learning* kits. Washington, DC: Author.

National Wildlife Federation. *Ranger Rick's Wildlife Magazine*. Washington, DC: Author.

National Wildlife Federation. *Your Big Backyard Magazine*. Washington, DC: Author.

Patterson, F. (1985). *Koko's kitten*. New York: Scholastic.

Paxton, T. (1996). *Going to the zoo*. New York: Marrow Junior Books.

Petty, K. (1997). *Carlos planta un girasol [Sam plants a sunflower]*. Barcelona, Spain: Destino.

Petty, K. (1997). *Marta planta un rabano [Rosie plants a radish]*. Barcelona, Spain: Destino.

Pienkowski, J. (1998). *La granja [The farm]*. Barcelona, Spain: Ediciones Destino.

Pienkowski, J. (1998). *Mis animals [My pets]*. Barcelona: Ediciones Destino.

Pilkey, D. (1997). *Big dog and little dog*. New York: Red Wagon Books/Harcourt Brace.

Pilkey, D. (1997). *Big dog and little dog going for a walk*. New York: Red Wagon Books/Harcourt Brace.

Pluckrose, H. (1995). *Exploring our senses: Hearing*. Milwaukee, WI: Gareth Stevens.

Pluckrose, H. (1995). *Exploring our senses: Seeing*. Milwaukee, WI: Gareth Stevens.

Pluckrose, H. (1995). *Exploring our senses: Smelling*. Milwaukee, WI: Gareth Stevens.

Pluckrose, H. (1995). *Exploring our senses: Tasting*. Milwaukee, WI: Gareth Stevens.

Pluckrose, H. (1995). *Exploring our senses: Touching*. Milwaukee, WI: Gareth Stevens.

Rice, M., & C. Rice (1988). *All about me*. Garden City, NY: Doubleday.

Silverstein, S. (1964). *The giving tree*. New York: Harper & Row.

Taylor, B. (1998). *Animal hide and seek*. New York: DK Publishing.

Udry, J. (1956). *A tree is nice*. New York: Harper & Row.

Urquhart, J. C. (1982). Animals that travel. In *Books for young explorers*. Washington, DC: National Geographic Society.

VanFleet, M. (1995). *Fuzzy yellow ducklings*. New York: Dial.

Venino, S. (1981). Amazing animal groups. In *Books for young explorers*. Washington, DC: National Geographic Society.

Waldrop, V. H. (ed.) (1983). *Ranger Rick's storybook*. Washington, DC: National Wildlife Society.

Wildlife Education, Ltd. *Zoo books* (series). San Diego, CA: Author.

Wood, A. (1984). *The napping house*. San Diego, CA: Harcourt Brace Jovanovich.

Audiocassettes, Records, and CDs

The circus. David C. Cook.

Creepy the crawly caterpillar. Children's Record Guild. (Record)

Dandy-lions never roar! Good Apple.

The farm. David C. Cook.

Folk song carnival. Hap Palmer Record Library (AR524 or AC524).

Folk songs for young folk—Animals (vol. 1). Scholastic Book Services. (Record)

Folk songs for young folk—Animals (vol. 2). Scholastic Book Services. (Record)

If a dinosaur came to dinner. The Child's World.

Listening. Newbridge Educational Publishing, LLC.

Singing fun. Bowmar-Noble.

The small singer (vol. 1). Bowmar-Noble.

The small singer (vol. 2). Bowmar-Noble.

Snoopycat. Scholastic Book Services.

Tick, tock, the popcorn clock. The Child's World.

Pictures

Animal homes. The Child's World. (Foldout)

Animals that help us. The Child's World. (Foldout)

Baby animals of the wild. The Child's World.

Birds. The Child's World.

Birds and other animals. National Audubon Society.

Birds and our land. David C. Cook.

Common birds. Society for Visual Education.

Common insects. Society for Visual Education.

Familiar fresh-water fish. Society for Visual Education.

Farm and ranch animals. Society for Visual Education.

Farm animals. Eye Gate Media.

Fishes. The Child's World.

Forest. The Child's World.

Insects. The Child's World.

Insects and spiders. The Child's World.

Insects and spiders. National Audubon Society.

Kinds of animals. The Child's World. (Foldout)

Learning with your ears. Coronet Films.

Mammals. The Child's World.

Moths and butterflies. Society for Visual Education.

Pets. The Child's World. (Foldout)

Pets. David C. Cook.

Pets. Society for Visual Education.

Plants and seeds. The Child's World. (Foldout)

Plants and seeds. David C. Cook.

Plants that provide food. The Child's World. (Foldout)

Reptiles and amphibians. Society for Visual Education.

The story of corn. The Child's World. (Sequence chart)

Tree study program. National Audubon Society.
Trees. National Audubon Society.
Trees and plants. National Audubon Society.
Trip to the farm. David C. Cook.
Trip to the zoo. David C. Cook.
Wild animals. Society for Visual Education.
Zoo animals. Society for Visual Education.

Multimedia Kits

Amphibians and how they grow. National Geographic.
Animals and how they grow (CD-ROM kit). National Geographic.
Birds and how they grow. National Geographic.

Dinosaurs: Giant reptiles. National Geographic.
Farm animals. National Geographic.
Mammals and how they grow. National Geographic.
Reptiles and how they grow. National Geographic.
The senses. National Geographic.
Spiders. National Geographic.
Whales. National Geographic.
What is a plant? National Geographic.
What is a seed? National Geographic.
A world of animals (CD-ROM kit). National Geographic.
A world of plants (CD-ROM kit). National Geographic.

Videos

The Human Senses Series (National Geographic)

In touch with the world
Learning to see
Listen! Hear!
A matter of taste
On the nose
Senses: How we know. National Geographic.

Computer Software

The house is bugged! Sunburst.
Learn about plants. Sunburst.
Learn about the senses. Sunburst.
Muppetville. Sunburst Communications (Macintosh, Windows).
Sammy's Science House. Riverdeep.
Science blaster Jr. Davidson.
Thinkin' Science. Riverdeep.
The treehouse. Broderbund.

Chapter 12

Problem Solving and Mathematics

"High-quality teaching in mathematics is about challenge and joy, not imposition and pressure. Good early childhood mathematics is broader and deeper than mere practice in counting and adding" (Clements, 2001, p. 270). The early years are the time for every child to develop a solid foundation of mathematics understanding and knowledge, the ability to solve problems, and to develop positive beliefs about mathematics. Teachers in early childhood should look at mathematics growth and learning like they do literacy development, as emergent and mathematical concepts develop by being exercised and stimulated (Geist, 2001). Developing understanding of mathematics is best achieved in a context where children are expected to reason, problem solve, and communicate their ideas and thoughts to others (Wood, 2001). A working definition of mathematics that will serve as an educational focus throughout this chapter is this: the science of mathematical understanding achieved through learning to solve problems. The National Council of Teachers of Mathematics (NCTM, 2000, p. 16) suggests six principles for school mathematics: equity, curriculum, teaching, learning, assessment, and technology. These principles are issues or features that need to be considered for high-quality math education.

- **Curriculum.** A curriculum is more than a collection of activities: it must be coherent, focused on important mathematics, and well articulated across the grades.

- **Teaching.** Effective mathematics teaching requires understanding what students know and need to learn and then challenging and supporting them to learn it well.

- **Learning.** Students must learn mathematics with understanding, actively building new knowledge from experience and prior knowledge.

- **Assessment.** Assessment should support the learning of important mathematics and furnish useful information to both teachers and students.

- **Technology.** Technology is essential in teaching and learning mathematics; it influences the mathematics that is taught and enhances students' learning.

National Council of Teachers of Mathematics, 2000, p. 16.

Principles of School Mathematics

- **Equity.** Excellence in mathematics education requires equity–high expectations and strong support for all students.

Early childhood classrooms should be communities of inquiry, problem posing, and problem solving, where children perceive that in math lessons they are expected to offer their thoughts about questions posed and to find resolution to these problems (Schifter, 1996). Young children should sense the application of mathematical ideas in everyday life. At this level, mathematics learning should be "active, rich in natural and mathematical language, and filled with thought-provoking opportunities" [National Council of Teacher of Mathematics (NCTM), 2000, p. 77]. Early childhood teachers should develop a positive attitude toward math remembering that mathematics learning builds on curiosity and enthusiasm (NCTM, 2000). Everyday activities, games, and questions can encourage mathematical understanding (Geist, 2001). Since early impressions are often lasting impressions, children need to sense the satisfaction of developing math and number skills as they participate and think about their world (Clements, 2001). Many activities throughout life rely on the use of math concepts and the ability to use numbers.

In problem solving and mathematics, teachers traditionally "have been more concerned with getting the 'right' answer than with 'how' children arrived at an answer" (T. L. Anderson, 1996, p. 35). Classroom focus should be on thinking, analyzing, understanding, and reasoning, not just facts (Schifter, 1996). It is too easy for children to be "inundated with the facts but starving for understanding" (Wurtman, 1989, p. 1). Memorizing facts is not the same as understanding the processes.

Problem solving should begin with natural and informal problems such as:

- How many children are in our class today? How many boys? How many girls? How many people?

- Be sure you take enough crackers so that everyone at your table gets four.

- Do you want a big helping of mashed potatoes or a small helping?

- Do more children like chocolate or strawberry ice cream?" (Charlesworth, 1997, p. 63) How do you know and what would it look like in a graph?

Engaging problems and mathematical conversations should be a part of every day, naturally integrated into all parts of the day. Problem solving is related to all areas of learning and involves four basic steps (Diffily & Morrison, 1996):

1. Identify the problem.
2. Brainstorm possible solutions.
3. Choose one solution and try it out.
4. Evaluate what happens.

Problem solving and mathematical thinking are invited when teachers ask thought-provoking and open-ended questions that lead to thinking and discussion (Frakes and Kline, 2000). For example, after making a graph, instead of asking a pointed or specific question, the teacher may ask a more open-ended question, such as "What do you see on the graph?" (Frakes and Kline, 2000). We should teach children to identify, classify, infer, observe, compute, measure, predict, solve problems, think through possibilities, and understand the process.

The use of mathematical thinking is preferred to planned, sequenced mathematics activities in discovering concepts and solving problems in everyday life (Clements, 2001; Clements, Swaminathan, Hannibal, and Sarama, 1999; Greenberg, 1993; Mills, Whitin, & O'Keefe, 1993). A simple problem-solving experience might evolve naturally at snack or lunchtime. If there are not enough forks for everyone, there are more solutions than just having an adult retrieve additional forks. Allowing children to determine various solutions may take more time, but it will increase their problem-solving skills. Children's possible solutions might include using plastic forks, borrowing from another classroom, eating with spoons for a change, taking turns eating, or washing some used forks (Diffily & Morrison, 1996). We need to realize that the children can complete many of our problem-solving concerns in the classroom.

Remember: Experiencing the process of problem solving is more valuable than arriving at a solution! Emphasize the thinking, rather than a specific answer. And look for the thinking that students demonstrate, not just the skills (Frakes & Kline, 2000).

> The ability to solve problems leads to new and more innovative thinking and inventions and prepares children to face the future. (Blake, Hurley, & Arenz, 1995, p. 82)

Therefore, teaching mathematics is most often done through thoughtful questioning, clarifying, or rich mathematical conversing. In addition, the use

These children are learning about the concepts of same–different, alike–not-alike. The teacher is assisting them by pointing out specific differences.

of materials such as books and manipulatives supports mathematics learning in the early years. However, mathematical concepts can also be taught in units, lessons, and projects. For example, units, lessons, or projects could be planned on shapes, calculators, recognizing numbers, or measurement notions. Units should be developmentally appropriate and match the interests and needs of the children. Research informs us that young children are capable of complex and sophisticated learning. All children, including those from low-income and minority populations, are interested in and capable of grappling with "big" ideas in mathematics (Clements, 2001).

GUIDELINES FOR INCORPORATING PROBLEM-SOLVING AND MATHEMATICS COMPETENCIES IN THE EARLY CHILDHOOD CURRICULUM

Teachers should avoid gender bias regarding math and must nurture confidence in and enthusiasm for math, problem solving, and reasoning activities in *all* children. If the concepts are geared to their particular level of interest and ability and if the emotional inhibitions that promote a feeling of inferiority are removed, all children are capable of mathematical reasoning and problem solving (Piaget, 1974). Teachers can use specific strategies to improve the performance of girls in problem solving (Casey, 2001). For example, use concrete manipulatives to calculate solutions, and use modeling and counting strategies to clarify problems.

Teachers should recognize that opportunities for teaching math abound in children's daily experiences as they encounter concepts relating to time, distance, measuring, weight, number recognition, and other math notions. During the early childhood years, many understandings of math concepts grow out of experiences with objects, food, play materials, nature, the outdoors, time, and space, in effect, their everyday experiences. Teachers should use children's unique experiences as springboards for learning math. Math concepts are often acquired in a spontaneous, natural way because children are normally curious about and interested in them (NCTM, 2000).

However, many math concepts require substantial experience and development time before they can be incorporated into the child's thinking. For example, young children often misunderstand time concepts such as today, tomorrow, and yesterday, and comments such as "I don't want my bath today, I want to have it yesterday" or "I already did that, I did it tomorrow" are very common among young children.

Math in early childhood should be concrete and manipulative. Young children develop abstract reasoning through numerous experiences with manipulative and concrete objects. Teachers should be cautioned against the use of workbook pages and dittos when teaching math in early childhood. "Where children are required to sit down, quiet down, and write it down, excitement about math may never have a chance to emerge" (Stone, 1987, p. 16). Many math understandings grow naturally from experience (NCTM, 2000). Teachers should provide the kinds of mathematics experiences that teach children to be problem solvers and thinkers and at the same time make math inviting. When math is intriguing, children will seek it out. We should make math fun, not just a drudgery of learning facts and figures. Children need to learn the intrinsic rewards of problem solving. Objects and manipulative toys and materials must be an integral part of early childhood math programs. It is difficult, for example, for young children to understand money concepts without opportunities to actually use money. However, although teaching and learning should begin concretely, research warns that concrete manipulatives do not guarantee meaningful learning; manipulatives do not transmit the meaning of a mathematical notion (Clements & McMillen, 1996). Ideas become meaningful through good mental activity, be it objects, materials, visuals, or an excellent computer program, and students build these ideas from working with and thinking about their actions on such materials (Clements & McMillen, 1996).

Math should be taught and integrated into all curriculum areas, although math learning centers can be set up and specific times allotted in the curriculum for math activities. Math is often a bridge to related fields of the curriculum (Charlesworth, 1997) and should be integrated (Mason & Lloyd, 1995). Problem-solving skills are related to all areas of learning, not just to math and science. For example, while on field trips, children spontaneously learn concepts relating to money, time, numbers, and other aspects of math; in food experiences, children are exposed to measuring, number concepts, fractions, and other math and problem-solving skills. These skills or concepts include matching (quantities, numbers, shapes, forms, sizes, etc.); making patterns; classifying, ordering, or seriating in order on the basis of size, number, ordinal position, or weight; and making comparisons. Recognizing and using patterns is a valuable problem-solving tool, as is classifying, which helps develop analytical and logical thinking and abstract concepts (Carr, 1988; Day, 1988). Classification relies on the recognition of likenesses and differences.

Children's literature can provide a springboard for teaching math concepts and thereby integrate math with reading and language arts (McMath & King, 1994; Thatcher, 2001; Thiessen & Matthias, 1992). A wide assortment of picture books and children's literature teaches math concepts and help young children understand how math is used in the real world (Welchman-Tischler, 1992; Whitin & Wilde, 1992).

It is important to begin with simple concepts and then move to the more abstract. Once a child has had experiences with beginning number concepts (that is, recognizing numbers, counting, understanding the meaning of numbers, and even some simple addition concepts), begin to teach more abstract math concepts, such as time, money, and space. Preschool children have difficulty with math concepts of these kinds because they are in the stage (preoperational) in which their understanding depends on how something appears to them (Katz, 1983). Consider Piaget's example of conservation: Five buttons, pennies, crackers, or other objects of uniform size are placed close together in one row; in a second row, five like items are spread apart. When children are asked whether both rows contain the same number of items, most preschool children will indicate that the row that is spread apart or is longer has more because it *appears* to have more. After 5 or 6 years of age, most children are able to focus on actual numbers and can separate length from number. Math notions should always be built on prior understanding and children's informal knowledge (Charlesworth, 1997).

Children learn best when allowed appropriate freedom to explore through their senses of touch, sight, sound, taste, and smell. Therefore, a good early childhood education environment for developing math and other problem-solving concepts should include literature and storytelling; blocks and construction; art; science; water and sand; music; language; food and nutrition; interactions with peers and adults; and other activities suitable for young children.

USE OF COMPUTERS IN MATHEMATICS AND PROBLEM SOLVING

Computers are a great asset in learning math skills and enhancing problem-solving competence. Young children can increase such skills as counting, number recognition, one-to-one correspondence, and understanding the relationship between quantity and symbol through the use of computer exploration. Many counting and math computer games are available for young children, and the thinking processes involved in using the computer often utilize mathematical reasoning, problem solving, or even manipulations (Clements, 2001; Clements & McMillen, 1996). Computer manipulatives increase attention and motivation, as well as facilitate precise explanations; they often go beyond what can be done simply using physical manipulatives (Clements & McMillen, 1996). Websites such as *standards.nctm.org* provide electronic examples that give children practice in the standards and expectations outlined by the National Council of Teachers of Mathematics. There are many excellent examples of software that are developmentally appropriate and give children experiences in mathematical notions and problem solving. Some examples are shared at the end of this chapter.

The National Council of Teachers of Mathematics suggests that technology is one of six principles of high-quality mathematics education. According to the NCTM "Technology is essential in teaching and learning mathematics; it influences the mathematics that is taught and enhances students' learning" (NCTM, 2000, p. 16). Specifically in the early years, NCTM (2000) suggests that work with calculators provides an opportunity to explore number and pattern and to focus on the problem-solving processes. Computers provide feedback and connections between various representations. Computers are especially valuable for students with physical limitations and also for those who prefer technology learning (Clements, 1999b).

TEACHING MATHEMATICS

Mathematics and problem solving involve more than learning about numbers and how to add, subtract, multiply, and divide them. The National Council for Teachers of Mathematics (*Principles and Standards for School Mathematics, Prechool Through 2nd grade*, 2000, pp. 78–136) suggests 10 curriculum standards for Pre-K through second grade. These standards provide a guide for early childhood curriculum planning (reprinted with permission from the National Council of Teachers of Mathematics). Five of them address mathematics *content standards*:

- Number and operations
- Algebra
- Geometry
- Measurement
- Data analysis and probability

    The other five are *process standards*:

- Problem solving
- Reasoning and proof
- Communication
- Connections
- Representation

Number and Operations Standards: Pre-K through Grade 2 Expectations (NCTM 2000, p. 78)
Understand numbers, ways of representing numbers, relationships among numbers, and number systems.   In prekindergarten through grade 2 all students should:

- Count with understanding and recognize "how many" in sets of objects
- Use multiple models to develop initial understandings of place value and the base-10 number system

- Develop understanding of the relative position and magnitude of whole numbers and of ordinal and cardinal numbers and their connection

- Develop a sense of whole numbers and represent and use them in flexible ways, including relating, composing, and decomposing numbers

- Connect number words and numerals to the quantities that they represent, using various physical models and representations

- Understand and represent commonly used fractions such as $\frac{1}{4}$, $\frac{1}{3}$, and $\frac{1}{2}$

Understand meanings of operations and how they relate to one another. In prekindergarten through grade 2 all students should understand:

- Various meanings of addition and subtraction of whole numbers and the relationship between the two operations

- The effects of adding and subtracting whole numbers

- Situations that entail multiplication and division, such as equal groupings of objects and sharing equally.

Compute fluently and make reasonable estimates. In prekindergarten through grade 2 all students should:

- Develop and use strategies for whole-number computations, with a focus on addition and subtraction

- Develop fluency with basic number combinations for addition and subtraction

- Use a variety of methods and tools to compute, including objects, mental computation, estimation, paper and pencil, and calculators

Algebra Standards: Pre-K through Grade 2 Expectations (NCTM 2000, p. 90)
Understand patterns, relations, and functions. In prekindergarten through grade 2 all students should:

- Sort, classify, and order objects by size, number, and other properties

- Recognize, describe, and extend patterns such as sequences of sounds and shapes or simple

numeric patterns, and translate from one representation to another

- Analyze how both repeating and growing patterns are generated.

Represent and analyze mathematical situations and structures using algebraic symbols. In prekindergarten through grade 2 all students should:

- Illustrate general principles and properties of operations, such as commutativity, using specific numbers

- Use concrete, pictorial, and verbal representations to develop an understanding of invented and conventional symbolic notations

Use mathematical models to represent and understand quantitative relationships. In prekindergarten through grade 2 all students should:

- Model situations that involve the addition and subtraction of whole numbers, using objects, pictures, and symbols

Analyze change in various contexts. In prekindergarten through grade 2 all students should:

- Describe qualitative change, such as a student's growing taller

- Describe quantitative change, such as a student's growing two inches in one year

Geometry Standards: Pre-K through Grade 2 Expectations (NCTM 2000, p. 96)
Analyze characteristics and properties of two- and three-dimensional geometric shapes and develop mathematical arguments about geometric relationships. In prekindergarten through grade 2 all students should:

- Recognize, name, build, draw, compare, and sort two- and three-dimensional shapes

- Describe attributes and parts of two- and three-dimensional shapes;

- Investigate and predict the results of putting together and taking apart two- and three-dimensional shapes

Specify locations and describe spatial relationships using coordinate geometry and other representational systems.   In prekindergarten through grade 2 all students should:

- Describe, name, and interpret relative positions in space and apply ideas about relative position

- Describe, name, and interpret direction and distance in navigating space and apply ideas about direction and distance

- Find and name locations with simple relationships such as "near to" and in coordinate systems such as maps

Apply transformations and use symmetry to analyze mathematical situations.   In prekindergarten through grade 2 all students should:

- Recognize and apply slides, flips, and turns

- Recognize and create shapes that have symmetry

Use visualization, spatial reasoning, and geometric modeling to solve problems.   In prekindergarten through grade 2 all students should:

- Create mental images of geometric shapes using spatial memory and spatial visualization

- Recognize and represent shapes from different perspectives

- Relate ideas in geometry to ideas in number and measurement

- Recognize geometric shapes and structures in the environment and specify their location

Measurement Standards: Pre-K through grade 2 Expectations (NCTM 2000, p. 102)
Understand measurable attributes of objects and the units, systems, and processes of measurement.   In prekindergarten through grade 2 all students should:

- Recognize the attributes of length, volume, weight, area, and time

- Compare and order objects according to these attributes

- Understand how to measure using nonstandard and standard units

- Select an appropriate unit and tool for the attribute being measured

Apply appropriate techniques, tools, and formulas to determine measurements.   In prekindergarten through grade 2 all students should:

- Measure with multiple copies of units of the same size, such as paper clips laid end to end

- Use repetition of a single unit to measure something larger than the unit, for instance, measuring the length of a room with a single meterstick

- Use tools to measure

- Develop common referents for measures to make comparisons and estimates

Data Analysis and Probability: Pre-K through grade 2 Expectations (NCTM 2000, p. 108)
Formulate questions that can be addressed with data and collect, organize, and display relevant data to answer them.   In prekindergarten through grade 2 all students should:

- Pose questions and gather data about themselves and their surroundings

- Sort and classify objects according to their attributes and organize data about the objects

- Represent data using concrete objects, pictures, and graphs

Select and use appropriate statistical methods to analyze data.   In prekindergarten through grade 2 all students should:

- Describe parts of the data and the set of data as a whole to determine what the data show

Develop and evaluate inferences and predictions that are based on data.   In prekindergarten through grade 2 all students should:

- Discuss events related to students' experiences as likely or unlikely

Understand and apply basic concepts of probablity.   The following are the five *process standards* suggested by the National Council of Teachers of Mathematics (2000, pp. 116–135):

Problem Solving (NCTM 2000, p. 116).

Instructional programs from prekindergarten through grade 12 should enable all students to:

- Build new mathematical knowledge through problem solving

- Solve problems that arise in mathematics and in other contexts

- Apply and adapt a variety of appropriate strategies to solve problems

- Monitor and reflect on the process of mathematical problem solving

Reasoning and Proof (NCTM 2000, p. 122).

Instructional programs from prekindergarten through grade 12 should enable all students to:

- Recognize reasoning and proof as fundamental aspects of mathematics

- Make and investigate mathematical conjectures

- Develop and evaluate mathematical arguments and proofs

- Select and use various types of reasoning and methods of proof

Communication (NCTM 2000, p. 128).

Instructional programs from prekindergarten through grade 12 should enable all students to:

- Organize and consolidate their mathematical thinking through communication

- Communicate their mathematical thinking coherently and clearly to peers, teachers, and others

- Analyze and evaluate the mathematical thinking and strategies of others

- Use the language of mathematics to express mathematical ideas precisely

Connections (NCTM 2000, p. 132).

Instructional programs from prekindergarten through grade 12 should enable all students to:

- Recognize and use connections among mathematical ideas

- Understand how mathematical ideas interconnect and build on one another to produce a coherent whole

- Recognize and apply mathematics in contexts outside mathematics

Representation (NCTM 2000, p. 136).

Instructional programs from prekindergarten through grade 12 should enable all students to:

- Create and use representations to organize, record, and communicate mathematical ideas

- Select, apply, and translate among mathematical representations to solve problems

- Use representations to model and interpret physical, social, and mathematical phenomena

The NCTM standards give a detailed overview of math content and processes for prekindergarten through second grade. The focus in early childhood will be on understanding numbers and the number systems and understanding operations, specifically addition ("putting together") and subtraction ("taking apart") (Kline, 2000). Implementing the NCTM standards has required teachers to alter their teaching role from transmitter of information and knowledge to the more constructivist approach of facilitator:"one who engages the class in mathematical investigations, orchestrates class discourse, and creates a learning environment that is mathematically empowering" (Herrera & Owens, 2001, p. 90).

Children become aware of numbers early in life, because daily experiences involve various uses of numbers. Soon after children begin to speak, they use words relating to numbers. But understanding the meanings of these number words comes later, as the child matures, experiences, and develops.

Young children are very interested in exploring and experimenting with numbers; math should be concrete and manipulative (Charlesworth, 1997). Intuitively, they like to count and rehearse the sequence of number names. Many experiences with self-correcting manipulatives should be provided for children throughout the early childhood years. Those working with young children should take advantage of opportunities that frequently arise in a child's play: pegboards, snap beads, abacus, clay, nesting cups, cooking, taking turns, sharing, climbing stairs, fingerplays, snack time, music, and so on. Children can best learn numerical combinations and relationships in the context of their play experiences, rather than with worksheets and skill and drill time (Clements, 2001; Kline, 1999). After children learn to associate a quantity with a number (idea), adults can begin to write down number symbols, or numerals, so that the children can associate the quantity with the numeral.

The classroom and activities of young children abound with opportunities for using numbers that include counting and simple number reasoning concepts; but many of the understandings that children have of number are incomplete or even misunderstood or confused. For example, children may enjoy counting, but the cognitive understanding of one-to-one correspondence comes some time later, developmentally, than rote counting ability. Children's understanding of numbers develops as they match, compare, sort, combine, separate, group, question, and order.

Various number concepts, including classification, comparison, ordering, sorting, ordinal and cardinal number, one-to-one correspondence, rational counting, number recognition, and conservation, can be explored through children's books and literature. However, for the early childhood teacher to be successful in teaching math concepts, the teacher must know the level of understanding of individual children and teach to their needs (NCTM, 2000).

Mathematical and number concepts can be taught in a unit theme or in individual or group activities, but must also be an integral part of the entire curriculum or preschool day. Mathematical understanding can be interwoven with literacy learning combined with drama to personalize the story and the math and to relate the literature to real-world activities, as well as to apply and extend the new concept (Harris, 1999).

Children can be given engaging problems to solve in cooperative learning groups. For example, in preschool each group could be given a set of beads or buttons and a set of numeral cards. Each group counts its objects and finds the numeral representing that quantity. For first or second grades, once a day in a cooperative group the children could have a story problem to solve relating to the math concept that they are learning. For example, if they are working on beginning addition, give a problem such as "There are three goldfish in the aquarium, and a class member brings in two more fish. How many fish are there in the tank all together?" Cooperative learning helps children to share, refine, and include all children in elaborating on information. It is important that adults use math terms correctly in their vocabulary, while listening for any misconceptions that children may have in their striving for understanding.

Birthdays and ages are constantly items of importance to children. They become measures of time, abilities, and achievements.

Often in children's speech we hear references to ages and birthdays.

"I already did this—when I was only three."

"Yesterday I was three, today I am four—and tomorrow I will be five!"

"My sister is 14 and I am 4, so we are the same age."

A 3-year-old was involved in a discussion with her 4-year-old brother. He had told her that she could not go to preschool because she was not yet 4. She said, "Someday I'll be 5," to which he replied, "Then I'll be 6." She said, "Someday I'll be 10"; he said, "And I'll be 11." They continued on and finally she said, "Well, someday I'll be 100," and he confidently said, "And then I'll be 101!"

Frequently, the importance of the child's age is apparent in responses to seemingly unrelated stimuli. A 3-year-old may not be satisfied with one cookie or with four cookies—just three. Since that age of 3 years is so important, the child can usually count to 3 and desires things in that amount. A soldier was visiting the classroom and explaining to the children about independence and being free. Richard, intently listening, suddenly retorted, "I am not free, I am 4!" The children were being divided into groups for an art activity, the groups being named "ones," "twos," "threes," and so on. The teacher said, "Destry, you are a 'two,'" to which he indignantly responded, "I am not 2, I am 5."

To a young child, age and size are directly associated, since the child assumes that the larger and bigger a person is, the older that person is. Children also directly associate age and authority: The more authority a person has, the older that person is. Only after gaining more experience and understanding does the child realize that a large

5-year-old child is younger than a small 8-year-old child or that a 40-year-old parent is older than a 30-year-old fire fighter. References to height and weight are often heard as children continue to experiment with their new vocabulary. "I ate 2 pounds of bacon for breakfast; now I weigh 37 pounds." "I weigh 65 feet."

The children were being measured and weighed, and these amounts were being recorded on a chart. Melissa observed the other children for a short time and then declared, "Pound me next."

Numbers are also familiar to children because they appear in telephone numbers, addresses, speedometers, speed limit signs, mileage distance signs, page numbers, clocks, calendars, and thermometers.

Calendars provide a natural avenue for learning basic concepts relating to numbers, counting, and time.

Here is a partial list of words and prefixes dealing with numbers with which children can become familiar:

dozen	uni-	less than
few, fewer	mono-	more than
many	bi-	same as
more	tri-	none
decade	quad-	pair
century	single	couple
equal	double	triple

characteristics; kinds of transportation; and animals by kind, category, size, or color.

Classification

Classification is a beginning math concept that can be taught in many ways, in different areas of the room, and in various curriculum areas. To classify means to sort or group by some common characteristic, such as size, shape, number, color, or other category. The objects being sorted are not as important as the child's own selection of object relationships. The younger the children, the fewer the sorting groups should be. Older children will determine more ways to categorize. For example, young children would sort buttons by color, and older children would sort by size, shape, number of holes, and so on (Micklo, 1997). Examples of classifying are workers by things that go with their jobs; fruits, vegetables, or flowers by kind or other

Seriation

Whereas classification refers to separating objects, *seriation* involves ordering them. As children experiment with objects, they will compare, sort, and group, but will not actually develop a logical system of ordering or seriating until they are 7 or 8 years of age (Micklo, 1997). The early years should have numerous experiences with comparing tallest to shortest, darkest to lightest, thinnest to thickest, heaviest to lightest, and so on. Even though only two objects are being compared, this is seriation at its beginning! Again, remember that the ideas of tallest–shortest, heaviest–lightest, and other descriptions may be difficult to comprehend because an item may be taller than some objects and shorter than others.

Words ending in "er" tend to make it easier to comprehend relationships than those ending in "est."

Spatial Relationships

The concept of *spatial relationships* at the early childhood level primarily involves using and understanding prepositional words. Spatial concepts answer *where* questions, *which way* questions, and *distance* questions. In other words, position, direction, and distance ideas are taught through vocabulary and actual experiences. Vocabulary words involving spacial relationships include *over, under, through, around, between, behind, next to, on, off, beside, in front of, outside, inside,* and *in the middle.* Remember to consider the developmental level and ages of the children when selecting activities involving spatial relationships.

Temporal Relationships

Temporal relationships refer to the quantitative measurements of time: minutes, hours, days, weeks, months, years, today, yesterday, tomorrow, morning, noon, night. As children begin to understand the concept of time, they usually refer to it in terms of events (VanScoy & Fairchild, 1993), such as holidays, birthdays, when a baby is born, attending kindergarten, and so on. (A more detailed discussion on time is presented later in this chapter.)

TEACHING NUMBER CONCEPTS

In the process of learning to understand numbers, some basic concepts must be learned. As children work on these understandings, they need the example and encouragement provided by the teacher so that misconceptions can be corrected. These concepts are not self-contained, and they may overlap. A child will develop many number concepts during the early childhood years. Some of the first concepts—becoming aware of the sound and sequence of numbers or counting and one-to-one correspondence—provide a basis for the acquisition of other number skills. The child then moves from counting to understanding what these numbers mean, and that "two" means two objects or things.

Becoming Aware of the Sound and Sequence of Numbers (Counting) and Developing One-to-One Correspondence

Children frequently hear counting, as steps are climbed, objects are stacked, foods are distributed, finger and toe games are played, familiar nursery rhymes and songs are enjoyed, and during many other activities (Clements, 1999a). This repetition reinforces the child's ability to begin memorization of the sequence and sounds of numbers even before the meanings of these numbers are understood. The recitation of numbers in the counting sequence has little meaning to very young children; in fact, they probably perceive it as just sound in a particular sequence. Songs, fingerplays, nursery rhymes, and stories utilizing the fingers as counting objects should be heard often. Because the correct number sequence is 1, 2, 3, 4, 5 . . . , these songs and fingerplays should utilize this particular ordering, rather than . . . 5, 4, 3, 2, 1. Learning correct counting is difficult enough for children to grasp; as their understanding increases, they are able to reason about the reverse counting sequences. It is not uncommon in this stage to hear children count 1, 2, 3, 4, 5, 6, 13, 11, 14, 5, 6. . . .

To rote count, verbalizing the number sequence, is one thing; but to count items correctly, one number per item, is more difficult. This requires skill in one-to-one correspondence. Often when a young child is given a series of items to count, the child may count two numbers for one item or one number for two items. Thus, children need to be given much time to learn to count; once this concept is mastered, the skill of one-to-one correspondence can be acquired. One way to foster the development of this skill is to have children record what they are counting, using symbols such as rocks, coins, beads, or punched holes in a card to represent numbers of items. They could count cars in a parking lot, children in the group, birds that fly overhead, or many other objects in their environment. Other daily opportunities for fostering one-to-one correspondence include table setting or passing papers or other supplies to class members. There are many children's counting books that can be read and objects counted to give further practice.

Understanding the Meaning Behind Numbers

As this memorization takes on meaning, the one-to-one correspondence necessary for actual counting is understood; the child learns that "three" means three objects or items. Even though a child may not yet be able to recognize the numeral, as objects are counted the child can correctly ascribe a number to it and understand what that number means. To understand the meaning of numbers, the child must be able to associate quantities with symbols. Puzzle matches, in which the numeral is on one side of the block or card and items representing that quantity are on the other side, provide good practice and can be geared to the developmental needs of the child. For example, a child just learning this concept may be given only matches 1 through 4, whereas another child may be ready for 1 through 10.

Zero, or the empty set, is also a rather difficult concept for children to grasp. Zero is less than 1; but when the numeral 1 precedes zero (10), then the numeral has 10 times the value of the 1.

Eric had a 6-month-old brother and was asked, "How old is your new baby brother?" After thoughtful consideration, he answered, "Zero."

Recognizing Numeral Symbols

Children memorize the sequence of numbers, and this sequence broadens into one-to-one correspondence between object and number. Now the task of recognizing the symbol representing the number (the *numeral*) must be mastered. Suppose that you were told to learn the symbols shown in Figure 12–1, which represent the numbers 1 to 5. This makes the child's position easier to understand. Now, if these numerals are written into mathematical problems, the task becomes even more difficult (see Figure 12–2). Through repeated experiences and opportunities, children learn to recognize the numeral symbols and say the names. The old adage that a single experience is not enough to build a reliable concept certainly applies in learning to recognize numerals. It is an exciting accomplishment for children and demonstrates much work and study on their part.

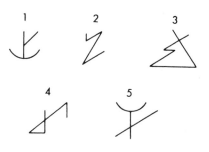

FIGURE 12–1
Example of Symbol-Learning Task

Many manipulative toys and materials can be used effectively in teaching numeral recognition. For example, separate cards for each numeral, with the numeral cut from sandpaper, are effective because they encourage tactile learning; the child feels the shape of each numeral as it is being learned. Numerals can be cut from felt to be used at a flannel board, made from wood to give three-dimensional shape, or cut from index cards or other heavy paper. To make a self-correcting number lotto, numerals can be cut and put on oak tag or poster board; then matching numerals that are exactly the same can be cut and put between clear plastic sheets so that each numeral for matching is separate. As the children match the numerals in plastic to the ones on the board, the plastic allows them to see through and correct themselves if the numerals have been matched backward or upside down. There are also many excellent commercial toys focusing on numerals that can be used in the early childhood classroom.

Once these skills are mastered, not only are the numerals correctly ordered and sequenced, but the child is able to place them so that they are

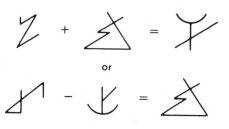

FIGURE 12–2
Sample Symbols in Problem Form

positioned correctly. The numerals are not backward, sideways, or upside down; and the numerals 6 and 9 are distinguished.

When teaching numerals, it is helpful if other concepts (such as size and color) are kept constant. For instance, it is easier for the child to concentrate on learning the numeral itself if all the numerals are the same size and color. If the numerals are of various colors, the child might think that the red numeral is a 4 and the blue numeral is a 5, rather than learning that the 4 is a 4 and the 5 is a 5, regardless of color. Varying the color, however, adds an element of difficulty to be introduced later in order to increase the challenge and motivation to the children. Once children understand the meaning of numbers and recognize numerals, they can associate the numeral with the number in the set. For example, the child can now match a set of four peanuts to the numeral or symbol 4.

Ordering Numerals and Sets

Once the numeral is recognized, the skill that often follows is the ability to order the numerals in sequence. As the children observe a collection of numerals, they are able to select first the 1, then the 2, the 3, 4, 5, 6, and so on, in correct order.

In addition, they develop the skill of putting sets of objects in order, from those with the fewest number of objects to those with the greatest number of objects. The children should also be able to make comparisons such as *more than, less than,* and *as many as.*

Once children master these basic mathematical concepts, they are ready for more advanced number skills and usually show signs of wanting to write the numerals.

Comparing and Conserving Numbers

In mathematical comparisons, children learn to make comparisons such as those that relate to size and measurement and to quantity, such as *more than, less than,* and *as many as.* Before children begin adding and subtracting, they should have many experiences comparing sets in terms of *more than, less than,* and *as many as.*

Conservation means that if two sets are compared and found to be equal, when they are rearranged to look not the same, the child can still determine that the two sets are equal. For example, if two rows of buttons, five in each row, are arranged in such a way that each button on one row corresponds with a button on the other row, it may be obvious to the child that they are the same or equal. If they are arranged so that the second row is more or less widely spaced than the first row, this concept will not be as obvious. However, the child who can conserve numbers will still recognize that the sets are equal. Number conservation experiences can also be planned with rows of unequal items, making them look either the same or different.

Conservation relates to judging the amount; as with number, the child recognizes that the arrangement of items does not change the number. Conservation of volume is more challenging, since the child must recognize and understand that changing the shape of something does not change the volume. To understand conservation of weight, the child must recognize that changing the shape or size of something does not change its weight, as long as nothing has been added or subtracted in the transformation.

Ordinal Numbers

As the child develops concepts of ordinal numbers (1st, 2nd, 3rd, etc.), he or she is also able to order items using ordinal numbers and to match ordinal numbers to cardinal numbers (1, 2, 3, etc.).

Adding Sets

As children develop skill in this aspect of mathematics, they are able to determine the number of items in a set when two or more sets are combined. Begin by having the child identify numerals that are one more than a particular number. Use real objects for early experiences. The child can then visualize that two buttons in one box and three buttons in another equal the same as five buttons in a box. Many games focus on addition. Frakes and Kline (2000) suggested a game or activity titled Total of Six. Numeral cards from 0 to 6 are put face up in three rows with four cards in each row. Additional cards are put face down in a pile. As players take their turns, they look for combinations of number cards to total 6. When a player finds a combination equaling 6, he or she places these cards together and then adds new cards to the rows. This activity could be adapted for combinations of 5, 7, and so on.

Subtracting Sets

As children develop skill in this aspect of mathematics, they are able to determine the number of items in the set resulting when one set is taken away from another set. Again, begin by having the child identify numerals that are one less than a particular number. Initially, working with manipulatives helps children to "see" what is happening in this kind of operation. As development and understanding progress, story problems can be used to help children to apply this operation to real-life situations.

TEACHING ABOUT UNITS OF MEASURE

We use measurements whenever we want to know "How far?" or "How much?" We use units of measure to determine length, quantity, temperature, weight, and time. Young children easily confuse different standards or units of measurement. For example, a mother was trying to get her 4-year-old child to sleep when Kyle said, "Do you know how much I love you, mother?" When she responded with "How much?" he hopped out of bed, pointed to a numeral on a nearby clock, and said, "This much, 87 pounds!" Another 4-year-old child was weighing herself on the bath scales; reading the numeral 40, she said, "I weigh 40 inches!" It takes time and experience for young children to use units and standards of measurement correctly. We must also point out that early childhood teachers should be familiar with metric units of measurement and vocabulary and understand how to convert standard units to metric units.

Fractions are also a part of measurement. Children during the early childhood years can begin to understand fractional terms such as *one-half* and *one-fourth* and to recognize that these terms indicate a part of a whole. An effective and natural way to introduce fractions to children is through many experiences with recipes. Fractions can also be taught by making a whole circle in one color; making a circle the same size in another color and cutting it in half; making the same size circle in a third

This boy is filling a cup of water that is going to be added to flour and salt to make play dough.

color, and cutting it in thirds; and making a circle the same size in still another color, and cutting it in fourths. Depending on the developmental level of the children, you could also do a circle for sixths and one for eighths. Another idea is to put the children in cooperative groups and give each group the same amount of clay. One group is to divide their clay in half, another group in thirds, and another in fourths, extending as far as developmentally appropriate. Still another possibility is to divide the class into halves, thirds, fourths, and various other parts of the whole.

Time, another unit of measure, is discussed in more detail later in this chapter. For more specific information on teaching measurement of temperature and weight, see Chapter 9 or the index.

Linear Measure

Learning linear measurement means understanding that length is measured in terms of inches, feet, and yards and understanding and using tools for linear measurement (for example, ruler, tape measure, or yardstick). Teachers should supply tools for linear measurement in the woodworking area, and it is helpful to add a ruler when using pencils and paper. A tape measure can be included in the dramatic play area for measuring height.

Liquid Measure

The concept of liquid measurement includes understanding that quantities of liquids are measured in terms of teaspoon, cup, pint, quart, and gallon and having experiences using containers that equal these amounts. Even more challenging is learning the number of cups in a pint, quart, and so on; the number of pints in a quart; and the number of quarts in a gallon. In addition to sensory media in the trough, add cups and jars for measuring, comparing, and problem solving.

TEACHING ABOUT MONEY

Because of the importance of money in people's lives, children are made aware of its value long before they understand the value meanings. Most young children's concepts of money relate to the understanding that we earn it by working and use it to pay for things that we purchase. Since it is easy for misconceptions to occur, many experiences should be provided that allow children to work with various amounts of money. When a child has the opportunity to use money, it becomes meaningful. Many games and types of play involve play money, and certainly play money has value as the child learns about payments, cash exchanges, and other concepts. But it is also important that the child experience the use of real money so that the various sizes, amounts, and markings become familiar. Because the child associates size with value, both the nickel and the penny seem to be worth more than the dime. Children are often able to identify different coins, even though the value of the coins is not known. The vocabulary attests to the child's understandings. "I need two-seventy pennies." "It costs sixty-eleven monies." George asked his mother for a tricycle. She answered that they did not have any money to buy a tricycle. Being accustomed to seeing the store clerk return change, George answered, "Well, let's go to the grocery store for some money."

It is important for children to experience shopping for food, toys, and clothing. Children will learn that not all items cost the same amount of money, that different items may have the same cost, and that the same item may have various costs. They often see change being returned to the buyer, but they need to learn that the buyer paid for the item before change was made. Perhaps an item costing 79 cents was paid for with a dollar. The change of 21 cents would be returned to the buyer as two dimes and one penny. It is difficult for children to understand that one piece of money ($1.00) is of more worth than three pieces of money (21 cents), since 3 is greater than 1.

The use of checks and credit cards further hinders a child's understanding of the value of money. Often, if a parent responds to a child's request for money with the comment "We don't have enough money," the child will reply, "Then write a check."

Concepts and Ideas for Teaching Numbers, Units of Measure, and Money

1. The words *number* and *numeral* have different meanings. *Number* is the idea, or what is being thought. *Numeral* is the name or symbol of this idea, or what is being written. The numeral, then, represents the number.
2. The correct numeral sequence is 1, 2, 3, 4, 5, ... Therefore, it is important that songs, fingerplays, nursery rhymes, poems, and games utilize this sequence.
3. A group of objects such as buttons, beans, or chips is called a *set*. An *empty set* is 0 (zero).
4. Numbers are used in many ways.
5. We use different items for measuring: clocks, rulers, measuring tapes, scales, measuring cups and spoons, calendars, and thermometers.
6. Money is used to purchase things. Coins and dollars are U.S. money, and coins have different names and different values.

Activities and Experiences for Teaching Numbers, Units of Measure, and Money

1. Select two pages from a calendar. Leave the numerals on one intact, and separate the numerals of the other. The single

numerals are then matched to those on the whole page.

2. Cut playing cards in half (make the cutting lines different on the separate cards, so that only the two correct halves will fit together). Then the cards are matched together as puzzles. A variety of number puzzles can be made matching the numeral or symbol to objects and the written name of the numeral to either objects or the numeral symbol. These can be constructed and geared to the developmental levels of the children.

3. Draw a line with numerals in the proper sequence on the floor. Tell the child to stand on a numeral and "move ahead four numerals—now move back two. What numeral are you standing on?" (This exercise also develops basic math understandings of addition and subtraction.)

4. Make a set of cards from pictures on seed packets. These cards can be grouped by flowers and vegetables; classified by kinds of flowers, by vegetables, or by colors; or used to present even more advanced concepts, such as vegetables that grow above the ground as opposed to those that grow beneath the ground.

5. Use a calendar. Children enjoy either marking off each day or adding the days to the calendar.

6. Use a calculator. Children enjoy seeing the numeral appear in response to the button that they have pushed. Older children can do simple addition and subtraction.

7. Make a classroom directory with each child's name, address, and telephone number. Put this list by the toy telephone so that the children can practice dialing numbers.

8. Use the flannel board with felt numerals and felt shapes such as stars, trees, flowers, apples, and others. Challenge the children to organize these shapes into sets representing each numeral. For example, for the numeral 1, one star; for the numeral 2, two apples; and so on.

9. Make a series of cards (at least 5 by 8 inches) with a tree cut from felt glued on the cards.

Cut apples from red felt. Children can put apples on the trees and then order them in sequence or make comparisons between trees, such as *more than, less than,* or *the same as.* They can also match the number of apples on a given tree to the numeral.

10. Do a variety of fingerplays, songs, poems, and stories that focus on rote counting.

11. Adapt pages from worksheets and workbooks to make learning games for number concepts. For example, make a matching game from a sheet on money or time on which the children are expected to write in the time or the amount of money. Write the times or money amounts on cards for the children to match to the clock faces or sets of money on the worksheet.

12. Place pairs of items (shoes, socks, earrings, dice, mittens, cymbals) in a bag and then have the children remove them and match them. Trace right and left hands on various wallpaper patterns (matching patterns for left and right), then cut them out, mix them up, and have the children match them (Stone, 1987).

13. Mark a numeral (2, 3, 4, 5, . . . 10) on a card. Have the children use paper clips, staples, hole punches, paper reinforcements, clothespins, or other objects to create sets: five staples on a "5" card, 8 holes punched on an "8" card, and so on (Stone, 1987).

14. Prior to an outdoor walk, give paper sacks to pairs of children and assign specific sets to collect: two pinecones, six leaves, eight rocks, and so on (Stone, 1987).

15. Ask your class, "How many class members have brothers? How many brothers? How many class members have sisters? How many sisters? How many have no brothers or sisters?" Now make a graph of the results. Make other simple graphs for color of hair or eyes, ages, number in family, favorite colors, favorite foods, kinds of pets, favorite books, number of books read, weather for a month, number of letters in name, number of buttons on clothing, and a comparison of the number of seeds found in a variety of fruits.

Do a graph of the class members' birthday months. Across the top of the graph, write the months of the year; then, to make the graph, have the children draw pictures of their faces and sign their names. How many birthdays in each month? Which month has the fewest? The most? What does this graph tell us?

16. Have the children play a game using a board such as the one shown in Figure 12–3. Each of two to four players has a marker such as a button. The object is to move from square 1 to square 12 and back to 1 again. There are three dice, and each player gets a chance to roll. The child must roll a numeral 1 before being able to move to square 1. Each player can add numbers together to try to get the needed numeral. For example, if the child rolls a 1, a 4, and a 2 and is on square 3, the child can move to squares 4, 5 (4 + 1), and 6 (4 + 2).

17. Play a game called "What's My Rule?" in which the children give you a number and you give it back to them, applying your rule. They try to guess the rule, but they do not shout it out. If they think that they know the rule, another child gives them a number and they apply the rule. For example, the rule could be to add or subtract a particular amount, or it could be to always add 10 to the number. You will need to make up rules according to developmental levels. Once the children understand the game, they can divide into cooperative learning groups and take turns thinking up a rule and applying it to numbers given to them by members of their group.

18. Divide the children into cooperative learning groups, and give each group a handout of developmentally appropriate math problems for which they will need to identify the pattern and determine the rule in order to select the number that comes next. For example:

    a. 1, 3, 5, 7, What is my rule?
       What comes next?
    b. 15, 12, 9, What is my rule?
       What comes next?
    c. 10, 20, 30, What is my rule?
       What comes next?

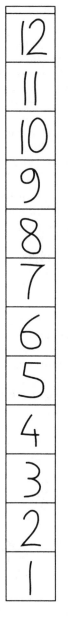

FIGURE 12–3
Board Game

19. Cover 10 soup cans with solid-color contact paper. Using small adhesive circles from an office supply store, put one on the "1" can, two on the "2" can, and so on. Children can put the same number of popsicle

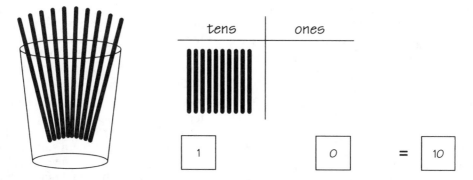

FIGURE 12–4
Sample Number Card Showing the Place Value of 10

sticks or straws in each can as there are circles on the can.

20. Number Rainbow is a good game for children to play in cooperative pairs while they develop skill in adding and subtracting. Each child has a card with a rainbow with numerals 2 through 12. The pairs take turns throwing two dice. If a player throws a 4 and a 3, a 7 (4 + 3) or a 1 (4 − 3) on the rainbow can be covered with an object such as a button. As the children take turns, if they throw the dice on a pair of numerals for which they have already covered the answers to the addition and subtraction problems, then they lose that turn. The player who first covers all the numerals on the rainbow wins.

21. This activity is for children in first or second grade as they begin to study place value (numbers above 10). To make this concept concrete, they need to see it and work with it manipulatively. Use the soup cans created for activity 19. Show the children that the 10 can, or 10 sticks, is equal to one number 10. Write the numeral on a number card as shown in Figure 12-4. Now do this with a higher number such as 14. Put 10 sticks in the "tens" can and 4 in the "ones" can so the children can learn that 10 + 4 = 1 ten and 4 ones = 14. You can do this same activity with blocks and numeral cards (see Figure 12-5). As children become developmentally ready, you can increase your tens' place value to 2, 3, and so on.

22. Give each child a number line to learn the number sequence from 1 to 10. Then, for addition and subtraction, have the children use buttons or poker chips on the number line as

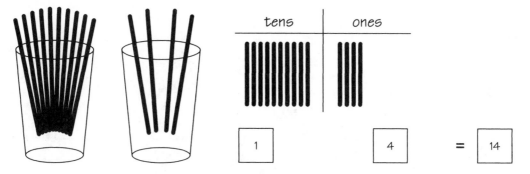

FIGURE 12–5
Sample Number Card Showing the Place Value of 14

manipulables to compute problems such as "Find 4 more than 1" or "Find 3 less than 5."

23. Make the points of a triangle with empty circles, and place another circle on each of the sides. Ask the children to figure out how to make each row of three circles total 9 (or any number) (Charlesworth & Lind, 1990). This is called a "magic triangle" (see Figure 12-6).

24. Take advantage of math experiences arising from the background, experiences, and knowledge of the individual children. In one class, the children illustrated and wrote math equations because of one child's response to his experience of losing some of his teeth. The child drew a picture of his smile and left spaces where he had lost teeth. He counted

and drew all the rest of his teeth. Then he made a math problem on his paper to show how many teeth he had left. The whole class then wanted to illustrate their smiles and figure out how many teeth they had (Mills, Whitin, & O'Keefe, 1993).

25. Play Target Addition with the class. Choose a target number such as 10, 20, 25, or whatever seems appropriate. There are two to four players with a board similar to the one shown in Figure 12-7. Players can work with one board (which would necessitate picking a smaller target number), or each player can have an individual game board. The object of the game is to pick two numbers, add them together, and cover those two numbers with

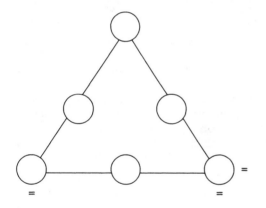

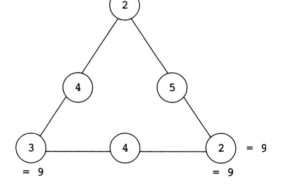

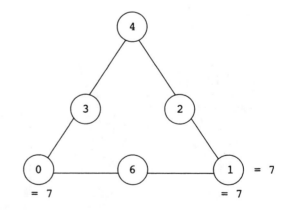

FIGURE 12–6
Magic Triangle

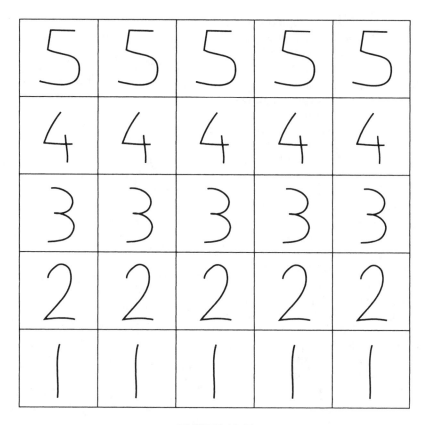

FIGURE 12–7
Target Addition Game Board

beans or buttons. The next player must start with what the last player's numbers added up to so that each player adds numbers on to the last player's. For example, the first player might select 1 + 1 = 2; the second player, 2 + 1 = 3; the third player, 3 + 2 = 5; the fourth player, 5 + 5 = 10, the fifth player, 10 + 5 = 15, and so on. Once you pass 5, players are only able to cover one of the board numerals since they only go to 5. The first player to reach the exact target number wins (Stenmark, Thompson, & Cossex, 1986).

26. Using dice, children can either add or subtract the numbers shown on two dice. Dice can also be used to find the different ways that a certain number can be made: 5 and 1, 4 and 2, or 3 and 3 can make 6. *Variation:*

Face cards can be used to work with the same concepts.

Note: Some stores carry dice with numbers higher than 6.

27. Cut a pig from heavy paper, and make a square hole near the top of it. Cut a circle about the size of the pig's body, and fasten this circle underneath the pig with a paper fastener. Glue various quantities of money on the circle where they will show through the hole. Turn the wheel so that the different quantities show through the square hole. Write each of the represented quantities on a small card so that the children can match the two. Include a small box or bag of change so that the same amount of money can be shown in ways other than that represented on the wheel or through the hole. For

example, if a dime is shown through the hole, the child should find the 10-cent card and also combinations equaling 10 cents (10 pennies, 2 nickels, or 1 nickel and 5 pennies).

28. Newspapers can be used to cut out advertisements on different items for making comparisons. For example, the children could cut out items and their prices and order them from least to most expensive. The children may need assistance in separating items by price per pound and price per individual item.

29. Money Math (ACEI, 1995/1996): As players take turns rolling a die, they get as many pennies as they roll. As soon as the players get 5 pennies, they exchange them for a nickel and 10 pennies for a dime, and so on, depending on the desired difficulty.

30. Whale on a Playground (adapted from *Learning*, 1994b): This activity helps children to apply measurement concepts as well as understand the size of a whale. Research the sizes of several different kinds of whales. Working in groups for each kind of whale, have the group members use chalk and tape measures to mark on the pavement the length of the different whales and measure them in yards or feet. Then they can use a long piece of string to form the outline of the whale. Inside the classroom they can make comparisons of the sizes of the whales and determine the difference between the largest and smallest one.

31. Each child picks an object such as a foot, box, piece of paper, pencil, or crayon that will be his or her unit of measure. Using the object, each child should "measure" several things, such as a desk, a door, or a table, and then record the answers. For example, the desk might be "9 pencils in length" and "7 pencils in width."

32. Using cups, pints, 2-liter bottles, and other containers, have children count the number of cups of water, sand, or other media that it takes to fill a pint, quart, or 2-liter bottle. How many pints will it take to fill a quart? How many quarts to fill a gallon?

33. Measure each child's height using cash register tape, yarn, or string.

34. One-Half: To teach the concept of *one-half* (or any other fraction concept), demonstrate one-half of an apple, cup of sugar, glass of water, licorice stick, and other examples that you choose. Then divide the children into pairs and give each a small candy bar. Let each pair determine how to cut the bar in half to be shared, but the person who cuts takes his or her piece of candy after the one who did not cut.

35. Fair Share: This activity teaches beginning concepts of division and also encourages sharing. In cooperative groups, give each group a container of cereal, crackers, or pretzels. Challenge the children to find a way to divide the treats to ensure that everyone gets an equal amount. Have one person in the group record how many of the treat each member of the group got and whether there were any left over. This activity can be repeated using nonedible items such as buttons, pennies, paper clips, or other items (*Learning*, 1994b).

UNIT PLAN ON NUMBERS, MEASUREMENT, AND MONEY

Field Trips

- Store: weight of items, cost of items, number of objects in each item (12 eggs in one dozen), money exchanges
- Bank
- Telephone company and telephone numbers
- Ride that includes seeing the speedometer, mileage signs, speed-limit signs, house numbers
- Weather station, thermometer
- Bakery: numbers of ingredients and baking time
- Carpenter shop
- A place where the children ride an elevator

Art

- Numeral collage: children supplied with cut numerals, glue, and paper; numerals pasted randomly or matched to predrawn numerals on background paper

- Block printing, with the raised numerals glued on blocks: numerals glued backward to be correct when printed; blocks dipped into liquid paint, then pressed onto paper or other background material

Visitors

- Store clerk, with items showing weight and cost
- Bank teller
- Telephone operator
- Police officer: importance of speed limit and mileage signs
- Weather forecaster with thermometer
- Chef, baker, or parent to prepare a food item requiring numbers in amounts and measurements
- Carpenter with measuring tape, yardstick, and ruler

Food

- Food experiences requiring recipes with specified amounts and numbers of ingredients
- Food experiences requiring baking and cooking time
- Numeral cookies: numeral shapes cut from rolled cookie dough

Music

- Musical footsteps: footsteps with numerals put in a circle on the floor; children skip, hop, and jump around the circle until the music stops; children name the numerals that they are standing on
- Clapping rhythms: record with definite beat, clapping varieties of rhythms ("This time we will clap three times, then pause one time, then clap three times again.")
- Clapping rhythms of nursery rhymes and familiar songs; clapping the numbers of dots placed on a chalkboard

Science

- Experiences with scales and balances using numbers for measurements

- Activities with yardsticks, rulers, measuring tapes
- Activities with liquid measurements
- Experiences with a thermometer

Language and Literacy

- Make number booklets with pictures from magazines or workbooks, photos, or the children's own drawings. Have the children write or dictate a sentence or two for each page.

TEACHING ABOUT TIME

Time is a temporal relationship; and because it cannot be seen, felt, heard, or touched, time is an abstract concept. The notions of *past, present,* and *future* are complicated for young children.

> Children begin to sense the importance and value of time early in their lives, but "have little concept of conventional time, nor will they be ready for instruction in time until well over 7 or 8 years of age" (Seefeldt, 1997).

Every day children hear references to time as they cook, listen to stories, and hear comments regarding time. However, understanding the meanings of these references is a relatively long and difficult process. To understand quantitative time, children must realize that time flows at a uniform speed that can be divided into equal intervals (VanScoy & Fairchild, 1993). It is important to remember that counting is the basis of time concepts.

Many of the phrases that children hear do not refer to given lengths of time or points in time, and it may be an awesome task to grasp the actual meanings. Some of these phrases are "time to go to bed," "time for a bath," "time to eat lunch," "hurry up," "we don't have time to," "not now," "maybe later," "just a minute," "just a second," and "in the olden days."

"Time to have a bath" may be at 6:30 one evening and 8:00 another evening. "Just a minute" could be 50 seconds, 3 hours, or possibly never. To a 5-year-old, "in the olden days" might be only 4 years ago, or it could be a long time ago. This phrase has different meanings for a 30-year-old and to an 80-year-old. Thus, it is easy to see why the concept of time is challenging both to teach and to learn.

How long is a minute? Specifically, it is 60 seconds, or one-sixtieth of an hour. Generally, however, the length of time varies in relation to experience. The way a person feels may make this minute feel either long or short. If you are anticipating an important long-distance telephone call, the minute seems much longer than if you are engrossed in an exciting novel—then the minute becomes much shorter. This phenomenon also presents difficulty as children try to grasp time understandings. Also, we often use the word *minute* without meaning the precise time interval of a minute. Young children are just beginning to understand time concepts, and they are often confused. They may know "today" but are still confused that "tomorrow," when it comes, is also "today." Such words as "later" or "after awhile" may mean very little to them. While taking every opportunity to introduce the words and ideas of time, the teacher must also keep in mind that "in a little while" may seem like an eternity to a frightened child waiting for her mother to return (Murphy & Leeper, 1970, p. 14).

As children get older, their concept of time also undergoes changes. To a young child, 18 is old; to an 18-year-old, it is young. To a first-grade child anticipating a summer out of school, the summer may seem a long time. But to a 20-year-old college student who is weary of studying, the summer may be much too short. Generally, however, the older a person becomes, the faster the time passes. Because of these varying concepts of time, a preschool child might ask, "Were you alive with the cowboys and Indians?" or "Did you know Abraham Lincoln?"

Children invent vocabulary words that are appropriate for their reckoning of time, for example, "yesternight" or "tomorning." It is difficult to put words in their proper context when "*to*morrow" does not refer to the same day as "*to*day" or "*to*night." If today is Wednesday, does "next Saturday" refer to the approaching Saturday or the Saturday following? A visit to the circus may be three sleeps, rather than three nights, away.

Teachers can direct children's attention to time and recognize that time words may need to be defined, such as "Yesterday is the day before this day." "Since children understand time concepts

based on a sequence of events before they understand those based on intervals, the use of such words as *before, after, fast, next, last, soon,* and *later* will enable them to further their ideas of temporal order" (Caplan & Caplan, 1983, p. 90).

Other Vocabulary Words Relating to Time

yesterday	second	short time
today	minute	long time
tomorrow	hour	never
last night	week	forever
morning	month	past
afternoon	year	present
evening	decade	future
noon	century	new
midnight	B.C.	old
day	A.D.	now
night	early(-ier)	then
spring	late(r)	next
summer	soon(er)	next time
autumn	A.M.	before
winter	P.M.	after

As children work with the calendar in the classroom, they begin to understand the names of the days of the week, the months, and the concepts that there are 7 days in a week, 28 to 31 days in a month, and 12 months in a year. Calendars promote various number concepts: There are 365 days in a year; these 365 days are grouped into 12 months; many months have the same number of days, but some do not; months are divided into weeks, and each week has 7 days; the days of the week have names; calendars tell of special days coming.

Calendars should not be overused in early childhood, but "only as they are functional and of immediate use to children" (Seefeldt, 1997, p. 181). It is not necessary to spend time every day going over calendar concepts, but more meaningful to use the calendar to anticipate and record special events (Seefeldt, 1997). Through conversations and experiences, children also develop concepts relating to reading the time on the clock and understanding hours, minutes, and seconds. It is usually around first grade that children begin to use clocks and watches to tell time (Patri-rarca & Alleman, 1987).

Various cultures and groups structure time differently. Some cultures live life slowly and deliberately, whereas others maintain a rapid pace. Some families have time to relax and participate in recreation, whereas others are much too busy to allow for these luxuries.

Understanding time is much more than being able to "tell time." Often elements other than the clock readings tell of the general time: darkness, overhead sun, snow, jack-o'-lanterns, children playing during recess in the schoolyard, a rooster crowing, and other events and circumstances indicate the possible seasons, hours, and holidays. Children learn that a specific ordering system exists among units of time.

Concepts and Ideas for Teaching Time

1. Time is measured progressively in seconds, minutes, hours, days, weeks, months, years, decades, and centuries.

   a. 60 seconds in a minute
   b. 60 minutes in an hour
   c. 24 hours in a day
   d. 7 days in a week
   e. About 4 weeks in a month
   f. About 52 weeks in a year
   g. 12 months in a year
   h. 10 years in a decade
   i. 100 years in a century

2. The clock has an hour hand and a minute hand (short hand shows the hour, long hand shows the minute), and they move clockwise on the clock.

3. Both the clock and the calendar are measurements of time.

   a. Clock: seconds, minutes, hours
   b. Calendar: days, weeks, months, years

4. Even though time is specific, it is flexible; there are 24 hours in 1 day, but a person can structure what will be done within these 24 hours.

5. Time regulates what children do.

   a. School around 9:00 A.M. on weekdays
   b. Church on Sunday for some children
   c. Bedtime around 8:00 P.M.

6. Time influences the food that we eat.

   a. Breakfast food generally different from dinner food
   b. Snacks during favorite television programs
   c. Plentiful and inexpensive vegetables in season
   d. Shortage of fruit supply during spring frosts

7. Time influences recreation.

   a. Basketball in winter, baseball in spring, football in fall
   b. No skiing if the season is sunny and warm
   c. No picnics when the weather is cold or rainy
   d. Outdoor movie theaters are often closed during winter

8. Time influences the clothing that we wear.

   a. Different clothing styles than 20 years ago
   b. Warmer clothing in cold seasons
   c. Cooler clothing in warm seasons
   d. Bedtime clothes different from daytime clothes
   e. Different clothing at home and at work
   f. Warmer clothing in late evenings and early mornings; cooler clothing in afternoons

9. Time is an element of measurement in holidays, birthdays, and other events.

   a. Operation on child 3 weeks ago
   b. Child's lost tooth on the night of a favorite movie
   c. Christmas always on December 25
   d. Child's birthday on same date each year
   e. New baby expected the first part of October
   f. Visit from a child's grandmother on April 4

10. Time is an element of measurement in seasons, weather, lightness and darkness, and speed.

   a. Four seasons: spring, summer, fall, winter, which always begin on the same dates and follow the same sequence
   b. Car traveling 45 miles per hour (45 miles traveled in an hour)

c. Distance of lightning indicated by lapse of time between observing lightning and hearing thunder

d. Warnings of approaching storms usually given in lengths of time

e. Inches of precipitation said to accumulate in a specific period of time

f. Rotation of Earth in 24-hour period, resulting in lightness and darkness: contrary to the usual childhood ideas that the sun makes the day light and the moon makes the night dark, and that the sun and moon come up and go down

Activities and Experiences for Teaching Time

1. Make a year's calendar and include dates of importance to the children: their birthdays, closing date of school, holidays, and special events. Refer often to the past, present, and future and how these time perspectives change from day to day.

2. Make a clock with movable hour and minute hands. Have it show appropriate times at the beginning and end of the school day, lunch, snack, outside play, and so on. Match digital times to a traditional clock's time, or vice versa.

3. Measure a 60-second length of time at two different times, one while the children are sitting with nothing to do and one while they are listening to a good story. Discuss the differences that they felt and why.

4. Make a sundial. On a large cardboard circle, attach a perpendicular straw or narrow stick. Leave it in the sun so that the straw will cast a shadow on the circle for 12 hours. Every hour on the hour, mark the position of the shadow of the straw. At the end of 12 hours there will be 12 appropriate marks, but these markings will not be equal distances apart. Then, at the mark indicating when school begins, place a picture or a drawing representing that time. Lunch, school ending, and other events of the day may be designated by drawings or pictures at the appropriate marks. As

the day progresses, the children observe the nearness of an event by the shadow of the straw cast on the dial. (This sundial will be accurate for only a few days; then another one must be constructed.)

5. From a calendar, take two month pages. Leave one page as is and cut the day numerals apart on the other page. Then have the children use the cut numerals to match the numerals on the page that has been left intact.

6. Measure the time of different egg timers.

7. Do language experience stories titled "Times I Like" and "Times I Do Not Like."

8. A favorite calendar activity is to use 31 sheets of paper, about $5\frac{1}{2}$ by 4 inches, representing each day of the month. Number them from 1 to 31 and put them up in correct order, representing a calendar. As each day arrives, a different child can write and draw a picture for that day. For example, on May 2, when Daniel announces that his dog had puppies in the middle of the night, he is invited to draw a picture on the paper with the 2. Either the child or the teacher, depending on the child's level of writing skill, then writes a related sentence on the paper. When the month is finished, the ordered pages are attached to a name-of-the-month cover sheet. The resulting book will be read over and over again. If saved for an entire year, the sheets can be put together into a school yearbook.

9. Read a story that has a definite time sequence such as *Caps for Sale* (Slobodkina, HarperCollins, New York, 1947); then go back through the story and label the sequences in terms of the time of day.

10. Using a kitchen timer, have the children first guess how many things can be done in a certain length of time, such as "In 1 minute, how many times can you bounce a ball?" "In 1 minute, how many times can you hop on one foot?" Then set the timer to 1 minute and actually count these out.

11. Take a picture of the children under the same tree at various times during the year to see the changes that result in both the tree and the children. Explain how the passage of time changes things.

12. After the children are able to read hour and half-hour times, teach them how to count by 5 and tell time to the nearest multiple of 5. Teach them to read both traditional hand and digital time.

UNIT PLAN ON TIME

Science

- Chemical garden: observation of changes
- Seeds planted: observation of growth over a specific length of time; comparison with original seed size
- Potato left on a table for a period of time: observation of changes
- Sundial

Music

- Musical chairs: music played for varying lengths of time
- Creative movements: being in a hurry, going slowly; pretending to be the hour, minute, or second hand of a clock; dramatizing a day from awakening through going to bed
- Rhythm sticks played along with a metronome, with variation of the beats per minute

Field Trips

- Clock sales and repair shop
- Science center with fossils
- Historical museum
- Bakery: time the baking time of breads, rolls, and other bakery goods
- Weather station
- Any business that uses a time clock for employees to punch in and out of work

Art

- Individual sundials made and decorated
- Clock face made by each child: paper plate and all numerals needed; numerals pasted on the plate in order or matched to a numeral previously drawn by the teacher

Food

- Any food activity requiring a specific cooking time: cookies, cakes, candies, casseroles, puddings, breads, pies
- Medium- or, hard-cooked eggs, depending on the cooking time

Visitors

- Grandparent, teenager, baby
- Person from museum of history: objects from the past
- Person with a fossil
- Baker: explanation of the time element in baking
- Person who sells or repairs clocks
- Weather forecaster

TEACHING ABOUT SHAPE

As early as 3 weeks of age, children begin to distinguish patterns of shape and form. Color is an important aid for identifying shape, but it is also possible that the form or shape of almost any object, for instance, a chair or a table, is more significant than its color.

By the age of 5 or 6 years, children can differentiate geometric shapes: squares, triangles, and circles. Concepts and understandings are formed from observation and manipulation of models and diagrams, rather than by mere definition (Fuys and Liebov, 1997).

Shape and form are important concepts to teach for a number of reasons. "Shape knowledge underlies algebra, geometry, and other domains of higher mathematics" (Diffily & Morrison, 1996, p. 28). Children are interested in the shapes of things: objects in their environments, the shape of their bodies, the shapes that they can make with their bodies, and geometric shapes. They also learn early that most things have a shape and that the shape of something helps to determine what it is or how it is different from other objects in the same category. One of the most important reasons for teaching the perceptual awareness of shapes and noticing fine differences in shapes is that a

A mixture of white liquid glue and liquid starch makes a putty-like textured medium that is excellent for rolling various lengths of ropes.

child's reading readiness will depend in part on visual perception of shape and form. Wide exposure to shapes and forms in the environment can also be enhanced through fine art, which involves more than geometric shapes and combines both regular and irregular shapes.

If a child has been taught to notice differences and to look for differences in the shapes and forms of things, he or she will be more able to read and master other academic skills. For example, in math a child must recognize the differences between the numerals 9 and 6 and learn the correct forms of other numerals in order to recognize them and comprehend their meanings. Work and study on shape and form transfer to other areas and assist the child in progressing in academic understanding.

Objects are identified by shape or form, and the recognition of various forms depends on previous visual experiences with the objects. The shapes illustrated in Figure 12–8 symbolize a concept or organized thought, even though verbal labels have not been ascribed to them. When the shape is observed, it is recognized and identified as having a particular meaning.

Although most things have a shape, it must be remembered that liquids and gases assume the shapes of their boundaries or containers. In teaching shape and form, it is also important to include shapes in addition to the common geometric shapes of a circle, triangle, rectangle, and square. Since shapes aid in or are sources of identification, limiting instruction to the basic shapes excludes from the learning environment the important aspects of recognition of shapes in general. Before uncommon shapes are taught, more familiar ones must be assimilated and understood. Recognition

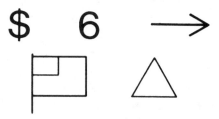

FIGURE 12–8
Examples of Shapes That Symbolize Concepts

of unfamiliar shapes depends on previous shape identification and recognition. Based on an understanding of simple shapes, the child is able to build more complex structures.

The children were on a field trip observing shapes, and the teacher inquired about the shape of the window in the back of the bus. (The window was rectangular, with rounded corners.) After thinking for a moment, Eric replied, "It isn't a rectangle, because it doesn't have any sharps!" As with the teaching of any idea, various shapes must be found in numerous ways in the child's environment, with many opportunities for manipulation and problem solving.

Words defining shapes should be used often, and words that are usually relied on, such as *that, there,* and *it,* must be accompanied by more detail. Everyday language should include such statements as "That is a square box," rather than "That is square"; "The clock is round," rather than "This is round"; and "Put the book on the square table," rather than "Put it over there." From such sentences, both the object and its characteristic shape become separate and unique ideas. Later more dimensions such as color, size, texture, and number may be added.

When unfamiliar shapes are introduced, a review of already familiar shapes should precede the introduction. Children need many experiences with shapes and with making comparisons between shapes before focusing on naming shapes. Then the children's thinking can be stimulated with such statements as "How is this new shape the same as . . . ?" or "How is this new shape not the same as (or different from) . . . ?"

Comparisons provide reinforcement and review of shapes already learned. Too often we begin with naming shapes. This is also true of letters: Children need experiences and opportunities to observe and compare before learning the names of the letters.

Before attaching specific names to shapes, ask such questions as "Who has a shape like this one?" However, do not leave the problem solving there. Follow with, "How do you know?" or "How is it alike?" (Micklo, 1995, p. 25). Identifying similarities and differences is a critical skill that prefaces being able to master reading, writing, spelling, and mathematics. Learning how to solve problems is more important than the solution itself!

To learn about shapes, children need to play with them through games, toys, art activities, fingerplays, songs, poems, and stories. Developmentally appropriate (Bredekamp & Copple, 1997) literature, materials, experiences, games, and toys, selected carefully and deliberately, stimulate and increase a child's ability to perceive shapes and forms in the environment. Children's literature is very important in enhancing the learning of prenumber concepts in the early years. The more difficult abstract concepts to grasp, such as "time, distance, size, mass, color, [and] shape . . . need to be clarified and amplified in books as well as in conversation" (Sutherland & Arbuthnot, 1986, p. 99) and in activities.

Concepts and Ideas for Teaching Shape

1. Most things have a shape, and we tell what they are by their shape.

2. Some objects are geometric shapes: circle, square, triangle, and rectangle. (Add the oval, diamond, pentagon, octagon, hexagon, rhombus, ellipse, and other names of specific geometric shapes for older children.) Three-dimensional geometric shapes include the sphere, cone, and cylinder.

3. The same items or objects may be found in different shapes.

   a. Flowers
   b. Hats
   c. People
   d. Dogs
   e. Automobiles
   f. Shoes
   g. Houses
   h. Pasta
   i. Telephones

4. The same shapes may be found in different objects.

   a. Circle found in a clock, marble, orange, basketball, coin, plate
   b. Square found in a book, fabric pattern, checkerboard, block
   c. Triangle found in a tent, house, bridge, musical instrument, highway sign

5. The same shapes may be found in different sizes.

   a. Suitcases
   b. Crayons
   c. Shoes
   d. Apples
   e. Picture frames
   f. Cans
   g. Balls
   h. Pizza
   i. Fish

6. Shape can be modified.

   a. Growth and aging: shape of a seed compared to that of a plant; a fresh fruit or vegetable to an old, shriveled one; a baby to an adult
   b. Movement: various shapes achieved by moving different parts of the body or by changing elastic or rope boundaries
   c. Pressure: applied to a tomato, egg, drying mud, wet cement, rough wood, or inflated balloon alters the original shape
   d. Temperature changes (heating and freezing): shapes changed by turning solids into liquids, as well as some liquids into solids
   e. Cutting, crumbling, crushing, bending, folding: not only change the original shape, but also may create identifiable new shapes
   f. Natural changes in nature: wind, water, and so on
   g. Pouring: liquids take the shape of the containers into which they are poured

7. One shape, by adding different dimensions, becomes another shape; for example, combining a triangle and a circle results in a face with a hat or an ice-cream cone.

Activities and Experiences for Teaching Shape

1. Shape identification. Circulate containers of objects to be identified by shape; the child feels the shape within the container and then reports the item felt.

2. Silhouette identification. Display outlines of various shapes (simple shapes, such as an umbrella, shoe, chair, or fish, and more complex shapes, such as different shapes of shoes, animals, and flowers, depending on the age level) for the children to identify.

3. Shape collage. Paste variously shaped pieces of paper on a background. Then distribute to the children matching shapes that have been cut smaller than the background shape. As the shape is matched, it is pasted on the background.

4. Sensory exploration. Put objects of various shapes (of the same category or a different category) in a trough or similar container so that the children can feel and see the various shapes. For instance, objects with circle shapes could include a ball, marble, coin, magnifying glass, and others.

5. Same shape collection. Place a large shape (for example, a circle) on the table or bulletin board. Then invite the children and their families to find photographs, pictures, or objects that are the same shape as the example (for example, a button, ball, coin, mirror, or plate).

6. Pegboard shapes. Supply the children with geoboards or pegboards and pegs and elastic. By stretching the elastic around various patterns of pegs, the children can form shapes. To make a geoboard, sand and finish a board 8 by 8 by 1 inch. Pound small finish nails at equal intervals using five rows of five nails each and leaving about $\frac{1}{2}$-inch space between the board and the head of the nail. (Since older children can draw shapes on paper, provide them with pencils and paper on which dots have been placed or drawn. Then they may draw shapes by connecting the dots.)

7. Shape classification. Cut various shapes (geometric and/or objects) in different colors and sizes from felt. The children classify or sort the items according to shape (for example, all the squares together, all the rabbits together).

8. Copying shapes. The 2-, 3-, and young 4-year-olds may have difficulty in copying even such shapes as circles and squares. Most 5-year-olds can begin to copy some shapes. Making a perfect copy will be difficult and

challenging, yet enjoyable, for many. By the time children are 6 to 8 years of age, they can copy many-sided geometric shapes and unusual shapes. One way to encourage copying shapes is to draw a particular shape on a series of evenly spaced dots and then, next to this, provide a similar series of dots on which the children can copy the shape.

9. Supply magazines for the children to go through and find objects with obvious geometric shapes. The children can cut these pictures out and make a shape book with a page or pages for each shape.

10. Make individual puzzles from cereal boxes by cutting out the entire front panel from the rest of the box. Then, leaving the four side borders of this panel intact, cut out shapes (triangle, square, circle, etc.) from the center area. Store these puzzle pieces in sealable plastic bags (Stone, 1987).

11. Prior to cooking pasta for a food activity, mix uncooked pasta of various shapes (shell, elbow, twist) in a bowl. Then have the children sort these into separate bowls. The pasta is later cooked, and the shapes of the cooked pasta are identified and compared. Various shapes of Styrofoam packing pieces can also be used for shape and form sorting and identification (Stone, 1987).

12. Assign the children to cooperative learning groups, and give each group a sheet with various geometric shapes drawn on it. The children in each group are to cut out their shapes and glue them on one picture that they work on as a group.

13. Discuss the general characteristics of quadrilaterals (four-sided shapes) and triangles by counting the sides of various figures in order to select the category to which they belong (Clements & Sarama, 2000).

UNIT PLAN ON SHAPE

Field Trips

- Bakery
- Shape walk
- Furniture store
- Shoe store
- Hat store
- Bus ride
- Construction site
- Art gallery

Art

- Sponge printing (geometric or other shapes)
- Shape collage
- Easel paper cut in various shapes
- Box sculpture: see unit plan on size and seriation
- Tracing around objects similar in shape
- Clay molding
- Different-shaped buttons in a collage
- Shakers of various shapes
- Marshmallow sculpture
- Circle or other shape drawings: Draw several circles on a sheet of paper and have the children make something different with each one.
- Various cutout shapes put into patterns or used to make figures

Music

- Twister with shapes, using music
- Playing instruments of varied shapes
- Comparison of sounds from instruments of various shapes
- Musical shapes: pass shapes around; identify or describe them when the music stops
- Different ways we can shape our own bodies
- Ways of moving around shapes or a particular shape

Food

- Variously shaped crackers with juice
- Shaped sandwiches
- Napkins folded in shapes
- Cakes baked or decorated in different shapes

- Rolled, shaped cookies
- Gelatin in molds
- Popcorn balls "sculpted" into various shapes
- Bread, molded and then baked
- Hotcakes cooked in various shapes
- Various shapes of pasta, uncooked and cooked

Visitors

- Carpenter
- Glassblower
- Person from hat store
- Person from shoe store
- Highway flag signaler or police officer
- Artist
- Flower arranger
- Family (comparison of body shapes)
- Parent to make cookie or bread shapes
- Pizza expert
- Wood carver

Science

- Shape changed by cutting, crumbling, and so on
- Shape changed by adding yeast
- Demonstration of erosion
- Water and air: take the shape of containers
- Balloon experiments
- Observation of snake after feeding time
- Crushing, then releasing of plastic
- Identification of objects from cut silhouettes
- Matching of shapes by feeling
- Bubble blowing ($\frac{1}{2}$-cup liquid dishwashing detergent and $\frac{1}{4}$-cup sugar, or 8 ounces of liquid detergent and 1 ounce of glycerin; either recipe can be diluted with a small amount of water, if necessary)

Literacy

- Make a booklet composed of pictures of various shapes. Add sentences created by the children (written by the children or teacher, depending on the children's writing ability). Even the booklet pages can be cut into shapes; either each page is different, or all pages within the booklet match.

TEACHING ABOUT SIZE

Although color and form are more functional than size in children's perceptions, size distinctions are still an integral part of early learning. Children learn to classify size through many experiences involving actual objects and construct new knowledge based on previous observations and manipulations (Clements & Battista, 1990; Kamii & Lewis, 1990; Micklo, 1995). Children realize how much they have grown as they compare their size with that of young infants. They see themselves as big. Activities with size can help them to learn to make comparisons and understand size. These activities must be developmentally appropriate for children, with both age and individual differences being considered (Bredekamp & Copple, 1997).

Teaching size involves making comparisons between the sizes of two or more objects. Seriation is arranging items in a specific order according to a specific rule, such as size. When children seriate with regard to size, they arrange items from smallest to largest.

It is important to remember that size is relative or comparative; in other words, the size of a particular object may be larger or smaller, depending on the size of the object to which it is compared or seen in relationship. An exciting brainstorming session can emerge as children are asked, "What is the largest object in the room?" Then they could be asked what would make that object smaller by comparison, then even smaller. The questions could continue until the final answer might be the universe. Since size is relative, it is better to use relative size words: *larger* rather than *large, smaller* rather than *small, bigger* rather than *big,* and so on. With the addition of the suffix *-er,* these words become comparative.

In teaching size and seriation, teachers should give children daily experiences in making size comparisons and in seriating objects. Motivating questions and statements should often be used, such as "Which is the smallest fish in our aquarium?" or "Put

Cans and hands seem big, but look even larger when seen through a magnifying glass.

the cars in order from smallest to largest as you put them away today." Not only is it important to ask such questions as "Which is larger?" but a follow-up question of "How can you tell?" helps children to further solve problems and determine correct attributes (Kilmer & Hofman, 1995, pp. 43–63).

Many opportunities for becoming familiar with size vocabulary should be provided. As a child has repeated exposure to words and their meanings, they soon become possessions and are an active part of the vocabulary.

Children often relate size to themselves or their own bodies. The distance an object is from a child affects how the child judges the object's size, and children have difficulty making comparisons and judgments as the distance between themselves and an object increases or decreases. Objects larger than themselves are "big," and objects smaller than themselves are "little." Concepts of age are tied to physical characteristics of size. To a child, the larger people are, the older they are. Children become aware of size early, since they are constantly reminded that they are "too big to . . ." and "too little to . . .," as well as being told that "when you are bigger you will be able to . . . ." Thus, children begin to feel that with size and age everything becomes possible, but in the meantime they have to wait because they are too young—and too small.

Many children, especially those who are shorter or smaller than their peers, equate their size with their character, which strongly influences their self-concept. These children not only feel shorter or smaller physically, but also emotionally small, inadequate, and unimportant. Teachers have a responsibility and obligation to all children to focus size remarks on objects rather than children. For example, instead of saying, "You are too small to reach the light switch," it might be better to say, "That light switch is too high—let me help you." Children should be frequently reminded that they *can* do many things because of their size. All too often, they are constantly reminded of things that they *cannot* do because they are either not old enough or not big enough. It is no wonder that some children are discontented with their size, age, and particular stage of life.

Examples of Words Relating to Size Aspects

larger/smaller	deeper/shallower
bigger/littler	taller/shorter
wider/narrower	gigantic/tiny
longer/shorter	fatter/thinner
higher/lower	thicker/thinner

Over 50 years ago, Davis and Havighurst (1947, p. 28) explained the child's desire to grow up, and their description is still realistic today:

Age is the ladder by which the young child hopes to climb to his Arcadia. . . . Very early he discovers that other children, whether in his family or his nursery school, measure his prestige by his age. On the ladder of age each step will lead him to higher privileges at home and at school, to sweeter triumphs over more and more "small fry," and to more dazzling signs of prestige. . . . Everything good, he is told by his parents, comes with age.

More than anything else, therefore, the child yearns to become bigger and older....To the young child ...age seems to be the key which unlocks all the forbidden doors of life. It is the magic gift of adults, which brings power and social acceptance. It lifts the barriers to the most inviting and mysterious roads, opening toward freedom and adventure. . . . As long as he is young he must be the underdog, he must yield, he must obey. It is not easy for a child to be always inferior, simply because he is inferior in size.

As children initially make comparisons of size, it is important to focus on only one aspect or attribute. Micklo (1995, p. 25) refers to "attribute materials" as those items that can be sorted in various ways, such as size, color, shape, or thickness. For example, if sizes of coins or buttons are being compared (larger versus smaller), do not add the comparison of thicker versus thinner. It is also wise to keep other concepts constant, such as color and shape, since changes in these attributes may confuse the child. A piece of equipment such as the familiar stacking cone often fails to focus on size, because the child memorizes the color sequence and knows that the top ring goes on the top because it is orange, not because it is the smallest. This stacking cone actually has at least four attributes for children to learn: small, round, red, and thin, or whatever adjectives are appropriate for the object. Depending on the desired concept focus, concentrate on only one attribute and gradually add the others as children expand their reservoirs of understanding. Care should be taken to avoid this confusion when selecting pieces of either commercial or handmade equipment. However, for some pieces of equipment relating to size, variation in color is appropriate. Color can serve as an aid in these kinds of toys, rather than as a distraction. An example is a set of different-sized dowels in which each dowel is a different color.

Concepts and Ideas for Teaching Size

1. The child is bigger than some things and smaller than others. This fact often determines what the child can and cannot do.

2. Size may stay the same, even though it appears to change.
   a. Child growing out of a coat thinks that the coat has changed in size.
   b. Size changes in terms of perspective; the farther away one goes from an object, the smaller it looks.
   c. Airplane in the sky appears smaller and then disappears.
   d. Use of magnifying glass, microscope, binoculars, telescope, or spotting scope

3. We feel different sizes even though our physical size does not change.
   a. When do we feel big?
   b. When do we feel small?

4. Things do not always look the same when size changes.
   a. Distortion mirrors
   b. Items viewed under a magnifying glass
   c. An inflated balloon compared to a deflated one

5. The same items come in various sizes.
   a. People
   b. Trees
   c. Flowers
   d. Automobiles
   e. Buttons
   f. Macaroni
   g. Cans
   h. Houses
   i. Marbles
   j. Balls

6. Size can change.
   a. Physical growth and aging: size of a seed in the growing process (fruits, vegetables, plants, etc.); aging fruits or vegetables as they shrivel up; a baby compared to an adult
   b. Cooking: some foods, such as rice, macaroni, and bakery products, become larger during cooking; others, such as meats, become smaller, or shrink.
   c. Subtracting: as air is taken out of a balloon, it becomes smaller; as wood is sawed, the pieces become smaller.

d. Adding: air in an inner tube; water to a dry sponge

e. Chemical changes: combining ingredients such as vinegar and soda changes their size; combining the ingredients that make Styrofoam causes a chemical reaction in which the material foams up and becomes much larger in size.

f. Cutting: changes the sizes of materials and items.

g. Temperature: freezing water expands.

h. Bending or folding

i. Instruments: microscopes, magnifying glasses, and binoculars all change the apparent sizes of items.

Activities and Experiences to Teach Size

1. Have the children seriate Styrofoam balls from smallest to largest or match duplicate sizes.

2. Put rods or dowels in matched pairs into containers; the child relies on the sense of touch to match two that are the same size.

3. Use materials such as buttons, gummed stars, lids, beads, feathers, and nails as sensory media, as collage material, or to seriate in order of size. Also, have the children make size comparisons between two or more of the objects.

4. Have the children seriate cans or boxes from smallest to largest by placing them inside one another.

5. Have the children seriate or match washers, plastic rings, or other materials in graduated sizes.

6. Cut geometric shapes in seriated sizes out of wood, felt, or cardboard. Cut two of each size for matching pairs; use one of each size for ordering size.

7. Put lima bean seeds or similar seeds on a glass slab on a damp piece of cotton each day. After several days, the changes in size are evident. The seeds can also be put in a glass between a paper towel and the outside of the glass; moisture is maintained by means of a continually dampened sponge in the center of the glass.

8. Give the children clay or play dough and have them roll balls of various sizes; then seriate these balls according to size.

9. Observe pieces of fine art (in books, calendars, postcards, galleries, etc.) and have the children compare lines, shapes, and spaces in terms of sizes and seriations.

10. Fill a shopping bag with pairs of objects that are similar except for size. The bag is emptied, and the children match and sort pairs of one big and one little object.

11. Supply greeting cards and envelopes or boxes and lids that are all mixed together. Have the children match the cards to the correctly sized envelopes or lids to the appropriate boxes.

12. Cut and compare various lengths of paper tubes (from toilet paper, paper towels, gift wrapping paper) for size matching.

13. Divide children into cooperative groups and give each group an orange. Using a string, measure the circumference of the orange. Each group determines how long its string is in inches or centimeters. On the chalkboard or chart paper, each group graphs its results. Comparisons are made. Each group then takes its string and finds at least three objects in the room that are the same measurement as the string or the same size as the circumference of the orange (adapted from Misifi, 1993). *Variation:* Adapt as an activity for estimating the circumference of, for example, a watermelon.

14. Place a hoola hoop on the floor and have children put the smaller of item pairs inside the circle and the larger items on outside the circle (Micklo, 1995).

15. Set a vegetable or fruit, such as a carrot, on the table. Every few days, compare its size with the size of a fresh carrot that has the same length and diameter as the original carrot. Continue this for an extended period of time. *Variation:* At Halloween time, graph the circumference of a carved pumpkin for several weeks, watching its change in size over time.

UNIT PLAN ON SIZE AND SERIATION

Field Trips

- Sports store: observe balls of various sizes.
- Clothing store: clothing too large and too small for children; clothing to fit parent(s)
- Grocery store: different items of the same size; the same items in various sizes
- Cycle shop: cycles of different sizes
- Carpenter shop: drill bits, pieces of wood, nails, and screws in various sizes
- Tire store: tires and inner tubes of various sizes
- Bakery: to observe process of bread baking
- Greenhouse: many kinds of plants in different stages (sizes) of growth
- Shoe store
- Art gallery

Visitors

- Mother and baby
- Grocer with canned goods of various sizes
- Baker to make doughnuts
- Service station attendant to fix an inner tube
- Teenager to inflate tires on bicycle
- Sports store clerk: seriation of balls (golf, baseball, softball, volleyball, basketball)
- Scientist with microscope or magnifying glass
- Carpenter with saw and boards
- Two grandfathers of different sizes
- Clothing store clerk with some clothes too small, some just right, and some too large for the children

Science

- Planting seeds: compare growing seeds and plants with the size of the original seeds
- Mixing vinegar and soda together

- Two similar sponges: allow one to become saturated with water and then compare the sizes of the two sponges.
- Freezing of water: draw a line on a clear bottle, fill to the line with colored water, let freeze, observe level of ice, and then let thaw and observe as the liquid returns to the original mark.
- Planting young tree: caring for it and watching its growth over an extended period of time
- Lighting a candle: observe the change in size (have two candles originally, so that the lighted candle can be compared to the unlighted one)

Food

- Bread: mix and bake, cool, eat
- Raised doughnuts
- Hamburgers
- Marshmallow squares: butter and marshmallows change size as they melt.
- Popcorn
- Cookies
- Ice cream: size changes in ice, salt, and amount of ice cream mixture
- Whipped cream or egg whites
- Egg soufflé
- Rice, spaghetti, or macaroni dish
- Snapping spaghetti into various lengths prior to cooking
- Cake
- Hotcakes cooked in various sizes

Art

- Collage with paper circles of various sizes, either of the same color or of different colors
- Button collage: buttons of many sizes pasted on Styrofoam trays
- Various lengths of straws, cut and strung
- Papier-mâché applied to an inflated balloon and allowed to dry; the balloon then popped and the resulting ball decorated

- Box sculpture: boxes of various sizes pasted together, allowed to dry, and then decorated
- Clay modeling of balls or ropes
- Smallest to largest pictures: draw pictures of objects, ordering them from smallest to largest; or pictures of animals, comparing smaller animals to larger animals.

Music

- Creative movements: of a child or seed growing, bread or cake baking, ice cube or icicle melting, balloon being inflated and popped, sponge absorbing water, vinegar and soda being mixed

- Music shakers: of varying sizes or of the same size, containing unlike sizes of materials (sand, berries, rocks, wheat, rice)
- Small musical instrument (such as a harmonica) compared to larger musical instrument (such as an accordion)
- Similar musical instruments of varying sizes (violin, cello, bass violin)

Literacy

- Write stories titled "As Big As . . . ," "As Small As . . . ," "As Tall As . . . ," or use other size words as similes.

Summary

As we have discussed problem solving and its relationship to all aspects of the early childhood education curriculum, we have stressed that the critical thinking required to reach a solution to a problem is much more valuable than the solution itself. This does not minimize the importance of learning facts, but it does maximize the lifelong rewards of being able to assess problems and evaluate possible solutions. Problem solving is particularly a necessary ingredient when working with mathematics and numbers.

Even though children become aware of numbers early in life through daily experiences, the actual understanding of number words depends on experiences, maturation, and intellectual development. Generally, number concepts are best acquired through incidental learning, rather than from formalized structured lessons. Research has found that teachers who learned math in the traditional drill-and-practice and memorize model have difficulty changing their beliefs to more constructivist, developmentally appropriate practice (Battista, 1994). However, developmentally appropriate lesson plans, carefully planned and prepared, assist children in assimilating concepts relating to numbers. For children in preschool and the early primary grades, math studies are most effective when the activities and experiences include concrete objects that relate to the concepts

being taught and are individually and age appropriate (Charlesworth, 1997).

Math activities should be enjoyable and challenging, worked on gradually, and repeated often. Although often informal and integrated into the entire curriculum, math learning is not "unplanned or unsystematic" (Clements, 2001, p. 273). As children gain experience and knowledge in measuring, counting, ordering, telling time, matching, comparing, estimating, and so on, their ability to recognize and ascribe appropriate ideas with number concepts increases.

Concepts relating to time and telling time are abstract, but they develop in early childhood as a result of daily experiences with time words and concepts and clocks. Children will learn that time exists in units and, as they understand specific units, their mathematical thinking and reasoning will be extended.

Two other specific attributes that involve problem solving were presented in this chapter, shape and size. Even in their first few months of life, children are able to distinguish shapes. While they are relatively young, they also demonstrate interest in the various shapes in their environment. Familiar and common shapes should be discussed and taught before more unfamiliar and uncommon shapes are introduced. Not only are objects identified by shape, but the recognition and perception of shapes are also basic ingredients in reading readiness. Children should have numerous experiences with the shapes in their environment. They should be encouraged to notice the differences and similarities among various shapes.

Size and seriation involve both making comparisons between two or more objects of different sizes and ordering items from smallest to largest. Size is relative; the size of an object depends on the size of another object with which it is being compared. In teaching size and seriation, provide children with many opportunities for practicing size comparisons, seriating objects, and hearing related vocabulary words.

Student Learning Activities

1. Discuss why you agree or disagree with the authors' premise that the critical thinking required to reach a solution to a problem is more valuable than the solution itself.

2. Visit a preschool, kindergarten, or first- or second-grade classroom. From the equipment and materials in the environment, list the opportunities that you see for teaching concepts relating to numbers, shape, and size. For example, you may see unit blocks of various sizes that could be compared on the basis of size or even seriated according to size.

3. With a group of children, implement at least one of the activities and experiences related to number, shape, or size concepts in this chapter. The children may be a classroom group or simply a small group of relatives or neighborhood children. Evaluate your experience.

4. Observe and talk with a preschool child, listening for comments and understandings related to numbers. Ask such questions as "How old are you?" "What is your favorite number?" "How far can you count?" and "Where do you see numbers?" Now make a comparison. Then observe and talk with a child between ages 5 and 6 and ask some of the same questions. You will want to ask additional questions, such as "Show me how you can add some items. Here are three pencils, and what will you have if you add three more pencils?" You may wish to relate problems to money, time, weight, measurement, and other concepts. Challenge the child with number questions and problems. Now compare the differences in the two children that you observed, keeping in mind the differences in their ages.

5. In this chapter are listed words and prefixes dealing with numbers, time, and size with which children 3 to 8 years old could become familiar. Brainstorm and add to these three lists.

6. List and draw the geometric shapes that children 3 to 8 years of age can learn. Find examples of three-dimensional shapes for children to manipulate and handle.

7. To help you to understand the challenge in recognizing numeral symbols, develop a set of symbols for the numerals 0 to 9, such as those suggested in Figure 12–1 for numerals 1 to 5. Learn these symbols or teach them to a friend. Several days later, see if you remember what each symbol represents, and try some addition and subtraction problems with them.

8. Visit a classroom and observe an activity or lesson for teaching numbers, shape, or size. Evaluate the activity. Was it appropriate for the age of the children? Was the emphasis on thinking and understanding the mathematical process(s)? Would you have made any changes in the lesson or activity? Was it effective? Did the teacher use materials? Was a ditto or workbook sheet used and, if so, was it effective?

9. Prepare a 5-day activity plan on shape, size, or number.

10. Make a game or piece of equipment to teach time, size, shape, or number to children 3 to 8 years of age.

11. Visit a children's library and add additional appropriate children's books to the Suggested Resources list for teaching time, shape, size, and number.

12. Visit a store or a school supply house or study an equipment catalog selling toys and learning materials that focus on time, size, shape, or number. Select three toys or materials and describe and evaluate them for their effectiveness in teaching.

13. Think of additional ideas for the Activities and Experiences sections and for the unit plans on time, shape, size, or number. Create a web or plan a child-centered project if you prefer.

14. Implement at least one of the activities that you planned in activity 13 with a group of children. Evaluate your experience.

Suggested Resources

Websites

http://www.terc.edu/investigations
http://www.gse.buffalo.edu/org/ conference
http://www.ncsmonline.org/
http://www.nctm.org
http://www.ed.gov/pubs/EarlyMath

Math Resources

Hurst, C. O. (1997). *Picturing math: Using picture books in the math curriculum* (prekindergarten through second grade.) DeSoto, TX: McGraw-Hill Learning Materials.

Children's Books on Counting and Numbers

Anno, M. (1977). *Anno's counting book.* New York: Crowell.

Anno, M. (1982). *Anno's counting house.* New York: Putnam.

Astley, J. (1990). *When one cat woke up: A cat counting book.* New York: Dial.

Baker, K. (1994). *Big fat hen.* New York: Harcourt, Brace.

Bang, M. G. (1983). *Ten, nine, eight.* New York: Greenwillow.

Burns, M. (1994). *How many feet? How many tails?* Jefferson City, MO: Scholastic.

Burns, M. (1997). *Spaghetti and meatballs for all! A mathematical story.* New York: Scholastic.

Carle, E. (1974). *My very first book of numbers.* New York: Harper-Collins.

Crews, D. (1986). *Ten black dots.* New York: Greenwillow.

Duke, K. (1985). *Seven froggies went to school.* New York: Dutton.

Ehlert, L. (1992). *Fish eyes: A book you can count on.* San Diego, CA: Harcourt Brace Jovanovich.

Feelings, M. (1971). *Moja means one.* New York: Dial.

Fleming, D. (1992). *Count!* New York: Henry Holt.

Foreman, M. (1995). *Dad! I can't sleep.* New York: Harcourt, Brace.

Fujikawa, G. (1981). *One, two, three: A counting book.* New York: Putnam.

Gag, W. (1928). *Millions of cats.* New York: Putnam.

Giganti, P. (1992). *Each orange had 8 slices.* New York: Greenwillow.

Gordon, M. (1986). *Counting.* Morristown, NJ: Silver-Burdett.

Hague, K. (1986). *Numbers.* New York: Henry Holt.

Hartman, W. (1994). *One sun rises: An African wildlife counting book.* New York: Dutton.

Hoban, T. (1990). *Exactly the opposite.* New York: Greenwillow.

Keats, E. J. (1972). *Over in the meadow.* New York: Scholastic.

Kitchen, B. (1991). *Animal numbers.* New York: Dial.

Kopper, L. (illus.) (1990). *Ten little babies.* New York: Dutton.

Langstaff, J., & F. Rojankousky (1967). *Over in the meadow.* New York: Harcourt, Brace, & World.

Leonni, L. (1962). *Inch by inch.* New York: Astor–Honor.

McMillan, B. (1992). *Eating fractions.* Jefferson City, MO: Scholastic.

McMillan, B. (1997). *One, two, one pair!* Jefferson City, MO: Scholastic.

McMillan, C. (1986). *Counting wild flowers.* New York: Lothrop, Lee & Shepard.

Milstein, L. (1995). *Coconut Mon.* New York: Tambourine.

Nelson, N. (1994). *Writing and numbers: Non-verbal communication series.* New York: Thomson Learning.

Nozaki, A. (1984). *Anno's hat tricks.* New York: Philomel.

Onyefulu, I. (1995). *E Meka's gift: An African counting story.* New York: Cobblehill.

Russo, M. (1986). *The line up book.* New York: Greenwillow.

Schlein, M. (1996). *More than one.* New York: Greenwillow.

Sendak, M. (1962). *One was Johnny: A counting book.* New York: HarperCollins.

Seuss, Dr. (1960). *One fish, two fish, red fish, blue fish.* New York: Random House.

Sloat, T. (1991). *From one to one hundred.* New York: Dutton.

Sturges, P. (1995). *Ten flashing fireflies.* New York: North–South.

Sullivan, C. (1992). *Numbers at play.* New York: Rizzoli.

Tafuri, N. (1986). *Who's counting?* New York: Greenwillow.

Tudor, T. (1956). *I is one.* New York: Rand.

Wahl, J., & S. Wahl (n.d.). *I can count the petals of a flower.* Reston, VA: National Council of Teachers of Mathematics.

Wildsmith, B. (1984). *One two three.* Topsfield, MA: Merrimick.

Children's Books on Money

Belov, R. (1971). *Money, money, money.* New York: Scholastic.

Hoban, L. (1981). *Arthur's funny money.* New York: HarperCollins.

Rockwell, A. (1984). *Our garage sale.* New York: Greenwillow.

Schwartz, D. M. (1989). *If you made a million.* New York: Scholastic.

Viorst, J. (1978). *Alexander, who used to be rich last Sunday.* New York: Macmillan.

Children's Books on Time

Barrett, J. (1976). *Benjamin's 365 birthdays.* New York: Atheneum.

Brown, M. W. (1947). *Goodnight moon.* New York: HarperCollins.

Flournoy, V. (1978). *The best time of day.* New York: Random House.

Flournoy, V. (1985). *Patchwork quilt.* New York: Dial.

McMillan, B. (1993). *Time to . . .* Jefferson City, MO: Scholastic.

Ross, T. (1995). *Bedtime.* New York: Red Wagon/Harcourt, Brace.

Rutland, J. (1976). *Time.* New York: Grosset & Dunlap.

Schlein, M. (1955). *It's about time.* New York: Young Scott.

Schwerin, D. (1984). *The tomorrow book.* New York: Pantheon.

Slobodkina, E. (1947). *Caps for sale.* New York: HarperCollins.

Wood, D. (1995). *Bedtime story.* New York: Western.

Children's Books on Shape

Bruna, D. (1984). *Know about shapes.* Los Angeles: Price Stern.

Budney, B. (1954). *A kiss is round.* New York: Lothrop, Lee & Shepard.

Carle, E. (1974). *My very first book of shapes.* New York: Crowell.

Gardner, B. (1980). *The turn about, think about, look about book.* New York: William Morrow.

Gordon, M. (1986). *Shapes.* Morristown, NJ: Silver-Burdett.

Groening, M., & M. Groening (1991). *Maggie Simpson's book of colors and shapes.* New York: HarperCollins.

Hoban, T. (1983). *Round and round and round.* New York: Greenwillow.

Hoban, T. (1986). *Shapes, shapes, shapes.* New York: Greenwillow.

Lerner, S. (1970). *Square is a shape: A book about shapes.* Minneapolis: Lerner.

Mackinnon, D. (1992). *What shape?* New York: Dial.

Micklethwait, L. (1995). *Spot a dog.* New York: Dorling Kindersley.

Ross, T. (1995). *Shapes.* New York: Red Wagon/Harcourt, Brace.

Russo, M. (1986). *The line up book.* New York: Greenwillow.

Sullivan, J. (1963). *Round is a pancake.* New York: Holt, Rinehart, & Winston.

VanFleet, M. (1995). *Fuzzy yellow ducklings.* New York: Dial.

Wildsmith, B. (1981). *Animal shapes.* New York: Oxford University Press.

Children's Books on Size

Anderson, L. C. (1983). *The wonderful shrinking shirt.* Niles, IL: Whitman.

Barton, B. (1981). *Building a house.* New York: Greenwillow.

Brenner, B. (1966). *Mr. Tall and Mr. Small.* Menlo Park, CA: Addison-Wesley.

Hoban, T. (1985). *Is it large, is it small?* New York: Greenwillow.

Hoban, T. (1996). *Just look.* New York: Greenwillow.

Holl, A., & S. Reit (1970). *Learning about size.* Indianapolis: Bobbs-Merrill.

Kohn, B. (1971). *Everything has a shape and everything has a size.* Upper Saddle River, NJ: Prentice Hall.

Krauss, R. (1947). *The growing story.* New York: Harper & Brothers.

Lenski, L. (1959). *Cowboy Small.* New York: Henry Z. Walck.

Lenski, L. (1979). *Big book of Mr. Small.* New York: McKay.

Lenski, L. (1979). *More Mr. Small.* New York: McKay.

Lionni, L. (1968). *Biggest house in the world.* New York: Pantheon.

McMillan, B. (1986). *Becca backward, Becca frontward: A book of concept pairs.* New York: Lothrop, Lee & Shepard.

Medearis, A. S. (1995). *Poppa's new pants.* New York: Holiday House.

Russo, M. (1986). *The line up book.* New York: Greenwillow.

Spier, P. (1972). *Fast-slow, high-low.* Garden City, NY: Doubleday.

Videos

It's about time. National Geographic.
Opposites. National Geographic
Shapes. National Geographic.

Teaching Videos

The Math Factor. Films for the Humanities & Sciences.
Math and Literature. Films for the Humanities & Sciences.
Whole Math. Films for the Humanities & Sciences.

Pictures

Colors and shapes. The Child's World (Panorama).
Counting and ABC's. The Child's World (Panorama).
Earning and using money. David C. Cook (74476). (Set of 20 pictures)
Learning about money. David C. Cook (51904). (Set of 12 pictures)
Learning to measure in metric units. David C. Cook (83287). (Set of 16 pictures)

Multimedia Kits

Disneyland magical metrics tour. Walt Disney.

Disney's basic math program. Walt Disney.

Disney's telling time program. Walt Disney.

Musical math I: Beginning concepts. Cheviot.

Telling time with Donald. Walt Disney. (Computer software)

Audio Cassettes, Records, and CDs

Addition and subtraction. Hap Palmer Record Library (AR541 and AC541).

Counting games and rhythms for the little ones. Scholastic Records.

Learning about numbers. David C. Cook (DC-44685).

Learning math with rods. Educational Activities (AC28).

Learning with circles and sticks. On *Learning basic skills through music* (vol. 2). Hap Palmer Record Library (AR585 or AC585).

Magic monster mix: Magic monsters count to ten. The Child's World.

Magic monster mix:Magic monsters look for shapes. The Child's World.

Money, money, money. On *Ooo we're having fun.* Cheviot (T-306).

The number march. On *Learning basic skills through music* (vol. 1). Hap Palmer Record Library (AR514 or AC514).

One shape, three shapes. On *Learning basic skills through music* (vol. 2). Hap Palmer Record Library (AR522 or AC522).

Sing a sum ..., Grade 1. Educational Activities (AR711 or AC711).

Sing a sum ..., Grade 2. Educational Activities (AR711 or AC711).

Triangle, circle, or square. On *Learning basic skills through music* (vol. 2). Hap Palmer Record Library (AR522 or AC522).

Walk around the circle. On *Learning basic skills through music—vocabulary.* Hap Palmer Record Library (AR521 or AC521).

Computer Software

Alligator alley. DLM Teaching Resources.

*Clock works.*The Learning Company.

Coin works. Nordic Software.

Colors, shapes & size. World Book Educational Products.

Combining and breaking apart numbers (designed by *Tenth Planet©*). Sunburst.

Combining shapes (designed by *Tenth Planet©*). Sunburst.

Creating patterns from shapes (designed by *Tenth Planet©*). Sunburst.

Early games match maker. Counterpoint Software.

Easy street. MindPlay.

Elevator magic (designed by *Software for Success*). Sunburst.

Exploring measurement, time, and money. IBM Educational Systems.

First shapes. First Byte.

Get up and go! (designed by *Software for Success*). Sunburst.

Graphers. Sunburst.

Grouping and place value (designed by *Tenth Planet©*). Sunburst.

Introduction to Patterns (designed by *Tenth Planet©*). Sunburst.

Jump start toddlers. Knowledge Adventure.

Kidsmath. Great Wave Software.

Kidstime. Great Wave Software.

Lemonade for sale (designed by *Software for Success*). Sunburst.

Mastering skills & concepts I: Preprimary mathematics. Riverdeep Interactive Learning.

Mastering skills & concepts II: Primary mathematics. Riverdeep Interactive Learning.

Math and me. Davidson.

Math blaster (K-2). Sunburst.

Math blaster (1-3). Sunburst.

Math rabbit (1997). The Learning Company.

Math van (1997). McGraw-Hill School Division.

Math workshop (1995). Broderbund.

Mathkeys: Unlocking geometry. The Learning Company.

Mathkeys: Unlocking measurement. The Learning Company.

Mathkeys: Unlocking whole numbers. The Learning Company.

Memory fun! Sunburst.

Mighty math carnival countdown (kindergarten-2nd grade). Riverdeep Interactive Learning.

Mighty math zoo zillions (kindergarten-2nd grade). Riverdeep Interactive Learning.

Millie's math house (preK-2nd grade). Riverdeep Interactive Learning.

*Money works.*The Learning Company.

Number meanings and counting (designed by *Tenth Planet©*). Sunburst.

Numbers undercover. Sunburst.

The penny pot (designed by *Software for Success*). Sunburst.

The playroom. Broderbund.

Preschool pack. Nordic Software.

Sequencing fun! Sunburst.

Shape up! Sunburst.

Spatial relationships (designed by *Tenth Planet©*). Sunburst.

Splish splash math. Sunburst.

Sunbuddy math playhouse. Sunburst.

Thinkin' things: Collection I (preK-3rd grade). Riverdeep Interactive Learning.

Thinkin' things: FrippleTown (K-3rd grade). Riverdeep Interactive Learning.

Trudy's time and place house (preK-2nd grade). Riverdeep Interactive Learning.

Turtle math. Logo Computer Systems

Zap! around town. Sunburst.

Part Four

Aesthetic and Creative Development

The two chapters in this part address the aesthetic development of young children, especially in the areas of creativity in music and art. The Educate America Act places dance, drama, music, and the visual arts at the very center of the curriculum (Thompson, 1995). Perhaps it would be wise to define what is meant by aesthetics and creativity.

Aesthetic awareness involves the ability to discern and be sensitive to things in the environment and to human creations. Aesthetic development encompasses the young child's individual taste, love of beauty, and criteria for judging beauty. There are numerous definitions and approaches to describing creativity, but whether it is being defined in terms of art, thinking, writing, or any other activity, certain words and ideas come to mind. *Creativity* appears to involve intuition, elaboration, fluency, flexibility, originality, evaluation, and divergent thinking. Most researchers believe that all human beings possess the capacity or potential for creativity. Teachers need to believe that all children possess creativity. When children express thoughts, feelings, or actions in original, self-initiated, or inventive ways, they are being creative.

During a unit on fish, the children were participating in an art activity in which they were making a collage of fish cutouts. One child put a group of them together, and the teacher, thinking this would be a great time for discussing the meaning of the word school of fish, asked the child if she knew what a group of fish is called. The child confidently responded, "Of course, it is a bouquet of fish!"

Remember, *all* children are creative. Children who are the most creative will often manifest a determination to express their creativity. Highly creative children, it has been suggested, often manifest characteristics such as the following:

- Have the ability to perceive unusual and broad relationships
- Have a different time–space perspective
- Have a sense of humor
- Enjoy inquiring and asking questions, as well as problem solving
- Show great ingenuity and imagination
- Offer many ideas and a variety of valid alternatives in problem solving
- Enjoy taking risks and participating in adventure
- Are often persistent in reaching a goal
- Enjoy firsthand investigative activities that provide the opportunity to probe, explore, discover, and create
- Use elaborate language and often express themselves in unique ways

Creativity is a continual process, and the best preparation is creativity itself. The joy of discovery is its own reward and provides the incentive for continuing exploration and discovery.

Too often our schools are not designed to promote or encourage creative thinking or creative art. Frequently, children's thinking and artwork must be exact and must fit into a mold or pattern. Many times there is no room for individuality, but only the opportunity to give back to the teacher the "right" or expected answer. Convergent thinking, arriving at the same "right" answer, is often the type of conformity encouraged and rewarded. This type of thinking is uncreative, less time consuming, easy to evaluate, and, in some areas, essential to education. However, a balanced view makes room for divergent thinking, too. We must continue to struggle to understand and find use for that powerful catalytic agent children have at their command—imagination!

To make any activity educationally meaningful, we should stimulate imagination (Egan, 1989), which is "the creation of possible realities" and the source of all creativeness (Smith, 1990, p. 45). Imagination can be a part of all mental functions, giving them "heightened capacity" (Egan, 1992, p. 65). Our schools need to be designed to encourage children to think, for all children can think both competently and creatively. Society and schools seem to be against divergence, and pressures on children often cause them to surrender their natural creativity. Teachers frequently cover too much material and do not ask enough questions or give children adequate time to think and respond verbally, with questions, in speaking or writing, or in art expression. Our schools often expose children to the constant fear of evaluation.

Researchers suggest that there is only a small relationship or correlation between intelligence and creativity (Torrance, 1976). Children can be taught in such a way that their creative thinking abilities become useful in attaining educational competencies. These creative skills and abilities are very different from those measured by intelligence and scholastic aptitude tests, but they are important to both mental health and vocational success. It is imperative that teachers strive to foster creativity during the early childhood years, because it is the child's creativity that sparks or kindles a new idea, that motivates the child to accept a challenging task or assignment, or that fosters the spirit of independence. Creativity offers the child the chance to change things that are or have been to things that might be or may yet be discovered. Ideas for better ways of doing things do not exist in computers or machines, but rather in the minds of humans. It is only when children are given the opportunity and even the responsibility to release their creative potential that these changes and new ideas are born.

Children grow, work, and learn better when there are periodic times set aside for self-expression. Creativity is not just for thinking, art, and music; rather it is an aspect or part of all areas in the curriculum (Smith, 1996). It has been suggested that three key ingredients are necessary for creativity to flourish in any classroom and in any part of the curriculum: (1) appropriate teacher attitude, (2) appropriate classroom atmosphere, and (3) appropriate activities and materials (Smith, 1996).

The ability to create new ideas and solve problems is one of the most important competencies for children to develop. Yet only a small percentage of the time in schools is spent encouraging students to think at the higher levels necessary for problem solving (Goodlad, 1994). Music and creative arts provide numerous opportunities for solving problems with creative thinking. Specific conditions that facilitate the development of creativity in the classroom include the following:

- Giving responsibility and independence

- Valuing the expression of feelings and individual divergence

- Emphasizing self-initiated exploring, observing, and questioning

- Creating a feeling of freedom and openness, and encouraging spontaneous expression

- Developing an accepting atmosphere

- Providing a wealth of stimulation from a rich and varied environment

- Asking provocative, thoughtful questions

- Valuing originality

- Providing many opportunities for achievement

- Providing differentiated, meaningful interaction

Experiences and activities in the creative arts reduce stress, enhance development, facilitate learning, and balance the often hurried lives of children (Elkind, 1988). The arts provide children opportunities for creative thinking as well as creative production. Children love to experiment with words, paints and other materials, and music; they find it enjoyable to dream and to create something of their own, something unique and original. Music and creative arts can give children opportunities for a creative outlet to use divergent, as opposed to convergent, thinking. Teachers must be careful not to teach these art areas in rigid, structured ways, thereby stifling children's creative potential. Teachers' techniques, approaches, and activities need to be open ended, giving children the opportunity to use their creative imagination.

Chapter 13 provides many different approaches and techniques for using songs in the classroom. In addition, a variety of suggestions for rhythm instruments and creative movements is given. Children in the early childhood years enjoy creative art activities. They enjoy them for art's sake. Both making art projects and also learning about art are integral parts of the early childhood curriculum (Seefeldt, 1999). Art activities take extra effort to prepare and clean up, but the effort is worthwhile. Care must be taken not to provide structured art activities, but rather the kinds that give children the experience of creating, planning, imagining, and exploring; many suggestions for these kinds of activities are given in Chapter 14. A variety of kinds of dramatic play experiences is also suggested in Chapter 14. "Preparing for and engaging in sociodramatic play provides a nonthreatening, child-centered environment where children teach, learn, and experience real-life roles" (Cooper and Dever, 2001, p. 62).

Children need experiences that allow them to use creativity and originality in expression or thought. Some children exhibit more potential for creativity than others, but the challenge comes in encouraging *all* children to use the creative potential that they have. Music and creative arts are areas that can encourage imagination, self-expression, and creativity; they should have an important place in every early childhood curriculum.

Teachers model and teach those things that they value and feel are worthwhile. When teachers respond emotionally and verbally to the aesthetic qualities in the environment, children learn to enjoy and appreciate things of an artistic nature. "Through a balance of academics and the arts, we will be able to graduate creative, disciplined, *whole* young men and women" (Lazdauskas, 1996, p. 23).

Chapter 13

Music and Movement

Children want to express themselves through music, and it is a meaningful and legitimate means to develop cognitive, physical, emotional, and social traits (Neely, 2001). Recent neuropsychology research suggests that music, as well as other strategies, integrates the functions of both hemispheres of the brain, making learning more fun and easier, and creating optimal learning (Davies, 2000). Although music promotes learning, it "is usually ignored as a talent for the select few or indulged as fun-time diversion. Musical illiteracy is all too often accepted as the norm" (Kenney, 1997, p. 104). But, according to Gardner (1983, 1991b), music is one of the basic intelligences possessed by all humans and, as such, is an aspect of human potential. There is a musical impulse in young children, and their potential and aptitude for music are nurtured by the musical environment provided them during infancy and early childhood (Kenney, 1997; Stellaccio & McCarthy, 1999). However, too often those involved in early childhood education appear less well prepared to use music, and programs lack musical direction (Scott-Kassner, 1999).

Reasons for Including Music in Early Childhood Programs

- Music can foster appreciation of various cultures, as well as one's own heritage. It is a part of every culture's uniqueness (Lazdauskas, 1996). Children enjoy learning songs and dances from various cultures and nations.

- Through music children experience pleasure, joy, creative expression, and other emotional responses.

- Music is one of the acceptable avenues for release and expression of feelings, moods, and emotions. Music can reduce stress (Davies, 2000).

- Music fosters self-esteem. It allows for the development of desirable feelings and moods and for dissolving undesirable feelings and moods.

- Music can quiet or calm children, create listening moods, or soothe hurt and troubled feelings.

- Music has therapeutic value and, as a result, can also enhance the child's feelings of self-worth. Songs can be sung that include the child's name, or children can write words, phrases, or verses of songs. Children should be permitted to interpret music in their own style and to make up new words, new melodies, and new movements.

- Children's listening skill, attention span, auditory discrimination, and memory develop through music. Listening to songs that tell a story (ballads) or give directions to follow provides an excellent opportunity for careful concentration and attention.

- Language and concepts can be developed through music as children sing using correct language form. New songs often introduce new words, concepts, and cognitive skills. Music can wake up the brain and increase the child's productivity (Davies, 2000).

- Research supports the notion of the physical and psychological advantages of music on the body and mind (Davies, 2000; Neelly, 2001).

- The rhythm and rhyme of music make it easier to remember factual information. Putting concepts and ideas to music often commits them to memory, since music aids recall (Davies, 2000).

Music can do many things for young children. Songs can call attention to clothing worn by the child or physical attributes possessed. Children can sing about their activities. They can name a locomotor skill or other activity and dramatize it while singing about it. Reading and singing are closely connected, because as songs are sung, language is whole and correct. When children show an interest in print, the songs can be printed in their entirety; children sense the meaning of the print as the songs are sung (Barclay & Walwer, 1992). Also, concepts can be better committed to memory when they are attached to melodies.

Music skills such as rhythm, meter, pitch, and tone are introduced to young children through music. Opportunities for participation should always be available for individuals; however, the sense of belonging to and functioning with a group is always enhanced through music participation (Neelly, 2001). Most of all, children enjoy music. They enjoy the intricate tunes and melodies; the words, which often tell a story or capture their sense of humor; and the rhythms, which often create spontaneous body movements such as toe tapping or hand clapping. Music in early childhood classes is a must; it is a teaching tool and has aesthetic qualities. Through fingerplays, action songs, music games, writing words for songs, composing melodies, and other music-related activities, children are able to utilize creative thinking in problem solving. Musical experiences are bridges to children's overall growth (Neelly, 2001).

MUSIC GOALS

Since music should be an integral part of the early childhood curriculum, its main objective for this age group is the child's enjoyment of music. Therefore, emphasis should be on the child, not the teacher; the enjoyment, not the skill; the process, not the product. "A child centered curriculum is based on the assumption that the learner is more important than that which is being learned. The child is more important than the music; music has the power, however, to make the child's life more important" (Andress, 1995, p. 100). Musical experiences defy time limits, exacting goals, and expectations. The time for music is any time!

Benefits of the Music Program in Early Childhood Education

- Success, joy, and pleasure through participation
- Opportunities to experience music through a variety of relevant activities, materials, instruments, and movements
- Acquaintance with a variety of types of music
- Provision for listening activities to foster music understanding
- Awareness of contrasts in music, such as fast and slow, high and low, loud and soft
- Responsiveness to simple rhythms through locomotor movements, body movements such as clapping, or the use of rhythm instruments
- Opportunity to sing a variety of songs
- Ability to express the mood or feelings of a musical selection through body movements, and opportunity to express emotion through music

The teacher should individualize these goals for the particular group and also for the individual children within the group. Too often teachers plan from an activity approach; they think of a "fun" activity instead of a music activity that is developmentally appropriate for the children (Andress, 1991). While working, if all the students do not want to listen to music or a particular type of music, those who do wish to listen can use headphones (Davies, 2000). The teacher should know each child's functioning level with regard to musical skills and interests. A good music program should incorporate the goals of music in singing, rhythm experiences, movement, and listening and through active involvement. These music activities must be developmentally appropriate (Bredekamp, 1986; Bredekamp & Copple, 1997) if they are to be effectively incorporated into all curriculum areas. The Music Educators National Conference (MENC, 1994) also advocates that music in the curriculum be consistent with appropriate practice, and, according to Kenney (1997, pp. 106–107), that means it demonstrates the following principles:

- Age appropriateness, individual appropriateness, and context must be taken into account when planning music learning environments.
- Play is a primary vehicle for musical growth.
- Every student should have access to a balanced, comprehensive, and sequential program of study in music.

Teacher's Role in Music Education

- Show an interest in the spontaneous beginnings of music that the child creates.
- Make time available for music and not just listening to music; active involvement is best (Fox, 2000). The power and benefit of music are in "doing" the music (Guilmartin, 2000).
- Be confident in your own musicianship (Palmer & Sims, 1993).
- Plan for every day, but also use music spontaneously to support other parts of the curriculum, to create variety, and to provide transitions to activities (Achilles, 1999; Lazdauskas, 1996).

- Provide adequate space for musical activities, particularly during creative movements and expressions.
- Allow for freedom of expression, as well as some freedom regarding participation. Young children should be free to become involved in music and to express their own feelings, moods, and interpretations.
- Avoid criticism and demands for perfection in performance skills.
- Create an appropriate music learning environment by planning activities that will encourage music participation and expression, as well as providing materials and experiences that will stimulate creative thinking and action.

Since young children are highly motivated by praise, the teacher should further motivate musical competencies by praising individuals. Comments such as "Jimmy has found a different way to use the rhythm sticks" or "Lori has learned that you can even jump sideways" provide individual motivation.

An important part of the teacher's role is planning the music curriculum.

According to Kenney (1997, p. 108), as adapted from the MENC (1994), "The music curriculum should be conceived not as a collection of activities but rather as a well-planned sequence of learning experiences leading to clearly defined skills and knowledge."

The experiences should be challenging, but reflect the joy and personal satisfaction that are inherent in music. The purpose of studying music should be to enable children to enhance the quality of their lives by participating fully in their musical culture.

Teacher-initiated activities include teaching songs and musical games, planning music activities that support and relate to curriculum areas, planning musical dramatizations, using rhythm activities and rhythm instruments, and encouraging

Using puppets and other visuals with music activities helps increase interest and facilitate concept development.

creative body movements. Since play is the primary vehicle for music experiences in early childhood, the teacher should also take advantage of child-initiated, child-directed activities (MENC, 1994). The children may begin singing or chanting during play. They may sing familiar songs, make up their own tunes, or use new words to familiar melodies. A child may begin spontaneously to hum or move rhythmically; the teacher should take advantage of the opportunity to praise the effort and encourage the child to continue. Musical experiences then should be both structured and open-ended (Hildebrandt, 1998).

Teachers should create opportunities for increasing their own musical competencies. They should develop enthusiasm for the music program, since their own feelings will be *caught* by the children, rather than *taught* to them. Although teachers may not see themselves as musicians, music can still be a valuable part of the program; being a musician is not a prerequisite for helping young children to enjoy music (Jalongo, 1996). Positive music attitudes are the key. Teachers who enjoy music and sing with enthusiasm, regardless of ability or training, are the ones who receive the greatest re-

sponse and involvement from children. Music is a universal language; we do not have to understand the terminology or musical mechanics to enjoy it. It is most effectively approached as an experience to be lived, rather than a subject to be taught. Gharavi (1993) provides five suggestions for expanding music and singing in the curriculum:

1. Singing at a comfortable pitch for young voices

2. Expanding our own musical repertoire

3. Becoming familiar with quality music available for young children

4. Providing a variety of musical styles, especially ethnic music

5. Providing opportunities for quiet listening

SONGS AND SINGING

Honig (1995) proposes that songs soothe, express love, promote cooperativeness and learning daily routines, help to smooth transitions, ease separation, build trust and self-esteem, encourage enjoyment for poetry and imagery, stretch memorization skills, develop humor, build motor skills, and increase group cohesiveness. Playing music and singing to young babies tends to nourish an early enjoyment for music and enhances the relationship between the infant and the singer. "Singing can be a powerful tool for letting a baby know that you care, that you understand her feelings or his needs" (Honig, 1995, p.73). Tiny infants enjoy listening to soft, melodic singing; and even before babies are 1 year old, they bounce their bodies or arms in rhythm to music. Learning songs and singing are probably the most common musical experiences in the early childhood years. The key to the child's total musical growth is cheerful singing. Again, the attitudes of enthusiasm for and enjoyment of singing are of the utmost importance. Teachers should build a repertoire of songs, and it is imperative that they use caution and wisdom when selecting songs to teach to young children. "Singing should be included in the daily activities of preschool children, but expectations of achievement should be based upon knowledge of the developmental nature of their ability. Songs for classroom use should be chosen with careful consideration of tonality, range, melodic configurations, and vocal developmental stages of the children" (McDonald & Ramsey, 1982, p.188).

Toddlers imitate singing and often tag on to the end of a phrase or song. They move to the music and enjoy very simple songs (Wolf, 1992). During preschool and early school years, singing becomes more ritualized and group oriented (Wolf, 1992). As 5-year-olds learn songs, they "first learn the words, followed by rhythm, then melodic contour, and finally intervals" (Kenney, 1997, p.112). Music preferences are formed by the age of 5, but can be changed as a result of music in the environment and by the caregiver's love for various kinds of music (Kenney, 1997; Peery & Peery, 1986).

Guidelines for Teaching Songs in Early Childhood

1. Competition has no place in teaching children to sing; often it distorts their voices and makes the melodies unpleasant. Comparisons between children should not be made.

2. Know the song well yourself, and then sing it to the children several times while they listen. Listening to good singing is a significant factor in children's vocal development (Haines & Gerber, 1996). Do not teach a song by repeating the words separately from the music. You might play a recording of the song for the children to hear; then they can join in and sing with the recording and the teacher. When selecting records or tapes, make sure that the voices are in tune and the instrumentation is uncomplicated (Wolf, 1992).

3. Some songs should be taught in sections: phrases, sentences, or short verses at one time. This is particularly true of longer songs that are more difficult to learn. Then these sections can all be put together. However, when the children are first introduced to the song, they should hear it in its entirety so that they experience it as a whole unit.

4. Use a variety of approaches and teaching techniques (discussed throughout this chapter) in teaching songs and singing familiar songs. Do not always teach songs in the same way. Use pictures, hand and finger actions, and simple props that will involve the children to assist them in remembering the words.

5. Do not force children to sing. Often a child does not sing at school, but sings all the songs at home. For some children, it takes time to feel comfortable singing with the group, and pressure to sing does not make them more willing to participate. However, involve the reluctant singer whenever possible. The more involved the children become in a song, the more the words become a part of the activity (Bayless & Ramsey, 1991).

6. Eye-to-eye singing, like eye-to-eye teaching, is most effective. The mood and feeling of the song, along with the teacher's enjoyment of singing, will be caught through the expressions that you convey to the children.

7. Sing songs to the children in a lower range (A or B below middle C to G or A above) (Wolf, 1992).

8. Make sure that children understand the meanings of new words in the song, as well as the meaning of the song. However, make certain that the content of the song is on the level of the children's understanding and interest.

9. You may want to discuss the feeling, mood, repetition of melodies or words, tempo, or rhythm of the song.

10. As you teach songs, enunciate clearly and distinctly.

11. If there is a part of a song that is particularly difficult for the children to learn, isolate this part and sing it to the children while they listen. Also, sing this part of the song much more slowly until the children have learned it. Other suggestions include having them clap the rhythm or use their hands to show how the melody moves.

12. To motivate children to listen to a song, ask questions about the song that prompt them to attend to the words (Brudnak, 1997).

13. Use instruments often to accompany the children's singing, but *teach* the songs without accompaniment (Wolf, 1992). Even if you are not skilled in music reading, there are still many instruments that can be learned or played easily (autoharp, baritone or tenor ukelele, guitar, rhythm sticks, other rhythm instruments).

14. Children enjoy songs with simple and clear melodies, although they are also eager to learn longer and more intricate tunes. When selecting songs for young children, remember that those with repetition of melody and words are generally both easy and enjoyable to learn.

15. When teaching new songs, hum and sing the song spontaneously to the children as they work and play; they may also hum along.

16. Songs with half-steps in the melody line, unusually large intervals between tones, or a broad range should be avoided because they are often too difficult for very young children to learn.

17. Whenever simple actions, motions, or dramatizations are appropriate, incorporate them into the singing time.

18. Sing confidently, and do not apologize for your singing.

19. When involved in a singing time, you may invite the children to sing along; usually you need only begin to sing and they will join in. Beware of asking, "Do you want to sing this song?" unless you are prepared to accept a negative answer.

20. Sing songs about familiar things or feelings.

21. Make a tape recording of favorite classroom songs, and add new favorites to it. Encourage parents or children to take it home for listening and singing along.

Variety in Singing

Routine approaches or techniques in any curriculum area tend to become boring to children. Thus, we need to become aware of possible ways to add variety to singing songs.

Ways to Add Variety in Singing

1. Use visual aids (such as overhead transparencies, movie boxes, charts, posters, chalk talk) to help teach a song. The children will also enjoy assisting with the visual aids. Puppets (finger, sack, stick, commercial, cone) add friendly interest. Stories that tell the content of the song can be used. As you tell stories about animals, places, or things, sing songs about them also.

2. Make up guessing games to utilize variety in songs. Say, "I'm thinking of a song that tells me to put my finger in different places" ("Put Your Finger in the Air"). Or start the singing time with a question that will arouse interest and gain attention (see item 12 in this box).

3. Put the names of songs on the backs of objects or pictures pinned to a chart or bulletin board, or put the names of songs in a sack or box. The children select the object from the chart or the paper from the box to determine the songs to be sung. Also, many songs that utilize action words such as skipping, painting, and so on, can be depicted in pictures.

4. Have children sing songs, or parts of songs, as a solo, duet, or trio.

5. Where accompanying chants are appropriate, have some of the children chant, and others sing the song. For example, in the familiar folk song "I've Been Working on the Railroad," some of the children chant "choo, choo, choo, choo." In the familiar folk song "Little White Duck," have some of the children accompany with "quack, quack, quack." In "Hush, Little Baby," have the accompaniment of "hush, hush."

6. Use sounds or instruments as accompaniment. Some of the children accompany while others sing.

7. Sing a song and pause while the children sing the end of the line, the next phrase, or the end of the sentence; the children fill in the words.

8. Write the words of a song on the chalkboard or a chart. Erase or cover words or phrases as the children are learning the song.

9. Have children pantomime a song for the rest of the group. Follow up with singing the song.

10. Have the children add new words to a familiar song in order to make or weave nonsense into them. For example, when singing "London Bridge," change "Build it up with iron bars" to "Build it up with bacon and eggs" or "Build it up with cats and dogs." In the song "Mary Had a Little Lamb," ask what silly thing Mary might have instead of a lamb (a centipede, for example).

11. Use pitch-level conducting in teaching a song. In other words, use your arm and hand to show the changes in pitch level.

12. Before you sing or play a new song, create a listening experience by asking the children the following kinds of questions:
    a. Who? ("Listen to this song and tell me *who* it is about.")
    b. Where? ("Listen to this song and tell me *where* the animal is going.")
    c. What? ("Listen to this song that I am going to sing for you and tell me *what* new word you hear" or "*What* words rhyme?" or "*What* parts of the melody or tune are alike?" or "*What* words are repeated?")
    d. How? ("Listen to this song ['Michael Finnegan,' a familiar folk song] and tell me *how* Michael Finnegan's whiskers got in again.")
    e. Why? ("Listen to this song ['Cindy'] and tell me *why* Cindy should go home.")

13. Incorporate a variety of other teaching methods, such as role playing or dramatizing a song.

14. Hum the song or parts of it.

15. Sing a song from a record or a tape by a children's recording artist such as Ella Jenkins, Joe Wayman, Raffi, Miss Jackie, Hap Palmer, Steve Millang, or Greg Scelsa. Discover your favorites at educational toy stores or at your library, where they can be checked out. Include them in your classroom for easy sing-alongs!

16. Teachers can use song picture books such as *The Lady with the Alligator Purse* (Westcott, 1990), *I Know an Old Lady* (Karas, 1995), *Six Little Ducks* (Conover, 1976), *The Itsy Bitsy Spider* (Trapani, 1993), *I'm a Little Teapot* (Trapani, 1993), and *Five Little Monkeys Jumping on the Bed* (Christelow, 1989) to link songs to literacy. The song can be sung, the picture song book read, and then a variety of activities in other curriculum areas planned to extend the learning (Barclay & Walwer, 1992). Song picture books facilitate literacy growth in young children and contribute to aesthetic development in music, art, literature, and creative writing (Jalongo & Ribblett, 1997).

17. See Figure 13–1 for a web for one of the song picture books called *The Wheels on the Bus* (a variety of authors and illustrators have done this song in picture book form). For complete references for the titles given here, see the Suggested Resources.

Specific Kinds of Songs

Literally thousands of excellent songs can be selected for teaching young children. Some of the categories of songs from which teachers should surely make some selections are discussed here.

FIGURE 13–1
Web for the Song Picture Book *The Wheels on the Bus*

There are songs to teach almost every one of the concepts discussed in this book. A teacher who desires a song about a specific concept for which a song cannot be found should write new words about the concept to a familiar tune or make up both the words and melody for a new song. The following categories of songs are valuable in teaching young children.

Expandable Songs. Expandable songs offer opportunities for children to help to create the songs, thus creating a sense of pride and enhancing self-worth. Since songs are language, they can be used to study parts of speech as one particular part of the song is "expanded" or changed each time it is sung (Kenney, 1997). For example, they can change the nouns in a song, or they often change the verbs or "doing" parts of a song. For example, the familiar folk song "If You're Happy and You Know It" becomes an expandable song as children add their own phrases: "If you're happy and you know it (blink your eyes)." Another way of changing this song is to change the word *happy* to different moods or emotions, such as "If you're mad and you know it, take a walk."

Suggestions for Songs That Contain Expandable Phrases and Words

"Mary Wore a Red Dress"

"Look Around the Room"

"I See a Boy"

"Sing with Me"

"My Little Soul's Gonna Shine"

"Over in the Meadow"

"Bumble Bee"

"The Wheels on the Bus"

"Come On and Join into the Game"

"Put Your Finger in the Air"

"Rig-a-Jig Jig"

"Johnny Works"

"Blue, Blue"

I Went to Visit a Friend

(To the tune of "Oats, Peas, Beans, and Barley Grow")

Underlined words and phrases are those that can be changed by the children.

I went to visit a friend one day,

She only lived across the way.

She said she couldn't come out to play,

Because it was her <u>cleaning day</u>.

This is the way <u>she cleans</u> away,

This is the way <u>she cleans</u> away,

This is the way <u>she cleans</u> away,

Because it was her <u>cleaning day</u>.

To the tune of "Mary Had a Little Lamb," sing the following:

Pass a napkin to your friend, to your friend, to your friend.

Pass a napkin to your friend. Now take one yourself.

or

It's time for us to go outside, go outside, go outside.

It's time for us to go outside, for soon we're going home.

or

Jimmy has some jingle bells, jingle bells, jingle bells.

Jimmy has some jingle bells, that he plays for us.

or

Martha brought a pair of skates, pair of skates, pair of skates.

Martha brought a pair of skates to our sharing time.

or

Eric has a shape that's blue, shape that's blue, shape that's blue.

Eric has a shape that's blue. What shape and color can you find?

or

Now it is cleanup time, cleanup time, cleanup time.

Now it is cleanup time, I will need your help.

To the tune of "Lazy Mary" (also "Here We Go 'Round the Mulberry Bush"), sing the following:

What is the color of the shoes, of the shoes, of the shoes?

What is the color of the shoes you're wearing on your feet?

or

Stand up if you are wearing red, wearing red, wearing red.

Stand up if you are wearing red, and show us what to do.

or

This is the way I nod my head, nod my head, nod my head.

This is the way I nod my head; you can join me too.

or

We are getting ready, ready, ready.

We are getting ready, to go outside and play.

or

Jimmy and Susie, you can go out, you can go out, you can go out.

Jimmy and Susie, you can go out; Bobby, you can go too.

or

We are working stirring the batter, stirring the batter, stirring the batter.

We are working stirring the batter, soon our cake will be done.

Many of the songs that you already know and sing are expandable, and they provide a valuable exercise in creative thinking and problem solving as children create their own words and phrases.

Nursery Rhymes. Preschool and kindergarten children delight in singing nursery rhyme songs. The simple melodies and short verses (most of them four-line songs) make them very appropriate for these young children. The familiar, simple, and catchy tunes also make them easily adapted to new words. These suggestions should only serve to stimulate your own imagination. Think of additional possibilities for other nursery rhymes. Some of the favorite nursery rhymes follow:

"Twinkle, Twinkle, Little Star"

"Old MacDonald"

"Sing a Song of Sixpence"

"Hickory, Dickory, Dock"

"Baa, Baa, Black Sheep"

"Jack and Jill"

"Peter, Peter, Pumpkin Eater"

"The Muffin Man"

"Three Blind Mice"

Old Traditional and Folk Songs. Children's musical heritage surely must include many of the songs that have been sung by children for centuries. We need only consult favorite songbooks and observe the citations in the upper-right corner of the music to realize that a majority of children's songs are traditional or folk songs from around the world. Jalongo and Collins (1985, p. 20) suggest learning a few traditional tunes that can "lead to many different songs because folk music has many parodies."

Some Favorite Traditional and Folk Songs

"This Old Man"

"Pop Goes the Weasel"

"Eensey-Weensey Spider"

"Where Is Thumbkin?"

"Rig-a-Jig Jig"

"If You're Happy"

"Little Peter Rabbit"

"My Pigeon House"

"I'm a Little Teapot"

"Yankee Doodle"

"B-I-N-G-O"

"Six Little Ducks"

"Michael Finnegan"

"The Noble Duke of York"

"The Bear Went over the Mountain"

Lullabies.   Lullabies often have a quieting and calming effect on children. Have preschool and kindergarten children pretend that they have a baby that they are trying to get to sleep. They may rock it in their arms or pretend to rock it in a cradle. How quiet they will be to make sure that the baby is not awakened! The following lullabies are suggested:

"Hush, Little Baby"

"Brahm's Lullaby"

"Rock-a-Bye Baby"

"All Through the Night"

"Kum Ba Yah" (African folk song)

Ballads or Story Songs.   These traditional songs have been handed down from generation to generation and enjoyed by many. Children love them because of the stories that they tell. After a ballad was sung to a group of children, Rachel immediately said, "Oh, sing me that story again!" Some of the following will be enjoyed by the children time and time again:

"Hush, Little Baby"

"I've Been Working on the Railroad"

"Frog Went a-Courting"

"I Know an Old Lady Who Swallowed a Fly"

Haines and Gerber (1996, p. 163) suggest an approach that they call "add-a-song": Children role play or dramatize favorite fairy tales or nursery rhymes, then add "a song or two, with simple words and a familiar tune," and repeat them when certain actions occur or recur in the story line. This approach combines music and storytelling and adds a new dimension to storytelling.

Rounds.   Even preschool children enjoy singing simple rounds, and they like to hear different words sung at the same time. However, when using rounds in early childhood, it is important that you have an adult leader for each group. For younger children, usually two groups are adequate, even though some songs have more parts to them. One of the simplest ways to sing a round with the very young is to combine two songs with different tunes: Have one group sing one song while the other group sings another song. Examples of such combinations include "Three Blind Mice" with "Row, Row, Row Your Boat" and "Are You Sleeping" or "The Farmer

Songs become favorites when they are sung frequently so children are able to identify the tunes, sing the words, and do the actions.

in the Dell" with "Skip to My Lou." You can also have the children sing rounds by combining two or more songs that have the same melodies:

> "Twinkle, Twinkle, Little Star" with "Baa, Baa, Black Sheep" or "The ABC Song"

> "The Farmer in the Dell" with "A-Hunting We Will Go" or "I Put My Right Foot In"

> "Frère Jacques" with "Are You Sleeping?" or "Where Is Thumbkin?"

> "The Mulberry Bush" with "Lazy Mary" or "The Wheels on the Bus"

> "The Bear Went over the Mountain" with "My Thumbs Are Starting to Wiggle"

When teaching rounds sung in the traditional way, make sure that the children know the song well first before trying it as a round and remember to have a leader for each group. Some rounds that can be sung in parts and are simple enough for children in the early childhood years include the following:

> "Frère Jacques" or "Are You Sleeping?"

> "Row, Row, Row Your Boat"

> "Sweetly Sings the Donkey"

> "Kookaburra"

Writing and Creating Songs. New words can be written to familiar old tunes or melodies. Children will also enjoy learning new words to familiar melodies of television commercials. They hear these melodies so often, and they are so catchy, that children will not have any difficulty with them! Children and teachers can also enjoy writing new words to new tunes. It is amazing how easy it is to create original words and a simple, original melody to go with them. Just be sure to record or write the words and melody, because they are often difficult to remember until they become familiar. Choose a topic, and then begin brainstorming short phrases about that topic. A small group of children could work cooperatively on an appropriate melody for these short phrases. The entire group could work on the words and then in small groups, each group being responsible for one or two lines; then the melody could be developed and finally recorded.

A simple way of creating songs is to work with *scale* songs. The melody is the scale, beginning at middle C, or lower, and then climbing to upper C (or

to the note on which you began). Then go back down the scale. For each scale song, you will need a sentence or phrase with eight syllables to go up the scale, and then a sentence or phrase with eight syllables to go down the scale. For example, the following words could be sung up and down the scale:

> Mr. Jones, the carpenter, came.

> He showed us how to build a cage.

Musical Games

Young children enjoy the involvement that comes with musical games, which spark enthusiasm and excitement. Musical games can be taught and carried out in a number of ways. Some are simple enough that the children need only follow along and do as the words tell them. However, others need careful instruction, and it may be wise to role play or go through these games before combining music and game. Also, the musical background can be provided in a number of ways. For familiar songs, the children can sing as the game is played. Sometimes a piano or other musical instrument is available for accompaniment. Many of these musical games are also on records.

Some of the Most Popular Musical Games for Young Children

"Hokey-Pokey"

"Here We Go Looby-Loo"

"Bluebird"

"Skip to My Lou"

"Oh Where, Oh Where Has My Little Dog Gone?"

"The Farmer in the Dell"

"The Mulberry Bush"

"Sing a Song of Sixpence"

"Pop Goes the Weasel"

"The Muffin Man"

"A-Tisket, A-Tasket"

"Put Your Finger in the Air"

"Did You Ever See a Lassie?"

"Come On and Join into the Game"

The more a child's body is involved in the musical activities, the more creative the possibilities become.

RHYTHM ACTIVITIES

In many ways, each musical experience that a child has will be a rhythm experience, because children begin to feel the rhythm pattern of music very early. Even infants begin to sense the beat, or rhythm, of musical selections. By age 3, children will repeat musical patterns, and by 5, they are able to demonstrate a steady beat (Kenney, 1997). However, it is not at all unusual to find a young child who has difficulty in sensing the rhythm pattern of music, or children might have a keen sense of rhythm and still not be able to carry a tune. Care should be taken not to make such a child feel uncomfortable or pressured, which will take away the enjoyment of the music. Children's first experiences in finding or experimenting with rhythm patterns will probably be with clapping or other spontaneous body movements and then playing the beat on a simple rhythm instrument (Stellaccio & McCarthy, 1999).

Initially, some children may simply enjoy the experience of hand clapping or playing the instrument and may not be aware of the rhythm. The teacher should not be concerned. The teacher's role in these early rhythmic experiences should be to encourage sound and rhythm exploration and participation, not duplication. During rhythm experiences, the teacher can pat the beat on the child's knees. Being able to keep time to music develops gradually, and there is much individual variation among children.

Early exposures to rhythm should involve simple and definite sounds, with even or steady rhythm patterns. A good beginning to rhythm activities is the exploration of sounds in the environment, not necessarily actual musical sounds. For example, encourage the children to listen for sounds that have definite beat patterns, such as a clock ticking, a water faucet dripping, or a jackhammer drilling. Then encourage them to listen to the sounds twice and try to reproduce them by clapping hands or tapping feet. Another possibility is to listen to the sound of different rhythmic vocal sounds. Select a particular vowel or consonant sound and sing it to a familiar melody. Other vocal sounds that can be set to rhythm patterns include buzzing, laughing (ha-ha-ha or ho-ho-ho), hissing, and chanting. Games can be made out of this kind of rhythm experience. In one game, the children sit in a circle, and as a beanbag or ball is thrown to a child, that child creates a vocal rhythm pattern and then tosses the beanbag or ball to another child. The second child must repeat the same rhythm pattern. Then the beanbag or ball is tossed to others, and they must come up with new patterns.

Chants can also be used for early rhythm exploration. Four- or five-word sentences can be made into chants and different rhythm patterns clapped or beaten out as the children repeat the sentences. For example, the sentence "You can't catch me!" can have a variety of patterns. Emphasis may be put on the first, second, third, or fourth words (*You* can't catch me; You *can't* catch me; You can't *catch* me; You can't catch *me*). Chants can be altered in other ways: they can be soft or loud, fast or slow, steady or wavering. Chants adapted from rhymes, stories, or fingerplays can be developed for children's actions, including jump-rope chants. If young children are not familiar with the chants, invite a person into the classroom to teach some of them to the children. After they listen, they can play the rhythm patterns of these chants on rhythm instruments or use "body instruments" such as hand clapping.

Children can pretend to do some of the following activities and develop a rhythm pattern by clapping or beating the rhythm pattern of each sound: chair rocking, clock ticking, washing machine agitator turning, water dripping, knocking on a door, hammering a nail, sawing a log or piece of wood, sweeping the floor, shining a window.

Many excellent tapes and CDs can give children experience in rhythm exploration. Some can be used for basic introduction to rhythm, and others are used for more advanced explorations (see the Suggested Resources at the end of this chapter).

Hissing	Head tapping, head nodding
Snapping fingers	Stamping feet
Clicking tongue	Gasping
Blinking eyes	Sh-h-h-h (gentle, or explosive and loud)

In addition, the children could take just one part of the body, such as the hands, elbows, or feet, and discover ways of using that body part to beat rhythm. For example, the hands could be used to clap, tap on the floor, or tap some part of the body such as the chest or back. The tapping could also alternate from head to floor or from shoulder to knees.

Body Instruments

Clapping is probably the most commonly used body rhythm instrument, and we have cited it often. However, other body instruments can be used in rhythm activities:

Whistling	Speaking
Humming	Thigh slapping (patting)

Rhythm Instruments

Give children frequent experiences using rhythm instruments. Many early childhood teachers do not like to use them because the children become difficult to control when the instruments are brought out for use. If these instruments are seldom used, the children may become too excited about them.

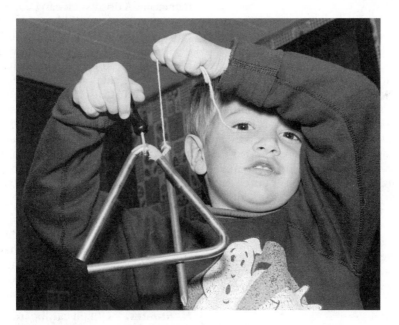

Using musical instruments to accompany singing encourages children's participation and is an excellent way to involve those who might not feel comfortable singing along.

Lack of variation in presentation and direction also encourages lack of control. When introducing an instrument, make sure to use its proper name, and give the children ample opportunity to become familiar with it. Freedom to explore instruments should be provided in various ways, not always in a rhythm band marching around in a circle and following a leader. The teacher might even allow exploration during free play.

Instruments can be purchased, collected, or made by the teacher or children. They can be as easy as collecting dried gourds or seed pods. Usually, school budgets determine the kinds and amounts of rhythm instruments purchased. With handmade instruments, it is usually possible to have greater numbers of the same kinds. The following is a discussion of many rhythm instruments that can be obtained in a variety of ways.

Bells.   Bells and jingles can be made simply by lacing bells on a cord and tying the ends of the cord together. Another method is to sew bells onto a mitten or glue them across the top of a wide elastic band. You can also drill holes in bottle caps, string them on a cord, and then tie the ends of the cord together.

Clappers.   The effect of castanets can be obtained by selecting a stiff piece of cardboard approximately the size of a matchbook (an empty matchbook could be used). Fold the cardboard piece in the middle, just as a matchbook is folded. Tape or glue a bottle cap on each inside end, but do not put the tape over the outside of the caps. The clapper is held between the thumb and the index and middle fingers and then is secured in this position with a rubber band. As the fingers and thumb are brought together, the bottle caps should strike each other, making the sound of castanets (see Figure 13–2).

Corrugated Cardboard Washboard.   Pieces of heavy corrugated cardboard (or lighter pieces pasted on heavy cardboard or wood) are strummed with a spoon, dowel, or nail for a washboard sound effect.

Cymbals.   Kettle lids or other lids with knobs attached will serve as cymbals. (Small pieces of wood screwed onto the lid will also serve as knobs.)

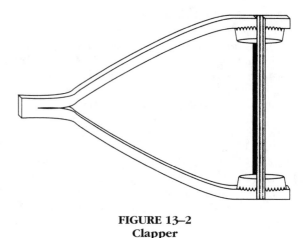

FIGURE 13–2
Clapper

Drums.   Use coffee cans, or obtain from cafeterias their largest metal cans. On the open end, stretch inner-tube rubber, chamois, Naugahyde, or similar material as tightly as possible, and secure it with wire or cord. When making a drum, the tighter the ends, the sharper the sound. Wiring is recommended over lacing, since lacing does not seem to be tight enough and the lacing holes may tear easily. A drumstick can be made out of a dowel or stick, to one end of which a piece of fabric-covered foam rubber is secured. The drum can be decorated by dipping magazine scraps and pieces of tissue paper into liquid starch and then placing them on the sides of the can.

Drums can also be made out of oatmeal or hat boxes, nail kegs, or large barrels; or two different-sized cans may be tied together to make bongo drums. Drumsticks that can be improvised include a dowel, spoon, eraser end of a new pencil, wire brush, rubber spatula, drawer-pull nailed to a dowel, or dowel inserted in a Styrofoam ball.

Gongs.   The sound of a gong can be obtained by setting a steel or brass hubcap on a block of wood to strike it or by drilling a hole in the hubcap and attaching a wire or rope as a handle. The sound will differ according to where the gong is struck and what is used to strike it. Possible strikers include a dowel, stick, spoon, or nail.

Hummers.   Obtain cardboard tubes from the inside of paper rolls (waxed paper, paper towels, toilet paper, etc.). On one end of the tube, punch a hole, using a paper punch and punching down as far as possible. Cover that same end of the tube with either waxed paper or aluminum foil (about a 3-inch square is adequate for each hummer). Secure this covering with a rubber band, but make sure that the punched hole is not covered. The tube can be decorated in any desired way.The children put their mouths up to the open ends of the tubes to blow and hum at the same time.

Jingle Clogs.   These instruments can be made by flattening bottle caps and then making a hole in the middle of each bottle cap with a nail. (This hole should be larger than the nail used to attach the tops to the dowel so that the tops can jingle.) Loosely nail the bottle caps to the ends of a 4- to 6-inch dowel. Bells may be used in place of bottle caps. Decorate them. Small wooden wheels, buttons, or metal washers could be used in place of bottle caps. Also, a nail could be pounded in one end of a piece of wood, bells joined loosely on a string, and the string tied to the nail (see Figure 13-3).

Hollow Clappers.   Two same-sized paper cups are provided for each child. They may be decorated. They are played by bringing together either of the two ends or alternating them—the larger ends together, then the smaller ends together. When using a coconut, cut it in half, hollow out the meat, and then strike the cut ends of the halves together.

Plucked Instruments.   Drill a hole through the bottom of an old washtub. Fasten a screw eye or a large bolt through the hole. Secure a heavy wire to the bolt; attach the other end of the wire to the top of a broomstick or long dowel. Secure the lower end of the stick or dowel in the bottom of the washtub by drilling a hole in the tub. Play it by plucking the wire; obtain pitch variations by tightening the wire by pulling on the broomstick. A rubber-band banjo can be made by obtaining a sturdy open box and stretching a few rubber bands of different sizes, spaced widely, around it. The box may be placed on a wooden table for more resonant tones.

Rhythm Sticks.   Cut dowels of any width into lengths of 8 to 12 inches. Cut them all the same length, and make enough to provide the children with two each. These sticks can be struck together or tapped on an aluminum pie plate, a steel bowl, or the floor. One stick could be ser-

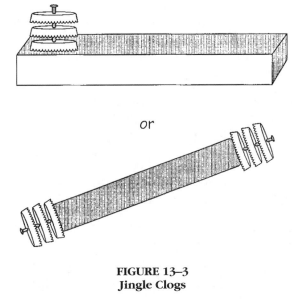

FIGURE 13–3
Jingle Clogs

rated so that a different sound would be made by rubbing the smooth stick over the serrated one (see Figure 13-4).

Shakers.   Dried seed pods or gourds often make the sound of maracas or shakers. Empty containers such as gourds, metal cans, or film containers; small boxes or cartons such as gelatin boxes, cottage cheese cartons, or half-pint milk cartons; paper plates stapled together; baby food jars; plastic bottles; or empty bandage boxes can be

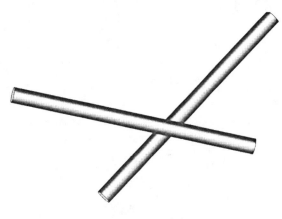

FIGURE 13–4
Rhythm Sticks

partially filled with sand, rice, dry beans, macaroni, pebbles, shells, paper clips, or similar items. Small amounts of these items are used. The shakers can be decorated (see Figure 13–5).

Tambourines. Tambourines can be made using either two lightweight paper plates with the rims attached together or one heavy paper plate. Bells or bottle caps are attached to the edges. Aluminum pie plates also work well.

Chimes. A chime can be made by obtaining a 3- to 5-inch length of metal pipe and a piece of heavy string 10 to 15 inches long. Run the string through the pipe and tie the ends of the string together. The children hold the string and strike the suspended pipe with a nail or other metal implement. Nails also make good instruments, producing the sounds of chime bands or triangles. Purchase one nail 5 inches in length or longer for each child in the class (a variety of lengths or the same length may be used). In addition, purchase a striker nail approximately 4 inches in length for each child. To the head of the longer nail, tie a string to be used as a handle for the nail. A horseshoe suspended by a string, with a nail for a striker, can also be used (see Figure 13–6).

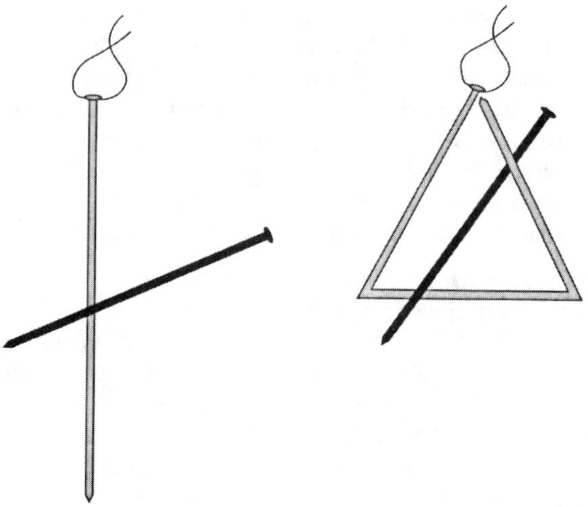

Tuned Glasses or Bottles. Fill glasses, soda bottles, or other glass bottles with water to different levels. If the water levels are properly varied, the tones achieved will represent a scale. Tap the

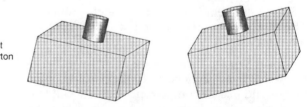

FIGURE 13–6
Chimes

bottles lightly with a spoon to produce the sound. (If these bottles are covered, the measured water will not evaporate as readily.)

Tuning Fork. A tuning fork, which can be obtained commercially, will vibrate and produce a certain tone, depending on the size of the fork.

Wooden Blocks. Wooden blocks are made of hardwood and provided in pairs. They can be cut into any shape, including geometric shapes, and sanded. Handles of spools, knobs, or wooden pieces can be bolted or screwed on. For variations, materials such as corrugated cardboard, sandpaper, or foam rubber could be thumbtacked on or attached to create different sounds (see Fig 13–7).

Xylophone. Obtain electrical conduit pipe from a hardware store. It should be cut into the following lengths, but the cutting must be exact.

JUICE   Juice can   Film can

SPICE   Spice can   MILK   Half pint milk carton

FIGURE 13–5
Shakers

FIGURE 13–7
Wooden Blocks

Therefore, it is best to use a power saw. (If the hardware store has a power saw, have the pipes cut there.)

middle C $12\frac{1}{2}$ in.   G 10 in.

D $11\frac{3}{4}$ in.   A $9\frac{1}{2}$ in.

E 11 in.   B♭ $9\frac{3}{8}$ in.

F $10\frac{3}{4}$ in.   B 9 in.

F♯ $10\frac{1}{2}$ in.   C $8\frac{3}{4}$ in.

Make a wooden xylophone using balsa wood $1\frac{1}{2}$ inches wide in the following lengths:

middle C 9 in.   G 7 in.

D $8\frac{1}{2}$ in.   A $6\frac{1}{2}$ in.

E 8 in.   B♭ 6 in.

F $7\frac{5}{8}$ in.   B $5\frac{1}{2}$ in.

F♯ $7\frac{3}{8}$ in.   C 5 in.

Other Rhythm Instruments

1. Hair-comb harmonicas or kazoos (waxed paper over the edge of a comb)

2. Pots and pans

3. Pages of a book ("strummed")

4. Wooden rungs of chair

5. Vegetable grater

Specific Activities with Rhythm

There are many delightful ways of using rhythm activities in the classroom, and the teacher should incorporate rhythm activities into the music curriculum, as well as into other parts of the curriculum.

Rhythm Activities

1. Have the children use body instruments or rhythm instruments to beat the rhythm of nursery rhymes, poems, names, colors, places, or songs. Alternatively, rhythm patterns can be suggested by using marks on the chalkboard or felt pieces on the flannel board. The following patterns could be put on the chalkboard and the children asked to clap them:

// //

/// ///

/// // /// //

More difficult patterns can be given as children's experience increases. Tell the children that you are clapping the name of a child, and have them stand if they think their name is being clapped. For example, the pattern for Allison McKean would be /// //. You could combine names such as Brandon and Marilyn (// / ///). As the children grow in experience, substitute note patterns for the marks or felt pieces. For example, Mary Lou Smith might be (♫♩); Phillip White might be (♫♩). The children will learn that the pause indicates the separation between words. Also, make guessing games by using the rhythm patterns of songs, familiar poems, nursery rhymes, animals, and other categories.

2. Give each child one rhythm stick or dowel. On the verse of the song, use locomotor movements to move around or over the dowel. On the chorus, the dowel is picked up and the rhythm tapped out on the floor. For example, on the first verse of the song "Rig-a-Jig Jig," the children find some way of walking around or over the dowel (backward, sideways, forward, or other), and on the chorus the children pick up the dowel and tap the rhythm. On the second verse, the children might hop as they sing, instead of walking; thus they must find a way of hopping around or over the dowel. Songs can either be sung by the children or played on records.

   Directions could be given to find a way to go *around* the dowel on the first verse and *over* the dowel on the second verse. On the third verse, encourage the children to find a different way of moving, but always on the chorus they pick up the dowel and tap out the rhythm.

3. Have the children pretend to be conductors, inventing their own arm and hand movements. They could use a dowel for a baton.

4. As the children are given an instrument, they can be encouraged to find two different ways of playing it or holding it.

5. As an accompaniment to the children's singing of or a recording of "Horsey, Horsey," provide each child with a pair of paper cups. As they play or beat the rhythm of the song, first striking the tops and then the bottoms of the paper cups together, the sound will resemble the "clip-clop" of horses' hooves.

6. Accompaniments for stories, songs, poems, and nursery rhymes can be devised. For example, drums of three different sizes could be used to tell the story of "The Three Bears." The larger, deeper-sounding drum would be the papa bear; the middle-sized drum, the mama bear; and the smallest drum, the baby bear. As an alternative, on a four-line song, one instrument (such as a triangle) could play the first line, wooden tone blocks could play the second line, the maracas could play the third line, and all could join in for the last line. For a nursery rhyme such as "Hickory, Dickory, Dock," some of the children could pretend to be the pendulum on a grandfather clock and "tick-tock" back and forth to the rhythm of the rhyme or song. On the first line, tapping instruments (such as wooden blocks or triangles) could "tick-tock"; on the second line, when the mouse runs up the clock, the xylophone could be played up the scale; on the third line, when the clock strikes one, the cymbal or gong could strike; also on the third line, when the mouse runs down, the xylophone could play down the scale; and on the last line, the tapping instruments could again "tick-tock."

CREATIVE OR EXPRESSIVE MOVEMENTS

"Adding movement to your day brings a light-hearted spirit to everything you do and creates an atmosphere that encourages divergent thinking and individuality" (Rodger, 1996, p. 6). To the young child, music and movement are often one and the same. Movement to music gives children another way to explore music. Whenever possible, involve some kind of finger, hand, or body movement or rhythm with songs.

> When children hear music, they move spontaneously.

Movement and dance are children's play and they naturally respond to music by moving (Kenney, 1997). Even adults often nod heads, tap feet, and move bodies to the rhythm and sounds of music. Teachers need not try to "teach" children creative movements, but rather help them to discover and release the creative movements that already exist. Creative movement to music enhances children's balance and coordination, rhythm and beat, ability to predict what happens next, self-esteem, and body awareness (Diffily & Morrison, 1996). "Movement to music provides children with opportunites to occupy their own kinesphere, to express the qualities of the music, to respond to rhythm and melody, and to interact musically with other children" (Neely, 2001, p. 37).

Creative movements require limitations and rules that must be explained carefully to the children. When and if they break a rule, they need to be reminded that if they choose to participate they must abide by the rules; if they cannot abide by the rules, they must be watchers. One basic rule of any movement experience is that children must move in their own space and not touch others. This rule helps children to become responsible for their own behavior. Another basic rule is to stop when the signal is given (music stops, hands clap, whistle blows). You may need additional rules, depending on your space, materials, and the children that you are working with. To add movement to your curriculum, you need no special equipment, just imagination, bodies, and the willingness to try (Rodger, 1996).

Guidelines for Effective Creative Movements

1. Children need as much space as possible; therefore, if a game room, gymnasium, or similar space is available, use it. If you must

stay in the classroom, move furniture aside to give adequate space. If you are planning the experience for outside, provide some limitations as to space.

2. Inhibitions can be avoided more easily if the teacher is not inhibited and is an active participant. Teachers can describe, suggest, and model for children (Andress, 1991). Do not press a child to join the group; sometimes shy children need to observe several times before joining. This is one of the values of having movement activities during free play. Inhibitions may begin with too much adult interference or with negative comments from either children or adults. Build confidence and give individual praise, especially to children who show some signs of hesitation.

3. Do not set up yourself or any child as a model to be copied by others. Rather, the modeling is a suggestion; and to be successful, the teacher must be aware of the children's motor capabilities (Andress, 1991). Do not make comparisons among children. In creative movements, the idea is to develop individuality of expression.

4. Do not use music as the only stimulus for creative movements. Sometimes no music at all is appropriate. Perhaps a story or poem will give a suggestion for creative movements, and sound effects made by the children could serve as the background for these movements.

5. As children become involved in movement explorations, try to redirect, challenge, and stimulate their discoveries by suggestions such as "Do what you are doing now in a slower way," or "Try moving in a different direction or at a different level," or "Try the same thing you were doing, but make it smoother or lighter." Verbalize or describe to the child what she or he is doing.

6. Avoid trite phrases such as "light as a feather." Instead, use phrases such as "Move as if you were a feather," "as if snow were hitting your nose," or "as if you were a butterfly landing on a flower." Children will make their own suggestions.

Movement Interpretations

Movement explorations and creative movement experiences can be used to interpret nearly every experience, thing, or phenomenon. (See the music sections in the unit plans in various chapters.) One teacher has her kindergarten children use their bodies to model the shape of alphabet letters as they are learning them (Brudnak, 1997).

Suggested Movement Interpretations

This list can be easily expanded.

1. Life cycle of the butterfly
   a. Caterpillar crawling
   b. Caterpillar eating milkweed
   c. Caterpillar hanging very still from a branch or twig
   d. Chrysalis hanging very still
   e. Butterfly emerging from the chrysalis
   f. Butterfly drying its wings
   g. Butterfly flying

2. Piece of cellophane or lightweight plastic
   a. Plastic crumpled in the teacher's hands without children seeing; children encouraged to guess what it might be, interpreting their guesses through movement
   b. Teacher's hands opened, with children watching plastic move, and then interpreting what they see through movement
   c. Piece of plastic used for movement exploration

3. Shaving cream

4. Airplane sequence
   a. Starting motor
   b. Taking off
   c. Flying
   d. Coming in
   e. Landing safely

5. Popcorn
   a. Butter melting
   b. Popping
   c. Everyone ending in a ball shape on the floor, all "popped"

6. Water
   a. Dripping
   b. Flooding
   c. Flowing in a fountain
   d. Freezing
   e. Melting
   f. Spilling
   g. Sprinkler

7. Laundry
   a. Inside a washing machine
   b. Inside a dryer
   c. Being scrubbed on a washboard
   d. Being pinned to a clothesline
   e. Drying in a breeze

8. Fishing
   a. Casting out
   b. Reeling in
   c. Pretending to be a fish
   d. Fly fishing
   e. Pretending to have a hooked line
   f. Frying and eating fish

These suggestions offer opportunities for sequences and a number of interpretations relating to a single idea. Also, many items, activities, and experiences allow for a single possible interpretation, such as "Move like a pair of scissors," "Show me how you would move if you were a needle on a sewing machine," or "Show me how your dog moves when you have just come home after being gone for a while and the dog is glad to see you." As teachers train themselves to become aware of movement opportunities, they will be amazed at the daily experiences that lend themselves to these kinds of activities.

Although materials are not necessary for movement interpretations, they can add variety, and for some children they may stimulate more movement exploration (Andress, 1991).

Suggested Materials for Movement Exploration

1. Plastic or cellophane (with a rule that the plastic cannot be put up to the face)

2. Scarves, drapery materials, or pieces of lightweight fabric

3. Ribbons, pieces of string or yarn, strips of crepe or tissue paper

4. Hoops
   a. Placed on floor to determine space
   b. Children do movements inside the hoop or around the outside
   c. Used with a partner
   d. Children moving in and out of a hoop in different ways

5. Balloons
   a. Children throwing and catching them with music
   b. Children following movements
   c. Balloon let go and deflated, and then movements followed

6. Balls
   a. Many different kinds
   b. Different parts of body moved to represent a bouncing ball
   c. Comparison of movements of different kinds of balls (e.g., Ping-Pong, foam)

7. Ropes

8. Batons

9. Boxes

10. Rubber or elastic bands

11. Feathers

12. Crumpled paper

13. Tubes (from waxed paper or paper towel rolls, decorated as desired)
    a. Story told, with children allowed to respond, imitate, and move with tubes
    b. Many different kinds of objects created for interpretations: oar, ski pole, telescope, fishing pole

14. Parachute
    a. Children encouraged to move around the parachute, using locomotor movements or any kind of movement patterns
    b. Parachute moved up and then down, with children and adults gathered around; then movements interpreted without the parachute

c. Ball placed on top of the parachute, with each person trying to prevent it from going out or off the parachute at a particular spot

Musical Dramatizations

Musical dramatizations also tie in closely with creative movements; children again move and interpret something. Many stories have possibilities for excellent dramatization, or parts of stories can be dramatized as the children interpret some situation, action, or incident. Songs also have possibilities for musical dramatization, since they allow opportunities for children to interpret through body movements. Many music books for early childhood provide musical dramatizations and tell stories interspersed with music (Haines & Gerber, 1996). Children also enjoy dramatizing poetry and nursery rhymes and often wish to repeat the same activity over and over again.

MUSICAL INSTRUMENTS

Whenever possible, children should be exposed to musical instruments. We have mentioned the use of rhythm instruments because children will enjoy playing them. However, if other musical instruments can be played by the children, their use is encouraged. A tuba was placed in one preschool classroom to be explored and tried out during free play. Although many of the children had difficulty getting enough wind into the tuba to produce sound, they enjoyed having an adult blow into it while they pushed the buttons to alter the sounds. Other kinds of instruments can be explored by the children, and including visitors in this objective broadens the many possibilities.

We also hope that if the teacher plays an instrument he or she will use it often as accompaniment or for listening experiences. There are many instruments that a teacher can learn to play with relative ease: the ukelele, guitar, autoharp, resonator bells, song bells, recorder, or Orff instruments. Children should be exposed to a variety of instruments, and many visitors are delighted to perform for children. In one preschool classroom, a grandfather who played the fiddle entertained the children with his music for 45 minutes. Another group of children were entertained when a visitor played a saw. Take the children on field trips to places having instruments and musicians: music stores, junior high school band period, high school orchestra period, a concert or concert rehearsal. A group of Head Start children visited a nearby high school during the orchestra period and listened to the orchestra practice for a performance. Then they were invited to wander among the musicians, who encouraged the children to touch and explore. The children could begin to classify or sort instruments into groups such as stringed, percussion, wood, and metal instruments, or even to organize them by size.

Pictures of musical instruments have been produced by Bowmar Publications, Inc. (Glendale, California). Each instrument is photographed individually, with educational material printed on the back of the photo. Also, young children can become familiar with musical symbols and notes through matching or lotto games. It is not intended that music theory be taught in early childhood, but rather that children be encouraged to become acquainted with such symbols as the bass and treble clef, rests, whole notes, quarter-notes, half-notes, and so on (Dumtschin, 1987). Music and stationery stores often carry stickers, posters, and other items with pictures of musical symbols or instruments.

LISTENING AND DEVELOPMENT OF APPRECIATION FOR MUSIC

Research findings indicate that infants hear and respond to music before birth (Kenney, 1997). If music is made an important part of the curriculum, children should develop an appreciation for music and its many assets and should learn to listen carefully. In addition to the planned musical activities, it is hoped that teachers will see the value of music used spontaneously throughout the day and in different areas of the curriculum. Often, all that is needed is to provide a setting and materials and an encouraging comment. It is also hoped that

Listening to music and stories should be frequent activities in the early childhood classroom.

throughout the day music will provide a background for play and activities; music often has a calming influence on young children. However, music should often be really listened to, without distractions. Children should listen to others, to themselves, to live music, and to recorded music (including marches, polkas, and waltzes). They should eventually learn to listen to various elements of the music. "Creativity exists both in the performance and enjoyment of listening to the music of others" (Matter, 1982, p. 305). Children can be exposed to the masterpieces in music directly through listening experiences. (If you do not have them in your classroom or library, they can often be borrowed from the public library.) These masterpieces can provide a musical background for free play, art activities, science activities, or other desired projects. Children can listen to and learn to appreciate the music of different cultures, which provides a link among people (Wolf, 1992). All these associations with good music assist children in developing appreciation for music.

> Music, a universal language, is a most important element of the early classroom curriculum.

Summary

Music should be developmentally appropriate and meet the needs of individual children (Guilmartin, 2000). According to Gardner (1983), music is one of the human intelligences, and recent research indicates that *all* people possess some degree of musical competence.

Performance should not be the focus in early childhood music; however, early experiences with music should be varied and should consist not only of listening, but more significantly of active participation (Guilmartin, 2000). Teachers also need to be active participants, whether they are skilled musicians or music novices.

Music can be the springboard for units and projects for study or it can be integrated into every part of the curriculum. Music allows and encourages enjoyment, attentive listening, moving to the beat, pleasure, creative expression, emotional balance, positive self-concept, music appreciation, and development of musical-related skills (that is, rhythm, meter, pitch, melody, tone). The most important emphasis on music, however, should be enjoyment!

As teachers' own musical competencies and abilities increase, they become much more capable of providing the kinds of activities that result in the development of children's own musical competencies and abilities.

Although songs and singing are the most common experiences, there are many others: musical games, rhythm activities, fundamental locomotor movements, musical instruments, and the development of musical appreciation. Music engages children and fosters developmental growth in other areas such as socialization, emotional satisfaction, cognitive growth in language and math, and opportunity for physical activity and movement. It is an integral part of the early childhood curriculum and should be experienced by each child every day.

Student Learning Activities

1. Examine why music is an important part of the early childhood curriculum. How do you plan to implement it as a part of your curriculum? How could you improve your music skills? Are there particular areas that you could work on?

2. Begin a music file of songs that you plan to use in your curriculum. Include folk songs and rhymes for a variety of ages and from a variety of cultures. Use the resources suggested in this chapter for both records and books.

3. Using at least one of the suggestions for providing variety in singing given in this chapter, teach a song to a group of children between 3 and 8 years of age.

4. Collect or make visuals for at least three different songs. You may use pictures or objects.

5. Visit a preschool, kindergarten, or first-grade classroom and observe how music is included in the curriculum. Are music tools and instruments a part of the learning environment? Are appropriate tapes and/or records available and used? Does the teacher sing to and with the children? Did you see any musical games, rhythm activities, or creative movements being used with the children? Were rhythm instruments available? Were they teacher made or commercial?

6. Make a list of music equipment and supplies that you would want in your classroom. Evaluate some commercial musical toys and instruments.

7. Listen to and evaluate at least three recordings suggested either in this chapter or by your instructor. How would you use these recordings?

8. Evaluate at least three of the music books suggested as references and resources for this chapter. What do you like and what do you not like about each book?

9. Make at least two rhythm instruments out of simple materials.

10. Add to the list of suggested movement interpretations or creative movements given in this chapter. With a group of children, use one of the suggestions and evaluate your experience.

11. Plan a musical dramatization.

12. Do a web, project, or unit plan for an early childhood song or song picture book, or evaluate and add to the one illustrated in this chapter (see Figure 13–1).

13. Develop a series of strategies and activities to educate parents about using music with their children.

Suggested Resources

Children's Books, Early Childhood Music, and Songbooks

Many excellent early childhood songbooks are no longer in print. However, they are often available and have good selections of songs. Consult libraries, book stores, schools, and other sources for out-of-print books and for those currently on the market.

Adams, P. (1973). *There was an old lady*. New York: Child's Play.

Adams, P. (1975). *This old man*. New York: Child's Play.

Aliki (1968). *Hush little baby*. Upper Saddle River, NJ: Prentice Hall.

Anderson, W. A. (ed.) (1991). *Teaching music with a multicultural approach*. Reston, VA: Music Educators National Conference.

Andress, B. (1998). *Music for young children*. Forth Worth, TX: Harcourt Brace.

Andress, B. L. (ed.) (1989). *Promising practices: Prekindergarten music education*. Reston, VA: Music Educators National Conference.

Andress, B. L., & L. M. Walker (eds.) (1992). *Readings in early childhood music education*. Reston, VA: Music Educators National Conference. (Articles focus on the role of music in the education and development of young children.)

Baby's book of lullabies and cradle songs (1990). New York: Dial.

Barbaresi, N. (1985). *Frog went a-courtin'*. New York: Scholastic.

Baum, S. (1992). *Today Is Monday*. New York: HarperCollins.

Beal, K. (1990). *Big book package* (4 vols.). Reading, MA: Addison–Wesley. (Multicultural sing-along big book program series.)

Bennett, P. D., & D. R. Bartholomew (1997). *Song works I. Singing in the education of children*. Belmont, CA: Wadsworth.

The big book of children's songs. (1990). Milwaukee, WI: H. Leonard.

Bonne, R. (1961). *I know an old lady*. New York: Scholastic.

Bullock, K. (1993). *She'll be comin' 'round the mountain*. New York: Simon and Schuster.

Burton, R. (1994). *My best shoes*. New York: Tambourine.

Campbell, P. S., & C. Scott-Kassner (1995). *Music in childhood: From preschool through the elementary years*. New York: Schirmer.

Carle, E. (1992). *Today Is Monday*. New York: Scholastic.

Cassidy, N. (1990). *Kids' songs jubilee*. Palo Alto, CA: Klutz.

Cassidy, N. (1991). *Kids' songs: Sleepyheads*. Palo Alto, CA: Klutz.

Child, L. M. (1974). *Over the river and through the woods*. New York: Coward.

Christelow, E. (1989). *Five little monkeys jumping on the bed*. New York: Houghton Mifflin.

Clark, K. B. (ed.) (1993). *Traditional black music*. New York: Chelsea House.

Conover, C. (1976). *Six little ducks*. New York: Crowell.

Cooper, D. (1992). *Recycled songs*. New York: Random House.

Davol, M. (1992). *The heart of the wood*. New York: Simon & Schuster.

Fox, D., & C. Marks (1987). *Go in and out the window: An illustrated songbook for young people*. New York: Metropolitan Museum of Art/Henry Holt.

Galdone, P. (1986). *Over in the meadow*. New York: Aladdin.

Glazer, T. (1982). *On top of spaghetti*. Garden City, NY: Doubleday.

Glazer, T. (1983). *Music for ones and twos: Songs and games for the very young*. Garden City, NY: Doubleday.

Glazer, T. (ed.) (1988). *Tom Glazer's treasury of songs for children*. Garden City, NY: Doubleday.

Glazer, T. (1990). *Mother Goose songbook*. Garden City, NY: Doubleday.

Goode, D. (1992). *Diane Goode's book of silly stories and songs*. New York: Dutton.

Gurney, J. S. (1992). *Over the river and through the woods*. New York: Scholastic.

Gutmann, D. P. (1990). *Nursery songs and lullabies*. New York: Putnam.

Hague, M. (1992). *Twinkle, twinkle, little star*. New York: Morrow.

Hale, S. J. (1995). *Mary had a little lamb*. New York: Orchard.

Hall, L. O., N. R. Boone, J. Grashel, & R. C. Watkins (eds.) (1997). *Strategies for teaching: Guide for music method classes*. Reston, VA: Music Educators National Conference.

Hallworth, G. (ed.) (1996). *Down by the river: Afro-Carribean rhymes, games, and songs for children*. New York: Scholastic. (Illustrated song collection.)

Hammerstein, O., & R. Rogers (1993). *My favorite things*. New York: Simon & Schuster.

Hoermann, D., & D. Bridges (1988). *Catch a song*. Nashville, TN: Incentive.

Ivmey, J. (1990). *Three blind mice*. Boston: Little, Brown.

Jeffers, S. (1974). *All the pretty horses*. New York: Scholastic.

Jones, C. (1990). *This old man*. Boston: Houghton Mifflin.

Karas, G. B. (1995). *I know an old lady*. New York: Scholastic.

Kennedy, J. (1983). *The teddy bears' picnic*. LaJolla, CA: Green Tiger Press. (Includes Bing Crosby's recording of the song.)

Kovalski, M. (1989). *The wheels on the bus*. New York: Trumpet. (Big book.)

Langstaff, J. (1974). *Oh, a-hunting we will go*. New York: Atheneum.

LaPrise, L. (1997). *The hokey pokey*. New York: Simon & Schuster.

Leventhal, D. (1994). *What is your language?* New York: Dutton.

Marzollo, J. (1990). *Pretend you're a cat*. New York: Dial.

McGee, S. (1992). *I'm a little teapot*. Garden City, Doubleday.

Mettler, B. (1976). *Creative dance in kindergarten*. Tucson, AZ: Mettler Studios.

Mettler, B. (ed.) (1979). *Materials of dance as a creative art activity*. Tucson, AZ: Mettler Studios.

Mettler, B. (1980). *The nature of dance as a creative art activity*. Tucson, AZ: Mettler Studios.

Morgenstern, C. (1995). *Lullabies, lyrics and gallows songs*. New York: North–South.

Music Educators National Conference (MENC) (1995). *Prekindergarten music education standards* (brochure #4015). Reston, VA: Author.

Nelson, E. L. (ed.) (1986). *The fun-to-sing songbook*. New York: Sterling.

Nelson, E. L. (1992). *Musical games for children of all ages*. Woodstock, NY: Beekman.

Orozco, J. (1994). *De colores and other Latin-American folk songs*. New York: Dutton.

Palmer, M., & W. L. Sims (1993). *Music in prekindergarten: Planning and teaching*. Reston, Va.: Music Educators National Conference.

Paxton, T. (1996). *The marvelous toy*. New York: William Morrow.

Pearson, T. C. (1985). *Sing a song of sixpence*. New York: Dial.

Peek, M. (1981). *Ten in the bed*. New York: Clarion.

Peek, M. (1985). *Mary wore her red dress and Henry wore his green sneakers*. New York: Clarion.

Quackenbush, R. M. (1974). *Clementine*. New York: Lippincott.

Rae, M. M. (1988). *The farmer in the dell*. New York: Viking/Kestrel.

Raffi (n.d.). *The Raffi singable songbook*. Toronto: Chappell.

Raffi (1986). *The second Raffi songbook*. Toronto: Chappell.

Raffi (1987). *Down by the bay*. New York: Crown.

Raffi (1989). *The Raffi everything grows songbook*. New York: Crown.

Raffi (1992). *Baby Beluga*. New York: Crown.

Raffi (1995). *Raffi's top 10 songs to sing*. New York: Crown.

Ramsey, M. E. (ed.) (1984). *It's music*. Wheaton, MD: Association for Childhood Education International.

Richards, M. H. (1985). *Let's do it again!* Portola Valley, CA: Richards Institute of Music Education and Research.

Roth, K. (1992). *Lullabies for little dreamers*. New York: Random House.

Rounds, G. (1989). *Old MacDonald had a farm*. New York: Holiday House.

Rounds, G. (1990). *I know an old lady who swallowed a fly*. New York: Holiday House.

Sale, L. (1992). *Growing up with music: A guide to the best recorded music for children*. New York: Avon.

Scelsa, G., & S. Millang (1992). *Dancin' machine*. New York: Random House.

Scelsa, G., & S. Millang (1992). *The world is a rainbow*. New York: Random House.

Schroeder, A. (1995). *Carolina shout!* New York: Dial.

Seeger, R. C. (1992). *American folk songs for children*. Hamden, CT: Shoe String Press.

Shannon, G. (1995). *April showers*. New York: Greenwillow.

Sharon, L., & B. Sharon (1985). *Mother Goose*. Boston: Atlantic Monthly.

Sims, W. L. (ed.) (1995). *Strategies for teaching prekindergarten music*. Reston, VA: Music Educators National Conference.

Smith, R. B., & J. W. Flohr (1984). *Music dramas: For children with special needs*. Denton, TX: Troostwyk.

Stauffer, S. L., & J. Davidson (eds.) (1996). *Strategies for teaching K-4 general music*. Reston, VA: Music Educators National Conference.

Thiele, B., & G. D. Weiss (1995). *What a wonderful world*. Littleton, MA: Sundance. (Big book.)

Trapani, I. (1993). *I'm a little teapot*. Boston: Whispering Coyote.

Trapani, I. (1993). *The itsy bitsy spider*. Boston: Whispering Coyote.

VanLean, N. (1995). *In a circle long ago: A treasury of native lore from North America*. New York: Apple Soup.

VanLean, N. (1995). *Mama rocks, Papa sings*. New York: Random House.

Warren, J. (1987). *Mini-mini musicals*. Seattle, WA: Warren.

Watson, W. (1994). *Fox went out on a chilly night*. New York: Lothrop, Lee & Shephard.

Weikart, P. (1988). *Movement plus rhymes, songs, and singing games*. Ypsilanti, MI: High/Scope.

Weiss, N. (1987). *If you're happy and you know it*. New York: Greenwillow.

Weissman, J. (1984). *Sniggles, squirrels, and chicken pox*. Overland Park, KS: Miss Jackie.

Westcott, N. B. (1987). *Peanut butter and jelly: A play rhyme*. New York: Dutton. (Big book version available from Trumpet Book Club.)

Westcott, N.B. (1989). *Skip to my Lou*. New York: Trumpet.

Westcott, N. B. (1990). *The lady with the alligator purse*. New York: Little, Brown.

Westcott, N. B. (1990). *There's a hole in the bucket*. New York: HarperCollins.

Wickstrom, S. K. (ill.) (1988). *Wheels on the bus* (Raffi songs). New York: Crown.

Williams, V. B. (1988). *Music, music for everyone*. New York: William Morrow.

Winn, M. (ed.) (1974). *The fireside book of fun and game songs*. New York: Simon & Schuster.

Wirth, M., & V. Stassevich (1983). *Musical games, fingerplays, and rhythmic activities for early childhood*. Upper Saddle River, NJ: Prentice Hall.

Wiseman, A. (1979). *Making musical things*. New York: Macmillan.

Wolff, A. (1990). *Baby Beluga*. New York: Crown.

Zeese, D. (1988). *Sing a song of concepts*. Washington, DC: Looking Glass.

Zeitlin, P. (1982). *A song is a rainbow: Music movement and rhythm instruments in the nursery school and kindergarten*. Glenview, IL: Scott, Foresman.

Zelinsky, P. O. (1990). *The wheels on the bus*. New York: Dutton. (Pop-up book.)

Audiocassettes, Records, and CDs

We believe you are familiar with a variety of musical records, CDs, and cassettes and have achieved musical successes in using them. We have chosen not to list specific selections because there are so many excellent ones from which to choose. Wisely purchase musical recordings, remembering that they serve various purposes: teaching a song, playing a game, experiencing rhythms, providing background music, or moving creatively. Include a variety of selections in your school or classroom library.

Multimedia Kits and Programs

Young Voices (1997). *Early Childhood Music Kits*. Fremont, CA: Author. (A series of ten kits that are part of an early childhood music enrichment program. Each kit includes games, hands-on activities, songs and art projects for music, dance, theater, and visual arts.)

Videos

Bringing multicultural music to children. Music Educators National Conference.
Cooperative learning in the music classroom. Music Educators National Conference.
Dance with joy. Documentary Films.
Peter and the wolf. Pyramid Films.

Sing! Move! Listen! Music and young children. Music Educators National Conference.
A young children's concert with Raffi. A&M Records.

Computer Software

Magic melody box. Human Touch.
Math workshop. Broderbund.
Muppet math. Sunburst Communications.
Muppetville. Sunburst Communications.

Chapter 14

Creativity, Art, and Dramatic Activities

Matthew, a preschool child, ran to the teacher excitedly one morning and announced: "Come over to the easel. I just painted a red bird with yellow eyes, and it looks like it is *really* flying!" As the teacher went to the easel, she beheld a red bird with yellow eyes that did indeed look as if it were *really* flying. The freeness of Matthew's painting created an impression of movement—a red bird with yellow eyes, in flight!

"Creative expression develops creative thinking" (de la Roche, 1996, p. 82). In addition, if presented properly, art offers great potential for developing the child's creativity, imagination, thinking, and emotions. Creative art is *not* imitation; rather, it is self-expression, individual, like no one else's work (Clemens, 1991). "Children are consciously working to express their ideas through symbols and images" (Colbert, 1997, p. 201). Developmentally appropriate art for children is personal, spontaneous, inventive, imaginative, unique, therapeutic, and fun (Diffily & Morrison, 1996).

Kay (1992) proposed that the arts are necessary because of their contributions to children's intelligence. When original ideas with art are encouraged, children's motivation, confidence, and self-esteem are reinforced (de la Roche, 1996). However, not all children respond to art experiences and materials in the same way. Most who have studied the responses of children to art believe that they respond naturally and with an intrinsic desire to express themselves (Colbert, 1997). Unfortunately, in early childhood, as well as at every educational level, the emphasis on accountability and higher standards has taken the forefront and the role of art in the curriculum has been challenged. Children need art for art's sake, as well as for their understanding of their world; it has many advantages (Balke, 1997; Seefeldt, 1999).

Art materials should be readily accessible to young children and carefully introduced to them. Markers, paste, clay, crayons, and paints should be in a place where children have access to them whenever they desire (Clemens, 1991). "Three-dimensional activities, whether with clay, cardboard, paper, fabrics, found-materials, cannot be overstressed in the art instruction of young children" (Baker, 1991, p. 136). Not only is it important to provide appropriate art materials and the opportunities to freely explore them, but we must also provide support, instruction in skill and technique, and direction (Edwards & Nabors, 1993; Seefeldt, 1999). As children draw, they learn about such art qualities and properties as color, line, shape or form, space, design, mass or volume, pattern, and texture (Dyson, 1988; Feeney & Moravcik, 1987; Schirrmacher, 1986). "When children draw, they are not simply communicating about their experiences; they are solving visual problems as well" (Dyson, 1988, p. 26). As children paint and draw their ideas on paper, they "think and talk their way through a picture" (Throne, 1988, p. 13). The main goal in creative art should be to communicate an idea, not to please the teacher.

The creative materials that can be used with glue are limitless: all kinds and sizes of boxes, paper plates, wood, fabric and string, carpet scraps, and so on.

Even though we often are unable to recognize and identify objects or symbolism in a child's particular drawing or painting, the progressive steps and understandings are valuable. Much of young children's art is personal, experimental, and not intended to look like something. As the young artist smears, brushes, dabs, and swirls paint or glue, we must remember that the efforts and process are more important than the product. Appropriate comments, sincerely and carefully expressed, provide encouragement and support to young children in their art endeavors and explorations.

Art pieces do not always need to be discussed. Our responses to children regarding their artwork must be genuine and directly related to the product. This will increase the child's self-esteem, interest in painting, and possible incentive to continue personal expression through art (Engel, 1996). Engel suggests six questions to consider that help us to look more carefully at a young child's art (p. 78):

1. What is it made of?
2. What does the observer see (lines, angles, colors, etc.)?
3. What does it represent?
4. How is it organized?
5. What is it about (humor, sadness, experimentation)?
6. Where does the idea come from (a story, an outing, imagination)?

ART AND CREATIVITY GOALS

As with all areas of the curriculum, art needs to have purpose and meaning. Too often in early childhood education, art is added to the curriculum for fun and creativity only, without thought for deeper purposes. The Consortium of National Arts Education Association (CNAEA, 1994) outlined the national standards for arts education, which are organized around content and achievement and advocate that children should:

- Understand and apply techniques and processes of media

- Use knowledge of structures and functions of art

- Choose and evaluate a variety of subject matter, symbols, and ideas

- Reflect upon and assess the characteristics and merits of their own work, as well as the work of others

- Make connections between visual arts and other subjects and curriculum areas

For each art experience planned, teachers should reflect on the purpose and intent of the activity. Teachers should know how the activity will affect the students' learning and achievement.

VALUES OF CHILDREN'S ARTWORK

Young children have "a very special need for the kind and quality of learning instruction that the visual arts and art-like activities provide" (Baker,

1991, p. 140). The child's artwork has many values, and art should be included as an important area of the curriculum. However, the art curriculum and environment need to be assessed to determine if they are developmentally appropriate for young children (Bredekamp, 1986), and art time should be integrated into the curriculum, not isolated from other subjects (Dever & Jared, 1996). Colbert (1997) addresses both appropriate practice and inappropriate practice from the perspective of the National Art Education Association's (NAEA) policy statement, *Developmentally Appropriate Practice for the Visual Arts Education of Young Children*, stating that in appropriate practice "the visual arts are used to enhance other areas of the curriculum and at other times the other areas are used to enhance the visual arts" (p. 211). On the other hand, with regard to inappropriate practice, "art is taught as a separate area of the curriculum. It is approached as a 'make and take' activity, one that warrants little discussion or attention" (p. 211). Our desire is that creative art follows developmentally appropriate practice (DAP).

Creative experiences require careful preparation on the part of the teacher, as well as close supervision, and they may be messy; nevertheless, they have great worth in programs for young children. The teacher's role in art is to provide for experiences and to encourage participation and reaching toward potential in art, "looking at art, and talking about art" (Colbert, 1997, p. 202). In addition, an "atmosphere of trust, comfort, and acceptance for children and their work" is needed to facilitate children's artistic efforts and development (p. 203). Often art is avoided because of lack of conviction regarding its value or because of messiness and the cleanup requirement. Early childhood teachers should recognize the great values of children's artwork and provide many varied art experiences.

Benefits of Art Experiences for Young Children

1. Art offers opportunities for self-expression and individualism. For some children, art media experiences may be one of the few means of self-expression (Clemens, 1991; Seefeldt, 1999). Young children's art expresses their thinking *and* feelings. There are children who do not communicate feelings well through verbal language, music, physical activities, writing, or other areas; however, they are able to express themselves through art media. For every child, art materials should offer the opportunity for self-expression, for celebrating individual uniqueness.

2. Art activities and experiences can deepen children's comprehension of the world, their perception of it or the way they view it, and can enrich their lives and understanding (Epstein, 2001).

3. Art experiences are satisfying to most children. They enjoy creating, working with the raw materials, the processes involved in the art activity, and the product achieved through creative art endeavors.

4. Art activities are therapeutic. Whatever the kind of art project, it offers a catharsis for the child's feelings and emotions that may not be expressed in any other kind of activity. Art activities provide a time to relax from the structure and sometimes the rigidity of the school day. They can be the means by which many children free themselves of pent-up tension and frustration and create feelings of pleasure and joy.

5. Art activities offer training, skill, and development in eye–hand coordination. Children learn to use scissors, manipulate and handle glue and paste, and work with a paintbrush and other tools, all of which promote eye–hand coordination. Most art activities require small-muscle skill and, as the child practices, this skill is improved.

6. As children mature and advance through the stages of art, they devote more thinking, planning, and organizing to their projects. Thus, the way that they interpret ideas, solve problems, and think through concepts can be reflected in their artwork. Much can be learned about a child's feelings and knowledge through artwork.

7. Art activities provide opportunities for language and communication skills as children listen to directions, talk to one another as they work, and describe their efforts and products as they finish.

8. Science skills and concepts are often demonstrated before their eyes as they work with and combine various media. For example, finger painting provides (literally) hands-on experience in combining colors or making shades of colors. Substances such as glitter, sand, or spices added to art media such as paints add texture and smell to artwork (Brudnak, 1997).

Children find great satisfaction in sensory exploration with the various media provided in art activities. Their satisfaction in the process and their pride in the product can make valuable contributions to boosting self-esteem in young children. There must be some wonderful, inherent, positive reasons why young children approach creative art activities with the drive, interest, and eagerness that is so often seen. Creative art is a vital and important part of the early childhood curriculum.

FOSTERING CREATIVITY THROUGH THE ARTS

The following are guidelines for teachers in using art as a method of fostering creativity in the young child.

Guidelines for Using Art to Foster Creativity

- Avoid patterns, ditto outlines, and coloring books.

- Through art, help the children to develop positive views of themselves. Let them know that you have faith in their efforts.

- Give affirmation and praise of the children's work. Let them know that you value uniqueness, diversity, and difference.

- Do not do the children's artwork for them, do not edit their work, and do not provide models for them to follow.

- Expose children to quality artwork through visits to art shows, bookstores, and museums.

Avoid patterns, ditto outlines, and coloring books. They do not promote creativity (Clemens, 1991). Children enjoy experiencing freedom and risk taking with art materials and media, and in appropriate practice they are encouraged to create their own drawings based on their own ideas (Colbert, 1997; Dighe, Calomiris, & Van Zutphen, 1998). In developmentally inappropriate practice, children are given examples and models to follow and told what to do with materials (Colbert, 1997). Children express their feelings, communicate, and make sense of their world through drawing. We do children a disservice when we require them to work with prefabricated, uniform pictures (de la Roche, 1996).

The young child who has not been exposed to the rigid structures of dittos and coloring books or the structured expectations of adults or older children enjoys the freedom of expression that unstructured art activities offer. Only when art activities are unstructured and utilize raw materials does the child have an opportunity for creative expression. Teachers can and should teach skills and model and support techniques that encourage artistic growth and teach graphic representation (Dighe et al., 1998).

Structured art experiences do not recognize the value of art as both a process and a product in the curriculum. The *process* of making art allows children a creative activity in which they learn to manipulate and use art materials. The *product* can be enjoyed by others and provides a means for communication and expression (Dever & Jared, 1996). If approached in the right way, every art project offers possibilities for encouraging creativity. Unfortunately, when activities are structured (coloring, painting, or collaging dittoed or precut patterns), art becomes a powerful force that works *against* the child's creativity. "Must all snowflakes and shamrocks and turkeys be the same shape? . . . Is regularity and sameness what we want from preschool, kindergarten and first-grade children?" (de la Roche, 1996, p. 82).

When children become dependent on the lines or patterns of others, they begin to think that they cannot perform on their own. For example, when a pattern of a horse is given to them to color, they will notice the sophistication of the drawing and how much it really does look like a horse. When they next try to make a horse, the pattern comes to mind, and since they might not be able to duplicate it, they say, "I can't draw a horse." Perhaps not long before they colored the horse, they had happily and confidently sketched a picture of a horse. To many adults it may not have looked exactly like a horse, but they had enjoyed the freedom of using their self-expression in creating their horse. This freedom, this creative expression, becomes lost for many children when they become dependent on the outlines of adult artists. Children may enjoy coloring books because they are not required to think for themselves. They become dependent on someone else's art, impression, or outline and in so doing become less confident in their own expression. The outlines of others so closely resemble the actual objects that children no longer consider their own efforts correct or worthwhile.

Art is an activity that is a personal expression of one's own ideas or reactions. "The children care more, learn more, and enjoy an activity more when they produce their own creations—not copies of ours" (Diffily & Morrison, 1996, p. 38). Note the individualism expressed in the following poem:

Patterns

by Jean Warren

Too soon
The patterns
Tell us how
To move.
Too soon
Leave your dreams
Outside the door.
All sit!
All stand!
Listen now!
The sky is blue.
Cut the line.
Make a star.
Stop!
Story time.
Too soon
And soon
The patterns
Tell us how
To think
To feel.
Too soon

The originals are gone
And in their place
The pattern of a single face.

Through art, help the children to develop positive views of themselves. Let them know that you have faith in their efforts. Tell them often, "You can." Discourage the use of models and patterns, and particularly praise their own unique efforts. Help the children to know that what they create is their own and that they should strive to please themselves—not you, not other children, and not other adults. When a child has a positive view of self, he or she can risk taking chances. A positive view of self allows the individual to be creative.

Provide affirmation for and praise of the children's work. Let them know that you value uniqueness, diversity, and difference. As you praise and talk to the children about their work, do not force or pressure them into telling you what it is; it may not be anything at all, but rather an exploration of the materials (Clemens, 1991). This is particularly true with younger children. In visiting with them and discussing their work, you can comment on design, shape, and color and invite them to tell you about their picture or tell them how it makes you feel. Teachers should let children either talk or be silent about their artwork, whichever they choose. If they describe it, an adult or older child may wish to write their descriptive words (exactly as they are said) on the picture, but you must have their permission to do so.

It shows interest, appreciation, and affirmation for their work to put their names on their pictures (if they are unable to write their names themselves) and display them. However, it is unwise to display any of the pictures unless they can all be displayed, particularly if only the "best" ones were to be selected. It is also best to display artwork at the children's eye level, not the adult's.

Do not do the children's artwork for them, do not edit their work, and do not provide models for them to follow. This can result in frustration for young children (Healy, 2001). You may want to show them how to use the materials provided, but then allow them to explore, experience, try out, and manipulate the media themselves. In addition, you can help them think and see the parts of what they are trying to draw or create (Healy, 2001). As you observe children working, there may be times for needed assistance, especially if the materials are being presented and used for the first time.

Do not evaluate the children's artwork. Teachers are conditioned to evaluate, but children should be free in the art area to express themselves without fear of being evaluated. The teacher's role is to provide the appropriate attitude, time, materials, and encouragement for children and then allow them the dignity of doing their own work (Smith, 1996). Do not grade art; rather, collect a sampling of their artwork for their portfolio.

Help parents to value their children's creative efforts. For young children, the product, the artwork itself, is not as important as the process used in the art project (Smith, 1996). However, children not only enjoy the process, but are very proud of the product.

Shane had painted his first finger painting, but he was unable to take it home because it had not dried adequately. It was difficult for him to leave the painting at school, and he made sure that he knew where it would be waiting for him the next day. His first words after arriving at school the following day were, "Do I get to take my picture home today?"

Young children are proud of their work; teachers should also be proud of the work, and parents can be helped to gain an appreciation for it as well. Many parents do not understand that children go through stages of development in art just as they do in every other aspect of growth. Children universally progress through the same series of stages in their early art development, but individual children go through these stages at individual rates and have unique results (Colbert, 1997). Scribbling begins at age 2 or earlier, extending up to the age of 4 or 5, at which time the child begins to draw symbolically (Kellogg, 1967). Kellogg (1970) has described at least 20 basic scribbles used by children, such as vertical, horizontal, and diagonal lines and other lines and patterns.

Parents may not understand that scribbling is a valuable stage of art. Many times they do not value children's artwork as an artistic and creative effort and part of artistic development. Sharing with parents guidelines for fostering creativity in art is therefore a worthwhile educational endeavor. Most often they will appreciate the insight and enlightenment given to them. It is difficult to measure the long-term effects that this new appreciation may have on promoting the child's creativity.

Expose children to quality artwork through visits to art shows, bookstores, and museums (Diffily & Morrison, 1996). Visit galleries and borrow from your public library reproductions of paintings by famous artists and display them in your room. Comment on the art or illustrations in picture books. Using postcard-sized reproductions of artwork available from museum gift shops, have the children match or pair those that are identical. The cards can also be grouped into such categories as subject, color, artist, size, or others. If the children know how to read, they can learn the names of artists and the titles of paintings. Young children can begin to develop artistic taste during their impressionable years.

PREPARING AND ORGANIZING ART ACTIVITIES

Art activities require careful planning and preparation on the part of the teacher. Very often, the success of a project rests on its preparation, not on the project itself. The following guidelines are useful:

Guidelines for Planning and Preparing Art Activities

1. Establish rules with the children concerning the care and use of art materials. They need to know that supplies and materials cannot be wasted. They cannot damage school property or other children's property with art supplies. Young children must be taught that art supplies are not for eating; many children cannot resist eating the tempting school paste.
2. Have all the materials and supplies needed for the project set up and organized. Since you have also carefully thought about what will be needed, all the supplies and materials are available.

3. Try out art activities ahead of time so that you know how to use the materials and can assist the children in learning how to use them. A student teacher was planning an art activity using plaster of Paris. She had not worked with it before and was not familiar with its properties. In making preparations for the day's activity, she carefully mixed the plaster of Paris before class began. Two hours later, the children were prepared for their art activity, but the plaster of Paris had already set! The teacher should know, for each activity planned, what kinds of materials are needed, what thickness of paint is desired for a particular activity, how long the string should be for string painting, or whether glue or paste works better with a button collage. All these questions and others need to be answered before the children begin; they are best answered when the teacher tries out the project ahead of time.

4. Cleanup should be organized and made as easy as possible. For many art activities, tabletops can be covered with butcher paper or old newspapers for rapid change and cleanup. Containers of soapy water can be provided for glue brushes or paintbrushes as soon as children are finished with them. Aprons or old short-sleeved shirts should be worn by the children to protect their clothing. A sponge, soapy water, and other necessary cleanup materials should be available for the children to use; they can be encouraged to clean up when they are finished.

5. The children should have adequate working space during the activity. If no large space is available, perhaps the activity can be done in smaller groups during free play. Or the children could be divided into groups; while one group is participating in the activity, the other children are involved in other projects.

6. Art activities need plenty of time—time for setting up, time for exploring and creating with the raw materials provided, and time for proper cleanup. Too often art experiences become rushed, taking the enjoyment and even some of the creativity out of the projects.

7. If paintings need to dry, plan ahead of time for a drying place. A place for finished products should also be provided. If one child's picture is displayed, all the other children should have their pictures displayed.

MATERIALS FOR ART ACTIVITIES

Materials for art activities should be handled carefully and should not be wasted. Children need ample supplies. Thus, if costly supplies are desired, use them less frequently, but when they are used, supply an adequate amount! Teachers can be on the lookout for discarded items that may be collected and stored in clean containers in an art-supply storage area. Empty plastic containers, aluminum containers and plates, aerosol lids, and so on are useful for many art projects. Some of the supplies may belong to an individual child, whereas other materials are shared by several children.

Many of the materials discussed in the following sections can be combined with other media. For example, instead of using finger paint alone, add sand, confetti, or glitter. Combine crayon drawings with finger painting for an interesting effect. First make crayon drawings and then finger paint over them. Or use cut-up tissue paper with paint at the easel. Let the child first paint a picture or explore with the paints and brush and then place pieces of tissue paper on the paint before it dries.

Surfaces

Include butcher paper (cut into individual pieces or left longer for murals), construction paper, paper bags, paper towels, newspaper, sandpaper, newsprint, cardboard, and scraps of wood. Styrofoam meat or pastry trays, paper plates, wallpaper, wrapping paper, print-shop end rolls (often available from newspaper printers), boxes (any kind or size), cans, and ice-cream cartons can also be used.

Variety so often increases interest! Vary the surface of the child's artwork; the novelty makes the activity and the product exciting for the child. Vary the size and shape of the paper. Art activities can be done on various sizes of paper, from very small bits to large pieces. Murals may be displayed

Children working on creative activities need plenty of time to explore and create with the materials.

either outside or inside the building. The individual child's portion may be cut out for taking home, or the mural may be done as a class project, with none of it taken home. Use simple geometric shapes and unusual shapes and designs of paper, as well as shapes and designs cut into the paper.

Finger Painting

Using fingers and hands in a paint medium is called finger painting. Some children are hesitant to become involved in this kind of activity and are concerned about being messy. Provide encouragement for these children, but do not force them to become involved. Heather was not willing to join in the first three times the class finger painted. However, the fourth time the activity was provided, she painted with one finger; the next time, she became completely involved with all her fingers. Finger painting must be well organized and supervised, and children should wear aprons. The painting can be done on many of the previously mentioned surfaces. Some kinds of paper should be either taped down or dampened on the underside so that they will adhere to the table. The entire table can be covered with butcher paper on

which the children can fingerpaint. Children will enjoy finger painting directly on the tabletop and then will not worry about sliding, slipping, or tearing the paper. If the child wants a product to save, you can print a reverse simply by blotting the design onto paper. Children may sit or stand while painting, depending on the freedom of movement desired. The following are possibilities for finger paint mixtures:

1. Soap flakes: water added and the mixture beaten to the desired consistency

2. Cream: shaving cream or other cosmetic creams; food coloring or dry, powdered paint added for color

3. Liquid starch: dry, powdered paint added for color

Foot Painting

Using any of the media mentioned under Finger Painting, have the children paint with their feet instead of with their fingers and hands. After the children remove their shoes and socks, the desired kind of paper can be put on the floor, which has previously been covered with newspapers. The paper should be taped down at least on the corners. One successful method is to put two rows of children's chairs parallel and facing one another. Then put one long strip of large-sized butcher paper between the two rows of chairs. Put a spoonful of finger paint in front of each chair. While painting, the children should stay seated in their chairs so that they do not slip. When they are finished, a plastic tub of water and a bar of soap can be brought to their chairs so that their feet can be washed. This activity can also be done outside in warm weather, with a hose handy to wash the feet.

Painting and Printing

Although liquid paints may be purchased from commercial supply houses, mixing paint from powder is more economical and provides many opportunities for child involvement. Vary the color and the consistency of the paints. Sometimes provide only one color; at other times, provide two or more colors. Combine some of the colors to obtain more unusual colors. Try adding small amounts of dark colors to darken the colors, or add white to make pastel colors.

The consistency of the paint will often be determined by the project. Straw painting requires fairly thin paint, whereas other paintings require thicker consistencies. Various media can be added to change the consistency of the paint. A frequently added medium is soap or detergent, which makes the paint go farther, makes cleanup easier, and makes the paint adhere to waxy surfaces (such as milk cartons). Other added media include sand, sawdust, and confetti, which vary in both consistency and texture. One teacher added strong spices to the paint during a unit on smells.

Paints are used differently for painting and printing projects. In painting, the tool (brush) is used to rub or brush the paint on the surface. In printing, the tool is dipped into the paint and then applied to the paper with no movement to leave the imprint of the tool shape. In this case, a sponge or paper towel saturated with paint may work better than a container of paint. Often printing turns out to be painting, but the wise teacher is not concerned, since interest and involvement are of much more value than the end product.

Art activities offer practice, skill, and development in eye-hand coordination as children learn to work with art materials.

- *Brush Painting.* Probably the most frequently used type of painting is brush painting. Although it is often done at the easel, it can be done in different areas and on a variety of surfaces. Vary the size of the brush and the consistency of the paint.

- *Sponge Painting.* Cut sponges into small pieces; clip each piece inside a clothespin for a handle, or tie it to a tongue depressor or stick. Sponges can be used for both painting and printing.

- *Feather Painting.* Use several feathers clipped inside a clothespin, a feather duster, or a single feather of any size or kind dipped into paint and used similarly to a brush. If single feathers are used, they may be attached to the picture, resulting in both a painting and a collage of feathers.

- *Cotton Swab Painting.* The cotton swabs are dipped into the paint and used as brushes, pens, or sponges.

- *Vegetable and Fruit Printing.* Pour the paint over a sponge or absorbent paper placed in a small dish or container. The fruit or vegetable is pressed into the paint and then onto a surface. Oranges, lemons, apples, grapefruits, onions, potatoes, green peppers, celery, pieces of corn on the cob, corncobs, and others work well. When potatoes are used, designs may be cut into the potatoes, or the potatoes may be cut around the design. (Use vegetables and fruits that are no longer edible.)

- *Button Printing.* Using epoxy glue, glue buttons onto small wooden dowels, and then use the buttons for printing. Vary the sizes, shapes, and designs of the buttons.

- *Spool Painting.* Empty thread spools are attached to a handle made from an old coat hanger or other wire. Small nicks can be made on the ends of the spools to create variation in the design.

- *Yarn-on-a-Metal-Can Painting.* Yarn or string is glued with a strong glue to a small metal can. Paint is brushed over the yarn, and then the can is rolled over a surface.

- *Fabric Printing.* Small pieces of burlap, nylon netting, or other textured fabrics ($2\frac{1}{2}$ to 3 inches square) are wrapped over a sponge that has been attached to a clothespin or secured to a dowel with a piece of string or elastic. The fabric is then dipped into paint and printed onto a surface.

- *Pinecone Printing.* Whole pinecones or pieces can be rolled in paint then rolled over a surface. The large ones with flat bottoms can be dipped into paint to make an impression of the bottom on a surface.

- *String–Block Printing.* String, yarn, rickrack, lace, or similar materials are glued onto small wooden blocks or scraps of wood. The blocks are dipped into the paint (or the paint is brushed on), and the design is printed onto a surface.

- *Blot Painting.* The paper or other material is folded in half; small amounts of paint are dropped with either a spoon or an eyedropper on one inside half. The paper is then folded over, and the halves are blotted together and then opened up.

- *String Painting.* One end of a piece of string or yarn, 8 to 10 inches in length, is attached to a clothespin. The string is dipped into the paint. The string is then placed in a design on one inside half of a piece of paper or other material that has been folded in half. The paper is folded over the string. One hand presses on the paper and string, and the other hand pulls the string out in different directions to make a design. If desired, the string can be dipped into paint of a different color and the same procedure repeated.

- *Straw Painting.* Paint is dropped onto a surface with an eyedropper or spoon. Then the paint is blown in different directions with a short straw.

- *Gadget Printing.* Gadgets (washable only) found around the house are dipped into paint and then onto a surface to make the design. Gadgets such as forks, potato mashers, jar ring tops, and rubber door stoppers make interesting choices.

Collages

When collages are made, some materials or combinations of materials are glued onto a surface. Many different kinds of materials and scrap items can be used for collages. Children can tear or cut their collage materials out of paper.

Glues.   A variety of substances can be used for glue or paste. For gluing paper of any kind, an inexpensive paste may be used, such as *library* or *school paste*. It can be thinned, if desired, by whipping or beating with a rotary beater. Do not add water. It can also be used directly out of the jar. For heavier items, such as scraps of fabric or macaroni, *white glue* is suggested. Homemade *flour paste* can be used as a glue, along with homemade *cornstarch paste* (flour or cornstarch mixed with a small amount of water). *Wheat paste* can be purchased inexpensively. *Plaster of Paris* can be purchased economically in bulk and mixed to a thick consistency. A small amount can be put on a base and then various collage items pressed into it. Tissue paper, cut-up scraps of magazines, or similar light media can be glued to any kind of surface with *liquid starch*. The pieces are dipped into the starch and then pressed onto such surfaces as plastic aerosol caps (two of the same size could be glued together, with some objects placed inside, to make a musical shaker); empty baby food jars (to make banks, vases, pencil holders, etc.); or half-pint milk cartons (to make musical shakers). Although a little more difficult to use, *rubber cement* is another possibility. The kinds of glues and pastes mentioned can be put as a blob on waxed paper, aluminum foil, a metal lid, or a paper towel (easily cleaned up) and applied with the finger or a brush; or the collage items can be dipped into the paste or glue and then onto the surface.

Suggested Media.   When children make a collage, they arrange, on a surface, a medium or combination of media in desired ways. Often their designs become intricate and unusual. Collage media can be found anywhere, including in the garbage can, and practically everywhere indoors and outdoors. Paper can be torn or cut for collage work; three-dimensional objects also offer good possibilities. Collages can become part of class murals in various sizes and shapes. Be sure that the glue is strong enough to hold the medium or media chosen. The following list of suggested media is only a beginning; use your own imagination, along with the materials and discarded items on hand in your environment. You can use combinations of items, one item, a variety of one item such as buttons, or even a category of items such as beans, seeds, sewing items, or wood.

Styrofoam	Dried flowers and
Wrappers from candy	weeds
bars	Leaves
Wood chips	Lace
Toothpicks	Hardware items
Labels from cans	Yarn scraps
Small rocks and/or	Carpet scraps
gravel	Linoleum scraps

Sculpturing

When children sculpt, they pile on, build high, pat, roll, flatten, poke, and squeeze, depending on the materials provided.

Clay Sculpture.   The most frequently used sculpture medium is clay. It should always be available in every early childhood classroom. Clay must be neither too sticky nor too dry. It should be pliable and workable. Children should be exposed to different kinds.

1. Play Dough

2 cups boiling water
food coloring (about 4 to 6 drops)
3 T. oil
$2\frac{1}{2}$ cups flour
$\frac{1}{2}$ cup salt
1 T. alum

Mix the food coloring with the water, then add the oil. Add the liquid ingredients to the dry ingredients and knead them together well. Form the material into balls and refrigerate in an airtight container. This play dough must be kept covered and refrigerated when not in use. It will not dry out like other salt-flour doughs. The texture and consistency are excellent!

2. Salt-Flour Clay or Dough

3 cups flour
$\frac{3}{4}$ cup salt
$\frac{1}{2}$ tsp oil

Water to achieve the right consistency

Mix together the dry ingredients with dry powdered paint for coloring, or add food coloring to the water. Gradually add water, and continue kneading

Suggested Media for Collages

Elastics	Confetti
All kinds of paper	Old jewelry
Keys	Feathers
Wallpaper	Spices
Sequins	Bottle caps
Tissue paper	String
Any kind of tape	Fabric scraps
Crepe paper	Brads
Gummed stars,	Beans
reinforcements,	Canceled stamps
or labels	Colored salt or sand
Newspaper	Eggshells, including
Magazine scraps	dyed
Cotton balls	Seeds
Straws	Sawdust

There are many kinds of play dough, both commercial and homemade, that allow for creating, cutting, measuring, rolling, squishing, stacking, sculpturing, and molding.

and mixing until the clay is the desired consistency. This clay can be mixed and stored in an airtight container for a long period of time. It can be used for making beads by rolling it into small balls and poking holes through each bead with a nail and then drying. The clay can also be used for making handprints, or it can be molded around a can, with collage items pressed into it for decoration. The clay can be left out to air-dry or can be baked until hard.

3. Oil-based modeling clay is very pliable and workable. It can be purchased from school stores or art-supply stores. It can be used over and over and should be stored in plastic bags so that it retains moisture.

4. Pottery clay is a moist clay used by potters. It can be purchased from art-supply stores or from a college art department. It should be stored in plastic bags so that it remains moist and workable.

5. Bread dough can be molded like clay and baked in the oven like ordinary bread and then eaten.

Wood Sculpture. Small scraps of wood (obtained from a mill or construction site) are combined with other items and glued or nailed to a wood base. Paint the dried sculpture.

Box Sculpture. An assortment of boxes of different sizes and shapes is glued together. A cereal box makes an excellent base, and then smaller boxes may be used to complete the sculpture. The sculpture can be painted; if powdered detergent is added to the paint, it will adhere to a wax-coated box.

Styrofoam Sculpture. A structure can be built with a Styrofoam base and scraps and pieces of Styrofoam attached with toothpicks.

Miscellaneous Art Activities

Necklaces. Children enjoy making things that they can wear. Both boys and girls delight in constructing necklaces. Make sure that a piece of tape is put on one end of the string or a small object tied to it to hold the objects on. The end being used for stringing should be stiff; yarn or string can be dipped in wax, glue, or nail polish, or tape can be wrapped around the end. A combination of the following are suggestions for stringing media.

1. *Colored macaroni.* Use smaller-sized macaroni, because it will go farther and the child can spend more time stringing it. If large macaroni is used, the necklace will hold only 6 to 10 pieces. To color macaroni or similar media,

put rubbing alcohol and food coloring in a jar. The darker and more intense the desired color, the more food coloring that should be added. Put the macaroni in the jar and shake it for a few minutes. Then spoon it out onto paper towels to dry. (Use macaroni that is too old to eat.)

2. *Paper*. Use small pieces of paper cut into shapes or designs with holes punched in the middle. Flower shapes are easily made this way.

3. *Horse chestnuts or small blocks of wood*. Drill holes through each for stringing.

4. *Plastic straws*. Cut into varying lengths for stringing.

Hats.   Various kinds of hats can be made for use in parades, games, musical activities, and so on.

1. *Paper plate hats*. Paper plate hats work best if a smaller paper plate is stapled to the back of a larger plate so that they are back to back. The smaller paper plate may have a hole punched on each side, with ribbons or strings attached to make the ties. The smaller plate then fits around the child's head and is not decorated. The larger paper plate will appear to sit on top of the head and can be decorated with collage paper flowers, cotton balls, flowers, or other objects.

2. *Crowns*. Cut a crown pattern for each child out of heavy paper such as poster paper. The paper can be decorated by painting, collaging, or printing. Add such items as gummed stars, glitter, aluminum foil, or old jewelry stones. Staple bands of the heavy paper to the crown, and then staple these two ends together to fit the child's head.

3. *Newspaper hats*. Fold newspapers into various hat shapes and then decorate them.

4. *Spring hats or bands*. Make a band of paper about $1\frac{1}{2}$ inches wide and long enough to extend about three-quarters of the way around the child's head; attach string or ties to the ends. Paper flowers can be cut out and glued on. Flowers can also be made by forming 1-inch squares of crepe paper over the eraser end of a pencil to make a flower formation, which is then glued to the headband. Bows can be made by twisting rectangular-shaped

crepe paper in the middle and then gluing the bows to the band. Another spring band can be made by cutting out the inside portion of a paper plate, decorating the rim, and attaching ties.

5. *Wigs*. A brown paper bag may be used to make a wig. Cut a face hole in one side of the bag, and then cut the rest of the bag into strips. Roll each strip on a pencil, crayon, or pen to curl it.

Cotton-Ball Painting.   Dip cotton swabs or balls into dry, powdered paint and smear them on paper. Pastel colors or shades work best. When the picture is finished, spray it with lacquer hair spray so that the paint does not rub off.

Melted Crayon Pictures.   Using a vegetable grater or a small plastic pencil sharpener, make crayon shavings using old crayons. Do not use many of the darker colors. Mix the shavings together and put them in small containers for each child. Sprinkle a few shavings onto half of the inside of a folded paper. Waxed paper works especially well because the finished picture is transparent and the two sides of the paper are sealed together. After the crayon shavings have been sprinkled onto one side of the paper, the other side is folded on top of the shavings. The picture is then placed between several layers of newspaper and ironed with a hot iron. The heat will melt together the crayon shavings. If waxed paper is used, the two portions will melt together. Small collage items may also be added with the shavings. For example, at Christmastime, cut holiday objects and shapes from tissue paper and add them, with glitter, to the shavings. Things from nature and the outdoors could be collected and added with the shavings. For example, one group of children made place mats in the fall by adding small seeds, dry weeds, and other outdoor fall treasures to the crayon shavings.

Salt or Sand Painting.   Although termed *painting*, this process is actually a collage activity. Glue is spread onto a surface, and then sand or salt that has been put in salt shakers or other containers is sprinkled onto the wet glue. The excess salt or sand is then shaken off. (Color the salt or sand by adding a few drops of food coloring or powdered paint.)

Paper Plate Crafts. Some suggestions for using paper plates have already been presented. Three paper plates of varying sizes can also be stapled together and then decorated to make snow figures. They can also be decorated to make turtles or masks. Eye holes can be cut out, with big, floppy bunny ears and a bunny nose and mouth added, to make a bunny mask.

Egg Carton Crafts. Egg cartons can be used to make insects, ants, caterpillars, or other animals. They can be painted and then items glued on to make faces. Pipe cleaners can be used for legs and feelers.

Coffee Filter Butterflies. Dip the filters in water colored with food coloring. After they dry, they are pulled together across the diameter of the circle and attached with a clothespin. Glue a head on and attach pipe cleaner feelers for a completed butterfly.

Milk Carton Crafts. Milk cartons can be decorated and used to make the sections of a train or to make other vehicles such as boats or wagons. They can also be decorated as planting boxes or as baskets.

Ice Cream Tub Crafts. These containers can be made into wastebaskets, flowerpots, drums, curler boxes, helmets, hats, or storage containers by collaging, painting, or finger painting them.

Paper Cup or Aluminum Can Crafts. Paper cups or aluminum cans can be decorated with desired media and used for pencil holders, planting containers, flowerpots, clay gardens, or musical instruments.

Rock Crafts. Rocks can be painted and decorated as animals, pets, or other objects. They can also be glued together for sculpturing.

Cameras. Provide each child with a box that has holes punched in the longest sides so as to create a lens hole through which the child can see. The boxes can be decorated with collage items or using marking pens. Put a picture of the child inside the box, along with cutout magazine pictures of other people. Decorate the cameras. When dry, put a rubber band around the box. As the children peer through the punched holes, they pretend to take pictures by snapping the rubber band. Then they can take out the picture inside that has already been "developed."

Soap Bubbles. Make blowers out of old coat hangers bent to the desired size, or use the plastic holders that link six-packs of sodas. Mix one of the following two recipes and give each child a small portion in an aerosol lid or similar small container. Let them blow bubbles outside; it prevents a sticky film from collecting on the floor.

Recipe 1

$\frac{1}{2}$ cup liquid dishwashing detergent
$\frac{1}{4}$ cup sugar
A little water to dilute solution, if necessary

Recipe 2

8 oz liquid detergent (quality brand)
1 oz glycerin

Crayon and Felt-tip Pen Art. These art tools are easy to obtain and offer great creative opportunities for children when used on a variety of surfaces. Use water-based markers, rather than permanent markers, because the permanent markers may contain toxic solvents and can stain clothes.

Chalk Art. Chalk can be used dry and then sprayed with lacquer hair spray to prevent it from rubbing off. Wet a paper with water, buttermilk, or liquid starch, and then use the chalk. Using these dampening methods makes the paintings much more brilliant, and the chalk sticks better to the paper. Chalk can also be dipped into sugar water (a few tablespoons of sugar mixed with half a cup of water), buttermilk, or water for the same results.

Box Crafts. Large boxes can be painted, sculpted, collaged, or decorated for play. A train could be made from a number of boxes, with ice cream tubs being used on the front box to make the engine.

DRAMATIC PLAY

"Dramatic play is the most highly developed form of symbolic play, in which the child begins the incredible process of using objects as symbols for objects and events in the real world" (Stone, 1995,

p. 47). Dramatic play is one of the great joys of childhood, helping children to develop interpersonal skills of conflict resolution and cooperation and improve their problem-solving and language abilities (Diffily & Morrison, 1996). There are many types of dramatic play activities, and each offers opportunities for all children to talk and listen, thus developing the language arts. They promote socialization and release of feelings and attitudes. The importance of dramatic play in the early years should not be underestimated (Stone, 1995). Dramatic play encourages creativity and offers the opportunity for children to play out their own personal culture and world.

Dramatic play allows children to act out stories, fingerplays, songs, and other sources of themes. It is easy for children to become police officers, firefighters, parents, or farmers.

Because young children love to pretend, and because dramatic play is pretending, this is an important value. The following experiences are valuable in incorporating dramatic play in the classroom curriculum:

1. Provide children with opportunities to create and explore in dramatic play centers.

2. Use drama in both large- and small-group situations in all curriculum areas.

3. Provide children with opportunities to act out stories that they have dictated to the teacher or that have been read to them.

4. Use drama to help to resolve conflicts, express emotions, and extend social skills (Howell & Corbey-Scullen, 1997).

Free Dramatic Play

During the early childhood years, children naturally engage in much dramatic play, acting out various play themes and dramatically portraying characters (Bronson, 1995). Dramatic play activities, often referred to as *free dramatic play*, or, more informally, "let's pretend," are set up during individual play for children who choose to participate. An area of the room is set up with desired materials. The children need not be told what to do, since the materials will suggest possibilities to them. To pretend, children "picture experiences in their minds" (Diffily & Morrison, 1996, p. 35), and their own experiences and imaginations will be all that they need. Dramatic play is especially enjoyed by 3- to 8-year-olds because they like pretending. Playing house seems to be the preferred theme, perhaps because it provides familiar roles for the children to use and expand (Griffing, 1983). It is easy for a child to become a police officer, farmer, mother, father, beautician, or whatever role the materials suggest. Teachers must encourage diversity of roles and watch for stereotyped comments and behaviors. It is suggested that an area of the room be set up for dramatic play and that this area be changed often to suggest various kinds of dramatic play.

Large, hollow blocks provide a great chance for dramatic play in which children "shape their own learning environments" (Cartwright, 1990). The children choose whether the play is housekeeping, farming, aviation, fishing, boating, or something else. When the accessories are unstructured, even more imagination and creativity can be tapped. For example, fabrics can be furnished for dressing up; small-unit blocks for small accessories; paper, tape, and crayons for signs. All are unstructured and leave what they become to the child's imagination (Cartwright, 1990).

Suggestions for the Dramatic Play Area to Be Used During Free Play

1. Housekeeping: Any housekeeping and domestic tools and equipment, such as brooms, mops, stove, table, refrigerator, dress-up clothes for boys and girls (child sized), hats, purses, shoes, gloves, ties, and eyeglass frames; in addition, towels, washtub, and dolls (of both genders and diverse ethnic and racial backgrounds), along with dishes, cooking utensils, equipment, and pretend foods

2. Barbershop and beauty shop: Actual materials and cosmetics, such as rollers, combs, brushes, hair dryer, mirror, fingernail polish, nail file, cotton balls, old makeup, perfume, lotions, shaving cream, play razor, and aftershave lotion, together with soap and water, as well as cleansing cream, if possible

3. Camping: Sleeping bags, small tent, backpacks, canteens, mess kits, compass, hiking boots, rope, flashlight, food, as well as rocks and wood to represent a campfire

4. Picnic: Tablecloth, napkins, picnic basket, jug for drinks, sandwiches, cookies, rocks and wood to represent fire, other equipment

5. Carpenter shop: Hammers, saws, other tools, nails with large heads, scrap lumber, sandpaper, woodworking bench

6. Plumbing: Pipes of all lengths, widths, and shapes; monkey wrenches, plungers, hose and nozzles, and box for tools

7. Restaurant: Small tables set up with matching tablecloths; old menus obtained from restaurants; placemats, napkins, place settings, and any other restaurant supplies obtained from local places that might be willing to give you these materials; an area where food is prepared, with both pretend and real foods available to serve customers

8. Grocery store: Foods and empty cartons, as well as empty metal cans with labels; large-unit blocks or small tables, with aisles and shelves set up for display of grocery items; cash register, real money (small change), cart or carriage, bags and/or boxes

9. Hospital: White shirts, stethoscope, adhesive bandages, elastic bandages, cotton balls, cots, pillows and sheets, scales, tongue depressors, flashlight, syringes, masks, rubber gloves, crutches, pill bottles for medicine, supplies donated from the disposable items used by hospitals and doctor's offices (sterilized before using, disposed of or sterilized after using)

10. School: Desks, chalk, chalkboard, erasers, paper, pencils, crayons, books, flannel board and flannel figures, any other school supplies

11. Office: Typewriter, paper, pen, pencils, telephone, briefcase, and any other office supplies available

12. Post office: Envelopes, both new and used, rubber stamp and ink pad (perhaps discarded from a post office), scales, used stamps, any kinds of stamps such as trading stamps, mailbag (old newspaper bag or large purse with shoulder strap), mailboxes (small and large shoe boxes), mail sorting box (box with cardboard sections in it)

13. Bakery: Bowls, rolling pins, playdough or clay, cookie cutters, muffin tins, cookie sheets, baker's hat, aprons

14. Gas station: Air pumps, boxes, ropes, hoses for pump, tools such as wrench and screwdriver, oil can, cash register, sponges and paper towels

Additional possibilities for dramatic play areas include a shoe store (complete with shoeshine area), dentist's office, television station, dress shop, men's clothing store, airport, space station, gardening center, farm, circus, fashion show, greenhouse, and pet store. Even a few materials will promote dramatic play with children. Another idea is to have a couple of suitcases ready to pack for trips. Line up chairs for an airplane, boat, automobile, bus, train, or whatever means of travel has been chosen. In many early childhood classrooms, the only dramatic play area ever set up is a housekeeping area. After many weeks, the children tire of it and do not use it as often. Try setting up new areas and you will be amazed at the interest and enthusiasm sparked in both the children and yourself.

Various sizes and shapes of blocks provide opportunities for children to create their own learning environments to support their dramatic play.

Creative Dramatics

Types of Creative Dramatics in Early Childhood:

- *Pantomime*: students act out situations within their own self-space using only actions and gestures as a means of expression

- *Story Dramas*: acting out whole stories or parts of stories

- *Role Playing*: various events, people, stories, and situations are acted out and they are usually spontaneously acted. By acting out roles, students are able to think, feel, and act as other persons. They are effective for resolving conflicts, practicing appropriate behavior, and creating empathy.

- *Choral Reading and Choral Speaking*: the oral interpretation of literature. Choral speaking refers to experiences in which students recite passages from memory, and in choral reading the students read text, such as poetry or stories.

- *Readers' Theater*: minimal theater in support of literature and reading. Usually, there is no full memorization and scripts are held during the performance. It is rather informal without full costume and no full stage sets.

Creative dramatics is more sophisticated than free dramatic play. Davis and Behm say, "Creative dramatics is an improvisational, non-exhibitional, process-centered form of drama in which participants are guided by a leader to imagine, enact, and reflect on nursery rhymes, folktales, and other stories" (quoted by Cline & Ingerson, 1996, p. 4). It is planned by the teacher, but acted and played out by the children. Creative dramatics has more form than free dramatic play (McCaslin, 1996). However, both free dramatic play and creative dramatics involve the children "in improvised dialogue, identification with a role, and minimal use of props" (Mandelbaum, 1975, p. 88). Creative dramatics is creativity, whole language, cooperative learning, and problem solving combined (Cline & Ingerson, 1996). A great benefit of creative dramatics is the full participation and involvement of all children. As children try out various roles, they learn about others and about themselves. Ideas from all aspects of the curriculum can be used to stimulate creative dramatics.

Skills That Children Acquire Using Creative Dramatics

1. Problem solving
2. Literacy (reading, writing, speaking, listening)
3. Analyzing
4. Planning
5. Self-confidence
6. Courage
7. Creativity
8. Empathy
9. Communication
10. Social interaction

Dramatizations can be stimulated and motivated in many ways. They must be geared to the ages of the children, and younger children will need more coaching and help from the teacher. Even though these children enjoy dramatizations, they do not often have the know-how to carry them out without guidance and assistance. The teacher may need to participate or simply give much prompting and assistance. As an example, one kindergarten group was dramatizing "The Three Billy Goats Gruff." The teacher first told the story and then parts were assigned, with children not having parts being the audience. A plank was set up between two chairs to represent the bridge, the troll wore an old coat and hat, and the three billy goats wore simple paper-sack masks. As the teacher helped the children with this dramatization, she used such motivating questions as "What happened next?" "What did the first billy goat do then?" and "What did the troll say?" If the children taking the parts could not remember, they were coached by the audience. They enjoyed participating, and it was not important that each "actor" have the part memorized or even remember it. What was important was that the children were involved in making the story come to life for them. For older children, fewer suggestions, along with the main plot or idea, will enable them to dramatize, or act out, the story.

Suggestions to Prompt Creative Dramatizations

1. Stories: read in class or in a reading group
2. Poems
3. Musical stories
4. Situations: a friend unwilling to share a toy with you, what to do if a friend gets hurt, being lost
5. Field trips: to the farm, to the zoo, or elsewhere
6. Events: a birthday party, a hike, a hunting expedition; trips to outer space, to Mexico, or any other place
7. Dramatizations centered on an object or series of objects: an object or objects put in a bag, with the children making up stories about the object(s)
8. Pretend activities: pretending to be seeds growing or sprouting, a worm crawling along a branch, or the like (especially enjoyed by younger children)
9. Plays
10. Role playing: specific role or character for an individual child or a story role played by the entire group to promote understanding of feelings and actions
11. Puppet shows

Choral readings can easily be organized and "cast" using either poems or simple stories. The following are different examples of how poetry might be organized for very simple choral readings:

Almost
By Leland B. Jacobs

Girls: I almost caught a honeybee,

Boys: I almost caught a fly,

Girls: I almost caught a beetle

Boys: But I didn't really try!

Day Dreams
By Aileen Fisher

Group 1:   In the middle of the summer
Wouldn't it be nice
To get a day of winter
Full of snow and ice?

Group 2:   In the middle of winter
Wouldn't it be fun
To get a hazy, lazy, blazy
Barefoot-day of sun?

Kites
By Emily Megow

Girls: Oh, how I'd like to be a kite
And skim across the sky

Boys: And dip and whirl and twist and whirl
And with the swallows fly!

Solo 1:   I'd climb into the tallest tree
And find a brown bird's nest,
And maybe she'd invite me in
To sit a while and rest.

Solo 2:   I'd fly as high as eye can see
Above the tall churchspire
And chase the moon and stars about
And never, never tire.

Girls: It seems to me that birds and kites
Have such a lot of joy

Boys: That it's mighty hard to have to be
Nothing but a boy!

Puppets

Use of puppets is a kind of dramatic play, and it offers many opportunities for both speaking and listening. "Young children are fascinated by puppets, and readily accept the apparent magic that is responsible for giving them life" (Smith, 1979, p. 4). Puppets are attention getters. They can be used in unstructured situations such as individual play; but sometimes children become aggressive when using them, particularly if animal puppets are being used, and limits and guidelines must be established. Puppets can be used to capture attention in a discussion, tell a story or poem, teach a song, give children directions, or assist in numerous other sit-

uations. Puppet skits can be used to help children to develop problem-solving skills such as sensitivity to problems or alternative-solution thinking. Younger children use puppets in less formal and structured ways.

Examples of Using Puppets

1. Storytelling
2. Play acting
3. Puppet show
4. Singing songs: puppets used by one or more children when singing songs; often helps shy children to sing or speak out more
5. Children in stories: participation by children in parts of stories
6. Stimulation of a dialogue or conversation between two or more children
7. Television shows: television set made out of a large box such as a store or refrigerator box; puppets used for quiz shows, talk shows, movies, or even commercials

Puppets can be made in numerous ways. The puppets that children make should be simple in design and easy to use, such as those made from paper sacks, sticks, felt, socks, vegetables, paper plates, cardboard cylinders, or gloves.

Summary

So many values emerge from children's creative art activities. A great deal of freedom lies within the bounds of limits, rules, and responsibilities. Individualism flourishes, self-expression flows, and there is satisfaction in both the process and the product. Art activities also have sensory qualities, often involving several of the senses at one time.

As teachers foster creativity in art during the early childhood years, children's abilities to dream and kindle new ideas, accept challenging tasks, and discover horizons not yet imagined are expanded. Ideas for better ways of doing things

exist in the human mind, not in computers or other machines. The sooner the mind is encouraged and invited to create, the more able it will be to expand its capabilities and the more time it will have to reach its potential. It should be easy for teachers to defend the value of art experiences in the curriculum. What is most important in art expression is "to ensure that each child grows and develops, learns to think and express his feelings and ideas, and creates new and original responses within an environment that is supportive, validating, and inclusive" (de la Roche, 1996, p. 83).

Dramatic activities have also been included in this chapter. Their value has been clearly defined, and they can be defended for their cognitive, emotional, and social benefits. They encourage creative thinking and doing and can be integrated into all aspects of the curriculum, but are particularly relevant and so easily stimulated during free play.

Student Learning Activities

1. Visit an early childhood classroom when children are participating in an art activity. Evaluate how effectively creativity was fostered. Notice individual children and their various stages of art. Was the activity well planned and set up, implemented, and cleaned up?

2. Collect art samples from children and study the various stages of art. One way to do this is to have a group of children draw a self-portrait, or simply give the children each a circle or paper plate and have them draw face portraits of themselves. What did you learn from this activity?

3. Make a list of the art supplies and equipment that you would want to have in your classroom.

4. Begin an art portfolio of children's art activities by completing a sample of at least two art activities suggested for each section in this chapter. For example, do at least two finger paintings, two paintings, two printings, two collages, and so on. Label them, and describe the materials needed on the back. Add to the collection each time a new art activity is done.

5. Prepare and try out at least one of the play dough or clay recipes. Evaluate your results. Do you like the texture and consistency?

6. Visit several early childhood classrooms and evaluate the kinds of art experiences that the children are having based on your observations and the children's artwork that you see displayed in the rooms.

7. Observe in a classroom where a dramatic play area is set up. Describe the area, the play that occurred during your observation, and the benefits for the children from this kind of play.

8. Plan, implement, and evaluate at least one creative dramatics activity with a group of children aged 2 to 8 years.

9. Make three different types of puppets. Plan how you will use them.

Suggested Resources

Creative Art References

Bos, B. J. (1982). *Don't move the muffin tins: A hands off guide to art for the young child*. Roseville, CA: Turn the Page Press.

Chenfield, M. B. (1983). *Creative activities for young children*. New York: Harcourt Brace Jovanovich.

Cherry, C. (1976). *Creative play for the developing child*. Carthage, IL: Fearon Teacher Aids.

Cherry, C. (1990). *Creative play for the developing child: A teacher's handbook for early childhood education*. Carthage, IL: Fearon Teacher Aids.

Colbert, C., & M. Taunton (1990). *Discover art: Kindergarten*. Worcester, MA: Davis.

Colbert, C., & M. Taunton (1992). *Developmentally appropriate practices for the visual arts education of young children*. Reston, VA: National Art Education Association.

Copple, C., I. Siegel, & R. Saunders (1984). *Educating the young thinker: Classroom strategies for cognitive growth*. Hillsdale, NJ: Erlbaum.

Davis, G. A. (1997). *Creativity is forever* (4th ed.). Dubuque, IA: Kendall/Hunt.

Davis, J., & T. Behm (1978). Terminology of drama/theatre with and for children: A redefinition. *Children's Theatre Review* 27(1): 10–11.

Gardner, H. (1983). *Frames of mind: The theory of multiple intelligences*. New York: Basic.

Herberholz, B. (1985). *Early childhood art* (3rd ed.). Dubuque, IA: William C. Brown.

Jalongo, M. R. (1997). *The arts in children's lives: Aesthetic education in early childhood*. Boston: Allyn and Bacon.

Jenkins, P. D. (1980). *Art for the fun of it: A guide for teaching young children*. Upper Saddle River, NJ: Prentice Hall.

Johnson, M. (1992). *Understanding and appreciating your child's art: How to enhance confidence in drawing, ages 2-12*. Los Angeles: Lowell House.

Koster, J. B. (1997). *Growing artists: Teaching art to young children*. Albany, NY: Delmar.

Lasky, L., & R. Mukerji (1980). *Art: Basic for young children*. Washington, DC: National Association for the Education of Young Children.

Lowenfeld, V. (1988). *The nature of creative activity*. Irvine, CA: American Biography Service.

Schirrmacher, R. (1998). *Art and creative development for young children* (3rd ed.). Albany, NY: Delmar.

Smith, N. R., C. Fucigna, M. Kennedy, & G. L. Lord. (1993). *Experience and art* (2nd ed.). New York: Teachers College Press.

Taylor, C. W. (1986). Be talent developers. *Today's Education 57*: 67-79.

Torrance, E. P. (1987). *Save tomorrow for the children*. Buffalo, NY: Bearly.

Wankelman, W., P. Wigg, & M. Wigg (1989). *A handbook of arts and crafts* (7th ed.). Madison, WI: Brown & Benchmark.

Wigg, P. R., J. Hasselschwert, & W. F. Wankelman. (1997). *A handbook of arts & crafts*. Madison, WI: Brown & Benchmark.

Davis Mass, 50 Portland Street, Worcester, MA 01608, specializes in creative art activities and has many materials available. By writing to this company, you can obtain a complete list of its available art publications as well as information on its periodical, *School Arts*.

Videos

The Arts and the Aesthetic Intelligence, Elliot Eisner (#Y1692-ISBN 1-57517-133-3). Skylight Professional Development.

Computer Software

The art lesson. The Learning Company.
Color me. Mindscape.
Color 'n' canvas. Wings for Learning.
Picture perfect. MindPlay.
Rainbow painter. Queue.

Web Sites

http://www.storycart.com   This website has great readers theaters for beginning readers.

http://tqjunior.thinkquest.org/ 5291/resources.html   This website, Children's Creative Theater Resources, has many suggestions for incorporating creative dramatics into the curriculum.

Lesson Plans

The following concepts or themes are included in this appendix as examples of lesson plans:

Emotions
Water
Wheat and Flour
Community helpers
Fruit
Light (shadows)
Texture
Sound
Numbers
Honeybees
Fish
Trees

LESSON PLAN ON EMOTIONS (FOUR DAYS)

Objectives

- Each child will become more independent in putting toys and other materials away, cleaning up, and putting clothes on.
- Each child will gain a better understanding of himself or herself, particularly his or her emotions and the expression of them.
- Each child will become more aware of the kinds of things that stimulate emotions and how to work with them.

Note: Many of the whole- and small-group activities in this lesson plan work well as cooperative learning projects, especially those that address happy and unhappy emotions, curiosity, fear, anger, and so on.

Day 1

Whole-Group Activity

Introduction to Unit on Feelings and/or Emotions
- Place felt cutout faces representing various moods or emotions on the flannel board and discuss them with the children. Afterward, tell the children a story about feelings and discuss it with them.

Small-Group Activity

Art—Construction Paper Collages
- Provide school paste, a sheet of white construction paper, and many cutout shapes of colored construction paper for each child. Divide the children into small groups after the introduction to the unit. The cutout shapes (similar to the felt ones used in the introduction) can be put together to represent faces with different moods. The children may wish to make faces, or they may want to paste the shapes in any collage design.

Individual Activities
- Large trough with wheat
- Paint at the double easel

Day 2

Whole-Group Activities

Discussion and Story on Happy Emotions— Love, Joy, and Excitement
- Show the children a picture of a child with a happy expression and ask them such ques-

tions as this: How do you think this child feels? What could have caused the feeling? Have you ever felt happy, excited, joyful? What told you that this child was happy? Share a story about love between a parent and children, and then follow it with a discussion on love. Emphasize that loving others or being loved by others makes us happy.

Visitor—Clown

- Have a visitor come dressed in a clown costume. While the children are gathered as a group, the visitor puts on the greasepaint and makes up a clown face. The clown discusses the concept that dressing up as a clown makes people happy.

Discussion and Story on Unhappy Emotions—Sadness, Loneliness

- Tell an open-ended story to the children and, with a partner or in cooperative groups, encourage them to supply possible endings. Show the children a picture of a crying child, and use the same kinds of questions listed in the preceding discussion. Tell a story to the children that will elicit how it feels to be rejected.

Individual Activity

- Large trough with snow or ice

Day 3

Whole-Group Activities

Discussion and Introduction to the Emotion of Curiosity

- Use an unfamiliar book, a pair of magnets, and a picture of children observing and playing with a frog to stimulate interest in the emotion of curiosity. Since the word *curiosity* will probably be new to the children, describe what it is: wondering about, investigating, and exploring something. Use questions to stimulate thought and discussion.

Discussion and Open-Ended Story about Anger, Frustration, and Jealousy

- Tell an open-ended story about a girl who is angry. The children will discover that the girl is angry; have them describe what made her feel that way. Show several pictures of angry children to the children, and have them discuss what might have made the children angry and

what can be done to solve the problem. Also, introduce *frustration* to the children as a new word, and have them talk about things that frustrate them and how they may become angry about them. Show the children a picture of a new baby and discuss jealousy. (These pictures could be distributed among cooperative groups so that more children would have an opportunity to participate and share ideas.)

Music—Creative Movements with Plastic

- Music of various moods will be played. Give the children a scarf or piece of colored plastic, allow them to move about the area, and encourage them to interpret the music and how it makes them feel. Ask them whether the music makes them feel afraid, curious, happy, excited, or sad. Accept any answer or response.

Small-Group Activity

Making Up Stories for Pictures

- After the discussion on anger, divide the children into small groups for cooperative learning. Send the groups to various areas of the room, where they will be given several pictures of children depicting specific emotions. In the groups, have the children make up stories for their pictures. If they want the stories written down, make lined paper available.

Individual Activities

- Trough with sawdust
- Magnets on science table

Day 4

Whole-Group Activity

Science—Discussion on Fear

- Have the children discuss some of the situations that stimulate fear: going to the doctor or dentist, getting shots, taking medicine, going on an elevator, hearing loud noises, being near animals, being in the dark, parents leaving. Discuss how to overcome these fears, mainly by having more experiences with the things feared. Afterward, discuss and display some things that the children should be cautious with: fire, matches, poisons, broken glass, medicines, and so on.

Small-Group Activity

Food—Popcorn with Cheese
• See recipe in Appendix B.

Individual Activities
• String painting
• Trough with manipulative toys

LESSON PLAN ON WATER (THREE DAYS)

Objectives

• Each student will recognize that humans have many uses for water: to dissolve some things, to drink, to cleanse some of the foods we eat, to swim, to wash our own bodies, to wash automobiles, to cool our bodies on a hot day, to put out fires, to cook, as an ingredient in many substances.
• Each student will name five of the preceding uses of water by humans.
• Each student will identify the three forms of water.

Day 1

Whole-Group Activity

Introduction to Unit
Tell a story about a child who went swimming. The story leads into a discussion about some other uses humans have for water. Put pictures illustrating some of these uses on a flannel board as they are discussed.

Music: Rhythm Sticks
Give each child a pair of rhythm sticks and have the children tap the rhythm as an appropriate record is playing that imitates the falling of rain and then the sound of thunder.

Small-Group Activity

Field Trip to a Gymnasium
When the children first arrive, give them the opportunity to take a drink from the water fountain. At the gymnasium, lead the children on a tour and give them an explanation of the swimming pool, shower room, and steam room. Take special precautions to ensure the safety of the children. Soon after returning, hold a discussion on the field trip.

Day 2

Whole-Group Activity

Discussion
Review some of the uses of water discovered yesterday and discuss how we use water in our homes: for cooking, for drinking, for bathing, for watering yards, and so forth. Do role plays of some of the activities involving the use of water.

Small-Group Activity

Food: Vegetable Soup
Form cooperative learning groups for making homemade vegetable soup. Provide each group with a large bowl, scrub brush, paper towels, peeler, cutting board, and small knife. The children in each group will take turns doing the various steps. First, they will wash and scrub the vegetables in a large dishpan. Then, under close supervision, they will peel and slice the vegetables. One child will take the group's sliced vegetables to a large pan placed on a hotplate in the classroom. When all the groups are finished, add several quarts of hot water to the vegetables. Caution the children that the pan will soon be hot. Allow the soup to simmer for several hours to be eaten the next day.

Individual Activities
• Watercolor painting with primary colors at the double easel
• Water in the trough with sponges and other materials

Day 3

Whole-Group Activity

Science Experiment
Show ice cubes and ask the children if they know what they are. Using a hot plate with a pan of boiling water, put the ice cubes in a pie plate and put this above the boiling water on the hot plate. Observe what happens as the heat from the boiling water changes the ice cubes to liquid. When the ice has changed to liquid, with the pie plate still on the boiling pan of water, put another pie plate over the water and as it heats watch it change to steam and then collect onto the second pie plate. Explain

that they have observed three forms of water: solid (ice), liquid (water), and gas (steam).

Small-Group Activity

Food Activity and Discussion
Eat soup made day before and review the concepts learned about water: the uses of water and the three forms of water.

Individual Activities
- Books and stories about water
- Water and ice cubes in the trough

LESSON PLAN ON WHEAT AND FLOUR (ONE DAY)

Overall Goals

- Each student will describe the following basic concepts of wheat:

    What wheat is

    What it looks like. Wheat has three basic forms: seed, greens (sprouts), mature shaft.

    How it tastes, feels, smells

    How it grows; where it grows

    Flour is ground wheat.

    Uses as food: whole wheat, cracked wheat, sprouted wheat, as well as flour (a basic element in many products)

- Each student will recognize what *growing* is by watching wheat sprout.

Whole-Group Activities

Discussion
Show kernels of wheat to the children and ask if they know what wheat is or from where it comes. Explain that these are wheat seeds taken from a mature shaft, and the shaft was grown on a farm and comes from a seed (the kernel). When the wheat is mature, it is harvested, and the kernels are removed from the wheat shaft and then ground into flour. If a wheat grinder is available, demonstrate how the wheat is ground into flour. Ask the children what the flour is used for? Explain that flour is a plant product that is vital to our diet. We use it in tortillas, breads, and many other foods that we eat everyday.

Demonstration of Forms of Wheat
Gather the children at the rug covered with a large tarpaulin. Have containers of whole-kernel wheat, sprouted wheat (greens), and mature-shaft wheat. Explain to the children the relationship among the three forms. To reinforce this concept, separate the wheat from the chaff of the mature wheat so that they can see that it is a whole kernel of wheat and begin to grasp the cycle. Give each child the opportunity to explore a shaft of wheat and extract the kernels onto the tarp. Put some kernels of wheat on a piece of gauze and put this over a jar of water. Keep the gauze moist and over a period of days and observe the kernels sprout.

Rhythm and Creative Movement Activity
Gather the children at the rug and have them participate in several well-known fingerplays and songs. Have them play the game The Farmer in the Dell, and then introduce them to the following new song by singing it several times to the melody of "I'm a Little Teapot":

> I'm a little wheat stock, short and stout.
> Here is my kernel, and here is my sprout.
> When I get all grown up, then I'll shout—
> Just pick me, farmer, and shake me out.

Small-Group Activities

Art-Painting with Wheat Shaft
Divide the children into groups by color squares, and ask each child to go to the table that has the appropriate color of paint. Provide the children with white paper on which their names have been printed and a bundle of three wheat shafts tied together to serve as a form of paintbrush. The paint is put on the paper in drops with a spoon (it should have a rather thick consistency), and the children paint with wheat. They may create whatever design they wish.

Food: Cooked Whole-Wheat Cereal
Cook the cereal beforehand, and divide the children into small groups by means of their names placed on small disposable bowls. Give each group containers of milk and brown sugar. Serve the cereal from the pan in which it was cooked. Give

each child a very small amount, along with a spoon, and encourage them to try it. Serve juice also.

Individual Activities

- Trough filled with whole kernels of wheat
- Role playing of various occupations

LESSON PLAN ON COMMUNITY HELPERS (FOUR DAYS)

Objectives

Each student will:

- Demonstrate involvement in the functions of a community so that a realistic understanding of community helpers will be gained
- Show awareness of how community helpers aid us and the necessity for the skills that they possess
- Describe ways of assisting the community helpers
- Identify a variety of tools and equipment used by community helpers
- Appreciate each occupation and respect the worker for the job that is done, eliminating fears and misconceptions

Note: Activities in this unit plan are listed in order of schedule.

Day 1—Farm Day (Food Sources)

Small-Group Activity

Food—Making Bread
As the children come in, greet them and give each one a name tag in the shape of either stalks of grain, a loaf of bread, a sack of flour, or a grocery store. Set up four centers in the room, and instruct the children to go to any one of them and see what the teacher is doing. At the tables are small amounts of bread dough, one for each child, and the teachers instruct the children to knead and fold it. Give the children adequate time to work the dough until all the children have arrived; then show them how to shape the dough into a small loaf and place it in their own individual small bread pans. Each group will take its bread to a

warm place to rise and then go over to the rug and sit down. The bread will rise and bake while the children listen to the record containing farm animal sounds.

Whole-Group Activity

Farm Discussion.
Begin singing the song "Old MacDonald Had a Farm" as the children begin coming over to the rug, and encourage them to join in. When everyone gets to the rug, tell a story about a vegetable and then lead into a discussion of farms. Talk about what is grown on farms and why they are important. Emphasize that wheat is grown on the farm and is later made into bread.

Transition

Tell the children to look at their name tags. In the classroom, there is a table with some stalks of grain on it, a table with a flour sack on it, a table with a loaf of bread on it, and a table with a miniature grocery store on it. Tell the children to go to the table that corresponds to their name tag.

Small-Group Activity

Art—Puppets
Spread out on the table materials with which the children can make sack puppets of farm animals, including pigs, cows, chickens, and horses. They can have their choice, and creativity is the key. The basic patterns are there for them to cut out and use; what they do is up to them. Also make available construction paper, blunt-end scissors, and glue. As the children finish, they will assist in cleaning up.

Individual Activities

- Stage on which to play with puppets
- Table with seeds, grains, feathers, and eggshells for making a collage
- Cups, dirt, and seeds that can be worked and planted
- Playhouse

Whole-Group Activity

Farm Record.
Put on a record of farm animal sounds while children clean up and come to the rug. Then read stories and sing songs about cows. Talk about how the cream in the milk turns into butter, and show the children how it is done by bringing out a churn.

Let them all take a turn at churning for a little while. When everyone has had a chance and the butter is all churned, add some salt for flavor. Then all the children will be able to eat their small loaf of bread with some of the churned butter on it and have a small glass of milk. After finishing, they will go outside to play until it is time to go home.

Day 2—Our Health Helpers

When the children arrive, give them name tags that are like little Red Cross badges. Ask them to hang up their coats and explore the different areas in the room.

Individual Activities

- Area with collections of books about community helpers

- Housekeeping area with hospital arrangement (bandages, small pillows, adhesive bandages, empty spray cans, gauze, syringes, and tape)

- Art area, constructing nurses' or doctors' hats from available materials

- Dentist's office, complete with magazines, reception desk, phone, office chair, teeth models, white coats, cloth to go over patients, and tongue depressors

Whole-Group Activity

Discussion on Checking and Maintaining Health
Use a large freezer box that has been previously decorated so that it looks like an ambulance. Make a siren noise and have the children hook onto the teacher's back like a train. Go around the room for everyone, and then go to the rug. After watching a filmstrip about health helpers and safety, have a discussion about the ambulance, doctors, nurses, and dentists. Stress the point that they are available to help us, not to harm or hurt us. Pull out a satchel and begin taking items out of it. The items should include a microscope, slides, and instructions for use; measuring tape; elastic bandage; reflex hammer; tongue depressor; stethoscope; sphygmomanometer; balloons; thermometer; and a dental hygiene kit. Discuss what each item is and how it is used. Also explain how to make microscope slides. As soon as everyone knows what the items are and how to use them, send an equal number of students to each of the four different areas for the science experiences.

Small-Group Activities

Science Experiences
Each group will spend about 10 minutes in each interest center, and the signal to change will be a siren. (1) Set up microscopes with certain prepared slides, and provide materials for the children to make their own slides showing such items as salt, pond water, sugar, and others. They will be able to see the slides under the microscopes. (2) Place a long piece of butcher paper along one wall. Set up a scale to weigh each child, and mark the child's height by a line on the butcher paper. On that line, write the child's name, height, and weight. These measurements are not mandatory, and children who are reluctant and do not want to participate should be allowed this choice. During this process, the others can occupy themselves with wrapping each other up in elastic bandages, checking each other's reflexes, and looking at each other's tonsils using the tongue depressors. (3) Provide several stethoscopes so that the children can hear each other's heartbeats. Set up a sphygmomanometer to take blood pressure. Have the children blow up balloons so that they can see what their lungs do, and provide thermometers so that they can take their own temperatures. (Properly sterilize or provide disposable plastic sheaths or covers for thermometers.) (4) By the sinks, provide a tooth brushing kit for each child, and set up mirrors. Have the children brush once and then chew the little red tablets to see where they have brushed their teeth inadequately; then have them brush again. Show them how to brush their teeth properly.

Art—Mobiles or Ambulances
In a large group, discuss the doctor, dentist, and first-aid kit. Make sure the children understand that both males and females can be doctors and dentists. Then divide into smaller groups. At the tables, the children will have materials before them for one of two activities: (1) making mobiles of teeth out of string, paper, cardboard, crayons, sticks, tape, pictures of teeth and mouths, glue, and marking pens; or (2) making ambulances out of matchboxes and white paper by adding details such as wheels with black construction paper, doors, a red beacon light, stripes, headlights, and so on. (Ambulances could also be made out of rectangular-shaped

pieces of Styrofoam, with red gumdrops for the sirens and black circles for wheels.)

Day 3—The Mail Carrier

The children's name tags today will be in the shapes of business envelopes, letter envelopes, packages, or stamps. As the children come in, direct them to tables where there is cookie dough. They may all help to drop the dough on cookie sheets and bake them in the oven while waiting for everyone to arrive.

Whole-Group Activity

Introduction to the Mail Carrier
Have everyone gather on the rug. Read a story about the mail carrier, and talk about the forthcoming field trip to the post office and some of the things to observe. Explain that both males and females can be mail carriers and postal workers. Assign the children to cars and adults according to their name tags. Before going, they will first go over to tables where there are certain materials.

Small-Group Activity

Wrapping Cookies and Field Trip to the Post Office
At the tables, each child finds a small box, some brown wrapping paper, and some string. Give the children two of the cookies to put in their boxes and wrap like presents. Then put the children's names on their boxes. When they are finished, have each group get into a car for the field trip. When they are all out of the room, put the packages in a big bag to be used later, after returning.

After returning from the post office, go to the rug and discuss the day and the mail carrier. Then have another teacher bring out the bag and pass out the packages of cookies and juice to each child; the cookies are eaten with the juice.

Day 4—The Fire Fighter

This morning welcome the children and encourage them to explore freely the different areas of the room.

Individual Activities

• Trough filled with wood and twigs
• Housekeeping

• Easel for painting
• A tape playing a story about a fire fighter
• Blocks for constructing a fire station; ladders and trucks, along with striped overalls, bell, fire hats, and long hose

Whole-Group Activity

Visitor—Fire Fighter
When the sound of the siren begins, gather all the children in the center of the room and ask them what they think it is. Then go to see that it is a fire fighter who has come to visit and has brought the truck. The fire fighter will tell the children all about the truck, show them all its parts, and then come in to talk to them. The fire fighter will discuss safety measures and how to prevent forest fires, house fires, and accidents. Emphasis will be placed on the fact that, although some fire is good for heat and cooking, it is harmful when it gets out of hand. Emphasize that fire fighters can be women or men. When the visitor has gone, make a long fire engine "train" and drop off "fire fighters" at the different tables.

Small-Group Activity

Food—Fondue
At the tables are fondue pots over small Sterno fires. Each child will prepare several kinds of fondue and have juice.

Whole-Group Activity

Dramatization
Have the children, in three groups, pretend that they are on fire and must find a way to extinguish the fire. The fire fighter comes to the rescue and saves the people. The fire fighter demonstrates the ways to put out clothing fires. This should include these three main ways: (1) put a blanket around you, (2) lie down on the rug and roll, (3) lie on the ground and roll. Emphasize the phrase "Stop, drop, and roll." Stress walking, rather than running. Talk about how water is important in putting out fires. Then tell the children the story of Smokey Bear.*

After the fire fighter is finished, the three groups will be ready for the art activity.

---

*Teacher's Forest Fire Prevention and Conservation Kit. Forest Service. U.S. Department of Agriculture and your state Forestry Department.

Small-Group Activity—Working Cooperatively
Art—Making Smokey Bear
Place art supplies at the tables for the children to construct a Smokey Bear on a piece of contact board. Materials available will include fuzzy fur for the body, which will be cut in the proper shape, and construction paper, string, yarn, and glue for the features. Have each group work together on one Smokey Bear. After the children finish, have them go over to the rug, where someone will be reading stories until all groups have finished the art project.

LESSON PLAN ON FRUIT (TWO DAYS)

Objectives

The students will:

- Label a variety of fruits, both familiar and unfamiliar
- Recognize that fruit comes in many different sizes, shapes, colors, textures, and tastes
- Recall that fruit has seeds and match the fruit with its seed
- Explain that fruits can be eaten: how they can be eaten, which parts of the fruit we eat, and which parts we throw away
- Review that fruit must be preserved to avoid spoilage

Day 1

Whole-Group Activities

Introduction and Labeling
Have an apple, orange, and banana at the rug. Talk about each one with the children. Determine whether the children can identify fruit as a category. Discuss each fruit with the children: what it is, what part we eat, what part we throw away, whether it is soft or crunchy to eat, where it is seen on the bulletin board, where it grows, how many seeds it has, and whether it tastes like anything else. (The bulletin board will display several familiar fruits in several different forms: on the tree, in a bottle or can, peeled, cut, sectioned, and so on).

Visitor—Demonstration of Making Fruit Juices
Have the children gather at the rug and watch as the visitor makes a variety of juices. (The visitor's demonstration should precede the children's own juice-making experience.)

Small-Group Activities

Food—Making Fruit Juice
Divide the children into four cooperative learning groups. Have enough grapefruits, juicers, knives, strainers, and cups for one group; enough oranges and equipment for another; enough limes and equipment for another; and enough lemons and equipment for the fourth group. Each group makes its own kind of juice, adding sugar if necessary. They then go to the rug to taste the various juices and talk about the experience.

Music—Musical Chairs
Divide the children and teachers into two groups to create more room for each group. Place fruit shapes in a circle around each group, one for each person. The fruit shapes that are being used should be presented first to the children; use only familiar fruits at this stage. Play music, and when the music stops, all sit down. Ask the children what fruits they are sitting on.

Individual Activities

- Red sand in trough, together with funnels, utensils, and bottles
- Science bench with dried fruit, jar of moldy fruit, jar of good fruit

Matching Fruit Lotto
Set out lotto games and dominoes made with various fruit pictures from seed packets or catalogs.

Day 2

Small-Group Activities

Field Trip—Fruit Stand or Store
Divide the children into groups, and assign to cars and an adult. First, check with the store or stand and notify the owner before you go. Tell the children that they may each choose one piece of fruit to buy and that the fruit that they choose will go into a fruit salad that they will help to prepare. At the stand, have one supervisor for every few children to watch them for safety reasons and to supervise what they choose for the salad.

Let each group buy its fruit separately so that the children will have more individual involvement in the buying process. Each supervisor should tell the children something about the fruits that they see at the stand.

Fruit Stand Center

Set up an actual fruit stand with fruit on it for the rest of the unit during free play. Make shopping bags and money available to create a more realistic situation.

LESSON PLAN ON LIGHT (SHADOWS) (FOUR DAYS)

Objectives

Each student will:

- Describe the concept of shadows and their origin.

- Recognize types of shadows, and then generalize the knowledge that a shadow's size and darkness are changeable, according to the light source and the distance from the object

- Identify the shapes of objects by their shadows

- Create interest in and appreciation for poetry

- Increase body awareness through creative movement, body shadow pictures, and rhythm activities.

- Because of the nature of this unit plan, one corner of the room will be darkened to be the "shadow corner," where many of the individual activities throughout the unit will be performed. The plans may have to be altered or changed if the weather is not sunny.

Day 1

Whole-Group Activity

Introduction to Unit on Light and Shadows
As an introduction to this unit, give a slide presentation. The slides will consist of many delightful pictures of shadows dealing with children's lives and what causes shadows. A cassette tape may accompany the presentation. Questions that may concern the young child will be answered during this presentation. Such topics as the causes of shadows, the shapes of shadows, the light source,

and the size of shadows will be illustrated during this short presentation. Afterward, read a poem about shadows.

Small-Group Activities

Science—Shadows

After dividing the children into cooperative learning groups, tell them to go outside. Each group will have a dowel or stick to place in the ground; then they will measure its shadow. Later in the morning, each group will go back to its own stick and again measure the shadow. A marker will be placed at the locations of both shadows to allow the children to see how shadows change as the day progresses.

Art—Paper Hats

Have the children as groups make pointed paper hats, which will be used for the "shadow parade" on day 2. They can decorate the hats with paint, crepe paper streamers, scraps of paper, and other materials.

Individual Activities

- *Tracing Shadows Outside.* Provide butcher paper and trace each child's complete body shadow while the child stands still and watches. Encourage the child to find a unique position or stance. Emphasize the body parts and help to increase the child's body awareness during this experience. Cut out the bodies so that the children can paint them on day 2. Each picture must be carefully labeled.

- *Object Printing.* Have the children make printings with various types of objects using a variety of colors of paint.

- *Lotto Shape Games.* Develop a set of black shadow shapes as a lotto game for matching and discrimination purposes. This game can be used at any time, but it will be especially effective during this unit or a shape unit.

- *Bubble Blowing.* Place the trough in the shadow corner. Mix 1 cup of granulated soap in 1 quart of warm water. Small open-ended cans and straws should be available for each child. It is interesting for the children to observe the bubbles that they blow and see whether the shadows are cast on the wall when the light in the shadow corner is switched on.

Day 2

Whole-Group Activity

Music—Shadow Parade

Have the children participate in a "shadow parade" with musical instruments. They wear the hats that they made on day 1 and carry a flag, baton, or rhythm instrument. Beat a rhythm on a drum, and encourage the children to beat out the rhythm as they march around the playground and especially to watch their shadows during the parade.

Small-Group Activity

Food—Fruit Salad (Cooperative Learning)

Ask the children to guess the shapes of certain fruits from their shadows. Place the fruits behind a sheet, with a light shining from behind. Each fruit will be guessed separately. Show the following fruits (easily identified): grapes, pineapple, watermelon, cantaloupe, bananas, and apple. They will be combined to make a fruit salad in each group. Each child will have a chance to cut some fruit into pieces and then each group's salad will be shared among the group. Since sharp knives will be used, this activity must be carefully supervised, and the children must be thoroughly cautioned about the dangers of sharp instruments.

Individual Activities

- *Painting the Shadows Outside.* Hang the traced shadows on the fence on the playground to be painted. Offer several colors of paint. Leave the pictures on the fence to dry.

- *Shadow Puzzles.* Cut the silhouettes of certain objects into puzzles, which the children will have the opportunity to put together and use, along with the other manipulative toys.

- *Puppets and Overhead Projector.* Set up an overhead projector in the shadow corner. Here the children can have creative play with the puppets and their shadows on the wall. Music may be played to stimulate creative movement.

- *Science.* On the science table, place several shoe boxes with balls of clay, a small flashlight, and a pencil. The pencil is supported in the shoe box by the clay. The flashlight is then used at various angles and distances from the box to produce different types of shadows. Help the children to observe the various angles of shadows that can be produced, making the pencil shadows both long and short.

Day 3

Whole-Group Activities

Visitor—Person to Demonstrate Shadow Plays

Ask a visitor to show a variety of finger shadow plays on a screen or wall in the classroom. In these plays, use simple shapes that children can quickly learn to imitate, such as those of a rabbit, duck, elephant, or dog. A light shining on the wall helps to produce the dark shadows. Encourage group involvement and have the children practice some of these shadow plays while the visitor is there to assist.

Discussion—Shadow at Night

Encourage discussion of the kinds of shadows that the children see at night in their bedrooms. Talk about how quiet, dark, and dim the shadows are. Help the children to talk about their fears, but minimize this aspect of the darkness. Discuss how shadows are not always what they seem to be. Emphasize the positive.

Small-Group Activity

Shadow Tag

Divide the children into small groups and have them go outside. There each group will play Shadow Tag. In this game, one person is "It" and tries to step on another child's shadow. When he or she does step on another child's shadow, that child then becomes "It." Several children can be "It" at once. Be sensitive to each child and careful not to let anyone feel that he or she is not a part of the game. Another variation to this game is Shadow Touch Shadow, in which the children try to let their shadows touch hands, feet, and so on.

Individual Activities

- *Trace Silhouettes.* Trace the children's profiles on black paper as silhouettes (with a sheet and light). Later, cut the silhouettes out and mount them on pieces of white paper. Provide a learning experience on day 4 with the silhouettes, and then let the children take their own silhouettes home.

- *Shape Collage.* Cut all kinds of shapes out of black paper, and have the children paste collages on white paper. Provide scissors if the children want to cut.
- *Shadow Plays.* Place the screen in the shadow corner so that the children can experiment with the shadow plays that they have been taught. Other media and shapes may also be provided to increase experimentation with the light and shadows.

Day 4

Whole-Group Activities

Prepare a Shadow Play
The shadow play will be performed completely behind a sheet, so that the children will see only shadows of what is happening. The shadows might be activities such as jumping rope, directing music, using a fly swatter, or a variety of motions. When the play is over, talk about what happened and remove the sheet so that the children can actually see the actions taking place.

Music—Creative Dramatics
Give each child a piece of plastic to move creatively with the music. Place a light behind the children to cast shadows on the wall. Encourage discussion about the shadows and why the plastic shadows are so much lighter than the children's shadows.

Small-Group Activity

Silhouette Game
Divide the children and their silhouettes made the previous day into small groups, and have each child try to guess his or her own silhouette.

Individual Activities

- *Shape Game.* Cut shapes of familiar objects out of black Pellon®, and have the children match pictures of them to the actual objects.
- *Trough.* Set a trough full of sand in the shadow corner. Put figures of animals and people in it to promote play. The children can observe the shadows cast from the animals and other objects.

LESSON PLAN ON TEXTURE (FIVE DAYS)

Objectives

Each student will:

- Describe textures that are common to his or her environment and attach descriptive language labels to textures
- Differentiate and identify various textures
- Identify basic concepts related to textures

Day 1

Whole-Group Activity

Introduction to the Concept of Texture
To lay a foundation for the study of textures, introduce the word *texture* to the children, along with the meaning of the word. Items having various textures will be available for the children to feel, see, and hear. Adjectives such as *rough, hard, soft, smooth, bumpy,* and *velvety* will be applied to the texture feelings.

Small-Group Cooperative Activity

Making Clay
The children prepare clay in three small groups. Each group has 4 cups of flour and 1 cup of salt, as well as water and some coloring. Since all the clay is approximately the same color, it can be put into one plastic container to ripen.

Individual Activities

- Autoharp
- *Material and Yarn Sewing.* Make various pieces of textured material, along with threaded needles, available for sewing and stitching.
- *Trough with Water in Various Forms.* Put containers of ice, snow (if available), and water in the trough, along with various measuring and pouring utensils.
- *Art—Crayons at the Easel.* Provide crayons to be used for drawing and sketching at the easel. Along with the regular easel paper, provide background papers of various textures. One

side of the easel has textured material underneath the easel paper; the other side has textured wallpaper and other materials.

Day 2

Small-Group Activity

Food—Gelatin
Have four groups of children make gelatin, each group making a different flavor. The gelatin will be set with ice cubes and then put into the refrigerator until firm. Later in the day, allow the children to eat the gelatin in a large group at the table.

Whole-Group Activity

Music with Texture Sounds
Demonstrate musical "instruments," such as sand blocks, corrugated cardboard, and washboards, that have various textures and that make sounds of various textures. Then let the children use the instruments to accompany familiar songs. Then the children go to the large table to eat the gelatin that they have made.

Individual Activities

- Small trough containing sawdust and wooden cars
- Double easel with sponges and brushes
- *Texture Collage on Styrofoam Meat or Pastry Trays.* Make materials and items having various textures available for pasting on the meat or pastry trays, which also provide an example of an unusual texture. Put paste into individual containers, and set out a jar of warm water for soaking the used brushes.

Day 3

Whole-Group Activity

Field Trip—Lumberyard
As the children arrive, attach an identification badge to each child's coat. Explain the reason for the visit to the lumberyard. Then divide the children into smaller groups according to their badges. At the lumberyard the children will feel and see the various textures of wood, glass, and other products. They will also be able to see ways in which texture may be changed.

Small-Group Activity

Stories about Field Trip
After the field trip, have the children return to the same groups that they had at the lumberyard. While the groups discuss the field trip, have a teacher or aide write down what the children say. Then read the "story" back to the children while they are still in the groups.

Individual Activities

- Finger painting
- Small trough containing bark, with wooden and rubber cars and trucks

Day 4

Whole-Group Activity

Science—Changing Texture
Demonstrate changes in texture by adding water to dry dirt or sand, by adding water to a very dry sponge, or by adding a smooth coat of paint to a rough surface. Have the children perform an experiment of their own as they make root beer floats.

Small-Group Activity

Food—Root Beer Floats
Divide the children into smaller groups to make and eat root beer floats. Put ice cream into the cups first, and then add the root beer.

Individual Activity

- Small trough with wooden blocks, hammers, and nails

Day 5

Whole-Group Activity

Visitor
Have a person who has various materials and items of similar and different textures visit the classroom. Explain the uses of the items and review appropriate texture labels.

Small-Group Activity

Texture Books
Give each child a sheet of poster paper and a sample cut from fabric. Each child in each group will have a different textured fabric. Have the children

discuss the texture and how it feels and then paste it on the paper. Their ideas will be written on their own sheets as they suggest them. If children are able to write, they should write their own ideas. These sheets will then be combined to form a book for the children to read.

Individual Activities

- Small trough with dolls and sponges
- Xylophone

LESSON PLAN ON SOUND (FIVE DAYS)

Objectives

Each student will:

- Discriminate among sounds and categorize them

- Recognize the loudness–quietness and highness–lowness that can be characteristic of most sounds

- Explain the emotional qualities of sound (happy, sad, fearful, light, comforting sounds)

- Identify and classify sound further by the object or objects that created it, such as human, animal, farm, and city sounds

- Detect that sounds can communicate (for example, the sound of a siren can mean an accident or a fire; a car pulling into the driveway at the end of the day can mean that Mom or Dad is home)

Day 1

Whole-Group Activity

Discussion of Loudness, Quietness, Highness, and Lowness of Sounds
At the rug, sing songs (with fingerplays) loudly, then quietly, and then in normal voices. Then play several sounds that have been tape-recorded. These sounds will be high or low, and in some cases the same object will create both sounds. Then imitate the sounds and discuss which are liked or not liked and how they make one feel when they are heard.

Small-Group Activities

Sound Hunt for Treasure
This activity takes place outdoors if the weather permits, and each group has a different route to follow. This game is comparable to a treasure hunt. Each new clue is found only when the children answer questions on whether certain objects make high, low, loud, or quiet sounds. Show the children that some objects can produce all these sound qualities. The treasure could be hidden inside a large chest or buried in the sandbox, depending on what the treasure is.

Art—Starch and Tissue Sculptured Drums
Give the children an opportunity to create a collage on the sides of drums made from large empty cans obtained from cafeterias, with a piece of inner tube stretched over the open end and secured with wire. The drums will be used the following day during a story. Explain this plan to the children while they are making their collages. Tissue paper dipped in starch is the collage medium.

Individual Activity

- *Feathers, Hammers, and Water-Filled Pop Bottles.* Place the feathers in the trough, place the hammers on stumps with nails, and line up the pop bottles on a table. Vary the water level in the bottles so that a person blowing on the openings will be able to produce both high and low sounds. The hammers, when used to pound nails, provide a loud sound, and the feathers provide an almost noiseless quality, bordering on a soft sound, which is discussed along with the emotional qualities of sounds.

Day 2

Whole-Group Activity

Flannel-Board Story
Tell the story outside. Pass out the drums made the previous day before telling the story. Have the children help to tell the story by playing the drums when given certain signals.

Small-Group Activity

"Sound" Walk on the Playground and in the Classroom
Have two groups of children begin outside and two inside. With eyes closed and ears close to objects so that sounds can be heard, the children

strike or listen to various objects, such as a drum, an autoharp, a seashell, or a music box.

Day 3

Whole-Group Activity

Visitors—Human Sounds
Ask a small group of high school drama students to perform a segment of the children's theater version of *Hansel and Gretel*.

Small-Group Activity

Animal Sounds
Bring four animals (or figures of animals) to the class and place them around the room. For this activity, each group of children has an animal at its table. The children discuss the sounds that the animal makes and then use clay to sculpt either an animal or an object representing an animal sound.

Individual Activity

- *Recording the Children's Voices.* Provide two or more tape recorders in various areas of the room, such as in the block or manipulative area. Have teachers in these areas record the voices of the children there and then play the tape back to them. Emphasis is placed on the idea that children make human sounds and that these sounds are meaningful.

Day 4

Whole-Group Activity

Music—Rhythm Band
Provide each child with an instrument, and use several different instruments. Have the children accompany a musical selection on a record or their singing.

Small-Group Activities

Science—Guessing Objects By the Sound That They Make
Assign the children to cooperative learning groups. Give each group a wrapped, jewelry-sized box containing three or four objects such as a coin, marble, bell, and screw or nail. Have them listen carefully and then brainstorm possibilities for what is inside. After they have guessed, have them open the container to see what is inside.

Art—String Painting
Have small groups of children gather at the tables. The children dip strings into liquid paint and then put them between the two halves of a folded paper. With one hand, they press the two sides together; with the other hand, they pull the string out. Make sure they leave an end of the string protruding so that it can be grasped for pulling out.

Individual Activity

- *Matching Sounds.* Use small boxes or film cans and put duplicates of different objects inside pairs of containers. For example, in each of two cans, put six paper clips; in two others, put five buttons; in two others, put one tablespoon of rice. Ask the children to shake the cans or boxes and listen to identify which pairs match.

Day 5

Whole-Group Activities

Sirens
As the children brown meat for sloppy joes, turn on a recording of a siren. From the sound heard, have the children try to determine what it could have been. Have some pictures to show possibilities. A review of the week may be given at this time.

Food—Making Sloppy Joes
Have the children gather at the rug as you combine the ingredients. Use a hot plate or electric fry pan. (The hamburger will have been browned by the children in their small groups.) Call attention to the cooking sounds.

Small-Group Activities

Food—Setting the Table and Browning the Hamburger
Have the children set the tables while listening to the sounds of setting the table. After establishing the idea that the sounds made while setting the table are dish sounds, introduce the final concept for the week by asking, "What do we think of when we hear the sounds of dishes being set on the table?" Since these sounds usually mean food, begin browning the hamburger to be made into sloppy joes.

Food—Eating Lunch
Go inside and dish up the sloppy joes. Have the children eat them with carrots and juice, observing the sounds that the different foods make as they chew.

LESSON PLAN ON NUMBERS (FIVE DAYS)

Objectives

Each student will:

- Actively participate in whole-group, small-group, and individual activities
- Recognize that numbers are used in the environment
- Recall the sound and sequence of counting numbers
- Identify the correct position of numerals
- Match the numeral or symbol of the number with the meaning of it (that is, the numeral 7 will be matched to seven dots).
- Order numerals from 1 to 10 or beyond if they are ready

Day 1

Whole-Group Activities

Introduction to the Unit on Numbers
Have the children gather on the rug, and place a sack in front of them containing various items that use numbers. Ask the children to guess what is in it. It will contain some of the following items: clock, recipe, book, newspaper advertisement, measuring cup, and toy.

Flannel-Board Story.
While the children are gathered on the rug, tell a flannel-board story. One relating to number concepts would be especially appropriate.

Small-Group Activity

Numeral Collages
Divide the children into small groups, and give each child an ice cream tub, a dish of liquid starch, and various numerals cut from lightweight paper, such as gift wrap. The children will paste the numerals, using the starch as glue, on their cartons.

Individual Activities

- Paint at the single easel
- Soapy water in the trough
- Number manipulatives

Day 2

Small-Group Activities

Matching Numerals
Direct the children to small groups as they arrive. Give each child one calendar page with the numerals intact. Also give each child a set of numerals cut out of a page. Direct the children to match the cut-up numerals to the sheet of numerals. If they have difficulty, select the numerals 1 to 3 and then point to these same numerals on the calendar, asking the child to match them. It is the responsibility of the teacher in each group to simplify the task as needed for individual children. They will stay in these small groups until all the children arrive and have an opportunity to participate in the matching activity. Give books to each teacher in case the children arriving first tire of the matching activity.

Field Trip—Grocery Store
Have the children gather at the rug after their matching activity, and explain the field trip to them. Explain and discuss the use of numbers in the grocery store. Encourage the children to look at prices on food items, weights on food items, and the use of numbers at the checkout stand in determining the total grocery bill. Also encourage them to weigh some produce items. Divide into four groups. Give each group some money with which to purchase one large package of pudding, which will be used in a food activity later in the unit.

Whole-Group Activities

Discussion on Counting and Position and Ordering of the Numerals 1 to 10
Have the children gather on the rug, and count the number of boys, girls, and teachers separately and then all together to give practice in rote counting. After some counting songs have been sung, place poster paper with the numbers 1 to 10 outlined at the top where all the children can see it. Hold up individual numerals in correct order and match them to the corresponding outlined

numerals on the poster paper. Emphasize the correct order and orientation of the numerals as they are pasted on the paper. Point out that numerals have to go a certain way, or else they will be upside down or backward.

Art—Gadget Printing

Place gadgets that make a circular imprint on a large table, along with black and yellow paint and white paper.

Day 3

Whole-Group activity

Visitor—Father or Grandfather of One of the Class Members

The visitor will be invited into the classroom to measure and cut wood for a simple birdhouse. He will focus particularly on the use of numbers in measuring and the importance of measuring accurately so that the pieces of wood will fit together properly. He will point out the numbers on his tape measure. During this activity the children will be gathered around a sawhorse, with a drop cloth and plenty of room for the visitor to work. Weather permitting, the activity could take place outdoors. The birdhouse, when completed, will be put in the art center for the children to paint as they wish. When completed, it will be installed in a tree on the playground.

Small-Group Activities

Food—Making Pudding

After the visitor's presentation, while the children are still in a whole group, introduce and explain the food experience. Tell the children that the numerals on the package indicate the price and the weight. Then tell them how they will make the pudding that will be eaten the next day. Place particular emphasis on the use of numerals in measuring and timing the cooking of the pudding. Then divide the children into four small groups. Two of the groups will go outside while the other two groups stay in and make their pudding. One of the two groups that stays inside will use the hot plate in the room for cooking, while the other uses the stove in the kitchen. Then the groups will change places, and the ones that were outside will make their pudding. Pour the pudding into small bowls labeled with each child's name, cover, and refrigerate until they eat it the next day.

Discussion and Structured Collages: Matching Numerals and Determining the Meaning of Numerals 1 to 10

Using the poster paper with the numerals 1 to 10 printed across the top (used the day before), have the children review the orientation, counting, and sequence of numerals 1 to 10. Then explain the meaning of these numerals. Under each numeral, paste the number of squares representing that numeral. Then divide the children into smaller groups and give one piece of construction paper to each child. On one side, the numerals 1 to 5 will be outlined; on the other side, 6 to 10. Give each child numerals to match and paste, providing guidance and help where needed. Then give the children squares to paste below each numeral to represent the meaning of this numeral. Dots will be placed on the construction paper to aid the children in this task; they can match the square to the dot. For example, one dot will be placed below the numeral 1 for its matching square. This activity must be individualized to meet the developmental needs of each child. It is not expected that all children will be able to complete the activity as described.

Individual Activities

- Bubble blowing
- Trough containing number toys
- Number manipulatives

Day 4

Small-Group Activities

Eating Pudding

In the same groups as the previous day, allow the children to eat their bowls of pudding. During the interaction, review and reinforce concepts relating to numbers.

Reading Stories; Manipulative Play with Number Toys

Read various stories to the children. Then give each group several number toys for play and exploration.

Individual Activities

- *Measuring in the Trough.* Allow the children to play at the trough, filled with bits of paper such as confetti, hole punches, or computer punches, along with funnels, cups, spoons, and other measuring and pouring devices.

- *Locomotor Rhythms Using Numerals* Designate one area of the room for this activity, and tell the children that those wishing to participate may do so. Tape pieces of paper, each with one numeral on it, to the floor (use only numerals 1 to 10). Give each participating child a small card with a numeral or with dots representing one of the numerals on it. Put on a record, and have all the children do locomotor movements appropriate to the rhythm of the music (hopping, skipping, jumping, leaping, and so forth). When the music stops, the children are to stand on the numeral that either matches the numeral or represents the number of dots on their card. Cards can be exchanged and the activity repeated many times.

Day 5

Whole-Group Activities

Clapping Rhythms

Have the children first clap the rhythm of some familiar nursery rhymes. Then clap some simple rhythm patterns, such as / //, /// /, or ////. The children will listen to the patterns and then clap them. Then place some black dots on the flannel board in different rhythmic patterns, one pattern at a time, and have the children clap them.

Science—Addition and Balance Related to Number Concepts

Have the children gather on the rug, and by means of a balance stick (see Chapter 9), explain the concept of balance as equal weight on two sides. First, focus on placing a disk on, for example, the numeral 5 on one side, and make it balance with a disk on the numeral 5 on the other side. Then show another way to make it balance by putting, on the second side, a disk on 3 and a disk on 2. Use real objects to illustrate that 3 and 2 are the same as 5. Then, with five beans, show ways of grouping to make 5, that is, combinations of 4 and 1 and 3 and 2. Divide the children into four smaller groups, and give each child 10 beans. The teacher in each group asks such questions as "Show me six

beans." "Now show me another way of showing six, such as three and three."

Daily Activity

During the unit, put out a number-concept table so that children can go there during free play and participate in games and activities or play with pieces of equipment related to number concepts.

Individual Activities

- Painting with brushes and water outside
- Dramatization of nursery rhymes
- Number manipulatives

LESSON PLAN ON HONEYBEES (ONE DAY)

Objectives

Each student will:

- Describe the honeybee and its characteristics: habitat, body parts, food, reproduction, locomotion
- Recognize how the honeybee helps humans
- Recall some uses of honey
- Overcome fears of bees
- Know that bees and flowers are necessary to each other for survival

Whole-Group Activity

Introduction to Honeybees

Tell the children that bees are the only insects that provide any important part of our food. Include questions such as "What is the food that they provide for us?" "What body parts do bees have? Do they have a head and legs?" "Where do honeybees live?" Have flannel-board cutouts showing body parts of bees: head, thorax, abdomen, legs, wings, antennae. Point out fuzz, pollen, and baskets, and talk about the nectar or honey sack. Show pictures of honeybee farms and wild bee hives; compare the differences. Ask what bees eat? Emphasize that bees are constantly seeking flowers because they use the pollen for protein and the nectar for carbohydrates. They convert the nectar to honey inside the hive.

Small-Group Activities

Food—Sampling Bread and Honey

Following the discussion on honeybees and honey, each child will be given a piece of bread, some butter, and honey to eat. Teachers will reinforce that the honey has come from bees. They will also brainstorm and teach how we use honey (that is, on bread or rolls, as honeybutter, or in recipes such as in wholewheat bread).

Art—Making Beehives

Provide the children with yellow and brown flour clay, as well as a piece of Styrofoam in the shape of a beehive. Encourage the children to roll their clay into a "snake" and then mold it around the Styrofoam, layering the yellow and brown clay. When the children are finished, each child will be given a purchased bee (purchased by the teacher from a hobby store) to place anywhere on the beehive. Compare the texture of the clay to that of the Styrofoam.

Field Trip—Library

Divide the children into groups by pinning different-colored bees on them. Parents will drive the children to the library. The children will listen to stories about honeybees read by the librarian.

Individual Activities

- Easel with brown and yellow paint
- Bees in aquarium

LESSON PLAN ON FISH (FOUR DAYS)

Objectives

Each student will:

- Recognize different kinds of fish and their uses
- Name the body parts of fish such as fins, tail, scales, and gills
- Identify several uses for fish (food, pets, recreation)
- Recognize that although there are certain elements that all fish have in common (backbone, mouth, gills, swimming), there are many kinds of fish; fish differ in size, color, shape, habit, taste, and use, as well as kind

Day 1

Whole-Group Activity

Introduction to Unit

Introduce the topic of the unit, as well as some of the basic concepts, such as what fish look like, where fish live, and how fish are cared for and used. Ask questions concerning what to observe on the field trip, such as "Do all fish look alike?" "Are all fish the same size and color?" "What odor does a fish have?"

Small-Group Activities

Field Trip—Fish Hatchery

Divide the children into groups with badges shaped like fish that are the same except for the fins. The fins will distinguish the groups. Teachers help the children to label this part of the fish and discuss the number or shape of fins to enable the children to find their own groups. Drive to the hatchery and tour the grounds. A guide should be available to show the children the fish equipment and to answer questions. Point out the various things to be observed: smell, size, and variations of fish.

Experience Chart

Gather the children into groups to make experience charts. Title the piece. Let the children contribute the observations that they would like to remember about the trip. Write these observations on a piece of butcher paper as the children watch.

Individual Activities

- Aquarium with goldfish
- Paper and crayons at easel

Day 2

Whole-Group Activity

Story about a Fish

Read the story *Fish Is Fish* (Lionni, 1970) (see Suggested Resources, Chapter 11) at the rug, with special emphasis given to the fish characteristics that are common in the pictures. Point out and label these characteristics.

Small-Group Activities

Science—Air in Water

Divide the children into small groups to discuss why the fish in the story had to live in the water. Let the children express their knowledge of fish. Bring in the concept of gills, and reinforce any correct concepts that the children discuss. Then perform the following science experiment: Before the children arrive, clear glasses will have been filled with water, one for each group. As the children finish discussing gills, underwater breathing, and living on land and in water, fill other glasses with fresh water, one for each group. Show the group the glass that was previously filled with water. The air in the water will have formed bubbles on the side of the glass. Explain that just as people can breathe air, fish have special equipment, gills, to get the air out of the water.

Art—Paper Bag Fish

Provide the children with a paper bag taped into a fish shape, string for the tail, newspapers with which to stuff the fish, and paint to decorate it. Show the children how to stuff the fish with paper, and tie each bag to make the tail, with the child assisting. The children can then paint their fish. The fish will be set somewhere to dry until day 3, when collage items (eyes, gills, fins) will be added. Names will be taped to the fish.

Individual Activity

- Fish in the trough

Day 3

Whole-Group Activities

Art—Collage

As the children enter at the beginning of the day, direct them to the art activity of gluing collage items to their fish (made yesterday). The children can decorate their fish as they wish. Use this opportunity to reinforce knowledge of the parts of the fish.

Music—Rhythm

Gather the children at the rug for a rhythm activity. Pass out instruments so that the children can accompany songs, fingerplays, and records. Explore various beats.

Individual Activities

- Watercolors and salt at easel
- Water and objects in a container

Day 4

Whole-Group Activity

Discussion and Review—Film about Fish

At the rug, involve the children in a discussion of what they have learned about fish: physical characteristics, where fish live, how they breathe, the uses of fish. Then present that all fish are not alike. The class will discuss how the fish that they have seen have various characteristics (color, size, location, uses). Then show a film that presents many unusual as well as common fish. Allow for discussion and comments.

Visitor, with Tasting Experiences

Ask the visitor to demonstrate how fish is cooked, including the preparation required before cooking and the method of cooking. While the fish is being cooked, have the visitor show the children fishing equipment and tell them about fishing as a sport. Then divide the children into groups for a tasting experience. Set up prepared samples of fish at the tables, which have been carefully deboned. Use two or three different kinds of fish, including one prepared in class. Encourage the children to try each of the samples and compare the tastes.

Small-Group Activity

Dramatization of Poems, Songs, or Rhymes

Gather one-half of the children inside, and send the other half outside. Give the inside group a nursery rhyme, poem, or song to act out or perform as they wish. When they have practiced, have the other group come in and practice. Then each group will dramatize their selection for the other group, who will try to guess what is being dramatized.

Individual Activities

- Trough with balance scales and corn
- Pictures of various kinds of fish on display
- Fish specimens and aquatic insects

LESSON PLAN ON TREES (FIVE DAYS)

Objectives

Each student will:

- Recognize the different parts of a tree (roots, trunk, branches, leaves)
- Develop an awareness of the nature around them
- Recall the many types, uses, values, and products of trees (shade, ornamentation, fruit, nuts, lumber, homes)
- Define vocabulary terms relating to trees

Day 1

Whole-Group Activities

Introduction to Unit
Gather the children together at the rug. Sing a few songs about trees. Then tell the children about the different parts of the tree and show them pictures of many different kinds of trees. Read the book *A Tree Is Nice* (Udry, 1956) (see Suggested Resources, Chapter 11).

Discussion of Nature Walk
Gather the children at the rug to discuss the nature walk. Then guide them in a discussion on the uses of trees (shade, ornamental, building homes, fuel for fires). Use pictures as illustrations.

Small-Group Activities

Art—Leaf Collages
Assign the children to small groups at separate tables. Give each group a piece of construction paper and some glue. Make many different shapes and kinds of leaves available for the children to use. The children will glue them on the paper in any desired way.

Nature Walk
Divide the children into groups of three or four, with a leader for each group. The groups will walk through the area, looking at the many different trees. The leaders will obtain feedback from the children and help to clear up any misconceptions

that they might have. This is also a good time to reinforce knowledge of the parts of the tree.

Day 2

Whole-Group Activities

Visitor—Forest Ranger
Invite a ranger to talk to the children about forests and the trees in them. The discussion should include some of the problems involving trees, such as fires, diseases, winterkill, and insects that destroy the wood, as well as some of the uses of our national forests.

Music and Creative Movement
Gather the children at the rug; after a brief introduction, put on a record. Have the children use their shakers to keep time with the music, and encourage them to move like a tree on a hot summer day, in the wind, in the rain, when thirsty, and so on.

Small-Group Activity

Art—Shakers
At the tables, give each child two paper plates with holes punched all around the outside, as well as yarn, snips of colored paper, and liquid starch to use as paste. The children put seeds from a honey locust or other tree inside the two plates and then lace them up with yarn. They can decorate them with the paper snips. They will use these shakers for the music activity.

Individual Activity

Trough with Wooden Items
Possible items include wood chips, sawdust, toothpicks, wooden spoons, bark, and wooden boxes.

Day 3

Whole-Group Activities

Movie Explaining Logging
Show a movie as soon as all the children have arrived. It should be a short movie, so that the children will not lose interest.

Field Trip—Sawmill
In groups of three or four, the children ride with parents and teachers to the sawmill. Here they see how the trees are cut into usable sizes and

observe treatments used to cure the wood. The children see how many wood products are made (rough-cut lumber, planed lumber, sawdust, pressed plywood).

Small-Group Activity

Art—Sawdust Pictures
Give each child a piece of paper and some glue. Make sawdust available at each table in several different colors, to be used as desired.

Day 4

Whole-Group Activity

Discussion of Things That Grow on Trees
Discuss with the children the many types of trees and the different things that grow on them. Use pictures of the trees and items or the actual items if available. Read the book *Apple Tree! Apple Tree!* M. Blocksma, Children's Press, Chicago, 1983.

Small-Group Activities

Food—Nuts
Divide the children into groups with name tags shaped like different kinds of nuts. Give them the opportunity to crack many different kinds of nuts and see how they taste. Save the shells.

Art—Nutshell Animals
Have the children take the nutshells and sort out some that they would like to use. Make paint, pieces of paper, glue, and small pieces of yarn available. These materials will be used for making animals out of the shells.

Day 5

Whole-Group Activities

Music
Set out such things as wood blocks and log drums for the children to make music. They can also use these items with a record for variety.

Science
Set out many different preparations of apples so that the children will be able to see the results of some of the processes that can alter the form of food. Some of the items shown can include raw apples, canned applesauce, dried apples, and apple juice. The children will be able to see how the dried apple soaks up water and swells to a larger size.

Visitor
Invite a person with an apple press to come in and show the children how apple juice, or cider, is made. The children will then drink the juice.

Small-Group Activity

Art—Toothpick Sculpture
Give each of the children toothpicks, some fast-drying glue, and a cardboard base on which to put his or her sculpture. The children put toothpicks into the glue and stick them together.

Recipes for Food Experiences

Recipes are grouped under Fruit–Vegetable; Grain; Milk, Yogurt and Cheese; and Protein Groups to assist in planning a variety of selections from each group using the Food Guide Pyramid described in Chapter 7. Some recipes include foods from more than one group, and some include foods from all the groups. The "Quick and Easy" ideas at the beginning of each section, along with many of the recipes, have been taken from a publication on food and nutrition by the United States Department of Agriculture titled *Food.* This publication is not copyrighted and contains public information. We appreciate it as a source for nutritious food recipes for children!

In presenting recipes, the goals have been fourfold: (1) emphasizing ingredients that provide nutrients, (2) being practical in the selection of foods, (3) planning activities that are developmentally appropriate, and (4) allowing children to learn by preparing foods from scratch.

A modest number of recipes that are rich in fat, cholesterol, sugar, or salt have been included; these should be used sparingly. Also, meat and eggs should be adequately cooked, and children should not be allowed to taste preparations containing raw eggs.

Fruit–Vegetable Group

Quick and Easy

- Finger fruits such as grapes, apple sections, pear sections, and so on
- Dried fruits such as apricots, raisins, prunes, bananas, pineapple, or dried fruit leathers
- Mini kabobs of bite-sized fruit chunks strung on a toothpick
- Banana chunks dipped in orange juice; shaken in a bag with chopped peanuts; speared with toothpicks
- Juice cubes made by freezing fruit juice in an ice cube tray; other fruit drinks chilled with the cubes
- Grapefruit half, sprinkled with brown sugar and broiled
- Tomato half, sprinkled with bread crumbs and Parmesan or grated cheese, and broiled
- Tomato sections, cucumber slices, and cauliflowerets marinated in French dressing
- Raw vegetable sticks or pieces (radishes, celery, cauliflower, zucchini, green pepper, carrots, cucumbers, parsnips); cutting them in various shapes may be tried
- Mini kabobs of bite-sized vegetable chunks strung on a toothpick
- Celery stuffed with cottage cheese, cheese spread, or peanut butter; raisins added for "ants on a log"
- Sliced zucchini, cauliflowerets, broccoli, and alfalfa sprouts with greens such as lettuce
- Cooked baby lima beans, sliced mushrooms, and green onions, seasoned with oregano; serve with dressing as desired

Banana Smoothie

The children mash pieces of banana on waxed paper. Add this to vanilla ice cream and milk. Stir together.

Orange Frost

6-oz can frozen orange juice concentrate
1 cup milk
1 cup water
1/4 cup sugar
1/2 tsp vanilla
10 ice cubes

Place all ingredients in a blender. Cover and blend until smooth. Serve immediately.

Fruit Dip

10-oz pkg frozen strawberries
8-oz pkg cream cheese
1/2 tsp lemon juice

Thaw and drain strawberries. Combine all ingredients in a blender and blend until smooth. Use as a dip for bite-sized fruit pieces.

Fruit-Nut Snack

6 1/2-oz can Spanish peanuts, salted
1 cup raisins
4 oz chopped dates
(Other fruits and nuts such as dried banana slices, sunflower seeds, coconut, or other raw nuts can be added for variety or taste. Carob pieces can also be added if desired.)

Mix all ingredients.

Frozen Fruit Pops

1 cup frozen or fresh unsweetened fruit (strawberries, peaches, raspberries, blueberries, kiwis, mixed fruit)
1 cup plain low-fat yogurt
5 Tbsp honey

Put fruit in blender. Cover and blend for 45 seconds at medium speed until smooth. Pour into 1-quart measuring cup, add yogurt and honey, and mix well. Pour mixture into 3 1/2-oz paper or plastic cups (about seven) and put a wooden stick in the center of each cup. Freeze for 1 to 2 hours until firm. Remove cup from frozen pop and serve.

Apple Crisp

3 1/2 cups sliced apples
1 Tbsp lemon juice
2 Tbsp water
1/2 cup flour (may use whole wheat)
1/2 cup quick-cooking oats
3/8 cup brown sugar
3/8 tsp salt
1/4 cup melted butter
1 tsp cinnamon

Combine apples, lemon juice, and water. Place in baking dish. Mix together remaining ingredients and sprinkle on apple mixture. Bake at 375° for 35 to 40 minutes.

Applesauce

6 apples
4 Tbsp honey or brown sugar

Wash, core, and slice apples. Put in saucepan with a little water. Cook slowly until tender. Strain or force through sieve or food mill or puree in blender (if apples were peeled).

Pumpkin Drop Cookies

1/3 cup shortening
3/4 cup sugar
1 egg
1 cup canned pumpkin
2 1/4 cups flour (part whole-wheat)
4 tsp baking powder
1 tsp cinnamon
1/4 tsp ginger
1/4 tsp nutmeg
1/2 tsp salt
1/2 tsp vanilla

Cream sugar and shortening; add egg, blend well, and add pumpkin. Add dry ingredients, sifted together, and flavoring. One cupful of raisins and 1/2 cup chopped nuts could be folded in. Drop by spoonfuls on greased cookie sheet. Bake at 350°F for 15 minutes. (Makes about 3 dozen cookies.)

Raggedy Ann Salad

Fresh or canned peach halves
Celery sticks
Shredded cheese
Nuts and raisins

Use a peach half for the body, celery for legs, and cheese for hair. Make the face with raisins and nuts. Place on a lettuce leaf.

Stew

Vegetables
Liquid
Browned stew meat, if desired

Have each child bring a vegetable. Prepare vegetables and add liquid. If desired, add browned stew meat. Simmer for at least an hour and a half.

Vegetable Dip

1/4 cup chives or onion tops
1/4 cup parsley
1/6 pkg (3 oz) fresh spinach (not frozen)
1/2 tsp salt
1/2 tsp ground pepper
1 cup mayonnaise

Place chives, parsley, and spinach in blender with a small amount of mayonnaise. After blending, add remaining ingredients and run blender again. (Half-and-half cream can be used to make the dip thinner.) Dip zucchini slices, cucumber, carrots, celery, and other vegetables into the dip.

Tempura Vegetables (single portion)

Batter:
1 Tbsp water
2 tsp beaten egg
2 Tbsp flour

Combine to make batter. Put carrot strips, green pepper, raw green beans, or other vegetables on a skewer and dip into batter. Cook in hot oil and serve with soy sauce.

Coleslaw

4 cups shredded or finely chopped cabbage
Salt
1 cup plain yogurt or salad dressing

Mix together. (May add diced apples, raisins, pineapple, marshmallows, etc.)

Salads with Vegetable and Fruit Combinations

To grated carrots, add any or all of the following:
  Crushed or tidbit canned pineapple, drained
  Raisins
  Diced banana
  Coconut
  Salad dressing or plain yogurt to moisten
To chopped or shredded cabbage, add any or all of the following:
  Diced celery
  Diced apple
  Chopped peanuts
  Raisins

Grain Group

Quick and Easy

- Raisin bread, toasted and spread with peanut butter

- Sandwiches using a variety of breads: raisin, cracked wheat, pumpernickel, rye, black

- Date–nut roll or brown bread spread with cream cheese

- English muffins, served open faced for sandwiches such as hot roast beef or turkey, chicken salad

- Individual pizzas: English muffin halves topped with cheese slices, tomato sauce, and oregano and then broiled

- Waffles topped with yogurt and fruit

- Wheat or rye crackers topped with seasoned cottage cheese, cheese, meat spread, or peanut butter

Bread or Bread Sticks

1 cup milk
3 Tbsp shortening
1 Tbsp salt
1 cup cold water
2 yeast cakes
1 cup warm water
3 Tbsp sugar
8 cups flour (or 4 cups white and 4 cups whole wheat)

Scald milk, shortening, and salt; dissolve. Then add cold water. Soak yeast cakes in warm water and sugar in large bowl. Next, add 2 cups flour to yeast mixture and mix well. Add the milk, shortening, salt, and water mixture; add 6 cups flour. Mix well, pour out, and knead for 5 minutes on floured board. Place mixture back in bowl and let rise until double in bulk, about 90 minutes. Turn out on floured surface and knead for 5 minutes. Make two loaves, let rise in lightly greased pans until doubled in bulk, about 45 to 90 minutes, or let children shape into individual rolls or sculptures. Bake for 20 to 30 minutes at 425°F.

Navaho Fry Bread (Pahnelaquiz)

2 cups flour
1/2 cup dry milk
1 Tbsp baking powder
3/4 tsp salt
2 Tbsp shortening
3/4 lukewarm water

Mix flour, milk, baking powder, and salt together and then cut in shortening. Mix in water (more if necessary) and knead until smooth and elastic. Let stand at least 30 minutes or refrigerate overnight. Cut into pieces and deep fry in small amount of hot oil.

Fry Bread (single portion)

2 Tbsp flour
1/4 tsp baking powder
Pinch of salt
2 tsp water

Mix and then shape into thin pancake shape. Deep fry and drain on paper towel.

Grits

1/3 cup grits
6 2/3 cups boiling water
1 1/2 tsp salt
3 Tbsp butter

Pour grits into boiling water, add salt, and stir until it thickens (2 to 3 minutes). Cover and cook over low heat 25 minutes; stir twice during that time. Dot with butter and serve.

Hoecakes (single portion)

2 Tbsp cornmeal
Pinch of salt
1 Tbsp boiling water

Mix, form into pancake, and cook on greased griddle. Serve with syrup or molasses.

Popcorn with Cheese

1/3 cup popcorn kernels, popped
2 Tbsp melted butter or margarine
1/2 cup Parmesan cheese
1/2 tsp salt, if desired

Placed popped corn in a shallow baking pan. Drizzle with melted fat; mix. Sprinkle with cheese and salt, if desired; mix. Heat for 8 to 10 minutes in oven, stirring frequently.

Scones

2 cups unsifted flour
1/4 cup sugar
2 tsp baking powder
1/2 tsp baking soda
1/2 tsp salt
1/4 cup butter or margarine
2 eggs
1/3 cup sour milk (or combine 1 tsp vinegar or lemon juice with enough sweet milk to make 1/3 cup)

Grease a baking sheet. Mix dry ingredients thoroughly. Mix in fat only until mixture is crumbly, using a pastry blender, two table knives, or a fork. Beat eggs; add milk. Stir into dry ingredients, mixing just until moistened. Divide dough in half. Place on baking sheet and shape each half of the dough into a 7-inch circle about 1/2 inch thick. Cut each circle of dough into six wedges. Prick with a fork. Bake at 375°F for 12 minutes or until lightly browned.

Bran Cereal or Whole-Wheat Muffins

1 cup whole bran cereal
1/2 to 1 cup milk
1 egg, beaten
1/4 cup oil
1/4 cup honey, molasses, or brown sugar
1 1/4 cups unsifted whole-wheat flour
2 tsp baking powder
1/4 tsp baking soda
1/2 tsp salt

Grease muffin tins. Stir bran cereal and milk together in a bowl. Let stand for a minute or two, then add egg, oil, and honey. Beat well. Stir remaining ingredients together until well mixed. Add to liquid mixture and stir only until moistened. Put into muffin tins, filling only about two-thirds full. Bake at 400°F for about 20 to 25 minutes or until lightly browned. (*Option:* Eliminate bran cereal and increase whole-wheat flour to 2 cups. If bran is eliminated, mix milk with other liquids.)

Red Beans and Rice

1/2 cup chopped onion
1/2 cup chopped celery
1 clove garlic
2 Tbsp butter or margarine
16-oz can kidney beans
2 cups cooked rice
1 Tbsp chopped parsley
1/2 tsp salt
1/8 tsp pepper

Cook onion, celery, and garlic in fat until tender; remove garlic. Add remaining ingredients. Simmer together for 5 minutes to blend flavors.

Whole-Wheat Drop Cookies

2 cups brown sugar, packed
1 cup shortening
2 eggs, beaten
2 tsp baking soda, dissolved in 2 Tbsp water
1/2 tsp baking powder
3/4 tsp salt
2 1/2 cups whole-wheat flour
1 cup chopped dates or raisins
1/2 cup nuts (optional)

Cream shortening and sugar. Mix remaining ingredients and add to creamed mixture; mix to a soft dough. Drop about 2 inches apart on baking sheet. Bake for 8 to 10 minutes at 375°F.

Individual Carrot Cakes

1/3 cup grated carrot
3 Tbsp yellow cake mix
1/4 tsp cinnamon

Pinch nutmeg
6 raisins
2 Tbsp beaten egg

Mix all ingredients together. Bake in muffin tin at
375°F for 10 to 15 minutes. Frost if desired.

Recipes Using Refrigerator Biscuits

Pigs in a Blanket

Small sausages or hot dogs
Refrigerator biscuits

Fold refrigerator biscuits around sausages. Place in
pan and bake at 450°F for 8 to 10 minutes. Cool
slightly and serve with mustard or catsup, if
desired.

Doughnuts or Scones

Refrigerator biscuits
Cooking oil (approximately 1/4 in. deep in skillet)
Sugar, cinnamon–sugar mixture, or glaze

Poke small hole in biscuit with finger or thimble. Fry
in heated oil for about 2 minutes or until done,
turning once. Drain on paper towels. Roll in sugar
or cinnamon–sugar mixture, or glaze. (For scones,
eliminate hole in center.)

Bread Sticks

Refrigerator biscuits
Butter
Seeds, such as sesame seeds

Roll each biscuit into a long cylinder. Roll in butter and
then, if desired, in any kind of seed, such as sesame
seeds. Bake according to package directions. Serve
in a basket with any kind of preserves or honey, or
just butter.

Individual Pizzas

Refrigerator biscuits
1 lb ground beef
2 cups tomato sauce
1/4 cup finely chopped onion, if desired
Finely chopped small garlic bud, if desired
Grated cheese

On lightly greased cookie sheet, flatten biscuits and
press up rim on edge. Fill with mixture of tomato
sauce, browned hamburger, onion, and garlic. Top
with grated cheese. (Other ingredients that may be
used include sliced wieners, pepperoni, Parmesan
cheese, oregano, parsley flakes, onion, garlic, basil,
pepper.) Bake at 425°F for 10 minutes.

Milk, Yogurt, and Cheese Group

Quick and Easy

- Milkshakes with mashed fresh berries or bananas
- Parfait of cottage cheese, yogurt, or ice milk
  combined with fruit, sprinkled with chopped
  nuts, wheat germ, or crisp cereal
- Fruit-flavored yogurt
- Custard
- Ice-milk sundae topped with fresh, canned, or
  frozen fruits
- Cheese cubes plain, or speared with pretzel
  sticks, or alternated with mandarin orange sections on a toothpick
- Assorted cheeses with crackers or fresh fruits
- Dips for vegetables sticks (for fewer calories
  and more nutrition, substitute cottage cheese
  or plain yogurt for sour cream and mayonnaise
  in preparing dips).

Butter

1/2 pt whipping cream
Dash of salt
Yellow coloring, if desired

Warm cream to room temperature. Shake in bottle
until butter and milk separate. Pour milk off and
continue to separate the milk from the butter. Salt
to taste. Add yellow food coloring, if desired.

Chili con Queso Dip

16-oz box pasteurized processed cheese spread, cut in
cubes
3/4 cup canned tomatoes, chopped
1 Tbsp finely chopped chili peppers

Place cheese cubes in the top of a double boiler over
boiling water. Stir constantly until cheese is melted.
Stir in tomatoes and peppers until well blended and
creamy. Serve hot with tortilla or corn chips.

Eggnog

3 eggs, slightly beaten
1/2 cup sugar
1/4 tsp salt
3 cups milk
1 cup half-and-half
1/2 tsp vanilla
1 1/2 tsp imitation rum flavoring
Nutmeg as desired

Mix beaten eggs with sugar and salt in the top of a double boiler. Add milk and half-and-half. Cook over boiling water, stirring constantly, just until mixture coats spoon, about 10 to 15 minutes. Cool. Add vanilla and rum flavorings. Chill. Immediately before serving, strain eggnog. Beat with rotary beater until frothy. Pour into chilled cups. Sprinkle each serving with nutmeg, as desired.

Banana Smoothie (single serving)

Mash 1/2 banana, mix with 1/2 cup ice milk and 1/4 cup milk.

Banana-Orange Shake

4 ripe bananas, sliced
1/3 cup orange juice
6 Tbsp honey
Salt
1/4 tsp vanilla
4 cups reconstituted nonfat dry milk

Put in blender and beat until smooth.

Strawberry-Yogurt Pops

2 10-oz pkg frozen strawberries, thawed (conserve liquid)
1 Tbsp unflavored gelatin
16 oz plain yogurt
3-oz paper cups
Wooden sticks
Drain strawberries. Place drained liquid in a saucepan and sprinkle with gelatin. Cook over low heat, stirring constantly, until gelatin dissolves. Mix strawberries, yogurt, and gelatin mixture in a blender until smooth. Place cups on a tray or in a baking pan. Fill with blended mixture and cover cups with a sheet of aluminum foil. Insert a stick in each pop by making a slit in the foil over the center of the cup. Freeze pops until firm. Run warm water on outside of cup to loosen each pop from the cup.

Protein Group (Meat, Poultry, Eggs, Nuts, Fish, Beans)

Quick and Easy

- Nuts, sesame seeds, or toasted sunflower seeds
- Sandwich spread of peanut butter combined with raisins or chopped dates
- Peanut butter and honey spread on an English muffin, sprinkled with chopped walnuts and heated under broiler

- Grilled open-faced peanut butter and mashed banana sandwich
- Tomatoes stuffed with egg salad
- Melon wedges topped with thinly sliced ham

Toasted Sunflower Seeds

1 cup sunflower seeds
1 tsp oil, if desired
1/4 tsp salt, if desired

Mix sunflower seeds with oil only if salt is used. Spread plain or oiled seeds on baking sheet. Bake at 325°F for about 8 minutes or until lightly browned. (Watch carefully, these seeds brown quickly.) Sprinkle oiled seeds with salt while hot.

Quick-Cook Chili

1 lb ground beef
1/2 cup chopped onion
16-oz can pinto beans
1 can condensed tomato soup
2 to 3 tsp chili powder

Heat beef and onion in a skillet until beef is browned and onion is tender. Drain off excess fat. Stir in remaining ingredients, cover. Simmer for 30 minutes, stirring occasionally.

Chao Fan

Scramble eggs with a bit of chopped green onion. Add chopped ham and cooked peas. Serve over cooked rice. Add soy sauce, if desired. (Adapted from Kositsky, 1977, p. 30)

Wontons

Wonton skins
Hamburger
Soya sauce
Bean sprouts
Green onion

Combine raw hamburger, a little soya sauce, some cut-up bean sprouts, and a little minced green onion. Put a teaspoon of the mixture into the center of the wonton skin and fold in half to make a triangle. Dampen the edges so they stick together. Simmer in chicken soup, or deep-fat fry until meat is cooked (5–10 minutes). (Adapted from Kositsky, 1977, p. 30)

Chicken-Fruit Salad

3 cups cooked chicken, cut in chunky pieces
3/4 cup chopped celery
3/4 cup grape halves, seeded

20-oz can pineapple chunks in natural juice, drained
11-oz can mandarin oranges, drained
1/4 cup chopped pecans
1/4 cup salad dressing or plain yogurt
1/8 tsp salt
Lettuce leaves

Toss chicken, celery, grapes, pineapple, oranges, and
3 Tbsp of the pecans together lightly. Gently mix
salad dressing or yogurt and salt with chicken
mixture. Chill. Serve on lettuce leaves. Garnish with
remaining pecans.

Mexicale Hot Dog (single portion)

1 flour tortilla
1 slice cheese
1 hot dog
Salsa (optional)

Lay flour tortilla out. Put slice of cheese on tortilla,
spread with salsa, put hot dog on top, and roll up.
Microwave for 1 minute.

Open-faced Submarine Sandwiches

6 English muffin halves, toasted
1 Tbsp butter or margarine
6 slices meat
1 cup chopped lettuce
1/2 small onion, thinly sliced and separated into rings
1 medium tomato, thinly sliced
1/2 tsp basil leaves
6 slices pasteurized process American cheese

Spread toasted muffin halves with butter or margarine.
Layer meat slices, lettuce, onion, and tomato slices
on muffins. Sprinkle with basil. Top each sandwich
with cheese slice. Broil until cheese is melted and
lightly browned, about 5 minutes.

Refried Beans

1 lb pinto beans, dried
1 qt water
Salt to taste
Dash of cumin
1/4 cup lard or bacon fat (optional)

Sort and wash pinto beans. Cover with water
generously; let stand overnight. Next day, pour off
liquid. Put in large pot and add twice as much water
as there are beans. Stir in salt and cumin. Quickly
bring to a boil. Lower heat. Simmer for 2 to 3 hours
(until tender). Drain; mash beans. Heat lard. Add very
hot lard to beans. Stir and simmer until fat is
absorbed. Use as is or refry. To refry, fry mashed
beans in hot lard until completely dry.

Peanut Butter

1 1/2 Tbsp oil
1 cup peanuts
Salt

Put the oil in a blender and gradually add the peanuts,
blending well; sprinkle in a little salt.

Peanut-butter Balls

15 oz graham crackers
2 Tbsp corn syrup
2 Tbsp milk
1/2 cup peanut butter
4 Tbsp butter or margarine
2 tsp vanilla

Crush crackers with a rolling pin or in a blender. Cream
butter and add syrup, milk, vanilla, and peanut
butter. Add 1 cup of the graham cracker crumbs and
set the remainder aside. Mix the ingredients
thoroughly; then roll into 1-inch balls. Roll the balls
in the remaining cracker crumbs and serve.

Baked Kidney Beans

3 cups kidney beans, dried
2 large onions, sliced
2 cups canned tomatoes
3 Tbsp chopped green pepper
1 Tbsp salt
2 Tbsp brown sugar
3 Tbsp vegetable oil

Cover beans generously with water and soak
overnight. Parboil with onions in the morning and
then turn into bean pot. Add the rest of the
ingredients and bake for 5 to 6 hours.

Mexican Loaf

1-lb can kidney beans
1/2 lb cheddar cheese
1 finely chopped onion
1 Tbsp margarine
1 cup bread crumbs
2 eggs
Seasonings
Green pepper rings
Tomato sauce

Drain liquid from beans. Grind beans with cheese.
Saute onion in margarine. Combine beans, cheese,
bread crumbs, onion, eggs, and seasonings. Put in
buttered baking dish, cover with bread crumbs, and
bake in 350°F oven for 30 to 40 minutes. Garnish
with green pepper rings and serve hot with heated
tomato sauce.

Miscellaneous Group

Pudding Squares

5 envelopes unflavored gelatin
1 small pkg. vanilla or butterscotch instant pudding
1 1/2 cups boiling water
1 1/2 cups cold milk

In large bowl, combine unflavored gelatin and pudding mix. Add boiling water and beat with wire whisk or rotary beater until well blended; stir in milk. Pour into 8- or 9-inch square pan and chill until firm. Cut into squares to serve.

Gelatin Squares (sometimes called Finger Gelatin)

2 large pkg flavored gelatin
3 cups water
1/2 cup sugar
3 envelopes unflavored gelatin
2 1/2 cups cold water

Boil the first three ingredients together and add the unflavored gelatin that has been dissolved in the cold water. Pour all ingredients into a 9- by 13-inch pan. Let set for about 2 hours. Cut into bite-sized pieces and eat with fingers, or cut with cookie cutters into desired shapes.

References

Media and Software Resources

Davidson & Associates
P.O. Box 2961
Torrance, CA 90509
(800-545-7677)
(*www.education.com*)

Davidson Films
668 Marsh Street
San Luis Obispo, CA 93401-3951
(888-437-4200)
(*www.davidsonfilms.com*)

Films for the Humanities & Sciences
P.O. Box 2053
Princeton, NJ 08543-2053
(800-257-5126)
(*www.films.com*)

Insight Media
2162 Broadway
New York, NY 10024-0621
(800-233-9910)
(*www.insight-media.com*)

National Geographic
Educational Services
1145 17th Street, NW
Washington, DC 20036-4688
(800-368-2728)
(*www.nationalgeographic.com*)

Riverdeep Interactive Learning
P.O. Box 97021
Redmond, WA 98073-0721
(800-362-2890)
(*www.riverdeep.net*)

Sunburst
101 Castleton Street
P.O. Box 100
Pleasantville, NY 10570
(800-321-7511)
(*www.sunburst.com*)

The Video Journal of Education
8686 South 1300 East
Sandy, UT 84094
(878-350-6500)
(*www.schoolimprovement.net*)

Abruscato, J. (1992). *Teaching children science* (3rd ed.). Boston: Allyn & Bacon.

Achilles, E. (1999). Creating music environments in early childhood programs. *Young Children 54*(1):21–26.

Adams, G., & N. O. Poersch (1997). Who cares? State commitment to child care and early education. *Young Children 52*(4): 66–69.

Adams, M. J. (1990). *Beginning to read: Thinking and learning about print.* Champaign, IL: University of Illinois Press—Center for the Study of Reading.

Akaran, S. E., & M. V. Fields (1997). Family and cultural context: A writing breakthrough? *Young Children 52*(4): 37–40.

Allen, J., P. Freeman, & S. Osborne (1989). Children's political knowledge and attitudes. *Young Children 44*(2): 55–61.

Allington, R. L., & A. McGill-Franzen (1995). Flunking: Throwing good money after bad. In R. L. Allington & S. A. Walmsley (eds.), *No quick fix.* New York: Teachers College Press, pp. 45–60.

Althouse, R., & C. Main (1975). *Science experience for young children: Color.* New York: Teachers College Press.

American Medical Association (1996). *Physician guide to media violence.* Chicago: American Medical Association.

Anderson, M., with D. Weinhouse (1997). Learning disabilities—Twice blessed. *Young Children 52*(4): 29–31.

Anderson, M. P. (2001). ACT against violence. *Young children 56*(4): 60–61.

Anderson, M. P. (1996). Frequently asked questions about NAEYC's linguistic and cultural diversity position paper. *Young Children 51*(2): 13–16.

Anderson, T. L. (1996). "They're trying to tell me something": A teacher's reflection on primary children's construction of mathematical knowledge. *Young Children 51*(4): 34–42.

Andress, B. (1991). From research to practice: Preschool children and their movement response to music. *Young Children 47*(1): 22–27.

Andress, B. (1995). Transforming curriculum in music. In S. Bredekamp & T. Rosegrant (eds.), *Reaching potentials: Transforming early childhood curriculum and assessment,* Vol. 2, pp. 99–108. Washington, DC: National Association for the Education of Young Children.

Annie E. Casey Foundation (1995). *Kids count data book.* Baltimore, MD: Author.

Appl, D. J. (1998). Children with Down Syndrome: Implications for adult–child interactions in inclusive settings. *Childhood Education 75*(1): 39–43.

Armstrong, T. (1996a). A holistic approach to attention deficit disorder. *Educational Leadership 53*(5): 34–36.

Armstrong, T. (1996b). ADD: Does it really exist? *Phi Delta Kappan 77*(6): 424–428.

Arnqvist, A. (2000). Linguistic games as a way to introduce reading and writing in preschool groups. *Childhood Education 76*(6): 365–367.

Association for Childhood Education International (1995a). Establishing and maintaining a multi-cultural focus. *Childhood Education 71*(4): 224–C.

Association for Childhood Education International (1995b). Inclusion: One way a professional development school can make a difference. *Childhood Education 71*(4): 224–M.

Association for Childhood Education International (1995c). President's message: Reconsidering developmentally appropriate practices. *Childhood Education 71*(4): 224–A, 224–D.

Association for Childhood Education International (1995/1996). Money math. *Childhood Education 72*(2): 96–I.

Association for Childhood Education International (1996a). Floating grapes. *Childhood Education 72*(3): 160–G.

Association for Childhood Education International (1996b). Issues of diversity in teacher education. *Childhood Education 72*(3): 160–L, 160–O.

Association for Childhood Education International (1996c). Reduce, reuse, recycle. *Childhood Education 72*(5): 288–G.

Association for Childhood Education International (1997). True colors. *Childhood Education 73*(4): 224–G.

Baker, D. W. (1991). The visual arts in early childhood education. In D. Elkind (ed.), *Perspectives on early childhood education.* Washington, DC: National Education Association, pp. 133–140.

Baker, E. T., M. O. Wang, & H. J. Walberg (1994/1995). The effects of inclusion on learning. *Educational Leadership 52*(4): 33–35.

Bakley, S. (1997). Love a little more, accept a little more. *Young Children 52*(2): 21.

Balke, E. (1997). Play and the arts: The importance of the "unimportant." *Childhood Education 73*(6): 355–360.

Banks, J. A. (1993). Multicultural education: Development, dimensions, and challenges. *Phi Delta Kappan 75*(1): 21–27.

Banks, J. A., & C. A. M. Banks (1993). *Multicultural education: Issues and perspectives* (2nd ed.). Boston: Allyn and Bacon.

Barbour, N. H., & C. Seefeldt (1993). *Developmental continuity across preschool and primary grades.* Wheaton, MD: Association for Childhood Education International.

Barclay, K., C. Benelli, & A. Curtis (1995). Literacy begins at birth: What caregivers can learn from parents of children who read early. *Young Children 50*(4): 24–28.

Barclay, K., & L. Walwer (1992). Linking lyrics and literacy through song picture books. *Young Children 47*(4): 76–85.

Battista, M. T. (1994). Teacher beliefs and the reform movement in mathematics education. *Phi Delta Kappan 75*(6): 462–470.

Bauer, K. L., M. A. Sheerer, & E. Dettore, Jr. (1997). Creative strategies in Ernie's early childhood classroom. *Young Children 52*(6): 47–52.

Bayless, K. M., & M. E. Ramsey (1991). *Music: A way of life for the young child* (4th ed.). Upper Saddle River, NJ: Merrill/Prentice Hall.

Bear, D. R., & M. Invernizzi, S. Templeton, & F. Johnston (2000). *Words their way: Word study for phonics, vocabulary, and spelling instruction* (2nd ed.). Upper Saddle River, NJ: Prentice Hall.

Beatty, B. (1995). *Preschool education in America.* New Haven, CT: Yale University Press.

Beaty, J. J. (1992). *Skills for preschool teachers* (4th ed.). Columbus, OH: Macmillan.

Benelli, C., & B. Yongue (1995). Supporting young children's motor skill development. *Childhood Education 71*(4): 217–220.

Bennett, L. (1995). Wide world of breads in children's literature. *Young Children 50*(5): 64–68.

Bennett, W. J. (ed.). (1993). *The book of virtues.* New York: Simon & Schuster.

Bennett, W. J. (ed.) (1995). *The children's book of virtues.* New York: Simon & Schuster.

Berger, E. H. (1995). Reaching for the stars: Families and schools working together. *Early Childhood Education Journal 23*(2): 119–123.

Berger, E. H. (1994). *Parents as partners in education: Families and schools working together* (4th ed.). Upper Saddle River, NJ: Merrill/Prentice Hall.

Berk, L. E. (1994). Vygotsky's theory: The importance of make-believe play. *Young Children 50*(1): 30-39.

Berk, L. E., & A. Winsler (1995). *Scaffolding children's learning: Vygotsky and early childhood education.* Washington, DC: National Association for the Education of Young Children.

Bermudez, A.B. (1994). *Doing our homework: How schools can engage Hispanic Communities.* Charleston, WV: ERIC Clearinghouse on Rural Education and Small Schools (ERIC Document Reproduction Service No. 372 905).

Bermudez, A.B., & J.A. Marquez (1996). An examination of a four-way collaborative to increase parental involvement in the schools. *Journal of Educational Issues of Language Minority Students Special Issue, 16*: 1-16.

Berreth, D., & S. Berman (1997). The moral dimensions of schools. *Educational Leadership 54*(8): 24-27.

Billman, J. (1992). The Native American curriculum: Attempting alternatives to tepees and headbands. *Young Children 46*(6): 22-25.

Blair, S., & M. S. Morrow (1997). Surgeon general's report on physical fitness. *Health and Fitness Journal 1*(1): 14-18.

Blake, S., S. Hurley, & B. Arenz (1995). Mathematical problem solving and young children. *Early Childhood Education Journal 23*(2): 81-84.

Block, M. E., & K. Burke (1999). Are children with disabilities receiving appropriate physical education? *Teaching Exceptional Children 31*(3): 18-23.

Bloom, B.S. (ed.) (1956). *Taxonomy of educational objectives: The classification of educational goals: Handbook I, cognitive domain.* New York, Toronto: Longmans, Green.

Bodrova, E., D. J. Leong, & D. E. Paynter (1999). Literacy standards for preschool learners. *Educational Leadership 57*(2): 42-46.

Bomba, A. K., C. B. Oakley, & K. B. Knight (1996). Planning the menu in the child care center. *Young Children 51*(6): 62-67.

Bond, T.F. (2001). Giving them free rein: Connection in student-led book groups. *Reading Teacher 54*(6): 574-584.

Booth, D. & B. Barton (2000). *Story works: How teachers can use shared stories in the new curriculum.* Portland, ME: Stenhouse.

Borden, E. J. (1987). The community connection—It works! *Young Children 42*(4): 14-23.

Bordner, G.A., & M.T. Berkley (1992). Educational play: Meeting everyone's needs in mainstreamed classrooms. *Childhood Education 69*(1): 38-40.

Bosworth, K. (1995). Caring for others and being cared for. *Phi Delta Kappan 76*(9): 686-693.

Boutte, G. S., & C. B. McCormick, (1992). Authentic multicultural activities: Avoiding pseudomulticulturalism. *Childhood Education 68*(3): 140-144.

Boutte, G. S., I. VanScoy, & S. Hendley (1996). Multicultural and nonsexist prop boxes. *Young Children 52*(1): 34-39.

Bracey, G.W. (1996a). Change and continuity in elementary education. *Principal 75*(3): 17-21.

Bracey, G.W. (1996b). The impact of early intervention. *Phi Delta Kappan 77*(7): 510-512.

Bradley, D. H., & P. R. Pottle (2001). Supporting emergent writers through on-the-spot conferencing and publishing. *Young Children 56*(3): 20-27.

Brand, S. (1996). Making parent involvement a reality: Helping teachers develop partnerships with parents. *Young Children 51*(2): 76-81.

Brandt, R. (1994). On educating for diversity: A conversation with James A. Banks. *Educational Leadership 51*(8): 28-31.

Brandt, R. S. (2000). *Education in a new era.* Alexandria, VA: Association for Supervision and Curriculum Development (ASCD).

Brazelton, T. B., & S. I. Greenspan (2001). *The irreducible needs of children: What every child must have to grow, learn, and flourish.* Cambridge, MA: Perseus.

Bredekamp, S. (ed.). (1986). *Developmentally appropriate practices* (position statement). Washington, DC: National Association for the Education of Young Children.

Bredekamp, S. (1987). *Developmentally appropriate practice in early childhood programs serving children from birth through age eight.* Washington, DC: National Association for the Education of Young Children.

Bredekamp, S., & C. Copple (eds.) (1997). *Developmentally appropriate practice in early childhood programs* (rev. ed.). Washington, DC: National Association for the Education of Young Children.

Bredekamp, S., & T. Rosegrant (eds.) (1992). *Reaching potentials: Appropriate curriculum and assessment for young children* (Vol. 1). Washington, DC: National Association for the Education of Young Children.

Bredekamp, S., & L. Shepard (1989). How best to protect children from inappropriate school expectations, practices, and policies. *Young Children 44*(3): 14-24.

Brendtro, L., & N. Long (1995). Breaking the cycle of conflict. *Educational Leadership 52*(5): 52-56.

Brewer, J., & J. Kieff (1996/1997). Fostering mutual respect for play at home and school. *Childhood Education 73*(2): 92-96.

Briggs, N., M. R. Jalongo, & L. Brown. (1997). Working with families of young children: Our history and our future goals. In J. P. Isenberg & M.R. Jalongo (eds.), *Major trends and issues in early childhood education: Challenges, controversies, and insights.* New York: Teachers College Press, pp. 56-69.

Brodmann, A. (1993). *The gift*. New York: Simon & Schuster.

Broman, B. L. (1989). *The early years in childhood education*. Prospect Heights, IL: Waveland.

Bromer, J. (1999). Cultural variations in child care: Values and actions. *Young Children* 54(6): 72–78.

Bromley, K. D. (1996). *Webbing with literature: Creating story maps with children's books*. Boston: Allyn and Bacon.

Bronson, M. B. (1995). *The right stuff for children birth to 8: Selecting play materials to support development*. Washington, DC: National Association for the Education of Young Children.

Bronson, M.H. (2000). Recognizing and supporting the development of self-regulation in young children. *Young Children* 55(2): 32–37.

Brudnak, K. A. (1997). Thinking . . . through the arts. *Learning* 26(2): 42–46.

Bryant, D. M., R. M. Clifford, & E. S. Peisner (1991). Best practices for beginners: Developmental appropriateness in kindergarten. *American Educational Research Journal 28:* 783–803.

Buchoff, R. (1995). Jump rope rhymes . . . in the classroom? *Childhood Education* 71(3): 149–151.

Burns, P. C., & B. L. Broman (1983). *The language arts in childhood education* (5th ed.). Boston: Houghton Mifflin.

Butler, L. A. (1997). Building on a dream of success. *Principal* 76(5): 28–31.

Campbell, R. (2001). *Read-alouds with young children*. Newark, DE: International Reading Association.

Caplan, T., & F. Caplan (1983). *The early childhood years: The 2 to 6 year old*. New York: GD/Perigee.

Carr, K. S. (1988). How can we teach critical thinking? *Childhood Education* 64(2): 69–73.

Carson, R. (1956). *A sense of wonder*. New York: Harper & Row.

Cartwright, S. (1990). Learning with large blocks. *Young Children* 45(3): 38–41.

Cartwright, S. (1991). Interview at a small Maine school. *Young Children* 46(3): 7–11.

Casey, M. B. (2001). Spatial–mechanical reasoning skills versus mathematics: Self-confidence as mediators of gender differences in mathematics. *Journal for Research in Mathematics Education* 32(1): 28–58.

Casey, M. B., & M. Lippman (1991). Learning to plan through play. *Young Children* 46(4): 52–58.

Cecil, N. E. (1999). *Striking a balance: Positive practices for early literacy*. Scottsdale, AZ: Holcomb Hathaway.

Chaillé, C., & S. B. Silvern (1996). Understanding through play. *Childhood Education* 72(5): 274–277.

Chapman, M. L. (1996). The development of phonemic awareness in young children: Some insights from a case study of a first-grade writer. *Young Children* 51(2): 31–37.

The Character Education Partnership, Inc. (1996). *Character education in U.S. schools: The new consensus*. Alexandria, VA: Author.

Chard, S. C. (1992). *The project approach: A practical guide for teachers*. Edmonton: University of Alberta Printing Services.

Chard, S. C. (1994). *The project approach: A second practical guide for teachers*. Edmonton: University of Alberta Printing Services.

Charlesworth, R. (1997). Mathematics in the developmentally appropriate integrated curriculum. In C. H. Hart, D. C. Burts, & R. Charlesworth (eds.), *Integrated curriculum and developmentally appropriate practice: Birth to age eight*. Albany, NY: Suny Press, pp. 51–73.

Charlesworth, R., & K. K. Lind (1990). *Math and science for young children*. Albany, NY: Delmar.

Charlesworth, R., C. H. Hart, D. C. Burts, & M. DeWolf (1993). The LSU studies: Building a research base for DAP. In S. Reifel (ed.), *Advances in early education and day care: Perspective in developmentally appropriate practice* (Vol. 5), pp. 3–28.

Charron, E., & T. Jones. (1992). Straight to the source. *Science and Children* 30(3): 36–37.

Chavkin, N. F. (1966). Involving migrant families in their children's education: Challenges and opportunities for schools. *Children of La Frontera: Binational Efforts to Serve Mexican Migrant and Immigrant Students* (ERIC Document Reproduction Service No. 939 648).

Chavkin, N. F., & D. L. Gonzales (1995). *Forging partnerships between Mexican American parents and the schools*. Charleston, WV: ERIC Clearinghouse on Rural Education and Small Schools (ERIC Document Reproduction Service No. 388 489).

Checkley, K. (1997). The first seven . . . and the eighth: A conversation with Howard Gardner. *Educational Leadership* 55(1): pp. 8–13.

Chenfeld, M. B. (1990). "My loose is tooth!" Kidding around with kids. *Young Children* 46(1): 56–60.

Chenfeld, M. B. (1991). Wanna play? *Young Children* 46(6): 4–6.

Chenfeld, M. B. (1995). Do spiderwebs ever wake you up? *Young Children* 50(5): 70–71.

Chenfeld, M. B. (1997). Telling time. *Phi Delta Kappan* 78(6): 475.

Chesebro, J., R. Berko, C. Hopson, P. Cooper, & H. Hodges. (1995). Strategies for increasing achievement in oral communication. In R. W. Cole (ed.), *Educating everybody's children: Diverse teaching strategies for diverse learners*. Alexandria, VA: Association for Supervision and Curriculum Development, pp. 139–165.

Children and Adults with Attention Deficit Disorders (Ch.A.D.D.) (1995a). Attention deficit disorder in the classroom (on-line). Available: *http://www.chadd.org/*.

Children and Adults with Attention Deficit Disorders (Ch.A.D.D.) (1995b). The disability named ADD: An overview of attention deficit disorders (fact sheet). Plantation, FL: Author.

Children's Defense Fund (1990). *Children 1990: A report card, briefing book, and action primer.* Washington, DC: Author.

Children's Defense Fund (1991). *The state of America's children 1991.* Washington, DC: Author.

Children's Defense Fund (2000). *The state of America's children: Yearbook 2000.* Washington, DC: National Association for the Education of Young Children.

Children's Defense Fund (1997). *The state of America's children: Yearbook 1997.* Washington, DC: National Association for the Education of Young Children.

Chipman, M. (1997). Valuing cultural diversity in the early years: Social imperatives and pedagogical insights. In J. P. Isenberg & M. R. Jalongo (eds.), *Major trends and issues in early childhood education: Challenges, controversies, and insights.* New York: Teachers College Press, pp. 43-55.

Christie, J. F., & F. Wardle (1992). How much time is needed for play? *Young Children 47*(3): 28-32.

Clark, E. T., Jr. (1997). *Designing and implementing an integrated curriculum: A student-centered approach.* Brandon, VT: Holistic Education Press.

Clark, L., S. DeWolf, & C. Clark (1992). Teaching teachers to avoid having culturally assaultive classrooms. *Young Children 47*(5): 4-9.

Clemens, J. B. (1996). Gardening with children. *Young Children 51*(4): 22-27.

Clemens, S. G. (1991). Art in the classroom. *Young Children 46*(2): 4-11.

Clements, D. H. (2001). Mathematics in the preschool. *Teaching Children Mathematics 7*(5): 270-276.

Clements, D. H., & M. T. Battista (1990). Constructivist learning and teaching. *Arithmetic Teacher 38*(1): 34-35.

Clements, D. H., & S. McMillen (1996). Rethinking "concrete" manipulatives. *Teaching Children Mathematics 2*(5): 270-279.

Clements, D. H., & J. Sarama (2000). Young children's ideas about geometric shapes. *Teaching Children Mathematics 6*(8): 482-488.

Clements, D. H., & S. Swaminathan (1995). Technology and school change—New lamps for old? *Childhood Education 71*(5): 275-78.

Cline, D. B., & D. Ingerson (1996). The mystery of Humpty's fall: Primary-school children as playmakers. *Young Children 51*(6): 4-10.

Colbert, C. (1997). Visual arts in the developmentally appropriate integrated curriculum. In C. H. Hart, D. C. Burts, & R. Charlesworth (eds.), *Integrated curriculum and developmentally appropriate practice: Birth to age eight.* Albany, NY: SUNY Press, pp. 201-223.

Coleman, M. (1997). Families and schools: In search of common ground. *Young Children 52*(5): 14-21.

Coleman, M., & S. Churchill (1997). Challenges to family involvement. *Childhood Education 73*(3): 144-148.

Coleman, M., & C. Wallinga (2000). Connecting families and classrooms using family involvement webs. *Childhood Education 76*(4): 209-214.

Coles, R. (1997). *The moral intelligence of children.* New York, NY: Random House.

Collins, N. L. D., & M. B. Shaeffer (1997). Look, listen, and learn to read. *Young Children 52*(5): 65-68.

Collinson, V. (1995). Making the most of portfolios. *Learning 24*(1): 43-46.

Commeyras, M. (1995). What can we learn from students' questions? *Theory Into Practice 34*(2): 101-106.

Conlon, A. (1992). Giving Mrs. Jones a hand: Making group story time more pleasurable and meaningful for young children. *Young Children 47*(3): 14-18.

Consortium of National Arts Education Associations (CNAEA). 1994. *Dance, music, theater, visual arts: What every young American should know and be able to do in the arts.* Reston, VA: Author.

Conroy, M. (1988). Sexism in our schools: Training girls for failure. *Better Homes and Gardens 66*(2): 44, 46.

Cook, J. W. (2001). Create and tell a story: Help young children who have psychological difficulties. *Young Children 56*(1): 67-70.

Coontz, S. (1995). The American family and the nostalgia trap. *Phi Delta Kappan 76*(7): K1-K20.

Cooper, J. D. (2000). *Literacy: Helping children construct meaning* (4th ed.). Boston: Houghton Mifflin Company.

Cooper, J. L., & M. T. Dever (2001). Sociodramatic play as a vehicle for curriculum integration in first grade. *Young Children 56*(3): 58-63.

Cortés, C. E. (1996). Preparing for a multicultural future. *Principal 76*(1): 16-20.

Council on Physical Education for Children (1994). *Developmentally appropriate physical education practices for young children.* Reston, VA: American Alliance for Health, Physical Education, Recreation, and Dance (AAHPERD).

Crosser, S. (1992). Managing the early childhood classroom. *Young Children 47*(2): 23-29.

Cullinan, B., & L. Galda (1994). *Literature and the child.* Fort Worth, TX: Harcourt, Brace.

Cummings, C., & K. Haggerty (1997). Raising healthy children. *Educational Leadership 54*(8): 28-30.

Cunningham, P. (2000). *Phonics they use: Words for reading and writing* (3rd ed.). New York: Longman/Addison Wesley.

Curran, L. (1991). *Cooperative learning lessons for little ones: Literature-based language arts and social skills.* San Juan Capistrano, CA: Resources for Teachers.

Curwin, R. L. (1995). A humane approach to reducing violence in schools. *Educational Leadership 52*(5): 72-75.

Dahl, K. (1998). Why cooking in the classroom? *Young Children 53*(1): 81-83.

Daniels, H. (1994). *Literature circles:Voice and choice in the student-centered classroom.* York, ME: Stenhouse.

Danielson, L. C., & G. T. Bellamy (1989). State variation in placement of children with handicaps in segregated environments. *Exceptional Children* 55(5): 448-455.

D'Arcangelo, M. (1999). Learning about learning to read: A conversation with Sally Shaywitz. *Educational Leadership* 57(2): 26-31.

Darling-Hammond, L. (1996). What matters most: A competent teacher for every child. *Phi Delta Kappan* 78(3): 193-200.

Darling-Hammond, L. (1997). Quality teaching: The critical key to learning. *Principal* 77(1): 5-11.

DaRos, D. A., & B. A. Kovach (1998). Assisting toddlers and caregivers during conflict resolutions: Interactions that promote socialization. *Childhood Education* 75(1): 25-30.

Davis, A., & R. J. Havighurst (1947). *Father of the man.* Boston: Houghton Mifflin.

Davies, M. A. (2000). Learning . . . The beat goes on. *Childhood Education* 76(3): 148-153.

Day, B. (1988). *Early childhood education: Creative learning activities* (3rd ed.). New York: Macmillan.

de la Roche, E. (1996). Snowflakes: Developing meaningful art experiences for young children. *Young Children* 51(2): 82-83.

Demarest, K. (1996). Playing with color. *Young Children* 51(3): 83.

Derman-Sparks, L., & the A.B.C. Task Force (1989). *Antibias curriculum: Tools for empowering young children.* Washington, DC: National Association for the Education of Young Children.

DeSteno, N. (2000). Parent involvement in the classroom: The fine line. *Young Children* 55(3): 13-17.

Dever, M. T., & D. E. Hobbs (1998). The learning spiral: Taking the lead from how young children learn. *Childhood Education* 75(1): 7-11.

Dever, M. T., & E. J. Jared (1996). Remember to include art and crafts in your integrated curriculum. *Young Children* 51(3): 69-71.

Diffily, D. (1996). The project approach: A museum exhibit created by kindergartners. *Young Children* 51(2): 72-75.

Diffily, D., & K. Morrison (eds.) (1996). *Family-friendly communication for early childhood programs.* Washington, DC: National Association for the Education of Young Children.

Dighe, J., Z. Calomiris, & C. VanZutphen (1998). Nurturing the language of art in children. *Young Children* 53(1): 4-9.

Dillon, J. T. (1988). *Questioning and teaching: A manual of practice.* New York: Teachers College Press.

Dodd, A. W. (1996). Involving parents, avoiding gridlock. *Educational Leadership* 53(7): 44-46.

Dreher, M. J. (2000). Fostering reading for learning. In L. Baker, M. J. Dreher, & J. T. Guthrie (eds.), *Engaging young readers: Promoting achievement and motivation.* New York: Guilford Press, pp. 68-93.

Duarte, G., & D. Rafanello (2001). The migrant child: A special place in the field. *Young Children* 56(2): 26-34.

Dumtschin, J. U. (1987). Music across the curriculum: More than just circle time. *Day Care and Early Education* 15(2): 22-25.

Dunn, L., & S. Kontos (1997). What have we learned about developmentally appropriate practice? *Young Children* 52(5): 4-13.

Dunston, P. J. (1992). A critique of graphic organizer research. *Reading Research and Instruction* 31(2): 57-65.

Dyson, A. H. (1988). Appreciate the drawing and dictating of young children. *Young Children* 43(3): 25-32.

Dyson, A. H. (1990). Symbol makers, symbol weavers: How children link play, pictures, and print. *Young Children* 45(2): 50-57.

Eaton, M. (1997). Positive discipline: Fostering the self-esteem of young children. *Young Children* 52(6): 43-46.

Edmiaston, R., V. Dolezal, S. Doolittle, C. Erickson, & S. Merritt (2000). Developing Individualized Education Programs for children in inclusive settings: A developmentally appropriate framework. *Young Children* 55(4): 36-41.

Edwards, L. C., & M. L. Nabors (1993). The creative arts process: What it is and what it is not. *Young Children* 48(3): 77-81.

Egan, K. (1989). Memory, imagination, and learning: Connected by the story. *Phi Delta Kappan* 70(6): 455-459.

Egan, K. (1992). *Imagination in teaching and learning: The middle school years.* Chicago: University of Chicago Press.

Egeland, B. R., E. Carlson, & L. A. Sroufe (1993). Resilience is a process. *Development and Psychopathology* 5(4): 517-528.

Eldridge, D. (2001). Parent involvement: It's worth the effort. *Young Children* 56(4): 65-69.

Elias, M. (1996). Teens do better when dads are more involved. *USA Today*, 22 August, D-1.

Eliason, C. F. (1996). Pedagogical actions of kindergarten teachers vis-á-vis pupil questions. Unpublished doctoral dissertation, Brigham Young University, Provo, Utah.

Elkind, D. (1982). Piaget (Article 26). *Annual editions: Human development.* Guilford, CT: Dushkin, p. 134.

Elkind, D. (1986). Formal education and early childhood education: An essential difference. *Phi Delta Kappan* 67(9): 631-636.

Elkind, D. (1987). *Miseducation: Preschoolers at risk.* New York: Knopf.

Elkind, D. (1988). *The hurried child* (2nd ed.). Reading, MA: Addison-Wesley.

Elkind, D. (1991a). Developmentally appropriate practice: A case study of educational inertia. In S. L. Kagan (ed.), *The care and education of America's young children: Obstacles and opportunities.* Chicago: National Society for the Study of Education, pp. 1-16.

Elkind, D. (1991b). *Perspective on early childhood education.* Washington, DC: National Education Association.

Elkind, D. (1995). Schools and families in the postmodern world. *Phi Delta Kappan 77*(1): 8-14.

Elkind, D. (1996). Early childhood education: What should we expect? *Principal 75*(5): 11-13.

Elswood, R. (1999). Really including diversity in early childhood classrooms. *Young Children 54*(4): 62-66.

Engel, B. S. (1996). Learning to look: Appreciating child art. *Young Children 51*(3): 74-79.

Epstein, A. S. (2001). Thinking about art: Encouraging art appreciation in early childhood settings. *Young Children 56*(3): 38-43.

Epstein, J. L. (2000). *School and family partnerships: Preparing educators and improving schools.* Boulder, CO: Westview.

Epstein, J. L., & M. G. Sanders. (1998). What we learn from international studies of school–family–community partnerships. *Childhood Education 74*(6): 392-399.

Epstein, J. L., K. C. Coates, M. G. Sanders, & B. S. Simon (1997). *School, family and community partnerships: Your handbook for action.* Thousand Oaks, CA: Corwin.

Fadiman, C. (1984). *The world treasury of children's literature, Book One.* Boston: Little Brown.

Farlow, L. (1996). A quartet of success stories: How to make inclusion work. *Educational Leadership 53*(5): 51-55.

Favazza, P. C., & S. L. Odom. (1997). Promoting positive attitudes of kindergarten-age children toward people with disabilities. *Exceptional Children, 63*: 405-418.

Favazza, P. C., P. Kumar, & L. Phillipsen (1996, December). *Strategies for promoting the social relationships between young children with and without disabilities: Implications for research.* Paper presented at the International Division of Early Childhood, CEC Annual Conference, Phoenix, AZ.

Favazza, P. C., J. LaRoe, L. Phillipsen, & P. Kumar (2000). Representing young children with disabilities in classroom environments. *Young Exceptional Children 3*(3): 2-8.

Fayden, T. (1997). Children's choice: Planting the seeds for creating a thematic sociodramatic center. *Young Children 52*(3): 15-19.

Feeney, S., & N. K. Freeman (1999). *Ethics and the early childhood educator: Using the NAEYC Code.* Washington, DC: National Association for the Education of Young Children.

Fenton, G. M. (1996). Back to our roots in nature's classroom. *Young Children 51*(3): 8-11.

Ferguson, C. (2001). Discovering, supporting, and promoting young children's passions and interests: One teacher reflects. *Young Children 56*(4): 6-11.

Fields, M. V., & K. L. Spangler (1995). *Let's begin reading right* (3rd ed.). Upper Saddle River, NJ: Prentice Hall.

File, N. (2001). Family–professional partnerships: Practice that matches philosophy. *Young Children 56*(4): 70-74.

Finders, M., & C. Lewis (1994). Why some parents don't come to school. *Educational Leadership 51*(8): 50-54.

Finn, J. (1998). Parental engagement that makes a difference. *Educational Leadership 55*: 20-26.

Fitzgerald, R. (1995). Straight from the reader's mouth. *Learning 24*(2): 74-76.

Fleege, P. O. (1997). Assessment in an integrated curriculum. In C. H. Hart, D. C. Burts, & R. Charlesworth (eds.), *Integrated curriculum and developmentally appropriate practice: Birth to age eight.* Albany, NY: SUNY Press, pp. 313-334.

Flynn, L. L., & P. G. Wilson (1998). Partnerships with family members: What about fathers? *Young Exceptional Children 2*(1): 21-28.

Fountas, I. C., & G. S. Pinnell (1996). *Guided reading: Good first teaching for all children.* Portsmouth, NH: Heinemann.

Fox, D. B. (2000). Music and the baby's brain early experiences: *Music Educators Journal 87*(2): 23-27.

Frakes, C., & K. Kline (2000). Teaching young mathematicians: The challenges and rewards. *Teaching Children Mathematics 6*(6): 376-381.

Freeman, N. (1998). Using NAEYC's Code of Ethics: What happens when school/parent relationships aren't good? *Young Children 53*(6): 75.

Freidberg, J. (1989). Helping today's toddlers become tomorrow's readers: A pilot parent participation project offered through a Pittsburgh health agency. *Young Children 44*(2): 13-16.

Frey, K., R. Fewell, & D. Meyer (1989). Parental adjustment and changes in child outcome among families of young handicapped children. *Topics in Early Childhood Special Education 8*(4): 38-57.

Fromberg, D. P. (1999). A review of research on play. In C. Seefeldt (ed.), *The early childhood curriculum: Current findings in theory and practice* (3rd ed.). New York: Teachers College Press, pp. 27-53.

Frye, C. (ed.) (1993). Handwashing. *Mayo Clinic Health Letter.* Rochester, MN: The Mayo Clinic.

Fuchs, D., & L. S. Fuchs (1994/1995). Sometimes separate is better. *Educational Leadership 52*(4): 22-26.

Fuerst, J. S., & R. Petty (1996). The best use of federal funds for early childhood education. *Phi Delta Kappan 77*(10): 676-678.

Fuhr, J. E., & K. H. Barclay (1998). The importance of appropriate nutrition and nutrition education. *Young Children 53*(1): 74-80.

Fuys, D. J. & A. K. Liebov (1997). Concept learning in geometry. *Teaching Children Mathematics* 3(5), 248-251.

Galinsky, E. (1992). The role of the corporation in promoting early childhood education and care and family support systems. In D. A. Steglin (ed.), *Early childhood education: Policy issues for the 1990s.* Norwood, NJ: Ablex, pp. 117-133.

Gallahue, D.I. (1996). *Developmental physical education for today's children* (3rd ed.). Madison, WI: Brown & Benchmark.

Gallahue, D. L. (1995). Transforming physical education curriculum. In S. Bredekamp & T. Rosegrant (eds.), *Reaching potentials: Transforming early childhood curriculum and assessment* (Vol. 2). Washington, DC: National Association for the Education of Young Children, pp. 125-144.

Gambrell, L. G., & S. A. Mazzoni (1999). Emergent literacy: What research reveals about learning to read. In C. Seefeldt (ed.), *The early childhood curriculum: Current findings in theory and practice* (3rd ed.). New York: Teachers College Press, pp. 80-105.

Garcia, E. E. (1997). The education of Hispanics in early childhood: Of roots and wings. *Young Children* 52(3): 5-14.

Gardner, H. (1983). *Frames of mind: The theory of multiple intelligences.* New York: Basic.

Gardner, H. (1999). *The disciplined mind.* New York: Simon & Schuster.

Garman, C. G., & J. F. Garman (1992). *Teaching young children effective listening skills.* York, PA: William Gladen Foundation.

Garmezy, N. (1985). Stress resistant children: The search for protective factors. In J. E. Stevenson (ed.), *Recent research in developmental psychopathology.* New York: Elsevier, pp. 213-233.

Garmston, R., & B. Wellman (1994). Insights from constructivist learning theory. *Educational Leadership* 51(7): 84-85.

Garrett, J. N., & M. F. Kelley (2000). Early childhood special education: Workplace realities. *Childhood Education* 76(5): 257-276.

Garvey, C. (1990). *Play* (enlarged ed.). Cambridge, MA: Harvard University Press.

Gatewood, T. E., & S. H. Conrad (1997). Is your school's technology up-to-date? A practical guide to assessing technology in elementary schools. *Childhood Education* 73(4): 249-251.

Gatzke, M. (1991). Creating meaningful kindergarten programs. In B. Spodek (ed.), *Educationally appropriate kindergarten practices.* Washington, DC: National Education Association, pp. 97-109.

Geiger, K. (1993). *Violence in the schools.* Statement presented at a news conference by the president of the NEA. Washington, DC, Jan. 14, 1993.

Geist, E. (2001). Children are born mathematicians: Promoting the construction of early mathematical concepts in children under 5. *Young Children* 56(4): 12-19.

Gharavi, G. J. (1993). Music skills for preschool teachers: Needs and solutions. *Arts Education Policy Review* 94(3): 27-30.

Gillard, M. (1995). *Storyteller, storyteacher: Discovering the power of storytelling for teaching and living.* Portland, ME: Stenhouse.

Gillespie, C. W., & A. Chick (2001). Fussbusters: Using peers to mediate conflict resolution in a head start classroom. *Childhood Education* 77(4): 192-195.

Glascoe, F. P. (1999). Communicating with parents. *Young Exceptional Children* 2(4): 17-25.

Glasser, W. (1990). *The quality school.* New York: Harper & Row.

Glasser, W. (1997). A new look at school failure and school success. *Phi Delta Kappan* 78(8): 597-602.

Glazer, S. (1996). Educators debate "character education." *Post Register,* Idaho Falls, ID, Sept. 4, 1996, p. B6.

Goldberg, M. F. (1997). An interview with Dr. James P. Comer. *Phi Delta Kappan* 78(7): 557-559.

Goldberg, M. F. (2001). An interview with Linda Darling-Hammond: Balanced optimism. *Phi Delta Kappan* 82(9): 687-689.

Goleman, D. (1995). *Emotional intelligence: Why it can matter more than IQ.* New York: Bantam Books.

Gollnick, D. M., & P. C. Chinn (1998). *Multicultural education in a pluralistic society* (5th ed.). Upper Saddle River, NJ: Merrill/Prentice Hall.

Goodlad, J. I. (1994). *What schools are for.* Bloomington, IN: Phi Delta Kappa Educational Foundation.

Goodman, K. (1986). *What's whole in whole language?* Portsmouth, NH: Heinemann.

Gracenin, D. (1994). Reaching and teaching the homeless. *Education Digest* 59(6): 37-39.

Graue, E. (2001). What's going on in the children's garden? Kindergarten today. *Young Children* 56(3): 67-73.

Green, C. R. (1998). This is my name. *Childhood Education* 74(4): 226-231.

Greenberg, P. (1992). Ideas that work with young children: Teaching about Native Americans? Or teaching about people, including Native Americans? *Young Children* 46(6): 27-30, 78-81.

Greenberg, P. (1993). Ideas that work with young children. How and why to teach all aspects of preschool and kindergarten math naturally, democratically, and effectively (For teachers who do not believe in educational excellence, and who find math boring to the max), Part I. *Young Children* 48(4): 75-84.

Greenberg, P. (1995). Promoting excellence in early childhood education. *Principal* 74(5): 11-14.

Greenberg, P. (2001). The irreducible needs of children: An interview with T. Berry Brazelton, M.D. and Stanley I. Greenspan, M.D. *Young Children* 56(2): 6-14.

Griffin, C. C., D. C. Simmons, & E. J. Kameenui (1991). Investigating the effectiveness of graphic organizer instruction on the comprehension and recall of science content by students with learning disabilities. *Reading, Writing, and Learning Disabilities* 7: 355-376.

Griffing, P. (1983). Encouraging dramatic play in early childhood, *Young Children* 38(2): 13-22.

Griffith, P., & J. A. Leavell (1995/1996). There isn't much to say about spelling . . . or is there? *Childhood Education* 72(2): 84-90.

Grisham-Brown, J. (2000). Transdisciplinary activity-based assessment for young children with multiple disabilities. *Young Exceptional Children* 3(2): 3-10.

Guilaume, A. M. (1998). Learning with text in the primary grades. *The Reading Teacher* 51(6), 476-486.

Guilmartin, K. (2000). Early childhood music education in the new millennium. *American Music Teacher* 49(6): 40-41.

Gullo, D. F. (1992). *Developmentally appropriate teaching in early childhood*. Washington, DC: National Education Association.

Guthrie, L. F., & S. Richardson (1995). Turned on to language arts: Computer literacy in the primary grades. *Educational Leadership* 53(2): 14-17.

Haines, J. E., & L. L. Gerber (1996). *Leading young children to music: A resource book for teachers* (5th ed.). Upper Saddle River, NJ: Merrill/Prentice Hall.

Halford, J. M. (1996). How parent liaisons connect families to school. *Educational Leadership* 53(7): 34-36.

Hall, N. (1987). *The emergence of literacy.* Portsmouth, NH: Heinemann.

Hannaford, C. (1995). *Smart moves: Why learning is not all in your head.* Arlington, VA: Great Ocean Publishers.

Hanson, R. A., & R. Reynolds (1991). *Child development: Concepts, issues, and readings* (3rd ed.). St. Paul, MN: West.

Harding, N. (1996). Family journals: The bridge from school to home and back again. *Young Children* 41(2): 25-30.

Hardy, D., T. Power, & S. Jaedicke (1993). Examining the relation of parenting to children's coping with everyday stress. *Child Development* 64: 1829-1841.

Hardy, G. R., & M. N. Tolman (1993). The care and feeding of magnets. *Science and Children* 30(4): 22-23.

Harlan, J. D. (1996). *Science experiences for the early childhood years* (6th ed.). Upper Saddle River, NJ: Merrill/Prentice Hall.

Harris, J. (1999). Interweaving language and mathematics literacy through a story. *Teaching Children Mathematics* 5(9): 520-524.

Harris, V. J. (1991). Research in review: Multicultural curriculum: African American children's literature. *Young Children* 46(2): 37-44.

Hart, C. H., D. C. Burts, & R. Charlesworth (1997). Integrated developmentally appropriate curriculum: From theory and research to practice. In C. H. Hart, D. C. Burts, & R. Charlesworth (eds.), *Integrated curriculum and developmentally appropriate practice: Birth to age eight.* Albany, NY: SUNY Press, pp. 1-27.

Hartman, J. A., & C. Eckerty (1995). Projects in the early years. *Childhood Education* 71(3): 141-148.

Harvard Mental Health Letter (1995). Attention deficit disorder—Part II (1995). *Harvard Mental Health Letter* 11(11): 1-3.

Harvey, S., & A. Goudvis (2000). *Strategies that work: Teaching comprehension to enhance understanding.* Portland, ME: Stenhouse.

Hatch, J. A., & E. B. Freeman (1988). Kindergarten philosophies and practices: Perspectives of teachers, principals, and supervisors. *Early Childhood Research Quarterly* 3: 151-166.

Haugland, S. (1992). The effect of computer software on preschool children's developmental gains. *Journal of Computing in Children's Education* 31(1): 15-30.

Haugland, S. (1995). Classroom activities provide important support to children's computer experiences. *Early Childhood Education Journal* 23(2): 99-100.

Haukoos, G. D., & A. B. Beauvais (1996/1997). Creating positive cultural images: Thoughts for teaching about American Indians. *Childhood Education* 73(2): 77-82.

Hayes, L. F. (1990). From scribbling to writing: Smoothing the way. *Young Children* 45(3): 62-68.

Healy, L. I. (2001). Applying theory to practice: Using developmentally appropriate strategies to help children draw. *Young Children* 56(3): 28-30.

Heckman, P. E., C. B. Confer, & D. C. Hakim (1994). Planting seeds: Understanding through investigation. *Educational Leadership* 51(5): 38-39.

Hefflin, B. R., & M. A. Barksdale-Ladd (2001). African American children's literature that helps students find themselves: Selection guidelines for grades K-3. *Reading Teacher* 54(8): 810-819.

Helm, J. H., & L. Katz (2001). *Young investigators: The Project Approach in the early years.* Washington, DC: National Association for the Education of Young Children.

Helm, J. H., S. Beneke, & K. Steinheimer (1997). Documenting children's learning. *Childhood Education* 73(4): 200-205.

Helm, J. H., S. Beneke, & K. Steinheimer (1998). *Windows on learning: Documenting young children's work.* New York: Teachers College Press.

Henderson, A. T., & N. Berla (1994). *A generation of evidence: The family is critical to student achievement.* Washington, DC: National Committee for Citizens in Education (ERIC Document Reproduction Service No. 375 968).

Henderson, N., & M. M. Milstein (1996). *Resiliency in schools: Making it happen for students and educators.* Thousand Oaks, CA: Corwin Press.

Hendrick, J. (1998). Achieving emotional competence. In J. Hendrick (ed.), *Total learning: Developmental curriculum for the young child* (5th ed.). Upper Saddle River, NJ: Merrill/Prentice Hall.

Hendricks, C., & C. J. Smith (1995). Transforming health curriculum. In S. Bredekamp, & T. Rosegrant (eds.), *Reaching potentials: Transforming early childhood curriculum and assessment* (Vol. 2). Washington, DC: National Association for the Education of Young Children, pp. 65–79.

Herbert, E. A., & L. Schultz (1996). The power of portfolios. *Educational Leadership 53*(7): 70–71.

Herrera, T. A., & D. T. Owens (2001). The "new new math"?: Two reform movements in mathematics education. *Theory into Practice 40*(2): 84–92.

Heuwinkel, M. K. (1996). New ways of learning = new ways of teaching. *Childhood Education 73*(1): 27–31.

Heward, W. L., & M. D. Orlansky (1989). Education equality for exceptional students. In J. A. Banks & C. A. M. Banks (eds.), *Multicultural education: Issues and perspectives.* Boston: Allyn and Bacon.

Hildebrandt, C. (1998). Creativity in music and early childhood. *Young Children 53*(6): 68–74.

Hill, S. (2000a). *Guiding literacy learners.* Portland, ME: Stenhouse.

Hill, S. (2000b). *Phonics.* Portland, ME: Stenhouse.

Hillman, C. B. (1995). *Before the school bell rings.* Bloomington, IN: Phi Delta Kappa Educational Foundation.

Hirsch, A. R. (1992). Nostalgia: A neuropsychiatric understanding. *Advances in Consumer Research 19:* 390–395.

Hobbs, D. E., M. T. Dever, & M. Tadlock (1995). A curriculum planning tool: The learning spiral. *Transendence: The Journal on Emerging Adolescent Education 23*(2): 28–33.

Holden, G. (1997). Changing the way kids settle conflicts. *Educational Leadership 54*(8): 74–76.

Holt, J. (1989). *Learning all the time.* Reading, MA: Addison–Wesley.

Honig, A. S. (1986). Stress and coping in children, Part I. *Young Children 41*(4): 50–63.

Honig, A. S. (1995). Singing with infants and toddlers. *Young Children 50*(5): 72–78.

Honig, A. S., & A. Thompson (1994). Helping toddlers with peer entry skills. *Zero to Three 14*(5): 15–19.

Honig, A. S., & D. S. Wittmer (1996). Helping children become more prosocial: Ideas for classrooms, families, schools, and communities. *Young Children 51*(2): 62–70.

Hoover-Dempsey, K. B., & H. M. Sandler (1997). Why do parents become involved in children's education? *Review of Educational Research 67:* 3–42.

Howard, M. B. (1993). Service learning: Cooperative education applied. *Educational Leadership 51*(3): 42–43.

Howe, H., II (1993). Thinking about kids and education. *Phi Delta Kappan 75*(3): 226–228.

Howell, J., & L. Corbey-Scullen (1997). Out of the housekeeping corner and onto the stage—Extending dramatic play. *Young Children 52*(6): 82–88.

Huettig, C., & J. O. Connor (1999). Wellness programming: For preschoolers with disabilities. *Teaching Exceptional Children 31*(3): 12–17.

Huffman, A. B. (1996). Beyond the weather chart: Weathering new experiences. *Young Children 51*(5): 34–37.

Human Kinetics (2001). Why build physical activity into your curriculum? *Young Children 56*(3): 28 (advertisement).

Humphreys, J. (2000). Exploring nature with children. *Young Children 55*(2): 16–20.

Hunt, R. (1999). Making positive multicultural early childhood happen. *Young Children 54*(5): 39–43.

Huntsinger, C. S., P. R. Huntsinger, W. D. Ching, & C. B. Lee (2000). Understanding cultural contexts fosters sensitive caregiving of Chinese Americans. *Young Children 55*(6): 7–15.

Hurst, D. S. (1994). Teaching technology to teachers. *Educational Leadership 51*(7): 74–76.

Hurt, J. A. (2000). Create a parent place: Make the invitation for family involvement real. *Young Children 55*(5): 88–92.

Hyson, M. C. (1994). *The emotional development of young children: Building an emotion-centered curriculum.* New York: Teachers College Press.

Hyson, M. C., & A. Eyman (1986). Approaches to computer literacy in early childhood teacher education. *Young Children 41*(6): 54–59.

Individuals with Disabilities Education Act (IDEA) Amendments of 1997 (1997). P.L. 105-17, 105th Congress, 1st Session, 13 May 1997. (20 U.S.C. 1400 Et seq., 111 STAT, 37).

Inger, M. (1992). Increasing the school involvement of Hispanic parents. *ERIC/CUE Digest Number 80.* New York: ERIC Clearinghouse on Urban Education (ERIC Document Reproduction Service No. 350 380).

International Reading Association (IRA) (2000). *Make a difference means making it different: Honoring children's rights to excellent reading instruction* (A position statement of the IRA). Newark, DE: Author.

International Reading Association (IRA) & National Association for the Education of Young Children (NAEYC) (1998). Learning to read and write: Developmentally appropriate practices for young children. *Reading Teacher 52*(2): 193–216. Also in *Young Children 53*(4): 30–46.

International Society for Technology in Education (ISTE) (2000). *National educational technology standards for students: Connecting curriculum and technology.* Eugene, OR: Author.

Isenberg, J. P., & M. R. Jalongo (2001). *Creative expression and play in the early childhood curriculum* (3rd ed.). New York: Merrill/Prentice Hall.

Isenberg, J. P., & D. L. Brown (1997). Development issues affecting children. In J. P. Isenberg & M.R. Jalongo (eds.), *Major trends and issues in early childhood education: Challenges, controversies, and insights.* New York: Teachers College Press, pp. 29–42.

Jackson, B. R. (1997). Creating a climate for healing in a violent society. *Young Children 52*(7): 68–70.

Jaelitza. (1996). Insect love: A field journal. *Young Children 51*(4): 31–32.

Jalongo, M. R. (1995). Promoting active listening in the classroom. *Childhood Education 72*(1): 13–18.

Jalongo, M. R. (1996). Using recorded music with young children: A guide for nonmusicians. *Young Children 51*(5): 6–14.

Jalongo, M. R., & M. Collins (1985). Singing with young children! Folk singing for nonmusicians. *Young Children 40*(2): 17–22.

Jalongo, M. R., & D. M. Ribblett (1997). Using song picture books to support emergent literacy. *Childhood Education 74*(1): 15–22.

James, J. Y., & L. M. Kormanski (1999). Positive intergenerational picture books for young children. *Young Children 54*(3): 32–38.

Janzen, R. (1994). Melting pot or mosaic? *Educational Leadership 51*(8): 9–11.

Jenkins, J. R., S. L. Odom, & M. L. Speltz (1989). Effects of social integration on preschool children with handicaps. *Exceptional Children 55*(5): 420–428.

Jensen, E. (2000a). *Learning with the body in mind.* San Diego, CA: Brain Store.

Jensen, E. (2000b). Moving with the brain in mind. *Educational Leadership 58*(3): 24–27.

Jewett, J. (1997). Childhood stress. *Childhood Education 73*(3): 172–173.

Johnson, D. W., & R. T. Johnson (1995). *Reducing school violence through conflict resolution.* Alexandria, VA: Association of School Curriculum Development.

Johnson, D. W., R. T. Johnson, E. J. Holubec, & P. Roy (1986). *Circles of learning.* Alexandria, VA: Association for Supervision and Curriculum Development.

Johnson, D. W., R. T. Johnson, L. Stevahn, & P. Hodne (1997). The three Cs of safe schools. *Educational Leadership 55*(2): 8–13.

Johnson, J. E., J. F. Christie, & T. D. Yawkey (1987). *Play and early childhood development.* Glenview, IL: Scott, Foresman.

Johnson, N. L. (1983). *How to insure your child's success in school.* Fresno, CA: Mike Murach & Associates.

Johnson, R. T., D. W. Johnson, & E. J. Holubec (1987). *Structuring cooperative learning: Lesson plans for teachers.* Edina, MN: Interaction.

Johnson, T. (1993). New hope for families with infants and toddlers who have disabilities, or are at risk for developmental delay. *Merrill–Palmer Perspectives* Fall 1993: 9–10.

Jones, E. (1997). Play is my job. *Principal 76*(5): 18–19.

Judge, S. L., & H. P. Parette (1998). Assistive technology decision-making strategies. In S. L. Judge & H. P. Parette (eds.), *Assistive technology for young children with disabilities: A guide to family-centered service.* Cambridge, MA: Brookline, pp. 127–147.

Jungers, S. (1996). Teaching young children about nutrition. *Principal 75*(5): 26–27.

Kamii, C. (ed.) (1990). *Achievement testing in early childhood education: The games grown-ups play.* Washington, DC: National Association for the Education of Young Children.

Kamii, C., & R. DeVries (1993). *Physical knowledge in preschool education: Implications of Piaget's theory.* New York: Teachers College Press.

Kamii, C., & J. K. Ewing (1996). Basing teaching on Piaget's constructivism. *Childhood Education 72*(5): 260–264.

Kamii, C., & B. A. Lewis (1990). Constructivism and first-grade arithmetic. *Arithmetic Teacher 38*(1): 36–37.

Kamii, C., F. B. Clark, & A. Dominick (1994). The six national goals: A road to disappointment. *Phi Delta Kappan 75*(9): 672–677.

Karnes, M. B., & L. J. Johnson (1989). Training for staff, parents and volunteers working with children, especially those with disabilities and from low-income homes. *Young Children 44*(3): 49–56.

Katz, L. G. (1983). *Getting involved: Your child and math* (DHHS Publication No. OHDS 83-31144). Washington, DC: U.S. Department of Health and Human Services.

Katz, L. G. (1985). What is basic for young children? In J. S. McKee (ed.), *Early childhood education 1985–86.* Guildford, CT: Dushkin, pp. 12–15.

Katz, L. G. (1990). Impressions of Reggio Emilia preschools. *Young Children 45*(6): 11–12.

Katz, L. G. (1994). Perspectives on the quality of early childhood programs. *Phi Delta Kappan 76*(3): 200–205.

Katz, L. G. (1995). *Talks with teachers of young children: A collection.* Norwood, NJ: Ablex.

Katz, L. G., & S. Chard (1989). *Engaging children's minds: The project approach.* Norwood, NJ: Ablex.

Katz, L. G., & S. Chard (1997). Documentation: The Reggio Emilia approach. *Principal 76*(5): 16–19.

Katz, L. G., & D. E. McClellan (1997). *Fostering children's social competence: The teacher's role.* Washington, DC: National Association for the Education of Young Children.

Kaufman, H. O. (2001). Skills for working with all families. *Young Children 56*(4): 81–83.

Kay, S. (1992). Cognitive theory: An element of design for arts education. *Design for Arts Education 92*(2): 1–13.

Kellogg, R. (1967). Understanding children's art. *Psychology Today 1*(1): 16–25.

Kellogg, R. (1970). *Analyzing Children's Art.* Palo Alto, CA: Mayfield.

Kelman, A. (1990). Choices for children. *Young Children* 45(3): 42-45.

Kendrick, A. S., R. Kaufmann, & K. P. Messenger (eds.) (1995). *Healthy young children: A manual for programs.* Washington, DC: National Association for the Education of Young Children.

Kenney, S. H. (1997). Music in the developmentally appropriate integrated curriculum. In C. H. Hart, D. C. Burts, & R. Charlesworth (eds.), *Integrated curriculum and developmentally appropriate practice: Birth to age eight.* Albany, NY: SUNY Press, pp. 103-144.

Kich, G. (1996). In the margins of race and sex: Difference, marginality, and flexibility. In M. P. P. Root (ed.), *The multiracial experience: Racial borders as the new frontier.* London: Sage, pp. 263-276.

Kieff, J., & K. Wellhousen (2000). Planning family involvement in early childhood programs. *Young Children* 55(3): 18-25.

Kilmer, S. J., & H. Hofman (1995). Transforming science curriculum. In S. Bredekamp & T. Rosegrant (eds.), *Reaching potentials: Transforming early childhood curriculum and assessment* (Vol. 2), Washington, DC: National Association for the Education of Young Children, pp. 43-63.

Klefstad, J. (1995). Cooking in the kindergarten. *Young Children* 50(6): 32-33.

Klein, H. A. (2000). Self-esteem and beyond. *Childhood Education* 76(4): 240-241.

Kline, K. (1999). Helping at home. *Teaching Children Mathematics* 5(8): 456-460.

Kline, K. (2000). Early childhood teachers discuss the standards. *Teaching Children Mathematics* 6(9): 568-571.

Kline, L. W. (1995). A baker's dozen: Effective instructional strategies. In R. D. Cole (ed.) *Educating everybody's children: Diverse teaching strategies for diverse learners.* Alexandria, VA: Association for Supervision and Curriculum Development, pp. 21-43.

Kohn, A. (1993a). Choices for children: Why and how to let students decide. *Phi Delta Kappan* 75(1): 8-19.

Kohn, A. (1993b). *Punished by rewards: The trouble with gold stars, incentive plans, A's, praise and other bribes.* Boston: Houghton Mifflin.

Kohn, A. (1994). The truth about self-esteem. *Phi Delta Kappan* 76(4): 272-283.

Kohn, A. (1997). How not to teach value: A rational look at character education. *Phi Delta Kappan* 78(6): 429-437.

Kontos, S., & L. Dunn (1993). Caregiver practices and beliefs in child care varying in developmental appropriateness and quality. In S. Reifel (ed.), *Perspectives in developmentally appropriate practice: Advances in early education and day care* (Vol. 5). Greenwich, CT: JAI Press, pp. 53-74.

Korgen, K. (1998). *From black to biracial.* Westport, CT: Praeger.

Kositsky, V. (1977). What in the world is cooking in class today? Multiethnic recipes for young children. *Young Children* 33(1): 23-31.

Kupetz, B. N., & M. M. Twiest (2000). Nature, literature, and young children: A natural combination. *Young Children* 55(1): 59-63.

Ladson-Billings, G. (1994). What we can learn from multicultural education research. *Educational Leadership* 51(8): 22-26.

Lakey, J. (1997). Teachers and parents define diversity in an Oregon preschool cooperative: Democracy at work. *Young Children* 52(4): 20-28.

Lally, J. R. (1995). The impact of child care policies and practices on infant/toddler identity formation. *Young Children* 51(1): 58-67.

Lamme, L. L. (1982). Handwriting in an early childhood curriculum. In J. F. Brown (ed.), *Curriculum planning for young children.* Washington, DC: National Association for the Education of Young Children, pp. 109-116.

Larkin, B. R. (2001). "Can we act it out?" *Reading Teacher* 54(5): 478-481.

Larsen, J. M., & J. Haupt (1997). Integrating home and school: Building partnerships. In C. H. Hart, D. C. Burts, & R. Charlesworth (eds.), *Integrated curriculum and developmentally appropriate practice: Birth to age eight.* Albany, NY: SUNY Press, pp. 389-415.

Lazdauskas, H. (1996). Music makes the school go 'round. *Young Children* 51(5): 22-23.

Learning (1994a). Language arts. *Learning* 23(1): 38-57.

Learning (1994b). Math. *Learning,* 23(1): 58-68.

Learning (1994c). Parent pointers. *Learning* 23(2): 37.

Learning (1995). Take parents where they are . . . not where you want them to be. *Learning* 24(3): 43-46.

Lee, E., D. Menkart, & M. Okazawa-Rey (eds.) (1998). *Beyond heroes and holidays: A practical guide to K-12 anti-racist, multicultural education and staff development.* Washington, DC: Network of Educators on the Americas.

Leibler, S. (1999). Move over, Richard Simmons. *Children and Families* 18(3): 34-37.

Leppo, M. L., D. Davis, & B. Crim (2000). The basics of exercising the mind and body. *Childhood Education* 76(3): 143-147.

Levin, B. (1994). Improving educational productivity: Putting students at the center. *Phi Delta Kappan* 75(10): 758-760.

Levin, D. E. (1998). *Remote control childhood? Combating the hazards of media culture.* Washington, DC: National Association for the Education of Young Children.

Lickona, T. (1993). The return of character education. *Educational Leadership* 51(3): 6-11.

Lillard, A., & S. Curenton (1999). Do young children understand what others feel, want, and know? *Young Children 54*(5): 52-57.

Lind, K. K. (1997). Science in the developmentally appropriate integrated curriculum. In C. H. Hart, D. C. Burts, & R. Charlesworth (eds.), *Integrated curriculum and developmentally appropriate practice: Birth to age eight*. Albany, NY: SUNY Press, pp. 75-101.

Link, G., M. Beggs, & E. Seiderman (1997). *Serving families*. Fairfax, CA: Parent Services Project.

Little Soldier, L. (1990). Making anthropology a part of the elementary social studies curriculum. *Social Education 54*(1): 18-19.

Lopez, M. L., & T. Schultz (1996). Serving young children: Strategies for success. *Principal 75*(5): 21-24.

Lubeck, S. (1994). The politics of developmentally appropriate practice: Exploring issues of culture, class, and curriculum. In B. L. Mallory & R. S. New (eds.), *Diversity and DAP: Challenge for early childhood education*. New York: Teachers College Press, pp. 17-43.

Lucero, E. L. (1997). Promoting multiculturalism in the early grades. *Principal 76*(5): 5-11.

Lupkowski, A. E., & E. A. Lupkowski (1985). Meeting the needs of gifted preschoolers. *Children Today 14*(2): 10-14.

Malaguzzi, L. (1993). History, ideas, and basic philosophy. In C. Edwards, L. Gandini, & G. Foreman (eds.), *The hundred languages of children: The Reggio Emilia approach to early childhood education*. Norwood, NJ: Ablex, pp. 41-90.

Maloney, J. (1994/1995). A call for placement options. *Educational Leadership 52*(4): 25.

Mandelbaum, J. (1975). Creative dramatics in early childhood. *Young Children 30*(2): 84-92.

Manning, D., & P. Schindler (1997). Communicating with parents when their children have difficulties. *Young Children 52*(5): 27-33.

Manning, D., S. Rubin, G. Perdigao, R. Gonzalez, & P. Schindler (1996). A "worry doctor" for preschool directors and teachers: A collaborative model. *Young Children 51*(5): 68-73.

Margolis, H. (1987). Self-induced relaxation: A practical strategy to improve self-concepts, reduce anxiety, and prevent behavioral problems. *Clearing House 60*(8): 355-358.

Marion, M. (1995). *Guidance of young children*. Upper Saddle River, NJ: Merrill/Prentice Hall.

Marshall, C. S. (1998). Using children's storybooks to encourage discussions among diverse populations. *Childhood Education 74*(4): 194-199.

Marshall, H. H. (1989). The development of self-concept. *Young Children 44*(5): 44-51.

Marshall, N. L., W. W. Robeson, & N. Keefe (1999). Gender equity in early childhood classrooms. *Young Children 54*(4): 9-13.

Marx, E., & S. F. Wooley (1998). *Health is academic: A guide to coordinated school health programs*. New York: Teachers College Press.

Marxen, C. E. (1995). Push, pull, toss, tilt, swing: Physics for young children. *Childhood Education 71*(4): 212-216.

Maslow, A. H. (1968). *Toward a psychology of being* (2nd ed.). New York: Van Nostrand.

Maslow, A. H. (1970). *Motivation and personality* (2nd ed.). New York: Harper & Row.

Mason, M., & A. K. Lloyd (1995). Ramona and the fruit flies: An interdisciplinary approach. *Teaching Children Mathematics 1*(6): 388-392.

Massachusetts Mutual Insurance Company (1991). American family values poll. Cited in *Post Register*, Idaho Falls, ID, Oct. 14, 1992, p. 5.

Matter, D. (1982). Musical development in young children. *Childhood Education 58*(5): 305-307.

Maxim, G. W. (1997). *The very young child: Guiding children from infancy through the early years* (5th ed.). Upper Saddle River, NJ: Merrill/Prentice Hall.

McAfee, O., & D. Leong (1994). *Assessing and guiding young children's development and learning*. Boston: Allyn and Bacon.

McBride, S. L. (1999). Family-centered practices. *Young Children 54*(3): 62-68.

McCaslin, N. (1996). *Creative drama in the classroom: And beyond* (6th ed.). White Plains, NY: Addison, Wesley, Longman.

McDonald, D. T., & J. H. Ramsey (1982). Awakening the artist: Music for young children. In J. F. Brown (ed.), *Curriculum planning for young children*. Washington, DC: National Association for the Education of Young Children, pp. 187-193.

McDonald, W. F., J. K. Burns, & J. Esserman (1981). In-home interviews measure positive effects of a school nutrition program. *Journal of Nutrition Education 13*(4): 140-144.

McElveen, S. A., & C. C. Dierking (2000/2001). Children's books as models to teach writing skills. *Reading Teacher 54*(4): 363-364.

McGee, L. M. & D. J. Richgels (2000). *Literacy's beginnings: Supporting young readers and writers*. Boston: Allyn and Bacon.

McGerald, J., & J. A. Nidds (1996). Self-esteem or self-confidence? *Principal 76*(1): 55.

McKean, B. (2000/2001). Speak the speech, I pray you! Preparing to read aloud dramatically. *Reading Teacher 54*(4): 358-359.

McLeod, M. (1997). Once upon a time. *Readers Digest 42*(251): 267-277.

McMath, J., & M. A. King (1994). Using picture books to teach mathematical concepts. *Day Care and Early Education 21*(3): 18-22.

McMillan, J. H., J. Singh, & L. G. Simonetta (1994). The tyranny of self-oriented self-esteem. *Education Horizons 72*(3): 141–145.

Meier, D. (1996). Supposing that. . . . *Phi Delta Kappan 78*(4): 271–276.

Meisels, S. (1993). Remaking classroom assessment with the work sampling system. *Young Children 48*(5): 34–40.

Melchoir, A. (2000). Service learning at your service. *Education Digest 66*(2): 26–32.

Merkley, D. M., & D. Jefferies (2000/2001). Guidelines for implementing a graphic organizer. *Reading Teacher 54*(4): 350–357.

Meyer, J. (2001). The child-centered kindergarten: A position paper of the Association for Childhood Education International. *Childhood Education 77*(3): 161–166.

Micklo, S. J. (1995). Developing young children's classification and logical thinking skills. *Childhood Education 72*(1): 24–28.

Micklo, S. J. (1997). Math portfolios in the primary grades. *Childhood Education 73*(4): 194–199.

Miller, H. M. (2001). Teaching and learning about cultural diversity: A dose of empathy. *Reading Teacher 54*(6): 380–381.

Miller, J. (1990). Three-year-olds in their reading corner. *Young Children 46*(1): 51–54.

Miller, S. E. (1999). Balloons, blankets, and balls: Gross motor activities we use indoors. *Young Children 54*(5): 58–63.

Mills, H., & J. A. Clyde (1991). Children's success as readers and writers: It's the teacher's beliefs that make the difference. *Young Children 46*(2): 54–59.

Mills, H., D. J. Whitin, & T. O'Keefe (1993). Teaching math concepts in a K–1 class doesn't have to be like pulling teeth—But maybe it should be! *Young Children 48*(2): 17–20.

Minzenberg, B., J. Laughlin, & L. Kaczmarek (1998). Early childhood special education in the developmentally appropriate classroom. *Young Exceptional Children 2*(2): 10–17.

Misifi, F. L. (1993). A sense of science. *Science and Children 30*(4): 28–29.

Morgan, C., & M. E. York (1981). Ideas for mainstreaming young children. *Young Children 36*(2): 18–25.

Morgan, E. (1989). Talking with parents when concerns come up. *Young Children 44*(2): 52–56.

Morgan, N., & J. Saxton (1991). *Teaching, questioning, and learning.* New York: Routledge.

Morrison, G. (1997). *Fundamentals of early childhood education.* Upper Saddle River, NJ: Merrill/Prentice Hall.

Morrison, J. W., & T. Bordere (2001). Supporting biracial children's identity development. *Childhood Education 77*(3): 134–138.

Morrison, J. W., & L. S. Rodgers (1996). Being responsive to the needs of children from dual heritage backgrounds. *Young Children 52*(1): 29–33.

Morrow, L. M. (1997). *The literacy center: Contexts for reading and writing.* Portland, ME: Stenhouse.

Morrow, L. M. & J. K. Smith (1990). Introduction. In L. M. Morrow & J. K. Smith (eds.), *Assessment for instruction in early literacy.* Upper Saddle River, NJ: Prentice Hall, pp. 1–6.

Moscovici, H., & T. H. Nelson (1998). Activity mania to inquiry. *Science and Children 35*(4): 14–17.

Murphy, D. M. (1997). Parent and teacher plan for the child. *Young Children 52*(4): 32–36.

Murphy, L. B., & E. M. Leeper (1970). *The ways children learn, Part I Caring for children* (DHEW Publication No. OCD 73–1026). Washington, DC: U.S. Department of Health, Education, and Welfare, Office of Child Development.

Murray, C. D. (2000). Learning about children's social and emotional needs at snack time—Nourishing the body, mind, and spirit of each child. *Young Children 55*(2): 43–52.

Music Educators National Conference (MENC) (1994). *The school music program: A new vision.* Reston, VA: Author.

Nachbar, R. R. (1992). What do grown-ups do all day? The world of work. *Young Children 47*(3): 6–12.

Nahikian-Nelms, M. L., & C. N. Mogharrehan (1994). Pilot assessment of nutrition practices in a university child care program. *Journal of Nutrition Education 26*(5): 238–240.

National Association for the Education of Young Children (1988a). Position statement on developmentally appropriate practice in the primary grades, serving 5- through 9-year-olds. *Young Children 43*(2): 64–84.

National Association for the Education of Young Children (1988b). Position statement on standard testing of young children 3 through 8 years of age. *Young Children 43*(3): 42–47.

National Association for the Education of Young Children (1996a). *Guidelines for preparation of early childhood professionals.* Washington, DC: Author.

National Association for the Education of Young Children (1996b). Position statement: Responding to linguistic and culture diversity: Recommendations for effective early childhood education. *Young Children 51*(2): 4–12.

National Association for the Education of Young Children (1996c). Position statement: Technology and young children—Ages three through eight. *Young Children 51*(6): 11–16.

National Association for the Education of Young Children (1997a). Position statement on developmentally appropriate practice in early childhood programs serving children from birth through age 8. In S. Bredekamp &

C. Copple (eds.), *Developmentally appropriate practice in early childhood programs* (rev. ed.). Washington, DC: Author, pp. 3–30.

National Association for the Education of Young Children (1997b). Position statement on the prevention of child abuse in early childhood programs and the responsibilities of early childhood professionals to prevent child abuse. *Young Children 52*(3): 42–46.

National Association for the Education of Young Children (1998). Section II of Ideals and principles about our ethical responsibilities of families. *Young Children 53*(1): 65.

National Association for the Education of Young Children (NAEYC) & National Association of Early Childhood Specialists in State Departments of Education (NAECS/SDE) (1991). Guidelines for appropriate curriculum content and assessment in programs serving children ages 3 through 8 (joint position statement). *Young Children 46*(3): 21–38.

National Association for Sports and Physical Education (1995). *Moving into the future: National standards for P.E.—A guide to content and assessment.* St. Louis, MO: Mosby.

National Association of Elementary School Principals (1990). *Standards for quality programs for young children: Early childhood education and the elementary school principal.* Alexandria, VA: Author.

National Association of State Boards of Education (1988). *Right from the start: The report of the NASBE task force on early childhood education.* Alexandria, VA: Author.

National Center for Improving Science Education (1990). *Getting started in science, A blueprint for elementary school science education* (report). Colorado Springs, CO: Author.

National Commission on Excellence in Education (1983). *A nation at risk: The imperative for educational reform.* Washington, DC: U.S. Department of Education.

National Commission on Teaching and America's Future (1996). *What matters most: Teaching for America's future.* New York: Author.

National Council of Teachers of Mathematics. (1989). *Curriculum and evaluation standards for school mathematics.* Reston, VA: Author.

National Council of Teachers of Mathematics (NCTM) (2000). *Principles and standards for school mathematics.* Reston, VA: Author.

National Research Council (1996). *National science education standards.* Washington, DC: National Academy Press.

Neelly, L. P. (2001). Developmentally appropriate music practice: Children learn what they live. *Young Children 56*(3): 32–37.

Nel, E. M. (2000). Academics, literacy, and young children. *Childhood Education 76*(3): 136–141.

Neugebauer, B. (ed.) (1992). *Alike and different.* Washington, DC: National Association for the Education of Young Children.

New, R. S., & B. L. Malory (1994). Introduction: The ethics of inclusion. In B. L. Mallory & R. S. New (eds.), *Diversity and developmentally appropriate practices: Challenges for early childhood education.* New York: Teachers College Press, pp. 1–13.

New, R. S. (1999). An integrated early childhood curriculum: Moving from the *what* and the *how* to the *why*. In C. Seefeldt (ed.), *The early childhood curriculum: Current findings in theory and practice* (3rd ed.). New York: Teachers College Press, pp. 265–287.

Newberger, J. J. (1997). New brain development research—A wonderful window of opportunity to build public support for early childhood education. *Young Children 52*(4): 4–9.

Newby, T. J., D. A. Stepich, J. D. Lehman, and J. D. Russell (2000). *Instructional technology for teaching and learning: Designing instruction, integrating computers, and using media.* Upper Saddle River, NJ: Prentice Hall.

Newman, R. (1995a). The home-school connection. *Childhood Education 71*(5): 296–297.

Newman, R. (1995b). "It's winter at my house and spring at your house—and that's the way the world goes 'round!" *Childhood Education 71*(4): 235–236.

Newman, R. (1997). For parents particularly: Learning healthful habits for a lifetime. *Childhood Education 73*(4): 234–235.

Newman, R. (1997/98). Parent conferences: A conversation between you and your child's teacher. *Childhood Education 74*(2): 100–101.

Novick, R. (1998). The comfort corner: Fostering resiliency and emotional intelligence. *Childhood Education 74*(4): 200–204.

Novick, R. (1999/2000). Supporting early literacy development: Doing things with words in the real world. *Childhood Education 76*(2): 70–75.

Nunnelley, J. C. (1990). Beyond turkeys, Santas, snowmen, and hearts: How to plan innovative curriculum themes. *Young Children 46*(1): 24–29.

Oakes, P. B., & D. A. Caruso (1990). Kindergarten teachers use of developmentally appropriate practices and attitudes about authority. *Early Education and Development 1:* 445–457.

Odom, S. L., & M. A. McEvoy (1988). Integration of young children with handicaps and normally developing children. In S. L. Odom & M. Karnes (eds.), *Early intervention for infants and children with handicaps: An empirical base.* Baltimore, MD: Paul H. Brookes, pp. 241–267.

Oehlberg, B. (1996). *Making it better: Activities for children living in a stressful world.* St. Paul, MN: Redleaf Press.

Ogle, D. M. (1986). K-W-L: A teaching model that develops active reading of expository text. *Reading Teacher 39:* 564-570.

Ohanian, S. (1996). Is that penguin stuffed or real? *Phi Delta Kappan 78*(4): 277-284.

Olson, J., C. L. Murphy, & P. D. Olson (1999). Readying parents and teachers for the inclusion of children with disabilities: A step-by-step process. *Young Children 54*(3): 18-31.

Ornstein, A. C., & L. S. Behar-Horenstein (1999). *Contemporary issues in curriculum.* Boston: Allyn and Bacon.

Osborn, D. K. (1991). *Early childhood education in historical perspective* (3rd ed.). Athens, GA: Daye Press.

Owens, C. (1999). Conversational science 101A: Talking it up! *Young children 54*(5): 4-9.

Owens, K. (1997). Confident, competent kids. *Learning 26*(2): 48-52.

Palmer, M., & W. L. Sims (1993). *Music in prekindergarten: Planning and teaching.* Reston, VA: Music Educators National Conference.

Parette, H. P., & B. Petch-Hogan (2000). Approaching families: Facilitating culturally/linguistically diverse family involvement. *Teaching Exceptional Children 33*(2): 4-10.

Parten, M. B. (1932). Social participation among preschool children. *Journal of Abnormal and Social Psychology 27:* 243-269.

Parten, M. B. (1933). Social play among preschool children. *Journal of Abnormal and Social Psychology 28:* 136-147.

Patrirarca, L. A., & J. Alleman. (1987). Journey in time: A foster grandparent program. *Young Children 34*(3): 30-39.

Patton, M. M., & T. M. Kokoski (1996). How good is your early childhood science, mathematics, and technology program? Strategies for extending your curriculum. *Young Children 51*(5): 38-44.

Payne, V. G., & J. Rink (1997). Physical education in the developmentally appropriate integrated curriculum. In C. H. Hart, D. C. Burts, & R. Charlesworth (eds.), *Integrated curriculum and developmentally appropriate practice: Birth to age eight.* Albany, NY: SUNY Press, pp. 145-170.

Peery, J. C., & I. W. Peery (1986). Effects of exposure to classical music on the musical performance of preschool children. *Journal of Research in Music Education 34*(1): 24-33.

Pellegrini, A. D., & B. Boyd (1993). The role of play in early childhood development and education: Issues in definitions and functions. In B. Spodek (ed.), *Handbook of research on the education of young children.* New York: Macmillan, pp. 105-121.

Perkins, D., & T. Blythe (1994). Putting understanding up front. *Educational Leadership 51*(5): 4-7.

Perrone, V. (1994). How to engage students in learning. *Educational Leadership 51*(5): 11-13.

Perry, G., & M. Rivkin (1992). Teachers and science. *Young Children 47*(4): 9-16.

Phillips, C. B. (1994). The challenge of training and credentialing early childhood educators. *Phi Delta Kappan 76*(3): 214-217.

Piaget, J. (1952). *The origins of intelligence in children.* New York: International Universities Press.

Piaget, J. (1955). *Language and thought of the child* (M. Gabian, trans.). Cleveland, OH: World Publishing Co.

Piaget, J. (1970a). Piaget's theory (G. Gellerier & J. Langer trans.). In P. H. Mussen (ed.), *Carmichael's manual of child psychology,* Vol. 1 (3rd ed.) New York: Wiley, pp. 703-732.

Piaget, J. (1970b). *Science of education and psychology of the child.* New York: Viking.

Piaget, J. (1973). *The child and reality.* New York: Viking.

Piaget, J. (1974). *To understand is to invent.* New York: Viking.

Pica, R. (1997). Beyond physical development: Why young children need to move. *Young Children 52*(6): 4-11.

Pierson, C. A., & S. S. Beck (1993). Performance assessment: The realities that will influence the rewards. *Childhood Education 70*(1): 29-98.

Pinnell, G. S., & I. Fountas (1998). *Word matters: Teaching phonics and spelling in the reading/writing classroom.* Portsmouth, NH: Heinemann.

Planje, A. C. (1997). Playing with water in primary ways. *Young Children 52*(2): 33.

Poest, C. A., J. R. Williams, D. D. Witt, & M. E. Atwood (1990). Challenge me to move: Large muscle development in young children. *Young Children 45*(5): 4-10.

Pool, C. R. (1997). Up with emotional health. *Educational Leadership 54*(8): 12-14.

Powell, D. R. (1998). Reweaving parents into the fabric of early childhood programs. *Young Children 53*(5): 60-67.

Putnam, J. W. (ed.) (1993). *Cooperative learning and strategies for inclusion: Celebrating diversity in the classroom.* Baltimore, MD: Paul H. Brookes.

Rafferty, C. D. (1999). Literacy in the information age. *Educational Leadership 57*(2): 22-25.

Raines, S. C. (1997). Developmental appropriatness: Curriculum revisited and challenged. In J. P. Isenberg & M. R. Jalongo (eds.), *Major trends and issues in early childhood education: Challenges, controversies, and insights.* New York: Teachers College Press, pp. 75-89.

Raines, S. C., & R. J. Canady (1990). *The whole language kindergarten.* New York: Teachers College Press.

Raines, S. C., & R. Isbell (1988). Talking about wordless books in your classroom. *Young Children* 43(6): 24-25.

Rakow, S. J., & M. J. Bell (1998). Science and young children: The message from the National Science Education Standards. *Childhood Education* 74(3): 164-167.

Rambusch, N. M. (1962). *Learning how to learn: An American approach to Montessori*. Baltimore, MD: Helicon.

Ramsey, P. G. (1995). Growing up with the contradictions of race and class. *Young Children* 50(6): 18-22.

Raywid, M. A. (1993). Finding time for collaboration. *Educational Leadership* 51(1): 30-34.

Reutzel, D. R. (1997). Integrating literacy learning for young children: A balanced literacy perspective. In C. H. Hart, D. C. Burts, & R. Charlesworth (eds.), *Integrated curriculum and developmentally appropriate practice: Birth to age eight*. Albany, NY: SUNY Press, pp. 225-254.

Reutzel, D. R., & R. B. Cooter (1992). *Teaching children to read: From basals to books* (2nd ed.). Upper Saddle River, NJ: Merrill/Prentice Hall.

Riel, M. (1994). Educational change in a technology-rich environment. *Journal on Computing in Education* 26(4): 452-474.

Rinaldi, C. (1993). The emergent curriculum and social constructivism. In C. Edwards, L. Gandini, & G. Foreman (eds.), *The hundred languages of children: The Reggio Emilia approach to early childhood education*. Norwood, NJ: Ablex, pp. 101-112.

Rivkin, M. (ed.) (1992). Science is a way of life. *Young Children* 47(4): 4-8.

Rivkin, M. S. (1995). *The great outdoors: Restoring children's right to play outside*. Washington, DC: National Association for the Education of Young Children.

Rock, M. L. (2000). Parents as equal partners: Balancing the scales in IEP development. *Teaching Exceptional Children* 32(6): 30-37.

Rodd, J. (1996). Children, culture and education. *Childhood Education* 72(6): 325-329.

Rodger, L. (1996). Adding movement throughout the day. *Young Children* 51(3): 4-6.

Rogers, C. S., & S. S. Morris (1986). Reducing sugar in the children's diets: Why? How? *Young Children* 42(5): 11-16.

Rogers, C. S., & J. K. Sawyers (1988). *Play in the lives of children*. Washington, DC: National Association for the Education of Young Children.

Rogers, F. (1997). Different and the same (sidebar). *Principal* 76(5): 8.

Rosenthal, D. M., & J. Y. Sawyers (1996). Building successful partnerships: Strategies for parent support and involvement. *Childhood Education* 72(4): 194-200.

Ross, M. E. (2000). Science their way. *Young Children* 55(2): 6-13.

Rousseau, J. J. (1911). *Emile* (trans. B. Foxley). London: J. M. Dent. (Original work published in 1762.)

Rule, A. C. (2001). Alphabetizing with environmental print. *Reading Teacher* 54(6): 558-562.

Russell-Fox, J. (1997). Together is better: Specific tips on how to include children with various types of disabilities. *Young Children* 52(4): 81-83.

Sadker, M., & D. Sadker (1994). *Failing at fairness: How America's schools shortchange girls*. New York: Scribner's.

Sagor, R. (1996). Building resiliency in students. *Educational Leadership* 54(1): 38-43.

Samaras, A. P. (1996). Children's computers. *Childhood Education* 72(3): 133-136.

Sampson, M., M. B. Sampson, & R. V. Allen (1995). *Pathways to literacy: Process transactions*. Fort Worth, TX: Harcourt Brace.

Sandstrom, S. (1999). Dear Simba is dead forever. *Young Children* 54(6): 14-15.

Sang, D. (1994). The worry doctor comes on Thursdays: Clinical consultation in a kindergarten class. *Young Children* 49(2): 24-31.

Santos, R. M., B. Lignugaris/Kraft, & J. Akers (1999). Tips on planning center time activities for preschool classrooms. *Young Exceptional Children* 2(4): 9-16.

Saracho, O. N. (1999). The role of play in early childhood curriculum. In B. Spodek and O. N. Saracho (eds.), *Issues in early childhood curriculum*. Troy, NY: Educators International Press, pp. 86-105.

Sarison, S. B. (1995). Some reactions to what we have learned. *Phi Delta Kappan* 77(1): 84-85.

Sautter, R. C. (1995). Standing up to violence. *Phi Delta Kappan* 76(5): K1-K12.

Scherer, M. (1996). On our changing family values: A conversation with David Elkind. *Educational Leadership* 53(7): 4-9.

Schifter, D. (1996). The constructivist perspective on teaching and learning mathematics. *Phi Delta Kappan* 77(7): 492-499.

Schirrmacher, R. (1986). Talking with young children about their art. *Young Children* 42(5): 3-7.

Schultz, T. (1992). Developmentally appropriate practice and the challenge of public school reform. In D. A. Steglin (ed.), *Early childhood education: Policy issues for the 1990s*. Norwood, NJ: Ablex, pp. 137-154.

Schultz, T., & M. E. Lopez (1995). Early childhood reform: Local innovations in a flawed system. *Phi Delta Kappan* 77(1): 60-63.

Schwartz, R. M., & T. E. Raphael (1985). Concept of definition: A key to improving students' vocabulary. *Reading Teacher* 39( ): 198-203.

Schweinhart, L. J., J. Berrueta-Clement, W. S. Barnett, A. S. Epstein, & D. P. Weikart (1985). The promise of early childhood education. *Phi Delta Kappan* 68(7): 548-553.

Schweinhart, L. J., & D. P. Weikart (1992). The High/Scope Perry Preschool study, similar studies, and their implications for public policy in the U.S. In D. A. Steglin (ed.), *Early childhood education: Policy issues for the 1990s.* Norwood, NJ: Ablex, pp. 67–86.

Schweinhart, L. J., D. P. Weikart, & M. B. Larner (1986). Consequences of three preschool curriculum models through age 15. *Early Childhood Research Quarterly* 1(1): 15–35.

Seefeldt, C. (1997). Social Studies in the developmentally appropriate curriculum. In C. H. Hart, D. C. Burts, & R. Charlesworth (eds.), *Integrated curriculum and developmentally appropriate practice: Birth to age eight.* Albany, NY: SUNY, pp. 171–199.

Seefeldt, C. (1999). Art for young children. In C. Seefeldt (ed.), *The early childhood curriculum: Current findings in theory and practice.* New York: Teachers College Press, pp. 201–217.

Shade, D. D. (1996). Software evaluation. *Young Children* 51(6): 17–21.

Shanker, A. (1994/1995). Full inclusion is neither fair nor appropriate. *Educational Leadership* 52(4): 18–21.

Shantal, R. (1998). Age-appropriate ecology: Are you practicing it? *Young Children* 53(1): 70–71.

Shaver, J. P., & C. K. Curtis (1981). *Handicappism and equal opportunity: Teaching about the disabled in social studies.* Reston, VA: Foundation for Exceptional Children.

Sheldon, A. (1990). Kings are royaler than queens: Language and socialization. *Young Children* 45(2): 4–9.

Shepard, L. A. (1994). The challenges of assessing young children appropriately. *Phi Delta Kappan* 76(3): 206–212.

Sherman, C. W., & D. P. Mueller (1996). *Developmentally appropriate practice and student achievement in inner-city elementary schools.* Washington, DC: Paper presented at Head Start's Third National Research Conference, June 1996.

Sherman, J. L. (1979). Storytelling with young children. *Young Children* 34(1): 20–27.

Sidelnick, M. A., & M. L. Svoboda, (2000). The bridge between drawing and writing: Hannah's story. *Reading Teacher* 54(2): 174–184.

Silcox, H. C., & T. E. Leek (1997). International service learning: Its time has come. *Phi Delta Kappan* 78(8): 615–618.

Singer, A. (1994). Reflections on multiculturalism. *Phi Delta Kappan* 76(4): 284–288.

Skinner, B. F. (1953). *Science and human behavior.* New York: Macmillan.

Slaughter, J. P. (1993). *Beyond storybooks: Young children and the shared book experience.* Newark, DE: International Reading Association.

Smith, A. F. (2000). Reflective portfolios. *Childhood Education* 76(4): 204–208.

Smith, B. J., P. S. Miller, & S. Bredekamp (1998). Sharing responsibility: DEC-, NAEYC-, and Vygotsky-based practices for quality inclusion. *Young Exceptional Children* 2(1): 11–20.

Smith, C. A. (1979). Puppetry and problem-solving skills. *Young Children* 34(3): 4–11.

Smith, C. A. (1986). Nurturing kindness through storytelling. *Young Children* 41(6): 46–51.

Smith, F. (1985). *Reading without nonsense.* New York: Teachers College Press.

Smith, F. (1990). *To think.* New York: Teachers College Press.

Smith, K. (1993). Becoming the "guide on the side." *Educational Leadership* 51(2): 35–37.

Smith, L. (1995). Guess what: Fathers matter, too. *Kansas City Star*, 26 March, H-2, H-4.

Smith, M. K. (1996). Fostering creativity in the early childhood classroom. *Early Childhood Education Journal* 24(2): 77–82.

Snider, S. L., & T. L. Badgett (1995). "I have a computer, what do I do now?" Using technology to enhance every child's learning. *Early Childhood Education Journal* 23(2): 101–105.

Snow, C., M. S. Burns, & P. Griffin (1998). *Preventing reading difficulties in young children.* Washington, DC: National Academy Press.

Snyder, T. D. (1996). Trends in education. *Principal* 76(1): 57–60.

Solter, A. (1992). Understanding tears and tantrums. *Young Children* 47(4): 64–68.

Sorenson, M. R. (1991). Integrating the curriculum through literature-based teaching. *Utah Association State Curriculum Development* (UASCD). Salt Lake City: UASCD, pp. 31–34.

Sosa, A. (1993). *Thorough and fair: Creating routes to success for Mexican-American students.* Charleston, WV: ERIC Clearinghouse on Rural Educational and Small Schools (ERIC Document Reproduction Service No. 360 116).

Soto, L. D. (1991). Research in review: Understanding bilingual/bicultural young children. *Young Children* 46(2): 30–35.

Spaulding, S. (1994). Four steps to effective parent conferences. *Learning* 23(3): 36–38.

Spewock, T. S. (1991). Teaching parents of young children through learning packets. *Young Children* 47(1): 28–30.

Spinelli, C. G. (1998). Home–school collaboration at the early childhood level: Making it work. *Young Exceptional Children* 2(2): 20–26.

Spring, J. (1998). *American education* (8th ed.). New York: McGraw-Hill.

Stafford, S. H., & V. P. Green (1996). Preschool integration: Strategies for teachers. *Childhood Education* 72(4): 214–218.

Staley, L. (1997). What does purple smell like? *Childhood Education* 73(4): 240-242.

Staley, L., & P. A. Portman (2000). Red Rover, Red Rover, It's time to move over. *Young Children* 55(1): 67-72.

Stallman, A. C., & P. D. Pearson (1990). Formal measures of early literacy. In L. M. Morrow & J. K. Smith (eds.), *Assessment for instruction in early literacy.* Upper Saddle River, NJ: Prentice Hall, pp. 7-44.

Staub, D., & C. A. Peck (1994/1995). What are the outcomes for nondisabled students? *Educational Leadership* 52(4): 36-40.

Stauffer, R. (1970). *The language experience approach to the teaching of reading.* New York: Harper & Row.

Stellaccio, C. K., & M. McCarthy (1999). Research in early childhood music and movement education. In C. Seefeldt (ed.), *The early childhood curriculum: Current findings in theory and practice* (3rd ed.). New York: Teachers College Press, pp. 179-200.

Stenmark, J. K., V. Thompson, & R. Cossex, (1986). *Family math.* Berkeley: Regents, University of California.

Stomfay-Stitz, A. (1998). Using children's books to model conflict resolution in your peaceable classroom. *Childhood Education* 74(4): 224-M.

Stone, J. I. (1987). Early childhood math: Make it manipulative! *Young Children* 42(6): 16-23.

Stone, S. J. (1995). Wanted: Advocates for play in primary grades. *Young Children* 50(6): 45-54.

Stone, S. J. (1995/1996). Integrating play into the curriculum. *Childhood Education* 72(2): 104-107.

Stone, S. J., & K. Glascott (1997/98). The affective side of science instruction. *Childhood Education* 74(2): 102-104.

Sturm, C. (1997). Creating parent–teacher dialogue: Intercultural communication in child care. *Young Children* 52(5): 34-38.

Sutherland, Z., & M. H. Arbuthnot (1986). *Children and books* (7th ed.). Glenview, IL: Scott Foresman.

Swadener, S. (1995). Nutrition education for preschool children. *Journal of Nutrition Education* 27(6): 291-297.

Swick, K. J. (1991). *Teacher–parent partnerships to enhance school success in early childhood education.* Washington, DC: National Education Association.

Swick, K. J., G. Boutte, & I. VanScoy (1995/1996). Families and schools: Building multicultural values together. *Childhood Education* 72(2): 75-79.

Sylvester, R. (1994). How emotions affect learning. *Educational Leadership* 52(2): 60-65.

Sylvester, R. (1995). *A celebration of neurons: An educator's guide to the human brain.* Alexandria, VA: Association for Supervision and Curriculum Development.

Taylor, B. M., & E. H. Heibert (1994). Early literacy interventions: Aims and issues. In E. H. Hiebert and B. M. Taylor (eds.), *Getting reading right from the start.* Boston: Allyn and Bacon.

Teale, W. H. (1990). The promise and challenge of informal assessment in early literacy. In L. M. Morrow & J. K. Smith (eds.), *Assessment for instruction in early literacy.* Upper Saddle River, NJ: Prentice Hall, pp. 45-61.

Ten Boom, C. (1971). *The hiding place.* New York: Bantam.

Tener, N. (1995/1996). Information is not knowledge. *Childhood Education* 72(2): 100.

Thatcher, D. H. (2001). Reading in the math class: Selecting and using picture books for math investigation. *Young Children* 56(4): 20-26.

Thiessen, D., & M. Matthias (eds.) (1992). *The wonderful world of mathematics.* Reston, VA: National Council of Teachers of Mathematics.

Thompson, C. M. (1995). Transforming curriculum in the visual arts. In S. Bredekamp & T. Rosegrant (eds.), *Reaching potentials: Transforming early childhood curriculum and assessment* (Vol. 2). Washington, DC: National Association for the Education of Young Children, pp. 81-98.

Thorne, J. (1988). Becoming a kindergarten of readers? *Young Children* 43(6): 10-16.

Tiedt, P. L., & I. M. Tiedt (1986). *Multicultural teaching: A handbook of activities, information, and resources.* Boston: Allyn and Bacon.

Tomich, K. (1996). Hundreds of ladybugs, thousands of ladybugs, millions and billions and trillions of ladybugs—and a couple of roaches. *Young Children* 51(4): 28-30.

Tompkins, G. E. (1997). *Literacy for the twenty-first century: A balanced approach.* Upper Saddle River, NJ: Merrill/Prentice Hall.

Torp, L., & S. Sage (1998). *Problems as possibilities: Problem-based learning for K-12 education.* Alexandria, VA: Association for Supervision and Curriculum Development (ASCD).

Torrance, E. P. (1976). *Guiding creative talent.* Melbourne, FL: Krieger.

Trelease, J. (1995). *The read-aloud handbook* (4th ed.). New York: Viking.

Turbiville, V. P., G. T. Umbarger, & A. C. Guthrie (2000). Father's involvement in programs for young children. *Young Children* 55(4): 74-79.

Turner, S. B. (2000). Caretaking of children's souls: Teaching the deep song. *Young Children* 55(1): 31-33.

Turner, T. N., & T. Oakes (1997). Stories on the spot: Introducing students to impromptu storytelling. *Childhood Education* 73(3): 154-157.

U.S. Department of Commerce (1996). *Statistical abstracts of the United States, 1996* (116th ed.). Washington, DC: U.S. Government Printing Office.

U.S. Department of Education (1997). Fathers' involvement in their children's schools (on-line). Available: *http://www.ed.gov/NCES/pubs98/fathers/intro.html#intro.*

VanHorn, J., P. Nourat, B. Scales, & K. Alward (1999). *Play at the center of the curriculum* (2nd ed.). Upper Saddle River, NJ: Merrill/Prentice Hall.

VanScoy, I. J. (1995). Trading the three R's for the four E's: Transforming curriculum. *Childhood Education* 72(1): 19–23.

VanScoy, I. J., & S. H. Fairchild (1993). It's about time! *Young Children* 48(2): 21–24.

Vygotsky, L. S. (1962). *Thought and language* (trans. E. Hanfmann & G. Vakar). Cambridge, MA: MIT Press.

Vygotsky, L. S. (1978). *Mind in society: The development of psychological processes.* Cambridge, MA: Harvard University Press.

Vygotsky, L. S. (1993). The collected works of L. S. Vygotsky, vol 2. In R. W. Rieber, & A. S. Carton (eds.), *The fundamentals of defectology.* Hillsdale, NJ: Erlbaum.

Wadlington, E. M., & M. E. Partridge (1998). Stress management for teachers. *Childhood Education* 75(1): 32-F.

Wald, G. S. (2000). Moving from "I think I can" to "I know I can." *Young Children* 55(4): 14–15.

Walker, C. H., & F. R. Yekovich (1999). TRALEs to literacy. *Educational Leadership* 57(2): 57–60.

Wallinga, C. W., & P. Skeen (1996). Siblings of hospitalized and ill children: The teacher's role in helping these forgotten family members. *Young Children* 51(6): 78–83.

Ward, C. D. (1996). Adult intervention: Appropriate strategies for enriching the quality of children's play. *Young Children* 51(3): 20–25.

Wardle, F. (1990). Endorsing children's differences: Meeting the needs of adopted minority children. *Young Children* 45(5): 44–46.

Warner, L. (1999). Self-esteem: A byproduct of quality classroom music. *Childhood Education* 76(1): 19–23.

Washington, V., V. Johnson, & J. B. McCracken (1995). *Grassroots success! Preparing schools and families for each other.* Washington, DC: National Association of Education for the Young Children.

Wasik, B. A. (2001). Phonemic awareness and young children. *Childhood education* 77(3): 128–133.

Wasik, B. A. (2001). Teaching the alphabet to young children. *Young Children* 56(1): 34–39.

Watson, R. (1995). A guide to violence prevention. *Educational Leadership* 52(5): 57–59.

Webb, N. C. (1997). Working with parents from cradle to preschool: A university collaborates with an urban public school. *Young Children* 52(4): 15–19.

Weinreb, M. L. (1997). Be a resiliency mentor: You may be a lifesaver for a high-risk child. *Young Children* 52(2): 14–20.

Welchman-Tischler, R. (1992). *How to use children's literature to teach mathematics.* Reston, VA: National Council of Teachers of Mathematics.

Wellhousen, K. (1996a). Do's and don'ts for eliminating hidden bias. *Childhood Education* 73(1): 36–39.

Wellhousen, K. (1996b). Girls can be bull riders, too! Supporting children's understanding of gender roles through children's literature. *Young Children* 51(5): 79–83.

Werner, E. E. (1984). Resilient children. *Young Children* 40(1): 68–72.

Werner, E. E., & R. S. Smith (1982). *Vulnerable but invincible: A longitudinal study of resilient children and youth.* New York: McGraw-Hill.

Werner, P., S. Timms, & L. Almond (1996). Health stops: Practical ideas for health-related exercise in preschool and primary classrooms. *Young Children* 51(6): 48–55.

Whitin, D. J., & S. Wilde (1992). *Read any good math lately? Children's books for mathematical learning, K–6.* Portsmouth, NH: Heinemann.

Whitmore, K. F., & Y. M. Goodman (1995). Transforming curriculum in language and literacy. In S. Bredekamp & T. Rosegrant (eds.), *Reaching potentials: Transforming early childhood curriculum and assessment* (Vol. 2) Washington, DC: National Association for the Education of Young Children, pp. 145–166.

Wiencek, B. J. (2001). Teaching ideas: the daily news. *Reading Teacher* 54(7): 658–659.

Wiggins, G. (1992). Creating tests worth taking. *Educational Leadership* 49(8): 26–33.

Williams, D. L., & N. F. Chavkin (1990). Essential elements of strong parent involvement programs. *Educational Leadership* 47: 18–20.

Williams, J. A. (2001). Classroom conversations: Opportunities to learn for ESL students in mainstream classrooms. *Reading Teacher* 54(8): 750–757.

Williams, K. C. (1997). "What do you wonder?" Involving children in curriculum planning. *Young Children* 52(6): 78–81.

Williams, L. R. (1999). Determining the early childhood curriculum: The evolution of goals and strategies through consonance and controversy. In C. Seefeldt (ed.), *The early childhood curriculum: Current findings in theory and practice* (3rd ed.). New York: Teachers College Press, pp. 1–26.

Wilson, L. J. (1997). Technology in the classroom. *Childhood Education* 73(4): 249–251.

Wilson, R. A. (1995a). Environmentally appropriate practices. *Early Childhood Education Journal* 23(2): 107–110.

Wilson, R. A. (1995b). Nature and young children: A natural connection. *Young Children* 50(6): 4–11.

Wilson, R. A., S. J. Kilmer, & V. Knauerhase (1996). Developing an environmental outdoor play space. *Young Children* 51(6): 56–61.

Winn, D. D. (1988). Develop listening skills as a part of the curriculum. *Reading Teacher* 42(2): 144–146.

Winter, S. M. (1997). "SMART" planning for inclusion. *Childhood Education* 73(4): 212-218.

Wolery, M., & J. S. Wilbers (eds.) (1994). *Including children with special needs in early childhood programs.* Washington, DC: National Association for the Education of Young Children.

Wolf, A. D. (2000). How to nurture the spirit in nonsectarian environments. *Young Children* 55(1): 34-36.

Wolf, J. (1992). Let's sing it again. *Young Children* 47(2): 56-61.

Wolfson-Steinberg, L. (2000). "Teacher! He hit me!" "She pushed me!" Where does it start? How can it stop? *Young Children* 55(3): 38-42.

Wolk, S. (1994). Project-based learning: Pursuits with a purpose. *Educational Leadership* 52(3): 42-43.

Wolter, D. L. (1992). Whole group story reading? *Young Children* 48(1): 72-75.

Wood, T. (2001). Teaching differently: Creating opportunities for learning mathematics. *Theory into Practice* 40(2): 110-117.

Workman, S. H., & J. A. Gage (1997). Family–school partnerships: A family strengths approach. *Young Children* 52(4): 10-14.

Wortham, S. C. (1997). Assessing and reporting young children's progress: A review of the issues. In J. P. Isenberg & M. R. Jalongo (eds.), *Major trends and issues in early childhood education: Challenges, controversies, and insights.* New York: Teachers College Press, pp. 104-122.

Wurtman, R. S. (1989). *Information anxiety.* Garden City, NY: Doubleday.

Wyckoff, C. L. (2000). Children who care. *Childhood Education* 77(1): 43-44.

Ybarra, S., & J. Hollingworth (1996). Getting classroom assessment right. *Educational Leadership* 25(May-June): 30-31.

Yopp, H. K. (1995). A test for assessing phonemic awareness in young children. *Reading Teacher* 49(1): 20-29.

Zahorik, J. A. (1995). *Constructivist teaching* (Fastback 390). Bloomington, IN: Phi Delta Kappa Educational Foundation.

Zeavin, C. (1997). Toddlers at play: Environments at work. *Young Children* 52(3): 72-77.

Zeece, P. D. (1995). Laughing all the way: Humor in children's books. *Early Childhood Education Journal* 23(2): 93-97.

Zegans, L. (1982). Stress and the development of somatic disorders. In L. Goldberger & S. Breznitz (eds.), *Handbook of stress: Theoretical and clinical aspects.* New York: Free Press, pp. 134-152.

Zeitlin, S. A. (1997). Finding fascinating projects that can promote boy/girl partnerships. *Young Children* 52(6): 29-30.

Zero to Three/National Center for Infants, Toddlers and Families (1994). *Diagnostic classification on mental health and developmental disorders of infancy and early childhood.* Washington, DC: Author.

Ziemer, M. (1987). Science and the early childhood curriculum: One thing leads to another. *Young Children* 42(6): 44-51.

Zill, N., & M. Collins (1996). Approaching kindergarten: Family risk factors. *Principal* 75(5): 14-17.

Name Index

Dighe, J., 458
Dillon, J. T., 47, 50
Dodd, A. W., 60, 73
Dolezal, V., 139
Dominick, A., 83
Doolittle, S., 139
Dreher, M. J., 235, 240
Duarte, G., 131
Dumtschin, J. U., 449
Dunn, L., 27
Dunston, P. J., 256
Dyson, A. H., 258, 455

Eaton, M., 178, 182
Eckerty, C., 81
Edmiaston, R., 139
Edwards, L. C., 455
Egan, K., 426
Eldridge, D., 62
Elias, M., 60
Eliason, C. F., 47, 50
Elkind, D., 2, 9, 10, 15, 18, 25, 27, 28, 30, 48, 83, 126, 176, 285, 427
Elswood, R., 133, 135, 145
Engel, B. S., 456
Englehart, M. D., 82
Epstein, J. L., 60, 457
Erickson, C., 139
Erikson, Erik, 6
Esserman, J., 207
Estes, E., 243
Ewing, J. K., 45
Eyman, A., 120

Fadiman, C., 253
Fairchild, S. H., 394, 405
Favazza, P. C., 148
Fayden, T., 130
Feeney, S., 455
Fenton, G. M., 311
Ferguson, C., 78
Fewell, R., 59
Fields, M. V., 58, 238, 239, 248, 258, 259
File, N., 57, 63
Finders, M., 60, 63, 72
Finn, J., 61
Fitzgerald, R., 60, 63
Fleege, P. O., 28, 30
Flynn, L. L., 59
Fountas, I. C., 243, 256

Fox, D. B., 430
Frakes, C., 385, 396
Freeman, E. B., 27
Freeman, N., 57, 58
Freidberg, J., 250
Freud, Sigmund, 5
Frey, K., 59
Froebel, Friedrick, 4-5, 6
Fromberg, D. P., 31, 32, 36
Frye, C., 205
Fuchs, D., 146
Fuchs, L. S., 146
Fuerst, J. S., 8, 15, 18
Furst, E. J., 82
Fuys, D. J., 409

Gage, J. A., 58
Galda, L., 268
Galinsky, E., 15
Gallahue, D. L., 198
Gambrell, L. G., 230
Garcia, E. E., 133
Gardner, H., 53, 79, 428, 450
Garman, C. G., 249
Garman, J. F., 249
Garmezy, N., 181
Garmston, R., 10, 46, 48
Garret, J. N., 145
Garvey, C., 33
Gatewood, T. E., 120, 121
Gatzke, M., 20
Geiger, K., 176
Geist, E., 231, 384, 385
Gerber, L. L., 432, 438, 449
Gesell, Arnold, 6
Gharavi, G. J., 431
Gillespie, C. W., 178
Glascoe, F. P., 68
Glascott, K., 277
Glasser, W., 10, 18, 21, 35, 48, 53, 60, 106
Glazer, S., 183
Goldberg, M. F., 15, 21, 83
Goleman, D., 170
Gollnick, D. M., 137, 138
Goodlad, J. I., 427
Goodman, Y. M., 236
Goodson, B. D., 16
Gracenin, D., 12
Graue, E., 2, 29
Green, C. R., 175

Subject Index